The bagpipe is one of the cultural icons of Scottish highlanders, but in the twentieth century traditional Scottish Gaelic piping has all but disappeared. Few recordings were ever made of traditional pipe music and there are almost no Gaelic-speaking pipers of the old school left. Recording an important aspect of Gaelic culture before it disappears, John Gibson chronicles the decline of traditional Highland Gaelic bagpiping – and Gaelic culture as a whole – and provides examples of traditional bagpipe music that have survived in the New World.

Pulling together what is known of eighteenth-century West Highland piping and pipers and relating this to the effects of changing social conditions on traditional Scottish Gaelic piping since the suppression of the last Jacobite Rebellion, Gibson presents a new interpretation of the decline of Gaelic piping and a new view of Gaelic society prior to the Highland diaspora. Refuting widely accepted opinions that after Culloden pipes and pipers were effectively banned in Scotland by the Disarming Act (1746), Gibson reveals that traditional dance bagpiping continued at least to the mid-nineteenth century. He argues that the dramatic depopulation of the highlands in the nineteenth century was one of the main reasons for the decline of piping.

Following the path of Scottish emigrants, Gibson traces the history of bagpiping in the New World and uncovers examples of late eighteenth-century traditional bagpiping and dance in Gaelic Cape Breton, in Nova Scotia. He argues that these anachronistic cultural forms provide a vital link to the vanished folk music and culture of the Scottish highlanders.

This definitive study throws light on the ways pipers and piping contributed to social integration in the days of the clan system and on the decline in Scottish Gaelic culture following the abolition of clans. It illuminates the cultural problems faced by all ethnic minorities assimilated into unitary multinational societies.

JOHN G. GIBSON is a Scots-born writer-historian living in Judique, Cape Breton, Nova Scotia.

Traditional Gaelic Bagpiping, 1745–1945

JOHN G. GIBSON

NMS Publishing Limited
Edinburgh, Scotland

McGill-Queen's University Press
Montreal & Kingston · London · Ithaca

© McGill-Queen's University Press 1998
ISBN 0-7735-1541-0

Legal deposit second quarter 1998
Bibliothèque nationale du Québec

Printed in Canada on acid-free paper

Published in the UK, Eire, and Europe by
NMS Publishing Limited
National Museums of Scotland
Chambers Street, Edinburgh, EH1 1 JF
ISBN 1 901663 17 5

This book has been published with the help of a
grant from the Humanities and Social Sciences
Federation of Canada, using funds provided by the
Social Sciences and Humanities Research Council
of Canada.

McGill-Queen's University Press acknowledges the
support of the Canada Council for the Arts for its
publishing program.

Canadian Cataloguing in Publication Data

Gibson, John G. (John Graham), 1941–
    Traditional Gaelic bagpiping, 1745–1945
    Includes bibliographical references and index.
    ISBN 0-7735-1541-0
    1. Bagpipe–Scotland–Highlands–History.   2. Bagpipe–
    Nova Scotia–History.   3. Bagpipe music–History and
    criticism.   I. Title.
    ML980.G449 1998   788.4'9'094115   C98-900393-0

Typeset in 10/12 Times Roman by True to Type

Contents

Preface

I have always been interested in Scottish Gaelic society, and this book is an effort to present, from a Gaelic point of view, what is known about Highland Gaelic community bagpiping and bagpipers over the two and a half centuries since 1745. Most refinements to modern piping and to the small existing core of modern piping scholarship have occurred largely in ignorance of the foundations of the art and its history, which are to be found in the traditional world of Gaelic instrumental music and dance in the late eighteenth century. The almost extinct piping of Gaelic Nova Scotia presents the only example of rustic bagpipe music in combination with the traditional dance of the Gael in the second half of the eighteenth century. This old-style piping is undergoing its first revival, albeit under altered social and intellectual conditions.

In any study of the Highland bagpipe it is important to regard the fixed scale gappings of the Highland bagpipe chanter as essentially Scotch Gaelic, any variants reflecting either community preferences or the makers' incompetences or eccentricities. The fiddle, with its infinite flexibility, has always offered Gaelic-speaking Scots the opportunity to express, deliberately or accidentally, different scale spacings. The bagpipe, as long as it was a popular instrument, guaranteed the conservatism of Scotch Gaelic scale concept and presents scholars with an invaluable perception of an ancient musical notion.

Conducting comparative studies of bagpipe chanters over the years has remained beyond my scope. However, Col MacLean Sinclair, who owned the pipe chanter that is thought to have belonged to Iain Dall (Blind John) MacKay, the Blind Piper of Gairloch (who died around 1756 aged over ninety years), reported that the scale spacings of that instrument, which was brought to Nova Scotia in 1805 by the Blind Piper's grandson, Iain Ruadh (Red John) MacKay, were almost identical to a modern pipe chanter's. This suggests that the preference for the scale as played on the Scotch Highland bagpipe has endured with little change since Iain Dall's father's day in the early seventeenth century. The proposition that the nine-note bagpipe scale was just one formalized variant of a broad spectrum of Gaelic scale preference is refuted by the relatively strong adherence to elements of the pipe scale (with whatever variations different fingerings permitted) by the last Gaelic-speaking generations of Cape Breton fiddlers.

Presenting a Gaelic viewpoint of traditional Gaelic bagpiping is fraught with danger. To begin with, I take the position that piping and the bagpipe were not banned by the Disarming Act of 1746 or by its 1747 and 48 amendments. Because so few people with an interest in modern piping have seriously considered the Gaelic traditional roots of Scottish/world bagpiping, this is a radical position to work from and must be thoroughly expounded. Hence the length and density of the first part of this work.

There are also sizeable academic difficulties in the study of Gaelic piping after 1745. It was not until fairly late in the nineteenth century that folk culture attracted scholarly or academic attention. For the period under study, therefore, cultural data must be sought within the sterile matrix of estate, government, and court records as well as in the more general and personal tourist literature of the Highlands. Published tourist observations must be read with an understanding of the background knowledge, competence, and attitudes of the writers. Smollett and Burt must be read differently from MacCulloch and most of the later visitor-writers who were in the Highlands after Walter Scott's novels had become popular in Europe. Scott's brilliant condescensions about the Highland Scot touched Scots deeply, but they have often proved to be a barrier, at times a convenient one, to a thorough understanding of the Gael.

The Gaelic sources, while inherently more reliable, tend to be bardic and one has to deal with the use of stylistic phrases, often exaggerated, particularly in eulogistic and obsequial verse. Then, as one moves into the second half of the nineteenth century, the writing in English and Gaelic by people who were Gaels has to be assessed carefully for thought borrowings from English sources. The Reverend Norman MacLeod (1783-1862), for example, had been in a position to find out a great deal about the MacCrimmon pipers from the last two, now-famous brothers, Iain Dubh and Dòmhnul Ruadh, and from many other cousins in varying degrees in Skye and elsewhere in MacLeod country. But he missed his opportunity and eulogized them instead in almost worthless prose that was accepted, predictably, as valuable by his faithful and devoted Gaelic readership in the Highlands of Scotland and in Nova Scotia but that added little to our knowledge.

From the middle of the twentieth century, the various magazines devoted to piping approached the subject in the same non-scholarly fashion. The *Piping Times* seldom cited sources. The piping notice of Duncan Stewart, for example, suggests very strongly that the Raasay pipers John MacKay and his sons (whose collective piping experience spans almost a century, from c. 1770–c. 1860) used, or tolerated, a non-modern fingering system. Inasmuch as John seems to have had MacCrimmon, and possibly also Gairloch MacKay, training then this unusual fingering may have been devised by one or both of them. Yet the anonymous author of the article presents his information confusedly and cites no source that might lend credibility to what may have been a seminal fact.

The later chapters of the book, which deal with the New World piping essentially in the Cape Breton *Gàidhealtachd*, are easier reading. They treat, after all, of a living, albeit moribund, culture. Since traditional bagpiping – functional piping for traditional Scotch step-dancing – is showing signs of making a comeback in Nova Scotia and in Scotland, I left the second section with some confidence that the case for an important continuation of essentially traditional, mid-eighteenth century Scotch Gaelic bagpiping's having survived in isolation, and latterly uniquely, in a New World *Gàidhealtachd* had been made strongly enough and needed no further elaboration.

I hope, through this book, that Scotch music everywhere will be better understood, and that musicality in the traditional sense will come to be appreciated on its own terms rather than judged by modern literate and competitive non-Gaelic standards. After all, the retentiveness of the Scotch Gaelic memory for tales and songs is widely acknowledged; people who had heard a song once often knew it a year later. This sort of mental cultivation was characteristic of fiddlers and pipers, too, for as long as Gaelic consciousness dominated the musical scene. It is by no means dead yet in Cape Breton. Traditional Gaelic pipers are much less common today than they once were (in fact they are on the edge of extinction), and those still living are now influenced by the more intellectual approach of the few students who have sought them out as teachers in a way that the old, often illiterate, pipers who learned by ear were not. But once upon a time they too emerged as naturals, some of them with remarkable talent and vast repertoires, and they were ubiquitous in the New World *Gàidhealtachd*.

William Matheson, after listening to the Gaelic singing of Duncan MacDonald (1882-1954), wrote, "His intonation was sometimes in doubt, but always there was the uneasy feeling that one's own apprehension might be at fault, non-plussed by an archaic musical idiom unfamiliar to the modern ear."[1] Matheson's sensitive and scrupulous thinking should be taken as a guide when listening to traditional Gaelic bagpiping or fiddling, and when considering the Gaelic point of view on traditional music and dance. Had Matheson's attitude been common when the last of the traditional, ear-learned pipers were passing into oblivion in Scotland, and when traditional piping was waning in Cape Breton, how much more we might have known today, albeit through the printed word.

The terms *ceòl mór* and *ceòl beag* appear frequently throughout the text. The former, which means "great music," is used synonymously with classical bagpiping and covers a large repertoire of pipe music distinguished by theme and variation, very often several predictable variations. Pipers generally understand it also as *pìobaireachd*, an abstract Gaelicization through its (feminizing) suffix *eachd* of the word *pìobaire* (piper), which is often seen as *pibroch*. I have used *ceòl beag* to include the rest of pipe music, distinguishing between march, air, and dance *ceòl beag* piping when necessary.

When necessary, the group dance reel has been designated "Reel" in the upper case, whereas the reel tune played by a musician or danced by a stepdancer has gone by "reel," lower case. Full musical notes are likewise given in upper case while grace-notes are given in the lower, although the value of any distinction is often moot.

Here and there slightly varying Gaelic orthographies have been cited, often involving the dropping of vowel accents. These citations have not been altered and no comment has been made, except where clarification is required. I have generally followed an older Cape Breton understanding and usage of the word "Scotch" to signify, as a noun or an adjective, Gaelic Scottish. The "of" in titles such as "MacKenzie of Gairloch" denotes ownership; the absence of the "of," as in "John MacKay, Raasay," indicates the name and address of a non-landowner, wadsetter or tacksman. I have reluctantly given greater prominence to the English versions of Gaelic names.

This book grew, broadly, out of a curiosity about eighteenth-century piping that had long roots in the Scotland of my youth, where my oldest half-brother, Dr Charles W.M. Orr, left a practice chanter around the house near Glenfinnan in the 1940s, which I played by ear, right hand upper. The work solidified with the Nova Scotian field work I began in the 1970s. Then, as now, Cape Breton had the last native Gaelic-speaking communities in North America, so most of the informants lived or came from there. Hundreds of kindly Gaels gave generously of their memories. Space has permitted me to list only the most important of them in the appropriate places in the text. I wish to thank them all, named or not. My gratitude for unstinting and excellent service goes to the staff of Eastern Counties Regional Libraries in Mulgrave and Port Hawkesbury, Nova Scotia. While some of these are named below, many other librarians and archivists in Canada and abroad are not. They are very much appreciated nonetheless.

Among the many considerate people in Scotland to whom I am indebted are Hugh Cheape, Assistant Keeper, and Andrew Martin, Assistant Librarian, Museum of Antiquities, Edinburgh; A.S. Henshall, assistant secretary to the Society of Antiquaries of Scotland in 1979 for permission to cite correspondence from MacDonell of Glengarry to James Cummings, 16 November 1781; all of the National Museum of Scotland (NMS); Dorothy C. Laing, NMS Library, William G.F. Boag (1923–92), Assistant to the Keeper; Edith D. Philip and C.J. Burnett, Curator of Fine Art of the Scottish United Services Museum, Edinburgh Castle (NMS); the Trustees of the National Library of Scotland (for permission to cite from John Johnston's letters to Seton Gordon); Lt Col A.W. Scott Elliot, Argyll and Sutherland Highlanders; Thomas B. Smyth, Assistant Curator (Regional Head Quarters), the Black Watch, Perth; and Lt Col (retired) A.A. Fairrie, Queen's Own Highlanders (Seaforth and Camerons). George Moss (1903–90) and James Laidlaw, neither of whom I met, generously sent me correspondence that adds importantly to the manuscript.

My thanks as well to Dr Peter Anderson and Mrs Jane M. Hill, National Register of Archives (Scotland); Peter G. Vasey, Stuart Allan, Martin Tyson, Dr N.J. Mills, and Dr Tristram Clarke at the Scottish Record Office, HM General Register House, Edinburgh; Dr Louise A. Yeoman, National Library of Scotland; Colin A. McLaren, University Archivist and head of Special Collections, King's College, Aberdeen; Iain Gray, Aberdeen City Archivist; Roy Wentworth, Gairloch, Bridget Mackenzie, Lednabirichen, Dornoch, Tearlach MacFarlane, Glenfinnan, Ian Fraser, School of Scottish Studies, Dr C.W.J. Withers, Department of Geography, Edinburgh University; the late John Lorne Campbell and Margaret Fay Shaw Campbell, Canna.

I am also grateful to A.V. Griffiths, Keeper, and Paul Goldman, Assistant Keeper, British Museum (Prints and Drawings); Dr Frances Harris, Department of Manuscripts; R.J. Chesser, Assistant Music Librarian, British Library; and to several professional and amateur historians, librarians, and archivists, civil and military, who helped in various quests, notably the vain searches for certain military records that are known to have existed of James Wolfe's circuit of military policing with the 20th Foot in the Highlands in the early 1750s, and for the Forbes of Invererman Manuscripts which were extant c. 1895 but seem now to be lost also.

In Maritime Canada, Allan C. Dunlop, Public Archives of Nova Scotia, Halifax; Marilyn Bell, Public Archives of Prince Edward Island; Kathleen MacKenzie, Archivist, St Francis Xavier University (St FXU), Antigonish, Nova Scotia; Maureen Williams, Special Collections, St FXU; Dr Ken MacKinnon, Saint Mary's University, Halifax (for generous help with the Coll MacLeans and Rankin pipers and for personal insights into the piping scene in PEI in the later nineteenth century); Mary MacRory, Kirsten Mueller (retired), David C. Cumby, Eric Stackhouse, Mildred Carrigan *et al.*, Eastern Counties Regional Libraries, Mulgrave, Nova Scotia, and Irene Burns, Ann Campbell, Rilla MacLean and Therese Reynolds in Port Hawkesbury; Drs Edward Pencer and Ken Den Heyer, St FXU; Tom Kearsey, former Principal, Nova Scotia Community College, Nautical Institute Campus, Port Hawkesbury, and Betty Campbell (for use of computer equipment); Dr Ray MacLean, Lanark, Antigonish County; A.A. MacKenzie, Merigomish, Pictou County; Joe Neil MacNeil, East Bay and North Sydney, Cape Breton – the last great Cape Breton *seannachaidh*, MacNeil died on 14 October 1996; the late James MacKay, Kingsville, Inverness County; Effie Rankin, Mabou, Inverness County; and Ronald Angus MacDonald, Antigonish, Nova Scotia.

In Canada I wish to thank Timothy Dubé, military archivist (state and military archives, MS division), and Denise Rioux and Paul Lemieux, reference archivists, National Archives of Canada; Mary Bond and Michele Jackson, reference and information services, and Sandra Burrows, newspaper specialist, National Library of Canada; Benoît Cameron, and, earlier, Russell Spurr, Royal Military College, Kingston, Ontario; and Dr Gerry Redmond, Nanaimo, BC, whose studies of sports history are very valuable. I must also acknowledge the wise and kindly suggestions made concerning the first manuscript made by Prof. Hugh MacCrimmon, University of Guelph, Guelph, Ontario.

In the US I am indebted particularly to Jesse R. Lankford, Jr, Assistant State Archivist, Raleigh, North Carolina, who drew my attention to contemporary evidence of Highland pipers at and just before the battle of Widow Moore's Creek Bridge in 1776; to Michael J. McAfee, Curator of History at the West Point Museum, for a photocopy of a published photograph of the 79th New York State Militia in Manhattan in 1860 and for insights into pre-Civil War New York militia establishments, and to Peter Harrington, curator of the Anne S.K. Browne Military Collection at Brown University Library, Providence, Rhode Island.

The Mitred Minuet. Non-clergy: from left, John Stuart, third earl of Bute (1713-1792), piper, Lord North, and Lord Mansfield. The first two were prime ministers of Great Britain, 1762-63 and 1770-82. Part of the cartoon's point is that Bute was a Scot, born in Edinburgh, and the first Tory prime minister under King George. His widespread unpopularity in England is emphasized by his Highland habite, his curious bagpipes, and clearly inept fingering. Artist uncertain, c. 1774 (the time of the Quebec Act). National Archives of Canada, C-038989

Piper Robert Hannah in dress appropriate for 1934. The picture was taken at Cape Smith, Northwest Territories, on 30 July by D.L. McKeand. Collection of Indian and Northern Affairs, PA 102146

The bagpipes used by Colin Fraser, Sir George Simpson's piper. Fraser, lately from the Highlands, accompanied Simpson from York Factory to Fort Langley, New Caledonia, in the summer of 1828, a journey involving birchbark canoe and countless portages and treks. Taken in Chipewyan, Alberta, 1927. Photograph by G.H. Blanchet, PA020213

79th Queen's Own Cameron Highlanders, c. 1915, parading in Winnipeg. A mingling of caricature and brass. Photographer unknown. Used by permission of the Manitoba archives

The piper at the Clandonald picnic (Alberta). The National Archives has confirmed that the piper was holding the instrument under his right shoulder. Photographer unknown, 1928. National Archives of Canada, C-028456

At a picnic at Glendale(?), Cape Breton, in the early 1930s, three old-style Catholic step-dance pipers. From left, Aonghus Dubh Mac Dhòmhnuil (Black Angus MacDonald), Melrose Hill, Allachan Aonghuis Dhuibh Mac a' Pharlain (Little Allan Black Angus MacFarlane), Upper Margaree, and Aonghus Iagan Raonuil Peutan (Angus Johnnie Ranald Beaton), Mabou. Photographer unknown. Given to me by Angus Cù MacDonald, Mabou

Protestant piper Fearchar Beag (Little Farquhar) MacKinnon, Cobb Brook, East Lake Ainslie side. Photographer unknown

PART ONE

*Piping in the Eighteenth Century:
An Unbroken Tradition*

1 Introduction

Gaelic-speaking Scots began emigrating to Nova Scotia by the shipload in the early 1770s, when the rotting old *Hector* from Loch Broom put in at Pictou Roads and disgorged its cargo into the forest. About a decade later, from c.1783 on, these first arrivals were joined by significant numbers of Highland and other Loyalists; there were similar influxes to what later became New Brunswick (in 1784) and to the future province of Ontario. The early emigration to Nova Scotia in 1773 marked the beginning of a long period of British civilian immigration to North America and laid the foundations of what the English hoped would become a defiantly superior British North America that would show the rebellious colonials to the South the imprudence of veering from the British monarchical system.

Included in this transatlantic migration were thousands of Highland Scots who came to various parts of Nova Scotia from about 1790 to the 1840s. They sailed not only from Scottish ports and sea-lochs but, in the case of many Islay people, from Loch Foyle in the north of Ireland. Nobody knows how many there were. The Highlanders were loyal to the British Crown but culturally distinctive. By and large, the English settlers overlooked them and later denigrated Gaelic and discouraged its use in public places, particularly in the emerging education system. In some rustic settings the descendants of these immigrants maintained the Gaelic language for five, sometimes six, generations and with it many of the cultural attributes of their late-eighteenth-century Highland antecedents. It wasn't just the Highlanders' stubbornness that enabled their music and dance to survive into this century in rural Nova Scotia.[1] The strong inclination of the Scotch Gael to practise his ethnically distinctive music and dance was vitally strengthened in the

New World, as it had been in the old, by the participation in those elements of his culture by the Gaelic middle classes.

What is left of native Nova Scotian Gaelic musical pastimes, as Gaelic withers into history in the last decade of the twentieth century, is something of the old step-dancing and an echo of its traditional fiddle music. But in addition to this, and within the memory of most Gaelic-speaking native-born Nova Scotia Gaels, piping once had the same function as fiddling. The bagpipe, like the fiddle, played step-dance music for individual and group dancers. The speed and rhythms required are sufficiently different from the modern form to be remarkable. Often many variations on the same tune evolved and flourished, and those variations, along with the repertoire, contained material unpublished by the modern school. Except for a few modern exponents like Barry Shears and Jamie MacNeil, whose understanding of traditional Gaelic piping superimposes the standard modern form, it has all but disappeared. Unfortunately, few tape recordings were made of the old pipers, and no records; nonetheless, enough is known of the musicians and their music for an understanding of eighteenth-century West Highland piping to emerge. With it comes a new and broader view of pre-emigration Gaelic Highland society and what bound it together until long after Culloden, when many Gaels had had enough of diminishing economic returns and joined the movement west across the ocean.

Arguing the value to Gaelic studies of these anachronisms in music and dance, particularly those found in Nova Scotia, goes against a natural old-country inclination to discount the music and dance of peripheral *Gàidhealtachdan* as spurious, copied, or independently evolved. With few ex-ceptions, piping scholarship in Scotland has neglected the older, more traditional piping of the New World often because there are prominent vested interests in various modern piping forms that originate in nineteenth-century Scotland.

The fact remains, however, that New World piping forms have become unique anachronisms in terms of function, style, and speed (particularly of reel and strathspey playing). The phenomenon raises important questions: did a high proportion of the culture bearers leave the Highlands, and if so, did certain forms of Gaelic instrumental music and dance flourish in rural Nova Scotia until well into the twentieth century when elsewhere they had all but disappeared from Scottish practice and memory by the turn of the century, much earlier in some cases?

To suggest that traditional forms of music and dance were simply overwhelmed in Highland Scotland by newer forms may be true in a general sense but it is insufficient as an explanation, particularly in the light of recent work in both piping and traditional dancing. By 1850 there was a large *Gàidhealtachd* in Canada, particularly in Nova Scotia, whose natural cultural conservatism cannot be ignored. Even in Britain, where Highland society was affected by the vast social changes of the nineteenth century, pockets of proud conservatism remained in the Hebrides and on the mainland where outside cultural influences, such as quadrille dancing, were powerfully resented and effectively resisted. Were such places havens of an unstudied and now-unknown traditionalism in music and dance? Was the music and dance of South Uist, for example, the same as that of Inverness County in Nova Scotia (particularly in places like Bornish) until the early years of this century? If it was (as recent work has proved) how could it have disappeared without a whisper in Scotland? Could Gaels eventually have become so self-denigratory that they deliberately forgot?

A general answer must be sought in the Highland emigrations, and until the demographics of the Gaelic Scotch diaspora are properly studied from a sociological and cultural point of view, important questions must go unresolved. In many places some sort of linkage between Highland community population numbers and class make-up, and the ability and desire of those remaining to hold on to traditional cultural forms, may have to be established before there will ever be a proper understanding of Gaelic culture as it was lived and remembered until a century after English and Lowland Scots law were uniformly applied in Gaelic Scotland in the early 1750s. As a non-statistician, I can only examine the post-Culloden Highland musical scene and the piping of Gaelic Nova Scotia and make the connection between the two. I can make observations on the dances and dancing that piping promoted and thrived on, especially in Nova Scotia. I can infer what the findings mean, but that is all. The full extent of the emigrations, forced or otherwise, from the Highlands of Scotland has yet to be carefully studied. The economically motivated resetting of Highland tacks, or large leaseholdings, that began in many patrimonies soon after the crushing of Gaelic clan/political power in the Highlands and resumed in others much later still has to be properly evaluated from a cultural point of view.

In *The Catholics of Scotland*, Aeneas McDonell Dawson sheds light on one significant impact of the emigrations in Roman Catholic and Protestant Highland communities. He paraphrases a private letter to the Scotch agent at Rome in 1789 from Bishop Ranald MacDonald about the plight of Catholic clergy in the Highlands. His concern points to the simple but important fact that it was the poorest in the communities who were left behind and the middle and upper middle classes who were able to go:

500 Catholics had lately emigrated to St John's Island (now Prince Edward's) and Quebec; and that 600 of South Uist were ready to follow them in the spring. This emigration greatly diminished their congregations, and some of the Highland missionary priests were in consequence, reduced to great distress. A sufficient number

of their flocks remained to require their ministry; but these were themselves among the very poorest" ... "The emigrants to America, meanwhile, were not left spiritually destitute. The Bishop, yielding to the importunities of the Highland settlers in St John's Island, had permitted Mr Angus McEachern, "a valuable young man," to go out to them.[2]

Another Catholic clergyman, Bishop Hay, with much the same concern for the capacity of communities to support local clergymen, wrote the following to the Scotch agent in Rome on 18 February 1792:

Accounts have been received from our last Summer emigrants. They went to Nova Scotia, were kindly received, got a year's provisions, and so much land from Government for each family. This encouragement has set others upon following them, and we hear that subscriptions are going on for a new emigration this year. There are many, however, of the poorer sort, who, not being able to pay their passage, are left at home in great misery. Would you believe it? A door is likely to be open for them at Glasgow. Manufacturers there are advancing to such a degree that they cannot get hands to supply. Children of seven years of age may make half a crown or three shillings a week, and others more in proportion ... If ... the emigrations continue for a few years we shall have very few of our people either on the great estates of Clan Ranald or Glengary.[3]

Like Bishop MacDonald, Bishop Hay observes that it is the poor who remained behind, or made it to the the Lowland cities at best. This prompts the question how well leaderless rural Gaels living in an English-language urban environment could maintain their cultural traditions. In addition to the almost total depopulation of whole parishes/patrimonies, how many glens or communities like Strath Glass, Strath Naver, Glendessary, parts of Morar, Glenelg, Glenaladale, Coll, Tiree and Islay, Glenshee, Glen Tilt, Tay-side and Glenquaich, Ushinish and Bornish in South Uist, and many another community from Argyllshire, Perthshire, and Stirlingshire north to Cape Wrath and the Butt of Lewis, whether Catholic or Protestant, were permanently reduced to a handful, if any, of their original natives by the end of the emigrations to North America in the 1840s? When the Glenelg estate was sold in 1811 Coll MacDonell of Barisdale lamented, "Times are most alarming ... Glenelg is sold, the present race must leave it; our first-rate farmers have taken the alarm."[4] Many glens have remained empty for almost two centuries.[5]

Coll MacDonell's alarum about the best farmers came a generation after the emigrations led by the upper middle class had bitten seriously into the fabric of society in Glenelg and elsewhere, particularly during the 1770s and 1790s. Many tacksmen realized their capital and emigrated, taking their tenant farmers with them. Although there are examples from the 1730s,[6] the best known are those who left for "America" from c.1760 until the start of the French war in 1793. Kenneth MacLeod, a tacksman in Glenelg, led an emigration to Glengarry in Ontario in 1793.[7] Alexander MacLeod of Suardalan, Glenelg, left, apparently with his four sons, for Glengarry at about the same time.[8] Captain John MacDonald of Glenaladale, tacksman of Clanranald, who shipped out to Isle St Jean (PEI) in 1772-73, wrote to his cousin Alexander MacDonald that "emigrations are like to demolish the Highland Lairds, & very deservedly."[9]

Captain John, in what was apparently an underestimation of the facts, mentioned a Skye emigration to Carolina the year before his own and alluded to another the year after. Glenaladale's attention to the possibilities of starting again overseas was caught by "emigrations that were carrying on in Argyleshire about Campbellton."[10] John Sinclair's *Old Statistical Account* (1791) mentions an emigration of Appin people to North Carolina in 1775 and another in 1790, after the war. According to the *Weekly Magazine* of 12 August 1773, ten ships from Skye had already sailed or were engaged to sail for America in that year, carrying emigrants from Skye, the Long Island, Glengarry, Sutherland, Ross-shire and other points. When Sir Alexander MacDonald of Sleat renewed the tacksmen's leases in North Uist in 1769 they were higher than the market for kelp and agricultural produce could bear, so the tacksmen amalgamated into a cooperative, realized their capital, bought one hundred thousand acres in South Carolina, and shortly thereafter emigrated. Between 1771 and 1775 over two hundred men, women, and children removed in a typical Gaelic community emigration for the New World, and they were not the first to go to the Carolinas.[11] There are many examples of emigrations like these. Those who left had the choice of staying and paying a higher, but often still manageable, rent.

In 1847 Robert Somers, the *North British Daily Mail*'s special correspondent, found that, apart from a "club tenant" (traditionally Gaelic) farm at Iomair' a' Ghradain and countless coastal crofts, Glenelg proper had been given over to sheep farms. The whole was owned by a Bristol businessman. Somers found one hundred and forty-eight Gaelic families huddled at Kirkton of Glenelg; fifty-seven were landless, the other ninety-one had tiny one-half- to two-acre allotments. The selective removal to British North America by assisted passage of three hundred and forty-four of Glenelg's most destitute Highland people took place in 1849. This was one of many instances of assisted passages paid by a landowner (in this case James Baillie) after the potato famine of 1846-47. It was cheaper to allow or coerce the poor to emigrate than to provide welfare. Once culturally rich, Glenelg changed between 1810 and 1839 into a cultural wasteland.[12]

In Perthshire, which was much easier of access and thus more susceptible to "improving" ideas than some of the more distant and rugged parts of the Highlands, certain glens, such as Glenshee, had been stripped of their Gaelic populations by 1800. Thomas Newte, whose observations were published in London in 1791, saw the terrible effects of the clearances in Perthshire and was "struck with the most unequivocal proofs of depopulation."[13] Even the modern 1:50,000 Ordnance Survey maps, on which two centimetres represents one kilometre, that replaced the old scale of one inch to the mile show examples of shielings and settlements in the Perthshire and other Highlands that have been empty for several generations.

While statistics, formal or not, may show population increases in many communities over several decades from around 1755 until the Old Statistical Account in the 1790s, and from the first official census of 1811, they hide completely the fact that the old Gaelic middle class was altogether gone from these areas by 1820. The effect of this disappearance of the sponsors and supporters of the Gaelic community way of life was tantamount to the crossing of a cultural Rubicon. In an anonymous pamphlet published in 1784 entitled *A View of the Highlands*, it was claimed that between 1763 and 1775 more than twenty thousand Scotch Highlanders emigrated to North America;[14] there are many other estimates and interpretations of the estimates.[15] Given that these were largely tacksman-led family emigrations, the impact, both cultural and economic, on Highland Scotland was profound.

A poignant example of the effect of economic pressures on the cultural life of Highland communities in the early nineteenth century is inferrable from what Col David Stewart of Garth in Perthshire[16] reported of an interview he had with a veteran of the 42d Regiment (the Black Watch). In 1820 or thereabouts, the colonel visited a Highland glen and met a soldier who had served twenty-eight years in the Black Watch, some of that time under Stewart himself. The man's army pension made him one of the best off in his community. Others in the glen told Garth a tale of woe, of income insufficient to meet the increased rents. The old soldier said that when he had joined up around 1790, there had been no dissatisfaction with the ruling class and everyone was content; there was lots of piping and fiddling at the weddings. He said that many of his neighbours were sorry that they hadn't joined the army with him.[17]

Garth was expatiating on the wisdom of a stable policy on the paying of military pensions, saying that recruits (from those who hadn't emigrated) could be much more easily raised if people could see how well old soldiers were treated (which was not, in all cases, very well at all).

The tacksman emigrations from the Highlands tend to be treated as an eighteenth century phenomenon presaging the early-nineteenth-century exodus of thousands of ordinary leaderless Gaels.[18] But after the Passenger Act (1803), continued emigrations were inadequately recorded and the outflow of the Gaelic middle class after the end of the Napoleonic Wars was not officially described and was generally overlooked. The data are diffused through countless local and family histories in Scotland and in countless archives and other sources in the New World. Yet a look at these sources immediately dispels the widely held opinion that only poor, illiterate, and unilingual Gaels emigrated in the first half of the nineteenth century.

Gaelic middle-class emigrations, which continued through the first half of the nineteenth century, were more gradual and prolonged than important published work on the tacksman-led emigrations of the early century suggests. Substantial tenant farmers,[19] army officers, clerics and other middle-class Gaels came to North America in the first half of the nineteenth century. As a class they were variable in terms of wealth, importance, perceptiveness, and readiness to start afresh. While many important MacLeod tacksmen had left Skye and Glenelg by 1776, others were still quitting their traditional patrimonies in the 1820s. Aonghas Og, chief of Glengarry, sold the bulk of his encumbered estate in c.1840 and emigrated to Australia (later returning to Knoydart, which he had retained); Raasay went to Australia in 1846, after the majority of ordinary Gaels had been cleared from the community that Samuel Johnson had found so warmly traditional over seventy years earlier. And according to the Coddy, "all the Barra tacksmen emigrated to North America between 1780 and 1830, except the MacNeils of Vatersay."[20]

Where Australia is concerned, records of the Highland and Island Emigration Society, which show, for example, that five thousand Highlanders received assisted passages to Australia between 1852 and 1857, emphasize the post-1850 emigrations of the destitute and inevitably overshadow earlier movements. Brander's work in 1982, non-statistical as it is, stated that "throughout the 1820s there was a marked influx of small tacksmen with Highland retainers."[21] However minor these leaders were, they and their retainers were still eager and able to finance the much larger cost of sailing to Australia than to North America.

Broadly speaking, then, Highland emigration can be divided into at least three categories. Firstly, there are the emigrations led by the upper middle class that were studied by Bumsted, in *The People's Clearance* (1982), which was limited to Scots who went to America between 1770 and 1815. Then there are the chronic emigrations of the less well heeled middle-class Gaels whose emigrations are casually associated with the first half of the nineteenth century. Lastly, there are the emigrations of the poorest folk who were more or less forced to move. The expansion of sheepfarming is rightly associated with the first two categories, but the poorest Gaels also had to contend with the deer-forest/game-shoot syndrome described by journalist Robert Somers.

Somers theorized convincingly that the clearing and dumping of countless impoverished Gaels – either into tiny coastal communities where they were allowed to hold (without a lease) a pendicle called a "croft," or in planned towns like Kingussie, Kinloch Rannoch, and Newtonmore – was a blatant procedure offering people who, it was hoped, would emigrate a temporary place to live. He interpreted the setting up of crofts as a greed-induced expedient to get rid of the last embarrassing impediments to the new Gael-less Highlands. These people were written off as useless and without economic function. Thousands left at their own expense or at the expense of their landlords or the public.[22]

When non-chiefs bought the old estates, heartless greed combined with careless ignorance of the Gael prompted further emigration and the dispersal of an intricate web of kin around the world. Those who chose to stay in Scotland and rented holdings from the departed tacksmen must have suffered major disruptions. For many of them their security became fragile as the clan's military function disappeared. The abolition of the Heritable Jurisdictions did not always impose foreign law through an outsider; often, legal power was simply reinvested in the traditional landowner/chief, so really biting change only came when the latter decided to manipulate improver law for his own acquisitive ends. The abolition of ward holding, taxed (cash commuted) and black (simple), and its replacement by "blanch and feu holdings"(see the Act for taking away the Tenure of Ward Holding in Scotland, and for converting the same into Blanch and Feu Holdings, 20 Geo. 2, 1746), which began as a paper threat, marked the end of landholding for military service in the Highlands. All of this has to be reviewed before a truer picture of the emerging neo-Gaelic society in the Highlands can be formed. Sometimes, however, kin did manage to resettle in the Highlands, so that the old relatedness and social values survived. When such communities were sufficiently isolated from the industrial revolution, the old way of life quietly persisted until late into the twentieth century.

Traditionally there was a strong element of disinterested benevolence on the part of the powerful in old Highland society. Considerate treatment of the less fortunate was essential and commonplace in a hard agricultural/fishing environment. So too was the corollary, the reverential treatment given chiefly landlords and their middle-class representatives by Highlanders time and again after the 'Forty-five. Samuel Johnson applauded the idea of benevolent chiefs, an idea that still survived in places like Raasay in 1772, and excoriated those who forsook the old ties in favour of impersonal profit-driven agriculture.[23] This benevolence of leader towards led certainly was common to many tacksmen and their equivalents in the old Gaelic middle-class, including Catholic clergy, military officers, and large tenant farmers in the last forty years of the eighteenth century and on into the middle of the nineteenth.

In the early years under English law in the *Gàidhealtachd*, not all middle-class Gaelic-speaking leaders were bilingual or literate, which in part explains their cleaving to conservative social and economic habits. This is not to say, however, that they were utopians. Many retained the old Gaelic attachment to commissioned service in the army (not necessarily Britain's), for which it was beneficial to retain the old rural populations from whom soldiers were easily recruited and commissions obtained. (In Britain the last battalions raised under this system were the Second Battalions of the 78th Ross-shire and 79th Cameron Highlanders, both of which were raised in 1804. Colonelcies were equally appealing to many chiefs long after their Gaelic consciousness had deserted them. But by the end of the Napoleonic Wars in 1815 when, among other things, the British army was reduced in size, stocking the military was no longer a reason to retain rural Gaelic communities. In any case, new economic forces compelled further thousands of Gaels to emigrate to the New World, weakening forever the traditional ways of life and music in the Old World.

Thus, when more is learned of the emigrations of Highland families, and particularly of the socioeconomic make-up of the emigrants and their kinship relationships, a picture emerges of the gradual, rather than catastrophic, decline of Gaelic society and culture. When these data are combined with information on surviving traditional music and dance, which is unique now to the Nova Scotian *Gàidhealtachd*, then the subtle cultural forces that bound all classes of old Gaelic society together will be better understood.

As it is, the work of Scottish scholars has tended to be limited by a lack of (or lack of interest in) detail about New World immigrations. The underlying and controlling factors of British politics and economics, the improver philosophy in essence and in effect, are well known and the written record of actual emigrations is sufficient to make a credible starting case, but a hundred seemingly unimportant gaps remain. Walker's statistics,[24] Sinclair's *Old Statistical Account*, and local observations of emigrations from Gaelic Scotland are often mentioned but seldom as part of any complete study of Highland emigration. Scientifically imprecise, they form an inadequate foundation for inference or speculation without corroborating support from other sources.[25]

The best work done in North America has been as thorough but has taken a regional, or otherwise limited, approach. Valuable extrapolations about Highland society during the emigration years have been made, notably by Bumsted in *The People's Clearance* and in Mariane McLean's *The People of Glengarry* (1991), but accurate data from all available sources has not yet been put together. It may never be, since the underlying complexity has to do with genealogy, with an impossibly complicated web of relationships built up over hundreds of years. What we have is still a body of research waiting to be collated and assessed *in toto*. Those who write about diasporas face the problem of having to collate material from widely distributed sources. Highlanders went almost everywhere when they finally made the break and left Scotland, and to find out what really happened to the Gaelic way of life in the Scottish *Gàidhealtachd* and what their social world was like is going to require the assembling of an immense quantity of minutiae from far and near.

In the meantime, one introductory way to come to terms with the older Gaelic way of life is by scrutinizing the cultural anachronisms (spoken Gaelic, story and song, music and dance) retained by the foreign descendants of the emigrants found in places like Gaelic Cape Breton and deducing what once flourished in Highland Scotland. Of what must have been several thriving New World *Gàidhealtachdan*, from Australia to the Carolinas and north to Nova Scotia, it is only in Nova Scotia that Gaelic language and consciousness still survive, albeit in parlous condition. For there isolation has guaranteed conservatism and preserved some of the keys to the Old World.

It should be said that while the subject of this book is piping, it could just as easily have been about traditional fiddling or dancing. In fact, dancing is inextricably bound up with the popular Highland music of Gaelic Nova Scotia because it is the demands of the dance that gave traditional Scottish Gaelic instrumental (and often vocal) music in the province's *Gàidhealtachd* its now-unique distinctiveness. Alas for cultural diversity, the last of the old-time traditional fiddlers and dancers are dying out in Cape Breton, along with their mother tongue. Surface impressions of vibrant Scotch Gaelic fiddling are deceptive; the actual number of Gaels playing traditional fiddle music in Nova Scotia is very small. However happy the melodies the few last Gaels play, they are part of a civilization's keening. There are almost no Gaelic-speaking pipers of the old school left who can pipe for traditional Scottish step-dancing.

In this work I have chosen not to rely much on the names of famous pipe tunes, particularly pieces of *ceòl mór*, as being indicative of a piper, a piping family, or a tradition of piping in a certain area. Since pipe tunes were first published in about 1800, many have been renamed for one reason or another, so that the provenance and composer of many tunes are impossible to establish categorically. For example, there is no reason to think that piping was anything but popular in Cameron country during the period 1745-81, but the hard evidence is scanty and a case can only be made by inference from other data. Discussing the various pieces of *ceòl mór* associated in modern publications with Clan Cameron only repeats old legends and complicates matters. If, however, there is any new reason to forward the argument for piping, from unconsidered lore or from a military point of view for example, that I will use.

The background work in the first part of the book is complicated but it had to be. Some important documentation was either not made or is missing for the immediate post-Culloden period, a lack that has been repeatedly exploited by the wishful thinking and unscholarly, including a few eminent and well-educated Scotsmen, who promote a fanciful theory about piping. Assembling from other sources the evidence that any honest reader must consider has had to be very thorough and as nearly exhaustive as possible.

2 The Roots of Jacobitism and the Disarming Act

In 1755 Dr Alexander Webster calculated the population of Scotland to be over 1,265,000. From Webster, according to T.C. Smout, in that year "just over half the people had lived north of a line from the Firth of Tay to the Firth of Clyde."[1] Allowing for the small but growing towns of Aberdeen and Inverness and the rest of the mostly English-speaking eastern fringe from the Tay to Inverness and further north in Caithness, we are left to assume that the Gaelic-speaking population of Scotland was about half a million people, most of them unilingual.

Gaelic society was a class society like rural England's and Lowland Scotland's but with significant distinctions. Firstly, Highland society was, and remains, intensely preoccupied with kinship. Secondly, it enjoyed a refinement inasmuch as inter-class relations were familiar and governed by a system of hospitality, understanding, and kindness extending *de rigueur* from the better-off to the less-fortunate Gael, both civilly and militarily, as well as from everyone to visitors. Even natural enemies of the Gaelic Scot found themselves remarking time and again upon this exceptional mannerly generosity. Highlanders were proud of this trait. Unfortunately, their understandable pride, particularly in kinship and in military prowess, was a strong contributing factor to the widespread sense of *hauteur* that any occupying force soon discovered. The poorest adjudged themselves "gentle" enough by virtue of some distant ancestral link to someone prominent. This impenetrable sense of personal superiority generally deepened any vengeful cruelty meted out to defeated Highlanders in the 1745 rising of the Jacobites.

Although Lowland Scots and Englishmen generally were ignorant of Scotch Gaels, they had certain things in common. A background for the his-

torical and cultural affairs of the second half of the Highlands in the eighteenth century must focus on these similarities and linkages, which are
found primarily in political and religious philosophy.[2]

Gaels considered themselves the true Scots (and the earliest bringers of
Christianity to Scotland), while the Saxon elements in the Lowlands were
seen as newcomers. By and large they were right: after all, almost all linguistic and other obvious traces of late Mesolithic and Neolith people, Picts,
and Britons in Scotland were long gone, and the Scandinavian presence was
generally limited to the northern islands where Norn was spoken. Even Lowlanders who denigrated Highlanders as uncultured superstitious savages
(often papistic), thieves and tribalists, and who called them "Erse" as though
they were *Untermenschen*, were simply in their heart of hearts accepting the
Gaels' valid claim. From just as weak a psychological stance came the contradictory "We are all Scots together." This must have left Gaels with a feeling of cynical contempt since in 1707 the Saxon Scots had been instrumental in the union of the Scottish and English parliaments, throwing away centuries of hard-won Scottish independence. Union had been forced on Scotland by the threats of an English trade embargo, the legal taking of Scottish
trading vessels in English waters, and alien status for Scots. Under the threat
Scotland, noble and common, Highland and Lowland would have voted
Jacobite. The union was hated by most Highlanders and Lowlanders alike.[3]
Those Gaelic Scots who had little trade with England and who felt themselves ignored in all national affairs had strong reasons to be angered by
their political subsumption into Westminster.

The union of the parliaments was accomplished hurriedly and in slightly
clandestine conditions during the reign of deposed King James VII's daughter, the childless Queen Anne, who held the throne from 1702 to 1714. But
the roots of the problem were more complicated. The Stuart king James VII
of Scotland (James II of England) died in exile in September of 1701 when
the reigning monarchs of England, Scotland, and Ireland were William of
Orange (1650-1702) and his wife Mary, James VII's daughter and Charlotte's sister. While in exile, James VII signed a grand alliance with King
Louis XIV of France in which the French king recognized James's son as
James III of England (and VIII of Scotland). However meaningless the document was,[4] it encouraged Jacobite hopes in Britain to flourish, then linger,
because of the implied potential for French military help. In the same year,
William of Orange signed the very meaningful Act of Settlement, which
established the Protestant Hanoverian succession for England, Scotland, and
Ireland. This act became the cornerstone of Whig political rationale until the
late 1750s.

The Scottish reaction to the union was strident and the English Whig reaction was predictably fearful. Then in 1708 a French fleet set sail from
Dunkirk Roads for Scotland with 6,000 men and 13,000 stands of arms for

the Jacobites, only to be driven out of the Firth of Forth by Admiral Sir George Byng. In England there was panic and a run on the bank. French lack of conviction, however, doomed this first attempt for King James – an attempt that would have received by far the greatest Scottish support of all the risings. Men of substance were riding towards Edinburgh with a gleam in their eyes to effect change. When failure came, the immediate Whig reaction was to take repressive measures against the principals. Lowland peers and Highland chiefs went to prison in Edinburgh and Stirling Castles. The duke of Hamilton and other powerful Scots were taken to London but subsequently released. Among the Gaels incarcerated in Scotland were MacDonnells of Keppoch and Glengarry, Stewart of Appin, and Ewen Cameron of Lochiel (aged over eighty). Five Lowland lairds from Stirling were tried but eventually won "not proven" verdicts (something less than "not guilty" but liberating nonetheless). Highland and Lowland Scotland had common cause against a regally inspired régime that championed, by an act of the English, not Scottish, Parliament, the German son of a daughter of King James VII over his son.

One of the saddest realizations for the Highland and other Scots Jacobites who took arms for King James in 1745 was that there would never be any sizeable military rising of the English Jacobites. The Scots had had to force themselves into imagining thousands of English anti-Whigs and Roman Catholics and other Jacobites ready to join the cause. That belief was fuelled by knowledge of the attitudes and actions of the nervously dominant Whig party in English politics in the early decades of the century and its seemingly unshakeable position of power,[5] and by minor but encouraging English involvement in the 1715 rising.[6] (Under the union, Scotland was dominated by Whig governments in London until 1762, when the earl of Bute formed the first Tory government).

The Protestant Hanoverian succession began with King George I in 1714, and the Scottish, and some English, Jacobites rose. The dilatory attempt at the restoration of King James III in 1715, led by John Erskine, earl of Mar, came to nothing against the forces of the Hanoverian duke of Argyll. The Jacobite rising in 1719, which involved the landing in Glenshiel of Spanish Catholic troops that had sailed from Cadiz,[7] was easily snuffed out. Among those Gaelic tribes to take the lesson to heart and to stay out of future Jacobite dreamings were the few remaining Jacobite Campbells under Glenlyon and Glendaruel, the MacDougalls in Lorne, and the MacKenzies in Ross-shire and Lewis, as well as several chiefs whose clans ignored them and went "out" in 1745. These included Stewart of Appin, MacDonnell of Glengarry, MacDonald of Clanranald, and many Grants and MacIntoshes.[8]

The Protestant MacDonalds of Skye and North Uist stayed neutral in 1745, having been in the front line at Sheriffmuir in Scotland, where the main battle between Mar and Argyll occurred in 1715, under the leadership of two brothers of the chief, Sir Donald MacDonald of Sleat. Sir Donald, with a wary eye on his patrimony, was a Jacobite who had made his private arrangements and then wisely answered the official summons to Edinburgh. The Protestant MacLeods were also present at Sheriffmuir in substantial numbers, although MacLeod of MacLeod had been prevailed upon by Forbes of Culloden to stay out. Both the MacLeods and MacDonalds of Sleat kept their estates in 1715 while others, like Seaforth (MacKenzie) lost theirs. It was in reaction to the 1715 rising that the Whigs and Hanoverians enacted the first Disarming Act on 1 November 1716 (1 Geo. 1), on which the more notorious Disarming Act of 1746 was based.

By 1745 Jacobite hopes had shrunk, with reason, but were not even then confined to Gaelic Scotland. Thirty years had passed since Sheriffmuir. The Whigs were still in power but the Stuarts were still something of a rallying point as distaste for Whig government, unhappiness at serving a German king, and anger at the act of union persisted. Moreover, the first Disarming Act had proved ineffective, and during the second rising chiefs found ways to avoid forfeiture. Certainly the tenantry, from the middle class down, was not threatened by this measure. Many of the duke of Argyll's MacLean tenants from Mull and Morvern, for example, rose under their tacksmen to fight for Prince Charles (1720-88) in 1745. Appin and Glengarry men were present too, although not under their chiefs. It is true also that the 1745 rising was not by any means confined to that one group of Highlanders who were most unjustly treated in Britain, the Roman Catholics.

Roman Catholics were persecuted to the point where in order for clan lands to be legally handed down patrilineally, as was the custom, the leadership had to abjure its religion. In Scotland, however, there was also legal discrimination against Episcopalians. For Catholics in particular, relative immunity to Church of Scotland power and anti-Catholic laws was, as late as 1745, at times won by independent armies that Catholic leaders and leaders of Catholics could command.[9] The Highlands were all but *terra incognita* even to Lowlanders.

In philosophical terms, defining Whigism is more difficult than defining Toryism. The maintaining of the Act of Settlement and of bringing some kind of determined stability to British political and economic life from 1721 until 1742 preoccupied Sir Robert Walpole. It is generally held that Walpole's single-minded resolution in maintaining the Crown and its settlement, in the absence of any clear political principle and in an age of intrigue and corruption, was the necessary labour for a future time when there would inevitably be the luxury of political principles in a country that would join in the leadership of Europe. For his success in this, for his encouragement of trade and industry, and for his mercantilist colonial policy, the self-aggrandizing Walpole is praised. His and the Whigs' long tenure and their ability to ensure the Protestant settlement through whatever corruptions allowed for national distaste at the earlier political and religious disturbance in Britain. Almost everyone in England was bone-weary at the Stuart question. Nothing more than nostalgia for James could be stirred, except in the most fervid quarters.

Where religion is concerned the Scotch Highlander's situation could be especially difficult if he did not choose to belong to the Church of Scotland because Scotland's post-Reformation Christianity was more radically changed than England's. By reason of bloody and chronic religious strife since the Reformation in the sixteenth century, Scotland's Calvinistic Presbyterianism in the early eighteenth century gave to non-Presbyterians the strong appearance of being unforgiving, intolerant, reactionary, fearful, and dictatorial. The Church of Scotland nonetheless was the established church and was politically powerful by hard-won right.

Not all of Gaelic Scotland had been Presbyterianized, however, and Roman Catholicism had both survived and been effectively encouraged in the southern Outer Hebrides and, from Ireland in the seventeenth century, in pockets on the western mainland after the Reformation to the point where several populous Gaelic tribes were defiantly Catholic in 1745, and feared. Many others, including the MacKenzies and Appin and Glencoe people, clung tenaciously to Episcopalianism into the 1720s and on, in some places, into the early nineteenth century. The Episcopal church had deep Scottish roots and was also feared, resented, proscribed, and rigorously denied a right to full existence by the powerful established church. In 1746 an anti-Episcopalian act demanded that by 1 November 1746, all episcopal ministers had to prove that they had taken the oath of allegiance to King George II. Episcopal membership, like Catholic membership, was all but forced to be Jacobite.

Thus, while James's claim to the throne in 1715 and 1745 was obviously the superior claim, his association with Catholicism had ended the Stuarts as a dynasty in the male line. In Scotland, where even the mention of Catholic emancipation in the 1770s generated public rioting in Edinburgh and Glasgow, the Catholics were the most disaffected. Others who were likeminded included the unwise who had no legal claim to anything other than a renter's right to someone else's land. Among these were the MacLeans and Camerons in Mull and Morvern, the MacGregors in Hanoverian Campbell country, and the Keppoch MacDonnells who continued to hold their traditional lands in Lochaber by recourse to military threat.

However much cause Gaelic Catholics might have with English Catholics, the first obstruction was the established Presbyterian church in whose dominance England wisely preferred to acquiesce. The second vital problem was that Highland Catholics were keenly aware of European Catholicism, having had to educate their children in France, Italy, Spain, and elsewhere. Many Catholic gentlemen served overseas in the armies of Catholic European countries. In the eyes of settlement Hanoverians and Presbyterian Scots alike, Highland Catholics were a dangerous fifth column. In Presbyterian minds Episcopalians marched in the same column.

During Prince Charles's Jacobite rising of 1745 for his father, James VIII (James III of England), although his Scottish army was by no means completely Catholic, there was a sufficient Catholic presence to render the cause senseless without massive help from France. Such assistance would have to have coalesced anti-Whig and anti-union Britons, risen above the deepest religious divisions, and then left the people of two countries to effect governments, and that was the sort of selfless interference that no king or government could give. Even with French assistance, anti-French sentiment in England was everywhere refined and had been since Marlborough's European campaigns in Queen Anne's day, and the chance of a Tory rising as a Jacobite and fighting alongside Frenchmen was minute. Charles himself was nominally a Catholic. He claimed French Catholic support, which always was more tantalizing than real. France was deeply involved, under Marshall Saxe, in fighting the British under the duke of Cumberland (1721–1765) in northern Europe in 1745 when Prince Charles launched his attack on England from Hanoverian-occupied Scotland. France's animus against England (and others) in Europe, along with the gift of money, was all the help Prince Charles's Jacobites should reasonably have hoped for and all they got. Charles landed soldierless in Moidart in 1745, a risky move that could only result in military disaster.

That the defeat of the Jacobites in the 1745 campaign might play a part in the eradication of Scotch Gaelic identity – linguistic, political, legal, and cultural – was foreseen by no one. Had it been, then either many more Scotch Gaels would have taken up Charles's cause, with or without their chiefs, or none would have, the risk being much too serious. Nonetheless the belief has endured in Scotland and elsewhere that all of those cultural losses to Gaelic Scotland were more catastrophic than gradual in nature and were precipitated by the battle of Culloden and the failure of Prince Charles's attempt to restore his father to the throne of the United Kingdom. The convenient, and relatively unimportant, rationale for this erroneous notion is the Disarming Act of 1746, which I will come to below.

In England, from a Protestant Hanoverian standpoint, stirring up outrage and resistance in 1745 was a propagandist's dream. The English Catholics and Tories stayed at home, having shown no evidence that they would ever fight the Hanoverian Protestant settlement, now thirty-one years old, in numbers sufficient to make a difference. In Scotland there was ambivalence. The Stuart kings, after all, were originally Scottish and could promise the hope of preferment and restoration of a Scottish parliament; the Whigs, including the Campbells and Munros among the Gaels, not to mention the Scottish regiments of the line, were defending an alien who condescended to Scotland as a backward, insignificant, and troublesome place. Within living memory Scotland – or North Britain, as Englishmen and many a Scot contemptuously called it – had become a relatively unimportant part of England. Most Scots stayed clear of the rising, including the Protestant MacDonalds, MacLeods, and MacKenzies, while the duke of Argyll, Scottish political leader and Hanoverian appointee, involved the Campbells actively in cleaning up the inevitable mess. The Skye MacDonalds and MacLeods and the Ross-shire Munros (through independent companies) became active Hanoverians once the Jacobite threat had been largely disposed of in 1746. More will be said about ex-Jacobite loyalty to the House of Hanover in the next chapter.

In the European war of the Austrian succession(1740–48), France's Marshall Saxe fought King George II's son William Augustus, duke of Cumberland. When the essentially Highland Jacobite army rose, occupied some of Edinburgh, and routed Sir John Cope near Prestonpans outside Edinburgh in 1745, Cumberland was diverted from the European action to defeat his distant cousin who had managed, with almost no English or French assistance, to reach Derby, never having taken any Scottish military fort of any size. Edinburgh and Stirling were still garrisoned by Hanoverian troops, and later, when the Jacobites tried it, they couldn't reduce Fort William in the heart of Jacobite Lochaber.

When Cumberland reached Scotland in the winter of 1746 after General Hawley's signal defeat by Prince Charles's forces at Falkirk, he was determined to put an end to Jacobitism once and for all and get on with the European war. The policy he adopted was conciliatory to the common soldier if he turned himself and his arms in (the Duke's Proclamation, 24 February 1746). Otherwise Cumberland aimed at two things: the military defeat of the Jacobites and the chastising of the Jacobite leadership and soldiery through the legal process; and the immediate impoverishment of the leaders by destruction of homes, barns, boats, and agricultural equipment and the confiscation of family records.[10] Destruction of property began before Culloden and continued apace thereafter, legally and illegally (although the distinction is hard to define).

At Culloden near Inverness in April 1746, Cumberland finally did what Cope and Hawley had failed to do. He systematically destroyed enough of the Jacobite army to be able to march fairly confidently into the heart of Jacobite Gaelic Scotland, although he was aware of risks. Most of the MacDonalds took no action from their left wing at Culloden and marched off in main force, armed, protecting the remnant of Prince Charles's army from the pursuing dragoons (an estimate of Jacobite fatalities has been put at 1,200).[11] Many immobile wounded and many others on the run were brutally slaughtered, but many more of them were captured. The few French and Irish military people were liberated while the poor Highlander faced harsh imprisonment. Cluny MacPherson, chief of a smaller but dangerous mini-federation of Jacobite Gaels centred in the district of Badenoch to the south of Inverness, never arrived at Culloden and so survived, fully armed and flushed with the last Jacobite victory over southern Perth and Argyllshire forts held by the part of the Campbell militia that had not marched to Culloden. Cluny's men must have been as well armed as the MacDonalds, and there is no question but that Cumberland and his occupying successors understood where Culloden had failed and reacted accordingly.

The entire campaign, then, amounted to about five thousand Highlanders, deliberately and prominently tartaned, being chased by two Hanoverian armies twice their size in northwest England before the final issue was settled. Yet it engendered inordinate fear and trembling in Hanoverian circles. Intelligence was notoriously subject to imagination in 1745 and imaginations magnified both numbers and the vaunted military prowess and un-Christian bestiality of the Highland Scots.[12] Even the scrupulous adherence by Jacobites to Prince Charles's order that they show nothing but kindness to "his" captured subjects at Prestonpans and elsewhere could not refute Hanoverian propaganda.

The British Hanoverian army and its operations were very much Cumberland's and during his few months in the Highlands things went hard for Jacobites, both English and Scots. An act facilitating speedy trials was given royal assent on 19 March 1746. The writ of habeas corpus was cancelled for a further six months (royal assent, 15 April 1746). Captured military deserters from Cumberland's army were summarily hanged. A small number of Jacobite leaders (Simon Fraser, Lord Lovat, and Lord Kilmarnock among them) were caught, tried by British peers, and beheaded. About one hundred and twenty others were hanged at various places in England (at Tyburn, Tower Hill, Kennington Common, Carlisle, Brampton, Penrith, and York), while hundreds of rank and file were doomed to imprisonment in hulks anchored in the Thames and in other gaols. Many of them died. Hundreds of ordinary men were banished to British colonial America.

An Act of Attainder was quickly passed on the same day as an Act of Indemnity for Hanoverian excesses (royal assent, 4 June 1746). The second Disarming Act (19 Geo. 2) and the Anti-Episcopal (Scotland) Act received royal assent on 12 August 1746. Also in 1746 the Tenures Abolition Act became law.

In 1747 the Act of Indemnity (for Jacobites) was passed. It was also known as an "Act for the King's Most Gracious General and Free Pardon," or more simply, the "Act of Grace" (20 Geo. 2, cap. 52). The Vesting Act, which governed the surveying of the forfeited estates, was brought in in the same year, while the Heritable Jurisdictions (Scotland) Act (20 Geo. 2, cap. 43), was drawn up by Lord Hardwicke, lord chancellor of England; it became effective in 1748 at the end of the European war. Also in 1747, 20

Geo. 2, the first amendment to the Disarming Act,[13] extended the deadline for the wearing of Highland dress to 1 August 1748 (a further extension was made under 21 Geo. 2, which is discussed below).

In 1748 the Anti-Episcopal Act was rendered harsher and the Treason Outlawries (Scotland) Act joined the list. Yet another pertaining to treason, passed in May, ensured that treason trials were to be held in Scotland. Finally, 1748 saw passage of the second and last amending act (21 Geo. 2, cap. 34), "An Act to amend and enforce so much of an Act made in the nineteenth Year of his Majesty's Reign, as relates to the more effectual disarming the Highlands in Scotland, and restraining the Use of the Highland Dress." This amendment made no significant alterations to the basic Disarming Act of 1746 but it changed and relaxed some of the penalties pertaining to the arms and clothing clauses. Also in 1748, the king applied his sign manual to the de-weaponing clause[14] of the primary Disarming Act of 1746.

This amending act of 1748, like that of 1747, contained no mention of bagpipes. According to a librarian at the British House of Commons library, "apart from the Act of 1748 ... which qualified the 1746 act, no change was made to these acts in the seven-year term appointed [for weapons]."[15] Nor, according to the same source, was there any entry for pipes or bagpipes in the abridged *Statute Law of Scotland* (1757), which is widely accepted as an authoritative source.

The Disarming Act of 1746 and its two amendments of 1747 and 1748 were written to be as free of loopholes as possible; they are repetitive and difficult reading but, if nothing else, they are explicit. The already complicated subject is made more confusing in that the section of one of the amending acts dealing with cattle theft in Scotland is elsewhere entitled as if it might be a separate act, using the Short Titles Act of 1896, and is dated at 1747.[16] "The Cattle Theft (Scotland) Act, 1747 (Short Titles Act, 1896)" was originally drafted as part of 21 Geo. 2, cap. 34, the second amendment to the Disarming Act.

For some Jacobite landowners the forfeiture of their estates lasted until 1784. The heritable jurisdictions, guaranteed untouchable by article 20 of the Act of Union, were dissolved forever as of 25 March 1748, and that put an end to Highland chiefs' vice-regal military and juridical power.[17] The elimination of ward holding and of the heritable jurisdictions combined to put an end, on paper, to Scotch mini-armies (which originally had been part of government policy to conscript loyal soldiers cheaply). The cattle theft portion of the 1748 act was aimed at reiving and blackmail, elements of the sportive and criminal Gaelic life that, it has been argued, were on the wane by 1745 in any case, but it was also a legal nastiness to rub in the effects of Cumberland's military policy of economic impoverishment. However strict these calculated acts may appear, many of them were paper tigers to the extent that the Hanoverian government had to police them, which was never easy. What is more, the record shows an obvious Hanoverian fear of another Jacobite rising until the early 1750s, which implies a continued potential political and military coherence in occupied Jacobite Scotland.[18]

Once military skirmishing ended a few months after Culloden, and once the 1747 Act of Indemnity cleared them of the chance of answering treason charges, most Jacobite Gaels had become more or less aware of the spate of Hanoverian enactments. But the Disarming Act, which was designed to distress the ordinary Gael (and Scots overall), caught their full attention.

Of all the Hanoverian acts against the Jacobites, the hardest and most unforgiving was the Act of Attainder, which dealt with the movement's leaders. With the exception of the forfeitures act, with which it was closely linked, this was the best reflection of Hanoverian fears that all the legislation aimed at Scotland was either unenforceable or could become so, given a degree of political initiative. After all, the raising of clan mini-armies for service in the Seven Years' War in 1756–57 shows the acts had actually done very little to alter Gaelic consciousness, Gaelic traditional loyalties to chief and tacksman, and love of military adventure. The Act of Attainder condemned a person to outlawry, in this case for treason, quite legally, without any trial. It entailed further "corruption of blood," which meant that one so attainted *and* his descendants lost all rights to rank and title. The attainted forfeited his estate and effects and could neither inherit nor transmit property by descent. He lost all civil rights and, if captured, almost certainly went speedily to a barbarous death at the gallows.

The Act of Attainder affected some eighty Jacobites, including Cluny MacPherson, Lochiel and his brother, Dr Archibald Cameron, and Archibald MacDonell younger of Barisdale. Many escaped to France with Prince Charles. The act was enough to ensure Dr Cameron's execution in 1753 despite appeals to the Crown. Barisdale, in 1754, escaped with his life. Cluny thumbed his nose at the act and only left his native Badenoch in 1755, in deference to Prince Charles's wishes. He had been protected by his well-armed mini-army through whatever rigours there were of Hanoverian military occupation. Cluny's contempt for both the law and the occupying soldiery, which did its devious best to provoke his people to the use of military force, put the promulgated acts into an important perspective. Cluny (and possibly Barisdale) was the only attainted chief to show up the difference between the well-crafted acts of London lawyers and Scotch Gaelic reality. But, as I will demonstrate with reference to the Disarming Act, there were countless almost playful examples at all levels of Gaelic society of the Gael's virility, stubborn independence, and relative immunity to the pathetic occupying forces of the House of Hanover until its efforts were finally abandoned at the opening of the Seven Years' War in 1757.

Impoverished Jacobite Scotland, through all of Hanoverian reaction to the 'Forty-five, retained its pride and freedom to make choices. A potential, but only a potential, to rise again had never been completely extinguished by the military occupation. However, although acceptance by Jacobites of the Hanoverian régime was by 1757 a reality, pride dictated that it be shown voluntarily. It took a major European and American war to make this acceptance obvious to the House of Hanover. The majority of Jacobite clans signalled, particularly through the raising of Fraser's Highlanders by many feared Jacobite family representatives,[19] that the claim to Britain's throne by the Hanoverian line was fair enough. After 1763 there was no real doubt of the loyalty of the majority of Highlanders, and their fidelity to the Hanoverian king in America in 1776 comes as little surprise. Anyone ready to start civil war over rightful kingship had a profound vested interest in the institution.

Thus, scanning the titles of the many anti-Jacobite acts written and promulgated in and after 1745 gives an impression of blanket control and the swift eradication of Scotch Gaelic Jacobitism, perhaps even of some radical aspects of Scotch Gaelic life. But the truth lies elsewhere. My purpose is to consider only the influence upon bagpiping of efforts to put down Jacobitism in Gaelic Scotland, and to do this I must concentrate on the efforts in law to constrain the common man, the Disarming Act of 1746 and, to a lesser extent, its second amending document of 1748. It is the 1746 act that is blamed for the commonly held belief that bagpiping was proscribed under its terms.

Among the immigrants who made their way ashore into the primæval forests from the rotting old square-rigged *Hector* in 1773, there was a Gaelic-speaking Highland piper. In Patterson's history of Pictou County he is listed as "John MacKay, piper, History unknown."[20] Who he was is not certain, although there is speculation that he was a member of the famous Gairloch MacKay piping family.[21] Whether or not he was, the Highlanders who had already gone aboard thought so highly of him that they arranged to cover the expense of his journey to the New World. It is widely assumed that he was known to the majority of the emigrants and that he was a Gairloch man from their own parish.

This man's musical repertoire is unknown, but in light of the fact that the *Hector* settlers were not led by a prominent member of the Gaelic middle class in Gairloch,[22] that classical piping was of limited popularity in the New World, and that it withered away in Nova Scotia in the absence of chiefs, it is fair to assume that he played popular music on the bagpipes, particularly dance music. If he had been given his Gaelic *sloinneadh* (Gaelic naming) and if it had shown that he was a member of, say, the famous MacKay piping family of Gairloch, pipers to the MacKenzie landowners and chieftains there, then he would almost certainly have been trained to play the so-called "great music" of the bagpipes as well.[23]

The noble and classical form of piping has always had narrowly pre-scribed functions and probably a fairly limited audience even in Gaelic soci-ety, except in certain military situations and at funerals and other affairs of the noble class, and it is almost impossible that John MacKay, or whoever he was, would have had his passage paid for him on the strength of his mas-tery of that repertoire alone. The last thing a shipload of emigrants would have wanted was lugubrious music, however differently or faster it may have been played by Gairloch pipers of the time (if indeed it was played faster).[24]

What is more important from the point of view of traditional Gaelic pip-ing in Nova Scotia is that the piper was an active traditional Gaelic musician in the early 1770s. He may have been young enough to have learned his art after 1746, when the Disarming Act is still thought by many to have pro-scribed the bagpipe. In any case, he is an apt starting point for setting the eighteenth-century piping scene in the West Highlands. It is in this time, the second half of the eighteenth century, that Nova Scotian and other New World traditional piping has its origins.

Knowledge of bagpiping and bagpipers in the Highlands from 1746–82 is quite extensive. From a casual reading of the traveller literature it is quite obvious that pipers were ubiquitous. There were, among many others, the Skye MacCrimmons and MacArthurs, the Mull Rankins and the Gairloch MacKays, all of whom flourished during and after Culloden for at least two decades.[25] According to Aeneas Mackintosh of Mackintosh: "The piper had a piece of ground granted to him and his posterity, Rent free, which was secured him tho' the rest of the Estate might be sold or forfeited, for the late Ld. Lovat's piper possesses the spot formerly given him, tho' the rest of the Estate was forfeited."[26]

Then there were characters like Captain Malcolm MacLeod of Eyre, Raasay, and John MacGregor in Perthshire, active teaching pipers who were also prominent Jacobite veterans of Prince Charles's army of 1745–46 and who lived into the 1770s and later; for others only a name remains and for others still, not even that – merely a reference to an anonymous piper. Yet with abundant evidence of pipers in all parts of Gaelic Scotland, Jacobite and Hanoverian, from 1746–82, the misapprehension remains that the bag-pipe had been banned.[27] The belief is still widespread among pipers, who often state categorically and with some national pride that, simply by own-ing a set of bagpipes, one risked some very unpalatable punishment under the Disarming Act. To separate fact from fiction, we must look first at the various acts themselves.

THE DISARMING ACTS

The title of the 1746 Disarming Act begins, "An Act for the more effectual disarming the Highlands in Scotland; and for more effectually securing the

Peace of the said Highlands; and for restraining the Use of the Highland Dress; and for further indemnifying such Persons as have acted in Defence of His Majesty's Person and Government, during the unnatural Rebellion; and for indemnifying the Judges and other Officers of the Court of Justiciary in Scotland, for not performing the Northern Circuit in May, One thousand seven hundred and forty six; and for obliging the Masters and Teachers of Private Schools in Scotland, and Chaplains, Tutors and governors of Children or Youth, to take the Oaths to His Majesty, His Heirs, and Successors, and to register the same."[28]

The document had as its foundation the first Disarming Act of 1716 which, having been found inadequate, was strengthened by another (11 Geo. 1) in 1725. The 1746 act is thus very dense and inclusive. As noted earlier, it too was amended, in 1747 (20 Geo. 2) and 1748 (21 Geo. 2), but the areas to be disarmed remained the same, namely the shires of "Dunbartain" (specifically, "such parts ... as lie upon the East, West and North Sides of Lochlomond, to the Northward of that Point where the Water of Level runs from Lochlomond"),[29] Stirling north of the River of Forth, Perth, Kincardin, Aberdeen, Inverness, Nairn, Cromarty, Argyle, Forfar, "Bamff," Sutherland, Caithness, "Elgine," and Ross.[30]

Although the 1716 act listed "Broad Sword or Target, Poignard, Whinger or Durk, Side Pistol, Gun or other warlike Weapon,"[31] the 1746 act mentions only "Arms and warlike Weapons."[32] The acts specified "persons," regardless of sex. There were exceptions in the 1746 act, to wit, "Peers of this Realm ... their Sons ... any Members of Parliament ... any Person or Persons, who, by the Act above recited of the first Year of His late Majesty, were allowed to have to carry Arms," as well as anyone specifically permitted by the King.[33] In the 1746 document, a first offence was punishable by a fine of fifteen pounds sterling and imprisonment until payment was made. If payment was not made within one calendar month from date of conviction, the appropriate officer was empowered and required to have the perpetrator enlisted as a regular soldier to serve in any of His Majesty's forces in America. Those unfit to serve were gaoled for six calendar months and also until they gave security for two years' good behaviour. The punishment was the same for hiding arms and being an accessory or being privy to the hiding of arms, except that the fine was not less than fifteen pounds and not more than one hundred pounds. Women who had arms illegally were fined and sent to gaol for six months in the tolbooth of the head town.

Conviction for a second offence for having arms and warlike weapons made the perpetrator "liable to be transported to any of His Majesty's Plantations beyond the Seas, there to remain for the Space of Seven Years."[34]

Before looking at the procedure that necessarily preceded enforcement, another significant aspect of the de-weaponing part of the 1746 act (which is found in other words in the 1716 act also) was its effective duration. The

1746 act reads: "And be it further enacted by the Authority aforesaid, That the above Provisions in this Act shall continue in Force for Seven Years, and from thence to the End of the next Session of Parliament, and no longer."[35] No amendment changed this clause. Thus the Disarming Act, where it concerned the bearing of arms, was a dead letter at the end of the session of Parliament that followed 1 August 1753; this, according to the *Journals of the House of Commons*, occurred when the session of 1752–3 was prorogued on 27 September 1753.

Where the method of enforcement of this part of the act was concerned, the procedure was that "His Majesty, His Heirs, or Successors shall, by His or Their Sign Manual, from time to time ... authorize and appoint ... the respective Lords Lieutenants of the several Shires above recited ... [or if the king wished it] ... other Person or Persons"[36] to issue summonses under their respective hands and seals to certain local people directing them to post public notices to the effect that specific people, or any and all people living within the specified area, at a specified day, must "bring in and deliver up" all their arms and warlike weapons. The notices had to be affixed to the mercat cross of each head burgh town, giving eight days notice for delivery of weapons, and on the doors of the churches in the shire or area delineated in the order, between ten A.M. and two P.M. on a Sunday, giving at least four days notice of the delivery date.

Although the clothing part of the 1746 Disarming Act (19 Geo 11) is peripheral to the subject of piping, it cannot be overlooked. The following facts are important. The anti-clothing measures for all those except officers and soldiers in HM's forces were to take effect from 1 August 1747, but the 1747 act to amend the 1746 act prorogued the effective date for enforcement to 1 August 1748, and the exceptions (officers and soldiers) made in the 1746 act were extended in 1747 to include also landed men and sons of landed men. This extension was continued by the 1748 amendment which also extended the period of grace so that the date for enforcement became 1 August 1749, with this proviso: "That nothing in this Act contained shall extend, or be construed to give Liberty to any Person whatsoever to wear or put on those Parts of the Highland Clothes, Garb or Habiliments, which are called the Plaid, Philibeg or Little Kilt, or any of them; but the said recited Act shall, as to the Plaid, Philibeg or Little Kilt take Place, from and after the twenty-fifty Day of December one thousand seven hundred and forty-eight."[37]

The post reports of the occupying soldiery show that efforts at enforcement were made in 1748. Bear in mind also that the clothing clause affected every man and boy in all of Scotland, with the exceptions listed (soldiery and landed men and their sons). What was banned was specified as "the Clothes commonly called Highland Clothes that is to say) the Plaid, Philebeg, or little Kilt, Trowse, Shoulder Belts, or any Part whatsoever of what peculiarly belongs to the Highland Garb; and that no Tartan, or party-coloured Plaid or Stuff shall be used for Great Coats, or for Upper Coats."[38]

Under the 1746 act conviction for a first offence resulted in a prison sentence of six months without bail. A second conviction made the guilty "liable to be transported to any of His Majesty's Plantations beyond the Seas, there to remain for the Space of Seven Years."[39] These penalties, however, never became effective since the amending act of 1748 changed them to one of enforced enlistment in the army. Besides the fact that from 25 December 1748 all males throughout Scotland, except soldiers and landed men and their sons, were affected by this section of the act, the other distinction is that there was no time limitation on the clothing clauses. Notwithstanding, the clothing provisions of the act of 1748 were not long in becoming a dead letter *de facto*, but they remained on the books until 1782.[40] The House of Hanover had been much more frightened of the uniform than of the arms themselves. In light of the fact that the army was reduced by more than half after 1748, the real force of the clothing clauses becomes clear. In Aberdeen, for example, where some, perhaps all clothing infringements were dealt with in the Baillie Court, there are no details of the specific charges in the minutes of that court from 1748-50. The Baillie court records have yet to be analyzed but two sorts exist, the minute books dealing apparently only with civil cases, and the enactment books, which record in detail the bonds of good behaviour given by those arraigned in the Baillie Court in criminal cases. The Baillie court handed down sentences of banishment and transportation, suggesting that Disarming Act infractions probably were handled there and not at the Sheriff court. From 1748–50 only four cases of tartan wearing are included. Even assuming that other cases may remain undetected in the records, this is not a large number.[41] Otherwise, Sir John Carr astutely noted that the anti-clothing decree for the Gael "redoubled his attachment to it [Highland garb]."[42] The act proved very useful when the Seven Years' War began – many kilted Highlanders were impressed in 1757.

Four other facts are pertinent: 1) the act and its amendments make no mention of bagpipes or bagpipers, or any other musical instrument or musician; 2) although the king was entitled "from time to time"[43] to issue his order under his sign manual to the lord lieutenant(s) or others to initiate disarming, this was only done once, on 16 October 1747; 3) the date for the policing of clothing proscription of the 1746 act was prorogued, or postponed, by the act of 1747, and again by the amended act of 1748; and 4) neither the de-weaponing nor the clothing clauses of the act was policed until 1748.

THE MYTH OF PROSCRIPTION

The history of the idea that the bagpipes were proscribed under the Disarming Act, as it has been published in popular piping literature, is a long and interesting one that begins with Donald MacDonald, born in 1749, a piper and pipemaker in Edinburgh in the early nineteenth century. With *ceòl mór* in mind, MacDonald wrote in his preface that "after the Battle of Culloden the Bag-Pipe was almost completely laid aside. In this interval much of the Music was neglected or lost."[44] Without being explicit, MacDonald implied that the Disarming Act was to blame. Although he talked of the bagpipe's having been laid aside, he was discussing *ceòl mór* and not the entire range of pipe music. (Of course, when MacDonald wrote that, he considered himself to be a rare Edinburgh-based exception to the trend.)

One of the earliest statements, perhaps the first, that the Hanoverian courts effectively banned bagpiping in the Highlands came from James Logan (c. 1794–1872), secretary of the Highland Society of London from 1835–38. His book *The Scottish Gaël* (1831) remains an influential work. Logan, who had probably read the trial records of captured Jacobites, wrote that "some of the unfortunate pipers who were taken on the suppression of the rebellion, thought they could effectually plead that, being only pipers, they had not carried arms against his Majesty, but it was decided that their pipe was an instrument of war."[45]

In the present century I.H. MacKay Scobie (1883–1947), who served as a commissioned officer in, *inter alia*, the Seaforth Highlanders, remarked that piping had fallen on "evil days" after 1746 and that the British army had a lot to do with saving it later on.[46] And as late as 1974, the principal of the College of Piping, Seumas MacNeill, wrote, "the situation for piping changed drastically. From 1746 to 1782 to play the bagpipe was a criminal offence punishable by death."[47]

The first published doubt, however tentative, that bagpipes were proscribed under the Disarming Act appears more than a century after Donald MacDonald's first note in 1822, after Seton and Arnot's *Prisoners of the '45* was published in 1928–29. In the introduction to the third edition of *The Kilberry Book of Ceòl Mór* (1969), Archibald Campbell of Kilberry, in half-hearted deference to the obvious survival of Highland piping from 1747–82, wrote, "Whether the repressive act of 1746 [The Disarming Act] was interpreted authoritatively to include the Highland pipe among 'arms and warlike weapons' is not quite clear. But certainly during the earlier years of its enforcement the pipe was heavily discouraged, though possibly allowed to favoured people and to Highland regiments. After the repeal of the repressive legislation, the Highland Society in London instituted a bagpipe competition."[48]

Campbell offered no examples of this "heavy discouragement." What's more, he had to include possible exceptions to the act since he was well aware that at least something of the old traditional *ceòl mór* piping of Gaelic Scotland had obviously survived it, and not all by way of the human voice or the violin.[49] In 1962 Kilberry again straddled the fence when he empha-

sized what he thought to be the importance of the Highland regiments to piping:[50] "At the same time the Regiments became more than ever the mainstay
of Highland piping as they had been ever since the repeal of the Disarming
Act in 1782."[51]

The same notion about exceptions to proscription in the second half of the
eighteenth century features in Francis Collinson's *The Bagpipe* (1975). In a
sweeping generalization about piping after Culloden, he wrote: "The middle
of the eighteenth century brought a crisis in the history of the Scottish Highland bagpipe – a crisis that might well have ended its existence as the national instrument. This was the change in the old Highland way of life after Culloden, and the effects of the Disarming Act which followed the collapse of the
rising."[52] Thus, for Collinson, it is not just the Disarming Act but also the disappearance of the old Highland way of life that was responsible for what he
saw as a "crisis" in piping around 1750. Although he did not elaborate on
what kind of music gave the Highland bagpipes their status of "national
instrument," there is no doubt that Collinson was referring to the classical
form. Collinson's research shows that he was aware of many of the salient
facts about piping, especially *ceòl mór* piping, during the Disarming Act
years. He was aware of the many prominent patronized pipers who could be
found, along with their patrons, throughout the *Gàidhealtachd*, and he even
admitted that the Disarming Act never mentioned the bagpipes at all; but still
he felt constrained to repeat the theory that the bagpipes were a proscribed
weapon under the act. Since Collinson was convinced that the radical changes
in Highland piping were rooted in the second half of the eighteenth century,
he treats the history of the instrument in the nineteenth century as insignificant and overlooks the period from the last great MacCrimmon (Lieutenant
Donald) to the twentieth century, the time of the greatest emigrations.

Having at least partially blamed the act for bringing piping in Highland
Scotland to the point of near extinction, Collinson deliberately leaves his
reader to infer that pipers faced the same penalty for contravening the Disarming Act as men bearing arms or wearing any part of the "Highland
habite": "transportation to any of His Majesty's Plantations beyond the Seas,
there to remain for the space of seven years."[53] Collinson adds that this
amounted to banishment for life since few could ever hope to raise the
money to sail home. He fails to specify, however, that banishment was the
punishment only for second offences against the act, which made one "*liable
to be transported*" to an overseas plantation (my emphasis).[54] That punishment, as will become clear, was no threat at all to Highlanders until 1748;
and from 1748 to 1750 the "Highland Reports" show that the policing officers were doubtful whether even the six-month prison term would be applied
by Lowland legal authorities, many of whom clearly felt ashamed of this
treatment of the Gaels, who then made up a large percentage of Scotland's
population, under English law.

Collinson stopped short of allowing his readership to infer that all piping after 1782 was the novel creation of the Highland Society of London piping competitions and the British army (pipers in the Highland regiments of the period had no official recognition). To begin with, this would have limited his argument to classical piping (*ceòl mór*), although Collinson, like Kilberry, subscribes to the widespread but erroneous belief that the pipers who served, unofficially, in the Highland regiments from 1757 till 1782 were limited either by their officers or by themselves to the playing of classical pipe music, according to the dictates of Highland military tradition. In any case, Collinson eschews the notion that the link with the traditional past was sustained during this period by the many pipers who were old enough to have learned the instrument before Culloden. Like Kilberry he offers other theories but notes nonetheless that "the effect of the Disarming Act upon piping has probably been to some extent exaggerated."[55]

Kilberry (a piper) and Collinson (a non-piper) would both vigorously have defended the position that many pieces of *ceòl mór* originated before 1782 and rejected any suggestion that all twentieth-century piping was at a radical remove from the traditional forms that flourished before Culloden in 1746. Both men were well aware that the modern repertoire included an old core of dance music (for them in name since only recently has light been thrown on what eighteenth-century Scotch Gaelic dancing was), as well as air and march piping. This knowledge committed them to linking the revived forms with the pre-Disarming Act ones. Kilberry, who was the more circumspect about the act and its powers over the bagpipe, mentioned that piping had probably been confined to favoured people and to the Highland regiments from 1746–82. A commonly repeated assumption is that the favoured people were pipers from the Hanoverian clans.

Collinson acknowledged this idea but explains the survival of traditional piping into the nineteenth century at least in part by means of exceptions under the Disarming Act: soldiers in the regular army, fencibles (whose service was limited to the home front), and cattle drovers,[56] for all of whom the bearing of arms was essential and legal.[57] *Ipso facto* no court in the land could uphold any decision that stated that they could be barred from playing an instrument that after all wasn't even named in the act.[58]

Collinson knew that more than classical piping existed before Culloden and that it, too, had somehow survived the proscription. However, since the Highland Society of London was exclusively interested in the revival of classical piping, and since he assumed that regimental pipers must have been chiefs' and chieftains' pipers or else simple offshoots of chiefly pipers and therefore devoted to the classical form(s), he had to find some other explanation for the survival of *ceòl beag*. The one theory that answered his purpose was that of the Highland small-pipes, which will be considered in greater detail later. According to Collinson the chanter and the small-pipes (which he doesn't define) were not specifically proscribed by the Disarming Act, so that through them the art of *ceòl beag* was passed on by irrepressible piping civilians who weren't drovers (as well as by soldiers and drovers).

His two working hypotheses are that Reel dancing to piping in the *Gàidhealtachd* was commonplace during the Disarming Act years, and that Highlanders had a small bagpipe that fell outside the terms of proscription under the act and was used exclusively for dance music. The first hypothesis was correct, although whether dance-music piping was popular all over Gaelic Scotland isn't clear; it is possible that the fiddle was more popular in certain areas, Badenoch and Strathspey for example.

Regarded *in toto*, Collinson's second claim is far less plausible because it begs the question what exactly the instrument was, what its dimensions were, and how common it was. While a variety of bagpipe sizes was in use in Gaelic Scotland at the time, definitely including a smaller-scale bagpipe, the instrument (small-pipes) that, Collinon says, was "so often described in the traditional Gaelic songs of the Highlands"[59] is almost a complete stranger to contemporary Gaelic song.[60]

Any claim by Kilberry and Collinson that the bagpipes were proscribed by the Disarming Act is wrong. Collinson's appeals to the idea that the policing of the act led to profound cultural degeneracy are also incorrect and misleading. This claim rests on the stubbornly held belief that without general and effective schooling in English for Gaels, a small occupying force – first of Gaelic-speaking, then of English-speaking Hanoverian soldiers from the British army – could, in a few summers, virtually wipe out an integral element of Gaelic cultural life.[61] Those who adhere to this belief cite the hanging at York of the Jacobite piper James Reid of Ogilvie's Regiment on 15 November 1746.[62]

The case of James Campbell Macgrigor, piper to MacGregor of Glengyle, is also cited, though less often. He too was tried as a traitor, in this case at Carlisle between 12 and 26 September 1746.[63] He was one of thirty-two who "Pled Guilty when brought to be tried," which in most cases was tantamount to accepting a sentence of death. His fate is not mentioned in *Scots Magazine* but Seton and Arnot list him as prisoner number "409 James Campbell, alias M'Gregor, from Crieff, piper in Glengyle's regiment, tried at Carlisle and transported on 21 Nov 1748."[64]

The sentence of hanging bestowed on James Reid is unique among cases of pipers being tried for high treason in Great Britain, and indeed the significance of the case is misunderstood. Reid the piper was hanged three months and fourteen days after the Disarming Act of 1746 was promulgated on 1 August of that year. His conviction had nothing whatever to do with the act. He was being tried for treason, having been captured in Carlisle as one of that city's garrison.[65] It bears repeating that the act's mandate, where arms were concerned, involved a clearly specified area of Highland Scotland.

Moreover, while the terms of the act date to 1 August 1746 (politically) and 12 August 1746 (royal assent), application of the part of the act pertaining to arms did not begin in the limited area of Gaelic Scotland until the summer of 1748.

King George II applied his sign manual to the appropriate order, and as of 16 October 1747 Lt Gen. Humphry Bland, newly promoted commander of forces in North Britain, was empowered to issue letters of summons to the various justices of the peace of the areas to be stripped of weapons. Bland sent copies of his letter to the JPs on 25 April 1748.

James Reid had been captured in December 1745 as one of the Jacobite occupiers of the English city of Carlisle. Humble piper though he probably was, he had been in active rebellion and went to his execution for that treasonous crime, not for contravening the Disarming Act. However, the court at York ruled with the words that have distorted the history of piping for generations: that "no regiment ever marched without musical instruments such as drums, trumpets and the like; and that a highland regiment never marched without a piper; and therefore his bagpipe, in the eye of the law, was an instrument of war."[66] The harshness of the judge's decision in Reid's case has no doubt added to the confusion; after all, at least six Scottish officers who were left to garrison Carlisle when the Jacobite army retreated north to its final grave were reprieved[67] after being found guilty of treason at their trials, and James Campbell Macgrigor was transported; what's more, the English jury at Reid's trial had recommended mercy. In short, Reid was the victim of judicial inflexibility, outrage, and revenge.

Although it is nowhere stated, Reid's case has almost certainly been emphasized for another reason. If he was an ordinary unlanded man (and it is all but certain that he was), then he faced the choice of drawing lots to see who should be tried for treason and who simply transported without standing before a judge (under the lot system one in twenty of the common folk were chosen to stand trial as traitors, while the other nineteen were transported). As James Logan hinted, if anyone considered that a trial might enable him to avoid both the death penalty and transportation it was surely the non-combatant piper and the impressed man.[68] Reid's plea would appear the more pathetic (as it did to the jury) if he eschewed the chance of life in a foreign land by opting for trial rather than drawing a lot.

The proponents of the idea that the Reid case set a precedent for the Disarming Act enforcers erroneously link what was a post-rebellion trial in an English city for the capital crime of high treason with the application of a calculated, extremely explicit sixteen-page act of the British government that had nothing whatever to do with proscribing the Highland bagpipes and was not enforced until after the Treaty of Aix-la-Chapelle ended the duke of Cumberland's European war in 1748. Not only is there no mention of bagpipes or bagpipers in the act but no pipers were convicted as such under any of the act's published stipulations. The records of the northern circuit of the Justiciary Court for the period 1748-51, for example, show no apprehensions, trials, or convictions of pipers.

Concerning convictions for wearing Highland clothing, few Highlanders suffered impressment under this clause until the outbreak of the Seven Years' War, if the army post records are a fair indication of what happened in the field from 1748–53. And there is no reason to believe that the reports were inaccurate in reporting the obvious readiness to overlook clothing infractions in Scottish courts. The act was never much more than an unenforceable threat. The Justiciary Court records cited above, which deal with cases of rapine, murder, and other serious offences, did include cases demanding banishment, but no piper ever received this sentence during those critical years. No piper was even charged.

For the moment, however, during the period when martial law, or something approximating that, governed Jacobite Gaelic Scotland, when hundreds of ordinary Highlanders were rounded up and imprisoned as armed, and unarmed, traitors to king and country, it is impossible that pipers and fiddlers who were designated simply as soldiers (because that had been their primary occupation) were not among those Jacobite captives who had to endure, or died neglected in the hulks on the Thames and elsewhere. Apart from these unknowns, however, a handful of pipers and fiddlers are identified in *Prisoners of the '45* (they crop up elsewhere as well). Among the hundreds of ordinary men and gentlemen captured by Cumberland's army, only five pipers are listed as captives incarcerated during and immediately after the 1745 rising:

409 James Campbell, alias M'Gregor, from Crieff, piper in Glengyle's regiment, tried at Carlisle and transported on 21 November 1748.

1380 Robert Jamieson, piper in the duke of Perth's regiment, from "Annanshire"; no further information.

1952 Allan M'Donall, piper in Lord Nairn's regiment, "a blind Highland pyper." He was from Argyll and was released under the general pardon.

2800 James Reid, "'Piper Ogilvy's,' executed York 15.11.46.'"

3045 Sinclair, or St Clair, piper of Ogilvy's regiment and Arbroath's town piper. He claimed to have been pressed. He was discharged on 4 March 1747.[69]

Two other pipers are mentioned in *Scots Magazine* in 1746. Nicolas Carr, a piper in the regiment of John Gordon of Glenbucket, deserted at Carlisle on the march south. He claimed to have been pressed and *Scots Magazine* made no mention of his having been brought to court.[70] The other was John Ballantine, a piper in Captain James Stewart's company in Lord George

Murray's regiment, raised mainly from the Gaelic part of the Atholl estate in Perthshire. Ballantine was tried, court and time unspecified, and claimed, like Carr, to have been pressed. He was acquitted. (His reported reaction to the decision – "Pray God bless King George for ever; I'll serve him all the days of my life" – shows that he probably spoke English.)[71] As an interesting afterthought that sheds light on the social status at least of a Perthshire piper at the time, the "Return of the Rebel Officers and Soldiers now Prisoners in Inverness, 19th April, 1746" includes "'Lord John Drummond's Piper's Servant.'"[72]

As for the possibility that pipers had been singled out for specially harsh treatment during the initial post-Culloden period, it is worth noting that the designation of "piper" in Seton and Arnot's lists of prisoners of the 'forty-five is to be found under the heading "regiment." That, however, was certainly the result of editorial preference rather than any contemporary official effort to target pipers. Fiddlers and "servants" (a category that could have included pipers) are so described but in the "general remarks" column. But the court record speaks for itself: one execution, one banishment, two discharges, and one "no further information."

On the whole, fiddlers in the Highland army suffered more than pipers, if one excludes Reid's execution. Of the four listed in *Prisoners of the '45*, three were transported on 31 March 1747.[73] John Shaw, a fiddler "in Aberdeen," was with the Jacobite army in "Stonywood's (Lord Lewis Gordon's)" from Angus and went into England. He was among fifty prisoners held in the tolbooth at Aberdeen in 1746 and claimed that "he surrendered in terms of The Duke of Cumberland's Declaration."[74]

3 Policing the Gaelic Highlands after Culloden

The myth that the bagpipe was proscribed under the Disarming Act is attended by another fanciful notion: that the last Jacobite loss at Culloden (16 April 1746) and the occupation that followed caused a profound, chronic, and irreparable "crisis" in Gaelic culture in general and community bagpiping in particular. To dispel this idea it is necessary to consider 1) the influence of military law in the period from April 1746 till c. 1747; 2) the post-based efforts at stopping impoverished Jacobite Gaels from stealing cattle (1747–48); and 3) the post-based efforts to enforce the three major elements of the Disarming Act (against weapons, Highland clothing, and, by amendment, cattle stealing), particularly that part proscribing the having or bearing of weapons (1748–53). Available post reports eloquently corroborate the point that there never was proscription of the bagpipes under the Disarming Act. Hence they provide further ammunition against the combined notions of Kilberry and Collinson that the Disarming Act all but destroyed traditional bagpiping, or that a cultural "crisis" doomed most piping to a speedy death and the rest to artificial and military-sponsored resuscitation.

For generations the impression has persisted that Cumberland, younger son of George II, was a brute who condoned murder and rapine even, to quote a relatively modern historian, to the extent of overseeing the decimation of Jacobite Gaelic society after Culloden.[1] Between 1745 and 1748, before, during, and after Cumberland's brief period of military liberty at law (which I am unable to define clearly), several acts of parliament were passed, to try to stamp out any politico-military significance of Gaelic Scotland once and for all. These acts appear on the surface to be overwhelming of all aspects of Gaelic life. Where day-to-day life and culture are concerned the reality is otherwise. With the exception of the leading 1745 Jacobites who were listed in the exceptions to the Act of Indemnity (June 1747), some of whom were harshly used even in and after 1753, Gaelic Jacobite Scotland, in a linguistic and cultural sense, was not severely affected at all. The potential to rise again persisted in some quarters, albeit unrealistically, in a quiet, non-confrontational, and well-controlled way. The numbers of occupying soldiers were insufficient to their tasks and the will of the Scottish legal system was not firm even in convicting kilted Highlanders. Cattle theft became, and the indemnity exceptions always were, another thing.

Cumberland's policy for Jacobite Scotland was straightforward. It came in two parts, the first being to beat the Jacobites on the battlefield, capture the leaders and as many of the combatants as possible, and consign them, as far as possible, to English justice[2] to disarm former combatants. The second part, which was of overriding importance from the outset, was the use of "systematic devastation as a weapon to discourage rebellion." This phrase was Cumberland's and was issued on February 1746 to Sir Andrew Agnew, a Scot and commanding officer of the 21st Regiment (Royal North British Fusiliers),[3] and by inference to all of his commanding officers. A few days later, on 22 February, General John Campbell of Mamore, commander of HM's forces in the west of Scotland under Marshall Wade (1668–1748), repeated to Sheriff Deputy Archibald Campbell of Stonefield Cumberland's orders to him "that strong partys should be sent to burn and distroy all the rebells' country as far as they can goe, and drive their cattle."[4] In May, when General Hawley's order (which had the duke of Cumberland's approval) was passed on to Captain Charles Hamilton of Cobham's Dragoons, the aide-de-camp who conveyed the order, James Wolfe, only had to write, "You know the manner of treating the houses and possessions of rebels."[5]

The reporting of Jacobite losses of cattle and other property prove indisputably that the impact of the economic policy was severe. Cumberland knew that arms were easily hidden and that the MacDonalds and the MacPhersons were extremely well armed, and the knowledge spurred Hanoverian reaction. This economic aspect of the occupying forces under Cumberland and Albemarle, who succeeded Cumberland after 18 July 1746,[6] shaped the Jacobite Highlanders' immediate future after Culloden far more decisively than the rough wooing visited by Hanoverian forces over a period of months after Culloden. An interesting and vindictive thread runs through Hanoverian cattle policy, but it will be the reader's privilege to decide how premeditated this was, or how accidental.

Cumberland's first public statement in Scotland, the Duke's Proclamation, was made on 24 February 1746. It warned ordinary Jacobites "by order of his Royal Highness the Duke of Cumberland, Captain-General of all his Majesty's forces in the kingdom of Great Britain" to turn in their weapons to a magistrate or a Church of Scotland minister and to inform on others so armed, or else they would be "pursued with the utmost severity as rebels and traitors, by due course of law or military execution."[7] The proclamation also ordered that names of the "disaffected" be gathered by all sheriffs, deputes, stewards, justices of the peace, and burgh magistrates. For all of his statement Cumberland cited the "plenary power and authority" granted him by the king.

Whether military law ended when Habeas Corpus was restored (c. October 1746)[8] or when the Act of Indemnity forgiving Jacobites was passed (June 1747), elements of its arbitrariness were common immediately after Culloden, against persons and against property. When the lord president of the Court of Session for Scotland, Duncan Forbes of Culloden, one of Scotland's most formidable Hanoverians, appealed to Cumberland to rely on the laws of the land rather than military force, possibly after May 1746, the latter retorted, "The laws of the country, my lord! I'll make a brigade give laws, by God!"[9]

Cumberland was a hard and blunt young man of mediocre military talent compared with France's Marshall Saxe, perhaps. But where outrages actually committed in Highland Scotland are concerned, his brutality appears to have been confined to what many Scots believe was his order to murder the Jacobite wounded at Culloden.[10] The executions on and near the battlefield have sullied his one military victory in Scotland. After Culloden the worst that can be said of Cumberland is that he demonstrated a lack of interest in seeing that uniformity of treatment was meted out by his officers to the defeated foe (the Reverend George Innes at Forres told Bishop Forbes on 27 February 1750 that the slaughter at Culloden was "greatest ... in pursuit" by Ancrum's Dragoons and Kingston's Light Horse who spared few or none).[11]

Cumberland was unaware of, or insensitive to, the tenacity of Highland feuds and the potential for abuses done to rebels by his subordinate officers. He meanly or ignorantly allowed Skye and Argyll Hanoverians and other Hanoverian Gaels to be among those who prosecuted his immediate post-Culloden orders to devastate. (Their greedy readiness to visit hardship on fellow Gaels, dastardly as it was, shows that the leaders in no way foresaw any calculated threat to Gaelic culture, or didn't care.) Then again, the Hessians who garrisoned Perth and Atholl for a month after Culloden were gentle.[12] After Culloden, it has to be added, Cumberland did not, where his officers were concerned, berate the lenient.

Captain Duncan Campbell of the Auchlyne Campbells, a captain of the Argyll Militia, was praised by the Jacobite poet Alasdair MacDonald in the poem *An Airc* for his compassion to the poor folk of Arasaig and Moidart in 1746.[13] Campbell of Airds is said to have taken the edge off Captain John Fergusson's relish for spoils in Glenfinnan.

Just as often, probably more often, the barbarous and zealous went unpunished. The correspondence of General John Campbell of Mamore[14] shows that he knew that Capt. Caroline ffrederick Scott had hanged a man with no trial on Mingulay on 30 June 1746; Captain Miller of Guise's regiment had complained. The general did nothing.[15]

At times there are signs almost of decency by the Hanoverian leadership. Cumberland, for example, was not in favour of disarming all of Gaelic Scotland after Culloden while General Campbell was. And while the identity of the man who killed Captain George Munro of Culcairn on the track along the north shores of Loch Arkaig in Lochaber in 1746 was known to local people at the time, the matter of the killing of a Hanoverian officer was never followed up. The only reason can be that the earlier murder of an innocent man by the Hanoverian officer Grant of Knockando (in Moray-shire) was rightly seen as utterly shameful and deserving of retaliation. It is revealing that the retaliator, a relative who shot Munro having mistaken him for Grant, was not arrested. That sort of oversight, the murder of a British army officer, could not have occurred without Cumberland's or Albemarle's knowledge.

Word of this martial oversight was furnished by the author of *The Lyon in Mourning* (1975), Bishop Forbes. Rev. Robert Forbes (1708–75) was episcopal bishop of Ross and Caithness (1762) and an ardent Jacobite who had been caught at St Ninian near Stirling on 7 September 1745 and imprisoned at Stirling Castle while on his way to join the Jacobite army. He assiduously gathered eye-witness and other evidence of the brutality of Cumberland's army at and after Culloden. He reported the cold-blooded murder of the wounded at Culloden and documented every case of later brutality of the occupying forces in the Highlands that he could find, specifically in order to put the Hanoverian victory in its truer, darker light. His list of horrors includes the murder of some twenty-three people (the twenty-fourth was that of the Hanoverian officer, Munro of Culcairn, mentioned above). Having just suffered an invasion to restore a Catholic monarch, this sort of rough treatment cannot have been unexpected. The surprise is that so few were murdered and that the period of general vengeance was so short.

The 1746 "act to attaint" (19 Geo. 2), brought in before news of Culloden reached London, may suggest to the legal mind that the occupying Hanoverian army did not act despotically and capriciously, but from a Jacobite point of view this act, on record from the fifteenth century, was so alienating and outlawing that any distinction is lost. In essence the act stated that if forty-three leading Jacobites did not turn themselves in by 12 July 1746 and submit themselves to justice for treasons committed, they would, after 18 April 1746, stand and be adjudged "attainted of the said high treason."[16] The Act of Indemnity of 1747 excepted an even greater number of Jacobites, many of whom were in France.

Harsh as these measures were and aimed unerringly and unforgivingly at the Jacobite leadership, catching Jacobite leaders and applying the laws was not always simple. Cluny MacPherson, a deserter from Lord Loudon's regiment who is prominent in both lists, chose to remain in hiding in his native Badenoch and only left in 1755, at Prince Charles's suggestion.[17] Allan Breac Stewart, another turncoat, had no qualms about revisiting the Highlands into the early 1750s.[18]

The destruction and theft of Jacobite property (including important family records) was rampant immediately after Culloden. Cumberland was in haste to return to his European war, and his officers with him, since promotion lay there and not in the wet, poor, and alien Highlands. France had made remarkable military gains from the moment Cumberland's forces were diverted from Flanders to beat the Scottish Jacobites and the sooner the prosecution of the European war could be renewed the better. One side effect of victory, or something near victory, would be to lessen even further, through agreement or concession, any future interest France might have in supporting the Stewarts militarily in Britain (an interest already shown to be minimal).

Jacobite areas were often pillaged more than once and it was not only English and Lowland officers (like Lord George Sackville, Fergusson, Scott, Lockhart, and Cornwallis) and their soldiers who prosecuted the practice. Highland Scots such as Sir Alexander MacDonald of Sleat and MacLeod of MacLeod were deeply involved along with Grant, son of Knockando, Munro of Culcairn (briefly), a Captain Campbell who pillaged Strathglas, and a Lieutenant MacNeil who headed some of the Argyll militia in robbing Atholl. That some of Cumberland's subordinates[19] at times let blood and lust, cruelty and petty revenge motivate them little interested him. Bishop Forbes's work clearly suggests that, for generations, it has been the uninformed fashion to exaggerate the nature and duration of this brutality.

The following summary of Cumberland's policy, particularly in relation to cattle driving (and Highlanders were very much a pastoral people while Highland traditional society lasted), reveals one of the major motivations of future occupying Hanoverian forces, Gaelic and English, just before and during the Disarming Act years in the Jacobite Highlands.

On 22 April 1746 Lord Loudon[20] was ordered by Cumberland to march to Fort Augustus and "drive the cattel and burn the plowes of all those that either are or have been out in the rebellion and to distress them in every other way and to burn the houses of their leaders."[21] In June the nineteen-year-old brigade major Wolfe expanded on standard orders in a letter to Hamilton: "The general bid me tell you that when any seizures were made of cattle or otherwise in this part of the world, the commanding officer and every person concerned have shares in proportion to your pay."[22] The ordinary, poorly paid soldier's understandable greed for money ensured success of the cattle policy.

Alexander Ross, in a letter to Baillie written between Culloden and 30 June 1746 said, "There's no end of burning the rebell countrey and bringing in sheep, goats, cowes, horses, all qch are to be devided among the armie after they traverse the whole hielands ... pains with our people to containe till that ... be over and that they might have their shares ... it was hard that these coming up reapt the advantage ... I am sure there is not a soger in this highland army but will draw £5 stg. besides pay on the 1st of Jully."[23]

Among many other examples is a letter from James Robertson written in 1749 from the Aird of Coigach in Wester Ross.[24] Robertson reported to the commissary clerk that marines had come to the Ross-shire coast in 1746 and pillaged the country for their concern in the rebellion. One poor man had his house plundered and burnt and his sheep taken away. (In fact most MacKenzies and their dependent peoples stayed out of the 'Forty-five.)

In 1746 Alexander MacKenzie of Fairburn wrote to Baillie, "I fear poor Geordy will be ruined as are all to the south of this place that were concerned in ye Rebellion ... got 110 Knodart men to surrender their arms at Bernera and Knoydart, and as yet they remained unmolested[25] ... I sent only 30 good cows to that market as they are surfeited with rebel cattle."[26] "Geordy" was the Jacobite George Mackenzie, third and last earl of Cromarty (d. 1766). He was responsible for neutralizing Lord Loudon's and MacLeod of MacLeod's forces and driving them, along with Duncan Forbes, fifth chief of Culloden, to Skye in early 1746. He and his son, John MacKenzie, Lord MacLeod, were captured at Dunrobin by MacKay's forces the day before Culloden. An eight-day plundering exercise that was led by Captain Fergusson from "a fleet" anchored in "Loch Ceannard" and was ostensibly a hunt for the Jacobite MacKenzie of Langwell, a relative of the last earl of Cromarty, is described in the *New Statistical Account* of Loch Broom by Dr Ross.[27]

Further to the south, General Campbell, a cousin of Archibald, third Duke of Argyll, had the duty to pass along to Captain Duff, RN, of HMS *Terror* Cumberland's "positive orders" to waste the duke of Argyll's property of Morvern (whose MacLeans and Camerons were active Jacobites; "their houses and granaries were to be burnt, their boats impounded or destroyed, and their cattle driven off."[28] A little northward in Stewart country, General Campbell drove the cattle from Appin and sold them to the benefit of his men. The cattle he had thoughtfully left for Lady Ardsheal's use were later taken by Caroline ffrederick Scott. With two hundred men, Noble drove four hundred beasts from Arisaig.

This cattle policy cut at the heart of the Highland economic way of life. It tore deeply into the rural economies of Gaels from Angus and Perthshire to Wester Ross, wherever men had risen and, in some cases, had been made to rise for the Jacobites. Jacobites quickly learned to drive the cattle not already on hill pasture to the hills when people like Fergussone, MacLeod of MacLeod, Lord George Sackville, Lord Loudon, General Campbell, Noble or Scott appeared, but often the army returned specifically to flush out herds such as Kinlochmoidart's and the Stewarts' of Appin for example. This systematic thieving had the obvious repercussion, it drove many people to theft as soon as the way was fairly clear.

However long the army's martial thievery of cattle lasted, the Moidart people's term *Bliadhna nan Creach* (Year of the Pillaging) may be taken to describe not just the stealing of cattle by King George's army but also the period from August 1746 to August 1747 when it was desperate Gaels who were doing the cattle stealing. Moidart, remember, enjoyed the humane policing of Duncan Campbell; how much worse must matters have been in less gently occupied places. (Claims for losses made by Cameron of Lochiel's tenantry, almost all featuring cattle high on the individual lists, extend from 1745 to 1747, the preponderance being in and after June 1746.)[29]

After the period of depredations by the Hanoverian army was over and before the Gael-manned post system was resumed in the spring and summer of 1747, contact between the occupying forces and Gaels was less than oppressive, as the number of armed Jacobite Highlanders stealing cattle proves.[30] The non-threatening nature of the relationship can be seen in the case of Captain Richard Coren of Barrell's Regiment. In 1747 Coren was employed in recruiting and road making in Highland Scotland, and his men were making illegal profits selling powder and ball to Highlanders.[31] In the summer of 1746 Col Charles Dejean's and Mordaunt's regiment were dispersed, presumably in posts, in the northeast,[32] and in or just after August Barrell's 4th Foot was ordered to police the southern *Gàidhealtachd*, especially MacGregor territory in Perthshire.[33] The men were stationed in posts from the Ford of Frew in the East, eight miles north of Stirling, to Inversnaid,[34] an old Wade fort near the east shore of upper Loch Lomond.

A number of factors conspired to make this 1746–47 occupation even more innocuous. In July and August 1746, when Viscount Bury (George Van Keppel, later third earl of Albemarle) officially assumed the commander's mantle from Cumberland,[35] a redistribution of the regiments serving in Scotland was ordered. Cumberland's four military divisions of Highland Scotland continued but the occupying force dwindled. Many regiments were removed from the Highlands, some to Flanders for the reopening of the campaign (Pulteney's and Sempill's Regiments and Wolfe's 8th Foot),[36] some to England (Howard's Buffs, Cholmondley's and Kingston's Horse). Barrell's Blues (the 4th Foot), young James Wolfe's regiment at the time, was removed from Fort Augustus to Linlithgow, served for a few months in the southern posts, and then went to Flanders in February 1747. The Black Watch, minus its three additional companies, which were recruiting in Scotland, returned from Ireland in February 1747 to the Downs in southeastern England where it joined "a large body of troops, assembled to reinforce the army in Flanders."[37] Stewart of Garth noted that by April-May 1745 the military season was well advanced in Flanders,[38] and "the greater part of the troops that formed this reinforcement consisted of those who had been ordered from Flanders in consequence of the Rebellion. Lord Loudon's Highlanders, and a detachment from the additional companies of the Black Watch, joined this force, which sailed from Leith early in April."[39]

More tellingly, according to J.T. Findlay, most of the officers couldn't wait to get out of Scotland. It was impossible to keep the regiments there up to establishment and those that were left to watch and police the Highlands were undermanned.[40] According to one volunteer, "Cumberland was no more inclined than he had been before Culloden to venture his regular infantry among "those mighty and dreadful mountains" that afflicted some of them with "hypochondriacal melancholy."[41] The cry was "Now Billy, for Flanders!" Findlay wrote that the occupying regiments were undermanned through sickness and "war wastage," but in any case, "the civil war was over. What remained was a long-drawn-out and tiresome epilogue."[42]

Thus, the military presence during the winter of 1746–47 amounted to a relatively powerless, barrack-based threat against any further rising. European armies did not campaign in the winter months. Although neither Garth nor Findlay gave any numbers for soldiers remaining in Scotland (and Garth overlooked Loudon's two recruiting companies that stayed in Highland Scotland when the rest of the regiment sailed for Europe), both men paint the same picture of the skeleton military staff that was left in Scotland. In the Jacobite heartland there was a predictable flurry to try to mend the terrible economic damage done by Cumberland's men. The richer Lowland farmers were frequent victims of cattle theft and complained vociferously.

Scotland had to be garrisoned, as it had been since Wade's time in the 1720s after the first rising. As in the rest of Britain the army was the police force. In 1747 the concepts of policing and getting roads built to facilitate military movement were linked. The continuation of Wade's road-building work (begun in 1725) was superintended in 1747 by Lt Col David Watson, whose centre was the encampment at Fort Augustus.[43] Policing, which boiled down to dealing with the problem of cattle theft, was addressed by Watson and then General Blakeney and became the prime mandate of the five Gaelic-speaking Highland companies of the Black Watch (known also as Lord John Murray's Regiment) and Lord Loudon's. The model used was the old Watch of the six Independent Companies of Gaelic soldiers, which had policed the Highlands since Wade's time. Even if Highland soldiers were biased in favour of fellow Highlanders, the garrisoned regiments from outside were considered far less effective as any sort of police force. Highland soldiers knew the native language and were inured to Highland climate and geography. They were posted from Nairn to Angus and further south, to protect Lowland cattle.

The outraged voices of those who were losing cattle to desperate and needy Highlanders had a different timbre. They knew from experience about Highland cattle thieving in calmer times, but they also knew, significantly,

from exaggerated story. They knew, too, of the one or two systems of Highland blackmail/herd protection perpetrated by Cluny and Barisdale,[44] in one
of which the Hanoverian government is believed to have conspired. To the
epithets "ignorant" and "idle" they added the easy phrase "inveterate thief"
and would not look beyond that impression to the inevitable effects of Cumberland's stripping of the Highlands of Jacobite cattle and the miseries that
that caused.

The army's plan, which emerged in the spring and summer of 1747, was
spurred by uncounted complaints at "thieving and depredations in the Highlands of Scotland," particularly from farmers to the east and south of the
Central Highland massif. An appropriate general introduction to the subject
is the "Memorial anent the thieving and depredations in the Highlands of
Scotland, and the countries bordering thereon,"[45] which was probably written in 1747. The part that follows points up the economic preoccupation of
the depredated and has nothing to do with anti-culture.

It is very well known, not only to all the Scotch Members, in both Houses of Parliament, but to many Thousands of his Majesty's most loyal and dutyful Subjects (who
daily feel the effects thereof), what miserable havock there is made by the barbarous
thieving Highlanders, of but a few Countrys, upon all the rest of the more extensive
and fertile parts thereof, and also in the whole Low Countries bordering thereon, by
pillaging their Houses and Stealing and driving away their Horses and Black Cattle,
without any the least Notice taken, or remedy applied by the Government for said
grievance. The present great dissatisfaction, among such vast Numbers of People of
all Ranks upon that Account (if allowed long to continue) would no doubt grow, into
some disaffection to his Majesty's Person and Government.

It is obvious that there is none of his Majesty's Forces fit to be employed for rem-
edying this insufferable evil, but Highlanders, who having their own Dress and language are the only properest for the fatigue, of long and Night Marches through such
rough and Uncouth Places, and can by their Intelligence (having the Irish Tongue)
get these Thieves best ferreted out of their lurking Holes.

As there are at present no other Regular Forces in Scotland that are Highlanders,
but the Five Recruiting Company's of Lord John Murray's and the Earl of Loudon's
Regts., who are now said to be Augmented to 100 Men each, His Excellency Gen.
Blakeney, late Commander in Chief, of his great Wisdom and Prudence having
maturely considered the Urgent Necessity of giving some Curb to the present growing Wickedness, which he takes to be an insult upon the Government, and is like to
terminate in the Devestation of a great part of the Country, made Trial of making sevl
Detatchments this last Summer [i.e., 1747] of small Partys out of the said Companies
to the different dangerous Passes where Depredations used to be driven, which was
found to be of great use, and his Excellency in consequence thereof has since laid
down a Scheme how the whole Nation may be protected in the same Manner without putting the Government to any further Charges of New Levies ...

The few Villanous Countries that stand as Common Enemies to the rest of the Nation, and that commit those daily depredations (and who have been so time out of mind) are Roinach, Glenco, Lochaber, Glengary, Knoidart, Glenmoriston, and Glenavie and Laggan in Brae of Badenoch. It is humbly proposed by the Memorialist (there being a disarming Act already past) that the Wicked Possessors of those above named Countries be suddenly summoned and disarmed at first, before any of the rest of the Highlands; were it but for a few Months, that they may once perceive themselves distinguished for their Villany, they being the only Wicked Aggressors, and people that occasion the keeping up the Spirit and general use of Arms in all the Highlands of Scotland.[46]

An early order, from "Lieut Colonel Watson to Lieut Forbes Or Offr Commanding Capt. McPherson's Addl. Compy at Ruthven. Edinr. 18th June, 1747" points to the primary aim and to the method of enforcement; it ends, "You are to Act in Concert with the Justices of the Peace of the Heads of the Countys of Banff, Aberdeen, Kincarden and Angus for protecting as much as Possible His Majesties Peaceable Subjects and their Effects in the above Countys against the Depredations of the Rebell and Highland Thieves."[47]

The chapter in Allardyce's *Historical Papers* (1895, 1896) headed "Concerning Highland Depredations" in 1747 discloses military schemes to counteract the rustling. An anonymous adviser suggested military posts and also mentioned, almost as an afterthought, that "this practice of Thieving is the sure and known Means of training up a number of people to the use of Arms, who on the least prospect of plunder are ready to join in any Rebellion or Tumult. In order to correct this abuse it will be difficult Matter to bridle those parts of the Highlands, where the Thieves reside, and at the same time by a proper chain of Posts effectually secure the heads of those Shires opposed to their depredation."[48] The gist of the anonymous memorialist's presentation eventually becomes clear: the writer felt that the new system of guarding the Highland/Lowland passes and apprehending Highland cattle thieves was laudable but too defensive, a bandage treatment when surgery was required; what was needed, he claimed, was a policy of greater aggressiveness, of making hard examples.

All of this shows that the forces in the Highlands in 1746–47 were ineffective as any kind of police force. Highlanders, quite legally, still went about armed and wore traditional Highland clothing. It will be shown that cattle theft lasted well into the Disarming Act period after 1748.

THE POST SYSTEM

At the end of the northern European fighting season of 1747, and doubtless anticipating an end to the war,[49] King George triggered the enforcement of the refined Disarming Act. On 16 October 1747 he applied his sign manual to the appropriate order to Lt Gen. Humphry Bland, newly promoted commander of the forces in North Britain,[50] empowering Bland to issue letters of summons to the various justices of the peace of the carefully defined areas of Gaelic Scotland that were to be deweaponed. Bland sent copies of his letter of summons to the justices of the peace on 25 April 1748, while other copies were posted at the churches in most of the appropriate parishes. The date of delivery of weapons varied from 3 June (proclamation at Kilmonivaick and Kilmallie churches for delivery at Fort William) to 17 June (proclamation at the mercat cross, Inverness, for delivery at the church of North Uist), with one late date, 10 August, for delivery at Bernera.[51] As noted earlier, this order dealt only with arms and warlike weapons and nowhere mentioned the bagpipes.

While barracks-based troops remained in Scotland making roads, repairing forts, and attending to other tasks, the system used for policing the arms clauses of the Disarming Act was the post system.[52] It relied, as James Wolfe of Bury's (the 20th) noted, on the rotation of various non-Highland regiments, adding a moving patrol as a refinement. By good fortune, published copies of some of the records of the officers who managed the posts in 1749 and 1750 are extant.[53] The regiments for whom reports exist are Herbert's, Pulteney's, Ancram's, Guise's, Bockland's, and Bury's. The post system went into effect officially for the regiments policing the Jacobite Highlands with the general orders of December 1748. Therefore, since it was winter, the Disarming Act was first enforced by the post system in the spring of 1749. It was thus put into effect, however poorly, for arms and other warlike weapons, for five summers.[54]

Other sources must be relied on to discover something of what went on from 1750–53 and later. James Wolfe's records of the 20th's service in Highland Scotland, published in various books, are the most readily available.[55] It should be remembered, too, that by 1750 the army had been reduced from about 50,000 to 18,800 men, following the cessation of European hostilities in 1748.

Gauging the degree of cultural "crisis" created by the occupation of Gaelic Scotland from spring/summer 1749 is thus fairly easy to do. On the one hand are the post and other published reports, such as Wolfe's letters, with their understandable bias, as well as the justiciary court records; on the other are the remarks left us by the Gaels who lived through the period and wrote about it in verse.

To begin with, according to Millar, the orders for North and South Uist, Barra, and Harris were publicly posted only at the mercat cross in Inverness in breach of the exact dictates of the act, which explicitly stated that the notice be promulgated in the parishes involved, which further suggests that a full-time military presence in those areas may not have been anticipated.[56] In neither 1749 nor 1750 is there any mention of Hebridean posts' having been set up (nor does current opinion seem to claim that they ever were). One instance of prosecution of the law occurs in W.C. MacKenzie's *History of the Outer Hebrides* (1903). MacKenzie wrote that an English officer "arrived in the Long Island in 1753, on a hunt for arms, priests, and the Highland dress." He added that "the Long Island was not exempt from the effects of the upheaval which took place in the Highlands generally, after Culloden."[57]

In addition, the act was not uniformly applied. Nothing is known, for example, of what was going on in the parts of Ross-shire that had been occupied by Munro's company of Lord Loudon's in 1747–48. We do know that the forfeited estate of Lord Cromartie in Assynt, in the west of Sutherland, went unsold until 1757, and in a contemporary report of Assynt John Home noted that "even the aftermath of the Forty Five left little mark."[58] In the rest of Sutherland (which shire was included in the deweaponing clauses), Bishop Pococke found on his tours in 1747, 1750, and 1760 that most households enjoyed venison.[59] It would be foolish to assume that the beasts were felled by bow and arrow.

The "Highland Reports" in Allardyce's *Historical Papers* do not give the numbers of non-commissioned officers and men serving in and from Inversnaid, but otherwise the totals for the rest of the headquarters, posts, and moving patrols in 1750 were: five captains, 13 lieutenants or ensigns, 28 sergeants, 42 corporals, and 418 men. The average number of men and officers, non-commissioned and commissioned, per post, including headquarters and moving patrols, is 7.46. What could some four hundred and fifty soldiers, thinly spread, do during the summer months in mountain terrain that ruined a pair of shoes in three or four days against a Gaelic population of tens of thousands? To begin with the Highland *àiridh*, or hill pasture system, ensured that a high proportion of the young people were in the more remote and inaccessible mountain areas during the grain and hay-growing months – the only periods when the post and patrol system worked. The reports that Allardyce published betray a weariness and frustration seldom punctuated by success on the part of the post officers. Not only was their success in catching armed men modest but they discovered that the law cut both ways, and that Scottish justices of the peace, sheriffs, lawyers, and judges were stubbornly unwilling to prosecute, particularly in cases of clothing infractions.

The reports try to put a brave face on it. But with Highlanders robbing the posts themselves at times, the Disarming Act was obviously treated by some as a game. Of course the reports are quiet about fear of Jacobite Gaels, but government actions betray just that, in 1753 and later. In fairness, the government's superior design, to eradicate Jacobitism systematically, was working. It penetrated the Paris- and London-based Jacobite cabal using Alexander Macdonnel (Pickle the Spy); it never gave up hunting the leadership, hounding Cluny MacPherson, capturing and hanging Dr Archibald Cameron in 1753,[60] prosecuting the younger Barisdale (who had also been attainted) and "Young Morer." It also began to break the Highland habit of cattle theft, although in some minds the habit was already dying a natural death by the time of Culloden.[61]

In any case, Findlay's view that the Highlands were thoroughly demoralized after Culloden is patently untrue. Likewise James Wolfe's observation that Highland Scotland was "in perfect calm and quiet" in early 1750 owing to "abundant military force." This statement typically misread, as a condition of cowed subjection, many Highland leaders' patient control over a potential army. That the Jacobite Highlands, even in hard economic times, retained its remarkable *hauteur* and feistiness became evident at the beginning of the Seven Years' War.

During Disarming Act policing there were several instances in which guns, swords, and dirks were said to have been found (with or without their owners). Men wearing Highland dress – sometimes armed, sometimes unarmed, sometimes stealing cattle – were also frequently mentioned in the reports the officers sent in every two weeks. Sometimes, if cornered, they were caught; much more often they eluded the law. For all their extended mandate (to police the Disarming Act), the records of the officers manning the posts in 1749 and 1750 continue to show a strong preoccupation with catching livestock thieves. Officers, often expressed their thoughts specifically on the difficulties of the apprehending of cattle thieves, many of whom were obviously notorious repeat offenders.

When Captain Molesworth went into winter quarters at Fort Augustus on 15 November 1750, for example, he wrote only of cattle thieves. "The Thieves of Note whom I leave in the Country are John Kennedy, called Bricke, or Pocke or Pocpitted. He is a Deserter from the British Service ... and speaks a little English."[62] Kennedy always went armed and he led a gang comprising a MacArthur from "Glen Luigh" (a deserter from Lord John Murray's Regiment), Alister Dubh Cameron, and John McDonell (Kennedy's nephew). Molesworth also mentioned three other cattle thieves, "Ewin Oge," "Johne Oge," and "McPhie at Glen Kinna." These men habitually stole from Kintail and drove "generally into the Brays of Loch Arkeg."[63] Some seventeen thefts were reported with thirteen Highland cattle thieves caught in about twelve months of work (1749 and 1750) – roughly one capture per month of policing. As yet no record has been found of any hanging for the offence. Of the seventeen cases three offenders were kilted and armed and one escaped.

Through all the thieving some Jacobite Gaels behaved with a playful Highland contempt. One instance of theft occurred at the Inversnaid army headquarters (two sheep and one cow; nobody was caught). Another was committed in the Dunmaglas area, the victim being the landlady of a corporal serving a Lieutenant Cumine of Guise's Regiment (again, no one was caught). In June 1750 Captain Patton of the same regiment, stationed in Rannoch, reported that six Highlanders "in kilted plaids and Philebegs &c compleatly Arm'd, with fire lock, sword and pistols each, Broke into a sheiling belonging to M's Allan Stewart proprietor of Indeshadden."[64] These robbers stole all the cheese and butter as well as an unspecified number of cows. Mrs Allan Stewart was targeted because she had had the temerity to provision Patton's company. (At the same time, 15 June 1750, Patton reported that the lowlands along Loch Rannoch were empty of people, it being the sheiling season.)[65]

In the capture of armed Highlanders the army's record is feeble. The reported numbers of men seen bearing arms in 1749 and 1750 was over thirty-seven, of whom thirteen were kilted as well. Only three were caught. Of arms actually found there were three French bayonets, a gun barrel, three firelocks, a "Spanish piece," a "Tower piece" (antecedent of the Brown Bess), a "durk," and a "Bullet Mould."

If there is doubt about when the duke of Cumberland's plenary powers ended, by the time of the Disarming Act there was no doubt in the minds of Highlanders about how matters stood, and they were right. To reiterate, the law cut two ways. Although the fact is seldom emphasized, the soldiers had to operate under the rule of law and this often rankled. It is nowhere admitted by the army, but it would come as no surprise to learn that in some places negative judicial reaction may well have influenced the soldiery to overlook infractions of the Disarming Act as hopelessly unenforceable (there is abundant evidence of local officials refusing to prosecute the clothing clauses). Without martial law, soldiers could not rough people up, or kill them;[66] they could not appropriate buildings or transport or provisions and if they tried they could expect to face a Scottish judge and a caste of Scottish lawyers whom they thought, often correctly, were biased against them (the hated union of the parliaments in 1707 was well within living memory).

Where the army was concerned there was no longer any chance to ride roughshod over Highlanders' rights. On 22 June 1750 the MacPherson who owned the "Publick house" at Dalnacardoch applied to the duke of Atholl's commissary, Bisset, to have the posted soldiers turned out of his barn. He argued that they had to pay for everything "since all was settled."

If there is one case that highlights the legal difficulties the forces had in 1749 and 1750, it is Captain Molesworth of Guise's. Molesworth had his headquarters at Lagan Achadrom, between Loch Lochy and Loch Oich in Glengarry country an the Great Glen. He was not a popular man among Highlanders and not perhaps a very imaginative one. His biggest problem began when he came to find accommodations for his men. He tried to quarter his Hanoverian soldiers on Glengarry people and of course they too complained and remonstrated, with effect. Glengarry, who had stayed home during the 'Forty-five and whose estate had not been forfeited, had encouraged Molesworth in his scheme to build a sixty-foot-long "hutt" for his men, but when the captain proceeded to press into service local horses and tools for the job the native people rose in righteous indignation and sued him, his sergeant, his corporal, and four of his men in Inverness.

Molesworth railed at the Scottish lawyers and their "many threadbare invectives against officers of the Army, and [their demanding] a high pecuniary Mulct," and he voiced the opinion of many army officers serving the Crown in the Highlands when he reported to his superior the lawyers' "darling topick of abusing the Army." (When the Inverness judge dismissed the case the aggrieved plaintiffs threatened to take their case to the Lords and sought punishment for the sheriff).[67]

Earlier, in July 1750, Molesworth had despaired of the "impartiality of the acting sheriff of Inverness,"[68] and he might have complained about a number of magistrates in different parts of the Highlands and its environs. Soldiers often had particular trouble getting JPs and sheriff deputes to prosecute Highlanders for wearing any part of the Highland "habite," as the law required them to do. Nor was there certitude that kilted Highlander who was also armed would automatically be prosecuted.[69]

While it is true that foodstuffs were delivered to some of the posts from Fort William and Bernera, most of the detachments doing the policing were in the difficult position of having to get their supplies from the people whom they were detailed to police – not a happy position for either supplier or supplied. Their treatment varied but several posts, notably the one at Glencoe, were in angrier surroundings than others (MacDonald of Glencoe himself was freed from Edinburgh's tolbooth prison on 11 October 1749 and was not in a forgiving mood). There and elsewhere the soldiers had no alternative but to pay high prices for whatever provisions the local people were prepared to sell them. In places like Morar and Knoydart, where poverty was extreme after Cumberland's raids, provisions were a major problem.

In summary, the Disarming Act, where it dealt with arms and warlike weapons, was a failure. Where it dealt with clothing its effect was also token, as those wearing Highland dress at the outbreak of the Seven Year's War in 1757 proves. For many of the Jacobite clans (MacDonells, MacDonalds, Chisholms, MacGillivrays, MacPhersons, and MacGregors *inter alia*) the ties binding the leaders and the led were still strong enough for a renewed challenge to the House of Hanover to appear marginally feasible, with outside support, in some fevered minds (including the government's). Old traditional Gaelic political allegiances lasted through the late 1740s and into the 1750s and the government feared them, at times irrationally. The whole intent and drive of Hanoverian policy, however, was to eradicate Jacobite leadership. This was probably an easier job than the government anticipated, even given the knowledge that France had not really become involved in

1745. For all that, there was a scare of Jacobite plotting in 1753 and in 1757, notwithstanding Prince Charles's banishment by Louis from France on 10 December 1748, pursuant to one of the terms of the Treaty of Aix-la-Chappelle.

Nothing whatever is written about pipers or bagpipes, and no pipers are known to have been convicted as such under any of the act's clearly published stipulations. It is obvious that even had the bagpipes been a legitimate weapon, neither soldiers nor Scottish magistrates were paying the slightest attention to them. Those court cases that were reported in *Scots Magazine* contain no arrests, trials, or punishments of people for owning or playing the instrument and just one such case would have been a *cause célèbre* in a country where both races, Gael and Saxon, were partial to bagpiping.[70] Two court cases involving Gaelic-speaking Jacobite gentlemen in the 1750s included witnesses who were freely described in the courts as pipers or sons of pipers, with no adverse effects.

The records of the northern circuit of the Justiciary Court for the period 2 May 1748–51 show no apprehensions, trials, or convictions of pipers. Indeed, a "James Pyper" was a witness at the trial "in Kintessack" of a Thomas Findlater of Captain Higgison's company of Barrell's Regiment (in which James Wolfe served) for the crime of raping Katharine MacDonald, daughter of John MacDonald of Kintessack. Private Findlater was found guilty and sentenced on 29 December 1749 to be hanged at Gallow Muir between two and four P.M.[71]

Young Barisdale's treason trial of 1754, while occurring a year after the Disarming Act's weapons clause had expired, offers another interesting example of a Jacobite piper mentioned in the courts. The slated Barisdale house was razed by irate and vengeful "Monroes";[72] his estate had been forfeited. Both Barisdales, father and son, had been among the most wanted Jacobites of 1745. The younger was arraigned on treason charges in 1754, and to look back to Dr Archibald Cameron's recent execution on 7 June 1753 for having been a Jacobite courier must have tested Young Barisdale's mettle. He opted for what Fraser-Macintosh called a defence of "due surrender" and mustered more than thirty witnesses, including "Lord Loudoun; Macleod; Donald Macdonell, his late servant; Donald Macdonald, sometime servant to Coll Macdonell of Inverie; Donald M'Dougal, alias M'Ianoig, piper at Inverie; Allan M'Dougall, the piper's son."[73] The point is that in 1754 Barisdale had no compunction about naming as witnesses the family piper and the "piper's son." He had no need to mention the man's musical calling, and every light and shade of Barisdale's character points to his having punctiliously attended to the needs of those in his service. He would never have implicated a family servant as a criminal under Hanoverian law.

Between 1750 and 1760 pipes were played in the *Gàidhealtachd* as usual. Road building continued apace, while army occupation, probably under the established post system, outlived 1753. The wearing of Highland dress persisted along with the stealing of cattle, although the true death knell of cattle lifting was sounded with the first execution of a cattle thief in 1752, following on the cattle theft clause in the 1748 amendment to the Disarming Act. In Robert Wright's work on Wolfe's time in Scotland, much of it spent in the Highlands, in 1751–53,[74] there are two published cases of the capture of armed Highlanders. At Dunan in Rannoch the Jacobite "Sergeant Mor" (John Dubh Cameron), leader of an armed seven-man cattle thieving band, was caught and hanged; among his crimes were murder and cattle theft.

The first three years of the decade show a continuing fear that Gaelic Jacobite Scotland would rise again. There was known Jacobite plotting in France and contact with the Highland Jacobites, all of which is reflected in the local Scottish judicial scene. The public burning by the hangman in Edinburgh of Alexander MacDonald's *Aiseiridh na Sean Chánoin Alban-naich* (*Resurrection of the Old Scottish Language*) in or just after 1751 ranked as highly in paranoid unreason as the judicial murder in November 1752 by the duke of Argyll and his Campbell gentry of Seumas a' Ghlinne after he was judged part of a plot to kill Colin Campbell of Glenure.

The same jitteriness was evident in everyday life. In Dalnacleragh, Ross-shire, William Ross, son of Alexander, was imprisoned in the tolbooth at Tain in 1751. A sheriff's warrant noted that he had been "taken up and incarcerate for wearing and using the Highland dress and arms ... contrar to and in defiance of the Act of Parliament."[75]

However, not once in the "Highland Reports" or anywhere else in current literature in English, including the court records, is the bagpipe or a bagpiper mentioned. The same is true for Gaelic literature as it has been collected and published. As one would expect from Jacobite bards, many took the time to vilify the Disarming Act, often in most useful detail. In this work they were joined by poets in Hanoverian territory. Indeed, most of the Scottish population, Lowland and Highland, was affronted at the clothing clauses of the Disarming Act, which affected all of Scotland. All would have bitterly complained at any proscription of the pipes and none did.

From many corners of the Highlands there is an abundance of tales, poetry, song, and lore of the great pipers that is rooted firmly in the second half of the eighteenth century. But the best place to look for any enforced cracks in piping tradition is in the surviving *bàrdachd* of the Culloden and Disarming Act period and there is not even a hint of a break. The four most prominent Gaelic poets, Alasdair mac Mhaighstir Alasdair (c. 1690–1770), Donnchadh Bàn Mac an-t Saoir (1724–1812), Iain Mac Codrum (c. 1700–79), and Rob Donn MacKay (c. 1715–78), as well as a number of lesser well-known bards, including Iain mac Theàrlaich Òig[76] and MacPherson of Strathmashie, wrote popular songs against the Disarming Act, but once again, none said anything about piping's having been proscribed or even beginning to decline.

Alexander MacDonald's song "*Am Breacan Uallach*" ("The Cheerful Tartan") against proscription of the Highland dress has nothing to say about the bagpipes. MacDonald wrote "*Moladh air Pìob-mhoir MhicCruimein*" in praise of the MacCrimmon bagpipe (no date). The song "*Moladh Moraig*" ("Praise of Morag") is to be sung to the air of a pibroch and contains cantos arranged under the headings of *ùrlar* (ground or theme), *siubhal* (variations), and *crunluath* (crowning fingering; the spelling is almost certainly modern), all names of parts of a classical piece of *ceòl mór* that were first described c.1761 by Joseph MacDonald in his manuscript "Compleat theory of the Scots Highland Bagpipe."

Alexander MacDonald was the ultimate in Scottish Gaelic Jacobite patriot; his biting talent would have swooped on any outrage such as the Hanoverians' banning of the bagpipes and shredded it loudly and in public, damned be the outcome, and yet he was silent.

In Reay country where King George's writ was accepted in 1745, Rob Donn also wrote about the prohibition against Highland clothes in "*Oran nan Casagan dubha*" ("Song of the Black Cassocks") with no mention of the bagpipes. Two of his other works, "*Iseabail nic-Aoidh (air fonn Pìobaireachd* (Isobel MacKay {to the medody of a pibroch})" and "*Pìobaireachd Bean Aoidh* (Mrs MacKay's Pibroch)," are constructed, like MacDonald's "*Moladh Moraig*" along pibroch lines, or at least what the poet may have presumed to have been pibroch lines.[77] The first apparently was to be sung to the popular tune "*Fàilte 'Phrionns'* " ("The Prince's Salute")[78] and is broken down as many published pibrochs are with the following cantos: *an t-ùrlar* (the ground, or theme), *an ceud siubhal* (first variation), *an dara siubhal* (second variation), *an taobhluath*, and *an crunluath*. The other has an *ùrlar*, *siubhal*, and *crunluath* (spellings are modern). Rob Donn had as a patron the Reverend Murdoch MacDonald, the Durness (Sutherland) minister and composer of many "airs" who encouraged three of his children (Patrick, Joseph, author of Complete Theory, and Flora) to follow their musical interests.[79]

Duncan Ban MacIntyre, who contrived, by funding a substitute, to miss action as a Hanoverian soldier at Falkirk in 1746, and who eulogized several Hanoverian Campbell superiors, also railed against the Disarming Act in "*Oran do'n bhriogais*" ("Song to the Trousers") and "*Oran do'n Eideadh Ghàidhealach*" ("Song to the Gaelic Dress") but without the least whisper of indignation at the bagpipe's ban. In the first one he took care to specify the actual arms and appurtenances prohibited in Gaelic Scotland: "When he [Cumberland] has left us captive-like,/without dirks and without guns,/without a sword or shoulder-belt,/not even pistols can we get."[80] It is out of the question that Duncan Ban MacIntyre could have listed shoulder-belts and have forgotten the bagpipes.

Elsewhere in his published work, "*Moladh Beinn Dobhrain*" ("Praise of Ben Doran") was composed to be sung to a pibroch melody, using the same repeating of the ground after each variation outline that Alexander MacDonald did in "*Moladh Moraig*." MacIntyre, who is not known to have been a bagpiper, was also commissioned to compose a song/poem to Gaelic and the Great Highland Bagpipe in 1781–85 and in 1789, and in none of the six songs, as he struggled for fresh inspiration, did he ever mentioned any proscription of the instrument or persecution of its exponents. Nonetheless, Angus MacLeod, editor and annotator of *The Songs of Duncan Ban* (1952), commented gratuitously that "the Act of 1746 forbade the wearing of the Highland dress and the possession of arms; even the bagpipe, being classed as an instrument of war, was forbidden."[81]

The bard Iain mac Theàrlaich Oig (John son of Young Charles) in "*Oran an déidh Bhlàr Chuil-lodair*" ("Song after Culloden"), complained bitterly at having had to give up the sword, targe, and gun for just a stick; he railed at the injustice of the tartan's and plaid's having been banned; but he never said a word about the pipes or any policy discriminating against music and dance.[82]

The absence of any mention of a ban on bagpipes in Alexander MacDonald's work is perhaps the best evidence that there was none. John Roy Stewart, a Jacobite officer who was capable of poetic vitriol in English and Gaelic and who would certainly never have missed the chance to condemn such a measure, said nothing in his songs on the subject either.

On the positive side, MacCodrum's poem "*Diomoladh Pìoba Dhòmhnaill Bhàin*" ("Dispraise of Donald Ban's bag-pipe"), written around 1760, actually mentions the three greatest living pipers of the time, in his opinion: "*MacCruimein, Con-duiligh, is Teàrlach*." He included their names in casual terms assuming the hearer would automatically know to whom each name referred. If they are who we think them to be, Donald (or his older brother John) MacCrimmon and Charles MacArthur were alive and piping between 1748 and 1753. If "Con-duiligh" referred to the piper of that name specifically and was not a patronymic, he would have been old since he piped at Sheriffmuir in 1715. However, this "Con-duiligh" could have been a son or grandson. Indeed, everything about this poem-song proves that piping was commonplace and not practised clandestinely in the Highlands of Mull and Skye.

It is also worth summarizing the writings of Tobias Smollett (1721–77), a doctor and writer from the Cardross area of Dumbartonshire. Smollett visited his native heath from England twice in the 1750s, in 1753 and again in 1755–56. His best-known novel, *The Expedition of Humphry Clinker* (1771), contains a number of observations on life in Campbell country during the Disarming Act years based on Smollett's first-hand experiences before the outbreak of the Seven Years' War.

Briefly, what Smollett said was that Highlanders were disarmed by act of Parliament and also laboured against an unjust and deeply resented legal prohibition against their traditional clothing. He described ways in which the clothing clause of the Disarming Act was obviated, but he had nothing to say about bagpipes being banned as weapons. Smollett told and retold the story of visiting, presumably somewhere in Argyllshire, cadet of the duke of Argyll's line called "Dougal Campbell," a non-traditionalist who detested the bagpipes but had to put up with the traditional and hereditary family piper. Smollett wrote of Campbell that he

has travelled in the course of his education, and is disposed to make certain alterations in his domestic œconomy; but he finds it impossible to abolish the antient customs of the family; some of which are ludicrous enough – His piper, for example, who is an hereditary officer of the household, will not part with the least particle of his privileges – He has a right to wear the kilt, or antient Highland dress, with the purse, pistol, and durk – a broad yellow ribbon fixed to the chanter-pipe, is thrown over his shoulder, and trails along the ground, while he performs the function of his minstrelsy ... He plays before the laird every Sunday in his way to the kirk, which he circles three times, performing the family march ... and every morning he plays a full hour by the clock, in the great hall, marching backwards and forwards all the time, with a solemn pace, attended by the laird's kinsmen, who seem much delighted with the music – In this exercise, he indulges them with a variety of pibrachs or airs.[83]

Smollett's novel is known to have been true to his own travel experiences, though the names are changed. There are echoes elsewhere of one of Burt's letters in Smollett's descriptions of pipers at a Highland funeral, but the picture of Dougal Campbell almost certainly sprang from Smollett's personal experience. Smollett had been in Argyllshire and there the speculation must rest. It is likely that this visit to the unknown Campbell household occurred in one or both of the visits of the 1750s since, Smollett scholar Louis Martz has declared, Smollett was too ill to gallivant round the Highlands in 1766.

An old tune published in 1816 by Simon Fraser of Knockie sums up the clothing and disarming elements of the Disarming Act nicely; the tune is called "*O gràin air na briogaisean*" ("O hatred on the trousers") and like many another song it expressed its unknown maker's abhorrence of that garment. It refers to the 1748–57 period. Simon Fraser knew the words, but since his policy was not to provide words other than the title above the notes, these are lost to posterity. In the note to this tune Fraser wrote, "No. 159 is one of the genuine pipe-reels, as preserved through Culduthel's[84] singing, and contains a most humorous declamation against putting breeks upon the Highlandmen,' and against the proscription of their native dress."[85] The point is that the tune was originally a genuine pipe reel commemorating the most hated clause of the Disarming Act.

If the Disarming Act had any influence on the ordinary Highlander at all, it must be that it drove weapons from public view in a well-defined part of Gaelic Scotland until late 1753. It may also have put paid to the wearing of the tartan plaid by the early 1770s, except in the British army where by the late eighteenth century it had become a skeuomorphic caricature.[86] It began to end cattle theft. To the extent that Highland pipers had customarily borne arms and worn the plaid it affected them, but only to that extent. The Disarming Act had no implied musical clause and none was enforced except in latter-day heated imaginations.

4 Postscript on the Disarming Act

The last real scare of another Jacobite rising in Gaelic Scotland began in 1756 when Britain and France found each other on opposite sides in what was to become the Seven Years' War. It was typically a time of some Hanoverian nervousness, but more important, in retrospect, it clearly marked the turning point in Gaelic Scotland. The voluntary formation of several Gaelic regiments, all of which admittedly were raised by non-Catholic colonels, marks a trend to general Gaelic acceptance of the House of Hanover (and a diminishment of English unease over Jacobite Scotland) because many Catholic ex-Jacobites were involved. The Hanoverian perception of Scotland as a threat was further eroded by such displays of loyalty as the Frasers' dashing part in the victory at Quebec in 1759.

In March 1756 an "Act for the speedy and effectual recruiting of his Majesty's land-forces and marines" (29 Geo. 2) was passed, legalizing impressment of able-bodied men who did not have "any lawful calling or employment or have not some other lawful and sufficient support and maintenance." Since the earlier European war the penalty for being caught in Highland clothes was enlistment if fit, so the poor, disaffected Highlander was doubly in jeopardy now. The large number of kilted Highlanders who were forceably enlisted shows that there was a much-reduced tendency of local courts to defy the occupying soldiery and overlook dress-code infringements.[1] With forced enlistment Highlanders could not benefit from the bounty system that the government had instituted.

Even so, there was a great deal of Highland loyalty to the Hanoverian Crown in 1756–57, where eleven years earlier there had been hostility and uncertainty. Lack of French support had been depressingly salutary. Common cause with England and Prussia against Austria and France in many once staunchly Jacobite Highland areas replaced Scottish animus against the "Auld Enemy."[2]

The loyalty of ex-Jacobites to King George in 1757 was remarkable, coming in several instances from the forfeited estates.[3] In the Gaelic Highlands Fraser's Highlanders were raised in 1757 for service in British North America and elsewhere. Fraser was a perfectly safe agent to carry the King's commission; he had been made a burgess of Inveraray in 1750, the year he received a full and free pardon from the government;[4] he had been one of the prosecuting lawyers in the malignant case against Seumas a' Ghlinne (James of the Glen, or James Stewart) at Inveraray in 1752 and curried as much favour as possible. Among his officers, however, were Jacobites and people with strong Jacobite ties. Commissions to raise Montgomerie's Highlanders were granted a day or so earlier and with both regiments the story of general rather than specific Highland loyalty to the House of Hanover had begun.

Burt's *Letters from a Gentleman in the North of Scotland* (1754) show that between 1727 and 1736 English regiments were expressly forbidden to enlist Highlanders. Later, the government's (in essence the duke of Cumberland's) diffidence at allowing soldiers (excepting the Black Watch) in Highland dress, using the Highland battle technique of the broadsword and dirk charge, to represent its interests is seen in its mid-1756 military policy of drafting Highlanders into English regiments where there was no hope for the use of eccentric, obsolescent military techniques. In January 1756 the 57th Regiment, later called the 55th Westmorland Regiment (an English regiment), was raised in Stirling by Colonel George Perry and must have attracted a considerable number of Gaels. In the same year the 3d, 4th, 8th, 11th, 12th, 19th, 20th, 23d, 24th, 31st, 32d, 33d, 34th, 36th, and 37th regiments, all English, were ordered to raise second battalions. None of the one-battalion Scottish regiments, including the Cameronians (26th Regiment of Foot), was allowed to raise a second battalion in 1756 but the 19th (Beauclerk's, later known as "the Green Howards"), the 31st (the Huntingdonshire Regiment), and the 32d (Cornwall Light Infantry) were all sent to Scotland specifically to do that,[5] in a planned attempt to diffuse any Scottish nationalist military consciousness.

The main concession made to the ex-Jacobite Highlanders was the permission granted to the lawyer-chief Simon Fraser of Lovat to raise Fraser's Highlanders in 1757.[6] Fraser's and Montgomerie's Highlanders served in North America and not in the main theatre of war, which was in Europe.[7]

From an English point of view this edginess at the use of once-disaffected Highlanders must temporarily have seemed to be justified inasmuch as a French invasion was planned for 1759 in which Prince Charles had a sharp interest. The plan to invade was thwarted by the Royal Navy at Lagos (August 1759) and Quiberon Bay (November 1759), and although Prince

Charles waited in anticipation in France, nothing happened in Highland Scotland. To have presumed that a Jacobite invasion from Gaelic Scotland was primed and poised to invade from the North was certainly absurd.

Montgomerie's and Fascr's Highlanders, though the earliest, were by no means the only Highland regiments raised voluntarily during the Seven Years' War. Late in 1759 Keith's (87th) and Campbell of Dunoon's (88th), each comprising eight hundred men, were raised and served under Frederick the Great in continental Europe.[8] Both were raised in only a few weeks according to Stewart of Garth.[9] The officers of both were predominantly members of Hanoverian clans; the men were raised in Argyllshire, Perthshire, Inverness-shire (including Skye), Ross-shire, and Sutherland. Both regiments were reduced in 1763. The 89th (Gordon) Highlanders, commanded by New England-born Lt Col Staates Long Morris, were raised in October–November 1759 and served in India. The bulk of the men were from Gordon properties in the North-East and in Lochaber. However, the officers included members of once stoutly Jacobite families, MacGillivray of Dunmaglass and MacPherson.

In 1760 Johnson's Highlanders (101st) were raised in Argyll, Ross, and Inverness-shire, all but three of the men and officers Highlanders. They served in Europe with Keith's and Campbell's Highlanders and were reduced at the end of the war in 1763.

Major Colin Campbell of Kilberry raised a regiment embodied at Perth in 1761; numbered the 100th, it was stationed in Martinique until 1763. Also raised in 1761 was the 113th, Royal Highland Volunteers. It was commanded by a Major James Hamilton and served in Scotland. Colonel David Graeme of Gorthy raised two battalions of the Queen's Own Royal Regiment of Highlanders in 1762. They were numbered the 105th. Twenty-five of the thirty-nine officers were Campbells and of the rest, one was Archibald MacDonald (son of Coll Ban, Young Barisdale, who had recently been released from Edinburgh Castle). The last line regiment of Highlanders numbered during the Seven Years' War was Captain Allan MacLean of Torloisk's 114th. According to Stewart of Garth, Torloisk's was a feeder regiment for Highland regiments serving in Germany and North America.[10]

While many of the Highland regiments had been trained for service in European theatres of war, some, like the first recruits of Keith's were not. Neither were Fraser's who served in the American revolutionary war; they went into action with next to no formal regimental training whatever, except what they got aboard ship travelling to the fray. England's policy in using these people was callous and often perfidious, as the mutinies show; a common English attitude is summed up in James Wolfe's cynical remark to a friend that it would be "no great mischief if they fall. How can you better employ a secret enemy than by making his end conducive to the common good?"[11]

By October 1759 Britain knew of Wolfe's success at Quebec the month before, and even Englishmen were singing the praises of Fraser's Highlanders. A letter in the *Scots Magazine* (20 October 1759) from James Calcraft gives an admiring view of the regiment's part in Wolfe's victory: "The regiment of Lascelles, Kennedy's and Wolfe's grenadiers, did wonders; yet the highlanders, if any thing, exceeded them. When these took to their broadswords, my God! what a havock they made ... Those breechless brave fellows are an honour to their country. —— I cannot do them justice in my description of them"[12]

On the homefront two regiments of Fencible Highlanders were raised in 1759. The Fencible Men of Argyllshire and the earl of Sutherland's Battalion of Highlanders were formed for service in Scotland (a Scottish equivalent of the recently formed English county militias and an indicator of the Hanoverian government's readiness to trust armed Highlanders in Scotland). Both were reduced in 1763. Many independent companies of Highlanders were also raised by Highland officers taking up commissions in "new regiments formed in the south."[13] Whether or not these Fencibles, line regiments, and stray Highland companies had pipers is not always recorded.

In fact there was an overflow of would-be soldiers from Scotland.[14] In March 1757 there were no vacancies left for the men from Caithness, Sutherland, Orkney, and Skye who wanted to sign up in the standard line regiments then serving in Scotland. Bockland's could take no more so these volunteers were sent to Gibraltar and enrolled in a London regiment, the 7th Royal Fusiliers (Lord Robert Bertie's). The Highland supernumeraries from Fraser's and Montgomerie's Highlanders were sent to reinforce Colonel Ross's Regiment (38th Staffordshire) in Antigua.[15] An unknown number of Scotsmen also joined the Marines. On 20 October 1759 Lt Gen. Lord George Beauclerk tendered a return of the men raised in Scotland to serve King George in Germany. That return is no longer extant but a general estimate of the total of Scots soldiers, English and Gaelic speaking, who served in 1759, is twenty thousand.[16]

How many of these were impressed Highlanders? The number is certainly in the hundreds. Undoubtedly the government anticipated raising many men this way since it enacted legislation limiting the service of such impressed men to five years (the Recruiting Act of 1756–57, 30 Geo. 2, cap. 8). When the 19th, 31st, and 32d were raising their Scottish second battalions, Edinburgh Castle was unable to provide accommodation for all the impressed men who came pouring in. In January 1757 Beauclerk had run out of room at Edinburgh Castle and had to send one hundred and thirty men to Morpeth to join the three regiments, at which time the secretary-at-war advised that future excess be sent to Bockland's at York. Thereafter, three hundred and thirty were sent to Bockland's.[17] Edinburgh Castle held more than impressed recruits and doubtless there were other people impressed than Scottish Gaels wearing Highland clothes, but according to Maxwell, "the 2d battalion of the 32d became the 71st (in 1758). It included a large number of Highlanders, who, having been convicted under the Disarming Acts of the crime of wearing the kilt, were condemned to wear breeks in his Majesty's 71st."[18]

In June and July 1759, the year of the French naval effort to coordinate and convoy a fleet of soldiers across the channel to attack England, occupying forces were still retained and active in Jacobite Scotland. Marking this renewed fear of Jacobite activity in the Highlands, the current court records show a number of cases of interest. In June a "Neil M'Fie" was indicted at Inverness "as being a Popish priest, Jesuit, or trafficking Papist."[19] He was banished forever from Scotland, on pain of death should he return a papist. In July Donald Macalpin of Clifton in Perthshire was charged with wearing "a philebeg, or some other part of the Highland garb prohibited by law."[20] Macalpin claimed that he had been brutally used by an officer and won his case. (The people of Clifton had freed another kilted man in July 1749. Highland dress was obviously still available to some Highlanders even in Perthshire after eleven years of enforcement of the clothing clause of the Disarming Act).[21]

The Ross-shire record for 1759 shows that "in 1759 David Munro, Fearn, for having and concealing a firelock, is fined £15 stg., and sent to prison till he can pay."[22] This case stands as an anomaly. But if in 1759 it was unsafe to bear arms openly (or to be a Catholic priest), the court record gives proof positive (as well as negative) that it was perfectly safe to be a Highland piper. Two court cases in 1759 – one implicating MacLean of Loch Buidhe's piper, the other involving a vagrant, James Wilson, who, with two women vagrants (Helen and Jean Stewart), was convicted of house breaking – show, predictably, that the piper had nothing to fear. Facing the possibility of a death sentence for theft, Wilson, a self-professed Highland piper, petitioned the court in Edinburgh for banishment to the American plantations for life. The judge granted his wish, noting that as a "highland piper," he might "supply the place of some of his countrymen of that profession who have fallen in that part of the world."[23]

In fact the Seven Years' War, involving as it did the accession in 1760 of the first English Hanoverian king, George III, and the remarkable military service of Highland Scots around the world, marked the beginning of the end of the perception of Jacobite Highland Scotland as an internal military threat.

The Reverend Robert MacPherson of Laggan provided an early retrospect on the Disarming Act. Referring in a letter of 1771 to the act and its most urgent proscription, that against the carrying of arms, the Reverend Robert MacPherson of Laggan wrote: "That law is in thorough desuetude now in the Highlands."[24]

Looking back in 1779 on the Disarming Act and its absence of interest in Highland clothing after the Seven Years' War, David Stewart of Garth cited the cases of three Highlanders who were naturally habituated to wearing Highland garb and ready to mutiny if forced into trousers. These men were among a number of the 42d and 71st Highland regiments who had been told at Leith in 1779 that, having enlisted in Gaelic-speaking regiments that wore Highland garb, they were to be drafted into the 80th Regiment (the Edinburgh Regiment) and the 82d (Hamilton's), both of which were English speaking and trouser wearing. They claimed that "they were altogether unfit for service in any other corps than Highland ones, particularly that they were incapable of wearing breeches as a part of their dress."[25]

None of the three men had ever known anything else and had enlisted in the 42d and the 71st in order to be able to live in Gaelic and to continue to wear their traditional Highland clothing. None could have been born much after 1763 (but perhaps as early as the 1730s). Archibald MacIvor from Northern Argyllshire and Charles Williamson from Western Inverness-shire, both monoglot Gaelic recruits to the 42d stationed at Stirling, told the court that "they [had] always been accustomed to the Highland habit, so far as never to have worn breeches, a thing so inconvenient and even so impossible for a native Highlander to do, that when the Highland dress was prohibited by act of Parliament, though the philibeg was one of the forbidden parts of the dress, yet it was necessary to connive at the use of it, provided only that it was made of a stuff of one colour and not of tartan, as is well known to all acquainted with the Highlands, particularly with the more mountainous parts of the country."[26]

In the same court Robert Brydges, another non-English-speaking Gael from "the upper parts of Caithness" who had enlisted in the 71st (Fraser's Highlanders), explained that he also was accustomed to wear the Highland garb and was unwilling to wear Lowland clothing. John Prebble, relying on modern research, turned up slightly varying details but the point at issue, the wearing of Highland garb, remains the same.[27]

The next part of this book looks at the record of Scottish Gaelic pipers both within the established British military and in association with it. Chapter 5 provides a general outline of Gaelic military piping on the European stage in the seventeenth century and in British military groupings in the eighteenth. Chapter 6 looks in detail at four Highland regiments during the second half of the eighteenth century – the Black Watch, Fraser's, and Montgomerie's highlanders, and the Seaforths – while chapter 7 surveys the evidence for pipers in non-Highland regiments and in the American and East Indian wars.

As we go through the record in the following chapters, two points in particular must be born in mind. Firstly, all of these pipers in the British army

– hundreds of them, in Highland regiments and perhaps in Highland companies in Lowland or English regiments at home and overseas – particularly during the Seven Years' War but also in the American revolutionary and Indian subcontinental wars, were Disarming Act pipers before taking the king's shilling. Secondly, there was no discrimination against non-*ceòl mór* piping in the army at any level of piper in the period 1757–83 or at any other time. The matter of repertoire will be discussed at greater length in Part Three.

The pipers who served in the Seven Years' War all lived through Culloden and the anti-Gaelic constraints immediately afterwards, until the army returned to its wars in northern Europe for the most part in 1747. It was during that time and on into the 1750s that they were learning piping and building their repertoires. The piper-veterans of the American war and the campaigns in India learned their trade later but still well within the years of the act. Not one of these men was taught piping in any regiment, Highland or otherwise. They joined or affiliated themselves to the British army as competent pipers in the first place, proving that in a wide variety of Highland communities, Catholic and Protestant, Jacobite and Hanoverian, piping was popular, and socially indispensable in fact, all through the disarming Act years.

PART TWO

Military Piping, 1746–83

5 Military Piping in the Seventeenth and Eighteenth Centuries

THE SEVENTEENTH CENTURY

An early instance of piping in a body of Scottish soldiers focuses attention on Argyll-shire, although as yet without the pre-eminent family of Argyll Campbells. In 1627 a contingent of two hundred Scotch bowmen was sent, along with "a number of the MacKinnon clan," to defend Protestantism in France by order of Charles I. They were led by Alexander MacNaughton and their number included pipers and harpers.[1] Nothing is known about the private soldiers or musicians and the piper would have gone totally unremarked had he not rallied spirits during a dangerous confrontation with a French warship on the high seas. John Francis Campbell published contemporary correspondence from MacNaughton of Dunderawe to the earl of Morton in which the piper's name is given as "Allester Caddel"[2] and a harper is given as "Harie m'gra ... fra Larg."[3] MacNaughton's letter mentioned "our bagg pypperis and Marlit Plaidis," so it is fair to assume that many, if not all, of the pipers were Gaels born and raised on their leader's holdings.[4]

Scottish Highland pipers also served in the three-thousand-strong regiment (organized in fifteen companies) of Donald, chief of the MacKays (c. 1590–1649). They sailed from Cromarty for the Continent and the Protestant cause in 1626. In May 1629 the MacKay men (now more accurately known as Lord Reay's), beefed up by recruits from home, left King Christian of Denmark's service and joined Protestant Europe's famous "Lion of the North," King Gustavus Adolphus of Sweden (1594–1632). A warrant from Gustavus to Lord Reay, dated at Marienburg on 17 June 1629, shows that Lord Reay's regiment then had twelve companies (totalling twenty-three hundred men) each with three drummers and three pipers.[5]

In 1631 they were one of the four Scotch regiments (with Hepburn's, Lumsden's Musketeers, and Stargate's Corps) that Gustavus formed into the Scotch Brigade, also known as the Green Brigade and "Colonell Hepburne's Brigade." This amalgam of Scottish regiments was under the command of the Catholic Sir John Hepburn (c. 1598–1636) of Athelstaneford, in East Lothian,[6] until he resigned in June 1632 after Gustavus foolishly insulted him for being a Catholic. Hepburn then joined the French element of this brutal Christian war in 1632 and command of the Green Brigade devolved upon his cousin, the Protestant Sir James Hepburn, heir of Waughton (Athelstaneford's feudal superior).[7] From the winter of 1630–31 Lord Reay was continuously in Scotland raising men for new Green Brigade regiments. One of these was Monro of Obisdell's, which by July 1633 was reduced to two companies.

Obisdell's men were absorbed by Lord Reay's regiment. Having been reduced to only one company at the defence of Nördlingen in August 1634, what was left of Lord Reay's men (perhaps including both Monro of Obisdell and his more powerful relative Monro of Foulis), all under the command of the new Swedish leader, Bernard, duke of Saxe-Weimar, joined with Sir John Hepburn's and Jacques Nonpar's combined forces in France at Loudun. According to James Grant, who described the residue of MacKay's soldiers:

Among them was the remnant of the Green brigade, who hailed their old commander with joy, and beat the *Scottish March*[8] at his approach, while one solitary piper – the last of Mackay's regiment – blew his notes of welcome, and all the survivors of the long career of Swedish glory were now incorporated in the *Régiment d'Hébron*, as it was named in the French service, and with it the Swedish regiment, whilom of Hepburn.

The strength of the latter was given in 1637 at the following:- The Lieutenant-Colonel Munro; the major, Sir Patrick Monteith; 45 captains, one captain-lieutenant, 93 subalterns, 12 staff-officers, one piper, 664 non-commissioned officers, 96 drummers, and 48 companies of 150 pikes and muskets, making a grand total of 8,316 men, representing thus the Scoto-Bohemian bands of Sir Andrew Gray and all the Scotch corps of Gustavus Adolphus."[9]

Assuming the list to be ranked from the top down, the piper's position was medial between officer and man. The Scottish March was a distinctive national drum cadence that Gustavus occasionally ordered to be used by German troops to instill fear in the Imperial Catholic troops, who recognized it instantly and quaked. Whether it was associated with Gaelic Scots in particular or with all Scotsmen is unclear.[10]

The Sutherland and Ross names MacKay and Monro were common ones in the service of King Gustavus Adolphus of Sweden, but a third northern Scottish surname, Sinclair, has to be included.[11] Predictably, Monro-patronized pipers are not specified in the early seventeenth-century religious wars in Europe, but Monro wrote of "Murdo Piper" as having drowned while swimming ashore at Rugenwelt in the 1630s. Pipers from Lord Reay's estate appear to have been plentiful and it is known that pipers under the command of a Sinclair from the north served in Norway. In 1612, according to James Grant, George Sinclair, natural son of David Sinclair of Stirkoke and nephew of the Sinclair earl of Caithness, received permission from James VI to raise a body of men from his own country to serve the "Lion of the North." He raised nine hundred, sailed to join the Swedish king, who was then in Norway, and was sent into the mountains of Dovrefjell, south of Trondheim, as part of Gustavus's effort to conquer his neighbour. At the narrow pass of Kringellen, Sinclair and his force were almost utterly destroyed. Grant, citing Calder's *History of Caithness* (1861), noted that Sinclair had been warned of impending destruction by a ghastly forerunner. "Be that as it may, the Sinclairs marched on, and the air which their pipes played is still remembered in Norway, and it was certainly their own dead march."[12]

Calder offers no supporting evidence that there were pipers in Sinclair's regiment, but there certainly were pipers in Sinclair country or near it some years before Gustavus Adolphus's time. For example, the remission granted to the piper Donald McCruimien and John mac Rory in 1614 concerned the murders of Sinclair of Stirkoke and Arthur Smyth.

Out of the involvement of Charles I in Europe after his accession in 1625 came "the first regiment of the British line, and the oldest in the world," the 1st Royal Scots. Their first colonel was Sir John Hepburn, the man so heartily greeted by MacKay's piper, mentioned earlier. In 1633 Hepburn was given command of a corps of Scotsmen originally raised in 1590 to assist Henry of Navarre in his wars against the Catholic League. The men had been formed into independent companies and were trained and commanded by officers from the élite Garde du Corps Écossais and the Gendarmes Écossais. Under Hepburn, who had instructions to raise more men in Scotland, this group became Le régiment d'Hébron in 1633. At Hepburn's death in 1637 the regiment became known as (Lord James) Douglas's. In 1675 it became Dumbarton's Regiment (its quickstep "Dumbarton's Drums" dates from this period) and around 1684 they were named the Royal Regiment of Foot, hence simply Royals.

Knowing that the remnants of the Green Brigade joined Hepburn's 1st Royal Scots, this outfit must have had at least one Highland piper almost from its inception. And if MacNaughton's bowmen in France were also transferred into the Royals, then the first British regiment of the line would have had several Gaelic-speaking pipers as well as harpers to help it fight and pass the time. Later records suggest that piping continued in the Royals into the eighteenth century. Given a Highland presence among its officers, it might even have lasted until Waterloo.

When the regiment was in Ireland in 1679 it comprised twenty-one companies. Exclusive of staff officers, they were made up of eighty-two officers, sixty-three sergeants, sixty-three corporals, forty-two drummers, and eight hundred and ninety-one private men. The staff officers were "the adjutant, chaplain, surgeon, surgeon's mate, quarter-master and drum major [and] a piper major."[13] Major M.M. Haldane, the regiment's historian, wrote that the piper major was "struck off the establishment from motives of economy about 1764, and that, in spite of the remonstrances of the Marquis of Lorne and subsequent colonels."[14] The staff position "piper major" was never revived in this, the only regiment ever to have one, but the title re-emerges unofficially, in the Peninsular War. Adam Graham (c. 1790–1832), for example, was called "Piper Major" in the *Descriptive Roll Book* of the 93d Highlanders.

In 1680 there were so many Gaels in the Royals that they openly spoke Gaelic in British Tangiers to convey information that had to be kept secret from the Moors. As Col Clifford Walton noted, the Royals "had a Piper as the peculiarity of the regiment (Est. Lists, Harl. MSS),"[15] but it is premature, given the noticeable number of Gaelic speakers in the regiment, to take it for granted that the piper major was the only bagpiper in the regiment. In 1783 the enlistment of Big Samuel MacDonald suggests that Gaels were still enlisting, and as late as Waterloo the commanding officer of the Royals was a Major Robert MacDonald.[16]

Within the Highlands in the seventeenth century interclan troubles surely featured bagpipers, but one has to look further afield to get a reliable first glimpse of pipers at all. In the civil wars between the Royalist forces of Charles I and the Scottish Covenanting forces, pipers are known to have fought "for religion, the covenant and the countrie" (as the earl of Montrose's banner defiantly proclaimed, before he defected to the Royalist side). They marched into the northeast of England on 20 August 1640 with the Covenanting Scottish army under the command of ex-Gustavus Adolphus soldier Alexander Leslie. According to the earl of Lothian, who was there, "We are sadder and graver than ordinary soldiers only we are well provided of pipers."[17]

In *Montrose* (1928), John Buchan cited the "Calendar of State Papers, Domestic" for 1640 to prove that there were Highlanders in that invading army, but whether the pipers Lothian referred to were Highlanders, Lowlanders, or both has yet to be established. There was plenty of piping in Lowland Scotland. Forty-two years later, in 1682, the Foot Regiment commanded by Charles Erskine, the "Earle of Marre" (later the 21st Royal Scots and then the Royal North British Fusiliers), had three pipers. According to John

Buchan they were included in the ranks as "sentinells" and not separated as the two drummers in each company were.[18] That regiment was seventy-five percent Lowland and knowing that piping and patronized piping were common in the Lowlands too, whether or not any of the pipers were Highlanders is unknown.

An interesting and important additional remark attributed to the earl of Lothian was that the kirk-sponsored Covenanting army was accompanied by fiddlers who may or may not have been combatants (and who, according to Lothian, were "intolerably given to drink").[19] Their presence in that victorious seventeenth-century army can be linked with the known presence of fiddlers in the army of Prince Charlie in 1745. Although I only know of these two recorded examples of fiddlers in a Scottish army, it is tempting to think that aggregated clan armies on major campaigns, at least within Britain, took both kinds of musician with them, the fiddle for dance music and the pipes for excitation to fight, and both also for dancing. If one were to rely on information taken from any company of Gaelic-speaking Highlanders raised in Cape Breton for service in the Great War, one would certainly have found several fiddlers and pipers or chanter players. The same was true for Cape Breton companies in the Second World War when, even if piping had yielded somewhat to the alien idea of pipe bands, which had been introduced to Cape Breton perhaps as early as the 1890s and during the Great War, the large majority of pipers were still ear-learned and traditional in their style. An important number of them also played the fiddle.

Turning now specifically to piping in seventeenth century Argyll regiments, Archibald Campbell, eighth earl of Argyll (and first Marquis from 1641) raised a Regiment of Foot for the Covenant in 1639. This regiment was the mould for the Scots Guards. In 1641 Charles I was in Scotland when the Scottish Presbyterian planters in Ireland were attacked by the displaced Catholic Irish under Sir Phelim O'Neile. Charles, having distributed honours including Argyll's marquisate, sanctioned the raising of ten Scottish regiments to control the Irish rebellion. One of these was Archibald Campbell's, which now became known as Argyll's Regiment; another was that of a relative, Col James Campbell of Lawers's.

Argyll's men spent seven years in Ireland. Col James Campbell's was there until 1644. No pipers are on record from the first days of these regiments but each had a "Drumer major" and "2 drumers at 1/- a peece" in 1644.[20] Then in 1648 Lawers's regiment had "12 Drumers and Pypers."[21] There is no similar information for Argyll's regiment, the proto-Scots Guards, although in 1649 a piper and drummer were added to a regiment that the marquis raised in 1643 for the Solemn League and Covenant.[22]

In 1678 in the battle of Allt nam Mèirleach (Thieves' Brook) near Wick, a Campbell piper is actually named. Finlay MacIvor from the neighbourhood of Glenlyon in Perthshire was a member of the army of the first earl of Breadalbane, which was led to victory over the Sinclairs in the North by Robert Campbell, fifth of Glenlyon. According to Angus MacKay, the Campbell force was composed of men from Glenlyon, Glenfalloch, Glendochart, and Achaladair, supplemented by men of the laird of MacNab (Breadalbane's brother-in-law).[23] The piece of ceòl mór "Bodaich nam Briogais" ("The Old Men of the Breeks") is supposed to have been played at the Campbell victory by Breadalbane's piper.[24]

Little is known about piping in the Argyll regiment raised roughly a decade later in 1689, two companies of which, under the same Robert Campbell of Glenlyon, were responsible for the massacre of the Glencoe MacDonalds in 1692. Glenlyon's piper, Hugh MacKenzie, is reported to have piped "A Breadalbane rant in triumph" as a postscript to Captain Robert's winter massacre.[25]

Since Glenlyon's company was far from senior it is worth listing in a note the other company commanders so that readers may judge for themselves just how Highland they were and therefore how likely to have had a piper or pipers.[26] The regiment's six hundred men in ten companies were reduced in 1698 after service in the Netherlands. Detailed records exist but no pipers are specified except in lore.

For all their Gaelicness the Argyll regiment uniform was essentially the same as that of English regiments, although the soldiers wore long tartan waistcoats under their greatcoats, if they had greatcoats. In their first winter (1689) some of them were issued plaids in place of greatcoats, but this might have resulted from a shortage of greatcoats and the ready availability of the "Highland habite" rather than from a dominant wish to cleave to Highland culture. The primary weapons were also atypical of a Highland regiment. They reflected the ideas that Gustavus Adolphus had introduced and used with such success sixty years earlier and not Gaelic Scottish preferences. Each sixty-man company had twenty pikemen and forty musketeers.

Several other regiments raised in the 1680s and 1690s are prime candidates for having had pipers, given the Gaelicness of their commanding officers and their recruitment from known piping areas of the Highlands. These are Grant's (1689–90), and three Strathnaver regiments from Sutherland (1689–90, 1693–1717, 1702–13), the second of which served in Marlborough's spectacular wars. Following those there were Colonel Robert MacKay's two regiments (1694–97), each of seven hundred and fifty men; Tullibardine's, or John Lord Murray's (1694–97), made up of seven hundred men in thirteen companies; and Mar's Regiment (1702–13), with nine companies of twenty-seven men each. From 1706 Mar's served in Marlborough's campaigns under the colonelcy of Alexander Grant, son of the chief of the Grants. The same Alexander Grant, now a brigadier, raised a regiment of ten companies that policed Edinburgh from 1715 until they were disbanded in 1718.

The Scots Guards, mentioned above (known from 1650–1712 as the Scottish Regiment of Foot Guards and from 1712–1830 as the Third Guards), left Scotland, save for one company, in 1704. They did not return until 1911, although in the nineteenth century recruiting was carried on in Scotland. However, the company that remained was the Highland Company and it was stationed in Inverness from 1704 until 1714, when it too marched south to London, and oblivion. It had fifty-eight men, including three officers, under a Maj. Duncan McKenzie and for the first time mentioned "a pyper." They were all Highlanders dressed in Highland garb, and when they marched into London in early 1715 they were led by their piper.[27]

As a footnote, it should be mentioned that the military status of the piper was unofficial. Judging from Turner's *Pallas Armata*, originally published in 1683, this was true in Europe as well as in England. Turner wrote: "In some places a Piper is allowed to each Company: the *Germans* have him, and I look upon their Pipe as a Warlike Instrument. The Bagpipe is good enough Musick for them who love it; but sure it is not so good as the Almain Whistle. With us any Captain may keep a Piper in his Company and maintain him too, for no pay is allowed him, perhaps just as much as he deserveth."[28]

While the officers and foot soldiers were paid (not always regularly), the piper's allegiance to his chief, chieftain, or perhaps even tacksman was presumably binding enough for him to take his chances as an active supernumerary in his superior's chosen wars. This could only have worked because the piper already enjoyed respect and status in his own society and had enough of a rent break as a musician to eliminate any potential grousing at ill usage.

Interestingly, the English, French, and German armies of the 1670s throw up a possible model for a particular kind of supernumerary classification into which some pipers may have fallen. This was the "Gentleman of the Company," described by Turner[29] as something more than an ordinary soldier and his pay a little better; his duties did not include "centinel," although he marched and watched with arms. In France the "Gentleman of the Company" was called an *Appointe* and in Germany a *Gefreuter*.

The Highland regiment itself was, until long after the removal of the heritable jurisdictions in 1747, a basically Gaelic institution, reflecting the stratified Gaelic social system, the subtlety of Gaelic discipline based on appeal to honour and the duties of kinship, and its unique war music. The Scotch Gaelic social analogue had four obvious levels, the chief or chieftain, the tacksman and wadsetters,[30] the tenant farmer, and the sub-tenant. All of these levels can be identified one way or another in Gaelic, not in post-mediæval Gaelicized French or English. By the seventeenth century the French and British officer class was divided into many more classifications than the Gaels had social classes; all used French terminology, from ensign and lieutenant to general. When the French officer nomenclature was applied to the Scotch Gaelic officer class, either directly in Scotland or France, or indirectly through the English military, the additional terminology was conveniently borrowed into Gaelic (*caiptean, màidsear, còirneal, oifigeach*).[31] Since Gaels had served as soldiers in France since the late thirteenth century, there was ample opportunity to absorb French military terminology (and concepts) where required. Even the term *saighdear* (soldier) is a loan-word and a pallid version of *gaisgeach, mìlidh*, or *laoch* (warrior/hero), among others.

Apart from the term for company, which is *cuideachd* in Gaelic, the terminology for the larger bodies of fighting men are also all borrowings (*réisimeid, bratailian, arm*). Even if at least half, geographically, of the independent nation of Scotland in the seventeenth century was Gaelic speaking, all national military terminology was imposed by the non-Gaelic speaking half. Gaels were no strangers to variants of the system since in those days they fostered much stronger ties with Europe, in educational as well as military matters, than today. It was not really until Gaeldom had been thoroughly tamed in the nineteenth century (by which time Europe had lost political interest) that this Gaelic military overlap was accommodated and the term "piper" was accorded official acceptance. By that time the average piper, whatever his social status, no longer stood haughtily aloof; he joined the ranks.

THE EIGHTEENTH CENTURY

The early military tradition of using pipers continued into the eighteenth century. During the Seven Years' War (1756–63), the American revolutionary war, and the long war with France (1793–1815), the British army used all the Highlanders it could get, particularly once the taboo on Catholic and Jacobite soldiers was broken.[32] These groupings of Gaelic men and officers were not confined to the "Highland" regiments but were also found in English-speaking regiments, probably almost everywhere that Highland officers served. There were Gaelic-speaking officers in the Royal North British Fusiliers (initially and by transfer), in Thomas Frederick Humberston MacKenzie's 100th, in the 82d (the Duke of Hamilton's),[33] and in many other regiments. The normal method of obtaining a commission, besides buying it, was to bring one's tenantry in as soldiery. Whether or not these Gaelic-speaking companies in English regiments had pipers with them has yet to be established; there was no legal reason why a gentleman might not have his private servants with him. There certainly must have been pipers and fiddlers in the ranks of enlisted men, but whether it was legal to take an enlisted man out of the line and use him as a piper in times of action is not known.

Highlanders also swelled the numbers of non-Highland regiments by transfer. For example John Small, late of the 42d (Black Watch) in America, transferred to the 21st Foot (Royal North British Fusiliers) rather than go on half pay in 1763; when a much-reduced 42d was on the point of leaving North America in 1767, the men were given the option of transferring to another regiment in North America or going home to be reduced. Small's popularity with the rank and file attracted a large number of men of the 42d to the 21st, and given his understanding of and sympathy for Highlanders, it is almost certain that ex-Black Watch pipers functioned as normal in the new regiment.[34]

Throughout the period in question there was prominent use of Highland pipers in the British army. However, to prove their presence necessitates the use of non-official documentation, which is seldom satisfactory. As far as the official military record goes, there is often only the barest mention of a piper or pipers; names are seldom given. As noted earlier, the term "piper" was in any case quite unofficial in all but one regiment until 1854. It occurred only in the official rank of "piper major," a staff officer designation found unique- ly in the Royal Regiment of Foot (also known as the Royal Scots, or just "The Royals"). The "piper major" appeared first in the written record in 1679 and remained a feature of the regiment's personnel until the rank was discontinued in 1764 (if there was one he was the only official piper at Cul- loden). All the other pipers, hundreds of them, who served in the Highland regiments from the eighteenth century until 1854 are ignored, as pipers, by the official record.[35]

Luckily, since Gaelic-speaking pipers in the British army (if not pipers in general)[36] appear to have been a novelty for many non-Gaels, stray but im- portant observations by English officers and others crop up by the 1750s, almost always involving military action and the piper's extraordinary power to invigorate.

When Highland officers like Colonel David Stewart of Garth wrote of pipers playing during an action, it is obvious that they wanted to give credit where credit was due; their reasons for mentioning pipers was the more heartfelt since pipers hazarded their lives as musicians and made egregious targets for sharpshooters. The ambivalence of the ordinary piper's military status in British military service made his risk taking all the more praise- worthy. David Stewart of Garth, second son of a Gaelic family, included pipers with drummers in some initial regimental enlistments; at other times he seemed to assume that there were pipers in all Highland regiments, ignored them altogether in his descriptions of enlistments, and treated the subject casually afterwards. Garth may have known Donald Gunn, a piper in the 77th (Atholl Highlanders), the regiment in which Garth is first listed as a commissioned officer.[37]

The argument is still made that pipers fell into the "drummer" category, and although it may have happened here and there it is by no means established as a general practice. Army tactics of the time made the drummer absolutely vital to the various deployments and manœuvres of large numbers of men in the hellish din of Europe's wars. The piper's prime value was cleverer, more visceral, and profoundly psychological; his function was to animate when the pressure was at its height, especially during the charge and the "shock" (man-to-man fighting). That degree of subtlety in motivating soldiers was beyond the ken of many English officers, who preferred to motivate men, most of whom they considered contemptible, by fear of the lash and the gallows.[38] The juggernaut psychology of the English military, for whom piping and pipers were not a priority, was country miles behind its Highland counterpart.

The story of Fraser's Highlanders refusing, without pipes, to charge Montcalm's army on the Plains of Abraham in 1759 is apocryphal, but it underlines two of the several distinctive features of the Gaelic military machine in the early days of its grafting onto King George II's army that were lacking in other European armies – the use of the Highland bagpipe as a stimulus to fighting, and the inclination to break ranks and charge the enemy with broadsword and dirk when the accepted practice of the day was to stand, reload, and fire again no matter how close the enemy got.[39] There may still have been pipers attached to German-speaking and other regiments in Europe, but it is unlikely that they affected European soldiery as profoundly as they did Highlanders, and probably Lowlanders too. Many Scots were indeed profoundly impressed by the *brosnachadh*, or inciting, quality of pipe music in the Highland regiments during actual conflict and by the remarkable bravery of the pipers. Their various observations add important data to the unofficial subject of piping in the army. This casual reporting backs up what is available in I.H. MacKay Scobie's *Pipers and Pipe Music in a Highland Regiment* (1924) and the regimental histories published by David Stewart of Garth in 1822. Stewart's two-volume *Sketches of the Highlanders*, despite its errors and romantic Gaelophile bias, is a valuable secondary source.[40] His informants included men who served in the Independent Companies (c. 1729), Black Watch (1739), Loudon's (1745), Montgomerie's (1757), Fraser's (1757), and all the many other Scotch regiments of the line that were raised later in the eighteenth century; at least one informant was a relative, Mr Stewart of Bohallie, a granduncle by marriage and one of the gentlemen private soldiers in Campbell of Carrick's company of the Black Watch, or 43d (renumbered the 42d in 1749). David Stewart did not say who the piper to Carrick's company was, nor did he bother to name pipers in the Highland regiments from 1739. He also failed to specify cases where officers-gentlemen were pipers, as some may have been in the Black Watch. Stewart simply took pipers for granted as a *sine qua non* of all Highland regiments and only in exceptional circumstances, such as when a piper was shot or otherwise distinguished himself, did he bother to remark upon them. Nonetheless, he is one of the key sources for what follows.

6 Piping in Four Eighteenth-Century Regiments

THE BLACK WATCH

The regiment now best known as the Black Watch began in the seventeenth century as a police force for the Highlands, became the Independent Companies in c. 1729, and was embodied as a regiment of the line in 1739 under the earl of Crawfurd, a Gaelic-speaking Lowlander and protégé of John, duke of Argyll. It is nowhere reported that these Independent Companies had pipers, but given the aristocratic nature of even the private men in these select groups in the 1730s, and given the importance to a chief or chieftain's dignity of having a piper, it almost goes without saying that there were several. Stewart of Garth implied a natural continuity with the older Independent Companies when he described the two tartans chosen for the newly formed line regiment of 1739. When the Black Watch was embodied, "the pipers wore a red tartan of very bright colours, (of the pattern known by the name of the Stewart tartan,) so that they could be more clearly seen at a distance. When a band of music was added, plaids of the pipers' pattern were given to them."[1]

Stewart, however, could not and did not say that these pipers were officially recognized in any way or that they drew pay as regular soldiers, so it is quite conceivable that they were present at the wishes and expense of company leaders, all of whom had discretionary public money at their disposal through the pay system, which also allowed off-reckonings or dockings of the privates' pay.

A record of piping in Morar in 1746, perhaps one of the earliest recorded instances of a Black Watch piper playing, emphasizes the ambiguous status of the piper in Highland military society in the 1740s. On 4 May of that year Simon Fraser, Lord Lovat, chief of a clan that had produced hundreds of Jacobite soldiers, was discovered hiding in the bole of a huge tree in the South Morar estate.[2] The man who first found him was Captain Dugald Campbell of Achrossan who at the time was under the command of Captain John Fergussone, RN, of *HMS Furnace*. Fergussone, the nemesis of many a Jacobite in 1746, had eighty regular soldiers and a hundred and twenty of the Argyll Militia with him, all seconded from the garrison at Fort William. Campbell was in command of the Argyll Militia, though his captain's commission was held in the Black Watch under Sir John Murray. Lord Lovat, old and obese, "was put into his litter, and the soldiers made a run with him to the sea-side, the pipers playing 'Lovat's March,' with which he seem'd well pleased."[3] A tune called "Fraser's March" appears uniquely in the "Campbell Canntaireachd (1797).

It has been assumed that the pipers in question belonged to the Argyll Militia but in fact to whom they were attached remains unknown. Accepting that Captain Fergussone had no pipers in his naval personnel, these ones may have come from Lord Lovat's personal service, or from the Black Watch or the Argyll Militia (if the piper was an official soldier), while some may have been personal pipers to Hanoverian officers.

Lord Lovat's political deviousness ensured that he was not captured in South Morar as an active rebel, so those with him at the time may have been able convincingly to claim that they were servants and non-Jacobites (to which Lovat would have happily attested). Lovat is also known to have had a pride in piping and in his current piper, David Fraser, whom he had sent to be trained by Malcolm MacCrimmon in Skye and who may have been one of the pipers at Loch Morar. Lord Lovat is still remembered as the chief who stipulated in a codicil to his will that "all the pipers between Johnnie Groat's House and the town of Edinburgh be invited to play at his funeral" (they weren't).[4] It is possible that at least one of the pipers involved in the playing of "Lovat's march" was Captain Campbell's piper, from the Black Watch, who may have gone with his officer to the militia either as the gentleman's piper or under force of military secondment. Another probable candidate is a member of the Argyll Militia, although Fergussone's *Argyll in the Forty-five* (1951?) makes no mention of pipers having been raised or having served as such. In the last case a piper or pipers may have been attached by Gaelic usage to Campbell of Achrossan, to serve him in peace and war.

That the Argyll Militia had pipers as a matter of course can only be proposed by analogy with known seventeenth-century pipers in the Highland company of the Scottish Regiment of Foot Guards at Inverness and in those northern Independent Companies raised in Skye and elsewhere in the North under the ægis of Duncan Forbes of Culloden in 1745. The piper MacCrimmon in one of the Skye Independent Companies was the only casualty at

Moy. The Skye pipers Iain MacIntyre and Neil MacCodrum from two of MacLeod of MacLeod's companies may also have attended as pipers purely by the dictates of Scottish Gaelic gentlemanly practice (including rental agreement).

Although David Stewart of Garth served in the Black Watch, or 42d, from 10 October 1787 until 24 April 1804, he wrote very little about its pipers and piping. However, in an appendix to his second volume he described the regiment – then still numbered the 43d – at its embodiment at Aberfeldy as containing ten companies, each consisting of "5 serjeants, 2 pipers or drummers, and 80 men each," for a total of eight hundred and seventy.[5] Francis Collinson said only that there was no official provision for pipers in government-funded Highland soldiers until Duncan Forbes of Culloden's Independent Companies were raised in 1745. If both men are correct, then the case is strong that pipers were retained privately, their wages found, perhaps, in discretionary and unreported ways, for example through off-reckonings.

Three of these companies were raised for the 'Forty-five, served as military policemen in Scotland, and were reduced at the Peace of Aix in 1748. A second battalion, seven companies of which were raised in 1758, was reduced in 1767. Another company, the 21st, was raised in 1776 while the Black Watch was stationed in Glasgow. At that time the strength of each company was raised to one hundred and five men. In 1756, when there were thirteen companies, the men *had* to be Highlanders and a large majority of the officers were Gaelic speaking – *esprit de corps* was highly valued. In 1775 Lord John Murray, in Scotland for the first time since 1743, failed to prevail in an argument over the appointment of English officers to the Black Watch and three were admitted to the regiment. Their powers as cultural or linguistic dilutants were probably minimal. On 10 April 1776 the rank and file comprised nine hundred and thirty-one Gaels, seventy-four Lowland Scots, five English, one Welshman, and two Irishmen.

What Black Watch veteran Stewart of Garth wrote, quite ingenuously, about the regimental pipers being uniformed in a distinctive red tartan is as convincing proof as any that the Black Watch had pipers and that they were at least in one way subject to uniformity. Twenty-four companies were raised between the Black Watch's establishment in 1739 and its arrival in America to fight in the revolutionary war. By Garth's reckoning many pipers must have joined, maybe twenty or more barring transfers from other companies and men who rejoined. We must assume that their numbers were much the same as the numbers in Fraser's and Montgomerie's Highlanders. As an aside, that the five Englishmen were all "in the band"[6] dates the presence of such a thing at least to April 1776. The Royal North British Fusiliers, or 21st, a Lowland regiment recruited mainly from South West Scotland, had a band during its four-year stint in Nova Scotia 1789–93.

The first mention of a piper after the embodiment of the Black Watch comes in connection with an action near the little North American community of New York on 16 September 1776. In that affair, among others, "1 piper and 2 drummers" were wounded. A month later, in the same general area, the 42d were ordered to make a feint on Fort Washington from the east to set up the main attack from another quarter. The Highlanders effected the feint, drawing Americans to the undefended side of their fort, and then proceeded to scale the cliffs to mount a full-blown attack. "One of the pipers, who began to play when he reached the point of a rock on the summit of the hill, was immediately shot, and tumbled from one piece of rock to another till he reached the bottom."[7] Among the 42d's casualties were "1 serjeant and 10 privates";[8] presumably the piper was one of these, or else went uncounted.

The 42d's pipers receive no other mention during the revolutionary war, or indeed during their year's term in Halifax, Nova Scotia, and after that in Cape Breton and Isle St Jean, where two companies were stationed. They embarked for England in August 1789 with additional companies that had been added in 1787, in one of which was Ensign David Stewart (later Colonel Stewart) of Garth, drafted from half pay in the Athole Highlanders on 10 October.

Piping in the Highland regiments during the Seven Years' War is not clearly recorded, but as the next two section show, there can be no question that the prominent regiments, Fraser's and Montgomerie's Highlanders, were well endowed with pipers. They were also in large proportion officered and manned by ex-Jacobite Gaels. While their various military achievements have been justifiably praised, the English government reflected Lt Col James Wolfe's profound dislike of Highlanders. The raising of two thousand men in the Highlands was not entirely a matter of letting bygones be bygones; it was also a way to thin out their numbers and dilute any threat of future rebellion.

FRASER'S 78TH HIGHLANDERS (1757–63)

The first Fraser's Highlanders, or 78th, were raised in 1757 by the ex-Jacobite Simon Fraser, son of Lord Lovat *decollatus* and veteran of Prince Charles' army.[9] By December 1757, according to Col J.R. Harper, Fraser's Highlanders consisted of eighty-two officers, fourteen companies of one hundred and five men, sixty-five sergeants, and thirty pipers or drummers, making (somehow) a total of one thousand five hundred and forty-two men of all ranks. Stewart of Garth is Harper's most probable source of the "30 pipers or drummers,"[10] and once again, interpreters have long assumed that pipers were categorized as drummers. This was not the case. There is no doubt whatever that, through the gunfire and smoke, drummers were the officers' voices and gestures and that two per company, the normal number for an infantry regiment, were specified for Fraser's Highlanders in 1757.[11] That makes twenty-eight drummers for fourteen companies with two drummers left over. Thus, if pipers received a wage they were obviously regarded for pay purposes as privates or supernumeraries, not as drummers.

Colonel Harper stated on his own authority that Fraser's Highlanders had fifteen pipers, one for the colonel (Simon Fraser, who led a company), one for the adjutant (Hugh Fraser), and one for each "major" commanding a company. (By major he must have meant captains and majors together since the various companies of Fraser's Highlanders were typically led by captains.) Fifteen pipers is a guess but a fairly accurate one.

Writing of the Seaforths, MacKay Scobie said that the number of pipers in the regiment depended on the commanding officer's wishes but usually each flank company (i.e., the Grenadier and the Light) had one or two pipers and each battalion company one. Scobie, who was himself a piper, added that each company was allowed two drummers and the flank companies an additional fifer. In the first Fraser's Highlanders, those raised for active service in the Seven Years' War, the normal complement of pipers, using MacKay Scobie's formula, would have been sixteen (one for each of the twelve battalion companies and two each for the flank companies), but we know from the diary of Sergeant James Thompson that his grenadier company had "but one," which yields Harper's figure of fifteen by what seems to be a more plausible reckoning. Why, for example, should the adjutant have a piper unless he led a company?

Who the pipers were is unknown and there are difficulties in discovering from whose estates or tacks they were raised. One extant list names the one hundred and fifty-eight men who chose to settle in British North America in 1763, classifying them as sergeant, corporal, drummer, and soldier.[12] Assuming that MacKay Scobie was right, and earlier military piping history suggests he was, then a company of men was associated with two pipers. Inasmuch as most Highland companies were raised ostensibly by a gentleman who became at least a captain, pipers were associated with that captain, most likely farming on his holding. However, recruiting was by no means necessarily limited to the captain. As an example from the 1757 Fraser's Highlanders shows,[13] lieutenants raised men too, which opens the possibility of their also, on occasion, bringing pipers with them into the army; ensigns may have done so as well.

It made good sense to Gaelic officers that a soldier expected to face death be encouraged by the music and the musician(s) with whom he was intimately acquainted. It made equally good sense to ensure that the piper was paid. We do not know how much pipers in the 78th received, but the earnings of one piper in a later Fraser's Highlanders – the 71st, raised in 1775 by the same Simon Fraser who had raised the 78th in 1757 – are known from a personal letter of a William MacKenzie to "Petter," dated New York, 7 February

1777: "I am still in Capt Patrick Campbell's of Glenuir's company I am Piper to the 2 Battn 71 Regt I am as well as ever I was in my Life my Pay is as Good and 1 Shilling & sixpence Per Day and I hope my fortune within two years will be as Good that I will have 200 Acres of free Grownd of my own in this country ... if it had not been for this war this is the Best Country in the World."[14] To compare pay, John MacDonald, the Skerray schoolteacher, was paid "a shilling a day" as "pipe-major" in the MacKay of Bighouse Company of the Gordon Fencibles in 1778,[15] and a private in the New Brunswickers, 104th Foot, in 1811 was paid 1/- a day.[16] Glenuir may have been generous to the piper.) The flexible bookkeeping system used by the army, the deductions from men's pay by officers (the "off-reckonings" mentioned earlier)[17], and the payment to a regiment by establishment numbers rather than actual numbers of active men allowed plenty of room to remunerate extranumeraries. Almost certainly MacKenzie in Campbell of Glenuir's company of the 71st in North America was paid in this fashion, or in an equivalent roundabout way, as probably the vast majority of pipers were until the status of piper was officially recognized by the British army in 1854.[18]

The original ten companies in Fraser's Highlanders were led by Lt Col Simon Fraser, Master of Lovat; Maj. James Clephane; Maj. John Campbell of Dunoon, Captains; John MacPherson (brother of Cluny); John Campbell of Ballimore; Charles Baillie (from Ross-shire); Simon Fraser of Inverallochy; Donald MacDonald, brother of Clanranald; John MacDonell of Lochgarry; and Thomas Fraser of Struy. (MacPherson, MacDonald, and MacDonell, the last two of whom spoke French, Gaelic, and English, had fought for Prince Charles, like Simon Fraser himself. A similarly pro-Jacobite representation floods the lower levels of the commissioned officers,[19] and doubtless the men too.) Three additional companies from Cork arrived in New York in the first quarter of 1758 in time to leave for Louisbourg that summer, while the fourteenth arrived in Quebec on 4 September 1759 under Captain Alexander Fraser of Culduthel, an important recorder of music and song in the regiment.

The three most likely names of captains of the additional companies from Cork are Alexander Cameron of Dungallon (fourth of Dungallon, ex-ensign in Lochiel's Jacobite regiment in the 'Forty-five), Thomas Ross of Culrossie, and James Fraser of Belladrum. Several other officers served as captains for unknown durations until the regiment was disbanded in early December 1763. Those whose names appear among the list of lieutenants originally commissioned in 1757 and who were promoted were Captains Charles MacDonell of Glengarry, Alexander MacLeod, Ronald McDonald, son of Keppoch, John Fraser of Balnain, and Archibald Campbell, son of Glenlyon. The names of two new captains that appear as lieutenants in J.R. Harper's "Later List of Officers Granted Commissions" were Alexander Campbell of Aross and John Nairn. (Harper's list of officers is almost the same as Stewart of Garth's, though Steward wrongly stated that his list contained the names of the officers whose commissions were dated 5 January 1757.) Campbell and Nairn may have been lieutenants in the four additional companies. How Captain Sir Henry Seton of Abercorn and Culbeg, Captain Montgomerie, and Captain Wood are reflected in the numbers of regimental officers, or whose companies they took, is unknown. Captain Hugh Fraser was perhaps the original adjutant. Two captain lieutenants, John Crawford Walkinshaw and Simon Fraser, are also listed. Of all of these officers four company captains were killed at the three major actions, Louisbourg (June 1758), the Plains of Abraham (13 September 1759), and Quebec (1760). The influence on pipers of changes in officers in the fourteen companies is unknown. At least one piper fatality is mentioned by Harper: "During this battle [the second battle of Quebec, 1760] the 78th Fraser Highlanders lost the intrepid Captain Donald Macdonald, Lieutenant Cosmo Gordon and 55 non-commissioned officers, pipers and privates."[20]

The first breakdown of the origins of the recruited soldiers is given by Stewart of Garth (and repeated by Col J.R. Harper), who said that Simon Fraser personally raised eight hundred men, while "the gentlemen of the country and the officers of the regiment, added more than 700."[21] This, if correct, means that probably about eight of the pipers were from the forfeited Fraser estate, which was under the factorship of Capt. John Forbes of Newe, Aberdeenshire (Fraser was granted his forfeited estate in 1774 for his military efforts on behalf of the Crown in the Seven Years' War). In all likelihood other pipers included one from the MacPherson estate of Cluny (possibly James MacPherson, who had been with Cluny at Benalder after Culloden),[22] one from the MacDonalds of Clanranald, one from the Cameron's Dungallon holding, one from Ross-shire with Captain Baillie, one from Ballimore's patrimony, and a piper associated with Lochgarry.

When Montcalm's French army crossed the Sillery Road near Québec on 13 September 1759, the Languedoc and Sarre regiments advanced on the 78th, then commanded by Captain John Campbell of Ballimore (Simon Fraser was recovering from a wound received on 2 September at Montmorency). When the French were at twenty-five yards, Ballimore barked out, "Ready-Drums, Present-drums, Fire." Although they had reportedly been ordered to stand, reload, and fire again, the Highlanders were too near the enemy for such sang-froid. They dropped their fire-locks, drew their broadswords, and charged. Sergeant Thompson of Captain Donald MacDonald's grenadier company wrote in his diary:

Our company had but one piper and he was not provided with arms and the usual means of defence like the rest of the men as to keep aloof for safety. When our line advanced the charge, General Townshend observing that the Piper was missing, and he knowing well the value of one on such occasions, he sent in all directions for him and he was heard to say aloud, "Where's the Highland Piper? And "Five pounds for a piper," but de'il a bit did the Piper come forward. However, the charge by good chance was pretty well effected without him as all those that escaped could testify. For this business the Piper was disgraced by the whole of the Regiment and the men would not speak to him, neither would they suffer his rations to be drawn with theirs, but had them served out by the commissary separately and he was obliged to shift for himself as well as he could.[23]

Captain Donald MacDonald's grenadier company piper went unarmed and, at least in this instance, unpunished for not facing the enemy. Had he been a private in 1689, he would have been put to death under article 16 of the "Laws and Ordinances Touching Military Discipline" for refusal to obey an order; there is no reason to think that greater leniency would be shown to (ex-)Jacobites in 1759. All that happened to MacDonald's absent piper was that he was sent to Coventry by his fellows, which suggests that the piper in a Gaelic-speaking regiment as late as 1759 was there at the dictate, and possibly the expense, of the Gaelic officer-gentleman (MacKay Scobie wrote that company pipers in the Seaforths were "provided and maintained by the Captain," not the military establishment)[24] and was not subject to the disciplinary articles. Thompson's captain, Charles Baillie, had been killed at Louisbourg and the company command had devolved upon Clanranald's brother, Donald MacDonald, who may have felt he had no traditional right to coerce the man. He was killed at the second battle of Quebec in 1760 and replaced by John MacDonell of Lochgarry. The same piper who was sent to Coventry by the regiment for avoiding battle in 1759 redeemed his honour by rallying the men at the second battle of Quebec. It is almost impossible to imagine his having been piper in a company led by the brother of Clanranald at such a critical encounter as the Plains of Abraham and escaping recrimination for such blatant dereliction of duty, unless he had some immunity to military law. What did happen when a captain was killed or otherwise removed from active service? Did the new captain's piper replace the original one? Nobody knows, but in the case of the grenadier company, and all those companies that did not suffer losses in such high numbers as to change, through replacements from the pool of supernumeraries, the cohesive subclan identity of the private soldiers, a good guess is that he didn't.

Besides the unofficial data on pipers to be had from Stewart of Garth and Sergeant James Thompson, another important source of general information on piping in Fraser's Highlanders is Simon Fraser's Airs and Melodies Peculiar to the Highlands of Scotland and the Isles (1816). This work, despite various shortcomings, provides a valuable glimpse of the repertoire of pipers in Fraser's Highlanders and focuses unselfconsciously on the tastes in and depth of traditional musicality of both officers and men of the regiment during the years 1757–63.

According to "William MacKay Jun. Blairbeg, Glen Urquhart, 28th July 1874,"[25] Simon Fraser was born at Ardachie near Fort Augustus in 1773 but lived most of his life in Stratherrick, to the east of Loch Ness, the traditional home of his family. He died in 1852. He was a tenant farmer at Knockie and obviously had a strong interest in passing on to future generations, in "scientific" form, an echo of the native Gaelic music he had had, directly or indirectly, from older people. He was a violin player, not a piper, although he lived in the days of several well-known Gaels whose renown as Highland pipers in his area has survived.

Adding information taken from his notes in the appendix to what he said of his informants in the "Letters and Prospectus relative to the Airs and Melodies," Fraser had six main sources. He stressed that his collection was based on tunes gathered mostly between 1715 and 1745. The first two informants, whom he never knew but who were obviously steeped in the tradition of the period between risings, were his paternal grandfather (whom he never named), a grazier and cattle dealer, and his grandfather's business partner, Hugh MacKay of Bighouse, son of George, the third Lord Reay. Hugh acquired Bighouse in 1744, having married the eldest daughter of MacKay of Bighouse. Hugh MacKay died in 1770 in Bath. He had been a military officer and for years led the wandering life of a cattle dealer. His memory for Gaelic songs, whether exceptional or not, is an important instance of natural and proud absorption in purely Gaelic tradition at the highest social level in Reay country.

Simon Fraser's grandfather had been a member of the original Black Watch in the late 1720s, the days of gentleman privates and their attendants. One of Simon Fraser's indirect informants was Lachlan MacPherson of Strathmashy, who gave material to his grandfather. Simon Fraser's prime informant was another conduit for the first two men – his father, Captain John Fraser. However, Captain John added to what he had from the older generation by collecting songs and melodies himself from the rich reservoir that he found in Fraser's Highlanders during the Seven Years's War and at home. He himself joined the 78th in 1757 as an ensign. Simon Fraser also mentioned two other informants, Doctor Morison from Lewis who was assistant surgeon in Fraser's Highlanders,[26] and Alexander Fraser of Culduthel, whose name and designation are among those given by Stewart of Garth as a captain commissioned in January 1757. Whether Simon Fraser learned Morison's and Culduthel's music directly from them or indirectly through his father is unknown.

Of the hundred and twenty-one airs and melodies Fraser published, fourteen are described as pipe tunes either on the music page or in the appendix. All of them are called pipe reels but one ("*Ho! 'se mo rùn an t-òigear*") is given as "Strathspey Style". Each, barring this last, was described by Simon Fraser as a "Dance and Song". He presented these "pipe reels" in several keys with accompaniment and strayed, often remarkably, outside the pipe chanter's range (though one or two tunes are almost playable on a chanter as he gave them).

Writing technically for non-pipers as he did, it isn't hard to understand the license Fraser took, or retailed. Nor is it surprising that Fraser's Highlanders emerges as a very musical group of Gaels, rich in pipers, singers of Gaelic songs, dancers, and presumably fiddlers, with not a few collectors in tow. And Dr Morison "composed verses to many of the Highland melodies while on that expedition."[27]

The tune *"Nach beir thu air a'bhana mhearlach"* (roughly, "Won't You Take Hold of the Female Thief"), a common-time "Pipe reel"[28] collected by Captain John Fraser, was "one of the pipe reels mentioned in Note 13, many of which he acquired during his service in Canada, in a corps of Caledonians, inspired with their success."[29] Assuming that the dance-music pipers in Fraser's Highlanders were, by and large, the same men who piped encouragement in times of action and not just enlisted fighting men who occasionally took up the instrument for dance and diversion, these pipers played both forms of pipe music since they were acquainted with the classical repertoire that a practised (ergo military) gentleman's piper was evidently expected to know. These "Dance and Song" pipe tunes and many other tunes for the violin were transmitted by the playing or singing of the melody as well as the words. Fraser knew the words to many of the tunes but unfortunately didn't give them in his collection.

Words were the equivalent of canntaireachd for the passing on of dance-music pipe tunes. Anyone with the grasp of piping "rules" that Joseph Mac-Donald set down in his "Compleat Theory" (allowing readers to believe such a grasp was common to all competent players) would have all the information required from a song with words, and the same is true of the less intellectual piper who had only his own imagination. Words were also a powerful *aide mémoire*. Fraser wrote that "formerly in Uist all the dancers sung their own music."[30]

The last novel cluster of facts about Fraser's Highlanders that appears in Simon Fraser's collection concerns the regiment's band. In the note to tune number ninety-five, *"An t-aiseadh do dh'Eireann"* ("The Crossing to Eireann"), Fraser said that he found it "in an ancient manuscript in the possession of his father, of some of the band music of the 78th regiment, to which he belonged, raised by the late General Fraser of Lovat in the year 1757."[31] Written in 12/8 time, Fraser said that it seemed to be a quick-march and suggested that it was either the basis for Lord Kelly's strathspey or a derivative of it.[32] He went on to describe the band master as "M'Arthur," a man who had been instructed as the future "minstrel to the Kilravock family" (the

Roses of Kilravock in Nairnshire) in whose home he had access to the European classical music proper to his calling. The ancient manuscript apparently has not survived, but Simon Fraser's additional information about music in Fraser's Highlanders shows that it was in essence an amalgam of the music of the men from Fraser communities. The regiment typically depended for its amusement on its rich Gaelic folk tradition, with the requisite nod in the direction of the wider European musical scene. It is reasonable to expect that other Highland regiments were similar.

MONTGOMERIE'S HIGHLANDERS (1757–63)

Lieutenant Colonel Archibald Montgomerie's Highlanders, originally known as the 1st Highland Battalion of Foot and later numbered the 77th, was also raised to serve in America in the Seven Years' War. Like Fraser's Highlanders it contained "30 pipers and drummers," according to David Stewart of Garth.[33] The regiment was made up of thirteen companies of one hundred and five men each. Besides the lieutenant colonel, there were two majors, eleven captains, twenty-six lieutenants, and thirteen ensigns, which breaks down into one superior officer, two lieutenants, and one ensign per company. No piper is named in Garth's text but at least one, probably four, are mentioned in connection with Major James Grant of Ballendalloch's doomed detachment of the regiment. Of Major Grant's foolhardy attack in 1758 on the French Fort du Quesne (Pittsburgh) Garth wrote that, "when near the garrison, he advanced with pipes playing and drums beating, as if he had been going to enter a friendly town."[34]

Grant is reported to have had with him four hundred of Montgomerie's Highlanders and five hundred provincials. As far as the 77th are concerned, this appears from the casualties to have been four companies (i.e., Major Grant and three captains, eight lieutenants, and four ensigns). Grant himself was captured but lived to fight another day, dying a general in 1806.[35] Captains William MacDonald and George Munro were killed and Captain Hugh MacKenzie was wounded. Five lieutenants were killed (Alexander MacKenzie, William MacKenzie, Roderick MacKenzie, Colin Campbell, and Alexander MacDonald); three others were wounded (Alexander MacDonald, Jr, Archibald Roberston, and Henry Munro).[36] Two ensigns were wounded, John MacDonald and Alexander Grant. So, of the sixteen officers of four companies of Montgomerie's at the attack of Fort du Quesne, only two ensigns and one hundred and fifty men escaped unhurt. Two hundred and thirty-one were killed or wounded and the detachment leader was captured.

Assuming that all the companies involved had at least one piper, then Grant's, William MacDonald's, George Munro's, and Hugh MacKenzie's pipers were present at this forest fiasco. Since the total figures – thirteen dead or wounded officers and one captured – show four MacKenzies, four MacDonalds, two Munros, and two Grants, (as well as a Robertson and a Campbell), the indications are that each captain recruited his junior officers from among his own people. The logical extension is that the pipers and privates likewise came from the same estates. Given that Archibald Montgomerie's sister Margaret was married to Sir Alexander MacDonald of Sleat, William MacDonald, his company, and his piper were probably Skye men. Who served as Montgomerie's piper during the Seven Years' War remains a mystery, but he is known to have had Charles MacArthur as his piper in 1781.

While Grant, MacDonald, and MacKenzie could be expected to have pipers, Munro's is more important because the clan has no "hereditary" piping family associated with it and the evidence of piping on the estate is sparse. There were, however, several Munros who raised men from their estates for the British army, of whom more in its place.

Other Contemporary Regiments

Excluding five fencible regiments raised for home service, nine other Highland regiments were raised and reduced between 1745 and 1765: Loudon's (1745–48), Maj. Robert Keith's 87th (1759–63), John Campbell of Dunoon's 88th (1759–63), Maj. Staates Long Morris's 89th (a Gordon regiment, 1759–65), James Johnstone's 101st (1760–63), Maj. Colin Campbell of Kilberrie's 100th (1761–63), Col David Graeme of Gorthy's Queen's Highlanders 105th (embodied in 1762, reduced in 1763), Maj./Lt Col James Hamilton's Royal Highland Volunteers 113th (1761–63), which stayed in Britain, and Capt./Maj. Allan MacLean of Torloisk's regiment (used as a feeder regiment, reduced in 1763). In addition, Garth noted that "many independent companies were raised, and a great number of men recruited by Highland officers, for which they got commissions of different ranks in the new regiments formed in the south, in which the Highland recruits were embodied."[37]

The men and officers in these Scottish regiments were almost exclusively Highlanders. Loudon's were at Culloden and served in Scotland afterwards. Keith's and Campbell's, though untrained, fought in Germany, the 89th served in India, and five of the independent companies that became the 101st were used to reinforce Keith's and Campbell's (88th) in Europe. James Johnstone was not a Highlander but deigned to wear the Highland dress and, according to Stewart of Garth, thoughtfully indulged the men in their customs wherever possible. Kilberrie's Regiment saw service in Martinique and Graeme of Gorthy's in Ireland. Surprising as it may be, there is no mention in Garth's book of pipers or piping in any of these regiments or latter-day independent companies.

The two fencible regiments raised in 1759 (the Argyle and the Sutherland) and the three raised during the American revolutionary war (the Argyle, or West or Western, and the Gordon, both in 1778, and the Sutherland in 1779),[38] were also overlooked by Garth, from a piping point of view. However, the Argyle fencibles had at least "two Pippers," according to an article published in the *Piping Times* in 1967.[39] The article lists five of their tunes; all are the classical form now called *ceòl mór*, or "pibroch." Confirming the existence of one of the pipers, Angus MacKay's *Collection* notes that in the Highland Society piping competition at Falkirk in 1782, "the prize was voted to John MacAlister, first Piper to the West Fencible Regiment."[40] The author of a notice in *Piping Times* said that John MacAllister was also "town piper in Campbelltown" and that his winner's bagpipe was inscribed "*Ioin MacAlasdair ard Piobaire na 'h Alba*."[41] In 1783 he was described as piper to MacAllister of Loup. The source for the additional detail appears to have been "MacIntosh's History of Kintyre," a title not accessible to me. This data is the closest one can come to any recognized piper within earshot of Inver-era Castle at the time. Cosh's search through the records of the new castle from the time of the setting of its cornerstone in the 1750s shows no evidence that Argyll patronized a piper.

In his "*Oran do Reisimeid Earra-Ghaidheal*" ("Song to the Argyll Regiment") Duncan Ban MacIntyre wrote of the Western Fencibles under their colonel Lord Frederick Campbell, son of the duke of Argyll: " 'Tis a joy to look at those gay lads/spick and span and hearty,/when they raised pipe and banners/upon the Lowland plains".[42]

Another Seven Years' War Highland regiment, one about which very little is known but in which pipers doubtless served, was the 114th Foot, otherwise known as the Royal Highland Volunteers. This regiment was raised in 1759 by Captain Allan MacLean (son of MacLean of Torloisk in Mull), a veteran of the Dutch service who had joined Montgomerie's Highlanders in 1757 and who later raised a battalion on the 84th Royal Highland Emigrants, which defended Quebec in 1775–76. In the Army List of 1763 the 114th had five captains, one captain lieutenant, twelve lieutenants, and five ensigns who, together with Major Allan MacLean, were all Scots. It is logical to assume that there were at least five pipers and ten drummers among the men and that they were all raised in the traditional Highland way, from the officers' farms. The 114th ceased to exist at the Peace of Fontainebleau (10 February 1763) when all regiments including and beyond the 71st were disbanded.[43]

Most of these high-numbered regiments (e.g., 106th, 107th, 110th, 111th, and 113d), which were raised during the Seven Years' War and disbanded at the peace, were forbidden to recruit in the Highlands, although the 108th, for example, formed in 1761, was commanded by one Lt Col Patrick M'Douall, obviously a Gael. More problematic was the 113th Foot, raised in October

1761 by Major James Hamilton and officered by apparent non-Gaels. Short-ly after its formation it was given the proud title "The Royal Highlanders" but in November was promptly forbidden to raise men in the Highlands. Like the 108th, the 113d funnelled trained men to various theatres of war.

THE SEAFORTH HIGHLANDERS, 78TH REGIMENT

Four Highland regiments raised before 1781 lasted at least into the nineteenth century, the Black Watch (42d), Lord MacLeod's Highlanders (73d, known as the 71st after April 1786, and as the 71st Highland Light Infantry after 1809), the second battalion of the 42d (which became a separate regiment, the 73d, in April 1786), and the Seaforths, which began life as the 78th in 1778 and became the 72d in 1786. As one would expect in a lore-based society, where there was continuity in such an institution as a Highland regiment, linked over generations with a family or region, there was an accessible oral tradition as long as Gaelic survived.

Of all of the regiments with roots in the period before the Napoleonic Wars, the Seaforths are uniquely significant in that someone took the time to tap the record. This is the only Scottish Highland regiment whose pipers and piping form the subject of a monograph, MacKay Scobie's *Pipers and Pipe Music in a Highland Regiment*. This book, which was written by an officer-piper of the modern Scottish school,[44] provides vital and diverting glimpses of Highland community and military piping from the second half of the eighteenth century until the twilight of the nineteenth. These ingenuous and proudly fond glimpses cast military bagpiping in a light in which it is seldom seen that can only be fully understood by viewing piping from a traditional Gaelic standpoint. About this, and about the Seaforths' significance to the repertoire debate, more will be said in a later chapter.

The Seaforths, in the "Highland habite," served in India in the early 1780s under Coote against both the French and the Indian general Tipoo (Sahib). Like the other regiments they had pipers from their inception. Like Anderson some years before him, MacKay Scobie highlights a number of points about this essentially Ross-shire Highland regiment, but the most important and interesting is the function of the piper in a Gaelic-speaking Highland regiment. This emerges despite MacKay Scobie's understandable effort to convey the orthodox thinking of the 1920s about the ceòl mór orientation of military pipers and its primacy as military pipe music.

MacKay Scobie's description of a piper or pipers in each of the ten companies, with one or two in each of the flank grenadier and light companies, predates Colonel Harper's description of pipers in the Fraser's who served under James Wolfe and General Townshend at Quebec during the Seven Years's War. But the two observations are in essence notes from the same

tune (a tune that the simple chronology suggests was arranged, if not composed, by MacKay Scobie). MacKay Scobie made himself the more credible by admitting that he could cite no authority for this widely accepted distribution of pipers, one, sometimes two per company. He reminded his readers that pipers were not officially recognized in the army until 1854 and that
a lot of the knowledge of early pipers and piping came down in large part
courtesy of lore alone.

It should be noted that in keeping with the normal methods of signalling
movement in the field, each company was allowed two drummers, with the
flank companies having an additional fifer. Like most, if not all, other regiments the Seaforths had a brass band, called a "Band of Musick." This was
a feature of the regiment, "some years after the regiment was raised, which
for a time, as in other corps, had several foreigners (Germans or Swiss) in
it."[45] Thus, typically, a Highland regiment had a brass band, in the case of
the early Fraser's Highlanders almost a century and in that of the Seaforth
Highlanders over seventy years before any pipe band was ever formed. Pipe
bands were a novelty thought by some to have been introduced around the
time of the Crimean War in the mid-nineteenth century.

MacKay Scobie also wrote that in its early days the number of pipers in
the regiment depended on the wishes of the commanding officer and that
each company piper was "provided and maintained by the captain."[46] At
least in the Seaforths, then, the practice whereby each company captain was
responsible for paying the piper or pipers was identical to the practice
described in 1670 and 1671 by Sir James Turner in *Pallas Armata*. Whether
or not the pipers were described as "supernumeraries" and how their wages
were or were not shown on army accounts is not known, although MacKay
Scobie is responsible for the general observation.

Out of the ten companies that became the Seaforth Highlanders, nine hundred men, the whole of the Gaelic contingent, were raised in MacKenzie
country. About two hundred more were Lowlanders who hailed from Nairn
and Moray, officered by captains (four) and lieutenants (seven) whose names
at first glance are Lowland.[47] Of the nine hundred Gaels, more than half
were born and raised on the broad patrimony of Kenneth MacKenzie, earl of
Seaforth (restored to the title in 1771), on the mainland and in Lewis. For all
Bàrasdal Og's real or imagined efforts at recruiting in the southern reaches
of MacKenzie country for Prince Charles's army, Seaforth stayed out of the
'Forty-five. The forfeiture and exile of his ancestor after Mar's rising in 1715
had made Seaforth and all the powerful MacKenzies in 1745 (save Cromartie) profoundly circumspect about drawing a dagg or a sword against the
House of Hanover a second time.

From a purely piping point of view, MacKay Scobie's record of head
pipers and acting head pipers shows that Gaelic speakers prevailed in the
Seaforth Highlanders until after the Crimean War. However, by about the

1820s the base of recruitment, at least of the highest-ranking pipers, appears to have shifted away from Seaforth territory northward, in large part, to Sutherland.[48] Head pipers were no longer MacKenzies and MacRaes.

Although the tributary MacKenzie landholdings of Scatwell, Kilcoy,[49] Applecross, and Redcastle are also associated with the raising of officers and men for the Seaforths, the dominant clan name among the ordinary soldiers in the newly raised 78th was MacRae, a strain of Ross-shire Gaels who had owed allegiance to the MacKenzie chiefs for centuries. (Nonetheless, Lieutenant Kenneth MacRae was the only MacRae among the officers from ensign up at the time the regiment was raised.) However, when the 78th mutinied at Leith in 1778 and marched defiantly up Arthur's Seat just south of the old walled city of Edinburgh demanding justice, the event was called the "affair of the Macraes."

Piping first crops up in the Seaforths at this affair. Stewart of Garth described the mutinous Highlanders as having been led up (and later down) Arthur's Seat by regimental pipers. Only two regimental pipers' names are known for the time: the more certain is Roderick MacKenzie, who was the first head piper of the Seaforth Highlanders (1778–84) and by inference, if MacKay Scobie is correct, the earl of Seaforth's family piper. If Angus MacKay's notes on the MacCrimmons in his Collection are accurate, MacKenzie was piping heir of John MacCrimmon (Iain mac Phàdruig Òig) (his dates unknown but one of his brothers, Malcolm, Calum mac Phàdruig Òig, lived until the mid-1760s and another, Dòmhnul Bàn mac Phàdruig Òig, was killed by the Jacobites at Moy in MacIntosh country in 1746.) The other Seaforth piper was Archibald MacDonald from Invera, described in Angus Mackay's book as "late Piper to the 78th regiment." He won third prize at the Highand Society competition in 1789.

The first actual description of the music played by a Seaforth piper tends to prove that Roderick MacKenzie was a typical traditional patronized piper. While en route to India in 1781, Kenneth MacKenzie, the earl of Seaforth, died. In a typical expression of Gaelic respect and angst, Roderick MacKenzie composed a *Cùmha* (Lamenting) that was apparently so evocative and distressing that an order was issued stating that "no laments or melancholy tunes should be played, but only lively marches, jigs and strathspeys."[50] This is not to say that the chief's piper indulged his fancy, if he had one, for *ceòl beag*, but the example clearly shows that some, if not all, of the pipers in the 78th were versatile and played "lively" pipe music as well as the classical form.

When the regiment returned to Scotland in 1789 it was down to a skeleton of its starting strength since many men had been drafted to other regiments in India. What was left of it was based in Perth for the purpose of recruiting, but very few men were tempted to enlist. MacKay Scobie attributed this to the small number and poor appearance of the veterans, whom he

said bore the signs of hard campaigning. For all the potential Highland officer knew, disease and the enemy had carried off everyone else; tropical service was not the Highlanders' favourite. The unmentioned factor, of course,
was improvement of and emigration from the traditional homeland. The rich
reservoir of manpower even in loyal Seaforth country had already been
diminished by emigration (typically tacksmen-led) to the American colonies
before the revolutionary war; the records of the campaigns in the South and
the claims of the Loyalists show several officers from Kintail (Murchisons
and MacRaes). Patterson[51] shows the settling of people from Kintail and
Lochalsh at Middle River, Cape Breton, in 1821. These people may have
been just a portion of a much larger overall emigration from the mainland
part of the Seaforth estate to various New World destinations.

7 Highland Pipers in the American Revolutionary War and in India

The York judge's remark in 1746 at James Reid's trial that a Highland regiment never marched without a piper must be adjusted to read "a Highland company in the service of King George never fought without a piper or pipers." There is no reason to believe that this ceased to be true in the old traditional sense throughout the eighteenth century when pipers were still intimately associated with their companies. Although pipers are seldom mentioned in America and India, at least in the Highland regiments this is because they were commonplace rather than the opposite.

The following nine Highland regiments, some of two battalions, were raised from 1775 to 1780, all destined at one time or another for North America, India, or the East Indies: 71st Fraser's Highlanders (two battalions), 1775–83; 73d Lord MacLeod's (two battalions) 1778–83 and beyond; 74th Argyle Highlanders, 1778–83; 76th MacDonald's Highlanders, 1778–84; 77th Atholl Highlanders, 1778–83; 78th Seaforth Highlanders, 1778–83 and beyond; 81st Aberdeen Highlanders, 1778–83; 84th Royal Highland Emigrants (two battalions),[1] 1775–84; 42d, Royal Highland Regiment, or Black Watch (second battalion), later 73d, 1780–83 and beyond.

The 71st, 74th, 76th, and 84th served in North America; the 73d (First Battalion), the 78th, and the 42d (Second Battalion) served in India; and the 77th Atholl and 81st Aberdeen Highlanders served during the war in Ireland and otherwise were stationed in England and Scotland. (In 1783 the 77th and 81st, having met the terms of their enlistment – war having ended and their minimum service time having expired – resisted efforts to send them, respectively, to India and the East Indies, and both regiments were reduced in Scotland.)[2]

MacKay Scobie's model of one or more pipers per company in the 78th Seaforth Highlanders (see chapter 6) almost certainly held for the Scottish Gaelic companies in all of these Highland regiments, perhaps also for the Lowland and other companies found in some of them. Yet supporting evidence for the claim is sparse. In the 71st Fraser's Highlanders in North America, for example, William MacKenzie of Glenure's company said in his letter that he was piper to the Second Battalion, which unfortunately leaves a picture of only one piper in a battalion of many companies.[3] However, there is no reason to believe that the regiment diverged in any way from the Highland tradition of the company piper or pipers. After all, as noted earlier, the man who raised the 71st Fraser's Highlanders in 1775 for the American war was the same Simon Fraser who had raised the 78th Fraser's Highlanders of the Seven Years' War and their pipers were company-based.

Further, in the eyes of Highlanders the 71st was a high-status regiment, which increases the likelihood of pipers being present, even if in the unthinkable event that they were little or nothing more than necessary musical appendages to chiefly and subchiefly status. The majors in the two battalions were Robert Menzies; John MacDonell of Lochgarry, son of the hardened Jacobite of the 'Forty-five; Norman Lamont, son of the laird of Lamont; and Duncan of the Kilns, son of the Jacobite Cluny MacPherson,[4] whom James Wolfe, as a young lieutenant colonel of the 20th in Fort Augustus, tried to provoke into a violent rage such that Wolfe could murder him and his followers with impunity. The captains – the gentlemen who were likeliest to have brought a company of men including their own pipers to the army – included Donald Chisholm of Chisholm, Norman MacLeod of MacLeod, Charles Cameron of Lochiel (who died in 1776), Aeneas Mackintosh of Mackintosh, Charles Cameron, son of Fassafearn, George Munro, son of Culcairn, and other people of prominence.

If Aeneas Mackintosh was not an intimate of piping, MacLeod certainly patronized at least one piper on his estate in Skye (and since tradition thrived in those parts, there would have been many more to choose from), and he doubtless had one piper to serve his company. Nor was he an exception among his peers. There is no record of the Chisholms in the eighteenth century being without a family piper, although the story of Chisholm pipers, like that of the Keppochs and the Camerons, is not well documented. So many chiefs and sons of chiefs, however, bespeak the presence of the traditional war music of the Gael; yet to date there is only proof of two pipers who served in the 71st.

The first is the William MacKenzie discovered in his letter to "Petter," mentioned above; the second is Allan MacIntyre who, in July 1783, played "*Fàilte a' Phrionnsa*" ("The Prince's Salute") at Dunn's Assembly Rooms in Edinburgh in the second competition sponsored by the Highland Society that year.[5] Whom did Allan MacIntyre serve as a member of the 71st Regiment? The answer is elusive but there were a number of Campbells in the two battalions who might have taken a MacIntyre piper with them from their estates into the 71st. Major Robert Menzies of the Second Battalion, 71st, who died at Boston Harbour in 1776, is another possible, MacIntyre pipers being associated with the Menzies Perthshire family.[6] Allan MacIntyre might also have been one of the hundred and twenty men enlisted to ensure the captaincy of Cameron of Locheil since there were MacIntyres of long standing at Camas na h-Eirbhe to the east of the Cameron Callart holding in Mamore.[7] However, the Camas na h-Eirbhe MacIntyres are not associated with piping.

Much less is known about piping in the 74th Argyll Highlanders, but a Gaelic bardic source offers a unique and important glimpse of piping in this regiment. The lines "Were I to see your standard/Being unfurled to the hard pole/Chanter's shriek provoking you to put on fierceness" in an old song about a Highland regiment's being shipped to North America in 1778[8] show that the 74th had a piper or pipers. The song specifies no regiment, but of the Highland regiments only the 74th shipped for North America in 1778, landing in Halifax, Nova Scotia. That they were raised by Col John Campbell of Barbreck (on the north shore of Loch Awe), a veteran of the Fraser's Highlanders of the Seven Years' War in which pipers figured eminently, also encourages one to accept the Fraser's Highlanders piper(s)-per-company model for the 74th.[9]

A piper's name may be added to the little that is known about piping in the 76th, MacDonald's Highlanders, and this time the source is Nova Scotia. In *King's Bounty*, Marion Robertson described the Shelburne town "pipe and drummer" as "Duncan McLean, formerly piper for MacDonald's Highlanders."[10] McLean was an ancestor of her husband, and his name has come down through family history. While he is the only known piper of MacDonald's Highlanders, surely there were several.

Piping is also attested, contemporaneously, in the two bodies of Highland soldiers raised in North America. The first, a body of Loyalists almost all Scots-born, was raised in 1776 in the Carolinas where hundreds of Skye, Kintail, and other Highland people had recently settled. In the opening days of the American Revolution Captain MacDonald of Kingsborough had the service of Highland pipers in the small, essentially Highland, army that was defeated and dispersed at the battle against Casswell at Widow Moore's Creek Bridge on 27 February 1776. In "A Narative [sic] of the Proceedings of a Body of Loyalists in North Carolina" there are two references to pipes and piping. The first stated that "Mess.rs McLean & Fraser [Francis] were left with a few men a Drum & a Pipe to amuse Casswell as if the Army meant to cross the River." The second described the morning of the action, when "Signals for an Attack was [sic] given, which was Three cheers the Drum to beat the Pipes to play." The bagpipe, of which there was at least one, if it was actually used, served to provoke and incite; it appears not to have accompanied the cross-country hiking that is described as "marching."[11]

There is no telling which Highland patrimonies these pipers came from; however, Major Donald MacDonald, who headed the provincial Highland recruits of the Cape Fear area of North Carolina, had served as lieutenant in Montgomerie's Highlanders, a regiment that Garth stated categorically had pipers. Two of MacDonald's captains, McLeod and Campbell, were veterans of the French war and one of the main recruiters was Captain Allan Mac-Donald of Kingsburgh in Skye. One of Major MacDonald's officers who escaped the Moore's Creek rout was Donald MacCrumen, the famous piper to the MacLeods, who had emigrated not long before to North Carolina. He and his Skye friend Soirle MacDonald[12] rejoined the British army at Philadelphia and received commissions in Banastre Tarleton's British Legion.

There is no indication that Lieutenant MacCrumen ever played the pipes during the arduous campaign in the South (1780–81) when, at times, they fought alongside Fraser's Highlanders. It seems that the weight of MacCrumen's military duties, together with an essentially English army officer's superior attitude toward pipers, may have prevented this.[13] Oddly enough, one piper does come to light in the muster records of one of the Highland Scottish companies in Tarleton's Legion. A John MacKay appears in the musters, appropriately, of Lieutenant MacCrumen's company in the later years of the war but unfortunately was listed as dead in the Huntingdon (Long Island) muster of Christmas Eve, 1782. Who he was remains a mystery; it has been suggested that he may have been of the Gairloch MacKay piping family and the famous Hector piper referred to in Angus MacKay's notes.[14]

There can be no reason why the Gaelic companies of the 84th Royal Highland Emigrants should not have had their pipers, either but the evidence again is slender. The lists of the officers and men mustered out of the 84th Royal Highland Emigrants in Nova Scotia only mention pipers once. These are in Captain Murdoch McLaine's fifth company of the Second Battalion (December 1782–October 1783) and are denominated thus: "Drummers (2nd pipers)."[15] Their number is unknown.

Stewart of Garth mentions the presence of a piper at the battle of Porto Novo, inland from Madras in southern India, in July 1781 and confidently implied that the 73d had several bagpipers in India. The first battalion of the 73d Highland regiment, Lord MacLeod's Highlanders (1777), formed part of the British force facing the much larger army of Hyder Ali. General Sir Eyre Coote placed what was left of MacLeod's Highlanders (then reduced to about five hundred men) on the right under their colonel, James Crawfurd. Coote, according to one source, knew little about Highlanders and considered bagpiping to be a useless relic of a barbarous age, but when the action began he quickly saw the power of piping to Gaels in a tight corner;[16] "One of the pipers ... always blew up his most warlike sounds whenever the fire became hotter than ordinary. This so pleased the General, that he cried aloud, 'Well done, my brave fellow, you shall have a pair of silver pipes for this.' The promise was not forgotten, and a handsome pair of pipes was presented to the regiment, with an inscription in testimony of the General's esteem for their conduct and character."[17]

There is nothing to suggest that the 73d MacLeod's Highlanders were different in traditionally Gaelic musical terms from the Fraser's Highlanders who served Wolfe at Quebec or the Seaforth Highlanders (1778) that MacKay Scobie described in *Pipers and Pipe Music*. The "MS Journal of John MacDonald," an Argyllshire man who was a schoolteacher in Skerray near Tongue in Reay country, is reported to show that he served in the Second Battalion of Lord MacLeod's Highlanders in Gibraltar as piper and personal servant to General Elliot.[18] One of the corporals serving in the First Battalion, 73d, in India in the 1780s was John Donn MacKay, son of the Sutherland bard Rob Donn. He had been in the habit of singing his father's songs and lifting the spirits of the soldiers under the intense Indian sun. He was killed by a canonball at the battle of Arnee on 2 June 1782 and was much lamented.[19] Like the other eighteenth-century Highland regiments, Lord MacLeod's was made up of relatives from communities whose small pleasures were largely defined by Gaelic tradition. Stewart remarked specifically on the strong family character of the Atholl Highlanders.[20]

Stewart also described the service of the 78th Seaforth Highlanders under Coote in India from their arrival at Madras in 1782, but he mentioned nothing about pipers. There is no proof that pipers played for the main action of the 78th at Cuddalore in the Carnatic (coastal southeast India) in June 1783. But there is no reason why they should not have; for by then the regiment had returned to strength[22] and MacKay Scobie has convincingly demonstrated, from regimental sources, including lore, that there were several pipers in the regiment on that service.

The Second Battalion of the 42d Royal Highland Regiment began in 1780 as "1,086 men, including serjeants and drummers."[23] Like the Seaforth's, it arrived in Madras suffering seriously from scurvy but revived and saw action at Paniané and at the siege of Mangalore. There is no evidence, however, of pipers or piping in the battalion and one is left grasping at the usual straws of kindred and tradition. About half of the officers have Highland names[24] and several probably were Gaelic speakers. Of the Highland officers three names encourage credible speculation that they took pipers with them overseas: Lt Col Norman MacLeod of MacLeod (d.1801), Captain Colin Campbell, son of Glenure, and Lieutenant "Alexander Macgregor of Balhaldy, died Major of the 65th regiment in 1795."[25] "General" Norman MacLeod, the chief, belonged to a family still intensely interested in retaining its family piper. He was the chief whom Lieutenant Dòmhnul Ruadh McCrumen greeted at Dunvegan in 1799 with *"Fàilte Ruairi Mhoir"* when MacLeod returned to his estate.[26] Colin Campbell was a brother of the Patrick Campbell of Glenuir whose company of the Second Battalion, 71st Fraser's Highlanders in North America had the letter-writing piper William MacKenzie.[27] Lastly, MacGregor of Balhaldy, if a patrilineal descendant of the escaped Jacobite of the 'Forty-five, William MacGregor Drummond of Balhaldy (who was living at Bièvres in 1754), was the son or grandson of a tacksman piper.

Stewart, who began his military career officially in the 77th Atholl Highlanders (1778) as an ensign in 1781, only mentioned piping in MacLeod's Highlanders in India because Eyre Coote noticed one piper's brave dedication to duty. Although he did not serve for any known time (as an ensign) in the Atholl Highlanders,[28] Stewart wrote nothing about piping in that regiment. Nonetheless, according to a duke of Atholl before or in 1908, "in 1779 the pipers and drummers were given green coats and belted plaids of red Murray tartan."[29]

How many pipers there were in units raised between 1775 and 1780 is unknown but doubtless there were well over a hundred. They came from a wide catchment area in the Gaelic Highlands that is reconstructable from a study of the holdings of the officers involved from ensign up.

GLENGARRY PIPING, 1757–83

Glengarry, hotbed of Jacobitism in the 'Forty-five, is one of those Highland estates about which there is scanty information about piping after Culloden until the competitions. With the exception of the old "Ticanderego" veteran John MacDonald, who was Glengarry's piper into the 1780s, not much is known.[30]

The village piper of this period, who cropped up in the observations of many Highlanders and others in most parts of the Highlands, and who was recorded in Gaelic semifictionally by *Caraid nan Gàidheal* for Glendessary, must have been common in Glengarry communities until the rapacious clearances of the 1780s. It would be absurd to suggest that the piper was not integral to local life. However, the military model discussed here also allows the inference of a more realistic idea of piping on the estate. One approach is to consider John MacDonell of Lochgarry, son of that quintessential Jacobite leader of the Glengarry men in the 'Forty-five. Old Lochgarry's son joined Fraser's Highlanders as an officer in 1757 and went on to make a very successful career out of soldiering for the Hanoverian Crown, dying a colonel in 1789.

Young "Lochgary," who had been brought up in France, received a captain's commission on 5 January 1757 in Fraser's Highlanders, a regiment that could safely be called the first atonement regiment since it had so many former Jacobites among its officers[31] and men. Like Montgomerie's Highlanders, formed only a few days before, Fraser's had pipers from its inception. Assuming that John MacDonell, son of a Jacobite refugee in France, lacked the wherewithal to buy himself his commission (and his father would never have helped him), then the common avenue of entry at the company level was through the raising of men.[32] If Lochgarry raised Glengarry men for his commission, which is probable, it is also almost certain, that a piper from part of Glengarry was one of them.[33]

In 1775 Lochgarry was commissioned a major in the 71st, Fraser's Highlanders.[34] On his staff as captains were Donald Chisholm of Chisholm, Norman Macleod of Macleod,[35] and Charles Cameron of Lochiel (d.1776). Lochgarry was named lieutenant colonel of the 76th, MacDonald's Highlanders, in 1777 and while he never served with his regiment he was one of two MacDonells on the staff, the other being Lieutenant Aeneas MacDonell. Any strength of men drawn from the still well populated and thriving Glengarry estate must have included a piper.[36]

HIGHLANDERS IN NON-HIGHLAND REGIMENTS UNTIL 1783–84

Highland officers and soldiers served in the French, Spanish, Dutch, and other Continental armies during the eighteenth century, but the subject of piping overseas in the service of other nations may only be touched upon cursorily here. (In the 1590s when the Scots Brigade in Holland was made up mostly of Lowland officers and troops, only one of the companies for which details are available, William Balfour's, was listed as having a piper.[37]) Before the Seven Years' War ended (when British recruiting was suspended), Stewart wrote that "large bodies of Highland youth enlisted for the Scotch Brigade in Holland." He added that MacLeod of Talisker, "and the gentlemen of the Isle of Skye, who joined the brigade in Holland, were particularly successful. They always found a ready supply of young soldiers."[38] It seems reasonable to expect that pipers were among them, especially from the island of Skye.

There are instances of piping in some of the British non-Highland regiments before the Napoleonic Wars. Some of these musicians may have been Gaelic Scots, although MacKay Scobie reported that piping in the Scottish Lowland regiments was standard practice from early times.[39] Scobie mentioned the subject in connection with the establishment of pipers in the Highland regiments in 1854, noting that the Lowland regiments were not afforded the same treatment,[40] though they too had had pipers and presumably still did.

Agnew's Royal North British Fusiliers (21st) had at least one piper at Blair in 1746, and although the regiment was essentially drawn from southwest Scotland, which itself was not altogether non-Gaelic in origin, a Highland presence persisted into the early nineteenth century. According to John Buchan, Alexander MacKay, a son of Lord Reay, became colonel of the 21st in 1770 when Lord Panmure moved to the Scots Greys.[41] A Captain Neill MacLean of the 21st was among those who surrendered to General Gates in 1777. MacDonald of Kinlochmoidart died an officer in the regiment at Guadaloupe in 1794 and Alexander Campbell, a cadet of the Breadalbane Campbells, was killed in a notorious duel by a fellow officer around 1808. All of these people came from families that had long associations with piping. It is worth adding that "the old quickstep 'The Sheriff's March,'" named after the regiment's colonel, Andrew Agnew of Lochnaw, and the regimental music of the 21st, is nowadays known under the title "The Rock and the Wee Pickle Tow" (whose meaning is unclear) and is arranged for the bagpipes.

According to the English military historian Colonel C. Walton, between 1660 and 1700 "the musicians in our army were limited to trumpeters, drummers, hautbois, fifers, and pipers."[42] In describing the "First or Royal, or Scots Regiment of Foot," he noted that "they beat the Scotch March" and "had a Piper as the peculiarity of the regiment (Est. Lists, Harl. MSS)" serving in Tangier in 1661.[43] Prince Charles Stuart's Jacobite general, Lord George Murray, began his military career in the Royals, deserting to the Jacobites in 1715. Part of the Second Battalion was routed at Falkirk in 1746 and then served under Albemarle at Culloden. Known also as the Lothian Regiment, the Royals had a "piper major" among their staff officers, "the first of that rank borne on the establishment of the British army."[44] Economy removed the position in 1764.

In the period from 1768 until the end of the American revolutionary war, the Third (Scots) Guards contained many more Gaels than is often realized. Among them were Ensign Alexander Murray, Corporal Maclury, and Private Maclaughlin, all of whom were tried in 1768 for shooting at a riotous mob and killing a civilian. The rioters were out in support of the notorious John Wilkes, then in jail, and the latter's followers were quick to magnify the brutality of the soldiery, describing the slain man's death as "an inhuman murder by Scottish detachments from the army." (The Guards were acquitted and praised for their service.)[45]

Among their sergeants in 1779–80 were a W. Campbell and a J. Colquhoun, both of whom were promoted to commissioned rank at the time. The presence of Highland-named privates and non-commissioned officers is more an indication of Gaels in the ranks than Highland-named people at the highest level; but in any case the regiment's Highland flavour is enhanced by two of its commanders. From 1770 until 1782 its colonel was John, fourth earl of Loudon. He was succeeded by John, fifth duke of Argyll who held the position from 1782 until his death in 1806.[46]

The Cameronians, or 26th Foot (also known in earlier days as the Angus Regiment, later as the Scottish Rifles), were the only Scottish Lowland regiment to serve in Scotland in those critical recruiting years 1754–57 when Highlanders and Lowlanders were drafted in large numbers into English line regiments. Unlike the English regiments, they were forbidden to recruit. In the 1680s and 1690s the Cameronians had had a Gaelic contingent. From 1688 the colonel was Andrew Munro, fourth son of Sir Robert Munro, third baronet of Foulis. He was succeeded by Ferguson of Badifurrow. At the battle of Killiecrankie in 1689 there was an Ensign Campbell serving in the Cameronians as well as fifty-six private men whose names began with Mac or its equivalent. In 1693 the officer list included Captains Stuart, Campbell, and Munro, and the fallen at Blenheim (1704) included Capt. Alexander Campbell, Lt Col Livingstone, Lieutenant Ferguson and Ensign MacLean. Gaelic, it should be remembered, was spoken in upland Angus in the eighteenth century.

The King's Own Scottish Borderers and the Scots Greys were thoroughly Lowland in composition during the period 1740–84. Only an occasional Highland name shows up, these professional soldiers among the commissioned staff probably holding purchased commissions (whether by influence or money). The 82d Regiment, however, is a different matter. They were a Lowland regiment known as the Duke of Hamilton's that existed from 1778 to 1784 and served in North America. In northern Nova Scotia on the Gulf Shore to the east of Pictou, one hundred and fifty men of the 82d under Lt Col Alexander Robertson were granted land at Merigomish in 1784. Among them were seven MacNeils and nine MacDonalds.[47]

Lt Col Robertson was the son of Duncan Robertson of Drumachuine, who had been excluded in the Act of Indemnity and whose possession of the Strowan estate had been forfeited in 1752 because he had fought for the Jacobites.[48] Lt Col Alexander was restored to the Strowan estate in 1784, his father having died by then. It is hard to imagine that he had not raised at least a company of Highlanders for service of the king, taking the route followed by Simon Fraser and many other ex-Jacobites when the writing was on the wall for any descendant of King James.

Recourse to the British army military lists, genealogies, and local and military histories also show a presence of officers with Highland names in non-Scottish regiments in the service of the Crown throughout the eighteenth century. Assuming that many of them obtained their commissions by bringing men with them into the service, then in many cases these soldiers must have been Gaels.[49] Whether or not English commanding officers ever indulged the desire of Highland officers to have active pipers remains to be discovered. The most likely case occurred in 1757 when the supernumerary

volunteers for the piping regiments, Fraser's and Montgomerie's Highlanders, were sent to reinforce Colonel Ross's regiment, the 38th Stafford-
shires, in Antigua,[50] not at all what they had expected.

Hundreds of Gaels volunteered or were impressed into many English regiments during the Seven Years' War.[51] Of those hundreds a number were
overflow redirected to English regiments from the already-filled Highland
regiments of their choice. The impressed included men who had been conveniently convicted under the revived anti-Highland dress clause of the Disarming Act and it is unreasonable to think that English officers permitted
Highland bagpipers to have any battlefield function in their regiments.[52]
However, wherever Highland soldiers served, under Highland officers or
not, both bagpipes and fiddles doubtless had a social, if not a military, function.

In any case, all of this shows that any earlier efforts to proscribe Highlanders for wearing Highland dress had been relaxed by 1755 when so many
were caught, and also that there was a willingness on the part of Gaelic Scots
to enlist, since not all had been impressed.

In the war against Napoleon Bonaparte, when there was much less selec-
tivity in taking officers and men for the army, the military diffused its thousands of brave Highland soldiers through many non-Scottish regiments. The
Regency period and the three decades after the end of the Napoloenic Wars
thus not only included the expansion of the economic ideas of clearing and
improvement by landowners, even more thoroughly and callously, into the
Highlands but also exposed a large number of young Highland officers to the
English-speaking customs of the British non-Highland regiments. The effect
ingrained and deepened the nascent linguistic and cultural desertion of the
Gaelic officer class to English, weakening old community ties in the Highlands for ever.

PART THREE

Repertoire of Civilian and Military Pipers, c. 1750–1820

8 Exclusivity of Repertoire: The Evidence Against

Since, as shown in Part One, the bagpipes were never proscribed, it is not surprising that the literate record of civilian pipers in Gaelic Scotland during the period 1746–83 is extensive. Chiefly and gentlemanly patronage of piping was very common in the Highlands.[1] The classical form of piping may have lost some of its value as a statement of social status in some parts of Gaelic Scotland. But piping was still widely popular on the whole, and both of its primary forms, dance and classical, were being composed – the best sign of living tradition. As shown in Part Two, piping was also putting down roots in the British military, and by the Seven Years' War it had become a recognized British military asset.

The Jacobite clans do not all furnish a written testimony for this period,[2] possibly because of the theft by Hanoverians of family records. Then again, there are lacunae in the other clans' records as well, clans that might be assumed to have had pipers. In two prominent clans, the Argyll Campbells and the Munros, leaders/chiefs are not known to have patronized pipers, although pipers were common in Campbell country and at least one later Munro achieved prominence in piping.[3] Several Gaelic *bàrds* praise, dispraise, or simply mention piping as an integral element in Gaelic life.

The truth of the matter is that pipers were found where there were Gaels, in both Jacobite and Hanoverian settings, civilian and military. People like Smollett, Pennant, Boswell, and Johnson all mentioned civilian pipers in the Highlands from the 1750s to the 1770s. Boswell and Johnson actually met Captain Malcolm MacLeod, a piper and composer of *ceòl mór* who lived out his piping times on his native Raasay (where Boswell and Johnson met him in 1773, dressed elegantly in Highland garb). While MacLeod had been taken as an active Jacobite (never as a piper), John MacGregor, who had been Prince Charles's piper in the 'Forty-five, returned to live undisturbed in Perthshire under the patronage of Campbell of Glenlyon.

Where bagpipes and pipers are concerned, the critical elements from the overall story of Scottish Gaelic social life are the emigrations and the gradual rather than sudden nature of change, excepting, perhaps, the end of the Napoleonic Wars in 1815. Collinson and Kilberry were right in positing only the slenderest of links between modern *ceòl mór* piping and what they imagined existed before the Disarming Act. They were just as right in their tacit acceptance that, by their time, almost all traditional *ceòl mór* piping had disappeared. The error they made was in believing that there was a catastrophic explanation for the fate of all traditional piping.

By the report of a young Joseph MacDonald (1739–c.62), repeated by others later on, there was a decline in the cultural vigour of *ceòl mór*, or classical bagpiping, after Culloden. This was occasioned by the gradual disintegration of the link between the top stratum of chiefly pipers and their patrons. This rupture brought about the disappearance of two of the so-called piping "colleges" in the 1760s and inevitably robbed the classical form of piping of its most powerful *raison d'être*. The process was obvious to Joseph MacDonald in the 1750s, but it wasn't until the start of competitions in the Lowlands in 1781 that this noble form of bagpiping began to rigidify into an increasingly non-Gaelic museum piece. However, MacDonald was alone among Anglicized Gaels in publicly lamenting the loss between 1750 and 1780, and the earliest competitions simply accepted and encouraged what was left of the art (obviously a lot) without making any useful study of it.

Although well intentioned, the revival effort that came twenty years later through the Edinburgh *ceòl mór* competitions inevitably dealt in an increasingly non-traditional form. From this sprang a misunderstanding by many interested gentlemen of the spontaneous nature of traditional culture. Revival and caricature more often than not go together; this had certainly proved true of classical piping in competition settings by the twentieth century and might probably be said of competition piping as early as the 1820s.

Leaving aside for the moment the more difficult problem of the survival of classical piping outwith the revivalist forces in London, Edinburgh, and elsewhere, it is apparent that by the mid-nineteenth century the stuffing had gone out of the composition of classical pipe music, and this was a loss of serious proportions to Scottish folk culture. However, it had less to do with the early competitions – the gentry who attended, after all, were initially content to hear traditional music traditionally played, whether or not they appreciated it – as with the pursuit by Gaelic-speaking chiefs and tacksmen who remained after Culloden of the new industrial improver economy that was reaching into the Highland estates from the South.

What he believed to be the imminent disappearance of classical piping was luckily the concern of Joseph MacDonald, son of the Reverend Murdoch MacDonald of Durness in Sutherland[4] (one of Rob Donn's patrons) and younger brother of Patrick (1729–1824). Joseph MacDonald's "Compleat Theory of the Scots Highland Bagpipe," the seminal study of the classical piping of c. 1750, is said to have been written in 1760 on a journey to India where its author was to join the East India Company. It is an instructional book that deals extensively with the rules of *ceòl mór*, from whose theoretical foundations MacDonald was at pains to show that Highland "dancing Musick" also sprang. The manuscript was apparently left in India for decades, very poorly transcribed for publication in 1803, republished *comme tel* in 1926 and again in 1972, complete with all the ineptitudes. The manuscript is of inestimable value; it was obviously the product of a very intelligent mind, and it contains terminology, grace-notings, introductory runs, repeated internal embellishments, and preludes unpublished by any subsequent publisher of classical pipe music.[5] If anything can properly claim to represent the classical piping tradition of the first half of the eighteenth century, unaffected by artificial reviving forces, literacy, or competition, it is the "Compleat Theory, " although it may only be a limited view.

The subject will be dealt with in detail later, but suffice it to say at this point that MacDonald did not attribute the rapid decline in the playing of classical pipe music to the Disarming Act or to anything else. He himself must have begun to play the bagpipes in the late 1740s and been acutely aware of what was happening to piping during the decade of the 1750s. His manuscript mentions no piper by name and leaves the impression that Mull rated as high as Skye in the world of classical piping.

Those who believe that the Disarming Act did prohibit ownership of the bagpipe speculate that MacDonald left out names of pipers, patrons, specific geographical locations, and even the names of the tunes he excerpted (many of which are recognizable to pipers today) in fear of bringing official recrimination on these people. The fact is that he described what he described as a living form. He also wrote of dance-music piping in the present tense, proving again that in Sutherland and elsewhere in the Scottish *Gàidhealtachd* (for obviously MacDonald's knowledge was not confined to piping in Sutherland), piping went on as usual during the early Disarming Act years.

All piping that served the chiefly class sooner or later withered and either died or was sapped of tradition. All piping that served the needs of Gaelic-speaking Highlanders continued as before and, at least until the 1850s, was brought to the New World over a period of some eighty years.

JOSEPH MADONALD'S "COMPLEAT THEORY"
AND PATRICK MACDONALD'S *HIGHLAND
VOCAL AIRS*

I have persistently avoided the suggestion that the playing of *ceòl mór* meant *ipso facto* the eschewing of *ceòl beag* – an idea that has been popular for a long time and, in certain instances, is possibly accurate. In retrospect the repertoire of Gaelic Scottish pipers between 1750 and 1820 is the repertoire about which least is admitted and about which a great deal of nonsense is still talked. Now that repertoire has to be assessed more carefully.

The earliest and most informative manuscript study of piping in the second half of the eighteenth century is Joseph MacDonald's "Compleat Theory." The manuscript dealt primarily with *ceòl mór* for the simple reason that, according to MacDonald, it provided the most comprehensive and rational overview of Highland piping. All the fingerings for dance music fell automatically into the wider study, the *ceòl beag* grace-note clusters being but fractional parts of, if not identical to, the longer *ceòl mór* ones. Obviously all Highland pipers saw both forms as part of a larger whole. MacDonald's manuscript contains an index, but the following citation suggests that the author planned a collection of both marches and dance music for the bagpipes:

As the Pipe being as well Calculate for dancing Musick as any Instrument ever Contrived; there is the most Compleat set of Jigs & Reells composed on purpose for it by the first Authors of Pipe Musick (as it appears from the Style of them) than which nothing can be more truly Highland. They are the most Singular for wild Expression, Vivacity, Excecution [*sic*]. Having also the pipe Cuttings in the greatest Perfection & Variety, evry Single note being Cutt and performd according to the Strictest Rules of this Instrument. They are only dancd in the Highlands and Isles – being never introduced any other where, nor Can they be well executed by any other Instrument – being So much in the native^style^Taste of this Instrument.

As they are entirely Pipe Compositions they Shall be set down with the Collection or after the Marches.

The Pipe also plays all the Violin Dancing Musick (within its Compass) very well but as they deviate from its proper Style (a great many of them) they cannot be So properly Cut & chiefly on account of the small Dote & Tich [dot and tick] (♩♪) as this never is peculiar to the Pipe."[6]

Under the title MacDonald wrote that his work included "all the Terms of Art in which this Instrument was originally taught by its first Masters & Composers in the Islands of Sky & Mull."[7]

In Joseph MacDonald's time and for a century before, Skye and Mull were the preserve of the MacCrimmons, MacArthurs, and Rankins. Joseph

MacDonald named none of these, but they are unquestionably the great piping families he was referring to. These and other Highland (mainland) pipe-music composers were the makers of the essentially Highland classical as well as dance music. Neither type of music was the preserve of any class of piper.

By "Marches" MacDonald meant pieces of *ceòl mór*. After the "small Dote & Tich" MacDonald gave a couplet of a dotted quaver followed by a semiquaver in brackets, the opposite of a *tackum* or *snap*. This dotted quaver followed by a semiquaver is what MacDonald said was inappropriate for the piping of Highland dance music.

In this quotation MacDonald leaves the reader confidently to assume that the Highland bagpipe was the instrument used for both types of music. Since Joseph MacDonald is thought to have been born in 1739, the period when he learned piping lay within ten to twelve years of the implementation of the Disarming Act and its enforcement (General Orders to the military, 1748) in the Highlands. Through whom he learned the style of piping of the first masters in Skye and Mull is unknown. The same instrument, the Scots Highland bagpipe, was used for uniquely Highland dances/dance styles; Joseph MacDonald did not specify any particular instrument that was used for dance-music piping and made no qualitative distinction between the two kinds of music, although the classical form was the primary focus of his "Compleat Theory" for the reason already advanced. The manuscript also contains a coloured drawing of a Highland piper in Highland clothes, playing a three-drone bagpipe.

An earlier collection by Joseph MacDonald of "the different kinds of bagpipe music" was apparently lost. He had intended to include at least some of the dance-music pipe tunes in his "Compleat Theory" manuscript. He died, it seems before he could do this, but an unknown proportion of his fieldwork collection of *ceòl beag* was published by his older brother, Patrick Mac-Donald, minister of Kilmore in Argyleshire, in *Highland Vocal Airs* (1784).[8] In the section headed "North Highland Reels or Country Dances," all but three of the twenty-four tunes are pipe tunes (one of the three extends beyond the chanter's range and two are not in the chanter's key).[9] Tunes number one and two, four, five to seven, and nine to twelve are in six/eight time, numbers three, eight, thirteen, and twenty-four are in nine/eight time, while the remainder, jigs and reels, are in common time. Patrick MacDonald said in his preface that "almost the whole of the North Highland airs" were collected by his brother. He added that the tunes were taken down from the playing of a piper.

Joseph MacDonald asserted that the composers of dance music (jigs and reels) were the same people who composed the "marches" (*ceòl mór*), although when these "first Authors" flourished is anyone's guess. If they lived several generations before MacDonald in the 1750s, there cannot have been much composing from their times to his; it is as though the works of the "first Authors" had stood the test of time and people were satisfied with one particular style of dance music as well as a fairly circumscribed repertoire. It should be added that in many minds an essential feature of traditional music is that it is shared by several generations and relatively slow to accrete;[10] MacDonald thus intimated that there was a Highland dance-music style in the stasis essential to traditionalism but still capable of grafting in fiddle tunes and appropriate new pipe tunes. He mentioned, without describing, a form of dancing that he categorized as being limited to the Gaelic parts of Scotland, but he made no comparison with other dance forms in rural Scotland, England, or continental Europe for that matter, so it is impossible to say whether the Highland dancing that Joseph MacDonald knew was distinct in type or in degree. Lastly, jigs and reels present few problems[11] as popular late-eighteenth-century dance timings. However, whether or not Joseph MacDonald meant to include in the term "reel" the "strathspey reel" is uncertain, although his correcting of the "Dote & Tich" suggests that he did. The tick and dot is the "snap" couplet (short/long) called a "tackum" that is characteristic of bagpipe strathspeys, many of which in the eighteenth century were called "strathspey reels."

Interestingly enough, one of the two characteristic differences between modern Scottish and modern Scotch Cape Breton strathspey playing is precisely the dotting that MacDonald mentioned (the other is speed of playing, about which little exact information can be taken from early written music). In Cape Breton Gaelic step-dance music (now almost exclusively fiddle music), the first note in the couplet is almost always short and the latter long, a "tackum" in fact. Modern Scottish pipe-music settings use the form that MacDonald described as unsuitable, which suggests that non-Gaelic forces were responsible for the literate settings of bagpipe music now so universally relied upon and that were widely diffused to the increasingly musically literate piping public in the nineteenth century. The alteration in strathspey time stress will be considered later.

Patrick MacDonald's use of the phrase "North Highland reels or country dances" prompts three questions. If "North Highland reels" were not synonymous with "country dances," was MacDonald, who wrote some of the text with the modernist Ramsay of Ochtertyre, imposing the scheme of fashionable middle-class Lowland dance trends on his own Highland people? Granted that "country dances" (and minuets) were becoming popular in Lowland Scotland in the eighteenth century, how popular were they in the Gaelic-speaking Highlands? Assuming, for the sake of argument, that they had become popular with ordinary Gaels in some parts of the monoglot Highlands in 1784, what were the routes of entry? MacDonald's phrase has to be seen in the context of Topham's remark that in 1770s Edinburgh the Reel was still the prime delight of dancers. In Montrose in 1793 or 1794 the

Chevalier de la Tocnaye watched reels and strathspeys danced vigorously by young and old: *"C'est quelque chose d'original de voir l'espèce de fureur qui saisit toute l'assemblée ... Jeunes et vieux, grand'mères et petites-filles, ministres et médecins, chacun se lève et saute"* ("It's something novel to see the kind of fury that seizes all of them ... Young and old, grandmothers and grand-daughters, ministers and doctors, each gets up and jumps").[12]

In 1784, when Cluny MacPherson had his forfeited estate returned to him, Colonel Thornton, who described the banquet and ball held at the old coaching stage at Pitmain near Kingussie, took pains to note that "Minuets were exploded" in favour of a variety of good Scotch Reels.[13] (For reasons of pomp Cluny had a band play for dancing after the banquet.) Popular pleasure in Badenoch in the dance depended on the favourite Reel. The continued resistance of Reel-dancing Gaels in South Uist to quadrilles, a century later, points to Gaelic dance conservatism. John MacKenzie, however, noted in 1841 that he had seen *"Moladh Chabair-Féidh"* danced not "as a common reel, but as a sort of country-dance."[14]

He did not say where this apparent aberration occurred. It is possible that Patrick MacDonald used the term "country dance" simply in contradistinction to "court dance" but it is more likely that his usage bespoke some cultural pretentiousness, Scots aping English country dances. In either case, as a powerful example from modern Cape Breton shows, typically Scotch Gaelic setting steps can be integrated into non-Gaelic dance patterns, in this case into quadrilles and lancers, which were successfully introduced from New England into rural parts of Gaelic Cape Breton around 1890. Some earlier equivalent integration of Gaelic setting steps and alien travelling movements may have been what MacKenzie saw.

Allowing that Joseph MacDonald knew his subject and that the playing of dance-music piping brought with it no condescending opprobrium, it is still possible that stratification by repertoire existed in Gaelic Highland piping in the mid-eighteenth century. That certainly has been the retrospective view of many who impute to MacDonald a preference for the classical form when in fact his mandate in writing the "Compleat Theory" was not just to expatiate on one branch of the topic. Nonetheless, in fairness, any emphasis on *ceòl mór* was also a response to the writer's fear that classical piping was fast dying away. Remember that he had intended to include dance music later in the manuscript, or elsewhere. If such an exclusivity occurred at all in the Gaelic piping world it was certainly only at the rarefied level of certain top pipers, not necessarily all the "college" piping families. It is also most likely that this exclusivity happened not before or during but after Joseph Mac-Donald's time, at least in part in reaction to unthinking interpretations of his work.

So let us assume, for the sake of argument and the development of a better perspective, that the MacCrimmon pipers whose memory lay within reach of the last bearers of bagpiping lore in the Highlands played only *ceòl mór*: were they the only hereditary piping family in Gaelic Scotland to limit their playing to this form? While no one really knows, there is proof that they were among a very few top bagpiping families who imposed on themselves, or had imposed on them, this restriction. A letter from Sir James Cumming, secretary of the Society of Antiquaries of Scotland, to Sir Alexander Dick of Prestonfield, in 1781, shows that Glengarry's piper, John MacDonald, played "pibrochs" and Reel dance music at the society's first anniversary in Edinburgh. There is a fair case to be made that Simon Lord Lovat's piper, David Fraser, the man who had been MacCrimmon-trained in Skye in 1743, played dance Reels. Simon Fraser (1773–1852) wrote of the reel "*Prionns Tearlach*" ("Prince Charles"), a "Dance and Song": "This reel to Prince Charles was struck up by Lord Lovat's minstrel, at celebrating intelligence of some of the Prince's successful movements in the south."[15]

Fiddlers don't commonly "strike up" and Lovat is not immediately associated with any other "minstrel" than his piper(s).

To the west, John MacKay, born in the early 1750s and the last hereditary piper to the MacKenzies of Gairloch, was reported by John H. Dixon as having gone "to Reay county, the native land of his great-grandfather Rorie, and there received tuition on the little pipes, which are often used for dance music."[16] If true, this happened because John MacKay's father Angus, son of the Blind Piper, died in the early 1770s, presumably before he had imparted all of his *ceòl beag* to his son.[17] It is reasonable to assume that John MacKay or his MacKenzie patron would have sought tuition from a high-status piper (unnamed, he may have been the George MacLeod mentioned by Rob Donn),[18] one who may have had some connection with Joseph MacDonald. There are many other examples from the tacksman's piper level, people who played both forms of pipe music. However, an even better example with which to call into question the exclusivity theory is John MacKay's famous paternal grandfather, the Blind Piper of Gairloch, Iain dall mac Ruairidh, who is said to have been born around 1656 and to have lived into the Disarming Act years until c. 1754. John H. Dixon, who lived in Gairloch in the 1880s and tapped the memories of the last lore bearers there (including a descendant of Iain Dall), repeated that the Blind Piper composed, along with "twenty-four pibrochs," and "numberless strathspeys, reels, and jigs, the most celebrated of which are called '*Cailleach a Mhuillear*,' and '*Cailleach Liath Rasaidh*.' "[19]

It is perfectly conceivable that the Blind Piper composed strathspeys long before such things were called strathspeys in English (in writing, the term first appears in the mid-eighteenth century). Simon Fraser was categorical that the "Strathspey" "*A' Chaora chrom*" ("The Ewie wi' the Crooked Horn" a dancing set) predated his own collection, *Airs and Melodies*, by a century, i.e., that it was composed around 1715; Fraser strengthened his argument by giving the names of three Nairnshire neighbours, Mr Rose of Kilravock, Mr Campbell of Budyet, and Mr Sutherland of Kinsteary, who produced the set he published. David Johnson identified the tune "Macpherson's Testament," which appeared on page 5 of the unpublishd "Sinkler MS" (1710) as being the earliest fiddle tune in strathspey rhythm.[20] Simon Fraser dated the incident that occasioned the composition by Lord Lovat's "attendant Minstrel and Bard" of "*Breacan ùr Fhir Ghortuileic*" ("Gorthleck's Highland Plaid")" to 1746, quite plausibly since Thomas Fraser of Gorthleck was Simon Fraser's maternal grandfather. He also included in his collection "*Tighearna Chuil Fhodair*" ("Lord President Forbes") in "Slow Strathspey Style," which he said commemorated an effort of Lord Lovat to kidnap Lord President Duncan Forbes (d.1747).[21] Simon Fraser wrote that the best dancers of the Strathspeys came from "the Highlands of Banffshire, extending south of the Spey." He also associated the origins of strathspeys with Aberdeenshire in his notes to tune no. 48, "*Nighean bodach an Raoinaitinn*."[22]

For all that, Dixon's reporting on the Blind Piper Iain Dall MacAoidh was in the main unthinking; having written that the Blind Piper "was sent to the celebrated MacCrimmon in Skye to finish his musical education" (presumably having been taught piping by his father Rory), Dixon said that the finishing course took seven years to complete.[23] No one is prepared to argue that even in the second half of the seventeenth century, when Iain Dall, presumably had his MacCrimmon tuition in Skye, the MacCrimmons were not the master-class teachers of piping to Gaels over a number of generations. The unquestioned assumption, of course, is that they taught only *ceòl mór*. Joseph MacDonald throws that into doubt, but the point here is that, judging from the records that exist, it took a matter of weeks rather than years to "finish" a pupil. In the case of Lovat's minstrel, David Fraser, in 1743, it was certainly only weeks; in the case of John MacKay, Raasay, it was possibly in six-month segments believed to have been between c. 1783 and c. 1823, but there is no verifying evidence. (It must be added too that the Blind Piper's authorship of one of the two dance tunes mentioned above, "*Caileach liath Ra'arsa*," was questioned in 1992 by Allan MacDonald, Glenuig.)

Dixon or his informant(s) obviously didn't pay much attention to accuracy. In this case Dixon retold what James Logan wrote in *The Scottish Gael* in 1831 about a seven-year finishing period for pipers with the MacCrimmons. The subject was untouched by John MacKenzie in his prefatory notes to Iain Dall's poetry in *Sar-Obair nam bard Gaelach* (1841), and MacKenzie, being a native of Gairloch, has more credibility. But it is still impossible to assume that the great Gairloch piper and bard followed what is popularly taken to have been the MacCrimmons' lead and restricted his piping to *ceòl mór*. The unthinkable may, after all, be true; he may have polished his dance-music technique, as well as his *ceòl mór*, during his stint in Skye.

It is worth mentioning that no Scotsman has ever suggested that the Blind Piper restricted his repertoire to classical piping. Nor has any Scotsman ever suggested that he toadied to the simple tastes of the Gaelic masses in Gairloch and elsewhere, or debased his remarkable talent by composing and playing *ceòl beag*. The Blind Piper stands out, among others, as a prominent but conveniently overlooked anomaly in the exclusivity theory concerning the repertoire of the great pipers.

It is also likely that Dixon took the phrase about the Blind Piper's grandson, John MacKay (Iain Ruadh), Gairloch, going to Reay country to learn the small pipes, as well as the observation that the small pipes were used for dance music, from a published source. Dixon's words have the hollow ring of plagiarism. The most likely available works were Patrick MacDonald's *Highland Vocal Airs* (1784), or Joseph's MacDonald's *Compleat Theory* (edited for publication in 1803 by Patrick MacDonald). Dixon, however, may have had Alexander MacKenzie, editor of the *Celtic Magazine*, as his authority.

The son of the last of the Gairloch MacKay pipers, Angus MacKay (1780s–1868), who emigrated to Pictou, Nova Scotia, with his parents and siblings on the *Sir Sydney Smith* in 1805, played both kinds of music. He was taught piping by his father, John MacKay, the Blind Piper's grandson, and was obviously being prepared as the next "hereditary" Gairloch piper. In Nova Scotia, finding no audience for the classical form, he let it slide but kept up his *ceòl beag* and taught it to a number of his neighbours. Unfortunately, no identifiable musical anachronisms remain.

It might be argued that the Gairloch MacKay pipers, despite the original and brilliant bardic/piping talent of Iain Dall,[24] do not come out of the same social drawer as the MacCrimmon pipers of Skye or the Conduiligh Rankins, who branched from the original stock even earlier than their chiefs. Roderick Ross stated on etymological grounds that the MacCrimmons (Mac Cruimein, *cruime* being a feminine noun from the adjective *crom*, crooked or bent) had sprung illegitimately from the loins of MacLeod chief Alasdair Crotach (Gibbous Alasdair), who ruled from 1480 to 1540 and whose distant noble record is dimmed by the massacre of the inhabitants of Eigg. The Conduilighs' origin is just as ancient and elevated. The assumption that the MacKay pipers were of commoner background is now being challenged. An unpublished Nova Scotia manuscript, "All We Know about Our Grandparents," written by a schoolteacher and descendant of the Blind Piper, Annie MacKay (1879–1938),[25] mentions in passing without elaboration that the Blind Piper was a grandson of Lord Reay. She is the only written source for this information, which is not part of Nova Scotia lore among the male line descendants of the Blind Piper in Pictou County. Nor can her claim be confirmed through *The Book of MacKay*, which explores the genealogies of important MacKays in Scotland and Holland down to the twentieth century. Nonetheless, what Annie MacKay says is not implausible. Both the first and second Lords Reay are candidates for regular or irregular paternity, particularly the first, Dòmhnul Duaghal MacAoidh, for whom, if title and tune are correctly assigned, a very beautiful classical lament was made, author unknown. This chief, the man who raised thousands of men for the wars in the Protestant cause in Europe from the 1620s to the 1640s and who served valiantly under Gustavus Adolphus, was married an uncertain number of times and fathered many children.

Gairloch MacKay bagpiping lore has survived longest in Nova Scotia, where almost all of the last hereditary piper's family came in 1805, and many other Gairlochers besides.[26] Only one girl of John MacKay's family remained in Gairloch and she is nowhere described as a piper. Her son, Iain Buidh Tàillear (Fair-haired John the Tailor), was among Dixon's informants. Annie MacKay's manuscript treats the subject of early MacKay pipers in Gairloch very briefly but from the point of view of a descendant of a little-known granddaughter of the Blind Piper, Ann MacKay, Annie's namesake. The manuscript is in English, although Gaelic, the natural medium for the retention and passing on of family lore, was still very much a spoken language in rural Pictou County in the last quarter of the nineteenth century. MacKay's work is sound, well researched, and verifiable in all other respects. Her longhand manuscript gives every appearance of being a reproduction of family knowledge (see appendix 2).

For all the Blind Piper's putative social status in the wider *Gàidhealtachd*, however, it could be argued that Gairloch was the realm of an hereditary chieftain rather than a chief (MacKenzie of Seaforth was the chief of the MacKenzies, however independently others of his name acted), and that in West Highland society it was not for the leader of *Clann* Eachuinn Gheàrrloch (the children of Hector Gairloch) to demand that his retained piper play only highly cerebral music. Yet it seems likely that Roderick MacKenzie, the principal piper of the newly raised Seaforth Highlanders and presumably Seaforth's family piper, played dance as well as classical pipe music since it is unlikely that the temporary ban on the playing of *ceòl mór* by regimental pipers aboard ship *en route* to India, when the earl of Seaforth died in 1781, could in fairness have influenced Seaforth's principal piper more strictly than the others in the regiment, who certainly played both types of pipe music.

The MacKay pipers in Gairloch, while they taught non-family as well as family members to play the pipes, are never in eighteenth- or early-nineteenth-century literature associated with any sort of "college."[27] The lore, however reliable it may be, describes three generations (Iain Dall, Aonghus mac Iain, and Iain Ruadh mac Aonghuis) as having had outside piping instruction, two with unnamed instructors.[28] A MacCrimmon, perhaps more than one, of unknown dates has been linked, possibly incorrectly, as a pupil (or pupils) of the MacArthurs; one each, maybe more, of the Conduilighs (date unknown) and of the MacIntyres are described as pupils of the MacCrimmons, while the MacKenzie chiefs' pipers, MacRaes or whoever they were, seem to stand aloof. Whether or not these college-running families, who appear to have shared among themselves at least some of the finest points of piping, played only classical pipe music remains to be seen.

As shown earlier, however, Joseph MacDonald claims that from some earlier time, the time of the "first Authors," until the 1750s, this exclusivity did not exist; therefore, the explicit social distinction made in the nineteenth century between classical and dance-music pipers reflects a divergence in thinking away from Gaelic tradition. It is a relatively modern and artificial distinction, and only (some of?) the MacCrimmons are exceptions, perhaps. (Iain Dubh and Dòmhnul Ruadh may have limited their teaching after 1781 to ceòl mór because the mystique had been created and demand fostered by the Highland Society of London, was limited to that kind of music.)

Whatever control the great chiefs and music patrons (like MacLeod of MacLeod in Skye) actually wielded over the repertoire of their most economically favoured pipers, the most plausible scenario is that in the days when it was to the chief's advantage to promote any and all beloved music of the Gael, played on whatever instrument, he did so. Joseph MacDonald wrote that "the Original Design of the [Scots Highland Bagpipe] ... was to animate a Sett of Men approaching an Enemy – To solemnise rural Diversions in fields, & before walking Companys – To play amidst Rocks, Hills, Valleys, & Coves where Ecchoes rebounded; & not to Join a formal regulated Concert." Along with providing "Dancing Musick," that was a wide mandate.[29]

The same was said more recently by Robert Glen, an Edinburgh maker of musical instruments (including bagpipes), in his "Notes on the Ancient Musical Instruments of Scotland" (1880). First cousin of David Glen, who will be mentioned later in connection with the collecting and writing down of new pieces of ceòl mór on Coll, Robert had an inclusive view of the repertoires of Highland pipers. Describing them as "hereditary," their function was to cheer on the march and provide music for battle. "In peace", however, the piper also "gave life and merriment to the wedding,"[30] which can only mean the playing of dance music of some sort. Glen overlooked what appear to have been pockets of chiefly élitism wherein the repertoires of family pipers were directed exclusively to the playing of classical pipe music. This trend certainly existed on Coll c. 1830 and marked the last phase in the story of Highland bagpiping there as people left the area.

In general, matters changed when modern economic ideas were embraced holus-bolus by many chiefs who had been Anglicized, if necessary de-Catholicized, and modernized as a result of an official campaign that began with the Statutes of Iona in 1609. No longer interested in encouraging community social cohesion, the Anglicized chief was content to take his ideas from the Highland Society of London, which was in the business of promoting exclusively the important dying tradition of classical music.[31]

THE VIEWS OF JOHN JOHNSTON REASSESSED

So what is the evidence for the piping repertoire exclusivity theory? In his four-volume traveller's description of the Highlands between 1811 and 1821, Dr John MacCulloch wrote of strathspey and reel-dance music: "Be it remembered, however, that it is *infra dignitatem* for a true Highland piper to play such music."[32] This is perhaps the earliest such observation. Interestingly, it belongs to the Regency period, a time of excess and significant middle-class attitude formation, that demonstrably touched many prominent Highland families. Moreover, MacCulloch was writing to Sir Walter Scott (1771–1832), novelist and poet, the popularizer of a new image for the Gaels. Scott organized the royal visit to Edinburgh in 1822 and was a friend of Alasdair Ranaldson MacDonell (Alasdair Fiadhaich, or Wild Alasdair) of Glengarry (?1770–1828), the revivalist character and unwitting fellow caricaturist of Highland culture. The remark almost certainly reflected MacCulloch's attitude more than any serious understanding of Highland traditional music. Its direct impact was limited to the literate in English and served only to underline the current thinking of the Highland Society of London, some thirty years after the organization had taken the *ceòl mór* bit between its teeth. Its perniciousness lies in the fact that a profound pro-Gael, John Johnston, was completely convinced of its truth a century later.

MacCulloch seems to have known the ground of a "pibrach" from its variations and thought the latter even "more abominable" than the former. The whole paragraph runs as follows:

"Though the pibrach is thus the proper music of the Highland bagpipe, and ... It is with far less propriety that this instrument is used to give life to the dance ... Nevertheless it is used for reels; and with bad enough success, if the ears are to be consulted: as a moving force however, it answers its purpose very effectually. In fact, there are very few dancing airs that lie within its compass; since the greater number of these have been composed on the violin: such as it can play correctly, it does however play very characteristically. Yet, even as a dancing instrument, it is defective; as no mode of cutting, or fingering, can give that spirit which is communicated by a genuine Highland fiddlestick. Six inches of Niel Gow's horse-hair would have beaten all the bagpipes that ever were blown. The reel and strathspey are wretchedly tame on the pipe, though noisy enough: but fortunately, willing heels serve to cover or repair all its defects. Be it remembered ..."[33]

MacCulloch was one of the many tourists who wrote books about the Highlands. He was a repeat visitor who lived on the mainland and islands for substantial periods over the years, but in many respects his observations were typically out of touch. He obviously didn't much like piping and doesn't seem to have interviewed any pipers, although he wrote so decisively about them.[34] His pontifications on the subject may be taken as the current views of his class and his up-to-date friends, whose piping tastes, if they really had any that were worth heeding, were shaped by the Highland Society of London, and even the Highland Society of Scotland, which was formed in 1784 to run the Edinburgh piping competitions.[35]

John Johnston (1836–1921) could not be accused of any lack of understanding of classical piping in its traditional form, although he wrote at almost a century's remove from MacCulloch. Johnston was a native Coll Gael and the last of his name on the island. Johnston, who had piping ancestors, was himself a *ceòl mór* piper who learned as a boy in Coll, and in North America, in the traditional manner, by *canntaireachd*; part of his contribution was to give David Glen hitherto unpublished pieces of *ceòl mór*.[36] Johnston held strong opinions about piping, some of which are sufficiently controversial and unsubstantiated to cause his ideas to be overlooked and, by some, discounted as fevered extravagances. Among them are certain general but unequivocal statements about the exclusivity of the repertoire of the great West Highland pipers: "As to the old Pipers playing marches, and reels, none of them did, nor were permitted to do. The chief of Coll, nearly dismissed one of the best Pipers he ever had, for hearing him play a march, on the sly. That tells the whole affair. Hardly any of them knew a note of a march, much less a reel. They called these The Tinker's Music."[37] "It will perhaps to (recte 'be') news to present-day pipers that the old famous ones did not play anything but 'Ceol mor'; not one finger of marches or reels, nor would they listen to such but held them in disdain, and so did the chiefs of the day."[38]

In 1919 a correspondent to the *Oban Times* asked Johnston for his reminiscences of some of the great pipers. On 10 November 1919 he responded with a letter about a piper to one or more of the lairds of Coll called "M'Master." This man, a friend and contemporary of Dòmhnul Ruadh MacCruimein (c. 1738–1825) and his pupil for the final polishing touches, had in Johnston's opinion been "one of the very best performers in Scotland."[39] By Highland Society standards at any rate, Johnston was correct; a Duncan MacMaster, piper to the laird of Coll, won first prize in 1805 in Edinburgh; conveniently adding to Dòmhnul Ruadh's reputation, a man who was his pupil at Glenelg in 1814, Alexander Bruce (1771–1840), won second place in 1807.[40] M'Master was the piping teacher of Johnston's own unnamed teacher. Johnston wrote: "M'Master was a native of the Lochaber district – somewhere in the vicinity of Fort William. He was esteemed as one of the very best pipers of his day, and that is saying a good deal, as the Highlands were full of noted pipers then, but it may be news to some of your anonymous correspondents, who claim to know so much about piping, that unlike them, he would not play one finger of marches or reels, which, like all his contemporaries, he called 'tinker's music.' The Chiefs to whom they played also held such music in complete disdain."[41]

It is obvious that John Johnston firmly believed in the truth of what he said. He was outspoken and the correspondence of the day in the *Oban Times* shows that he ruffled a few feathers in the piping community. He was keenly distressed about current trends in *ceòl mór* playing and said so:

Let me assure these people once again, as an old man who studied under a noted pupil of the M'Master, that their notation is quite wide of the mark in regard to the manner in which piobaireachd was originally played, and is not even an approach to it. I speak the truth in this matter and from actual experience; impugn who list. The late Mr David Glen, of Edinburgh, affirmed this in my presence, and he knew what he was talking about. He knew well how to take down piobaireachd when played before him in the original way. Specimans [*sic*] of this may be seen in his publication on the Clan Maclean music. I would ask several of your correspondents to compare some of the tunes seen there to the way they play themselves, and they will see the result ...

I would go many miles, old as I am, to hear your expert correspondents play "Allister Carrach's Salute," the oldest one known to the old pipers."[42]

A piece of pibroch contemporary with the Alasdair Carrach of the "Salute" would push the origin of the form back dramatically to the late fourteenth or early fifteenth century and might cast Joseph MacDonald's "first Authors" in a rather antique light.[43] John Johnston definitely believed that pibroch was a very old form of Gaelic music that had been specific to the bagpipes in the late Middle Ages. The mandate of the Highland Society of London, drawn up officially in 1778 under the ægis of Simon Fraser, shows that the London Society also considered *ceòl mór* piping to be of ancient origin. An equally speculative modern opinion suggests that *ceòl mór* as played on the Highland bagpipe was much more recent, shifting from its original instrument, the *clàrsach*, as recently as the second half of the seventeenth century, within living memory of people alive in Joseph MacDonald's time.[44] This opinion has opened the door to the idea that those few fiddle pibrochs celebrating pre-1665 people or events may have derived not from piping at all but from *clàrsach* playing.[45] The points are moot.

John Johnston also had a bagpipe *port* (tune) that he claimed commemorated the clan combat on the Inch of Perth in 1396 (and that he unwittingly allowed Seton Gordon [d.1977] to learn by ear). It is short but of variational form and *inter alia* contains *crunnludh a mach*, a complex grace-note pattern that many who don't take Joseph MacDonald's manuscript seriously assume to be the last and finest development in *ceòl mór* piping, and thus surely newish in 1650. It is puzzling that Johnston was not eager to pass this sort of material along as explicitly as possible, showing the fingering techniques, explaining every element that needed words; after all, he did teach his pupil "tunings" that as far as can be guessed, were just as close to extinction as this five-hundred-year-old tune, and he was the last person alive to know them (although he may not have known that). But apparently Seton Gordon had to commit them to memory from a few gratuitous renditions by the old man. Seton Gordon himself showed a similar furtiveness: he refused to allow Roderick Cannon to see his fingering when he reproduced one of Johnston's "tunings" for him. (According to John Francis Campbell, it was also the custom of John [Iain mac Ruairidh] MacKay to play *ceòl mór* tunes with his back to his pupil, John Ban MacKenzie [1796–1863], thus setting a precedent, perhaps, for John Johnston's and Seton Gordon's teaching technique.)[46]

John Johnston admitted to Seton Gordon that he knew little about piping beyond the classical form played in the West Highlands and islands. So devoted was he to the subject that he emigrated to North America in or just before 1864 to find classical pieces that he knew to be lost in Coll because of the emigrations. There, among other things, he is believed to have to sought out a well-known piping relative of his own, Hector Johnston, who left Coll in 1819 (see appendix 4) and from whom he hoped to fill the gaps in his learning.[47] However imperfect or limited John Johnston's point of view was – particularly given Joseph MacDonald's description of dance-music piping in the 1750s, and John H. Dixon's unchallenged public claim in 1886 that Iain Dall MacAoidh composed and played dance music on the pipes – there is firm conviction in the old man's statement. He is also the first person since Joseph MacDonald known from the published record to have used the term "finger" for bar.

John Johnston's claims to have known a late-fourteenth-century pibroch and old "tunings" are often met with doubt, while his contention that all modern pibroch was played incorrectly in the early years of the twentieth century has inspired outrage. Yet no one bothers to expose his one indisputably incorrect claim, the only truly vitiating claim he made – that all top pipers disdained the playing of *ceòl beag*. To date there is no record of a chief dressing down a delinquent piper who dared to play *ceòl beag* to substantiate Johnston's statement about the laird of Coll and his piper.[48]

The trouble is that Johnston put neither a name or a date to the chief.

Nonetheless, his assertion became a virtual article of piping faith. Johnston's credibility was enhanced by his Gaelic background, his forceful personality, and his having enjoyed the impressive trust first of Henry Whyte ("Fionn"), David Glen, and later of Seton Gordon, CBE, friend of royalty and a man long involved in the *ceòl mór* competition scene in Scotland. Unfortunately, John Johnston's remark retroactively affected all the great pipers from the dawn of classical piping music, which Johnston apparently believed to have antedated 1396 at least. So, for those who subscribe unquestioningly to Johnston's idea, its application can reach to some misty piping past. The result was that classical piping was elevated to a plateau that even John Johnston could not claim it had attained, for he, like many another, played the form as a boy. And although they are often unaware of its source, Johnston's idea frames the thinking of many pipers and gives the old "hereditary" piping families that they read about a nearly magical status.

The first of two explanations that exonerate Johnston is that what he said may have applied strictly to the man whom he described as the dominant piping force in the last years of the eighteenth century and the first of the nineteenth, Dòmhnul Ruadh MacCruimein, and by extension to his brother and perhaps contemporary cousins. Perhaps rightly Johnston cleaved to the view common among pipers of his time that the MacCrimmon pipers in all their perfection had only deigned to play *ceòl mór*. This position was certainly taken by Dr Neil Ross in 1929, a few years after Johnston's death.[49] It was obvious that pupils of Dòmhnul Ruadh would imbibe his values.

In Johnston's mind the great pipers of yore (an era he didn't bother to date) were set apart as rustic "classical" music geniuses (doubtless true of some, perhaps many) whose various playings of the same music were almost indistinguishable, so rigid were the rules of the great teachers; for him *port* playing reeked of a rare fragrance that certain tunes, "tunings" (preludes), and perhaps fingerings/grace-notings may have possessed. This attitude without doubt amounts to more than an old Coll man's nostalgia, but they have unfairly overshadowed the equally or more important traditional *ceòl beag* piping, which was common all over the *Gàidhealtachd* until well into the nineteenth century. *Ceòl beag* music was part of day-to-day life and bound together a far greater number of Gaels than the more élite classical form. The question is whether the patronized pipers played it, and the answer, by and large, is yes.

Had Johnston been circumspect he would have discussed with Seton Gordon the period in which, to his way of thinking, there really may have been an attempt at exclusivity of repertoire, or demand for such from the piper's employer. Had Seton Gordon confronted him with the quote from Joseph MacDonald's manuscript, there is no doubt that Johnston would have placed his remarks within a stricter frame of reference centring on the years during which the Highland Society ran its famous *ceòl mór* contests beginning in

1781, one year before the clothing part of the Disarming Act was officially abandoned. The interesting question remains to what extent was Dòmhnul Ruadh was influenced by the Highland Society's mandate to revive classical piping.

The second and more plausible explanation of the Johnston exclusivity theory is that Johnston was mirroring the attitudes to piping of a Coll laird, or lairds, living not long before and perhaps during his own time. M'Master, Coll's piper around 1800, was Johnston's pointer to and link with the old greats of *ceòl mor* and the piper whom he uses to defend his exclusivity theory. However, according to Johnston, M'Master was a contemporary and pupil of Dòmhnul Ruadh MacCrimmon, specifically for the finishing touches, at Dunvegan. Since MacCrimmon left for North America in the early 1770s, M'Master's tuition and playing with Dòmhnul Ruadh alternately at various occasions may well be before the Coll lairds became exclusivists. It is possible that both Dòmhnul Ruadh and M'Master played dance music. By the time MacCrimmon got back to Scotland (c. 1790), Johnston believed that none of the great West Coast chiefs brooked *ceòl beag* piping. If so, these chiefs, and their pipers who sought to make a living with the instrument, must have been almost blinded, in the last quarter of the eighteenth century, by the belief of the Highland Societies of London and Edinburgh that *ceòl mor* was doomed and required intensive care.

9 The "Revival" of *Ceòl Mór*

Despite the fact that *ceòl mór* continued to be transmitted in the traditional way through song until the late nineteenth century in the *Gàidhealtachd*, many Highlanders, including Joseph MacDonald,[1] believed that classical piping was an endangered species, and the closure of the colleges suggests that there were grounds for apprehension. Whether or not *ceòl mór* was moribund, it was to stop its anticipated extinction that the Highland Society of London competitions were begun in 1781 in Falkirk.[2] About a decade into the competitions the Society's drive to set up Lieutenant MacCrimmon as professor in a new college indicates a nostalgic revivalism using the old symbols (which the lieutenant rejected: no college ever materialized).

How many Scottish patrons of piping, Lowland and Highland, took up the challenge to resurrect classical piping on their own demesnes is unknown, but the competitions were the easiest means for pipers to get exposure to potential employers; a number of Coll lairds seem to have followed the trend, and probably many others (MacCulloch heard a lot of "pibrach" on his travels between 1811 and 1821, by which time many chiefs were largely severed from Gaelic tradition). Beginning at least in the early 1780s several Lowland lairds retained Highland pipers, James Cummyng in Edinburgh in 1784 had his own piper; Donald Gunn, formerly of the 77th Regiment,[3] was piper in 1784 to Sir John Clerk of Pennicuik,[4] a rural community south of Edinburgh; in 1786 Roderick MacKay was piper to Sir Hugh Dalrymple of North Berwick, a Lowland family whose Drummore branch (east of Musselburgh) retained a Lowland piper, Geordy Sym, in 1741.[5] Later, Sir Walter Scott kept John Bruce in his border barony as sometime piper.

The full extent to which, by 1800, *ceòl mór* piping had become a national predilection, however slightly understood by Lowlanders, is little considered.[6] (Fiddle "pibrochs," according to David Johnson, were a minor subject of experimentation for some Lowland and Highland fiddlers from c. 1710 and were still being composed into the 1750s.) Another unexplored element of the subject is the extent to which the sort of grace-notings that Joseph MacDonald recorded in 1760 were still being played by the traditional pipers, including those who competed in the early competitions. Few of those who judged and heard these performances in Edinburgh may have appreciated that they were hearing a G-F-E-D, introductory run and that it reflected the last days of an independent Gaelic tradition in Sutherland. However, as John Johnston wrote, perhaps the best of the latter-day Coll pipers, M'Master or whoever he was, also played *ceòl beag*. Obviously, the exclusivity theory on Coll at that time was an imposure of the laird's.

No MacCrimmon or Gairloch MacKay of the famous piping families[7] is known to have competed in the Highland Society piping competitions before 1815, but as already mentioned, Coll was represented at least once, in 1805, by Duncan MacMaster, piper to the laird of Coll and teacher of Johnston's piping instructor. Here may be the piper Coll chided and the source of John Johnston's influential pronouncement on repertoire exclusivity.

The competition system initiated in 1781 persists in one form and another to this day. There is perhaps still a split between the cultured and less cultured among pipers, the sort of split that Caraid nan Gàidheal's Finlay Piper and Joseph MacDonald seventy-five years earlier would have chided as phony. With these competitions, however, a piping Rubicon was crossed. In 1784, the year the Highland Society of Scotland was formed, Patrick Mac-Donald's *Highland Vocal Airs* was published, and it was in this work that Ramsay of Ochtertyre anonymously promoted, among English speakers and readers in Scotland, the idea that dance music was the exclusive preserve of the "small-pipes" – a peculiarly indefensible position. The scene was set for what in retrospect can only be described as a glaring lack of interest in and ignorance of dance-music piping in the Highlands of Scotland. How else could outsiders like John MacCulloch develop the conviction that the dance-music piping they were hearing all over the Highlands, in the fields, on the roads, at weddings and at *céilidhs*, lay beneath the dignity of the true Highland piper? Was Joseph MacDonald wrong? Was the Blind Piper a tinker?

The MacArthur's teaching establishment in Skye had ceased to operate about a decade before the competitions began. The Rankins' college in Mull was also defunct. Donald MacCrimmon, MacLeod's piper, whether or not he had taken any pupils before he quit Boreraig, had emigrated to North Carolina; in 1781 he was fighting his North American neighbours and was later barracked in Huntingdon Long Island waiting for patriation to Nova Scotia with the Port Roseway Associates. At Boreraig in the early 1770s he left his piper brother John in a position to charm MacLeod and anyone else and to propagate what he knew of piping. John was an important character in the *ceòl mór* story. His long-recognized contribution to classical piping was the transmitting of *puirt* (tunes) to the world through MacLeod of Gesto (a small Skye tack). Beyond that, however, there are strong suggestions that John MacCrimmon's influence as teacher while he piped at Boreraig (c. 1772–90) has been underestimated.

There is a tantalizing observation in the "Circumstantial Account" of the 1783 Highland Society competition in Angus MacKay's *Collection* to the effect that one of the four piper sons of John MacGregor (Prince Charles's piper from 1745–46) "was for some time at Dunvegan." Assuming that being "at Dunvegan" meant having been tutored by a MacCrimmon, and knowing that three of the sons were born in 1740, 1748, and 1750, then they, and per-haps their brother too, could have been taught by John MacCrimmon (d.1825) at any time, or, from 1790 onward, by Donald MacCrimmon after his time in the colonies. If "Circumstantial" was used to mean eye-witness, however, then the tutor could only have been Iain Dubh Mac Cruimein for the following reason: "Professor" John MacArthur, great piper of the old MacArthur school in Skye, pupil of his uncle Charles MacArthur (the great-est of the MacArthur pipers), grocer in Edinburgh, and one-time piper to the Highland Society of Edinburgh, was described in 1784 by a reporter as the "only surviving professor from the ancient college of Dunvegan, and piper to the Highland Society of Edinburgh."[8]

Still taking "Circumstantial" to have meant eye-witness, pipers generally accept that it was Dòmhnul Ruadh MacCruimein who closed the ancient MacCrimmon college at Boreraig when he left for the Carolinas around 1771,[9] so John MacGregor's son, whichever one it was, must have been tutored by Iain Dubh. The charge that the reporter was just repeating a flat-tering lie is unlikely since, immediately after making that public claim for "Professor" MacArthur's having been the last survivor of the ancient col-lege, the reporter listed the competition prize winners and the first was John MacGregor, "the eldest of five sons, taught by their father John MacGregor." What's more, among that year's competitors there were no fewer than five MacGregors. Professor MacArthur was probably a pupil of Malcolm Mac-Crimmon, father of the last two brothers, Donald and John.

The alternative interpretation of "at Dunvegan" is that, like the mysterious Angus Mór MacKay who is described as "piper to Dunvegan" in the early nineteenth century,[10] one of the MacGregors might have been a patronized piper to MacLeod. Pipers were plentiful in MacLeod's territory in Skye and historical records show that patronage, or at least the occasional financial indulgence, of more than one was perfectly normal.

Let us now consider how great a piper Iain Dubh MacCruimein was in the eyes of his Inner Hebridean fellow pipers. In the case of the Raasay piper

Iain mac Ruairidh, John MacCrimmon's cachet appears in one quarter to have been less than that of a young John MacKay of Gairloch (the man who emigrated to Nova Scotia in 1805). John MacKay, the Blind Piper's grandson, was the piping tutor selected by Captain Malcolm MacLeod, Fear Aire, for his precocious Raasay herd-boy pupil, John MacKay (Iain mac Ruairidh).[11] Malcolm MacLeod might have sent Iain mac Ruairidh to Mac-Crimmon. The Blind Piper's grandson himself was not sent to Iain Dubh for tuition as far as we know. There is no list of John MacCrimmon's pupils, which reflects the fickleness of historians or MacCrimmon's mediocrity. Lore has almost nothing to say directly about him in the eighteenth century when presumably he was at his best as a piper, but if he was the teacher of John MacKay, the Raasay herd-boy, and if he was the teacher of John Mac-Gregor's son, then his style and technique (mediocre or not relative to his younger brother Donald MacCrimmon) spread to many pipers and modern classical piping's debt to him is large.

In any case, to suggest that Dòmhnul Ruadh or Iain Dubh mac Cruimein or their piping ancestors let loose with a few reels on the bagpipes for a series of Four-hand Reels at Dunvegan is to lay out an almost heretical proposition that, in some circles, only the bravest would think to defend. Yet if some of the MacCrimmons were not only excellent *ceòl mór* players but also the last word in fingering technique, subtlety of phraseology, and the playing of the preludes (also called "tunings" by John Johnston) that Joseph MacDonald wrote about, would they not wish to display their brilliance in even faster music? The MacCrimmons, certainly after the 'Forty-five, are not associated with *ceòl beag* and there seems to be no establishable linkage between them and that form at this late date. There is not even a hint in Alasdair mac Mhaighstir Alasdair's poem "Moladh air Pìob-Mhóir Mhic-Cruimein" that Malcolm or any other current MacCrimmon of the mid-eighteenth century played dance music.[12] Parallel interests of contemporary European classical composers in folk music would be vainly presented when it comes to MacLeod's famous pipers (many of whom probably led a life of greater security, if not always comfort, than many of their patronized European musical counterparts).

It is a neglected fact that for generations some of the MacCrimmons were among the gentlemen of the Clan MacLeod, the most powerful of whom had a wider economic function in the Hebridean black cattle economy than the everyday tacksman-farmer elsewhere on the estate. The most militarily capable MacCrimmons were often strategically settled along the vitally important drove routes through Skye and through Glenelg on the mainland, through which cattle from the Outer Islands travelled on their way to Lowland markets.[13] (It is hard to conceive of MacLeod of MacLeod not having set up several profitable arrangements exploiting this position; he certainly was strategically placed to protect herds going through Glenelg, and the name MacCrimmon is long associated with that mainland holding).[14] Given the MacCrimmons' status among the Clan MacLeod gentry, is it reasonable to assume that their musicians cleaved exclusively to classical piping? Were there not other pipers in Gaelic Scotland of equal social importance for whom this exclusivity of repertoire should, by analogy, have held? What evidence is there that any stratum of Highland pipers played only *ceòl mór*?

While it is generally believed that the "schools" taught *ceòl mór* exclusively, this may not have been the case. They went out of business primarily because that sort of music was functionless in the new military and political system in the Highlands, but to limit them to this category, or to imply that they scorned it as inferior, is premature. If one accepts, for example, that the Gairloch MacKay teachers were on a rough par with these other, perhaps more famous, "colleges," there is no doubt that the Gairloch pipers were in a position to pass along instruction in *ceòl beag* and almost certainly did so. What is certain is that the competitions' mandate was solely to resurrect *ceòl mór*. They didn't mind if competitors played on two-drone pipes until 1821, and they didn't care that none of the known early competitors was musically literate, but from the outset they disallowed *ceòl beag* in competition.

As the Highland Society of London saw matters, single-mindedness was desperately needed if ancient high-class piping was not to disappear. Had this single-mindedness been combined with accurate reporting on paper of what the older competitors were playing, grace-note for grace-note, note for note, phrase for phrase, the world would have knowledge of any stylistic differences in the playing of *ceòl mór*, as well as a record of the decline of classical piping that Joseph MacDonald understood to be taking place. In the early days, unfortunately, understanding piping was not what the Highland Societies of Edinburgh and London were interested in, and their ignorance was responsible for the gradual adherence to the MacDonald/MacKay styles to the exclusion of others like that of Joseph MacDonald.

The success of the competitions has skewed piping thought away from Joseph MacDonald's simple but erudite observations. As a result, the less thoughtful consider that the dance-music piping that was reported from all over Gaelic Scotland from 1750 to 1850 was somehow trivial, the third-rate product of Highland pipers who barely deserved the name. It is important to restate, moreover, that several of the grace-note clusters described by Joseph MacDonald have only reached us on the printed page. Whether or not anyone from Sutherland or elsewhere played them during the competitions is unknown, although at least two pipers who learned long before 1745 took part, John MacGregor and Donald MacIntyre, both of whom were born before 1715. It is not inconceivable that their styles were even more complex, assuming what Joseph MacDonald described as something less than an apogee.

Assuming with the Highland Society organizers that artificial resuscitation was preferable to natural but imminent death, the influence of the High-land Society competitions on Gaelic Scotland has to be adjudged generally positive. A quite strong echo of a music was preserved that otherwise would have been lost through waning concern, like much mediæval *bàrdachd*. However, this dwelling on one form of piping worked to the detriment of the *ceòl beag* form. By the time the nineteenth-century emigrations had stripped the *Gàidhealtachd*, the door was opened to distorted reasoning along the lines that dance-music piping had been the sole preserve of some undefined "small pipe," that it had been persecuted to the point of death by the Dis-arming Act, saved exclusively by the military,[15] or, as the wildest postulate, that it had never really existed at all.

The lore surrounding Ruairidh Mac Aoidh, who lived in Eyre in Raasay, hints at the transition from traditional piping of c. 1780, with its more flex-ible attitude to repertoire, to Lowland/Anglicized Gaelic *ceòl mór* ideas about piping exclusivity. Ruairidh MacAoidh was the first of the MacKay family to settle on Raasay; whether he was married or had children at the time of the move is unknown. According to Angus MacKay, his most famous paternal grandson, Ruairidh was from Reay country and had had "training from his countryman and namesake the *Piobaire Dall* [Blind Piper] of Gair-loch" (by namesake the author can only have meant MacKay. Rory Mac-Kay, Raasay, was neither blind nor a contemporary of the sighted Rory MacKay, Gairloch).[16]

If Rory Raasay was a contemporary of the Blind Piper, then Rory Mac-Kay was old enough to have been sent to Gairloch from Sutherland before the Blind Piper died in the mid-1700s at the age of about ninety.

The dubious value of the texts in Angus MacKay's *Collection* has been firmly established, yet his words have to be given at least some credibility.[17] Garbled as the claim is, it is not unreasonable to suppose that Rory MacK-ay, Raasay, was taught by a Gairloch MacKay piper, perhaps the Blind Piper, perhaps his son Angus.

John, the son of Rory Raasay, was born c. 1767. When still a young boy he was orphaned and fell to the tender mercies of Captain Malcolm MacLeod, Fear Aire, who raised him. John was a herd at Eyre in South Raasay, showed natural talent on the chanter, and was taught by the bluff old Jacobite whom Boswell and Johnson had met on Raasay in 1773. John MacKay was not Fear Aire's only pupil, though no other names have sur-vived; Fear Aire also composed at least one piece of *ceòl mór*. What he imparted is unknown. He was typical of the Gaelic-speaking members of his class, interested in the whole culture of the Gael; he danced Reels to fiddling in Raasay when in his sixties, sang Gaelic song, and courted tradition.

John MacLean, in an article on the Blind Piper, wrote that Captain Mal-colm MacLeod was a cousin (probably second cousin) of John MacLeod (c. 1714–86), eleventh chief of Raasay. Malcolm was alive in 1782, by which time he had paid for John MacKay's more advanced tuition in piping with the MacKay pipers of Gairloch (unquestionably with Iain Ruadh, the man who emigrated in 1805).[18] MacLean does not mention that he learned only classical piping and it must be restated that the Gairloch MacKays were *ceòl beag* as well as *ceòl mór* exponents. John MacKay had subsequent instruction from MacCrimmon.

William MacLean is said to have described John MacKay as "the bottleneck through whom has come all that we know about piobaireachd."[19] Although MacLean may have had good reasons to say this, it is popularly assumed that John MacKay's fame depended on the famous "three six months" of training he had with MacCrimmon mentioned by his famous piping son, Angus MacKay. If popular assumptions are right, there are difficulties with William MacLean's statement; it overlooks, for example, other lines of piping knowledge that come directly from Dòmhnul Ruadh MacCrimmon, MacLeod of MacLeod's first choice as piper to replace his father Malcolm MacCrimmon in 1767. It also overlooks Gesto's collection of music taken down from Iain Dubh in the early nineteenth century,[20] as well as the contribution to the Raasay piper's training of the MacKays of Gairloch, who, through Iain Dall, were arguably the bearers and transmitters of the rich MacCrimmon piping tradition of Dòmhnul Ruadh and Iain Dubh's paternal grandfather, Pàdruig Òg. Indeed William MacLean may have been referring to the Gairloch genius in his statement. Inasmuch as Iain mac Ruairidh rose to become piper to James MacLeod, twelfth chief of Raasay, whose title ran from 1786 until 1823, 1786 is a plausible approximate date for his taking the job and also for his vaunted stints with MacCrimmon (these were doubtless arranged so that he might flatter Raasay). The question when the three six months happened is important. Before 1790 it could only have been Iain Dubh; after 1790 it could have been either or both of the last MacCrimmons.

According to the Army School of Piping's "Historical and Traditional Notes on Piobaireachd" (1964), the three six-month periods happened between 1783 and 1791, the latter being given as the year when Iain mac Ruairidh took up the job as Raasay's piper. Dòmhnul Ruadh MacCrimmon got back from Nova Scotia in 1790; he was in London in June of that year and in Inverness in September. At the time the twenty-third MacLeod of MacLeod, unconcerned about the feelings of veteran Boreraig piper Iain Dubh, was loudly touting Dòmhnul Ruadh as the greatest piper and the ideal candidate for the Highland Society of London to sponsor in Scotland as piping "professor." Dòmhnul Ruadh's domestic affairs appear to have been unsettled, however, and it was not until the resetting of tacks at Whitsun 1792 that MacLeod announced to the Highland Society that he had settled "Mr MacCremman, Professor of the Pipes in a farm on his estate in the Isle of Skye."[21] In 1793 MacCrimmon took up the tack of Boreraig, which he had pettishly quit in the early 1770s and which his older brother had just given up.

While it is not known why the Army School of Piping cites the years 1783–91, the case for Iain mac Ruairidh's having been a pupil of Iain Dubh MacCrimmon is strong. John MacLean, offering no evidence, wrote that Captain Malcolm MacLeod (Fear Aire) sent Iain mac Ruairidh to "Boreraig" in "about 1782 or so."[22] MacLeod of MacLeod's championing of Dòmhnul Ruadh may not indeed give a fair impression of the capacities of Iain Dubh as a piper but the fact that Captain Malcolm MacLeod sent Iain mac Ruairidh to Gairloch for the meat of his piping instruction may support the notion that Iain Dubh was low profile compared to the Gairloch pipers in the second half of the eighteenth century. It may also bolster the MacLeod chief's opinion in and after 1790 that as far as the living MacCrimmon pipers went, it was Dòmhnul Ruadh or nothing.

Along with the speculation, it is profitable to bear in mind that Iain mac Ruairidh did not quit Raasay until the twelfth chief, James MacLeod, died in 1823, so there were many years when he might have received tuition from Donald MacCrimmon either at the tack at Trien in Skye (1792–93), at Boreraig (between 1793 and the early nineteenth century), or at Glenelg. Donald MacCrimmon is known to have taught at least two other pipers, Sandy Bruce as late as 1814 and M'Master (date unknown). However, with or without Donald MacCrimmon's tutoring, Iain mac Ruairidh beat Robertson of Struan's piper and a twelve-year-old MacGregor boy piper for the Highland Society's first prize in 1792. If this represented the apex of his career he could only have had one six-month training period from Lt Donald Mac-Crimmon at that time.

It is additionally noteworthy that John MacKay (Iain mac Ruairidh) almost certainly knew dance music for the pipes as well as whatever pieces of ceòl mór he had absorbed. His son Angus certainly did, and Angus is not known to have had any early teacher but his father.

By now it should be clear that tacksmen's, chieftains', and many chiefs' pipers were dance-music as well as classical pipers in the second half of the eighteenth century. The evidence is presented in the next chapter through a look at the competitions in Edinburgh, 1781–1844, various civilian circumstances, and the army.

10 *Ceòl Beag* and Dance-Music Piping

Faujas de Saint Fond and the *Scots Magazine* reported on two of the earliest Highland Society *ceòl mór* piping competitions in Edinburgh and both discussed dancing. The magazine commented on dancing at the 1783 competition noting that this addition to the program was "so much to the satisfaction of the company, that we hear it is requested that premiums may be devised ... upon the next occasion of competition."[1] J.F. and T.M. Flett include in their article "Early Highland Dancing Competitions" the following quotation pertaining to the 1783 competition: "Several of the pipers afforded no small entertainment by giving a specimen of their agility or spirit in Highland dancing."[2]

De Saint Fond, at Adam Smith's invitation, attended one of the Edinburgh competitions, probably in 1784. Without the least understanding of what he was hearing, he hated the classical piping of John MacGregor senior of Fortingall (Perthshire), Donald Fisher (second piper to the Earl of Breadalbane in 1783)), and Dugald MacDugall and all the others who failed to rank in the top three. MacGregor (1708–89) was the man who had been piper to Bonnie Prince Charlie and later to Campbell of Glenlyon and whose style surely represented the early eighteenth century; MacDugall was piper to a minor West Coast chief, "Dugald MacDugall, Esq., of Gallanach."

De Saint Fond found the dance that followed lively and invigorating but hated the "unbearable noise" produced by "the union of all these bagpipes." The lively and animated dance was "formed by one part of the pipers, while the others played suitable airs, which had some melody and character."[3]

The names of the dancers and of those who piped for the them are not recorded. Nor is there a record of what they danced in these early events other than that the dance(s) were "Highland" and almost incontrovertibly Reels.[4] Adam Smith, the economist, may have anticipated de Saint Fond's reaction to piping, but that he made such an event part of his guest's stay in Edinburgh shows something of the Lowlander's interest in pointing out some of his country's uniqueness on the European cultural scene.

Once the organizers realized that dancing was popular it became a permanent feature of the *ceòl mór* competitions – understandably since *ceòl mór* requires some knowledge to appreciate, probably more then than now. As of 1785 dancing, once a post-competition feature, was interspersed throughout the program in much the same format described by James Logan in *The Scottish Gaël* (1831). What has always been taken for granted but seldom emphasized is that it was the competing pipers who provided bagpipe music for the dancing exhibitions probably until 1826, by which time they shared this duty with an orchestra. With one known exception – in 1799 a woman performer was brought in for entertainment – the dancers were always men. They were drawn for the most part from the competing pipers at least in the first thirty years of Reel dancing, but even in the 1830s pipers were among the dancers (the Fletts noted that in 1787 some of the dancers were non-pipers).

Up to and including the competition of 1798, pipers whose names were published in Angus MacKay's *Collection* (i.e., prize winners for the most part) as well as those sixteen competing pipers in the 1784 competition who are listed in the *Scots Magazine* of that year included those of the chiefs of the Grants, MacDugalls, MacNabs, MacDonalds of Clanranald, Breadalbane Campbells, Robertsons of Struan, Camerons of Lochiel, Lamonts, Menzieses, and MacAlisters of Loup. Also taking part at least once were the pipers to the earl of Eglinton, Lord Mountstuart, and the duke of Athol. Among the prominent tacksmen and chieftains represented by their pipers were Cameron of Callart, Campbell of Glenlyon, MacDonald of Lochgary, Campbell of Airds, and MacLeod of Raasay (whose piper in 1792 was Iain mac Ruairidh from Eyre); in addition, there were several military pipers with allegiances to landholding or controlling Highland(-based) families, names unspecified. In 1785 there were twenty-five performers and competitors in piping, so the chances are excellent that more than one chief's piper was among those piping for the dancing, and among those doing the dancing.

The *Scots Magazine* indicates that the dances done in 1789, 1791, 1795, and 1798 were exclusively Highland Reels and dance accompaniment exclusively bagpiping, so it is obvious that, once again, prominent, patronized pipers, played reels for group Reel dancing and were themselves dancing with their comrades. They clearly were not singled out for punishment by their employers, however Anglicized and ignorant of Gaelic tradition the latter-day Highland chiefs may have been. Like old John MacDonald, Glengarry's piper, who competed in 1801, these self-respecting Highland pipers were not bound by any notion that playing dance music was *infra dignitatem*. Joseph MacDonald's observation held true.

If the piper-dancers were not dancing reel setting steps individually, they were dancing the travelling and setting steps of the four-hand Reel until 1799. There is no doubt that the four-hand Reel was the most generally popular traditional dance performed by traditional Gaelic-speaking pipers and the dance that Gaels all knew in Sutherland, South Uist, Perthshire, and Kintyre.[5] Dancers who were often from quite different parts of the *Gàidhealtachd* may have had to decide upon the travelling figures beforehand, but with late-nineteenth-century Cape Breton "Scotch Four" dancing as the model, the variations were not startlingly different or difficult to adapt to in a short time. What the setting steps were is unknown from Scottish sources but distinctiveness did not interfere with the travelling movements. Despite the group nature of the dances, the prizes were given for individual rather than group performance. The prime criterion therefore was setting steps. In these early dancing competitions it was specialist pipers (but not always, given the number of boys competing), not specialist dancers, who were dancing and what they danced was exactly what one might have seen at any Gaelic *céilidh* or wedding, or even after a day's march in the army – foursome Reels, or the setting steps for those Reels.

It wasn't until 1799 that the competition organizers tried to introduce variety into the dance repertoire and to display people considered to be dance specialists, but even then Highland Reels remained the favourite at least into the 1830s and probably much longer. Changes, however, were coming.

In 1826 the dancing exhibition followed the piping. It was all Highland Reels but this time, according to Angus MacKay, the accompaniment alternated between "the Bag-pipe and the Orchestra,"[6] which Joseph MacDonald would have found most unsatisfactory. According to the Fletts, beginning with the second of the triennial competitions in 1832, the music for the dancing competitions and public exhibition performances was provided by "an ordinary instrumental band." By that time the program of dance had been altered so that from 1816 those dancers seen in public danced only exhibitions. In 1812 a "Twasome Strathspey" was introduced, but it was never popular. In 1829 the "Reel of Tulloch" was made compulsory as a test dance, although the exhibition was still the favourite four-hand Reel. In 1832 the "Gillie Calum" was introduced – the first time it had been seen in the Lowlands, according to Dalyell's *Musical Memoirs* (which gives an honest idea of the extent of Lowland ignorance of Highland culture, for all the two peoples shared the Reel). The "Gillie Calum" was popular, although only five took part in that branch of the competition in 1832, only three in 1838, five in 1841, and nine in 1844 (out of a total of forty-four dancers).

There remains another counter to MacCulloch's and John Johnston's fatuous observations. In 1832, when the dance-music production for competition and exhibition had inappropriately devolved upon "an ordinary instrumental band,"[7] a difference of opinion developed between the Highland Society of London and the committee of the Highland Society of Scotland empowered to run the annual event. Kilberry noted from the records held by the Piobaireachd Society (1948) that a letter had been written in 1832 by the appropriate committee of the Highland Society of Scotland to the parent organization in saying that there should be competition piping in strathspeys and reels.[8] The Scottish committee noted that piping competition in at least reel playing already existed in other places:

[Strathspey and reel piping] was a branch of the art which the Highland piper viewed with feelings approaching to contempt, accompanied with a strong prejudice against it, from a belief that the practice of it was incompatible with anything like perfection in the nobler and more important strains with which he is wont to salute the chief and his friends, or to summon his countrymen to battle. The Committee are of opinion that this is an unfounded prejudice, and they are confirmed in this belief by having in view the example of several first-rate performers, who have been persuaded to make the experiment fairly, and who are satisfied that the occasional practice of reel and strathspey musick does give an ease and freedom to the *fingering* in Pibrochs, which the Performer will in vain seek to acquire by any other means of equal facility."[9]

Bearing in mind that pipers had produced the Reel dance music exclusively until c. 1800, later sharing it with an orchestra, one can see here the origin of the *ceòl mór* exclusivity theory in the early nineteenth century. The extent to which this manipulation of Gaelic folk tradition was accepted by Scottish organizer and Gaelic piper alike and the degree to which the improver and other chiefs and chieftains took to heart the Highland Society of London's mandate to save classical piping, was as absurd as the wider caricaturing of all things Gaelic boosted by George IV in 1822 under the direction of Walter Scott.

The Highland Society of Scotland also received at least one complaint about non-Highland musicians being employed for Gaelic dancing. Allan Cameron MacKay, a dancer, suggested almost forlornly in 1835 that at least the sword dance hornpipe *"Gille Caluim"* be danced to the music of the bagpipe. In this the Highland Society of Scotland's committee acquiesced. After the 1835 triennial competition, the job was given to the champion piper, who presumably had to look as if he were swallowing his pride to get the work done.[10]

DANCE-MUSIC PIPING IN THE COMMUNITY

Turning now to the repertoire of the community piper in Gaelic Scotland and to his function (the two things being closely linked), getting a feel for the importance of instrumental music in the daily life of Gaelic Scotland around 1780–1820 or 1830 is fairly straightforward on a general level. However, finding the details underlying the generalities is remarkably difficult. Nowadays there is literate learning of piping and competition and the occasional peacock display to attract and sustain interest. But the period 1750–1820 was characterized by ear-learning, memory, and the different rhythmic needs demanded by a rural Gaelic population whose affection for (at times, addiction to) dancing was legendary. In those days the piper, like the fiddler (often one and the same person), was an integral part of his community in ways that are almost inconceivable in Scotland today.

From the 1750s until about 1850, when the emigration of Gaels to North America had largely dried up, the contingent semiphilosophy of Moderatism in the Kirk condoned a tolerance of music and dance in Highland and Lowland Protestant Scotland. This attitude was punctuated and offset, from about 1800, by an upsurge of evangelicalism, which turned a puritanical frown on music and dance in many Protestant areas of the *Gàidhealtachd* and the *Galltachd* (Lowlands). In the eighteenth century Moderatism also tried to open the door to the toleration of Roman Catholicism. When faced with the actual decision, however, it backed down in the face of a riotous and threatening populace imbued with a pathological fear of the papacy.

Moderatism, for all that, set a kindly breeze on music and dance in Protestant Scotland, Gaelic and English. Alexander "Jupiter" Carlyle, minister of Inveresk from 1748 to 1805, claimed to have been an unusually early son of the manse to take dancing lessons (1737), besides breaking other recreational ground for the established clergy.[11] At the same time Murdoch MacDonald, the minister in Lord Reay's country in Sutherland, was teaching his sons Joseph and Patrick, or having them taught, to play the violin and (in Joseph's case) the pipes as well, and to be literate in music. Later in the century the MacLeod manse in Morvern echoed to fiddling by the minister himself for his children's (Reel?) dancing.[12] MacLeod was by no means an exception as a parlour musician in the Highland Presbyterian church although his caste has been accused by the unthinking of cultural suppression.

The entire period was marked by a widespread Highland/Lowland, urban/rural delight in Reel dancing; there was also a sophisticated interest in the folk music of the fiddle.[13] It was the Golden Age, as some have called it, of strathspey and reel collecting, a time of committing to paper of age-old Highland folk music by the educated (many of whom added new material and altered names to suit whim), people who had been influenced by the brief upsurge in interest in classical music in Edinburgh (David Johnson placed the height of the period somewhere between 1760 and 1780).[14] It also appears to have been the time when the strathspey was transformed from a rhythm that originated c. 1700 in (we are led to believe) the Gaelic-speaking parts of Strath Spey and Aberdeen-shire, into an accepted branch of reel dance-music timing in Lowland Scotland.[15]

Traditional Gaelic music and dance in the Roman Catholic Highlands seems to have thrived during Penal Act days, which lasted into the nineteenth century, along with singing and storytelling. Quite apart from the fact that this persecuted branch of Christianity would have risked losing membership had it condemned its people's traditional pastimes, there is no evidence of any cultural repressiveness on the part of Catholic clergy (in fact the reverse was probably true). In the late eighteenth century any power to direct in matters of music and dance would have rested much more with what was left of the traditional Gaelic middle class (chieftains and tacksmen)[16] than with the clergy, and as John Ramsay of Ochtertyre said in the last decades of the eighteenth century, the degree of natural intimacy that existed between middle class and ordinary Gaels was remarkable;[17] theirs was a profoundly shared culture. Therein lay the essence of clan social and military cohesion. Examples of chieftains and tacksmen spontaneously integrating themselves in the music and dance pastimes of the people are found throughout the *Gàidhealtachd*.

The Catholic clergy (many of whom were the younger sons of the powerful) were often dependent on the gentlemen of society for their places of worship – private homes, much of the time – and for their protection from enforcers of the Penal Laws, especially during the pre-1792 period. In the New World, where in general there were owners of land (grantees) and squatters (potential grantees) rather than leasers (tacksmen, wadsetters, and the later improver-farmers), tenants, and subtenants, the Roman Catholic clergy often assumed, or perpetuated, the social and cultural role of the tacksman (in many cases the role of leader had already been assumed in the old country when the vacuum was perceived).[18] That meant priests involving themselves in and encouraging music and dance. This involvement in music certainly did not always begin in the New World; Father Allan MacLean (1804–77) was a piper and dancer as well as a *bàrd*. The Reverend A.A. Johnston's *A History of the Catholic Church in Eastern Nova Scotia* shows that MacLean was born in Arisaig and, after his education in Spain, served as a priest in Barra, South Uist, Fort Augustus, and Glasgow. Almost certainly his attachment to Gaelic tradition grew in the Arisaig of his boyhood. "He came to Cape Breton, and he was a great number of years labouring in the parish of Judique ... He was a good piper and dancer and he made many songs".[19]

Within this favourable atmosphere it is certain that, at least in the early

decades of the Highland Society competitions, many of those who competed in Edinburgh were still *céilidh* pipers whose functions in their communities were many and varied. Although the written record is thin, one can still
glimpse that old Gaelic world in marvellous richness and ubiquity of Gaelic rural music and dance that survived deep into the twentieth century in conservative Gaelic Cape Breton. Without the Cape Breton analogue, piping in
late-eighteenth-century Scotland would be all but unimaginable.

Why are detailed observations of piping in late-eighteenth-century
Gaeldom so sparse? In the first place, although Lowland Scotland was
exposed to innovation from the South, it too was essentially rural and culturally conservative and there were important music and dance similarities
between Lowland and Highland Scotland. Reel dancing, for example, was
common enough in English Scotland for Highland versions not to appear
remarkable, and therefore not to have been studied and described with care.
What was commonly seen was construed by the majority as eternal. In Gaelic Scotland the traditional ways changed at varying rates in different places,
so that the disappearance of certain forms, such as Gaelic dance setting steps
and the pipe and violin music that they demanded, was gradual and went on
largely unremarked. After all, the Outer Hebrides, the heartland of Gaelic,
remained an almost impenetrable mystery in a linguistic and social sense to
Lowlanders until the present century. In the Gaelic heartland and elsewhere,
for an outsider to experience the intimate warmth and cultural richness of a
céilidh was undoubtedly as difficult in 1820 as it would have been for a
tourist in 1970, even a Nova Scotian, in Cape Breton, to have discovered
Gaelic being spoken by native Gaels far less to have seen spontaneous step-
dancing in non-concert surroundings.

That simple tourist observation shifted to scholarly interest in Gaelic folkways is in great part due to the inspiring genius of John Francis Campbell
(1821–85), also known as Young John of Isla, or Young John of the Songs,
who set out with pen and paper to garner the stories that Gaels had told for
hundreds of years. He relied on thoroughgoing Gaels and people who could
insinuate themselves sympathetically into company that was often wary of
outside curiosity. Campbell was to Gaelic storytelling in the second half of
the nineteenth century what Joseph MacDonald was and could have been to
ceòl mór and to Gaelic piping more generally a century earlier. Like Mac-
Donald, Campbell feared that a large part, perhaps all, of a magnificent
repertoire of the most remarkable folk material would disappear if it were
not sought and recorded. Unfortunately, Campbell, whose first mentor was
his old piper-nurse John Campbell,[20] grandson of the Glenaladale piper who
fled Moidart after Culloden, had more than enough of a job collecting and
transcribing stories, so his work on piping is neither extensive nor systematic.[21] But he had been marvellously exposed to his own native Gaelic civilization by his old pocked piper-nurse, an experience he would have missed,

like most of his contemporaries but for the broadmindedness and wisdom of his parents.[22]

Campbell's *Canntaireachd: Articulate Music* presents the piping world with puzzles. The title page advertises "the old forgotten language of Mac-Crimmon, piper to MacLeod of Dunvegan; of MacArthur, piper to the Lord of the Isles; of '*The Piper o' Dundee*;' and of John Campbell, the Lorn piper, who taught me fifty years ago how to rouse men with strange words out in the Isles." What the language was is not presented systematically enough to be meaningful to me, but the quotation may confirm John Johnston's statement that the great music of the Scots Highland bagpipe came from the Hebrides.[23]

Campbell also reported his interview with the duke of Argyll's piper, Duncan Ross, at Argyll House.[24] This took place on 12 August 1880. Ross had been orally taught in Ross-shire by John Ban MacKenzie. Ross said that before his time, in the last quarter of the eighteenth century, the bagpipe was a two-drone instrument. Ross also reported that there were no grace-notes, those being a recent "improvement" there was no *ceòl beag* at all. He added inanely that he had often heard old women singing *canntaireachd* while out herding and that they had no grace-notes. But Joseph MacDonald's manuscript descriptions of complex grace-notings and "Dance Musick" bagpiping suggests that most of this is untrue and so misleading as to cast doubt on Campbell as a source of information about traditional *ceòl mór* bagpiping. Ross's uninterpreted information marred the great work Campbell did in all of his other Highland endeavours.

J.F. Campbell attributed his almost intuitive understanding of other European folk cultures to his childhood experiences of the extraordinary social freedom found in Gaelic society in Argyle. An earlier example of social freedom in the Highlands is found in the writing of Adam Ferguson (1723–1816). The son of a minister from Logierait in the Perthshire *Gàidhealtachd*, the Gaelic-speaking Ferguson was chaplain of the Black Watch from 1744 to 1754 and professor of Moral Philosophy at Edinburgh University from 1764 to 1785). His memories of the Highlands extended from the 1720s until the 1750s. A seasoned scholar who had travelled in France and talked to Voltaire, he wrote, "Had I not been in the Highlands of Scotland I might be of their mind who think the inhabitants of Paris and Versailles the only polite people in the world." In the Highlander he knew one who could "perfectly perform kindness with dignity; can discern what is proper to oblige ... [and who] having never seen a superior, does not know what it is to be embarrassed."[25]

In addition to its becoming increasingly rare for middle-class native sons like Campbell of Isla to be taught Gaelic in childhood, in Gaelic Scotland in 1800 and 1850 there were attitudes of superiority on the part of the anglicized élite that put unfortunate boundaries on scholarship. Even when curiosity had been aroused by Boswell and Johnson and Walter Scott, there was a regrettable lack of interest among most educated people living in the Highlands who might have left invaluable descriptions of piping and pipers and other aspects of Gaelic folk life. Memories of the late eighteenth century were left unexplored often because the belief in "improvement" was so ingrained that all else, Ossian excepted,[26] was unremarkable. Had it not been for Stewart of Garth's military history of the period from 1757–1822, the prevailing "North British" idea would have submerged Scotland's remarkable contribution to the United Kingdom's imperial growth.

The chasm that divided the English-speaking improver from the victim of his superior, rational ideas was immense. In 1859 John Francis Campbell felt this keenly and told his fellow Gael Hector MacLean (an Isla schoolmaster and one of Campbell's collectors of old Gaelic tales), "Do not trouble yourself to go to ministers and school-masters except for information as to the people. The educated generally know nothing of the amusements of the people."[27]

"Dr Prosody's" 1821 parody of tourist writings on the Highlands rightly drew attention to the superficiality of those works, but unfortunately there are few other places to turn to now. Luckily, what is available, taken together, throws some light on pipers and piping. Just beneath the surface of the travellers' daydreams lay a self-contained Gaelic culture suffused with music, story, and song. The effects of having been roughly absorbed into southern economic and juridical thought must have been felt almost everywhere. On the other hand, cultural affairs, guarded by the barrier Gaelic threw up around them, continued as usual in many Gaelic communities, to some extent even in the weakening Gaelic-speaking communities in Perthshire, into the twentieth century.[28] Everywhere in Gaelic Scotland, where the struggle for subsistence dominated day-to-day life, work and community social events went on much as they always had. People got married, people lived within the warm conservative Gaelic milieu of their grandparents, sharing their stories and melodies. In some places tradition disappeared with the emigration of entire communities, and there may have been divergences from tradition here and there near the Lowlands. Even further afield, in the monoglot heartland, there were agents of contact and of potential change, Gaelic people whose business took them into the wider world – soldiers, traders, and drovers for example. But by the 1780s, apart from the disappearance of the piping "colleges," the one change common to thousands of Gaels at all levels of society was that for the first time they had relatives living overseas.

As for the pipers, they were not unceasingly revered as the mystical pulse of genius celebrating some ethnic musical attar, although in some cases they merited and enjoyed that sort of reverence. Rather, in Gaelic-speaking Scotland the piper and his pipes were an everyday feature of life; the pipes were used to lighten many kinds of work and give it the benefit of rhythm, and they were at every social event.

Much of the music of the latter-eighteenth-century Highlands was written down by collectors, so melodies remain, but traditional dance is gone from Highland Scotland; and without both together, the function of piping (and fiddling) and the way that community life worked in the Highlands for at least a century after Culloden is hard to imagine fully. Rhythm in all its cleverness is impossible to commit to notation. But the pipes and the fiddle were everywhere and their players were vitally important to the communities they lived in.

The Reverend James Hall noted that "when the Highlanders mourn, they set the bag-pipes a-playing, and begin to dance, drink, and be merry."[29] Dr MacCulloch wrote that, "the jovial reel on the well-trod green would lose half its interest before any other tones than that of the pipe: and often have we all hailed with pleasure the long struggling column returning from the Southern harvests, with the piper marching at their head."[30] Stewart of Garth left an unaffectedly nostalgic note on the place of bagpiping and dancing in Gaelic society around 1822:

They were, and still are, enthusiastically fond of music and dancing, and eagerly availed themselves of every opportunity of indulging this propensity. Possessing naturally a good ear for music, they displayed great agility in dancing. Their music was in unison with their character. They delighted in the warlike high-toned notes of the bagpipes, and were particularly charmed with solemn and melancholy airs, or Laments (as they call them) for their deceased friends, – a feeling, of which their naturally sedate and contemplative turn of mind rendered them peculiarly susceptible; while their sprightly reels and strathspeys were calculated to excite the most exhilarating gaiety, and to relieve the heart, from the cares and inquietudes of life.

Such were some of the most striking and peculiar traits in the character of this people.[31]

Garth's description supports Joseph MacDonald's statement; Garth made no qualitative distinction between lament playing and dance-music piping. He implied no league of Highland pipers whose music was exclusive in its repertoire. He never mentioned "hereditary" pipers. He never mentioned any small-pipe, for dancing or anything else. For him and for his contemporaries, including Duncan Ban MacIntyre and John MacCodrum, the term *pìobaireachd* meant simply piping. When it came to dance music piping, he wrote in a footnote to the above citation that, "at harvest-home, hallowe'en, christenings, and every holiday, the people assembled in the evenings to dance. At all weddings pipes and fiddles were indispensable."[32]

The rich musical world of dance and song he described is a composite snapshot of his experiences but based on his early years in the Perthshire

Gàidhealtachd in the 1760s and 1770s when his mind was young and most impressionable and when major social disruptions still had a long, telling term to run. Although by 1820 whole Perthshire Highland communities had disappeared and changes had whittled away at traditional pastimes, as Garth said, music and dance were still extremely popular. He was pessimistic about Gaelic culture, he wrote in the past tense, because he had lived close to the new powerful, watching the erosion of his native culture. The shift away from the traditional functions of the Gaelic middle class, in Stewart's opinion, was a very significant factor in cultural change and emigration. He had seen communities disappear to the New World and bilingualism put down roots. Stewart was also sensible of the effect of war on people's visions and values. The French war had spanned twenty-two years. The dawn of pre-Industrial Revolution scientific thought had broken upon the United Kingdom, intensifying a preference for dwelling upon human reason. To many a Scotsman the old world must have seemed a distant unsophisticated place doomed to extinction.

Garth's understanding of and sadness at change can be seen in the following account of a military acquaintance, the twenty-eight-year veteran of the Black Watch living around 1820:

I met this man two years ago, when riding through a glen, where, if the people are to be credited, the rents are higher than the produce of the lands can pay. After the first salutation, I asked him how he lived. "I am perfectly comfortable," said he; "and, if it was not for the complaints I hear about me in this poor country, I would be happy. I vow to God, I believe I am the richest man among them; and, instead of having thirty-four pounds a-year, as I have, I do not believe a man of them has thirty-four pence after the rents are paid." The words of the soldier were, "times are sadly changed since I left this country to join the 42nd. We had then no complaints of lords or lairds, were all merry and happy, and had plenty of piping, and dancing, and fiddling, at all the weddings."[33]

Garth was here defending the wisdom of Wyndham's bill to grant fair pensions to army veterans. This, he argued, would encourage recruitment instead of alienating potential soldiers who saw veterans of years of military service often returning, perhaps disabled, "to their ancient homes in the improved and desolated districts, without a house or friend to receive them."[34]

As noted earlier, religious revivalism was another factor in public attitudes to gaiety in some parts of the Highlands, particularly in the one-time piping capital, Skye. In Gairloch, for example, the old traditional *céilidh* began to be discouraged in 1830. Henry Urquhart (Pool-Ewe) wrote to J.F. Campbell in 1860 telling him that the minister came to the village in 1830 and the schoolmaster soon after him, and together they "put a stop in our village to such gatherings."[35] Such dour influences would have coloured Stewart of Garth's gloomy prognosis for Gaelic culture, but economic policies were at the root of the changes. In Perthshire, even where people remained, community cohesiveness and traditional folkways suffered in the face of new ideas and indifference of those who manipulated the resources. Garth's opinions were those of a bilingual landed gentleman, but like a large percentage of Highland officers and gentlemen who knew the value of social bonds between officers and men, he shared in the social pastimes of the people on his estates and in the army. This feature of Gaelic society, the sharing of music and dance by leaders and led until long after Culloden, was an important criterion for the survival of tradition.

It was during the nineteenth century that the Gaelic-speaking middle class (exclusive of ministers and teachers) withered so dramatically in Highland Scotland, and Garth's awareness of this unquestionably gave his views of tradition a negative tint. The fact is that reel and strathspey pipe and fiddle music and dance retained their vigour in many monoglot communities in the northerly and westerly heart of Gaelic Scotland for many decades after 1820. There was resistance in the Outer Islands to the quadrille as late as the 1880s (about the same time as the dance in another guise was being accepted in Nova Scotian Gaelic-speaking communities). Illiterately learned Reel-dance piping survived into the twentieth century in South Uist. Wherever Gaels settled until the 1840s in Maritime Canada at least, they brought with them the pipes, the fiddle, and the Reel dancing that they had received through the age-old form of transmission that Peacock and his sort would have disparaged. Even in Perthshire, had Garth, like J.F. Campbell, gone out to look for what remained in action and memory, his pessimism might have been tempered.

Weddings, Work, and Funerals

The popularity of the bagpipes in Gaelic Scotland throughout the eighteenth century is attested in many other places. Burt, who was in the Highlands from 1727 until 1736, described the custom at weddings in one area: the newlyweds, at the end of the day, were turned out of the company with the requisite bedding while the guests had a fine time dancing to the piper all night long;[36] In Penny Weddings the money collected, he wrote, went to the feast and the fiddler.

David Stewart of Garth offers a slightly different description of weddings: "During the whole day, the fiddlers and pipers were in constant employment. The fiddlers played to the dancers in the house, and the pipers to those in the field."[37] Garth was adamant that the pipes were strictly an outdoor instrument – a point of view that may have been true of his Perthshire estate in the good weather but is clearly in error for other places. Piping and piping instruction were certainly indoor as well as outdoor affairs. Archibald Mac-Donald of Rhu and Lochshiel,[38] a fiddler and known reel-step dancer, when the weather was too bad for travel, habitually treated his guests in his home in Arasaig to fiddle and pipe music for dancing.[39]

Piping indoors was also normal in Kingussie in Strathspey around 1816. John MacKenzie, or Eileanach (1803–86), son of Sir Hector MacKenzie of Gairloch, whose piper left for Nova Scotia in 1805, wrote in his diary at the time that on his way south to school in Edinburgh from Inverness in the "Highland coach," the coach's "guard," a familiar old friend he called "dear Donald" (Mackintosh), asked the passengers if they would mind leaving Pitmain, the usual stop, a little late for the leg to Dalwhinnie; he wanted to join in the wedding celebrations of his cousin in Kingussie, half a mile to the south. "So, all the passengers being fonder of their fun than of their meat, we soon despatched our dinner and, pioneered by Donald, reached a house in the village and were made more than welcome by the marriage party we found dancing to the pipes. And we agreed that, as was right and proper in Strathspey, we had never seen such *famous* dancing, nor have I ever seen the like since. All seemed trained dancing masters."[40]

Duncan Ban MacIntyre (1724–1812) often sang of piping for dancing, and what he said of weddings confirms in Gaelic what Burt and Garth wrote and what Eileanach said of indoor wedding piping: "Twas blithe to be in winter there,/at weddings one had fun:/the pibroch's fluent harmony/–none wearied for its close;/then sound of strings from fiddlers,/who played the bars all through;/and their own lilt from maidens/of the most tuneful and sweet voice".[41] Outdoor dancing in the winter at weddings in Highland Perthshire was as improbable as it was anywhere else in Scotland. Elsewhere Duncan Ban wrote that the pipes were "esteemed at every wedding" (*measail air gach banais*) in the Rough Bounds.[42]

In the immediate post-Waterloo years it is quite apparent that the "quality," in places, still sponsored and shared happily in the common man's pleasures. Eileanach delightedly recalled the piping and fiddling for New Years' dances held at the Gairloch MacKenzies' eastern estate at Conan House near Dingwall.[43] And in his notes to the tune *"Feadan glan a' Phìobair,"* Simon Fraser said that the words to the tune championed the music of the "noisy rattling piper" over the fiddle at a country wedding; no broken strings, no stops for tuning.[44] Fraser's collection, which was first published in 1816, also includes two tunes, a strathspey and a reel, celebrating "Huntly's wedding" (1813). This was a big local occasion. Gentlemen celebrated in their homes while "others entertained their tenantry round a bonfire, with Highland cheer, and dancing to the bagpipe, – Lovat, in particular, had bonfires on all his hills."[45]

As a work instrument Highland bagpipes were popular in many parts of the Highlands in the period 1750–1843. Sir Aeneas Mackintosh, writing not long after the American revolutionary war, said that "frequently in the hearvast the Reapers cut the corn regularly to a tune, which custom is still preserved in the Isle of Sky, where the only good pipers are reared and to be found."[46] Although there aren't many harvest observations to report, one from Gairloch will serve to test the limitations of Mackintosh's field observations. Some time before the Free Church of Scotland became the accepted Christian church in Gairloch parish in Wester Ross (i.e., pre-1843) the minister's manse was at Cliff House. With the building went land enough for the man's living and this he farmed. Every autumn he was in the habit of rounding up as many youngsters as he could find to cut and bring in his grain for him, "and to cheer up his squad of perhaps not very willing workers he always had a piper to play to them."[47] The old minister placed markers where he expected his labourers to reach and then went trustingly home to his dinner. The workers as regularly moved the markers back and contented themselves with dancing to the piper's music. More generally Thomas Newte observed "in travelling through the Highlands, in the season of Autumn, the sounds of little bands of music on every side, joined to a most romantic scenery, has a very pleasing effect on the mind of a stranger."[48]

Harvesting, apparently as late as the early nineteenth century, drew an annual contingent of Gaels to work in Lowlanders' fields and with them went the piper. As early as 1548 Highland and Lowland fieldhands had worked to pipe accompaniment of some sort and had danced a ringdance on a hillock when the work was done.[49]

The Highland bagpipe relieved the monotony of labour for roadworkers and rowers as well. On his tour of the Highlands in 1776, John Knox observed that "at this time the inhabitants of Skye were mostly engaged upon the roads in different parts of the island, under the inspection of the gentlemen and tacksmen, and accompanied, each party by the bagpiper."[50] Queen Victoria's reporting of P. Cotes's[51] piping for the rowers who conveyed her across Loch Muich reinforced what Burt had written ten to fifteen years before Culloden. The queen noted that the rowers let out a shout when Cotes played a reel, which reminded her of a line from "The Lady of the Lake" by Sir Walter Scott. The bagpipe was used to accompany rowing, reaping, and washing work.

Turning to funerals and piping, this is an area in which the attachment of instrument to rite has never died out in Scotland or overseas, however much the interpretation of the lament may have changed. But in the mid-1730s in Perthshire the claim was made publicly that bagpipe lament playing was one of the casualties of Gaelic culture. Stewart of Garth, on the authority of an old man who had served Rob Roy and later Garth's grandmother and Garth's father, stated that the last time a pipe dirge was played at a funeral in the Highlands of Perthshire was at Rob Roy MacGregor's funeral in 1736.[52]

At much the same time Burt described a Highland funeral that was led all the way by a piper playing on his bagpipe, "which was hung with narrow streamers of black crape."[53] In the second half of the century Aeneas Mackintosh wrote that a piper "attended the Corps to the Grave."[54] Pennant outlined a rather strange funerary custom from Rannoch that he learned about or saw in 1769. Calling the event a "Late-wake," he said that the mourners danced and greeted (wept) violently at the same time, the music having been played on the bagpipe or fiddle.[55] This dousing of sadness with forced merriment was reported by Aeneas Mackintosh in Clan Chattan country for a period he gave as "up to 1740."[56] In that part of the world the nearest relative began the dance.

As far as dancing to the pipes in general is concerned, there are many references in poetry and elsewhere but one odd instance is worth including. Again it is by Thomas Pennant, who this time recorded dancing to bagpipes on board boats in Loch Fyne, Argyleshire, in 1769: "On the week-days, the chearfull noise of the bagpipe and dance ecchoes from on board."[57] Even in 1819 John MacCulloch, a bagpipe detester and one of the proponents of the Highland Society view that only classical music was played by the self-respecting piper, added an unwilling endorsement of the instrument's suitability as a dance-music instrument: "And the effects hence produced are such as no ear could be supposed to endure, were there not daily proof to the contrary in the joy that accompanies the national and characteristic dances, where the bagpipe is employed in executing the most refined of the dancing melodies."[58]

Highlanders, as several writers have remarked, loved dancing: how they must have shrunk from the ideas of Free Church ministers after the Disruption of 1843 when dancing was frequently proscribed by a church that had rebelled against chiefs' and landowners' rights to select pastors for their parishes.[59] Peacock and Logan both condescended to the Gaels' aptitude for his native dancing. Logan in 1831 tried to betray an intimate understanding of Gaelic folkways and traditional methods of passing on dances and setting steps in saying that they excelled with no tuition. But he made no effort to describe the steps his Highlanders were doing.

Before turning to the army, another class of Reel should be mentioned, namely those Reels that were always danced to the music of the pipes. The fieldwork on this subject was done by J.F. and T.M. Flett in the 1950s. Among the dances that were recalled for them were *"Ruidhleadh nam Pòg,"* *"Cailleach an Dùdain," "Cath nan Coileach," "Dannsa na Tunnag,"* and *"Coille Bharrach."* Some of these Reels, as one would expect, had words. The oldest was "Cailleach an Dùdain," which dated to 1804, but it and the others were arguably older dances going back well into the eighteenth century. As far as one can judge, these dances never formed part of the repertoire of Lowland dancing masters like Peacock. There is no record of any of them in Cape Breton. Other tune-specific dances, however, have survived in Gaelic Cape Breton, so a general template exists for this kind of dance.

CEÒL BEAG AND DANCE-MUSIC PIPING IN THE ARMY

Highland Regiments

At the core of MacKay Scobie's regimental history of the Seaforths is what the author reveals about the piper's repertoire. Leaving no room for doubt, what MacKay Scobie described from old memories and records (including Anderson's *Seaforth Songs, Ballads, and Sketches*) was a piping repertoire that included *ceòl beag* (primarily dance music) from its earlier days in the late 1770s. The fact, simple as it seems, is of the greatest importance to any understanding of Gaelic Scotch piping, certainly at the community or tack level but also at the highest level of chiefly patronage in the second half of the eighteenth century. From the point of view of piping in the New World *Gàidhealtachd* where the eighteenth-century traditions flourished continuously into the twentieth century, MacKay Scobie's and others' remarks about piping, especially piping for Reel dancing in the Seaforth in Highlanders, is of fundamental significance. They confirm firstly, the powerlessness of the Disarming Act over piping, and show secondly, that piping's widely appreciated social function (shared with the fiddle) of producing Gaelic dance music flourished during the post-Culloden eighteenth century.

The idea that Highland pipers in every company of Highlanders in the Highland regiments of the second half of the eighteenth century played only *ceòl mór*, no matter what the circumstances, has gradually come to occupy the high ground, despite abundant proof to contradict it, and despoiled the truth of Gaelic piping. It has magnified the importance of *ceòl mór* and focused attention on the top stratum of piper, the chief's piper, and within that relatively select group, on one kind of music that this piper is known to have played (although not necessarily exclusively) and at times to have composed. As a result, study of the actual range of repertoire of the chief's piper and of the wider social functions he performed has been neglected; likewise the social function of the tacksman's piper, the community piper, the sort of man typified in the fictional piper whom Rev. Norman MacLeod, in his *Caraid nan Gàidheal*, placed in Glendessary. Otherwise fair-minded people have chosen to ignore evidence by writers like Joseph MacDonald, to whom they gladly acknowledge an unquantifiable debt for that part of his work that they have accepted willingly. It has detracted from a dispassionate evaluation of piping in the diaspora *Gàidhealtachdan*.[60]

There is absolutely no doubt that *ceòl mór* was signally important and often ordered to be played in the Seaforths. MacKay Scobie cited an undated Order Book that he said was "probably compiled on the formation of the 72nd" (as the 78th was renumbered in 1786); it included ten pieces of music of which seven are of the classical variety, including *"Tulach Ard"* (signalling the gathering), *"Fàilte Mhic Coinnich"*, *"Blàr Sron"*, *"Cumha Mhic Coinnich"*, *"Siubhal Chlann Choinnich"* (played at sunset), *"Ceann Drochaid Aluinn"* (a tatoo), *"Blàr Ghlinne Seil"* (the warning, before dinner), and *"Cath Sléibh an t-Shiora"* (played at dinner). The remaining three, however, are not: *"An Cuilfhionn"* (a slow march, remembered in the 1930s by an ex-Seaforth in the 1870s as a march), *"Caisteal Donan"* (the quickstep), and the rouser *"Tormod Bàn MacLeoid's 'Cabar Féidh,'"* which was played at the charge.[61] The critical business of killing and being killed in the Seaforths was done to a fast piece of music. In my opinion this choice of fast piece of music for the charge and the "shock" was probably widespread. It was not time for the intellect.

The classical music, typically was order- and officer-related, was not the only kind of music acknowledged in this early officer's record. MacKay Scobie also said that "The MacKenzie Men," a quick-step, was composed shortly after the raising of the Seaforths in 1778 and that another "old quickstep" was "MacKenzie of Gairloch March." He ascribed the inspiration for the composition of "MacRae's March" to the mutiny at Leith and the march to Arthur's Seat, although this tune is almost certainly the piece of *ceòl mór* that goes by that name and not a piece of lighter music. He also said that three "ancient" slow marches were traditional Ross-shire melodies that had been played by Seaforth pipers since the beginnings of the 72d; he then named four tunes, *"Loch Duich"*, *"Theid mi dhachaidh"*, *"Chro chinn t-Saille"*, and *"Duthaich nan Craobh."*[62]

A picture emerges of several talented pipers in the Seaforths of 1778, people whose musical sense extended quite normally to the composition and playing of various sorts of pipe music to meet the occasion. The distribution of MacRaes among the men and MacKenzies among the officers of the Gaelic companies probably points to a roughly fifty-fifty split of pipers between Seaforth and his "suit of mail" (the MacRaes).

In early-twentieth-century deference to the mystical element of piping, *ceòl mór*, MacKay Scobie wrote that until about 1850 only this form of music was permitted to be played in the Seaforths, but it grows clear that what he really meant was that in certain prescribed situations before the Crimean War the duty piper had to play a piece of *ceòl mór*. He mentioned that the playing of this kind of stately, variational music was *de rigueur* for the duty piper outside the officers' quarters every night bar Sunday, half an hour before dinner, and in the messroom on guest nights.[63] This custom, he added, harked back to the old chiefly Highland custom of *ceòl mór* playing for the chief and his guests, a custom that is attested on many occasions in the Highlands by touring people like Pennant (1772), Johnson (1773),

Caraid nan Gàidheal (1791), and Walter Scott. MacKay Scobie's observations, based almost certainly on memories of the pre-Crimean Seaforths, also show that the playing of *ceòl mór* was not the sole preserve of the head piper. It was an expected part of the captain's (in other words, the community's) piper's repertoire as the Reverend Norman MacLeod had outlined in the music he had Finlay Piper play in Glendessary before the people left.

MacKay Scobie wrote of marches and quick-steps for march accompaniment (by marches he is believed to have meant, as Joseph MacDonald did c. 1760, *ceòl mór*) and also of reels, strathspeys, and jigs for dancing. These were by no means trivial, undemanding novelties introduced to some watered-down military piping scene in the post-emigration years when some hoary old Gaelic tradition of military *ceòl mór* could no longer sustain itself for want of exponents (an image tempting even to MacKay Scobie). This devaluation of non-classical pipe music was quite common in the 1950s. Indeed, the value-laden terms *ceòl beag* and *ceòl mór* are, appropriately enough, late Victorian in origin. This light-music repertoire was quite a matter of course, intensely functional, expected and enjoyed in the Seaforth Highlanders in the eighteenth century however much like Scobie and others preferred to overlook it.

Oblivious to the cultural significance of the words he took from Anderson's *Seaforth Songs*, MacKay Scobie retold an important incident that occurred in Madras in the summer 1783 when the Seaforth Highlanders had forded a river in the evening of a long tropical day. (This must have taken place on the march to Cuddalore, a coastal town to the south of Madras; in any case it happened when Dòmhnul Ruadh MacRae was head piper.) "When the other troops were flinging themselves on the ground incapable of further exertion, the pipers of Seaforth's Highlanders struck up a lively tune and the men of the regiment began to dance reels to the amazement of the onlookers."[64]

This is one of the earliest references to Highland soldiers dancing Reels to the music of regimental pipers. There are many others but they occur later in South Africa, in the Peninsula (Spain and Portugal), and in the more northerly European theatre of the latter stages of the Napoleonic Wars. To overlook the importance of dancing to Highlanders is to overlook something that was tremendously popular in ways that are all but unimaginable in modern Scotland. To isolate the ordinary Gael, the private soldier for example, as the only level of Gaelic society to indulge his or her passion for Reel and other dancing is to ignore the truth of the matter. All classes of Gaelic society, chief to commoner, in Highland Scotland in the Disarming Act years (as well as before and after) danced Reels as Caraid nan Gàidheal's letters from Finlay Piper and many other records in Gaelic song and English tourists' observations prove. Only in the conservative Cape Breton *Gàidhealtachd* is a surviving analogue to be found, at least of the setting steps danced in the late eighteenth century (the Eight-hand and Four-hand Reels no longer being danced spontaneously but only as exhibitions at summer festivals and the like). In 1783 the Seaforth Highlanders, death from sickness aside, were the same regiment of men that had been raised in 1778. Their music was still an an accurate reflection of what was going on in the Seaforth tacks, particularly in Kintail. Obviously dancing was inspiriting and piping for it common probably to all the regimental pipers.[65]

The British Army

The actual status of the military piper in a Highland or other regiment in the British army from the 1750s until 1820 is undefined, and what he played in various active situations is not well enough known to allow for generalization. But there is no doubt that not just many but probably all pipers, whether attached to patrons (officers and gentlemen) or actually enlisted in the regiment, played both classical and dance music. This is attested to by recollections of pipers with Fraser's Highlanders during the Seven Years' War in North America. Further evidence can be found in the Highland Society of London competitions particularly in the 1780s and 1790s but also on into the first decades of the nineteenth century; these show that *ceòl mór* competition pipers who had served, or were still serving, in the army must also have been dance-music pipers (and dancers of Reels).

An earlier example taken from the time of Mar's rising in 1715 has nothing to say about classical piping but a great deal to say about light-music piping of songs with English words of which Highland officers, at least, were aware. A letter from the Reverend William Trail to Rev. Robert Wodrow, dated Benholm, 11 April 1716, makes it immediately clear that Highland Scots soldier-pipers from Campbell country played *ceòl beag* and with particular effect.

When Argyle's Highlanders entered Perth and Dundee in the van of the government army that had defeated Mar in 1715, they did so in three companies, each of which had "their distinct pipers, playing three distinct springs or tunes, apposite enough to the occasion. The first played that tune, 'The Campbells are coming, oho, oho!' the second, 'Wilt thou slay me, fair Highland laddie?' the third, 'Stay and take the breeks with thee:' and when they entered Dundee, the people thought they had been some of Mar's men, till some of the persons in the tolbooth, understanding the first spring, sung the words of it out of the window, which mortified the Jacobites there."[66]

Further afield, in the campaign against the Dutch in South Africa in January 1806, after marching in the blinding summer heat the men of the Grenadier company of the Seaforth 72d commanded the pipers to, "play them their regimental quick step – Cabar Feidh, to which they danced a Highland reel, to the utter astonishment of the 59th regiment (2nd Nottingham Reg^t), which was close in our rear."[67] MacKay Scobie added a fascinating pagan touch: "Before the battle of Blawberg, in the Cape, on 8 Jan 1806, the pipers rose at daybreak and doffed their caps to the rising sun in the East before striking up and awakening the troops."[68] Later, between 1825 and 1827, the regiment served in detachments in various places in Ireland and MacKay Scobie said that the pipers were in great demand by the Irish, for marriages and dances. (The head piper at that time was a Sutherland man, Donald MacDonald, whose English was secondary to his Gaelic and who played a three-drone set of pipes and with pear-shaped drone terminals. Scobie described MacDonald as "a great character and a fine player of the old school." It is illuminating that Scobie more than once used the term "old school" for former pipers in the Seaforths but never elaborated on the features that made them different.)

In 1811 during the Peninsular War, Pipe-major Cameron of the 92d (Gordon Highlanders) hinted macabrely at his ability to play dance music on the pipes and at the same time gave evidence of why Gaelic pipers were generally much respected in Highland military society. A shot meant for him punctured the bag of his bagpipe. Enraged, he is said to have dangled the instrument around his neck, reached for a musket, and entered the fray uttering the ominous threat, "We'll give you another kind of dance music."[69]

On 28 October 1811 an unnamed piper struck up the contemptuous piece of *ceòl beag* "Hey Johnnie Cope" for the advance on Arroyo de Molinos, gaining, as Stewart of Garth noted, "additional celebrity" for the tune.[70]

In 1812, while the Gordons were in Spain, dances were arranged in which the Highlanders were initiated into the mysteries of the bolero and the waltz while their hosts learned the foursome Reel and the sworddance. At the battle of Puerto de Maya in June 1813, Pipe-major Cameron of the 92d played "*Pibroch Dhonuil Dhu*," presumably a piece of *ceòl mór*, to charge up the men while the French were massing to attack. At the battle of St Pierre on 13 December 1813, two of the pipers of the 92d were killed in turn while playing "*Cogag na Shee*" ("War or Peace") to encourage their friends.[71]

The other well-known instance in which "*Is coma leam cogadh no sìth*" was played was when Piper Kenneth Mackay of the 79th (Cameron Highlanders) stepped outside the protection of the square at Waterloo to inspire his fellow Highlanders. The tune, which is repetitive in a throbbing way and not hard to commit to memory, appears to have been known to all Highland military pipers. It was played in concert after the defeat at Culloden, as reported by Spanish John MacDonell, and, at Lord Cathcart's request, in Paris by nine pipers for Emperor Alexander I of Russia, who was curious about Scottish Highland dress and equipment.[72]

On 15 June 1815 a number of noncommissioned officers were invited by the duchess of Richmond, daughter of the duke of Gordon, to show her gentle and noble friends a specimen of Highland dancing at the famous pre-

Waterloo ball. In a letter dated 13 January 1889 Lady Louisa Tighe wrote, "I well remember the Gordon Highlanders dancing reels at the Ball ... There was quite a crowd to look at the Scotch dancers." The music they danced to was pipe music, according to "Circumstantial Account of Waterloo, 1816."[73]

One of the more unusual examples of military bagpiping happened on 23 June 1795 at the naval battle at Isle Groix between Lord Bridport and Vice-Admiral Villaret-Joyeuse. On the seventy-four-gun HMS *Colossus* were Lts John Hay and John Grant and seventy-nine noncommissioned officers and men of the 97th regiment (Inverness Shire Highlanders). When the action began a kilted piper was ordered to "the maintopmast staysail netting ... where he skirled merrily for the three hours the ship was in action."[74] The author of this account, H.B. Mackintosh, regretted the nonlisting of pipers' names at the time. What the piper played is unknown. In the same regiment, in Lt William Rose's company, were a number of Banff men, one of whom, Samuel Gray the piper, was wounded while serving aboard HMS *Orion* during the naval action on 23 June 1795.[75] Presumably the Banff soldiers were English speakers. The bagpipes for the 97th were bought from a James Munro in Inverness for five guineas apiece.[76]

Obviously *ceòl mór* and *ceòl beag* were part of the repertoires of most, if not all, military pipers thoughout the Napoleonic campaigns and afterwards. However the pipers of this massive campaign may have differed from those of Wolfe's campaign against the French in North America in the late 1750s and early 1760s, the differences were small. As far as the Gordon Highlanders were concerned, according to Lt Col C.G. Gardyne, author of that regiment's history from its inception in 1794 until 1816, the pipers were not recognized by the military authorities and had no rank, but they were held in the "highest esteem by officers and men."[77] How they were remunerated is not officially mentioned by Gardyne, but money was available.

Whatever people like MacCulloch and prominent members of the Highland Society of London thought about the repertoire of the "true" Scottish Highland piper, there is no doubt that pipers themselves considered that the instrument's repertoire included both *ceòl beag* and *ceòl mór* and that their normal function was to pipe for dancing when the occasion called. It is unlikely that even the MacCrimmons were exceptions to this rule, though some of the MacCrimmon family *may* have limited themselves in their famous "college" to the teaching of the classical form.

Despite the Highland Society of London's influence in promoting the ancient classical music of the bagpipes by means of Lowland piping competitions and in encouraging the literate transmission of piping from about 1800, and despite the opening up of the Scottish *Gàidhealtachd* to modern economic ideas, changes in traditional piping were few in the period

1750–1820. European court music was never important to eighteenth and early-nineteenth-century Gaelic-speaking tacksmen, chieftains, or chiefs in the *Gàidhealtachd*. As David Johnson has pointed out, by about 1750, prominent people with substantial land holdings in Gaelic Scotland such as the dukes of Argyll (Campbell), Atholl (Murray), and Gordon could all have kept a "ducal orchestra," but none did. They were educated to appreciate the contemporary classical forms and paid lip-service to the classical scene in Edinburgh, but "for them, as for the lower classes, it was Scottish music which really spoke to the heart."[78]

Johnson underlined his point by noting that the duke of Atholl patronized the fiddler Neil Gow at Dunkeld, and the duke of Gordon employed the fiddler-composer William Marshall of Fochabers. Elsewhere the duke of Atholl is said to have been the patron of a Perthshire Stewart family of "hereditary ear pipers" whose temporal origins are unknown.[79] However un-Gaelic or artifically Gaelic these relationships between master and musician may have been they draw attention to a sociological feature of truly Gaelic society that lasted as long as there was a Gaelic-speaking middle class in the Highlands to foster music and dance.

11 The Small-Pipe, the Quickstep, and the College

THE SMALL-PIPE CONTROVERSY

Francis Collinson, who discovered in Gilbert Askew's "The Origins of the Northumbrian Bagpipe"[1] a set of small-pipes that had belonged to some person or persons in Montgomerie's Highlanders (1757–63), was surprised to realize that a member of the regiment would have deigned to play "this set of miniature bagpipes." He reasoned that since the army piper was at liberty to play *a' phìob mhór* (the great pipe), he would find it demeaning to play a small-pipe. Collinson's surprise is founded on two misleading assumptions: first, that Joseph MacDonald had written that Scottish Gaels had a specific dance-music bagpipe in the 1750s, the small-pipe; and second, that MacDonald had implied that dance music was given over to this instrument because the great bagpipe was banned by a provision of the Disarming Act.

In the first case Collinson cites the published version of "Compleat Theory" as follows: "Though the Reels and Jigs peculiar to the Pipe are in large companies as at Weddings etc., played to good effect on the greater Pipe, yet they have besides, thro' the Highlands in general, a smaller Bagpipe, Compleat, the same in form and apparatus with the greater, differing only in size, and used for Dancing Music alone, altho' all other Music peculiar to the instrument may be played on it as truly, though not so grandly, as on the large Pipe."[2] This passage, however, does not occur in the orginal manuscript retrieved from Bengal by MacGregor Murray. As noted in chapter 8, Patrick MacDonald, Joseph's older brother and editor of the first published version of *Compleat Theory* editorialized where the need was felt without distinguishing or attributing the additions from the original. The gist of the small-pipe statement is found in a chapter headed 'Of the Influence of Poetry and Music' that was taken unacknowledged from Patrick MacDonald's earlier work, *Highland Vocal Airs* (1784), and written by John Ramsay of Ochtertyre. The overall work was superintended by Reverend Walter Young, Erskine, who wrote the preface. As for the Disarming Act, Joseph MacDonald said nothing of the bagpipe's having been banned, an oversight, it was earlier suggested, that some proponents of the prohibition theory advance as a proof for the virulence of the prohibition.

Whether Patrick MacDonald was reflecting what he knew himself from his own experiences of piping in Sutherland, Lochaber, and Argyllshire from the mid-1730s until 1784, or whether he was uncritically endorsing Ramsay of Ochtertyre's small-pipe thinking, his reader is left to infer a functional dichotomy in instruments. When, at the request of "many respectable subscribers" he added the four pibrochs after his dance music, Young wrote in the preface to *Highland Vocal Airs* that these pieces were played on "the large or true Highland bagpipe."[3] And although the small-pipes are seldom mentioned in Gaelic song, there are good grounds to assume that such an ill-defined instrument existed, Collinson notwithstanding.[4] Ochtertyre may have overstated his case for the general use of the small-pipes throughout the Highlands, but he can have had no motive for lying. It isn't impossible that by "small-pipes" he meant two-drone sets, which were common enough, apparently, in the second half of the eighteenth century and used in the *ceòl mór* competitions in Edinburgh. However, drones that were smaller than modern ones and that were almost certainly brought to Canada by immigrant Gaels in the first half of the nineteenth century have come to light in the Cape Breton *Gàidhealtachd*. It must be remembered that bagpipe manufacture must have been far less standardized before the formal recognition of pipers by the British army in 1854 and before pipes were played in unison as bands. Highland pipers played the pipes that were available to them, whether made in the Highlands or the Lowlands. The "Contullich Papers" show that in 1765, for example, MacLeod of MacLeod bought pipes, presumably for his piper, from R. Robertson, an Edinburgh turner who, in 1775, is known to have operated his business on Castle Hill.

The most modern reference to the small-pipes crops up in John H. Dixon's *Gairloch* (1886). Adducing no source or authority, Dixon reported that the Blind Piper's son's son Red John went as a young man "to the Reay country, the native land of his great grandfather Rorie, and there received tuition on the little pipes, which are often used for dance music."[5] Red John emigrated from Gairloch with his wife and family, including piping sons Angus and John,[6] and settled in 1803 in what later became New Glasgow in Pictou County. Apart from his signature on a legal document and what is said to be the pipe chanter of the Blind Piper, no detail marks his life in the province. His son John, later "Squire John," lived with him longer than anyone else in his family and was interviewed in Nova Scotia by the editor of *Celtic Magazine*, Alexander MacKenzie, in 1879. MacKenzie only mentioned that Red John, who "died a very old man," "continued to play the national instrument all his life,"[7] but it is possible that the interview was the source for small-pipe reference in Dixon. It remains a mystery why he needed specific tuition in an instrument that at least one person in 1803 described as "the same in form and apparatus with the greater, differing only in size."[8]

As far as almost all Gaelic bards were concerned, bagpipes were bagpipes, and indeed the term "great" may have done little more than distinguish the Highlanders' bagpipe from some alien instruments also known as bagpipes. Those Gaelic bards who liked piping, John MacDonald, Alasdair MacDonald, Duncan Ban MacIntyre, Rob Donn MacKay, and Archibald MacDonald, left no record of small-pipes.

Whether or not the two-drone bagpipe was mistakenly called the small-pipe or was lumped in with some definable small bagpipes that were used in Gaelic Scotland has yet to be resolved, but there is no doubt that from 1750 until 1821 both two and three-drone Highland bagpipes existed in Gaelic Scotland. John G. Dalyell reported in *Musical Memoirs* (1849) that in 1821 the two-droned pipes were barred from the Edinburgh competitions. This decision followed by nine years the report of an award of money to the Highland Society of London's piper and musical instrument maker, Malcolm MacGregor, "for essential improvements made by him on the Great Highland Pipe."[9] What these changes were is not mentioned, and when, if ever they reached the most Gaelic parts of the Highlands in the next fifty years, is unknown.

Given conservativeness of tradition, it is safe to assume, with Dr Duncan Fraser,[10] that the two-drone pipes and unimproved bagpipes continued to be played for decades afterwards in places where the influence of the Highland Society of London wasn't felt. There is some evidence, from the lore bearer Joe Neil MacNeil and J.M. MacDonald[11] for example, that two-droned bagpipes were played in the 1830s in Cape Breton.

Dalyell published a representation of a three-droned bagpipe said to have been played at Culloden, and the watercolour in Joseph MacDonald's manuscript shows a Highlander in contemporary banned middle-class clothing, playing a three-drone set, with pear-shaped terminals.[12] The 1803 published version claims that the three-droned Highland bagpipe was the original Highland bagpipe and that it was still (c. 1760) played in the North. If it is true that Red John MacKay, Gairloch, went to Reay country around 1770 to learn to play the small-pipes, then both instruments were played in Sutherland. The 1803 version accurately quotes Joseph MacDonald's manuscript as follows:

"Besides the smaller Drones of the Highland Bagpipe (two in number) there was, and still is, in use, with the Pipers in the North Highlands particularly, a great Drone, double the Length and Thickness of the smaller, and in sound, just an octave below them, which adds vastly to its grandeur, both in sound and show.

This Drone may be properly termed the Bass Drone, and, in proportion to the simplicity of the Instrument, has a good deal of the nature of a Bass accompanyment, Insomuch that to Persons of true Taste, accustomed to it; the want of it makes a most capital Defect in the martial Strain of Pipe music.

The reason given by the Pipers of the West Highlands for laying aside the use of the great Drone, was frivolous, and unfounded, namely that the loudness of it drowned the sound of the Chanter music, But this is a mistake, & should it happen so, it is easily rectified, by weakening the Reed of the great Drone."[13]

Had the West Highland pipers begun, by 1750, to use a cylindrical bore pipe chanter that used a weaker reed[14] (which would indeed have been drowned out by the noise of a bass drone), a knowledgeable writer like Joseph Mac-Donald unquestionably would have known.

The West Coast two-drone bagpipe is mentioned at least once in the Gaelic literature. In his "Elegy to Red John the Piper" Archibald MacDonald (c. 1750–c. 1815) writes, "The blow-pipe is stopped,/The two drones are deep-sleeping."[15] Red John MacQueen was a former soldier and a piper in the army, if the allusion in verse four of the same song is anything to go by. As his friend Archibald MacDonald described it, he would play his harp (*chluicheadh a chlàrsach*) and sing at the inn or at a milling/waulking. He was a dancer and a dance-music piper whose repertoire of grace-notings included the "*crunnluath.*" This was not necessarily to say that he played *ceòl mór*; Joseph MacDonald mentioned that the "*creanludh*" gracing was used in pipe reels, although he said that the more complex gracings he described were not. (With one exception that I am aware of, no pipe reel written since the appearance of staff notated pipe music even uses the "*crunn-luath*" or the "*edre*" upper-hand ending of the *crunludh*.)[16]

Joseph MacDonald's view that two-drone pipes were used by Gaels in the West Highlands is also vindicated in the Reverend Alexander MacRae's *History of the Clan MacRae.* Here Colonel Sir John MacRa (1786–1847) of Ardintoul in Kintail is wrongly credited with having added the third drone. Among many commemorative inscriptions on the instrument, there are three on the bass drone (suggesting two tuning slides) and one on the stock. The topmost bass drone inscription makes the claim that "all Highland bagpipes, till after the Battle of Waterloo, had but two or three short or treble drones." The second shield states that "Lieut.-Colonel Sir John Macra, K.CH., late 79th Cameron Highlanders, was the first to introduce (and it was on this set of pipes) the use of a big or bass drone."[17]

Colonel MacRa, in his Kintail retirement, was a wealthy yacht-owner and patron of the piper Archibald Munro (c. 1800–56). A piper himself, MacRa dabbled in making the instrument but Munro, his piper, preferred to play what in his time was considered to be an old-fashioned set (no description of which exists). Unlikely as it seems, it appears that MacRa was unaware of the three-drone bagpipe's popularity in the Northern Highlands in the mid-eighteenth century, well within living memory of his lifetime. The drones of MacRa's famous "silver-mounted black ebony set" date at least to the early nineteenth century. The chanter, which was the centrepiece and known as the *Feadan Dubh Chintaille* (the Black Chanter of Kintail), is claimed to date from the late eighteenth century, or possibly earlier.

John MacGregor (1708–89) from Fortingall in Perthshire, piper (teacher?) to Prince Charles in 1745–46, is believed also to have played a two-drone bagpipe, thus providing at least one example of the instrument's use in the south-central Highlands.[18]

THE QUICKSTEP AND THE COLLEGE.

Breaks with piping tradition appear to have been almost nonexistent in the Highland regiments in the second half of the eighteenth century and were probably insignificant roughly until the Crimean War in the 1850s.[19] However, there are two recorded observations of change in the late eighteenth century, both having to do with the Highland regiments, that must be acknowledged.

First, in *Highland Vocal Airs* Patrick MacDonald wrote: "One of the greatest improvements in the military art, that has been made in modern times, is the introduction of quick-step marches."[20] These lines occur in the essay "Of the influence of Poetry & Music upon the Highlanders," which was written by Ramsay of Ochtertyre. For all his wisdom and influence, Ramsay's firsthand experience of clan military music before the inception of most Highland regiments was probably insufficient to allow him to pontificate or to allow us to accept his statement unquestioningly.[21] Ramsay must have been aware of the various "quicksteps" associated with such Lowland regiments as the 2d Dragoons (Royal Scots Greys), the Royal Scots, and the 21st (Royal North British Fusiliers) and probably noted an extension of specific tunes into Highland regimental pipe music. Neither Ramsay nor MacDonald, however, offered a definition of a quickstep,[22] and while Ramsay may have accurately reported what was to him an apparent novelty in Highland military piping, there is no doubt, as we saw in chapter 10, that this sort of non-dance-music *ceòl beag* was used by Gaelic pipers in military settings, probably for clearly understood purposes, at least as early as Mar's Rebellion in 1715 and probably much earlier.

Alexander Nicolson's *Gaelic Proverbs ... based on MacIntosh's Collection* (1882) describes the chorus "Gabhaidh sinn an rathad mór/Olc no math

le càch e" ("We'll take the high road/whate'er the rest may say" my translation) as belonging to one of the "most popular Highland 'quick-steps,'" composed to commemorate the march through hostile (Scottish) country of a
number of Highland Royalist soldiers to join Montrose for the battle of
Inverlochy in 1645.[23] It is uncertain who collected this "proverb" since
Nicolson made additions to Rev. Donald MacIntosh's original collection, but
MacIntosh's dates were 1743–1808.

An equally plausible idea of the interrelationship between English and
Scottish military musical repertoires in the later eighteenth century appears
in the writing of P-N. Chantreau, who toured Scotland in 1788–89.
Chantreau noted hearing Scottish airs borrowed by English military musicians and played on the fife.[24]

Towards the end of Ramsay of Ochtertyre's lifetime there is an example
of an English regimental band that may well be a late example of the model
followed in 1756–57 by Fraser's Highlanders when they formed their "band
of musick." Harry Ross-Lewin, a commissioned officer in the 32d regiment
who fought at Vimiera in the Peninsular War on 21 August 1808, wrote that
early on that day the 43d (Monmouthshire) passed them by "in beautiful
order, with their band playing merrily before them. How many gallant fellows that we then saw marching to the sound of national quicksteps, all
life and spirits, were before evening stretched cold and stiff on the bloody
turf."[25]

Without defining quickstep it would be reaching too far to describe Gaelic military quicksteps as a late-eighteenth-century innovation. At the battle
of Vimiera, Ross-Lewin noted that the pipers of the First Battalion, 71st,
MacLeod's Highlanders, at the order to advance to the charge, "struck up a
national Scottish air, as is generally their custom."[26] The name of the air is
unrecorded. It might have been a Lowland tune for the 71st was quickly
being reinforced from its Glasgow-recruited Second Battalion. Although
even before the Napoleonic wars there were unilingual Gaels with ostensibly Lowland names, names are sometimes an indicator. One of the pipers
with the 71st at Vimiera was "a Highlander named George Clerk." He was
shot in the groin and had to let the 71st charge without him but he continued
to pipe. For his bravery Clerk was promoted to sergeant and given the title
"piper-major," a titular military honour based on the only known piper's rank
in the British army. However, Ross-Lewin also attributed to Clerk an outraged reaction to being denied the privilege of being up with his fellow
Highlanders.

Clerk's line from the pen of Ross-Lewin was a variant of one that James
Logan had published earlier in *The Scottish Gaël* in 1831. Both were given
in broad Lallans, suggesting that Clerk may have been a Lowlander,[27]
although his name has a perfectly good Gaelic equivalent (*Cléireach or Mac
a' Chléirich*). Four years later, details of 71st casualties lengthen the odds of

his having been a Highlander, except in name. Of the four officers killed at the battle of Vitoria in June 1812, only one, MacKenzie, bore a Highland name. Of the ten wounded only three, Grant, MacIntyre, and Campbell, had obvious Highland roots. One of the dead officers was Col Henry Cadogan; his piper, buried at Ardersier, was Piper D. Lamont who is described in his memorial as "field bugler" to Cadogan, suggesting dual musical function or broad interpretation of the term "bugler" to get a piper on the government payroll. The Lamonts are associated with Cowal in southern Argyleshire.

Apart from Clerk, the pipers of the 71st seem to have gone relatively unscathed during the Peninsular War or else were overlooked as Pipers and included with the rank and file. Buglers did not fare so well. The *Memorials of the Late War* cited by Keltie in his history of the Scottish Highlands show that six buglers of the 71st were killed between 14 June and 7 August 1812. Whatever its proportion of Gaelic speakers, when the best six companies of the First Battalion, 71st marched through Lisbon in 1810 they did so to concerted bugle music. Was this typically British military custom or just unimaginative instrumentation?

Two other pipers from the 71st are mentioned during the war against Napoleon. Kenneth Logan, also called a "piper-major" of the 71st in Angus MacKay's records, competed at the Edinburgh competition in 1813 and won third prize. (Clerk competed in 1815 when the organizers "thought proper to vote him a gold medal instead of considering him as a candidate for one of the prizes.")[28] The other is unnamed, but he played "Hey Johnnie Cope" at the attack on Arroya del Molino in October 1811. If this could be construed as a quickstep (and there is no reason to believe it couldn't), it is an example of a famous mid-eighteenth-century quickstep that Rev. Patrick Mac-Donald and Ramsay of Ochtertyre had presumably overlooked. The tune made its published début in book 9 of James Oswald's twelve-book series of five hundred and fifty tunes, published between 1743 and 1759, although the melody was attributed by Stenhouse to an earlier period.[29]

The second development is a continuation, in an unlikely southern part of the *Gàidhealtachd*, of the institution of the Gaelic "college" of piping at about the time that the Skye and Mull colleges were reported to be closing. The college in question was the MacGregors' in Gaelic Perthshire; James Logan placed it at "Rannach."[30] When it began is unknown but a guess would be at least in the late seventeenth century. Beyond doubt it relied on traditional teaching techniques probably for as long as it existed, since there was no staff notation in bagpipe music at the time. Whatever and whenever its origins, this institution was run by a MacGregor family in Perthshire in the southern Highlands. In its report on the October 1784 Highland Society of London piping competition held at Edinburgh's Assembly Hall, *Scots Magazine* said that the winner was "John MacGregor of Fortingall, who, with the additional merit of having already taught above 50 military pipers himself is the eldest of five sons, taught by their father, John MacGregor, together with 90 other pipers."[31]

The author of the competition notes in Angus MacKay's *Collection* gives the 1784 winner as "John MacGregor senior, from Fortingall," who, we are deliberately allowed to infer, was the same man described in the 1783 competition notes as being the seventy-five-year-old piper to Colonel Campbell of Glenlyon.[32]

According to David Burns's article "John MacGregor of Fortingall and His Descendants," the John MacGregor who won in 1784 was born in 1708 and died in 1789.[33] Burns, however, is at variance with *Scots Magazine* inasmuch as Burns gave John MacGregor's father as "Patrick McIN SKER-LICH." The John MacGregor reported as father of the 1784 winner in *Scots Magazine* presumably flourished around 1700. The 1784 winner, John son of John, was one of Prince Charles's pipers in 1745 and 1746. The notes in MacKay's *Collection* tell us that he was father of four sons (including a third-generation John), all pipers (one who was "eminent in that profession" and had been "for some time at Dunvegan,"[34] which may mean either that he had been employed there as a piper or had been good enough to be sent there for the MacCrimmon finishing touches appropriate to a great piper, or both). Using Burns's dates for these four piping sons of John MacGregor, the John who won in 1784 at age seventy-six was teaching his sons piping around 1750 and was available to teach pipers who enlisted for the Seven Years' War as well as the American revolutionary war.

The *Scots Magazine* article points to the vigour of piping in Highland Perthshire, even if graveside pibroch playing may have died out with Rob Roy. It shows a widespread interest on the part of youngsters who were presumably competing for positions that weren't even officially recognized, in the Highland regiments. But the claim also leaves the residual questions what the MacGregor school taught and how great a need there was for a school of piping.[35] Did the MacGregors' school mark a turning point after which Perthshire Highland piping revived from a 1730s low, or was there no critical break with Gaelic tradition? The 1784 *Scots Magazine* report strongly affirms the latter possibility with competent MacGregor piping going back unbroken from the 1800s to the late seventeenth century. Then, assuming that Edinburgh competitions were the benchmark accepted (and in large part set) by Perthshire MacGregor pipers of three generations, why does the name sink out of the prize lists around 1815? The answer is that Gaelic traditionalism in music, which relied on ear learning and was not bound by any all-encompassing technical or interpretative standard, was rapidly being replaced by literate learning and set standards at the *ceòl mór* competition level. The banning by competition organizers of the two-drone bagpipes may also have something to do with it.

Excluding the competition-dominant MacGregor pipers, who were associated primarily with the Campbells in Breadalbane and Glenlyon in Perthshire, the Edinburgh competition results of winners in the eighteenth century show that pipers were retained by the MacNab laird (1783 and 1785), Sir R. Menzies (1783), MacDonell of Lochgary (a boy piper, 1790), and Robertson of Struan (1792), all Perthshire gentry. In addition, there were pipers from the county who were unattached to any gentlemanly family. Between 1799 and 1817 George Graham, Donald Robertson, Duncan Mac-Gregor, and Donald Gunn competed in the Edinburgh competitions as members of the Perthshire Militia and (if it was different) the Royal Perthshire Militia. By the latter date Sir John MacGregor Murray's influence on Perthshire piping must have been strong, but the almost customary MacGregor presence in the prize list was gone. If there was a break with tradition in Perthshire piping it probably came in the 1820s, the same time that Stewart of Garth was writing of the Gaels' love of music and dance in the past tense and of the rapid disappearance of the old Gaelic-speaking middle class. A piper who strongly echoed this theory was Angus Cameron, Ballachulish (born c. 1776). What happened, for example, to people like "Alexander MacLean Piper in Wellhouse" in the parish of Kilmorack, county of Inverness, who was named in a Decreet of Removing, 16 May 1795?[36]

What model was used for Highland military pipers is a mystery. As far as we know, there was no official standard for pipers attached to the Highland regiments at the time. If the pipers who resorted to the MacGregor school were already fairly capable players, it might be that the school's job was to expand repertoires to include music that was specifically military, possibly national quicksteps and pieces of *ceòl mór* that were not common to all the *Gàidhealtachd* or among essentially dance-music pipers. Particularly in the case of *ceòl mór* playing, there is only Garth's passing observation about graveside pibroch playing in the 1730s to suggest an early decline.

PART FOUR

Tradition and Change in the Old World and the New

12 The Turning Point, 1790–1850: Innovation and Conservatism in Scotland

The critical time for the traditionally minded Gaelic-speaking population of the Highlands was the period 1790–1850, especially after the end of the Napoleonic Wars and the collapse of the kelping business in the 1820s. It became increasingly obvious to Scotch Gaels, from the Chisholm and Sutherland clearances, from the expulsions and leavings of Gaels from North Uist, Moidart, North and South Morar, South Uist, Eigg, Raasay, Knoydart, Skye, Assynt, from Barra, the Breadalbane lands in Argyll and Perthshire, Strathglass, and from many other places, that Gaelic traditional life must be replanted or adapt itself painfully to new utilitarian profit-oriented priorities, letting cultural elements live or die as they might.

These decades are the turning point, much more so than Culloden and the brief occupation after it. This was the time of large-scale emigrations to North America. By 1851, the end of the half-century, emigration to Cape Breton and Nova Scotia was all but over. At the same time emigration to Australia and New Zealand was picking up.[1] The most significant cultural corollary is that what remains of the spontaneous, informally learned music and dance of late-twentieth-century Cape Breton is anachronistic, harking back to the late eighteenth and early nineteenth centuries, while what is found in the antipodes is modern, originating in the mid- to late nineteenth century when a weakened traditional piping was more susceptible to change.[2] In Scotland the fact of emigration weakened tradition and bolstered the emerging dominance of modern piping and new trends in dancing.

In this period, for all that, the two elements – persistent tradition and introduced novelty – co-existed in Scotland, at times in stark contrast. Accompanying them were two different attitudes. The progressive improver often saw tradition as all but extinct; the traditionalist saw matters otherwise. Thus, Sir John Sinclair of Ulbster (1754–1835), president of the Highland Society of London in 1796, wrote that had it not been for the exertions of the society, the army would not have been supplied with enough pipers, "so rapidly was that species sinking into oblivion."[3] He gives no credit to the MacGregors, to the MacKays in Gairloch, to the last two MacCrimmons that we know about or to countless others including emigrant bagpipers mentioned in New World histories. Sinclair's questionable generalization however was a cornerstone of the idea that all eighteenth-century piping was saved from imminent extinction by the Highland Society of London competitions and, by implication, by the British army.

In contrast, Chantreau wrote in 1792 that to a Scotch Highlander or a Hebridean, it was "*le plus grand éloge que de l'estimer un bon joueur de cornemuse*" ("the greatest praise to consider him a good bagpiper").[4] Among a number of French visitors who had been inspired by the writing of Walter Scott (and perhaps by the Ossianic debate), the economist-banker Duclos who visited Perthshire, the Great Glen, Iona, and Staffa between 1814 and 1826 was reported to have detected in the Highland Scots "*un peuple demeuré fidèle à ses usages primitifs, à la langue de ces ancêtres ... leur cœur bat au récit des hauts faits de leurs aïeux, et chacun connaît par cœur les vers des bardes et des ménestrels ...*" ("a folk still faithful to its primitive customs, to its ancestral language ... their heart beats to the tale of the great deeds of their ancestors, and each knew by heart the verses of the bards and minstrels ...").[5]

The persistence of traditional Gaelic music and dance in Scotland into and after the middle of the nineteenth century is the more remarkable in light of the fact that the emigrations to North America had been so massive and disruptive. They were prompted by economic and philosophical factors already touched on, factors that inevitably came to operate in the New World too, although much later in rural communities like those of northeastern Nova Scotia, where at least partial self-sufficiency, and with it cultural conservatism, survived well into the twentieth century. However, there were other important influences in the first half of nineteenth-century Scotland that reinforced the Gael's decision to leave and guaranteed a much-altered future for piping (and fiddling and dancing) in the Old Country. These include the desertion from Gaelic language and social life of the Gaelic middle class from c.1790, the influence of the evangelical Protestantism in the Highlands, education and the growing acceptance of literacy in piping, the expansion of competition piping, and the beginning of Highland games. I will deal with the stubborn persistence of Gaelic traditional piping to 1850 in Scotland under similar but extended headings.

From about the start of the Napoleonic Wars, as Gaels were emigrating in increasing numbers to North America, the ability of traditional Gaelic life to resist change was gradually lessened by the growing presence of a Highland middle class that had a greatly diminished understanding of Gaelic life; fewer of them than ever spoke Gaelic and more of them than ever were interested only in the externals of Gaelicness, as they perceived them, if in anything Gaelic at all. With dwindling social and economic support of the middle class, and for many other reasons, Gaelic emigration grew to a torrent. Studies of those emigrations from 1790 to 1850 show that they were the last of the family and community emigrations of Scotch Gaels.

There is general agreement among historical demographers and emigration experts that the essential character of Highland emigrations changed around 1850 from this older family and community kind, which Bumsted described for 1770–1815 in *The People's Clearance*, to individualistic leavings. This general observation is substantiated repeatedly, although unscientifically, in the Gaelic record and explains cultural retentiveness of tradition in Nova Scotia and the ceding to modernity in Australia and New Zealand.

For the ordinary Highlander it didn't matter where the middle class went. A typical insider's view is presented by the Reverend Norman MacLeod, through his fictional character Finlay Piper. Writing probably in the 1830s, MacLeod had Finlay Piper lament the near disappearance of the old lairds and the rapid dwindling of the heart of the tenantry from the old Highlands:

But the lairds of the Gaeltachd have been destroyed – they're gone like the winter snows that melt away, and since the day they left, the honest country people, the brave stalwart who was in the country went too. And if some men denigrated great chiefs, I don't see great prosperity, or happiness since the *little* chiefs came, and the new men in the land. With them [the *tighearnan mòra*, or great chiefs] there was protection, and there was kindredness, warmth, and goodwill, and memory of days gone by binding poor and rich together; but a dispersal overtook them which I don't understand. There are no homes or families of the gentle-folk among us now, which may be compared to the hospitable, plentiful homes of the people who went before them. There's nought but scarcity, and meanness compared to what there was in my day ...[6]

The new middle class's lack of interest in piping is found elsewhere in MacLeod's writing: "Many of the Gaelic chiefs are indifferent about piping and the customs of their stalwart ancestors. They'd sooner hear the bleatings of the great sheep, and the English of lowland shepherds than the sweetest music of the pipes and the clarsach; but there linger still some who are fond of them, and it's no wonder to us."[7]

For many, retaining a piper and wearing tartan in novel and non-traditional ways were about the extent of their contact with the people who lived on their lands. The second marquis of Breadalbane,[8] for example, the proud employer of the piper John Ban MacKenzie, depopulated Loch Tay-side and Glenorchy in the 1830s and 1840s. Earlier, according to Somerled MacMillan, Donald Cameron, ninth of Lochiel, whose piper, Angus Cameron, won second place in the 1793 Edinburgh competition, oversaw the depopulating of Loch Arkaig and Glen Dessary and Glen Pean, among other places on his vast estate.[9] Without sophisticated social support, surviving Gaelic tradition turned in on itself and opened up only to fervent and sensitive scholars like the Gaelic-speaking Etonian John Francis Campbell and Alexander Carmichael (1832–1912), author of *Carmina Gadelica*.

This was a great change from the last quarter of the eighteenth century, about which Lowlander John Ramsay of Ochtertyre (1736-1814) wrote in his manuscript reminiscences: "The duinewassals and commons being bred together in the same sports and pursuits, and having the same friends and enemies, lived on the footing of familiarity which nowadays would be considered as mean and unbecoming."[10] Ramsay also remarked that the middle and inferior classes of Highlanders who had not been out of their own country retained "the domestic manners of their forefathers in great purity."[11]

In 1822 Stewart of Garth stated the case MacLeod later made but attributed some causes. Garth said that, compared to their fathers and grandfathers, the middle class of his day were relatively uneducated and "more degenerated" even than the peasantry.[12] He "knew several tacksmen of correct learning, who could quote and scan the classics with much ease and rapidity; while the sons of these men are little better than clowns ... When the Hessian troops were quartered in Athole in 1745, the commanding officers, who were accomplished gentlemen, found a ready communication, in Latin, at every inn." (By custom, inn-keeping was a middle-class occupation in the second half of the eighteenth century in the Highlands.)[13] Garth's more telling remark, however, was "that three-fourths of the old respectable race of gentlemen tacksmen have disappeared, and have been supplanted by men totally different in manners, birth, and education."[14] Garth did not elaborate on or substantiate this statement but three-quarters was probably right for MacLeod holdings in Skye by 1822; it would have been too small for Barra by 1842 where almost all the old tacksmen emigrated, and for Cameron country by 1847.[15] A similar disappearance of the old Gaelic middle class happened on many other estates. However, as late as 1866 improver and traditionalist lived side by side in Skye.[16] Sadly, too, eviction was not exclusive to those of non-traditional bent. A Gael like MacDonald of Lathaig was guilty of heartless evictions on Eigg.[17]

Garth, with an officer's bias, believed that the last representatives of the old school of tacksmen and their sons, the educated Gaelic-speaking people who shared the culture of their tenants with enthusiasm, were more and more found only in the army.[18] The incoming improver farmers had no legal obligation to former tenants or interest in Gaelic tradition and many of them, having applied the laws of property to their advantage, argued, callously but quite rightly, that the people they cleared would be far better off overseas.[19]

By 1850 the situation had inevitably worsened. Highland estates were changing hands more often as real and imagined British land values closed on each other. Emigration by then had raked many old patrimonies of the valorous old spine of Gaelic society, the substantial tenant farmer, and as emigration continued, a reflection was seen in the old Highland regiments, which, by the time of the Crimean War, were markedly less Gaelic and more Saxon.[20] What was a significant social collapse led to the traditional piper's becoming something of an anachronism in many parts of Highland Scotland and in the army, as his contemporaries adopted the alien, intrusive ideas of competition, literacy, and service of the non-traditional.[21]

For 1840–50 I have presented the image of a dramatically diminished, in some areas vanished, Gaelic-speaking middle class of arable and dairy farmers (who typically had let or sublet land to poorer Gaels). The idea is exaggerated and challenged by exceptions, but from the emigrants' point of view the notion is broadly valid. Another general image exists, that of the bulk of poor Gaels' being cleared off all profitable land and herded into economically non-viable "crofts" on the coast in places such as Plockton, Janetown, Dornie, Glenelg,[22] and the edge of Lochiel, or into planned towns in the interior such as Kingussie and Newtonmore. These generalizations point to the increasingly pathetic social isolation and cultural vulnerability of the poor Gael that Somers described in 1846 in *Letters from the Highlands*. Many living in the West and North, already displaced from their traditional places in the name of profit maximization, now found themselves living on tiny oceanside allotments enduring a very spare existence that depended on fishing, meagre gardening, and kelping. When kelping declined in the 1820s these people were devastated. They constitute the majority of the post-1850 emigrations.

THE INFLUENCE OF THE CHURCH

Inasmuch as Catholic South Uist, Barra, Eigg, Morar, Moidart, and other Catholic parts of Highland Scotland were the most culturally conservative, it is fair to say that there was no discouragement of traditionalism by the clergy in those communities during the century 1750-1850. Elsewhere the story changes. The period when Moderatism dominated over the popular or evangelical faction in the Church of Scotland began in 1752[23] and was weakening by the turn of the century. In the Highlands this was the time when traditionally musical ministers flourished – men like Norman MacLeod, Murdoch MacDonald (Joseph and Patrick MacDonald's father), and Patrick MacDonald himself. They sang Gaelic songs, played musical instruments for dancing, and apparently fostered tradition as socially beneficial.[24] Moderate Church of Scotland ministers had no quibble with folk culture.

At the turn of the nineteenth century more austere and less-trusting Protestant clerical attitudes to cultural pleasures began to appear, particularly in the emerging evangelical wing of the Church of Scotland.[25] Later these attitudes were more widely inculcated by the Free Church, which split from the mother church in 1843 at the Disruption. Where the Highlands are concerned there is a temporal link between the emergence of evangelicalism and the emigration of the Gaelic middle class, and between the emergence of a national Free Church in 1843 and the individualistic leavings. While it can't be proved, both links are more than coincidental.

The revival in evangelical religion at the turn of the nineteenth century, hardly a surprise under the economic and social circumstances, promoted in its votaries a gaunt and perverse sense of guilt at personal inability to cope with the improving, or capitalist, ethos; cruelly, it began to put up blocks to the Highlander's access to his traditional pastimes and pleasures, music, dance, story, song, and the cup that cheers and palliates.

Stewart of Garth sadly noted of Highlanders between 1782 and 1822 in Protestant communities that were familiar to him that "their taste for music, dancing, and all kinds of social amusement, has been chilled. Their evening meetings are now seldom held, and when they do occur, instead of being enlivened with the tale, the poem, or the song, they are too frequently exasperated with political or religious discussions."[26]

Free Church ministers were puritan sabbath keepers for many of whom the notion of traditional story was falsely imbued with mendacity. However difficult it may have been for EveryGael to adapt to their new social values, the willingness to adhere to the new ways, in some places, must have got a boost from the persecution of the Free Church in its first decade of existence by Highland landlords such as Fraser of Lovat, the duke of Athol, Lord Seafield (Grant), and Colonel MacLean in Ardgower.[27] For all that, the application of an unpromulgated anti-music and -dance policy in the Protestant Highlands by the evangelical and Free Church clergy, while already advanced in parts of Skye by 1843, cannot have been uniform; not all cultural memories were obliterated.[28]

The late Major C.I.N. MacLeod of Dornie and Antigonish, Nova Scotia, told me in 1972 that he found an old relative in Free Church Lewis in the 1950s who recognized the step-dancing that he demonstrated to her as typical of (and, in his mind at the time, exclusive to) Nova Scotia's Gaels. His relative told MacLeod, who had worked on his mother's family's shieling in Lewis in his boyhood summers, that they had done that kind of dancing long ago. Her memory could not have gone back much beyond 1860. Duncan Fraser found people in Free Church Assynt who could play the two-drone bagpipe for dancing in the 1880s, and a similar turning point appears in

Tiree.[29] Something of the sharp anti-cultural edge that is often associated with all Highland Free Church clergy may yet be dulled in some parishes by more searching scholarship.

THE INFLUENCE OF EDUCATION AND OF LITERACY ON PIPING

Piping, fiddling, dancing, story telling, and song also found an enemy within the evolving education system, but how widespread this was and how Church-related is not certain. Professor Kenneth MacKinnon has pointed out that Gaelic was fostered as the medium of Protestant and improver education from 1767 roughly until the Education Act of 1872, when Gaelic was systematically discouraged. MacKinnon showed that in the early years, as of 1767, the Society in Scotland for Propagating Christian Knowledge (SSPCK),[30] and the schools run by the commissioners for the forfeited estates taught in Gaelic (with a view to later Anglicization through literacy first in the mother tongue). This policy encouraged the formation of societies for the support of Gaelic schools in Edinburgh (1811), Glasgow (1812), and Inverness (1818).[31] From one of these comes a telling example of cultural discouragement.

A Gaelic bard who came to Canada, Ewan MacColl (1808–98) of Kenmore at the head of Loch Fyne, was raised in a traditionalist family, in a traditionalist Church of Scotland community where the *céilidh* was beloved. Canadian Gael Alasdair Friseal reported MacColl as saying, "Playing the pipes and fiddling were really common around the head of Loch Fyne and no company were complete without a piper or a fiddler".[32] Friseal went on to write:

Its ministers weren't looking gloomily on the diversions, the *ceilidh* or the shinty games of the men. This was before the time of the Gaelic schoolmasters sent out by the Edinburgh society to be broadcasting the Bible light in the *Gaidhealtachd* and to be teaching the people. These pious men set their faces harshly against the traditional practices that they condemned absolutely and upon which they fixed the mark of sin. They were men sincere in their moral conduct, hard, unbending in their opinions and zealous for belief. With them came many changes to the people's lifestyle but the Bard had grown up to young manhood before the new ideas got a bite on the place.[33]

The career of Dougald Buchanan (1716–68), composer of religious poems and hymns in Gaelic, as a teacher and catechist for the SSPCK in Kinloch Rannoch, Perthshire, between 1755 and 1768 offers an earlier example of righteous discouragement of "sinful amusements" including sabbath "foot-ball" playing.[34] He was strong, sternly and obsessively evangelical, and persistent, but whether or not he was typical of later SSPCK employees remains to be seen. What can be said is that Kinloch Rannoch was an atypical community, one of a number of villages planned by the commissioners of the forfeited estates in the early 1760s and peopled *inter alia* by "King's Cottagers." These were people who the government hoped would sow the seeds of improver agriculture among the local Gaels. The steadier social norms found in longer-established and more socially cohesive Perthshire Gaelic communities may have been in disarray in Kinloch Rannoch.

Where learning piping from written bagpipe music is concerned, apart from the published work of Patrick MacDonald in 1784, this is a nineteenth-century phenomenon. Angus MacKay's reports of the Edinburgh *ceòl mór* competitions wrote that "John" MacDonald's "On the Theory, Principle, and Practice of the Great Highland Bag-pipe Music" was awarded as an encouragement "to such of the performers as had made the greatest improvement."[35] From 1806, according to Angus MacKay, cash incentives were awarded, intermittently it seems, at the Edinburgh competitions for writing pipe music.[36] These facts strongly indicate a deliberate educational agenda on the part of the Highland Society of London (acquiesced in by the Highland Society of Scotland) quite out of keeping with tradition and carelessly or deliberately divergent from it. The impact of literate learning and of the competitions upon tradition in the sequestered *Gàidhealtachd*, however, was slight.

Until 1840 there were about seven publications of pipe music:[37] Patrick MacDonald's *Highland Vocal Airs* (1784), Joseph MacDonald's *Compleat Theory* (1803), Robert Menzies's *Bagpipe Preceptor* (1818), Donald MacDonald's *Collection* (c. 1822), Neil MacLeod's *Pibereach or Pipe Tunes* (1828), Donald MacDonald's *Collection* (1828), and Angus MacKay's *Collection* (1838). Until 1840 there were eighteen editions available to any would-be literately learned bagpipers. Patrick MacDonald's book was not specified as a book of pipe music. Menzies's work contained only fifteen pieces, all written one-fifth below the chanter sound, and went out of print after the first edition. It may be misleading but the fourth edition of Donald MacDonald's 1828 *Collection of Quicksteps, Strathspeys, Reels & Jigs* ran to only twenty-five copies.[38] If they were ever available to the ordinary Highland piper, all were prohibitively expensive, and the power of any or all seven publications to influence traditional piping beyond the Highland line was very small.

Two important points to re-emphasize are that many incompetent pipers[39] took part in the Edinburgh competitions, and that of the publications of pipe music, only three were of *ceòl beag* – Patrick MacDonald's, Menzies's, and the 1828 MacDonald collection. The rest were restricted to classical piping, the form exclusively promoted by the Edinburgh competition system of the Highland Society. These publications were aimed at a curious, literate urban market. Publications of pipe music became much more common after

1840[40], however, and from then until Thomason's *Ceòl Mór* in c. 1896 there is a preponderance of *ceòl beag* in them. This shift of content is allied with the decline in interest in classical piping in Edinburgh, the inclusion of *ceòl beag* in competition piping at Inverness and elsewhere (as well as in the new nineteenth-century phenomenon of Highland games), and the shifting trends in army piping from battlefield functional and inspirational to march accompaniment and simple ceremonial piping.[41]

With the first of his two collections, Donald MacDonald is accepted as having improved the writing of pipe music to the extent that he made gracenotes instantly recognizable by turning all tails upwards (and all melody notes downwards). While this is no obstacle to the piper who feels free to adapt from the written version to meet his needs, it encourages less-confident pipers, firstly, to distinguish grace from melody notes, and then to standardize the length of all grace-notes as short (often demi-semi-quavers). This can easily detract from traditional rhythms for dancing where the older-fashioned, less grace-noted page of music might not. Competition judging, as it grew to depend on the published scores, encouraged the purely mechanical aspect that Donald MacDonald's bright idea introduced to piping.

MacDonald's first pioneering collection laid the groundwork for Angus MacKay's 1838 collection of *ceòl mór*. MacDonald's place, however, is more in the improving than the preserving fold. Not only did he adapt *ceòl mór* for orchestral instruments but in his book of light music, by his own admission, he threaded his way through northern and western styles of piping, which he alone identified, offering no description of either and proudly announcing that his version struck out a new course. The degree to which MacDonald's publications influenced Angus MacKay's work of 1838 is unknown, but like MacDonald's, Angus MacKay's scores never include the post-*creanludh* grace-note complexes, such as the *barrludh*, that are found for *ceòl mór* in Joseph MacDonald's manuscript. What's more, Joseph MacDonald's unexplained introductory runs are all but absent from the later collector-publishers' books.[42] In *ceòl beag* Donald MacDonald's work does not include the *creanludh* that, according to Joseph MacDonald, was indeed used in light music.

However widespread among the few literate piping improvers was the thought of superiority in the 1820s, 1830s and 1840s, the modernized, standardized literately learned forms of piping have become the accepted ones. Even with easy access to Joseph MacDonald's manuscript in the Edinburgh University library there has been very little interest in duplicating his style.

The sharp increase in publications of piping music after 1840 and their emphasis on *ceòl beag* are contemporaneous with the more rapid disappearance and decay of traditional Gaelic community piping in Highland Scotland (South Uist, and doubtless other conservative communities, excepted). However, although the first edition of William MacKay's *Complete Tutor for the*

Great Highland Bagpipe in 1840 adhered to Donald MacDonald's grace/melody note distinction, it presented tunes much more simply with fewer grace-notes, along Joseph MacDonald lines, assuming competence on the part of the player.[43] When slightly complicated gracings are included, Cannon suggested that MacKay had taken the tunes containing them from MacDonald.[44] Apart from some incompetence in English that Cannon noted, one deduces from William MacKay's work the relative insignificance of some of the publications of pipe music from 1784 to 1850 as forces for manipulating and improving community piping. These relatively ungracenoted publications, in which modernists must find shortcomings, may have been deferring to an understood native Highland requirement for freedom of expression in embellishment. For this reason one cannot discount the use by traditional Gaelic pipers of appropriate published fiddle music.

THE INFLUENCE OF THE COMPETITIONS

From 1781 to 1783 in Falkirk and from 1783 to 1844 in Edinburgh the Highland Society of London sponsored classical piping competition in Lowland Scotland in a noble effort to reinvigorate what it conceived to be dying classical piping. The idea of exhibition and later competition in dancing Reels, or reel steps, by men at the same competitions was also introduced – all alien concepts in the Gaelic traditional world that would eventually have profound effects. But it was a time for improvement and societies. The Society of Antiquaries and the Highland and Agricultural Society were formed around 1784. However, despite the improving spirit that was abroad, the piping competitions in Falkirk and Edinburgh had about twenty years of relative freedom from manipulation. The music was not written down and the judges judged without scores. At least once, in 1783, the competitors appear to have equated their judges' subjectivity with incompetence, but otherwise the gentlemen's decisions were accepted. What their standards were and what their influence was – on which pipers were chosen to compete, on which tunes were played – is unknown. The instruments were not tampered with; the dances, with a minor exception in 1799,[45] were those performed spontaneously by Gaels to piping and were the more appreciated because they periodically alleviated the tedium of endless, often repetitive,[46] flooding of noisy, esoteric music that only the devotees in the audience could have understood.

The war with Napoleon undoubtedly drained away a lot of pipers who might otherwise have competed, but what exactly the quality of competition pipers ever was, and how accurately they represented the various threads of traditional Gaelic piping from 1781 until 1800, is debatable. The MacGregor family from Perthshire dominated the prize lists but boy pipers also competed successfully during those early years, and between 1800 and 1838. So much either for judging or for the vaunted mystique that now clings to classical piping. Reading between the lines, it seems fair to say that by about 1800 the strange, incomprehensible novelty of *ceòl mór* (and nothing but Reel dancing) had worn thin in Edinburgh and the organizers were casting about to make the competitions freshly attractive. *Ceòl mór* competition had to remain, for that was the Highland Society of London's primary piping concern, but inevitably, in the peripheral events the organizers extended the compass of the whole show and in some ways moved away from what can only have been Gaelic tradition.

By 1817 one man remarked that two-thirds of the audience showed up to see the dancing, not the piping. The variety of dances was widened and cash incentives were offered to dancers who by now did not necessarily come from the ranks of the competing pipers. In 1805 the (undescribed) broadsword exercise was introduced as an added diversion, and in 1809 five instead of three prizes were offered to pipers. In 1822 the degree to which caricature had entered the "Highland" scene is seen in reports of King George IV's visit to Edinburgh.[47]

In 1826 the bagpipe alternated with an orchestra in providing music for the dancing and in 1832 and 1835 the "*Gille Calum*" was danced exclusively to a Lowland orchestra, drawing at least one disgruntled letter from a dancer critical of the capacity of a Lowland band to produce suitable Highland dance music. This prompted the organizers to decree that the champion piper should pipe for that dance, a dubious honour if MacCulloch's opinion had any truth and quite contrary to what John Johnston said about the great pipers knowing nothing of "tinkers' music." There is no record of any winning piper refusing the job because he couldn't or wouldn't. The cynical would say that the prospect of a job in a stately home guaranteed compliance.

The trend to innovation in the competition arena continued. Angus MacKay's *Collection* mentioned prizes offered in 1838 at the Edinburgh *ceòl mór* and dancing competitions for the best-dressed, probably meaning best-dressed piper and/or dancer, and for the best-dressed in homemade tartan.[48]

The Highland Society of London's Edinburgh competitions were forty-five years old in 1826. Their novelty was staling and they became triennial; in varying degrees they had become the modern model and springboard for an expanding network of formal cultural and sporting events run in the Highlands, events that were obviously directed to contend in a superficial and condescending way with the generally unappealing idea of Scotland as North Britain, which had been seeded in 1707. The distinctiveness (perhaps already becoming a wan caricature) was Gaelic, the manipulation, Saxon. Archibald Campbell of Kilberry noted that "the fashion for 'competition' *ceòl beag* marches to which the soldier does not march, and dance tunes to which the dancer does not dance started in Angus MacKay's time. He is spoken of sometimes as the originator of it. If he was not, he, like other pipers in Deeside in Royal or other exalted employ, was an early devotee."[49]

The critically misleading effect, retrospectively, of the revivalist competition piping in the 1780s and 1790s as well as the 1800s is the fostering of the idea that the existence of competition is proof that *ceòl mór* piping was in remarkable decline all over Gaelic Scotland. Well-intentioned, if quite uncomprehending, incidents such as the offering of Joseph MacDonald's book to the most improved competitors at the Highland Society of London competitions in Edinburgh have encouraged the assumption that there was a wide range of piping skills in evidence at the competitions, and there probably was. But to go from there to arrogating to the Edinburgh competitions credit for the survival of all civilian and military classical piping is nonsense. To have loosed the bafflingly edited and poorly printed 1803 version of Joseph MacDonald's manuscript on learning pipers bespeaks less than intimate knowledge of *ceòl mór* on the part of competition organizers. How judging was done is anyone's guess. There was no published reference for standard of fingering until Joseph MacDonald's book. If there was standardization of tunes (and inasmuch as competition pipers played at least once in concert, there must have been, sometimes, some agreement, if only temporary,[50] it can only have existed within the *canntaireachd* system of passing the music of.

Gradually and for the most part unwittingly, the competition system permitted the intrusion of altered attitudes to piping when the traditional piper had learned to denigrate his type of skill. At the time (1781), however, detecting from London a slackening of interest in classical piping, there appeared to be no alternatives (short of restoring political power to chiefs and letting music rediscover its own levels) to making piping gradable and competitive. Over the nineteenth century, classical piping's traditional spontaneous functions were, in many quarters, replaced by artificial ones, competitions and the novel exigencies of the army and the new gentry. All of these agencies operated with the best of intentions but little flexibility and sensitive intelligence. As far as dance-music piping was concerned, there is no reason to believe that anything other than characteristically traditional r(R)eel piping continued for as long as bagpipes provided music for Gaelic dancing. Where competition and standardization of technique had no appeal, older traditional styles and repertoires of *ceòl mór* lingered into the twentieth century.[51]

HIGHLAND GAMES

Although quite different from the modern event, one starting point for the phenomenon of the Highland games is the Northern Meeting, first held in Inverness in 1798. It began its annual existence as a social event for the gentry featuring balls, card parties, dinners, concerts, and horse races. With the exception of horse racing it appears not to have been even remotely connected to Gaelic tradition and there is no reason to think that the race track was included as a sop to Highlanders, many of whom had been keen horsemen for generations. The Northern Meeting was an English-speaking society affair and it wasn't until 1859, after a fifteen-year hiatus, that the Edinburgh piping and dancing competitions were grafted onto it, giving it the Highland aura that it retains.

Just in its title, *Comunn nam Fìor Ghàidheal*, or Society of the True Gaels, created by Alasdair Ranaldson MacDonell of Glengarry, there is enough to explain its reactionary mandate. Its first organized games were held in 1815 at "Ionmhar-Lòchaidh,"[52] but they only lasted till 1820. One searches in vain for a precursor, or anything like them for that matter, in Gaelic Scotland, so this event, with its trials of strength, its piping and Gaelic recitation, which set the Northern Meeting at contemptuous defiance, is at least the partial template for the first Highland games.[53]

Out of Glengarry's novel "gymnastic games" and the Edinburgh piping competitions sponsored by the Highland Society of London emerge the first Highland games at Strathfillan (Perthshire) in 1817 and at Braemar (Aberdeenshire) in 1832. Competition piping was a feature in both and in all subsequent Highland games. Nothing is known of the persistence or otherwise of traditional bagpiping in any of these early Highland games but, at least in concept, they were countertraditional in that they extended the notion of competition piping into the fringes of southern and eastern Gaelic-speaking Scotland.

Despite its hardiness in rapidly changing times, Gaelic traditional culture suffered losses many of which cannot now be made up from isolated, culturally conservative Gaelic colonies like Nova Scotia's. Among the losses is the dance *"Mac an Fhorsair,"* which, according to Stewart of Garth, was extinct by 1822. If it was ever danced in Nova Scotia it is now lost there too. Simon Fraser wrote in 1816 that "Late Wakes and other Public Meetings" were disappearing and with them old popular melodies for the violin and the bagpipes. He described the local pipe reel *"An oidhche ro' na posadh"* ("The Feet Washing"), for example, as among many that were "hitherto neglected."[54] The losses apparently continued in Scotland, for Dalyell noted that the old tunes that had drawn an enthusiastic response from the dancers at the competitions of 1800 and 1810 were less widely known by 1840. In his opinion, "the true quality of the dance had greatly declined ... But many of the tunes most effectually enlivening the dance thirty or forty years ago, and then in highest vogue, have been gradually falling into oblivion."[55]

Simon Fraser's opinion that there were large losses in song and pipe-tune repertoires from 1715 until 1815 must be regarded as accurate, but with a caution. His comparison depended on the music collected between 1715 and

1745 by two droving forebears who ranged hither and yon in Gaelic Scotland collecting cows and music,[56] while his own area for collecting was much smaller. And, as he observed, his home community of Strath Errick east of Loch Ness was "at present ... divested by absence, death and other casualties, of every friend, but those who have forfeited all title to the appellation, and of every circumstance that could tend to render his residence in it agreeable or comfortable, though once the scene of his highest enjoyments, and still of his dearest local attachments."[57] Fraser tacitly acknowledged the importance of emigrations and leavings on tradition.

In contrast to Fraser, Stewart of Garth wrote nothing about change in piping repertoires, and from the 1780s until 1804 and beyond, he had had experience of pipers in the Black Watch (42d) and the Ross-shire Highlanders (Second Battalion, 78th). Nor did he ever mention small-pipes or two-drone pipes. However, his general remarks about music and dance are, as noted earlier, couched in the past tense. Gaels loved both with a passion, but Garth implied that their old-fashioned pastimes were doomed to extinction.

As with Sinclair of Ulbster's sweeping generalization about pipers sinking into oblivion, Fraser's and Garth's ideas were tainted by a pessimism compounded by their having become in large part English and improver in outlook. Dalyell's remarks, unique of their kind, are those of a Lothians-based observer not known to have understood Gaelic or to have travelled widely in the Gaelic heartlands of his times.

For all that, and despite the rampant economic changes in the Highlands, traditional Gaelic music and dance did endure until 1850 and beyond for the ordinary unilingual Gael. During the first half of the nineteenth century Gaelic traditional music and dance were still to be seen and heard within a day's walk of Edinburgh, although Lowlanders appear to have taken it for granted. Highlanders supplementing their dwindling incomes by Lowland harvest work took their musicians with them. To cite an old song written by a Gael in which the Lowland farmer is castigated as a suspicious, mean-spirited killjoy: "When we had been singing songs for a spell,/ and for a while telling silly stories,/ Squinting Rob put his pipes in order,/ and some folk began to dance."[58] This happened in a Lowland inn. The farmer's wife, possibly a Lowlander, openly chided her farmer husband for his surliness when he returned to the inn to find his wife and other women dancing with the Highlanders to Rob Cam's piping. Any implicit denigration of rich Lowland farmers is put into the mouth of the man's own wife: "I'd rather frolick with the Gael; piping and Gaelic, they were always more pleasing to me."[59]

Traditional pipe music and dance were also still appreciated by the remnant Gaelic middle class that kept up stronger linguistic ties to Gaelic than English. Had all these people suddenly bidden farewell to their ancestral language and tradition, they would have left themselves socially and culturally undefinable. Excepting the zealous convert, no one in his right mind rushes upon such dismal anomie. The collecting of tales and songs in the second half of the nineteenth century by John Francis Campbell, Alexander Carmichael, and Father Allan MacDonald (1859–1905) of South Uist eloquently points to a determined protection of Gaelic tradition in out-of-the-way places.

Where piping is concerned in 1800–50, the shift from tradition for most Gaelic-speaking pipers in the *Gàidhealtachd* was gradual. Proof of this will be adduced from the Protestant and Catholic communities. Monoglot Gaels were in the majority in Gaelic Scotland in the first half of the nineteenth century, and with Gaelic as a barrier to intrusive ideas and geographic remoteness as an added protection, there is no doubt that antiquated cultural traditions endured inland from the fringe areas. (Anachronistic cultural survivals in Gaelic Nova Scotia are the best proof of that.) Literacy and staged competitiveness in bagpiping were aberrations unknown to, or eschewed by, Gaels who managed to go on living in places like South Uist, North and South Morar, and Moidart, places where tourists did not go.[60]

The *canntaireachd* method of transmitting the classical form lasted into the early twentieth century in parts of the Gaelic heartland, a prominent exponent being Calum Johnston (1891-1972) in Barra. This was long after the decline of the Gaelic-speaking landlord-tacksman, and there is every indication that traditional ear-learned piping and traditional Reel dancing were flourishing in the Outer Hebrides throughout the first half of the nineteenth century.[61]

Despite the desertion to English language and values of many of the Gaelic middle class during and after the Napoleonic Wars, the traditionally minded tacksmen had not completely disappeared by 1850. In some parts of the Highlands, as Norman MacLeod noted in the 1830s and 1840s, there lingered Old World tacksmen who preserved the older, patriarchal social and cultural bonds.

On an unspecified New Year's Day at the Easter Ross Conan estate of Sir Hector MacKenzie of Gairloch (d. 1826), three miles from Dingwall, "after eating and drinking till full to the bung, fiddle and pipe kept every light fantastic toe busy till ten P.M."[62] Sir Hector, as Osgood MacKenzie wrote, may never have cared to keep another personal family piper when the Blind Piper's grandson, Red John MacKay, left for Pictou Roads in 1805,[63] but he was ready to indulge his guests' fancy in music, and it was not simply the bucolic and unlettered to whom he was catering. At the time there appears to have been no Presbyterian interference in Gaelic cultural affairs.[64] Dr John MacKenzie (1803–86), one of Sir Hector sons, wrote in 1819 while he was a medical student at Edinburgh University that "the amount of bowls of punch emptied and of bull reels danced after supper to Piper John MacKenzie – for we generally supped where we dined and too often went to cards till daylight – did not much promote study next day."[65]

In Catholic Clanranald country the story of conservative cultural retentiveness and middle-class involvement during emigration times is similar. Although the original date of composition is unknown, memories in song of Highland gentlemen dancing Reels to traditional Gaelic dance music in Clanranald country were alive in the Cape Breton *Gàidhealtachd* in 1937.[66]

Where sentiment was against music and dance, the inability of ministers and functionaries of evangelical and reformed Protestant Christianity to extirpate piping in the first half of the nineteenth century is best evidenced in the case of Skye. Although piping had withered dramatically by the twentieth century in the island of the MacCrumen and MacArthur pipers, survivals during the nineteenth indicate something less than catastrophic for the bagpipe and the piper. Although around 1800 Munro the catechist had railed against Gaelic instrumental music in Skye, the Reverend Roderick MacLeod was still preaching in the 1820s against the "seductive" effects of the bagpipes.[67] MacLeod, who was ordained in the Church of Scotland at Bracadale, Skye, in 1823, remembered that in his boyhood at Dunvegan, "as soon as the services, which were conducted in the open field, were ended, three pipers struck up music, and three dancing parties were formed on the green."[68] In the 1830s Kyleakin was the home of the pipers John MacKay from Eyre in Raasay and Dòmhnul Ruadh MacRae, showing that in the southeast of the island piping was a profoundly important cultural indulgence.

Furthermore, despite the preachings of two Church of Scotland anti-music zealots, there is evidence of traditional piping at mid-century in Skye, which suggests that religious attitudes varied depending upon the parish, the pastor, and the denomination.[69] Duncan MacPherson, a dance-music piper from Upper Breakish in Skye who was born around 1870, told the Fletts in 1954 that "the people of his parents' generation would happily spend an entire evening dancing Scotch Reels, and would have nothing to do with Country Dances, Quadrilles, and Lancers."[70]

As for education and literacy in piping music, the near absence of published or unpublished bagpipe music dating to the immigrant decades in culturally conservative Gaelic Scotland and in immigrant Gaelic Cape Breton is proof enough that the traditional way of learning by ear lasted through the emigration decades. The survival of the ear-learned method in Gaelic Cape Breton until roughly the Second World War will be considered later. The beacon light of bagpiping improvement from 1781 to 1838, with a few novel Highland games piping competitions as additions in the fringe of the *Gàidhealtachd*, shone from Edinburgh and was concerned exclusively with *ceòl mór*. The means of revival were always radical but the effect was long term and depended for its eventual success on the critical weakening of Gaelic society by the massive family-based emigrations. Modern piping did not triumph everywhere until this century, and to assume that before 1850 the dance-music piper in the monoglot Gaelic heartlands had his head turned by improving ideas from Edinburgh is wrong.[71] To overlook a Gaelic disdain for Lowland competitions run by the Saxon or Saxonized gentry would also be wrong. Literately learned and competition *ceòl beag* piping were insignificant in the Gaelic community setting in the first half of the nineteenth century, and until the early twentieth in some places.

Dr John MacCulloch's opinion that variational pipe music was superior to dance music, an idea that persists, derived from his knowledge that the Highland Society of London was trying to revive only the variational form.[72] There is no evidence that he knew anything about piping. Most pipers associated with the improved bagpiping in the first half of the nineteenth century were tempted by prizes and jobs in the homes of wealthy, often non-Gaelic, landowners. In the case of the Raasay MacKays and John Ban MacKenzie, their music can have differed very little from preliterate traditional piping and one wonders just how their playing was distinguishable, if it was.[73] Sinclair of Ulbster might have been right in stating that the competitions served the need for army pipers. His claim, however, neglects to mention that the gentlemen doing the recruiting often had no contact with Gaelic tradition and no knowledge of how to assess traditional Gaelic piping. Sinclair did not understand that something other than scarcity was responsible for the difficulty in recruiting pipers to fight England's war with Napoleon.

The British army's influence on piping since the 1850s has been intense, innovative, and eventually harmful to the little that remained of tradition, but there is evidence that traditional Gaelic piping lasted throughout the century. In March 1858, after the third and successful attack on the Indian "mutineers" at Lucknow, a private in Captain Baird's Number Six company in the 42d Regiment wrote, "But as we approached a big bungalow our hearts were cheered by the sound of the bagpipes playing a Foursome Reel. When we were halted and dismissed I went into the building, and there were four or five sets up dancing with all their might, Captain Macpherson and Sir David Baird footing it among the rest."[74] In that officers and men were involved, it is tempting to think that something of the old Gaelic bond between the classes remained.

THE PERSISTENCE OF PIPING IN KEPPOCH AND GLENGARRY

For Lochaber and Glengarry from 1800 until 1850 there is information on a surprising number of prominent pipers but no way of assessing the degree to which they cleaved to tradition. However, the fact that they all appear to have been ear-learned and that a number were dance-music pipers hints strongly at tradition. In Lochaber George Gordon, the fifth and last duke of Gordon (d.1836)[75] and the last Gordon landowner in Lochaber, retained Angus M'Innes as his piper. M'Innes was still piping in 1840, when he helped to celebrate the marriage of Queen Victoria with a typical repertoire that included *ceòl mór* and Reel-dance music.[76] The Fort William area also produced Duncan MacMaster, Coll's prize-winning piper in the 1805 competition and pupil of Dòmhnul Ruadh MacCruimein, according to the published writings of John Johnston.[77]

Another popular piper, apparently unsponsored, who flourished in the second quarter of the nineteenth century was John Campbell, who settled at Invermoriston in the Great Glen. According to the *Piping Times*, which did not disclose its sources, he was good at strathspeys, reels, and jigs, "had a style peculiarly his own," and "was a frequent performer at dances throughout the Great Glen."[78] Earlier a "John Campbell alias MacGlaserich, piper" is among several MacGlaserich Campbells living at Inverroybeg and Boline in Keppoch. Apparently he was cleared by Alexander Mackintosh, tacksman of Inverroy for Aeneas Mackintosh, twenty-third laird of MacIntosh and author of *Notes Descriptive*, in 1802 (other McGlaserish Campbells had been cleared by Aeneas Mackintosh from Tulloch in 1795 and were to be cleared from Inverroymore and Inverroybeg in 1804).[79]

In a four-page song Allan Dall MacDougal (c.1750-1828), bard from about 1798 to Alasdair Ranaldson MacDonald of Glengarry (d.1828), commemorated the/a successor to Alasdair Ranaldson's old Ticonderoga veteran piper John MacDonald. The song is entitled "*Oran ... Do Mhac-Pharlain, Piobaire Mhic-Ic-Alastair*,"[80] showing that the Glengarry piper, by 1798, was a MacFarlane, not a common name among Scotch pipers at any time. This MacFarlane was from *Urchaidh nam breachd tarr-gheala* (Orchy of the white-bellied trout) and the song strongly suggests that he had a military career.[81] In his later collection, *Orain, Marbhrannan agus Duanagan Ghaidhealach* (1829), MacDougal also mentioned MacDonell of Keppoch's piper, albeit only by his patronymic, Mac a' Ghlasraich. The name, which is synonymous with Campbell in Keppoch, appears in the song "Epitaph for Keppoch."[82]

To those pipers must be added Finlay MacLeod (Grant of Glenmoriston's piper), Archibald Munro (c. 1800-56), piper to Glengarry and then to Col Sir John MacRa of Ardintoul, and his piper-brother William Munro. Even without knowledge of the more local pipers, a powerful image of the popularity of piping from the Keppoch braes to Invermoriston in the first half of the nineteenth century emerges, one from which it would be foolish to postulate a dearth of pipers in the period 1746–1800. Dance-music piping was popular in the lower Great Glen into the middle of Queen Victoria's century. After that in Glenmoriston, and in many other Protestant parts of the Highlands, things changed.

Whether or not the Keppoch and Glengarry richness in pipers had any-thing to do with considerate landlordism remains to be seen, but the phe-nomenon of club farms offers one explanation for the survival of tradition, there and elsewhere, into the 1840s. Club farms, as described by the jour-nalist Somers in 1846, were arable and pasture farms run by kin groups of Gaels who had won leases on the open market. Writing of the huge farms of Mackintosh of Mackintosh and Walker of Loch Treig in Brae Lochaber, Somers reported that both contained two elements, the landlords' extensive sheep farms and "Highland townships ... [where] their mode of culture, their habits of life and principles of their social union, are true relics of the olden time, and may now be regarded as peculiar to the Highlands. The people, or club-tenants, as they are called, live together in small hamlets, containing ten or so chosen families each, who occupy the soil in common, and rear and divide its produce on principles which seek to harmonise individual rights with a community of interest."[83]

The Inverlochy estate (roughly, from Glen Nevis to Glen Spean and Glen Lochy), although since 1836 out of the duke of Gordon/marquis of Huntly's hands and owned by the Englishman Lord Abinger (Mr Scarlett), still showed traces of traditional and improved-traditional Gaelic arable and pas-ture farming, which Huntly had encouraged, particularly at Killiechonate under a "John MacDonald Esq."[84]

It is a statement of the strength of conservative Gaelicness that these town-ships still existed after all the clearances in the area. In the braes of Lochaber, as in Glenuig, Moidart, Gairloch, and elsewhere, given use of the traditional clan lands, those who hadn't been cleared or who hadn't moved or emigrated kept up the old pastoral life, and undoubtedly traditional music and dance lived on to mid-century. At Inverroy the marquis of Huntly's piper, M'Innes, was a near neighbour of all the Lochaber and Brae Lochaber communities.

From 1850, however, harder economic dictates governed Highland agri-culture and until club farms are studied, how long they lasted will remain unknown. There were pipers in Keppoch to greet Queen Victoria in 1873 but there is no comment on their traditionality. However, the richness of Bohuntin and other Keppoch music in Inverness County, Nova Scotia, gives an indication of the character and amount of what once existed.

13 Influences on Piping in Nineteenth-Century Nova Scotia: The Middle Class, the Church, and Temperance

The community rather than the individualistic nature of the emigrations from Gaelic Scotland to Canada, particularly to Nova Scotia, in the first half of the nineteenth century is more significant for the study of traditional piping (and fiddling and step-dancing) than the actual numbers of emigrants. By the middle of the nineteenth century when Scottish Gaelic emigration to Canada was drying to a trickle and thousands of Gaels were moving and being systematically cleared to Australia[1] and New Zealand (and to central Canada), new piping ideas – learning through musical literacy and non-functional competition piping the most radical of them – often within the embrace of the other influences discussed earlier, found themselves in a position to influence profoundly what remained of traditionalism in the *Gàidhealtachd*.

The middle of the nineteenth century was the cultural turning point for the ordinary rural class of Gael in Scotland and overseas. Before, wherever Gaels went and created rural communities that didn't have to, or preferred not to, rely on exogamous marriages to non-Gaelic speakers, the tradition was strong enough to be confidently transmitted to following generations (as in Cape Breton), given the language's survival and minimal interference from outside and from within. After, increasing exposure to the novel, caricaturist aspects of Gaelic culture ensured a break with the past. Outside of Nova Scotia, for example in Australia and New Zealand, the Gaelic language has not survived in a community setting and neither have traditional music and dance.[2] Even in Cape Breton, the last Gaelic-speaking part of the New World, it is a story of near death; since around the time of the Second World War the Cape Breton *Gàidhealtachd* has been in the sad process of making the last breaks with tradition. As Gaelic has withered, so its traditional music has increasingly strayed from Gaelic conceptualizing, forcing inevitable changes on traditional dancing.[3] Pipers, for years estranged from step-dancing, naturally look to Scotland for models and thus are drawn into modernism, with consequences for other aspects of folk culture.

The inference to be drawn from this radical shift in type of emigration around 1850 is that community cohesion was breaking down in many parts of the Highlands at mid-century. From a cultural point of view community-oriented bagpiping (and any other Gaelic traditionalism) had almost no chance for survival in the New World if community cohesion did not exist there and if Gaelic was quickly supplanted by English.

With today's worldwide vested interest in modern, literately learned, competition-oriented piping, it is difficult for many pipers in Scotland and in the diaspora *Gàidhealtachd* to look further back than 1850 to the music of the eighteenth century, unless it is to wonder unthinkingly at the greatness of certain popularized piping families and a few outstanding individual pipers.[4] The traditional non-literate piper's function in the community, from providing dance music for all to playing *ceòl mór* at the appropriate occasion, was overlooked as the literate form took charge and as changes cut deeply into the fabric of the old way of life. The notion that there might be many ways to make notes was increasingly put down to weakness, uneducatedness, and deviance. Joseph MacDonald's manuscript, in many of its complex grace-notings, is an inexplicable enigma that pipers ignore as unlikely, although the fingering he offered has been accepted as piping truth.

THE CULTURAL IMPORTANCE OF THE GAELIC MIDDLE CLASS IN NOVA SCOTIA

Many of the influences that caused a shift from traditionalism to modernism in Gaelic Scotland worked in Nova Scotia too but later and generally with less impact, given the exigencies of pioneer life. In the 1880s another rage for emigration, this time from Maritime Canada to the United States (notably to the Boston area), and seasonal contact with western parts of the Dominion exposed the Nova Scotia *Gàidhealtachd* to more English and other outside ideas. The education system, promoted English especially in the twentieth century, and there are hints that the Christian church, had it had the opportunity, might have been sterner about some kinds of dancing and, of course, about liquor than it was. However, inasmuch as traditional ear-learned fiddling and home-learned traditional step-dancing still exist with some vitality, albeit in an almost completely English environment,[5] obviously a strongly conservative element in Nova Scotian Gaelic society ensured cultural retention, which was not a feature of Highland society elsewhere to anything like the same extent, with the possible exception of Catholic South Uist.

What distinguished the Nova Scotian Gàidhealtachd was the presence of socially cohesive communities in which there was a representation of the old Gaelic middle class and the solid stratum of the old tenantry that Stewart of Garth and Rev. Norman MacLeod knew to be getting out of Scotland.

In dealing with the question of the middle class in Nova Scotia, there are three basic difficulties. First, there is a shortage of ships' passenger lists for the 1815–50 period. Second, there is a lack of detail in those that do exist. Third, there is the problem of defining the Gaelic-speaking middle class in Nova Scotia and assessing the part it played in cultural retention. Obviously any attempt to present statistically acceptable resolutions to these problems awaits the massive, collated study of local histories and all other primary and secondary materials that mention emigration/immigration, something that is in the genealogist's mind's eye but not mine.

According to T.M. Devine, many more Highland Scots left after 1815 than before. Also, the passenger lists for the late eighteenth century, insufficient as they are, do reflect the family and community nature of the emigrations while the later ones are aggregate statistics of total departures, as demanded by the Passenger Act. With exceptions, in the later lists place of origin and social make-up of the emigrants are missing.[6] In addition to the accepted causes, Devine mentioned the grain and potato failures in 1836–37 and in 1846–47, and that between 1848 and 1853 the Lowland Scottish economy was stuck in a depression. Other years of poor harvests, fear of cholera, smallpox and consumption and of a degrading life in the cities might be added to the list.

The surge of emigration to Cape Breton in the 1820s, almost the underlying theme of J.L. MacDougall's *History of Inverness County* and A.D. Mac-Donald's *Mabou Pioneers*,[7] and contemporary emigrations to other parts of Nova Scotia are unstudied from the standpoint of the social status of those who left Scotland. In the case of clearances of the Catholic and Protestant poor before and after 1815 (for example, of the Protestant poor from Sutherland between 1807 and 1821), the problems that arose were not just the physical ones faced by newcomers to the New World. The clearers, their descendants, and the tenants living on the cleared land had to come to an acceptance of the new *status quo*. However much the prevailing ethos condoned (and subsequent emigrant success in Canada justified) the clearers' actions, the cries of the poor cannot have gone unheard. In adapting to those cries of the cruelly usurped, the clearers erected psychological barriers to understanding the old Gaelic way of life, and rationales for denigrating it; these barriers have been passed down the generations and still work against a true knowledge of Scotland.

Furthermore, in dealing with emigrations of the Gaelic middle class, the good stock, it is incorrect to think that only Gaelic-speaking traditionalists emigrated, escaping the new economic order. Middle-class improver agriculturalists who were thoroughly Gaelic-speaking also left the Highlands, many bound for Australia and New Zealand. At a lower social level there are still memories in Inverness County of relative late-comers from the Highlands who were considered atypical because they were more knowledgeable farmers, as though they had almost become a new immigrant subtype.

Devine's point, however, is that by and large a bedrock native resistance to leaving the ancestral home was radically weakened by the economic realities after 1815. The new economics were concerned primarily with property and commodities. Clan land was legally vested in estate owners, making any Gaelic communal concepts of large-scale land use impossible, and the continuance of subsistence agriculture on what actually was allowed to the Gaelic peasantry completely dependent on the owner's will.[8] Cash economics continued systematically to create redundant populations in many parts of the Highlands until only the unadaptable near-pauper class remained by the 1850s. This is a generalization, but it is aptly defended in some communities through the records of landlords offering assisted passages to the poor folk willing to leave, and to coerce others.[9]

These deportations of the equity-less poor did not affect Nova Scotia where normal community immigrations continued into the 1840s.[10] In Nova Scotia even the third and fourth concessions far from the life-sustaining seas and more often than not on infertile Appalachian peneplain lands were settled by communities and attracted later immigrants.[11]

Despite the march of economic progress, traditional Gaelic kin communities continued to exist in Gaelic Scotland at, and despite, the owner's behest, generally in new economic circumstances that accommodated sheep farming, in places like Skye, Raasay, Gairloch, Moidart, Glenaladale, Knoydart, and parts of the Outer Hebrides until two and three decades after the Napoleonic Wars, often longer. Alexander Smith, for example, described the abrasion of the traditional and the modern worlds somewhere in Skye in or before 1866.[12] In such places there were relatively complete Gaelic sociocultural systems operating within the loose embrace of the outsider's political and legal imposure.

Among the people who came out to Nova Scotia in the family and community emigrations were many community pipers, some of whom played *ceòl mór* as well as the staple dance music. There were also representatives of the old rural/traditional Gaelic middle class and members of the better-off tenant farmers, all demographically well distributed. It is quite wrong to characterize these post-1815 emigrations to Nova Scotia as being only of the extremely poor, illiterate, and least socially sophisticated, although this opinion is still sometimes disseminated even in Inverness County.

What is more, throughout the times of the great Highland emigrations to the New World, very much more of Gaelic musical tradition than has been imagined owed its vigour and persistence to the patronage and attitudes of the Gaelic middle class. There can be no doubt that the people in positions of sufficient power in Gaelic Scotland to settle tenantry on the land had a pronounced interest in having popular traditional dance-music players among their tenants. In many instances these were the same people who organized and led the emigrations to the New World. The same mix of social strata occurred in Nova Scotia that had existed in Highland Scotland. The same Highland understanding and acceptance of many elements of social stratification continued to live in the minds of immigrant Gaels for as long as the primary language was Gaelic. The persistence of the idea of the force of patronage of the musically talented, as with the bardically gifted, is to be found in the New World *Gàidhealtachd*, as well as in the old, but the barriers to understanding that force in its modified New World form and at this distance from the immigrant generations are not inconsiderable, since land was not conferrable through the class system in the New World and the system of sinecures was new and limited.

In the New World the new land tenure system blurred, for a non-Gael, residual social distinctions that were obvious to the traditional Gael. Everyone owned land, or looked forward doing so. The deference owed by renter to owner was gone and what was left in colonial Canada was the British deference owed by the uneducated class to the educated and more powerful, a deference ingrained in Gaelic society in any case. Getting a feel for the transplanted Gaelic social system and its underpinnings, however, demands a readiness to imagine a world unsaturated with literacy and formal qualification and a pre-industrial rustic world in which overt and subtle social distinctions had already been of remarkably long duration. Little wonder that such concepts died hard. Stuart Macdonald's picture (redrawn from a volume of George Borrow) of a young man, Donald MacDonell, sitting with two friends on a dry stane dyke at Achnacrois near Spean Bridge in 1858 presents in metaphor the alien and non-material understanding one has to assume in order to come to terms with Gaelic social class consciousness in a largely foreign setting. The young man told Borrow the true but unlikely story that his uncle was the rightful Keppoch.[13]

In Nova Scotia, however, there were obviously middle-class Gaels who had known social prominence in Highland Scotland, as well as those reposing unpretentiously and often unremarked on the same size of granted acreage as the common man. And then there were plenty of ordinary Gaels from previously unprivileged families whose drives and talents gave them status that inflexible usages could seldom have permitted in the old country.

THE PROTESTANT OLD WORLD MIDDLE CLASS IN NOVA SCOTIA

Among the first group was Alasdair the Doctor MacDonald, born in 1782, a patrilineal great grandson of Lord MacDonald, the eleventh baron and fourth baronet of Sleat. The doctor was sent out to Prince Edward Island with a shipload of cleared people in the early years of the nineteenth century. His pedigree and social standing were undeniable. His life in the New World was spent for the most part in Antigonish County, Nova Scotia.

In North Ainslie in Inverness County, Cape Breton, one finds an Archibald Campbell, descendant of the Scalpay Campbell family and a school master in Duirinish, Skye, who brought his family out in 1830. He was married to Matilda MacLeod, a paternal granddaughter of Norman MacLeod, twenty-second chief of the clan MacLeod and a first cousin of Major General Norman MacLeod, twenty-third chief.[14] The Campbells had two hundred acres, which didn't distinguish them from many a neighbour of humbler origins in Cape Breton, but as a teacher at Whycocomagh, Campbell's social prominence was obvious. His son's typical middle-class aspiration to become a Church of Scotland clergyman also set this family apart.[15] Skye was a major centre of independent revivalism in the first four decades of the nineteenth century and Campbell was probably aware of the radical preaching of the catechist Donald Munro and certainly of the fire-eating reformer Rev. Roderick MacLeod, who was ordained in the Church of Scotland at Bracadale in the parish of Duirinish in 1823. Archibald Campbell's church was the one that condoned three pipers' playing for parties of dancers on the greensward at Dunvegan around 1800 immediately after an outdoor church service, something that Rev. Roderick MacLeod recollected from his boyhood,[16] and that he and the Skye revivalists in the 1820s would never have tolerated.

Dr Hugh (Hoodie) MacDonald was born at nearby East Lake Ainslie, the Gaelic-speaking grandson of four grandparents who emigrated, married, to the New World in 1820.[17] I have confined the extended genealogical data, under the broader middle-class heading, to Hoodie's family because it is fairly typical of both Christian communities, and because Hoodie's family information is less widely accessible than that for Catholic middle-class families who have been more thoroughly documented by local genealogists.

Hoodie earned his professional status at Queen's University in Ontario but was already confident in his social place by virtue of his ancestry. Much of his knowledge of his genealogy was given him by his two Scotch grandmothers, Mary MacLean, who died in 1879, and Ann Campbell. From their combined knowledge MacDonald paints a middle-class background for his family. It has been hinted that Hoodie indulged in a bit of wishful thinking, concocting a glowingly exaggerated family history, but his story is plausible although unverifiable at some points. It certainly shows where he thought he fitted and is a defence of the persistance of that kind of British class thinking in rural Inverness County.

The only two great-great-grandparents mentioned are Malcolm MacDonald and John MacKinnon. MacDonald is given as being of the Keppoch family, presumably the chiefly family into which Joseph MacDonald's brother the Reverend Patrick married; the family moved first to Ross-shire and then to Tiree where Hoodie's grandfather, Hugh son of John son of Malcolm (Eoghan mac Iain 'ic Caluim), was born. John MacKinnon is given as being "of the MacKinnons of Straith, Isle of Skye, Inverness-shire, and of the same family as the celebrated bard Lachlan MacKinnon."[18]

At the grandparent level, Hugh (MacDonald) of Tiree was, according to Dr Hoodie, a close relative of the father of Sir Hector MacDonald, "Fighting Mac,"[19] commander of the Highland Brigade, a well-known Scottish Highland hero in the Cape Breton Scotch community until not long ago. Hugh MacDonald was married to Ann Campbell, daughter, according to Hoodie, of "Col Dougald Campbell of the Argyleshire Highlanders"[20]; Ann Campbell lived in Saltcoats, Ayrshire. When Hugh was shipwrecked at the Strait of Canso in 1820 he spent a year at the Strait before settling at East Lake. Allan Ban MacKinnon (1786–1856) was married to Mary MacLean, daughter of Red Charles (Tearlach Ruadh), who was "a near relative of the Laird of Coll to whom he did not pay rent for lands occupied, no doubt owing to relationship and Scottish clannishness." (J.L. MacDougall reported an "Allain mac Thearlaich ... who had been a Laird for the landlord of Coll. Scotland, an uncle of his,"[21] as an early pioneer in the Port Hastings area of the Strait of Canso, on the Cape Breton side). The MacKinnons emigrated, married, in 1820, from Muck where they had settled after the family left Skye.

It bears repeating that two of the "great" Protestant pipers mentioned earlier considered themselves, with justification, to be members of the middle class. Lt Donald MacCrumen at Jordan Bay[22] had been a Dunvegan tacksman, a man of considerable property. Red John MacKay falls into the category of educated substantial tenant in Gairloch. The two warrant a closer look.

MacCrimmon's name is scarcely known in Nova Scotia although he leaves many traces in the Loyalist record. The MacCrimmon name in general is associated with various places in Ontario, including a MacCrimmon's Corner in Glengarry County, and in Alberta. Donald MacCrumen, as he spelled it in army musters, arrived in Nova Scotia, with family and servants, while the snow was on the ground in 1783 as a Port Roseway Associate – a large group of beaten Loyalists on whose behalf Guy Carelton organized the planned migration to and settlement of Port Roseway, now Shelburne. He left in 1790 broke, sought by the Shelburne sheriff, his fare paid by the Highland Society of London. The soil on his acreage on the east side of Jordan Bay in the south of Nova Scotia, like many other farms, had turned out to be hopelessly shallow, dioritic, and infertile, making Skye in the Hebrides look like an agricultural paradise. The ferry he operated across the bay obviously hadn't paid. The nearest Scotch name on the map lies a mile or two to the south, MacVicar's Rock. MacCrimmon's property is remembered locally not for the presence of one of the world's great pipers but as the place where Zane Grey docked his luxury fishing boat in the 1920s.

Although at least one other military piper, Duncan MacLean of the 76th (MacDonald's Highlanders), settled at Port Roseway at the same time, nothing has turned up to indicate whether piping was popular in early Shelburne. MacCrimmon's status as an ex-officer, along with what is known of his social habits once back in Britain, guarantee that he limited his socializing in Nova Scotia to his own kind. His closest military associate both in North Carolina and in Nova Scotia was a fellow British Legionary, Ensign Soirle MacDonald[23] whose record in Nova Scotia is tarnished by a brutal and arrogant physical attack on a man whom he considered an inferior. Whether or not Donald MacCrimmon kept up his piping is not recorded.

Norman MacLeod of MacLeod (d.1801) keenly touted MacCrimmon, one of his family's former tacksmen, as a potential professor of piping in the Highlands, an idea that the Highland Society liked and funded more than once, stretching it to bailing the old piper out of Inverness gaol for debt in 1808. MacLeod had fought as a captain in Simon Fraser's Highlanders (71st) in the American revolutionary war, at times alongside Tarleton's Legion in which MacCrimmon was a lieutenant, so he may have heard the piper play in the New World, perhaps at his own command.

MacCrimmon consistently disappointed the Highland Society, although he had a pupil in Glenelg in 1814 and probably many others there and elsewhere (including, according to John Johnston of Coll, Duncan MacMaster, piper to Coll in 1805). Using rural musical Cape Breton as an example, in its last Gaelic days, many of the gurus were keenly sought by the perceptive and the great MacCrimmon must have attracted his share. In Britain however, Donald MacCrimmon always showed more interest in recovering a career in the army and in mingling in English upper-class company. His son Patrick's will (1829) claims that the late duke of Kent owed his father £492:10:00.[24] According to Walter Scott, Donald MacCrimmon chose not to teach what he knew of piping to his family. Scott heard him piping to MacLeod at Dunvegan in 1814 but did not add much to his biography beyond the snide remark that he had "risen above his profession."[25]

As a footnote to the Donald MacCrumen case, among the MacCrimmons who came to North America there appears to have been at least one musical one, MacLeod suggests, who came about fifty years later to Cape Breton:

It's the "Midlothian" that took aboard the crofters from Lowergill, near Glen Dale, in the Island of Skye. The "Midlothian" sailed from Loch Snizort on the fourth day of August in 1830, and reached Sydney in Cape Breton Island, two months and two days after that. Captain J. Morrison [possibly MacGillivray] from Cataibh was the skipper on the vessel, and according to the information as I heard it, a MacCrumen man was aboard who made the tune they call "The Lowergill Crofters' Farewell to the Isle of Skye." The men got the removal order from government.[26]

According to a MacCrimmon who was interviewed in Scotland in 1898 and cited by W.L. Manson,[27] the Lowergill MacCrimmon family furnished the MacLeod chief with pipers for most of the nineteenth century. Presumably the emigrant piper belonged to this family. Neither John Johnston nor anyone else, including the MacCrimmon genealogists Poulter and Fisher, has left any observations of the family as pipers.

Unlike Donald MacCrimmon, Red John MacKay, the Gairloch MacKay piper who emigrated to Nova Scotia in 1805, lived, and, as far as we know, died (date unknown) in the province. Although his descendants gradually spread out from Nova Scotia (a grandson John MacKay, for example, is said to have died of injuries suffered in the American Civil War fighting for a Mississippi infantry regiment),[28] none are known to have returned and settled in Scotland. There are still many in Canada, among them the family of the late Lt Col John MacKay Sinclair, whom I interviewed in 1982 and who at the time was the owner of the Blind Piper's pipe chanter, which now belongs to one of his sons.

John MacKay Sinclair learned piping but did not demonstrably represent the oral tradition that his great-great-grandfather brought out. Sinclair's great-grandfather, Squire John MacKay, JP (1790s–1884), the younger son of the immigrant Red John MacKay, gave up piping in Nova Scotia. However the older son Angus (1780s–c. 1868), who Sinclair very reasonably maintains was being trained to follow in his father's footsteps as piper to the MacKenzies of Gairloch, continued piping in Nova Scotia and did some teaching.

Angus MacKay is known to have taught only one fellow Gael to play the pipes in Nova Scotia, and that was John MacPherson (1799–1883), son of Donald who, with his family, had sailed with the MacKays on the brig *Sir Sydney Smith* in 1805. The MacPherson family was from Gairloch. John MacPherson lived in New Gairloch and Angus MacKay lived in his early years in Nova Scotia in nearby Churchville (Angus was of age in 1811 when he petitioned for a government land grant independently of his father Red John, who settled nearer what is today New Glasgow).

MacPherson in his turn taught three MacKenzie brothers, neighbours in New Gairloch, Donald, Hector, and William. The MacKenzies were also originally of Gairloch stock. Donald MacKenzie, the best piper among them, was in demand for his music in Nova Scotia, New Brunswick and Prince Edward Island. His brothers Hector and William were fair pipers, but with two of William's sons, George and Alexander MacKenzie, the musical teacher-pupil line subtended by Angus MacKay of Gairloch and Nova Scotia continued. They were pupils of their uncle Donald MacKenzie. George, in the opinion of his niece Marjorie (MacKenzie) Hawkins,[29] was the best after Donald MacKenzie and John MacPherson, but he died young. His brother Alexander was one of the last New Gairloch pipers, according to his daughter Marjorie Hawkins. In the late 1970s Donald MacKenzie's practice chanter was in the possession of Betty (Ferguson) Hughes, his great-grandniece, a piper herself. Betty Ferguson, from Gairloch, Nova Scotia, was a pipe-band piper who had learned by the written note. Her music was of a typically modern character, serving a modern set of functions. For reasons to be considered later, the same may have been true of most of the MacKenzie pipers going back at least to the turn of the century.

Despite the fact that Gaelic, and with it cultural traditionalism, lasted longest in Pictou County in settlements like Churchville, Springville, and Gairloch, which were far enough away from the industrial area to be almost isolated, there is a lack of evidence that Gaelic traditional piping survived long into the twentieth century there. In various parts of Cape Breton, where Gaelic has not yet disappeared, the gathering of essentially Gaelic information is still possible. First, however it will be helpful to look at what is known of Angus MacKay, Red John's son and the paternal grandson of Angus MacKay, son of the Blind Piper, and his family and descendants in Nova Scotia to consider what may be learned of the Gairloch MacKay pipers before him and the implication, mentioned above, that the in-family traditional piping of the famous MacKays of Gairloch ended with him. Alexander MacKenzie, editor of *Celtic Magazine* who visited Nova Scotia in anticipation of finding the long-lost MacKay piping family, found the last of the Gairloch-born pipers, Squire John, JP, in November 1879 in New Glasgow. MacKenzie learned from the old squire that his older brother, Angus MacKay, had recently died.[30] Of the two sons of the last hereditary piper to the MacKenzies of Gairloch, Angus had kept his skills up at least for some time. MacKenzie reported that Angus "also played marches, reels, and strathspeys, but *pìobaireachd* not being appreciated in the land of his adoption, he practised that higher class music but little, and was not, therefore, up to the family standard of excellence in that department." Then, writing of the squire: "John himself also learned to play; but at the age of eighteen he finally gave it up, so that now not one of this celebrated family keeps up the name and reputation of the family ... He talked of things long ago as if they were but of yesterday; and I parted with him with very mixed emotions."[31]

Accepting uncritically that the MacKay pipers from Gairloch were from the top drawer of Highland bagpiping (as the notes in Angus MacKay's *Collection* imply, Logan having never mentioned the family), this ingenuous remark of MacKenzie's in 1879 is evidence that in at least one of the best piping families pipers in the second half of the eighteenth century played dance music. Angus was taught by his father Red John at the family home on the south side of Loch Maree in Gairloch, and it is reasonable to deduce that the father taught his sons dance-music piping as well as the classical form.

In 1886, a few years after MacKenzie's visit to Nova Scotia, John H. Dixon published "Gairloch,"[32] the sifted memories of many older Gaels in Gairloch, Scotland. There he described Red John MacKay as having been sent to the north of Scotland specifically to learn the small-pipes.[33] Dixon was also responsible for the claim made by then-current Gairloch lore that the Blind Piper had also composed and played dance music for the bagpipes.

According to Squire John MacKay's reminiscences (written for the most part in 1868), his father was literate and fluently bilingual while his (the squire's) older brother, Angus, had had schooling in English in Scotland. The old squire certainly spoke Gaelic with eloquence to MacKenzie in 1879, and there is no reason to think that Angus ever lost the use of his mother tongue. However, Angus's son Alexander (d.1927), was remembered in 1981 by a neighbour, Jessie (MacLean) Chisholm, born c. 1891, of Churchville, as having had no Gaelic, although there were still Gaelic church services held in Springville in 1879; MacKenzie attended one.

I corresponded with two of Alexander MacKay's daughters, Clara G. (born in 1901) and Lelia (born in 1899), in 1981 and 1982 respectively, and neither mentioned their parents' having spoken anything but English in the Churchville home. Alexander certainly was not a piper in their lifetimes and the sisters' awareness that the family had once contained at least one well-known piper is sufficiently disjointed to be almost certainly unoriginal. However, both old ladies, then living in Massachusetts, remembered seeing a set of bagpipes that were brought to their father's home when their paternal uncle, Angus Colin MacKay (born in 1869), died in 1920.

Clara MacKay wrote to me that there was a famous piper in the family in Scotland who emigrated to Nova Scotia "maybe on the *Hector.*" This idea probably came from that history of Pictou County that listed a John MacKay, piper, who had been aboard the *Hector*; but if it did spring from independent family lore it would confirm the notes in Angus MacKay's *Collection*, which mention that a MacKay piper emigrated to Nova Scotia around 1778, close enough to 1773 when the *Hector* reached Pictou Roads. Lelia (MacKay) Emerson, however, did not know her paternal great-grandfather's name and so her evidence is questionable.

Why no memory of the piping of Red John MacKay himself has survived even within the family in Pictou County, where he was almost a charter member of the New Glasgow community, is a puzzle. The squire, being the younger son, had helped him start the farm and must have known his father's music intimately, yet MacKenzie recorded nothing; the squire may have avoided the topic. As far as Alexander MacKenzie was concerned, Red John was the only celebrated Gairloch MacKay piper who was still actually rememberable in Scotland's Gairloch, as the last practising professional piper to the Gairloch chieftain, although people who might have recalled his playing must have been very long in the tooth in 1879. All that MacKenzie wrote, presumably on the authority of the squire, was that Red John MacKay played the pipes all his life. MacKenzie may not have been able to weasel information out of Squire John MacKay, whose own reminiscences say almost nothing about piping. He was a commanding presence in his community. It is possible, too, that before publication of the *Collection*, the MacKay pipers in Gairloch, the Blind Piper excepted, were less remarkable than nineteenth-century publications made them out to be. And MacKenzie himself may have had no understanding of piping. Whatever the case, there is no more lore about Red John MacKay than there is about Donald McCrumen in Jordan Bay, and very little more about John's son Angus.

THE ROMAN CATHOLIC MIDDLE CLASS IN NOVA SCOTIA

The Roman Catholic community in Scotland suffered social discrimination long after 1790 and had not had the same economic opportunities in Gaelic Scotland as the Protestant community, but the same typical sprinkling of its middle class is found in Nova Scotia and elsewhere in the Maritime provinces, as well as further afield.[34] MacDougall's *History of Inverness County* and MacDonald's *Mabou Pioneers* time and again describe families that were closely related to the powerful and once powerful in the old Highlands, sometimes even implying that Lord Lyon King of Arms' decisions in favour of Scottish chiefly pretenders have been premature. In the Mabou area and elsewhere the descendants of old middle-class families from Keppoch, the Bohuntins, Tullochs and Killiechonates (the last including the traditional piper Black Angus MacDonald), are numerous.

In Brae Lochaber, as in Glenaladale in Clanranald country and in all conservative parts of Gaelic Scotland, in the middle and lower ranks of society there was little exogamy.[35] Most Scotch families tended to be endogamous for the purpose of retaining land and social station. The *Mabou Pioneers* shows nothing if not a very complicated interweaving of marriage relationships among many of the families that emigrated, a complexity that would be deepened in Nova Scotia. In both the Old and New Worlds many of these immigrant families contain examples of traditional Gaelic middle-class status (often including, for example, traditional poet/singers) as well as examples of the commercial middle class (store owners and businessmen). Among them are the Ridge MacDonalds, of Bohuntin ancestry, who produced bards and musicians in Cape Breton and Nova Scotia. John "Lord" MacDonald, another immigrant, had been a hotel owner in Kinlochlaggan in the 1790s. In 1831 John "Baron" MacDonald and his family settled in South East Mabou where he ran a successful business in Hillsborough, east of Mabou. Of his seven children two were merchants in the Mabou area and one, Allan, was an artist, photographer, and musician. John "Baron" Mac-Donald's wife was Mary MacDonald, daughter of Alasdair Dubh (of the Killiechonate family) and Anne MacDonald of the Bohuntin family.

To understand the Cape Breton Killiechonates' appreciation of their status in Keppoch society, Katharine MacDonell, sister of Ranald MacDonell, seventeenth of Keppoch (who died c. 1798), was married to John MacDonald of Killiechonate. To add to the piping perspective, another of the chief's sisters, Barbara, was married in December 1757 (as his second wife) to the Reverend Patrick MacDonald, author/editor of *Highland Vocal Airs*, while a third sister, Charlotte, married Alexander MacDonald of Garvabeg in Badenoch, a son of Reverend Patrick MacDonald by his first wife (a daughter of MacIntosh of Balnespick).

In Cape Breton one can still identify Ardnamurach, Retland, and Stoull people from the Morar area. In Low Point, Inverness County, the late Dougal MacDonald was the direct descendant of the last MacDonald of South Morar.[36] Besides John MacDonald of Glenaladale and Dougal MacDonald from Meoble, many Catholic representatives of the old Clanranald middle class also settled in Nova Scotia and are alluded to in *The Clanranald Connection* and elsewhere.[37] The immigrant progenitor of the Upper Margaree MacFarlanes, Dougal, was married to a sister of Spanish John MacDonell of the Scotus family in Knoydart.

The officer and teacher class are also well represented. Captain Allan MacDonald, ancestry uncertain but from Moidart, settled in South West Margaree, Inverness County, and Captain Alexander MacDonnell "of Murlegan" lived in the area (on the west side of Mabou Harbour) from c. 1823. Two sons of a Morar MacLellan spent their lives teaching in Nova Scotia, John MacLellan eventually living in Mabou Coal Mines. The various local histories and genealogies give details of the many doctors, lawyers, clerics, educators, administrators, businessmen, politicians, and other Gaels, including the traditionally talented, who came to prominence in the province. One of the provincial politicians was John MacKinnon (b.1808) from William's Point in Antigonish County. His father was from Eigg. MacKinnon was a dance-music piper.

In both Christian denominations the family and community nature of the emigrations is clearly discernible. The Brae Lochaber emigrations were family emigrations, often comprising three generations. With the exception of a family of Beatons who came to Lochaber from Skye before 1745 (a number of whose members married into the Bohuntin lineage), and the Rankins whose origins appear to have been Glencoe, most of the Bohuntin and Bohuntin-related emigrations to the New World marked a first break with traditional glens and farms that the families had occupied for centuries. A large part of an entire community eventually resettled in the Mabou area.

It is a surprise to many people to discover, a century later, just how pro-British Nova Scotian Gaelic society was in the days when the language was still vigorous. British society was clearly stratified socially and Gaelic society was too, traditionally, but with some sophisticated ease of interclass relations to commend it. This Britishness was bolstered by various vice-regal and military visits to the Maritime provinces that were covered in old summertime newspapers. Nova Scotian Gaelic society was remarkably cohesive and interrelated in the nineteenth century. It was also almost devoid of common crime (overlooking home distilling and smuggling); there were clearly understood limits to the physical violence (which generally excluded metal armaments and fell short of homicide). The occasions when resort to brawling could be expected (such as over local pride and honour and at political meetings) were also understood. The legal system, with sheriff and justices of the peace (unpaid in colonial times) and no police force, was neither pervasive nor oppressive and the middle class deserves its share in the credit for promoting and sustaining the old traditional norms of behaviour.

However, in Gaelic Nova Scotia English-speakers had difficulty in identifying and setting apart the Gaelic middle class. Ray MacLean's recent book *The Casket* nicely reveals an Antigonish Gaelic middle-class testiness at being overlooked by British officialdom – through arrogance rather than incomprehension – in the mid-nineteenth century.[38] One difficulty, even for Gaels, looking at class stratification in the diaspora *Gàidhealtachd* is that the group is not known to have had a distinctive accent like the English and Lowland Scot.[39] Therefore, if landownership was an unreliable indicator and accent no indicator at all, one is left with education and occupation. Since education, or the lack of it, was itself an unreliable marker of class status, it was official and professional occupations that most clearly identified the middle class, particularly the neo-middle class. Sometimes an "Esquire" on a census provides the same evidence. Justices of the peace, merchants, religious and political leaders, teachers, occasional militia leaders, and "esquires" who were Gaels all form a strong, well-distributed, and respected class in rural Nova Scotia.

Where the intellectual characteristic is considered, Calum MacLeod, writing of Gaelic society in Nova Scotia from the earliest days, remarked that, "there were always well-known, excellent Gaelic scholars in Nova Scotia ever since the Gaels first came ashore from Scotland in Pictou county in 1773."[40] In its context Calum MacLeod's opinion could not have been expanded, but it is not to be casually put aside by the cynical as empty bragging or common devaluation of the notion of what constituted a "scholar."

However, the idea of Gaelic scholarship *vis-à-vis* English-language scholarship has to be seriously considered, so that people like Dougal MacDonald – the last Dùghal of the tribe in South Morar[41] and a staunch traditionalist, though he had very little formal education – not to mention local family historians and relatively uneducated poets, are classifiable as among those who enjoyed some privileged status.

A number of modernizing, or improving, forces ranged against cultural traditionalism in the nineteenth century, two of which it will be profitable to examine at this point. Firstly, there were the Protestant and Catholic churches' efforts to snuff out alcoholism, which sometimes touched music and dance; secondly, there were the Disruption ideas of purity that permeated the Free Church Presbyterian communities. (Even John Calvin's dictum "Who loves not woman, wine, and song,/Remains a fool his whole life long"[42] had only modified acceptance apparently).

THE INFLUENCE OF THE DISRUPTION IN PROTESTANT GAELIC NOVA SCOTIA

In the Cape Breton Presbyterian *Gàidhealtachd* all parishes aligned themselves with the Disruption Free Church in or after 1843. In some areas there was warm contact (excluding marriage, generally speaking) between the neighbouring communities; in fact, older Gaels are usually emphatic in their assurances that good Christian relationships bound the two elements of Christianity together in Cape Breton. It may be that overt cultural exuberance was more muted in the Free Church parishes, but only marginally.[43] Before the Disruption there was no cultural feature of the Catholic Cape Breton community that was not to be found in the Church of Scotland community, and the tradition persisted when the break with the mother church came in and after 1843. Among the immigrants to Scotsville, for example, was the dancing master Calum MacLean from Mull, one of whose descendants, Alice (MacLean) Freeman, sings Gaelic songs. Among the MacKinnons, and doubtless other families, there were many immigrant pipers and fiddlers until within living memory.

Evaluating the impact of the Presbyterian Disruption on traditional bagpiping, fiddling, and dancing in the Gaelic communities of Nova Scotia, it is fair to say that where the Disruption church emerged, there tended to be a growth in serious piety and in temperance. There is a temptation to believe that there was a downturn in traditional music, dance, and story telling, but in the case of the Presbyterian area from Strathlorne to Headlake via the east side of Lake Ainslie in Cape Breton, any downturn was slight. Protestant musicians and dancers did not disappear when the Church moved from establishment status (and doubtless those who preferred to shun music and dance continued in their ways). Many very musical Presbyterian families had emigrated from Scotland, some of whom certainly had no compunction about continuing to foster musical tradition.

The most musical family known from the record is that of the MacKinnons, known in Gaelic as Clann Ionmhuinn a' Chiùil (the MacKinnons of the music). The immigrant generation comprised siblings Captain Allan MacKinnon (1786–1856), Annie, Archibald (the Big Batchelor, fiddler, piper, lore bearer), and Donald (d.1887), violin player. The first Nova Scotia-born generation included Big Farquhar MacKinnon (c.1835–1923), piper (and pupil of his Scotch uncle, the Big Batchelor), fiddler and Kirk precentor, his brother John, a piper and fiddler who went to Prince Edward Island, and their sister Annie, piper and fiddler. In the next generation there were Hector MacQuarrie (1865–1904), piper, Allan B. MacDonald (Hoodie's brother), a piper who died at twenty,[44] and Big Farquhar's nephews, Little Farquhar MacKinnon (1868–1941) and his brother Hugh Fred MacKinnon (whose dates I do not have), both pipers (see chapter 15).

There are instances of Free Church clerical sternness over the years towards traditional Scotch music and dance, but by and large these were restricted to a reawakened interest in keeping the Sunday Sabbath and fighting to establish temperance. Clerical narrow-mindedness was more a personal than an institutional idiosyncracy and often remained unexpressed. Both religious communities shared a common music and dance culture in Nova Scotia and many Presbyterians at East Lake Ainslie, Glenville, Strathlorne, Kenloch, and Scotsville were still step-dancing to traditional music in the second half of the twentieth century.[45]

I found no evidence of pipers or fiddlers having been discouraged by the East Lake Ainslie Free Church clergy, although Sunday was probably bereft of non-religious music. Big Farquhar, the longtime precentor there, must have been his uncle's piping pupil in the 1840s or 1850s, and his fiddling was widely enjoyed.[46] But where liquor was concerned, the case of Archibald MacKinnon highlights the social thrust of Free Church clerical efforts at East Lake Ainslie. The Big Batchelor stuck by the older tradition and in providing for his funeral he left five gallons of rum; the first dram was to be taken at the house, the second at his nephew Neil Mor MacDonald's, and the last at the graveside. The minister's reaction is not recorded. All that Hoodie said was that the Big Batchelor's was the last funeral at East Lake at which liquor was served.

THE INFLUENCE OF THE TEMPERANCE MOVEMENT IN THE ROMAN CATHOLIC COMMUNITIES

There were many forces working against tradition, if not always deliberately, in the nineteenth century. The emerging education system of the late nineteenth century[47] and greater contact with the English world in Canada and the United States, taken with the passing of the immigrant generations, were powerful agents of change. These outside influences will be addressed in following chapters. Some gained strength and intensity in the twentieth century; in the classroom, for example, it was a direct goal of educators to extirpate Gaelic. However, from within Gaelic society the temperance movement had some negative effect and it is widely believed to have had some unpleasant repercussions in terms of tradition. Clerical attitudes towards drinking over a century, since immigrant days in Nova Scotia, are important to consider. To begin with, the Catholic clergy in the landlordless New World had a far greater capacity to influence society than in Scotland, where within living memory Catholicism had had to defer to the noblemen who had shielded it from its Christian enemies. (In the Catholic Nova Scotian Gaelic community tradition ably stood its ground, as countless stories show.)

Serious Canadian government control of liquor began in 1918, although the Canada Temperance Act was passed in 1878 and pre-Confederation statute law, certainly in the early 1860s, forbade distilling.[48] Nonetheless, in many rural areas the nineteenth century was something of an alcoholic free-for-all, the main driving force against alcoholism being the various Christian churches that laboured, often in vain, to encourage sobriety. Whisky, rum, alcohol, all were rooted almost as prerequisites of hospitality in the Highland mind and could never have been eradicated piecemeal. In Scotch Nova Scotia the earliest overt clerical attempts to banish liquor were made by the Presbyterian reverend Norman MacLeod at St Ann's, Cape Breton, in the late 1820s. He found a cooperative fellow spirit in Judge J.G. Marshall in Sydney.[49]

At least one Catholic priest had identified liquor as a societal problem even before MacLeod's settlement, but the first Catholic efforts to fight the evils caused by alcohol were generated by Bishop William Fraser in 1841 (his episcopal term ran from 1827–51). Later bishops, MacKinnon (1851–77) and Cameron (1877–1910), redoubled Fraser's fight. At the parish level there are notable temperance priests, including Fr Kenneth J. MacDonald at Mabou, who made temperance a big part of his life's crusade. Others in the diocese were obviously less preoccupied with liquor and its powers. In no case, however, was the fight ever won, and, given so much alcohol and given the application of the law in places like immigrant Scotch Cape Breton, the relative absence of serious crime, while not vindicating drunkenness, at least shows that Highland society was remarkably capable of policing itself.[50]

Mabou's case may not be typical but in its chiaroscuro nature, and because it was steeped in tradition, it is the best example to use. In Mabou there is no evidence of any clerical interference in the normal daily drinking and cultural life during the pastorate of its first resident priest, Father

Alexander MacDonald, a Bohuntin man who lived in Mabou from 1842 to 1865.[51] As of 1868, however, the clergy took aim at the drinking community and the moonshine business in the parish (although smuggling from the French islands of Saint Pierre et Miquelon off southeast Newfoundland continued, pretty much as a Highland custom from the Old Country, and required naval or coastguard intervention to stop). These clerical struggles went on into the 1930s. Fr Kenneth J. MacDonald, translated from Arisaig, Nova Scotia, brought a zeal against drink and drinking with him to Port Hood (1865–68) and then Mabou (1868–94). Fr (Dr) John Francis Mac-Master (1894–1937) kept up the crusade but in modified form and with less of the consuming passion.

Of the two leaders the first must have had much the greater challenge after generations of home stills and socially condoned heavy drinking in New and Old Scotland. He also faced the "modernist" trend in Catholic church music, which condoned vulgar instrumental music in the mass. He was not inconsistent but it is remarkable that, on the one hand Fr MacDonald attacked fiddle playing and the *céilidh* because they were associated with stills but presided over a mass that used local violins in church.[52] Nonetheless, throughout his pastorate fiddlers and pipers and traditional dancers were everywhere, however many were the violins that he confiscated.

Fr MacMaster's preoccupation with the drinking problem was coupled with the threat to his parishioners' morals, as he saw it, of the quadrille, a new group dance in which there was body contact. However, he was much more obviously in favour of Scotch music than Fr Kenneth, particularly piping, and appears never to have discouraged traditional step-dancing to traditional music. He organized picnics and bazaars and counted on local musical and dance talent to put on a show. But, he would not brook public quadrille dancing.[53]

In retrospect it would be unfair to overestimate Fr MacDonald and Fr MacMaster's success in eradicating home distilling. What's more, the *céilidh* was always central to Gaelic life whatever people like Kenneth Mac-Donald wished. Where church music was concerned, Pope Pius X promulgated the *Motu Proprio* in 1903, putting an end to inappropriate music in the Catholic mass. How much this edict de-Gaelicized the mass and touched confidence in traditional music is open to discovery.[54] Today, as Gaelic dies out, it is sadly moving to see the fiddle making its last Gaelic appearance in Catholic funeral services. Tears of sadness are purified one last time.

Whether or not the Catholic clergy made inappropriate use of its opportunity to flex more social muscle than was appropriate is debatable. The fact remains that the campaign against alcohol from roughly mid-century on was no great success. In Judique Fr MacLean was a fiddling, piping, and dancing priest, presumably into the 1870s. Later in Mabou, the temperance priest Dr MacMaster was a devotee of traditional music and a latter-day patron of

Black Angus MacDonald, the famous Melrose Hill piper (of whom more later). Any damage to musical tradition appears in Mabou's case never to have been more than accidental.

There is another, more modern notion that in the New World the parish priest deliberately usurped the role of a non-existent Gaelic middle class from the earliest times. This simple idea is a later twentieth-century one, the product of ignorance of Gaelic society, and is demonstrably incorrect, but it brings up the very important observation that the real shifts away from Gaelic and Gaelic traditional culture that occurred from about 1880 were caused by the deaths of the immigrant Gaelic generations. As the critical time in Gaelic Scotland was around 1850, in Nova Scotia the transition from deeply traditional to altered traditional occurred from about 1880 when outside and inside non-Gaelic influences found fertile ground to grow. From a class point of view the indication is that, after the immigrant generation of Gaels (presumably along with some of the grosser aspects of the old hard-drinking days) had died away, the native-born Gael was relatively unprotected and subject to certain countercultural clerical directives. In the Presbyterian communities also, the Big Batchelor's rummy funeral, the last of its kind at East Lake Ainslie, suggests that the old Gaelic shared social consciousness survived the Disruption of 1843 only to be weakened when the stalwart immigrant generations died away.

In the last days of Gaelic traditionalism in Inverness County in this century, a number of priests took a very active part in encouraging what remained of Gaelic traditional amusements,[55] but this must be acknowledged alongside the realization that the Church may have had a hand in certain cultural extinctions in the last years of the nineteenth century, notably of the old traditional dancing master and his end-of-term ball and the old "Wild Eight" (Eight-hand Reel), whose disappearance has been attributed to clerical repression.

Although Scotland's rediscovery of the Nova Scotia Gàidhealtachd in 1879 was probably accelerated by the *Celtic Magazine* articles that Alexander MacKenzie published in Scotland after his tour, it also happens at about the turning point for Gaelic tradition. By 1880 North American "Highland" games had had a fair run at Halifax, Antigonish, New Glasgow, and Charlottetown and environs, attracting modern-style pipers from many places and apparently there was a growing interest in Scotland to bring modernizing forces to bear on New World traditional piping. For all that, many Cape Breton communities have managed to support important cultural anachronisms and memories of anachronisms to the present and for generations have offered the world a rich field for study of Gaelic music and dance. The remarkable persistence of traditional bagpiping in Nova Scotia, which includes Alex Currie (1910–97) and a number of others, has to be understood in the light of various inside repressive measures (as yet not thoroughly defined or assessed) and the culture's increasing exposure, particularly in the twentieth century, to modern American thoughts.

The fundamental strength underlying the survival of traditional piping in Nova Scotia owes much to imperial neglect, remoteness, the persistence of the ear-learning method used by traditional pipers for centuries, the near absence throughout the century of contact with the imperial military machine and of competition piping in Nova Scotia until the twentieth century, and to the natural conservativeness of transplanted communities. But added to that is the confidence traditional musicians took from acceptance of their music, in essence traditional step-dance music, by the middle-class Gael. The crux of the matter, however, is that, in Nova Scotia, any idea of patronage that operated, outside the realm of sinecure, concerned the community musician, the sort of person who in Scotland had owed, in some degree as yet not adequately defined, his farm and his subsistence, or later a steady job, to his social function as one of the community's musicians.

In summary, the Gaelic language and culture survived the nineteenth century in Nova Scotia but with noticeable signs of decline and change in the last quarter. While Gaelic survives in Scotland but shorn of the traditional Gaelic instrumental music and dance, the opposite is true in Nova Scotia. The foundation of support for Gaelic in Nova Scotia began to erode after the immigrant generations died, and the decay has continued fast as unilingual English-speaking Everyman emerges, not into the old Victorian English-speaking world of subtle and unsubtle class distinction but into an English-speaking world enfilladed and dominated by post-revolutionary American ideas in which the notion of class is another matter. And yet the cultural elements were so deeply ingrained that vitally important cultural facets of the old Highlands have almost miraculously survived. As chapter 16 will show, traditional bagpiping made it to well within living memory and is not yet quite extinct, despite the modernist inroads discussed in the next two chapters.

14 The Transition to Modern Piping in Scotland and Nova Scotia

INTRODUCTION

It is generally held in Nova Scotia that the only piping of any significance in the province began at about the time of the First World War. The argument, quite a powerful one when one listens to old tapes of traditional bagpiping in Cape Breton, is that superior modern Scottish piping began about then to make its way into the rural piping scene. It came through various avenues, from immigrant Scots pipers and through contact in Europe between Gaels from rural Nova Scotia and modern Scottish pipers in the British army. Many rural pipers learned to denigrate their talent from a technical point of view, without bothering to consider the true Gaelic function of the piper in the community; examples of this self-denigration are still to be found in Inverness County.

Sandy Boyd (1907–82), the semi-itinerant Scottish piper who spent many of his forty years in Canada in Nova Scotia, was charitable in local company when discussing the traditional Gaelic piper but harboured contrary thoughts when among literately trained pipers. Then he dismissed rural pipers as "country pipers" and presumed an ignorant and inferior randomness to their fingering when different from his own. To Sandy Boyd Black Jack MacDonald of the Cape Breton Highlanders pipe band, for example, was a "rough" piper, as were pipers like Alex Currie. Currie, on the other hand, was glowing in his praise of Boyd, although he knew the Scotsman should be more carefully classified rather than compared. Currie, who filled just as many halls as Sandy Boyd, knew the value of his own piping and could never have been convinced otherwise. Very little is known about the opinions of Black Angus MacDonald (1849–1939) and Angus Campbell Beaton (1895–1971) of modern Scottish piping.

Sandy Boyd's opinions are typically limited by an ignorance of the rural Gaelic piper and his function in Gaelic society. They were limited by a hard-earned sense of self-confidence and superiority that would be difficult to gainsay when one considers the training he had, how well he played technically, and the company he piped in. However, his views were also limited by a lack of appreciation of the actual historical varieties of piping fingering used, even at the highest level of the art, in nineteenth-century Scotland. In 1815 Alexander Campbell, as an early example, watched and heard Dòmhnul Ruadh MacCrimmon[1] piping near Glenelg and remarked cogently that "the manner in which he moves his fingers seems peculiar to himself."[2]

For all his lack of knowledge, Boyd's opinions, typical Scottish piping thoughts, provide a useful introduction to an understanding of the influence of modern piping thought on the traditional world of piping in the Nova Scotia Gàidhealtachd, an influence that is still culturally corrosive, not just of Gaelic traditional bagpiping but beyond the confines of the art.

This influence is difficult to assess during the nineteenth century in Nova Scotia and Scotland, although the case for the Nova Scotia rural Gàidhealtachd's having been the more ignored and therefore longer retaining invaluable anachronisms of piping function and style of playing is undeniable. The subject is complicated by the fact that traditional piping survived in the British army long after 1850. Also, in the civilian sphere in Scotland people like John Johnston and George Moss both refused to kow-tow to what they saw respectively as the incorrect or too-narrowly prescribed modern competition ceòl mór playing styles. Who knows what else survived.

Concerning the other organized influence on piping, the Highland Games, there are signs that tradition rather than modernity thrived there in certain parts of the New World, as the next chapter will show. Here and there in Cape Breton it is probable also that the judging of ceòl beag piping competition in the 1920s was based on traditional rather than modern standards.

Many of the Highland regiments did their stints in Nova Scotia and elsewhere in Canada (until November 1871 when the last of the British regiments, the 78th, left).[3] Scottish Highland military pipers serving in Halifax, for example, competed in games competitions in the 1860s. However impermeable traditional Gaelic Nova Scotia, and traditional Gaelic Scotland, may have been to post-traditional (modern) piping trends in the nineteenth century, there is no doubt that one Cape Breton publisher's starting point for the sort of piping that he conceived as being worthy of study, a point he set at c. 1918, provides a useful parameter. It was about then, in the first two decades of the twentieth century, that the intense influence of modernity on piping that had touched Scotland since perhaps the 1870s began to be felt more deeply in some quarters in Nova Scotia and all over the Scottish world.

THE TREND AWAY FROM TRADITION
IN THE BRITISH ARMY

While on the social and community level charting the intrusion of modern literate piping is difficult even in Gaelic Scotland, there are plain indicators in the British army of a trend away from tradition. In this regard the reader should consult Diana Henderson's *Highland Soldier: A Social Study of the Highland Regiments 1820–1920*. To begin with, the old Highland regiments, both men and officers, spoke increasingly more English from Waterloo until 1850, and this Anglicizing process continued apace thereafter. The proportion of Lowlanders in the ranks had been increasing since the Napoleonic wars, as was the number of other non-Gaels, including Englishmen as officers (which forced some bilingualism on what existed of the Gaelic rank and file). Accepting that by 1850 Lowland piping was all but extinct and insignificant as an influence, the door was open in the Highland regiments with their increasingly English outlook for novel interpretations of Highland bagpiping.[4] Henderson discovered, for example, that after mid-century it was the officer class that began to take a serious interest in army piping. The traditional hold-outs were inevitably the Gaelic-speaking pipers.

With the old official army rank of piper-major having been in desuétude for nearly a century, the rank of piper became official in 1854, at least reflecting, for the piper, some belated rationalizing of the pay system. However, it appears that the same impetus that gave rise to the increased numbers of Lowlanders in the Highland regiments, namely, a shortage of Highland men ready "to hug Brown Bess," was touching pipers. (Many Highland military pipers emigrated to or settled in Canada during the nineteenth century, some after 1850, from the Seaforths, the 74th, and other regiments.) The desire to be a piper in a Gaelic regiment that had given a Perthshire Mac-Gregor a teaching job a century earlier was a much rarer thing now. For a larger number of Highlanders than ever, it is fair to say that emigration had acquired greater appeal than military service, the land base in Gaelic Scotland now being radically insecure, whatever a brave son might do. In 1848 the 74th Highland Light Infantry feared making its pipers give up their uniform kilt in favour of the trews that the rank and file had worn for three years lest they lose the pipers, who were, according to their Berwick-shire commander in chief John Fordyce, "not easily procured."[5]

Henderson noted that it was the officers of the 91st who met the cost of equipping a pipe band in 1860. The appearance of a pipe band with pipes and drums playing together (if indeed that is what existed in the 91st in 1860) in itself was a radical departure from Highland military tradition (not that Gaels piping in unison, perhaps even making and using their own drums,[6] was unprecedented) and signified a novel use for a class of soldier whose old function of musically accompanying his company's advance or charge was disappearing. After 1848, as disciplined line advance with a fixed bayonet replaced the minor disorder, under fire, of taking out and fixing a detachable bayonet after firing a flintlock and then joining in the less regular bayonet advance/charge, the piper's function in the army was changing. His power to incite and to scare, and his symbolic value, were still immense. But now ostentation and a broader Scottish, rather than purely Gaelic, identifying function were part of his job. As *ceòl mór* was losing ground (with more non-Gaelic-speaking officers and fewer Gaelic-speaking rank and file), he was also becoming the player of march accompaniment.[7]

The Highland games idea in the form of regimental games was common in the 1850s and 1860s and long after. In May 1852 at Weedon (Northants) and in 1853 at Chobham camp, the Sutherland Highlanders held their Sutherland Gatherings.[8] At the Weedon gathering the dancing events were the same as those at the Northern Meeting in 1856, reel (Reel?) dancing, Highland Fling and *Gillie Callum* (sic). There were also interregimental games. In one of these gatherings, held in the Crimea in August 1855, there was piping competition that fell into the following categories: pibroch, march, strathspey, and reel (either two, three, or four separate events). A two-day event was held in the Crimea in 1856 and in that year the Northern Meeting piping was divided into "Piping: strathspeys and Marches" and "Pibrochs" with military and civilian pipers competing in both.[9] There is, however, no indication of how to assess the competitors. Many, probably all, were ear-learned traditional pipers. The dances sometimes featured at some of these events, the reel and Reel, the *Gille Caluim*, and the Highland Fling to whatever instrument they were danced, may as easily have been a guarantee that the music was traditional in speed and timing rather than modern, since there are no descriptions of the steps.

Henderson developed the common old military opinion that the Highland regiments were the faithful preservers of Highland bagpiping by pointing to the involvement of the officer class as the main novel factor rather than of the rank-and-file Gaelic-speaking piper. In the Highland regiments, she wrote, officers, "played a considerable part in retaining, encouraging and preserving Highland music in the Highland battalions."[10]

This may be true but it is worth scrutinizing. After all, what is meant by "Highland music"? Although Henderson did not attempt to date officer involvement, she mentioned that by 1888 the bagpipes were the instrument for gentlemen to play. She named, by way of example, eight officers of the Cameron Highlanders who played the pipes well that year. She firmly, and plausibly, implied that this middle-class involvement was stimulated by Queen Victoria's fascination with Gaelic Scotland and its traditional music and dance.[11]

One example of the spread of Scottish officer involvement in bagpiping will broaden the reader's conception of what was happening, not just in the

Highland regiments but in British-officered foreign regiments. Lt Col John Peter William Campbell (1824–1901), third son of Sir Duncan Campbell, first baronet of Barcaldine and Glenure, who retired from command of the 1st Sikh Regiment in which he had served for sixteen years, having seen a total of twenty-two years' active service with the Punjab Frontier Force, "was responsible for the introduction of bagpipes into the first Sikh Regiment ... During 1875 bagpipes were instituted in the Regiment as an alternative with the band. The pipes were obtained from Edinburgh, and the number at first was fixed at four pipes."[12] Campbell may have been following in a fairly common Scotticizing custom in which Sir John MacRa had indulged in India at the turn of the nineteenth century. His paternal nephew, who chronicled the lieutenant colonel's career, did not state how the bagpipers were taught or used, or whether they were Europeans or Sikhs or a blend of each; that the four were the core of a band seems not entirely out of the question, although no drummers are mentioned. (They may have been used as the pipers seem to have been in the pre-American Civil War scene in New York, four heading a parade; see below). If the four pipers were not a band, then assuming that Campbell was up to date with trends in military piping, the band's appearance in the British army may date to the last quarter of the century. The spread of the standardized bagpipe, through British officers, to colonial regiments in this period is an unstudied subject.

As an example of middle-class officer pipers, among the many was I.H. MacKay Scobie, a Sutherland man whose aim, eventually fulfilled, was to serve with the Seaforth Highlanders.[13] He was a commissioned officer and a piper who served during the First World War. As we have seen, Scobie took a deep interest in Seaforth musical history, unlike his fellows. His published writing about the Seaforths shows that traditional and modern piping coexisted in the regiment for most of the latter part of the nineteenth century.

For a class of people that consisted of a decreasing number of Gaelic speakers and an increasing number who were strangers to any Gaelic tradition at all, the easiest way to become bagpipers was almost *de rigueur* by written music and some equivalent of the classroom.[14] Donald MacPhee's *Collection of Piobairachd* (1879), David Glen's *Collection of Ancient Piobaireachd* (1st edition, 1880), General Thomason's *Ceòl Mór* (1st edition, c. 1896), and the volumes of the Piobaireachd Society (1904–13 and then from 1925), all containing only classical pipe music, were aimed obviously at this market. From this effusion of published pibroch grew the idea that the form was esoteric and highly intellectual, thereby precluding all but the finest pipers. It was earlier observed that boy pipers were not uncommon in the winners' lists of the earlier Edinburgh competitions. According to Diana Henderson, the first formal classroom appeared in 1910 at the Cameron Barracks in Inverness under John MacDonald, whose job was to improve pibroch playing in the Highland regiments. The as yet unanswered question is how did the traditional piper view his own piping under these circumstances – as inadequate perhaps? Scobie's writing betrays no bias against ear-learned piping bias but P.-M. Willie Ross (Edinburgh Castle) who taught many aspiring officer-pipers in the 1920s and 1930s is known to have remarked on the improvement of Cape Breton piping since literate learning became more common in the 1920s.[15]

Earlier literate learning, however, or at least what the hypercautious might give as an explanation of some men's fingering techniques, was encouraged *inter alia* by the following compilers of pipe music and instruction: Joseph MacDonald (1803, 1927), Robert Menzies (1818), William MacKay (1840, and several subsequent editions, some enlarged and improved by Angus MacKay), and Thomas MacBean Glen (1843, or slightly earlier).[16] Moreover, there were countless collections of Highland fiddle music dating from the mid-eighteenth century that contained a quantity of music that was in essence pipe music, or readily adaptable as such. Since the sizes of a few printing runs of specifically bagpipe music are known,[17] perhaps it is fair to suppose that William MacKay and Angus MacKay's tutor collection, which went into so many editions, may have been the most influential. The question remains who formed the market for this material. Cannon did not cite many private holders, and in any case tracing the original owners would often be impossible.

As radical a departure from tradition as literate learning was the emergence of the pipe band, and then (if different) the pipe and drum band.

Common to the manufacture of most post-1850s bagpipes is the use of tropical hard woods. Given army tendencies to standardize, why, where, and when did the Highland bagpipe fall under any requirement for uniformity of dimensions? (The simpler, corollary question is, when did the band dominate regimental thinking about its piping?) Henderson suggested tentatively that the first pipe band was formed in a Highland regiment in 1833, fifteen years earlier than previously thought in some quarters; but Henderson's example was nothing more than unison piping, which in fact has a much longer pedigree going back at least to 1746.

The famous "evidence" for the next "first" pipe band is based on an that occurred in 1848 when the 79th Highlanders were en route to Quebec. Running into thick fog, the pipers were ordered to play on deck to alert nearby ships, by the discord, of their presence. D.J.S. Murray, whom Roderick Cannon cited in *The Highland Bagpipe and Its Music*,[18] gave the location as the Hudson River, which is very unlikely since the regiment's transport reached Quebec in July, an ice-free month in the St Lawrence. The production of bagpiping discord and the absence of mention of drummers prove only that this was hardly a pipe band, merely an interesting form of mobile foghorn, producing the kind of music that would have fascinated Charles Ives.[19]

Cannon, citing A.D. Fraser's *Some Reminiscences and the Bagpipe*

(1907), then mentioned the unison piping by the 93d of "The Campbells Are Coming" along the Crinan Canal to greet Queen Victoria in 1853.[20] This may be closer to an example of a proto-band, without drummers, but the pipers involved were still unofficial musicians and, as stated, unison piping was not unknown a century earlier, probably having been used militarily in 1715. When the 42d (Black Watch) marched out of the Citadel in Halifax, Nova Scotia, to board the troop ship *Resistance* to return to the United Kingdom in May 1852, they were led "by the fine band of the 97th and the music of the 42d." First, the 97th was not a Highland regiment. Second, there is no mention of any pipe band or even of bagpipes in the 42d on this occasion.[21] At this point it seems that the bagpipes' abnormal alliance with the drum lay in the future, and until one understands when the drum was sufficiently freed from its old function as a signalling device to be grafted onto a similarly displaced Highland bagpipe, the story will not be clearly understood.

A photograph of the 79th Regiment (originally of the New York Militia) taken on 4 July 1860 in Tryon Row, Manhattan, shows, according to M.J. McAfee from whose collection it comes, that this American Civil War regiment is being led by four kilted pipers. (In the copy of the photograph available to me, one set of what might be drones, held under the soldier's right arm, is clearly visible.) The leading lines of the parade formation show kilted soldiers, while another photograph, also from McAfee's collection, shows a non-commissioned officer of the 79th New York in glengarry, dark kilt, diagonally cut tartan hose, and a tasselled shaggy sporran.[22] The wearing of non-regulation uniform raised a controversy, but in fact the 79th did not wear it during Civil War actions, and as far as can be ascertained the regiment's only band, of which they were very proud, was a typical military band of music under a William Robertson. However, for present purposes there was no 79th New York pipe band or conjunction of pipers and drummers, and it is fair to say that had that model existed in the United Kingdom at the time, the 79th would have aped it; most of the men had been born in Scotland, the "stuff" of their uniforms came from Britain, and the author of the most accessible regimental history, William Todd (*The Seventy-ninth Highlanders*, 1886), was himself an English immigrant. Todd often referred to the seventeen-member regimental band but only once was a piper mentioned, a latecomer to the regiment from Michigan, during the war; Todd wrote in a letter that "we also have a new 'institution' attached to the regiment – nothing less than a Scotch 'piper' from Michigan, who joined us on our way down here [Vicksburg area, Mississippi]. He has a full suit of the kilts and so entertains us with his alleged tunes on the pipes, that we have several times threatened to 'fire him out,' and not allow him to perform again till he learns how."[23]

However, perhaps more important than speculation on proto pipe and drum bands is that Henderson noted that uniform pitch was established for British military bands in 1858. Cannon added that bandsmen in the British army began to be trained at an army college in 1874; nothing at this stage of musical instrument research about pipe bands but at least something about the overall wish to standardize and pipe bands are essentially about rather tricky standardization.[24]

An interesting case of attempted tax evasion in the port of Halifax, Nova Scotia, published in the *Acadian Recorder* on 20 July 1868, throws light on one purchaser's perceptions of certain bagpipes as belonging to a uniform class. Under the heading "Tilley and the Bagpipes," the story tells how a Highlander called Donald Ross[25] had imported a "set of No. 1 Military Bagpipes" from the celebrated pipe maker Mr Glen of Edinburgh. They had arrived in Halifax by the last steamer and the local customs officer had immediately allowed the instrument in duty free. However, Tilley, at the time Ottawa customs official of the year-old nation, was in Halifax and he saw matters differently. He imposed a duty of $6.33 on the bagpipes, despite Ross's protestations that he had bought and imported the instrument to donate to "a Highland or Scottish Society in Cape Breton" with the aim of preserving "the martial spirit, music, poetry, dress, and games of the Scottish Highlanders." Ross's claim fell on deaf ears, the exaction stood, and Tilley was derided for his meanness. The Glen company in question was either John's or Robert's or their uncle Alexander's.[26] The set of pipes has not been located.

The classification of this set of bagpipes particularly as "military bagpipes" is a rare instance of its sort to be found in Nova Scotia's published record, although the terminology may have been Glen's and common enough elsewhere. In any case the nomenclature suggests something new, something standardized, something to be coveted, especially by a would-be revivalist-benefactor, into which category I tentatively put Ross. From a slightly later period there are several sets extant that were bought from Scotland between 1875 and 1900,[27] and not a few of the older, much more valuable sets that they replaced. Even in the remotest Gaelic-speaking communities and perhaps as early as mid-century, pipers wanted the modern sets. Peter Henderson's, bagpipe makers in Glasgow whose pipes became popular in Cape Breton, opened for business in 1868.

THE SURVIVAL OF TRADITIONAL PIPING IN THE ARMY

The case to be made for the ubiquitous presence of traditional piping and dancing in 1850 is strong. By 1900 in Scotland it had certainly weakened. The price of those editions of bagpipe music that were available was, it is true, beginning to fall by mid-century, but it is still commonly believed that almost all pipers were still ear-learned by 1850 and most for much longer. This this was the point of view expressed by John Glen (1833–1904), son of Thomas MacBean Glen and continuer, with his brother, of the family musical instrument manufactury.[28] The dearth of published pipe music known to have been purchased (or borrowed) and used by Nova Scotian Gaels throughout the entire nineteenth century shows that Glen's opinion held for Nova Scotia too.

In Scotch Nova Scotia a file has yet to be made on Gaelic-speaking men from the province who served in the American Civil War, but they were much more numerous than those who went to fight in the Crimean campaign, or to join the British army at all during the nineteenth century. For all the occasional presence of Highland regiments in barrack towns like Halifax and Windsor as well as in Annapolis and Cape Breton, not to mention in Prince Edward Island,[29] there was little recruitment.[30] (In 1870, when serving in Halifax, the 78th Ross-shire Buffs were reduced in numbers and reorganized.) There is no evidence that local Gaels ever saw or were in any way influenced by pipe bands up until 1871 when the British regiments left for good. This is all but confirmed for Cape Breton Gaels by the fact that when the proto Cape Breton Highlanders were formed, the militia regiment's only band from 1875 until 1881 was a brass band.

In any case, there is convincing evidence that tradition survived in the mid-nineteenth-century Highland regiments that served in Nova Scotia and elsewhere in Canada. Citing the diary of Col J.W. Wedderburn for 15 April 1852, Diana Henderson found that Maj. George Burrell Cumberland, commander of the 42d in Halifax, objected to the pipes, pibroch, and Reels in the mess. This distaste ensured that more piping and fiddling went on. That the pipe-major of the 42d was in all likelihood of the old traditional Gaelic school emerges again from Wedderburn's diary. When the regiment was sailing for the United Kingdom from Halifax in 1852, he wrote, "The Band played after Mess also the Pipes and old McLean the Pipe Major danced and played the fiddle like a five year old."[31] (Interestingly, the Fletts discovered a record of the pipe-major of the 42d Regiment, Donald McTavish, in 1821. McTavish was described at the piping competition as a "capital dancer.")[32]

There is no description of McLean's steps but the fact that he played both instruments implies that his music was traditional and not learned in the classroom. (The ability to play both instruments was quite common among Nova Scotian Gaelic pipers like Allan MacFarlane, Black Angus MacDonald, Ranald Beaton (Raonul Màiri Bhàin), Angus Johnnie Ranald Beaton, and many others in the twentieth century. More will be said about some of these pipers in chapter 15. Pipers who fiddled are not unknown in Gaelic Scotland either.)[33] McLean, however, the 42d's unofficial pipe-major, was also competitive. Late in June 1852, with the Black Watch's service companies just home from Nova Scotia and ensconced at Stirling Castle, Colonel

Wedderburn left a brief report of a piping competition (as part of a military Highland games) at the "bowling green" in Stirling. This event appears to have been interregimental since Wedderburn noted that McLean and Ross were the best pipers while the pipe-major of the 79th (presumably Alexander MacLennan) had no chance. At the same event the dancing was "splendid" and the "Broadsword" very good.[34]

The other powerful clue that tradition survived is found in Maj. I.H. MacKay Scobie's *Pipers and Pipe Music*. Scobie wrote that the unofficial pipe-major of the Seaforths for an undetermined number of years up to 1828 was Sutherland Gael Donald MacDonald. On unknown authority but still significantly, Scobie described MacDonald as a great character and a fine player "of the old style."

Between 1840 and 1848 and at times between 1852 and 1856, the unofficial and (from 1854) official pipe-major in the regiment was Neil Mathieson, also from Sutherland, who enlisted in 1839. He spoke Gaelic and English, the latter with a heavily Gaelic flavour. Scobie wrote that he was "a first-rate performer of the old style."[35] Mathieson was in charge of the first five official pipers – Ronald Kemp from Glen Urquhart, Alexander McLean, John MacDonald, John Miller, and Donald Grant – who were created in 1854 when the regiment was in Halifax. (The other pipers associated with the regiment remained unofficial.) Mathieson was one of several pipers who settled in Canada; he remained behind in 1854 when the regiment left Halifax and then rejoined in 1855, only to be discharged to a pension in 1856 when he settled in Ontario.

One of the acting pipe-majors between 1854 and 1856 was John Mac-Donald, "*am pìobaire Frangach*," yet another Sutherland man. Scobie recorded that he was a fine sportsman, a good dancer, and "an excellent piper of the old style."[36] Another John MacDonald, a Tiree man who had won a piping competition in the Crimea in 1855, was pipe-major in 1856–1864. He came to Canada as Governor General Lord Lorne's piper. Other Highland regiments, including the 42d, the 71st, and the 74th, had pipers who emigrated to Canada in the nineteenth century.[37]

The interesting feature of Scobie's work is that he distinguished between old and new styles of piping even after 1850. Although he did not give sources, there is no reason to doubt that he interviewed veterans of the Seaforth Highlanders who had served from before the Crimea. Unfortunately, he left no indication of what marked this "old style," or whether it was peculiar to the non-officer class (which it appears to have been). Scobie also mentioned a former colonel's description of an old piper who appears to have had a good deal of traditional piping music that was clearly beginning to be forgotten by 1877. "Old Kenneth ... could play hundreds of rare old tunes, and was himself no mean composer, although such a modest and retiring Highlandman."[38]

The extent of Anglicization is seen in the 72d. In 1887 only 332 of the 814 members of the regiment were Scotch Highlanders; 337 were Lowland Scots, 115 were English, 29 were Irish and one was colonial. Since mid-century the pipers increasingly played *ceòl beag*. However, the case for piping's having moved by 1900 out of the realm of the traditional piper and into the world of the officer in the Seaforth Highlanders is not cut and dried. The Seaforths appear to have retained a stronger Gaelic flavour, although gentlemanly interest and influence were increasing. What is more, the fact that Pipe-Major James MacDonald from Caithness, tenured in 1880–88, refurbished the regiment's old sets of bagpipes and then introduced new sets suggests a move to the new standardization of the instrument, and perhaps to a band. Who actually stimulated the upgrading, whether James MacDonald or members of the officer élite, is unknown.

It is not clear how many traditional pipers in the Highland regiments played in the old style by the 1880s. However, it can be argued that the Seaforth pipe-major in 1893 and 1894, James Sutherland, was moving into the realm of literate modern piping. During the First World War James Sutherland, according to R.C. Strelley (1906–87), taught band piping at the Edinburgh Academy.[39] While still at school Strelley also took piping lessons from Pipe-Major Willie Ross (1879–1966) at Edinburgh Castle. Strelley had no knowledge of any older Gaelic style of piping and disdained fast *ceòl beag* piping, which he heard from time to time on Scottish city streets, as "tinkers' music." Moreover, when shown traditional Scotch Gaelic step-dancing from Cape Breton, Strelley found it novel.

THE EMERGENCE OF THE PIPE BAND IN NOVA SCOTIA

In Cape Breton and elsewhere in Canada, generally speaking, the recognizably modern military pipe and drum band appeared during the First World War, largely in response to the earlier emergence of the phenomenon in Britain. The British army pipe band was certainly one model. However, there were also civilian pipe and drum bands before the Great War in Britain and Canada. The civilian MacIntyre band, the first to be formed in Eastern Canada according to Barry Shears, was formed in urban Cape Breton in 1898, and a Pictou equivalent, the Pictou County Pipe Band, was photographed around 1906. Both bands had only one side and one bass drummer.[40] Even if pipe and drum bands occurred first in the Highland regiments in the British army (no date is ascertainable), the actual evolution of such bands in Canada may owe its origins as much to immigrant civilians who in Britain had been exposed to the earliest civilian or military equivalents. The degree to which immigrant Scottish pipers got pipe and drum bands going in Canada is still unstudied, as is their impact on Canadian Highland gatherings.

Another civilian pipe band in Canada that existed before the Great War was the old Edmonton Pipe Band. It enlisted *en bloc* and became the "Princess Pats" pipe band during the war (probably under Scots-born William Campbell). From the military side there is an early mention of a "Pipe and Drum Regiment Band," that of the 78th Nova Scotia Highland Regiment, which appears in the Charlottetown *Herald* (6 August 1913) in an advertisement for the annual Scottish gathering sponsored by the Charlottetown Caledonian Club and held at Vernon River Bridge that year.

According to Pipe-Major Stephen MacKinnon,[41] between twenty-five and thirty Canadian military pipe bands served overseas during World War I. MacKinnon reported from personal experience that "several great piping tourneys behind the lines" took place during the Great War and that in October 1917, at Camblain l'Abbé four or five miles west of Vimy Ridge, Sir Douglas Haig reviewed the massed pipe bands of the Canadian Corps. On 1 July 1918, Dominion Day, "all available pipe bands in the British Army met at 'Tanks' for a Highland Gathering such as would have gladdened the heart of a Roderick Dhu or Prince Charlie."[42] According to MacKinnon, an estimated five hundred pipers were present. MacKinnon rightly believed that a piping renaissance had been generated by the Great War.[43]

In the post-colonial as in the colonial Canadian setting, however, there was a general absence of sophisticated, urban middle- and upper-middle-class Victorian affectation among the officers in these regiments. Certainly in Gaelic Cape Breton this absence was remarkable and ensured that the character of the pipe band that emerged was in essence more traditional than modern, although the modernizing forces became more pronounced during and after the Great War when there was extensive contact with British Highland regiments and their musical standards.

In October 1871 the 94th Victorian, a militia regiment, was formed with regimental headquarters in Baddeck, Nova Scotia. Composed from its inception almost completely of Gaelic-speaking Highlanders, it was designated a highland unit in 1879 and took the subtitle Argyle Highlanders. The first music associated with the group was a brass band of fourteen musicians that was set up in 1875, there being and never having been any pipe bands to that point in Maritime Canada. In 1881, "in keeping with the change to a Highland Unit the band was composed of six pipers."[44]

In 1887 there were fifteen pipers. Whether or not these can be described as a modern pipe band remains to be found out. There may have been no drummers. The Cape Breton Highlanders hived off from the 94th to be formed into the 85th in 1915, and photography shows that in the pipe bands of the Great War, pipes and drums were united. There was at least one Gaelic-speaking officer in the Cape Breton Highlanders who also played the bagpipes, Captain Angus MacNeil from the Iona area of Cape Breton. He was a cousin of Stephen B. MacNeil, and according to Barry Shears, the "unit" had the highest percentage of Gaelic-speaking officers and men of any in the British army.

Although the majority of pipers in the early Cape Breton Highlanders played by ear, the likelihood is that Captain Angus MacNeil was a note piper. Barry Shears described Angus's cousin Stephen as a "competent *pìobaireachd* player" and arranger of light music, obviously musically literate. Shears also noted that Black Jack MacDonald was taught his piping, through the literate method, by Stephen. Black Jack from Soldier's Cove, was apparently not a fluent Gaelic speaker. A veteran of both world wars and sometime pipe-major of the Cape Breton Highlanders, he in turn taught the late George Sutherland (1909–84), one of the pipe-majors of the Cape Breton Highlanders during the Second World War. George Sutherland, whose mother-tongue was Gaelic and who was never anything but a note piper, was quite certain that Black Jack was a note player too, saying that he had the *obair ùrlair*, or ground work (meaning that he made the notes "correctly" and played the various gracings in the "correct" manner). Sandy Boyd the Largs (Ayrshire) piper knew Black Jack MacDonald and in a diplomatic moment said that he was typical of a piper who had not had the fortune to have been well taught, although he was "a good band piper." This was a category into which Boyd kindly placed several other local pipers. In light of Black Jack's commitment to literately learned piping, it is notable that, according to Sandy Boyd, Black Jack had confided to him that one member of his band, while he was pipe-major of the Highlanders, had been a very fine native Cape Breton piper. Boyd did not remember who this was.

From the point of view of traditional ear-learned bagpiping, the most important point to be emphasized is that the Cape Breton Highlanders pipe band, even during George Sutherland's tenure as pipe-major during the Second World War, continued to have mostly ear-learned traditional Scotch pipers. In fact the general impression George Sutherland left me with[45] was that most of his pipers had originally learned by ear and, with efforts to introduce them to note learning, had shown confusion. Of the four pipe-majors of the band during his time as a piper, including himself, Sutherland described two as ear-learned. Pipe-Major Alex "the piper" MacDonald (1892–1966) a Gaelic speaker "from Upper Margaree," was one; the other was Wild Bill Gillis (1914–95) from Inverness. Sutherland said that Alex the piper (also known as the Indian teacher) served with the Highlanders in Sydney, Cape Breton, and never went overseas. Sutherland described him as having had "leaky fingers." Wild Bill Gillis, known everywhere as "Willie the piper," was described as having had some Gaelic and originally being an ear piper.

Willie the piper eventually learned to read pipe music but initially he played traditional Scotch music in the old fashion, by ear. In corroboration of this he said himself that he and John Angie MacDonell (who died in 1980) of the town of Inverness, also a member of the Cape Breton Highlanders pipe band during the Second World War, often piped for step-dancing in and around Inverness.

Of the rank and file Cape Breton Highlanders pipers during the Second World War, Sutherland mentioned several who were traditional in style. John Angie MacDonell had no *obair ùrlair* but could "take a tune from the book." Sutherland said he was a good ear player who would put in what were, to Sutherland, indescribable grace-notings where grips or taorluaths (*tudhlud-han*) appeared in the music. Sutherland credited the Scotsman in Inverness, the immigrant piper-miner Sandy Russell from Dundee, with having taught John Angie what he knew of pipe music. Another piper in the band who was an indirect product of Sandy Russell's tuition was Archie Allan (Ack Ack) MacKay (b. 1920), a Protestant piper from Inverness County now living in West Vancouver. Sutherland said that MacKay in turn taught Gordon Mac-Donald to play the pipes.[46] Dan J. MacKenzie from Christmas Island but living in Sydney Mines at the outbreak of the war, a Gaelic speaker who was literate in the language, was another ear piper.[47] Archie MacPhail, a non-Gaelic speaker from Glace Bay, was to Sutherland "like the rest," half an ear-learned piper who was, typically, confused when confronted with having to learn tunes from sheet music. Another Gaelic speaker, Joe MacMillan of Reserve, who was too old for active service and left the regiment in England, was also an ear piper. (Joe MacMillan's son John Joe was a piper as well; he spoke no Gaelic and was remembered by Sutherland as having been a Highland dancer who danced the Highland Fling. Interestingly enough, during an interview given on 3 December 1976, Sandy Boyd included him among his rather short list of best Cape Breton pipers.)

Perhaps the most interesting of the rank and file Cape Breton Highlander pipe band pipers was Gordon MacQuarrie. Sutherland described him as an ear-learned piper who did not have the *obair ùrlair* (Sandy Boyd said that he had "an open style"). However, MacQuarrie fell into a quite different category from Sutherland and Boyd. MacQuarrie was both a reader and writer of music who was fluent and literate in both Gaelic and English. The original printing of *The Cape Breton Collection of Scottish Melodies*, compiled and arranged by Gordon F. MacQuarrie, was done in 1940. Sutherland told me that while the regiment was in Perth, Scotland, Red Gordon MacQuarrie wrote letters in Gaelic to the BBC in Scotland. MacQuarrie, like Black Angus MacDonald from Mount Young, obviously chose to continue to play the bagpipes by ear. For both men literate piping was an inadequate form of expression. As of September 1997, Alex Currie was the only one like them alive.

During the Second World War the Cape Breton Highlander pipers played bagpipes made by the same maker. According to his brother, Neil MacKay of Dunvegan, Inverness County, Archie Allan MacKay of Cape Mabou and Inverness never bought his own set of bagpipes, preferring always to rely on army issue, which during his roughly four years of wartime service was a Peter Henderson set.[48]

Inherent in these few sketches of Cape Breton Highlanders is the framework for an understanding of the interaction of traditional and modern piping in the military in Cape Breton during the first four decades of the twentieth century. One significant feature is the influence of the urban English-speaking industrial environment. In the Sydney area, even in Inverness and Port Hood, Gaelic withered more rapidly where there was industrialization. It is remarkable that in the MacMillan family in Reserve the father was a Gaelic-speaking ear piper while the son was a unilingual English-speaking "Highland" dancer (as well as a presumably literately learned piper).

Without a doubt, bagpiping in the British army had moved to the modern literate concepts, for most if not all pipers, long before the Second World War – any time after 1880, judging by MacKay Scobie. World War I was probably late in the process. However, even in the Scottish Highland regiments there is no question but that bagpiping was for long quite traditional and ear-learned, serving military and social needs that had not changed much from clan requirements in the late seventeenth century (excepting the part played by *ceòl mór*, which withered dramatically in the nineteenth century). There are also clear pointers to the influences that shifted British military piping away from that tradition. One of those influences was the piping-school system mentioned above, in Inverness for *ceòl mór* under John MacDonald, and in Edinburgh under Willie Ross for all forms of military piping.

As with many questions in piping, representative examples are too few to allow for reliable generalization, but the part played by the civilian pipe band in Scotland in the move to literate band piping deserves mention nonetheless. Although little is known about the emergence of the pipe band as either a military or civilian (semi-civilian, in the case of the Boys' Brigade bands of the late nineteenth century) phenomenon in Scotland,[49] the notion that the Highland regiments were the predominating force for modernity in piping should be tentatively moderated.

James Laidlaw, piper and founding member of the Stonehouse civilian Pipe Band near Lanark, Scotland, wrote the following in January 1977:

It was a good Band and made quite a name for itself throughout Scotland. Its leader Hector McInnes was an expert on Bagpipes and all its pipers for many years had been a product of his tuition.

Contests for Pipe Bands were becoming a yearly Event and in 1909 the first World Championship was played for at the Cowal Games—Dunoon.[50]

This event was open to Military and Civilian Pipe Bands, the Trophy being the family shield of the Duke of Argyll, previously it had been a Military affair – and on the same day was contested the Civilian Pipe Band Championship – the trophy being a Shield presented by then Harry Lauder. Also on this same day – the piping judges were for the first time put into tents and didn't know which Band was playing. After all the Bands had competed and the massed Bands had marched round the field and then lined up before the Grandstand to hear the Results read out, it was found that Stonehouse Pipe Band had won both Shields. I still remember the Band of the 1st Highland Light Infantry marching away playing "There is a Happy Land." It was a great day – then in 1910 we again won the Harry Lauder Shield – and once again in 1911.

We had some good times in the Band and our pleasure in the Summer time was being engaged to play at various gatherings such as Cattle Shows, Sports Events and other occasions which took us to different parts of the County and besides giving pleasure to others it was a pleasure to us also.

Outside the work of the Band, we would visit each others home[51] and do a bit of practice there or at a week-end take a walk round the farms and play for the dances amongst the farm workers[;] our pleasures were simple and home made ..."[52]

James Laidlaw, by 30 November 1976, was the last living member of the Stonehouse championship band, to his knowledge. When asked later where his old friend and fellow Stonehouse piper Jack Muir had got his handwritten pipe music (which I saw), Laidlaw wrote, "I would say without hesitation that it would have been written by our Pipe Major Hector McInnes, as he wrote out all our tunes. I had a book of them also which I passed on to a nephew."[53] (Roderick D. Cannon's grandfather similarly wrote out copies by hand of music for his Manchester Company Boys' Brigade pipe band, c. 1912. This was probably common practice.)[54]

The military bands that the Stonehouse civilian band competed against in 1909 and later may have been literately trained, but it is not to be overlooked that Hector McInnes aimed at uniformity of performance by handwriting his band's music, and his band won. (Hector's son Hector McInnes was brought out to Detroit to organize the Ford Pipe Band.) The other important feature of Laidlaw's letter is the two young men's piping for farmers' dances in the Stonehouse area. While it lies outwith my mandate, there can be no harm in suggesting that the dancing of the farm folk in rural Lanarkshire before World War I would have been traditional in nature and almost certainly akin to that of rural East Lothian and Kirkcudbrightshire. The "treepling" that J.F. and T.M. Flett described in *Traditional Dancing in Scotland*[55] and the dancing master's teaching of the rhythm "Peter-a-Dick's peat stack" were obviously step-dancing of a sort that was basically similar to the traditional Gaelic step-dancing, which survives, vigorously, in Cape Breton.[56]

Scobie's observation of piping anachronisms places the shift to modernity at mid-century, about which time, coincidentally, march timing began to dominate the world of literate bagpiping. The retention of traditional non-march piping in the army therefore is linked to the retention of traditional dancing. The half century of emigration from 1815 is the obvious feature of Scottish Gaelic society that facilitated change, perhaps even demanded it if anything at all were to survive in Scotland.[57] If there was an honest sense that it would be better to replace what was being lost in the "Highland" regiments and in Highland society by some literate form of piping than by nothing, then it is not difficult to understand the wish to spread the new piping wherever there were Scots. That, indeed, is the innocent and enthusiastic attitude that still flourishes in all parts of Canada.

15 Highland Games and Competition Piping

In the non-military sphere in late-nineteenth-century Scotland, other forces can be identified that detraditionalized Gaelic piping, particularly the emergence of competitive ballet-inspired "Highland" dancing. These dances were done to bagpiping, but a different notion of dancing grace evoked a different sort of timing and speed of playing, at least of specific tunes. A second influential phenomenon of the rural popular scene was the expansion of non-classical competition piping in mid-century. Competition piping and new forms of dancing comprise part of what is known as the Highland gathering, or games, which with one exception spread north and west from the Lowland/Highland fringe in the East and South (Perthshire and Aberdeenshire), eventually reaching Glenfinnan and the Outer Hebrides in the twentieth century.

Although by the 1850s so-called Highland gatherings were features of various Highland regiments, and aggregates of Highland regiments in the British army, my treatment of the phenomenon comes from a civilian point of view. In the all-male military environment where fitness for most was at a premium, sports appear to have become an important feature of recreation by about 1850, and at several points it is almost impossible to detach or extricate the military from the Highland games in the United Kingdom[1] or in Nova Scotia. However, the essential idea of Highland games originated in a civilian rather than strictly military setting in the Scottish *Gàidhealtachd*; there were no organized military games in the Highland regiments of the eighteenth century. Sifting through events that have been commonplace since the 1850s to discover what about them is Gaelic shows just how far Highland games are from traditional Scotch Gaelic pastimes and how alien the concept is.

Annually repeated, formal music and dance competitions are a nine-teenth-century accretion. Highland gatherings, Caledonian games, athletic games, or whatever title they are given, have all been studied, but no one has effectively rooted Highland games in true Gaelic culture except by wishful thinking. To begin with, unless under exceptional circumstances, competition would too often have been much too damaging to the Highland pride of the loser, and winner, if staged on anything wider than a community basis. To involve unrelated clans in competition would have been a risky proposition in the eighteenth century when Highlanders could be counted upon to fight at graveyards and over seemingly trivial points of honour.

The bridge between the Braemar Games of the mid-nineteenth century, the bridge even between some aspects of the Society of True Highlanders games staged in Lochaber by Alasdair Ranaldson MacDonald of Glengarry around 1820[2] and their Scottish Gaelic eighteenth-century antecedent, has yet to be built. Nonetheless, many writers have blithely assumed its existence and held up stray events in history as signposts showing a long continuous history (Queen Mary's hunt being one such event). This assumption creates another barrier to a fair understanding of Gaelic rural life and of the Highlander's conception of manliness. For that reason the subject generally has to be broached with great care. The real model for most athletic events in modern Scottish Highland games will almost certainly turn out to be Saxon, possibly infiltrating through the English regiments. Cumberland's games at Fort Augustus in 1746, inasmuch as they contained horse racing, were probably closer to West Coast Gaelic tradition than the modern games are; they may also point to a post-1746 origin for what really are modern athletics events, kilted or not.[3]

In the case of the military influence in Nova Scotia, the Nova Scotian and Maritime *Gàidhealtachd* was exposed directly to the Highland games quite early, around 1860 in Halifax and soon after in Antigonish and New Glasgow. The first annual gathering of the Caledonian Club in Charlottetown, Prince Edward Island, was held in 1863.[4] However, as with trying to assess the survival of Gaelic piping and dancing tradition in the Scottish Highland regiments, one cannot be certain as to how modern some of these events were when considering events of actual cultural significance. The Gille Caluim was the sword dance; but what was the Highland Fling in the 1860s, a step-dance hornpipe or a piece of pseudo-ballet that had evolved from one isolated characteristic of the reel setting steps? No one knows.

Yet in at least one case, that of New Glasgow, there is an argument to be made for initial confusion as to what dances to put on. In the New Glasgow event the published reports suggest that traditional reel (possibly Reel) dancing was a prominent feature. It is quite plausible that no one yet felt adequately prepared to dance the prescribed Highland Fling and Gille Caluim. In Prince Edward Island there is evidence that what was reported in the

Charlottetown *Herald* from 1893 was restricted to the usual official "Highland" events and that a good deal of non-competitive but culturally traditional things were going on, at least at two of the Caledonian Club games. In addition, were one looking for ideas in the 1830s, a similar perplexity could be found in New York, where organizers of the earliest Scotch games were apparently unaware of what Alasdair Ranaldson MacDonell of Glengarry had recently staged in Lochaber (or were repulsed by what they knew), or of what was going on the southern Highland fringes, and found themselves casting around for what was truly Scotch.

The death of the "oda" (horse racing) in Barra in 1828 marks the end of an old organized sporting tradition there, one that surely had ancient roots.[5] By contrast, there is nothing from Gaelic sources to foster the idea that foot races, throwing a hammer, or tossing a caber ever were organized in any recognizably competitive way, if indeed they existed at all in Gaelic Scotland (tossing de-limbed trees was definitely not indigenous to the Outer Hebrides). Local communities, possibly parishes, certainly pitted man against man in physical challenges such as wrestling (which has a long history in parts of Gaelic Scotland),[6] shinty, in stone throwing, lifting, and carrying, but there is no record of any major regularly repeated organized gathering until the nineteenth century. Until the first Antigonish Highland Games in 1863, I have found no record of any organized games being held in Gaelic Nova Scotia.

At the local level in Gaelic Scotland there are some eighteenth-century references to sports. When the Reverend Eneas Sage[7] took up his Kirk charges in Loch Carron, Gairloch, and Applecross just after he obtained his license in 1725, he met with resistance. The Episcopal church was strong in that area of Wester Ross[8] and the Kirk intrusion was heartily resented (one contemporary minister in Gairloch was roughly used and dared not live in his parish in the 1720s). Sage met initially with scant success, and few people attended his services. "After his settlement, to show their dislike, the people assembled every Lord's day in a plat of ground about twenty yards from the church door for the practice of athletic games. This unbecoming behaviour my grand-father had ... to witness weekly."[9] There is no description of the games themselves, but Sage's grandson, the writer, saw nothing untoward when he noted that the reverend eventually managed to entice a number of people to his services by bribing them with a pound of snuff.

Otherwise, eighteenth-century Gaelic writing often describes manly calf muscles, implying walking and running abilities above the average but it never commemorates organized athletics such as one saw in nineteenth-century Highland Games. The term "sportsman" connoted hunting by the privileged classes more than anything else. However, Gaelic stories of immense antiquity do mention contests of manly strength that must surely have persisted in rural Gaelic Scotland until 1800. The other main feature of

Highland sporting society, apart from deer hunting with deer hounds and (where possible) horse racing, was shinty, which all classes took part in. *Caraid nan Gàidheal* includes Finlay the Piper's description of the annual New Year shinty match held in the area of Glendessary.[10] This article was reproduced in the Antigonish *Casket* on 30 December 1852.[11] (The Reverend Norman MacLeod had Finlay the Piper summon the players from their homes with *"A mhnathan a' Ghlinne, nach mithich dhuibh éiridh."*[12] ("women of the Glen, isn't it time for you to rise"). When the forty players were being drawn up the piper played *"Ghlas-mheur"* ("Finger Lock"), and for the first dance after the day was over he played *"Ruidhle-thulachain"* ("Reel of Tulloch") followed by countless others. After the shinty match and refreshments, MacLeod wrote that *"chaidh a' cheathairne a chaitheamh na cloiche neirt"* – in my translation, "the group went to cast the stone of strength," which is the only other sport mentioned. There is no reason to think that the author had to purloin the idea of putting the stone of strength from any non-Gaelic source or that, some time after 1830 when the article was published, he had placed a nineteenth-century pastime into a late-eighteenth-century context (which is where the Glendessary shinty match fits). It was obviously a fieldstone, but nonetheless this element of the story may authenticate "stone of strength casting" as a rural late-eighteenth-century Gaelic pastime, the honest forerunner of the modern shotput.

In Gaelic Inverness County, Cape Breton, an early reference to shinty sticks (*caman*) appears around 1830 in the poetry of Alasdair MacDonald (Big Painter) (1829–1910), son of a Keppoch Bohuntin man. Referring to Broad Cove and Mabou Coal Mines in immigrant times, MacDonald wrote, *"S mo luaidh na fir nach 'eil beo/A bheireadh dhuinn duais/Bho fhuaim nan caman/Gu luath 's a' ghloin' air a' bhord."*[13] (Here the bàrd praises the kind old folk who quickly rewarded the young people who had been rattling their shinty sticks; how soon there would be a refreshing glass on the table.[13] Effie (MacCorcadail) Rankin, Mabou, suggested that this was a ritual of some sort rather than an actual game of shinty, a view that finds support in the "striking parties" referred to by Malcolm MacQueen in *Skye Pioneers & "The Island"*(1929). MacQueen drew on the memories of a Miss Margaret MacQueen of Orwell, Prince Edward Island, age eighty-four, daughter of a Skye woman from Uig who married in 1839. According to Miss MacQueen, striking parties were a New Year's Day custom of long standing when the young people in a Gaelic district went "armed with sticks" through the settlement, surrounding a house and beating the log walls with their sticks while singing a Gaelic song demanding the customary Highland exaction (whisky if possible). The author gave the traditional song in a Lallans translation as if to intensify its Scottishness.[14] According to Malcolm MacQueen the custom died with the disappearance of the log house.[15]

The earlier allusion to what was happening in New York concerns the "first Sportive Meeting," arranged in 1836 by the Highland Society of New York. Gerald Redmond discovered that "the activities seem to have been confined to games of *caman*, or shinty, followed by dancing accompanied by the bagpipes, but it represented an expression of Scottish patriotic feeling."[16] Perhaps if deer hunting, rowing, wrestling, stone throwing, and horse racing had been added, the New York sportive meeting of Caledonians would have covered the main elements of Highland sporting tradition (it was too late for indigenous Gaelic sword exercises, which would certainly have been part of any fair representation of Highland outdoor activities in 1740). Redmond, who had a declared preoccupation in exploring the origins of American track and field and the influence on it of what he believed to have been Highland sports, knew that "other professional runners" and foot races and walking contests had been common during the first half of the nineteenth century. It appears, however, that the organized nature of the Highland games may have been novel, and that the appearance of the New York Athletic Club in 1868 has, in that sense, to be seen as a product of the urban American Highlander organizers' later efforts at presenting a mingling of athletics and what was seen as Gaelic tradition. In post-Civil War America Scottish gatherings were held in New York, Newark, Boston, Philadelphia, and Providence and perhaps elsewhere.

By the 1860s Highland games included foot races, hurdle races, hop-step-and-jump, running high jump, standing leap, broad jump, vaulting with a pole and dancing competitions. The last most commonly involved the Gillie Caluim and Highland Fling but occasionally also Reel dancing (possibly dancing by individuals to reels) under various headings. The piping competitions almost certainly were traditional, as presumably were the occasional "singing of Gaelic songs"; the stone-throwing events may also fall into the category of tradition, although weights were by now standardized and metal. The best-dressed Highlander class was of course as contrived as the whole games idea. Where the long-hafted hammer and the caber came from is open to question. By the 1890s in Prince Edward Island, bicycle races and vaulting with a pole were standard fare. In 1895, for example, the three bicycle races were reported in the Charlottetown *Herald* of 7 August 1895 as the "most exciting" events of the day.

To assess just how inauthentic the Prince Edward Island Caledonian Club annual gatherings of the 1890s were, one has only to compare the listed events with those of the "Benevolent Irish Society Pincnic" (*sic*) held on Monday, 6 August 1894 at Scotchfort, Prince Edward Island. The events reported included the running long jump, pole vaulting, a hurdle race, running high jump, hundred-yard dash, putting the light stone, throwing the light hammer, and a tug-o-war (in which the Irish were beaten by an all-comer group made up mostly of Highlanders). The "pincnic" was only Irish in that it ran a "Best violin music (Irish air)" competition and a "Best Irish

step-dancing, championship of the province" competition, which one chari-
tably accepts as traditional. Otherwise, add the caber, the Highland Fling, the
Gille Caluim and piping and you have the standard Highland Gathering,
immediately recognizable to the organizers of the first Braemar Highland
Gathering thirty years earlier.

If the same few "Highland" events had been added to the Charlottetown
Labour Day games of 9 September 1903, for example, or to the sports of the
4th Regiment, which were held on the Halifax Common in June 1868, there
would have been Highland games.[17]

Generously interpreted, these were Highland games in which real and
imagined Celticism were reinforced; more accurately, they were alien athletic events with quasi- and sometimes real Gaelic cultural graftings. For my
purposes, however, the more important question is how, if at all, this highly
organized sporting event, which in its early days included some genuine elements of Highlandism, distorted understanding of Gaelic traditional piping
and dancing.

In the United States there was a hiatus in the staging of Highland games
in the 1880s[18] when, having perhaps introduced an organized format to professional sporting events in urban America, they were superseded by track
and field organizations took over.[19] By the 1880s a report from the *Scottish-
American Journal* stated that "the picnic features, which used to be so enjoy-
able have been abandoned ... people are getting tired of seeing the everlast-
ing Highland Fling and Sword Dance, to the exclusion of all others."[20]

The games met with this reaction in Nova Scotia as well. The Antigonish
Highland Games of 1898 attracted only about six hundred people, although
the weather was fine. The *Casket*'s reporter noted the fall-off, comparing it
with the crowds that had shown up "a dozen or so" years earlier. In mentioning that professional athlete W.F. Marsh of Boston, had been on a winning streak at the 1898 games, the reporter noted the importance of sporting
"stars" to Highland Games.[21] The same waning of interest appeared also in
Cape Breton in the first half of the twentieth century, but questions about the
continuity of Highland Games in the province would now certainly elicit the
proud example of the Antigonish Highland Games and their remarkable
durability.

Most people no longer question the authenticity of Highland games. But
the long-extinct competitions involving the Highland Fling in Sydney and
Inverness in the 1920s have been overlooked.[22] Neither the Gille Caluim nor
the Highland Fling as danced today has any traditional function, in Inverness
County or anywhere else in Gaelic Nova Scotia; they are display dances that
bear almost no resemblance to the traditional step-dancing that persists in
the province's *Gàidhealtachd*.

In Nova Scotia and elsewhere in Canada, the Highland games idea took
deeper root than in the United States by virtue of the British connection.

Highland gatherings often involved special visits by the vice-regal and the prominent, processions with pipers and military brass bands,[23] speeches, and committed Britishness in general. At times, the games even appear to have been presented as the leading edge of the new track and field sports.

In 1867 at the Scottish games sponsored by Jones's Wood New York Caledonian Club, "a sort of human kangaroo, from Canada – with the aid of a pole, actually leaped 9 feet and 3 inches from the ground" (this was probably Edinburgh-born athlete George Goldie, 1841–1920, who was known as the father of the pole vault).[24] Pole-vaulting was not indigenous to the Gaelic-speaking Scotch community. However, when the famous Antigonish Highland Games were begun in 1863, the organizers had another purpose in mind. Discussing the work of the Antigonish Highland Society in 1922, John L. MacDougall (c.1851–1928), a Gaelic-speaking Cape Breton lawyer, wrote, "The games held annually are only part of its work. The ambition of the society is to make the Antigonish Highland Festival the Braemar of Nova Scotia, to revive the ancient tongue and to perpetuate the ancient customs."[25]

The records of the games run by the Antigonish Highland Society are neither complete nor as detailed as they might be, but newspaper reporting (also incomplete, with major gaps in the 1860s) offers useful information that, combined with local family history, throws some of the games into a clearer light. They were in essence an English phenomenon but with Highland overtones that reveal an underlying and quite different Scottish Gaelic tradition, which the cynic would say had yet to be purged.

The Antigonish *Casket* of Thursday, 17 July 1862 reported that, three days earlier the Antigonish Rangers marched through the street headed by "Mr John McQuarrie, Piper, who played beautifully on the Bagpipes several martial airs of the Gael and wore the Highland dress which he won as a prize at the Scotch Gathering at Halifax two years ago. The Company were afterwards drilled in a neighboring field."[26]

In September 1862 John McQuarrie competed in "Highland Pipe Music" at the Halifax Caledonia Club Games held at "A. Downs Esq's, North West Arm." The usual procession marched from "Wallace's" to "Queen's Wharf" in "the garb of old Gaul," embarked on the "Micmac" and sailed "up the Arm." The band of the 17th Regiment (an infantry brass band) played and prizes were awarded by the Honourable A. Keith, chief of the Caledonia Club. The competition events were the usual ones, with an extra sack race and a wheelbarrow race thrown in. From the Highland point of view there were two categories of "Best Highland Costume," adults and boys; there was "Dancing Gillie Callum" (won by a W.H. Anderson) and the Highland Fling. The winner of the "3rd (extra)" prize for "Highland Pipe Music" was John McQuarrie, who got six dollars.[27]

John McQuarrie's third prize may mean nothing since there may only have been three competitors. But be that as it may, other family information about him shows that, at least in terms of piping, these Halifax games had not yet solidified in modern form. McQuarrie's music and his competition accomplishments were appreciated in Antigonish and beyond, in what was the county of Sydney, perhaps, because they showed tradition could stand up to modernity. John McQuarrie was an immigrant piper who had left Eigg in the 1850s.[28] His son, Hector Angus (who preferred to be known as Angus H.), born in 1862, married when he was fifty-two and in 1918 fathered my informant, Angus MacQuarrie, former warden of Antigonish County.

Angus, who had visited Eigg and talked family with local historian Hugh MacKinnon, said that his paternal grandfather, the piper John MacQuarrie,[29] was himself the descendant of a MacQuarrie who was known as "the big piper" and who flourished in MacCrimmon times. John MacQuarrie was nothing if not a traditional Gaelic musician. His grandson said that the old piper had more music than subsequent generations, and that he was part of the old Gaelic tradition, in no way connected with the modern literately learned school of piping.[30] Angus MacQuarrie volunteered that the immigrant would have been "rough on the top music." But in light of new thought on the playing of certain elements of *ceòl mór* (and of fingering), this observation may be questionable. The Halifax gathering, then, was ready to acknowledge traditional-style piping, grudgingly or not. In Antigonish society John McQuarrie had a prominent sponsor in the person of Bishop Dr Colin F. MacKinnon, who, according to the piper's great-grandson, A.M. MacQuarrie, imported a set of Glen bagpipes around 1858 for his fellow Eigg man.

The first Highland games sponsored by the Antigonish Highland Society, held on October 1863, were none too traditional; predictably, they included the light and heavy hammer, light and heavy stone, the twenty-foot caber, running high leap, standing (long) jump, running (long) jump, a foot race, playing the bagpipes, dancing the Highland Fling, and two novelty events, the wheelbarrow and sack races.[31] Perhaps it was only because they lacked the full slate of field events that they might be described, however optimistically, as slightly traditional. Nonetheless, noteworthy here as elsewhere is the absence of any pipe band.

Antigonish Highland Society treasurer and *Casket* editor John Boyd (son of Angus Boyd, an immigrant Gael from South Uist) wrote that he was "quite convinced ... that the 'sons of the heather' who might have witnessed these sports, would have good reason to feel proud of their countrymen and their descendants in this and the adjoining Counties."[32] This remark does not suggest that local Highlanders took no part in the event, but it does hint that the whole games were a major staged event that was at least as important to the watchers as to the participants, and that was intended to put "Highlandism" into a modern British framework, the sort of framework that permitted control and inevitably led to the denigration of the older Gaelic traditions. That the Antigonish organizers were themselves Gaels shows some of the problems facing the old way of life as little as a lifetime away from the earliest immigration.

Developing professionalism in athletics inevitably added to the non-community aspect of the Highland games, something that was completely missing from the local Glendessary New Year's Day event that Finlay Piper had described long before.

The excitement generated by the first Antigonish Highland Games is conveyed in an article that appeared in Boyd's *Casket* on New Year's Day, 1863. Members of the Highland Society of the county of Sydney, "attired in their Highland Garbs, recently imported from Scotland," met at one Duncan Chisholm's store on 30 December and set off in a procession that was led by banner and "cheered by the martial Pibroch of the Gael." They took a sleigh ride through Antigonish to Cunningham's Hotel where there were speeches, toasts, and conviviality until four in the morning. The *Casket* article goes on to mention the upcoming Highland Games, eleven months away.[33] A notice that appeared in the newspaper on 1 October 1863 lists the events for the games, but the issue that must have contained the report of the actual happening is missing and the winner and placers of the bagpiping contest are unknown. (The other events were also open to public participation, effectively barring no one except perhaps in the Highland Fling which few if any could have known. Even if that was a traditional step-dance "hornpipe" like the Flowers of Edinburgh in South West Margaree, its dancing may have been limited to those who had had formal Gaelic dancing tuition.)

The 1868 games added a number of events including the sword dance and the Highland Reel, and a prize was added for the wearer of the best Highland costume. The inclusion of the Highland Reel may have resulted from low turnouts for the modern dances. Presumably, with the local Highland Society setting the example, those competing for the best Highland costume imported their quaint dress patriotically from Scotland.[34] That Highland clothing should be given as a prize to John McQuarrie at Halifax games of 1860, indeed that the games were held at all, must surely have had a salutary effect on the middle-class pro-British Gaels of Antigonish at the time and led to their foray into the world of Highland games. Beyond the occasional presence of Highland regiments and a small and diffused population of settled Gaels, Halifax was emphatically not a Scotch Highland community; Antigonish, on the other hand, certainly was, although by no means exclusively.

As for the Antigonish Gaelic middle class, even there one found a persistent strand of Gaelic traditionalism. The standing member of the Nova Scotia Assembly for Antigonish County (as Sydney County was called after 1863) from 1851 to 1867 and member of the province's Legislative Council from 1867 until his death in 1892 was the Honourable John McKinnon of William's Point, outside Antigonish. McKinnon was the son of a Scots-born

Roman Catholic immigrant and the older brother of Archbishop Dr Colin F. McKinnon, the benefactor of piper John McQuarrie. John McKinnon was an "agriculturist"[35] as well as a dance-music bagpiper.[36] His granddaughter, Mary Isabel (Grant) Ormond, born to his daughter Margaret in 1860 and raised in Mabou from 1861, recollected: "Once upon a time, many years ago, – I was three – my mother went home to Williams Point, Antigonish, on a visit, taking me with her ... Grandpa MacKinnon played the bagpipes and the boys and girls in the neighbourhood gathered in at times, dancing to the reels."[37]

MacKinnon's part in the initiating and organizing of the first Antigonish Highland Games is unknown. So too is his musical involvement with his fellow piper John McQuarrie, but both families were from Eigg.[38] Furthermore, Bishop MacKinnon, John MacKinnon's younger brother, took a part in resolving John McQuarrie's difficulties over his land in Highfield, so it is unlikely that musical links did not exist, possibly going back to the Hebrides.[39] In clarification it must be said that Reel dancing in Antigonish in 1863, as in 1900 and 1940, was primarily the Scotch Four, with traditional step-dancing setting steps.[40] Even in 1995, when the Four is dead, reel timing is still the favourite in Antigonish for step-dancing, although suffering the constraints imposed on any free form by classroom transmission.

The sword dance I assume to have had genuinely Gaelic Scotch origins although I have seen no mention of it in eighteenth-century Gaelic literature and the Highland Reel, which is often mentioned in Gaelic sources in 1750–1800, could not have been anything but Gaelic. As noted above, what was meant by "Highland reel" in the Antigonish competition was almost always individual rather than group dancing, to one or several reels played on whatever instrument the Highland Society, or perhaps the competitor, chose for the dance. The available record shows that prizes were awarded to individuals, not groups. The "Scots Gathering" of the Highland Society of Nova Scotia held at Patrick Goulding's at Bedford Basin in 1868 included "Dancing Highland Reel,"[41] for which the prize was three dollars (for the Gillie Callum and the Highland Fling it was five dollars). The following year's games were held at McNab's Island off Halifax, and they too included reel dancing. This McNab's Island event was won by Piper-Major McKenzie of the 78th Regiment (he had finished second to one of his pipers in the Highland Fling). Obvious questions come to mind; was the reel traditional Scotch step-dancing, and what was the reason for its inclusion? The army may have been drilled in new Highland dancing, if such existed by that time, but in the case of Antigonish in particular, was the reel put in as something traditional to encourage public participation in these early games, or because not enough local Gaels had bothered to learn how to do the appropriate "Highland" dances (especially the Highland Fling) for the show, or both?

A similar adjustment to include a traditional pastime in the slate of events was made in Pictou County at much the same time. The first annual gathering of the Pictou Caledonia Club for competition in Highland games was held at or near New Glasgow on Tuesday 11 September 1866. The gathering was advertised in the *Eastern Chronicle* of 16 August above the signature of a John MacKay, secretary, and the results were reported by the paper on 13 September. The events were the usual ones with the addition of "Quoits – 10 competitors." There was also the "Pole Leap – ten competitors." From the Highland point of view these first games gave prizes in "Highland Fling – 4 competitors, Gillie Callum – 4 competitors, Highland Costume, Gaelic Song – 8 competitors,[42] Gaelic Reading – 3 competitors and Highland Pipe Music – 14 competitors,"[43] a fairly rich diet of "tradition" by comparison with the other games.

In the 1860s Gaelic was still a spoken language in Pictou County among all classes of Scots. "English is the prevailing language, but the Gaelic is universally spoken. The bag-pipe and spinning-wheel are still heard discoursing sweet music within their dwellings."[44]

The reporter of the 1866 games remarked on the "exceedingly good pipe music played by several little boys under 12 years of age. – A third prize was contributed for one of these by 'D. Ross Esq., Halifax'" (possibly the Donald Ross mentioned above, importer of the Glen military pipes), "to which contributions were added by several other gentlemen." Not all the games listed in the program could be fitted in for want of time, but there is no record of the cancellations.

From a traditionalist's stance, the relatively small number of competitors in the Highland Fling and the Gille Caluim in New Glasgow suggests that few local Gaels knew these dances. Both events were won by William H. Anderson of Halifax, but the more intriguing outcome is the second-place finish in the Gillie Callum by "John Cummings, Piedmont." Piedmont is in eastern Pictou County, at the time probably every bit as traditionally Gaelic as Inverness County (the Cummingses are long gone now and there is nothing to associate them with any dancing or dancing school). The piping results were John McKenzie, Halifax, first prize (ten dollars, the second highest sum of cash awarded as first prize), Hugh Fraser, second (four dollars), and nine-year-old David W. Beaton, third prize.

An earlier *Eastern Chronicle*, had mentioned under "local items" that a Scottish club had been formed (presumably recently), that games were imminent, and that "the Glengarry [Ontario] champion was also expected to be there and he would probably 'astonish the natives' by an exhibition of extraordinary skill and strength."[45] If nothing else, this exposes Ontario as another source for the form of such gatherings. It also lightly emphasizes an inclination on the part of the organizers to present these games as a spectator more than a competitor event.[46] The Ontario Glengarry champion was

R.R. MacLennan, who stood six feet eight inches tall.[47] At the 1866 gathering there was a crowd of about six thousand in the enclosed grounds at any given time, and about ten thousand in all entered the grounds, "the largest assemblage of people ever witnessed in Pictou County." The Scottish clubs of Halifax, Antigonish, and Prince Edward Island "were well represented by true 'sons of the Heather,' some in Highland costume, which added additional interest to the days' proceedings"[48] (presumably because they looked so unusual).

By 1867 the Pictou County games had dropped the Gaelic song but had become more traditional in another way. In that year there was professional competition in "Scotch Reels and Strathspeys" (musical instrument unspecified, group or individual dances also unspecified). In the "Reels and Strathspeys" first prize was awarded to J.D. Donaldson (five dollars), hinting that the competition was for individuals. The piping was won by John Patterson, second prize going to Donald MacKenzie[49] and third to David W. Beaton, aged 10. In the Gillie Callum first again was William H. Anderson, second, Duncan Robertson, and third, a MacKinnon boy aged 8.[50] That the third prize in piping went to a boy suggests that many adult pipers did not compete. An eight-year-old coming third in Gillie Callum proves early training in this dance but does not point either to traditional or formal method, although the latter is the more likely. If there was a formal "Highland" dance teaching system it may have been in old dancing schools run by the dancing masters, such as existed in Inverness County.

Formal instruction in the modern dancing elements of the Highland games appears to have been available in Ontario at much the same time as these early New Glasgow Highland games. In Lucknow, in western Ontario, the Caledonian Society of Western Ontario was formed in 1874 by Dr Donald Alexander McCrimmon, MD (1836–1917).[51] McCrimmon, who probably stood in cousinly relation to the famous piping families, was chief of this society until he left Lucknow. His family "were taught Highland dancing" and his sons "won many medals for their fine interpretations of the dances."[52] McCrimmon's adaptation to the novel Highlandism extended to inducing Donald Dinnie, the leading athlete of Scotland, and William MacLennan, the champion Scottish piper, "to visit America and be present at one of their gatherings."[53]

The first Pictou County gatherings were similar to the modern Highland games in certain prominent features. These were the invited presence of top Highland athletes as financial attractions, and the circuit of events on which men like W.H. Anderson, McLennan, and Dinnie travelled to compete. In 1869 and 1870 members of the 78th Highland Regiment did well in the Highland events at the Halifax gatherings,[54] but there was a civilian presence as well, Colin McGillivray and Dougald Cameron, both of Antigonish, earning good income for a day's sport.

In many of these early Maritime gatherings it appears that sops were thrown at expedient times through newspaper advertising preceding the event to true Gaelic tradition. When piping was involved, it could be argued that it was solidly traditional in any case, because literate learning of piping in Maritime Canada was still rare. For Reel dancing the same is almost certainly true, but for the Highland Fling and perhaps even for the mid-nineteenth-century Gillie Callum, there is room for doubt.

Records of the various Caledonian Clubs' Highland games in the Maritimes are poor; newspapers are often the best source of information. One difficulty, however, is that the newspapers tended to present a limited, socially acceptable, somewhat stereotyped image of what was going on. The frequency of visits to the events by prominent British personages even in the twentieth century[55] shows how keen the organizers were to establish the Maritime gatherings as socially acceptable in English terms. Even as a Dominion, the country was highly conscious of empire.

The *Acadian Recorder* of 4 September 1867 declared that, "all over the Provinces, at this beautiful season of the year, these Scotch picnics are being held, and appear to be decidedly 'the rage.' " The term "Pic Nic" pops up in the first Antigonish *Casket* in 1852, referring to an event held by the Sons of Temperance, and occurs often thereafter, but it connotes nothing of the structured formal competitiveness of the games, although there may well have been overlap in content. One "Pic Nic" that featured Highland piping was held in Westville, Pictou County, in August 1869; the weather deterred New Glasgow and Pictou folk but five hundred showed up from Albion Mines. "After partaking of the bounteous repast, the company separated to enjoy themselves, some to dance to the music of the pibroch, persistently if not skilfully played – others took a turn on a revolving swing."

In two instances, both almost within living memory, the *Charlottetown Herald* made comments in connection with the Highland games that point to the illusion of living Gaelic tradition in the big event. The first concerned the games sponsored by the Caledonian Club and held at Charlottetown on Thursday, 10 August 1899. The promotional advertising announced that the events would be enlivened by "banner and pageant, fife and drums,"[56] – formula writing. The reporting of the event itself mentioned that the club members and other clansmen marched to the venue from the club rooms in bonnet and plaid "wearing sprigs of heather," and that the "air resounded with the music of pibroch and violin, and the lads and lasses danced awa wi ae anither." The writer, who may have been a Lowlander, went on to report "Col Irving's prize for step-dancing – one of the prettiest events of the gathering. Miss Belle Paton was awarded the medal. The remaining contestants were Geo. Arbuckle Wᵐ McLean, D. Lamont, Springton."[57]

Although there is no definition of "step-dancing," this result followed the customary "Highland" gathering dances, "Dancing Highland Fling" (Belle

Paton; "city" was second), and "Dancing *Ghillie Callum*," so it is not unreasonable to assume the same meaning for the term then as today, and that this was the real cultural MacCoy.

Twenty years later, on 13 August 1919, the "Scottish Gathering," again held at Charlottetown, consisted of twelve published events. Although not one of them was "Highland" (no caber, no hammer, no stone), the *Charlottetown Herald* reported "Specialties – Highland Fling, Ghillie Callum, Reel of Tulloch, Reel of Four, Step Dances by Scottish Lads and Lassies" (the day's events ended with horse races, three classes of "trot" and one of "pace").

The "Reel of Four" had long been associated with the authentically Gaelic in the Maritime *Gàidhealtachd*. This one certainly was one of the several variants of the old Gaelic step-dance circular Reel. The casual mention of the violin for dancing in 1899 is a fair indicator of traditional Gaelic dancing. Another instance of dancing to the fiddle crops up at the Prince Edward Island games, which were held at the head of St Peter's Bay in August 1898. The report in the Charlottetown Herald states that "the best of order prevailed: the pipers and band enlivened the scene with choice strains, while the best of violin music was furnished to those who patronized the dancing booth."[58]

The mention of the dancing booth points to the picnic atmosphere of this gathering, an atmosphere that may have been pervasive in Highland games held in the more rural Gaelic-speaking areas of the Maritimes.[59] The St Peter's area was thoroughly Scotch Gaelic and at the turn of the present century, like all the rural Gaelic areas of Prince Edward Island, it was as culturally Gaelic as Inverness County. The kin relationships connecting the east of the island to the west of Cape Breton were still strong. Today Gaelic is no longer passed on in the family in Prince Edward Island, but, as in Cape Breton, Gaelic flavoured fiddling and step-dancing continue with a typically modern and at times commercial vigour.

Although it didn't happen often, at least two of Nova Scotia's urban Highland gatherings featured Highland regimental involvement. The annual Scottish gatherings of the Highland Society of Nova Scotia took place at Bedford Basin on 25 August 1868 and at McNab's Island in 1869 and 1870. In the latter two years official pipers of the 78th Highlanders took part.[60] In 1869 the military pipers were Pipe-Major R. MacKenzie[61] and pipers Alexander Cameron, Alexander Stalves, and a MacMillan.[62] In 1870 pipers J. Campbell and J. Matheson of the 78th competed,[63] making up, one assumes, the official regimental complement of six.

The writer who in 1867 classified the early Nova Scotian Highland games with picnics made the point, perhaps inadvertently, that in addition to the advertised events, other traditional activities were going on at these games. Unfortunately there is no research to suggest, for example, that the well-patronized dancing booth in the St Peter's Bay games was a widespread feature.

The view of *Celtic Magazine* editor Alexander MacKenzie of the Canadian Highland games, including piping, around 1880 appears in W.L. Manson's *The Highland Bagpipe* (1901):

"In Canada, says the late Mr Alexander MacKenzie, the jumping, tossing the caber, stone throwing, and various other Highland competitions, would do credit to some of the best athletes at home gatherings, although, he adds, the pipe music was nowhere. Since he travelled through Canada [1879–80], however, there have been great improvements, and the visits of leading pipers from home have borne good fruit. Canada now has her own Highland pipers and dancers, reared on her own soil but on the home model, not perhaps so good as the best at home, but better than the average. Scotland abroad is more Highland than Scotland at home, and the hope of the future of the language and music lies as much in Canada and Australia as it does in Argyllshire, Perthshire, or Inverness-shire."[64]

As noted earlier, MacKenzie's inadequate report of his conversation with Squire John MacKay in Pictou County betrays, among other flaws, a set of preconceptions about piping that precluded objectivity about tradition. Manson's remark that Canada "now has her own Highland pipers and dancers, reared on her own soil but on the home model" is typical of that last attitude. By the turn of the century the new "Highland" style had begun to be imported. Who the leading Scottish pipers were who came to Canada between 1880 and 1901 is not precisely known, but Dan Angus Beaton's repetition of the story that several top Scottish pipers adjudicated at the Charlottetown Highland games piping competition in 1895 suggests that it was true.

From Scots-born Pipe-Majaor Stephen MacKinnon's point of view – the literately trained piper's point of view – a renaissance of piping "swept not only Scotland and Canada but the United States as well."[65] He wrote that the old Highland gathering had taken "a fresh lease on life" as new gatherings were added to the "old games circuit once confined to Scottish centres in Quebec, Ontario and the New England States. [The old circuit] has widened to include all Canada. In the old days professional pipers and dancers made the round of the games, the tour proving a pleasant and profitable summer sideline for the topnotchers."[66] MacKinnon, it must be observed, omitted the only living *Gàidhealtachd* in North America from his "Scottish centres."

Stephen MacKinnon, who had emigrated in 1911, conveniently – and in a sense quite innocently – emphasized the clubby nature of competition piping, particularly the limiting of competition to the few, something that also occurred in many of the so-called Highland sports. The same old faces were seen meet after meet, year after year. As a pupil of MacDougall Gillies[67] in Glasgow, and like Sandy Boyd, a pupil of Glasgow-based John MacColl,[68]

MacKinnon accepted the primacy of technique in piping and assumed, along with modern competition piping judges, that the piping competitors were the cream of the crop. MacKinnon took the time to list some of the old pipers and dancers who had been prominent on the old Canadian games circuit – Willie MacLennan, Bob Ireland, Farquhar Beaton, Fred Riddell, and John Mathieson. Given his attitude, MacKinnon's statements about revival, particularly in Canadian band piping, were correct. He cited the existence in Canada of about sixty bands in 1932, doubtless a great increase since 1900.

Like Sandy Boyd later, MacKinnon was in every way the product of a feisty time and environment. Thomason's *Ceòl Mór* (1900) was new, the Pibroch Society was beginning to flex its literate muscles under Thomason's successors, and Glasgow had become one of the major, self-confident centres of new piping. It was a world stretching proudly to formularize piping at all levels, from the Boys' Brigade up. It is possible that, under these improver pressures, some of the famous pipers changed some of their fingerings in *ceòl beag*; Archie MacNeil, the blind piper from Govan, said that John MacColl, champion and (Highland) dancer, played doublings on B and C with two "d" grace-notes, as they were frequently written in William MacKay's *Complete Tutor* (1840), rather than with a "g" and a "d". Mac-Coll's pupil Sandy Boyd certainly played in the latter way.

16 Traditional Pipers in Nova Scotia

Although the forces for change from traditional to modern literately learned piping were strong, even within the Nova Scotia *Gàidhealtachd*, old-style piping thrived in the rural environment until well within living memory. The modernist, although often a Highlander, was typically English speaking, or at least bilingual Gaelic-English, and operated through the medium of English. The places where modern ways were promoted were the towns. Yet even in places like Sydney and Antigonish (and, to a lesser extent, New Glasgow), and especially at the country borders, the barrier of language was able to ensure confident cultural retention. Within walking distance of the site of Antigonish's Highland games, within walking distance of Port Hawkesbury, Sydney, and New Glasgow, there were hundreds of families for whom Gaelic and its old ways were amply satisfying. There are many memories in Cape Breton of returned relatives who were ridiculed for affecting the New England accent and who claimed to have forgotten their Gaelic.

It may be difficult to imagine proud self-confidence for a language and way of life that have been systematically denigrated, and that were turning in upon themselves in parts of Scotland with not a little baffled resentment in the 1860s, but is nonetheless what existed in rural Nova Scotia. For a century after the immigrations the security of relatively large (if not always fertile or manageable) acreages, undreamt of by most Gaels in Scotland, and supported a social confidence, including ideas of social superiority, still to be discussed, in Inverness County, but that had been common in eighteenth-century Highland Scotland.

Because the bagpipes had become Scotland's national instrument, known in every nook and cranny of Britain's empire, the direct and indirect forces ranged against traditional bagpiping, even in rural Nova Scotia, were vastly more formidable than those confronting traditional fiddling. Nonetheless, where the old society persisted the old traditional piping survived, long into the time of near-instant communications and easy travel. In what follows a small but important sample of these pipers is given, showing the character and function of their music in the dying days of a self-confident European culture transposed to the American New World.

In general pipers are more often mentioned than fiddlers in the published record of Highland immigrants to the New World. "Violinist" may have struck writers as pretentious and "fiddler" as devious, but "piper" was redolent of Highland Scotland and if only by name the immigrant piper is mentioned, whether in pioneer Nova Scotia or Saskatchewan.[1] Unfortunately, sources seldom mention more than a presence. Sometimes in this century there is a photograph. Lore conveys the descriptive "piper" down to the present quite often in Nova Scotia, attaching it to the non-piping descendants sometimes to the fourth and fifth generations of some early musician about whom next to nothing is known except that he must have been a piper. The "piper" families MacMaster and MacLellan in Judique are two examples.

In any case, immigrant pipers, fiddlers, and step-dancers in the Gaelic New World, especially Cape Breton, about whom nothing has been written far outnumber those who are mentioned in print. J.L. MacDougall, for example, who was in a position to elaborate on a fellow MacDougall, Donald MacDougall, who emigrated from Arisaig to South West Margaree around 1828, described him as an excellent piper but left his repertoire and musical functions to be guessed at.[2] Across Lake Ainslie from where the Protestant MacKinnon pipers later flourished, Allan MacCormack, an immigrant Gael from South Uist via Prince Edward Island, settled in 1808. MacDougall only gave his name and details of family but no musical detail; family information gives him as a piper.[3] Dr Hoodie MacDonald's cultural notes are probably nothing if not typical of many Highland immigrant families in the Gaelic Maritime provinces and further afield. In addition, the notion that one's family was gentlemanly, a characteristic of so many Highlanders in Scotland long after Culloden, extended to what is left of Gaelic Cape Breton and even now crops up time and again in what appear to be materially unprepossessing surroundings.

In nineteenth-century Gaelic Nova Scotia there were three discernible groups of traditional Gaelic pipers. First were what have come to be called the "hereditary," or great, pipers, almost certainly all ear/*canntaireachd* learned though tutored, one presumes, in fingering, complex grace-notings, and in repertoire. Secondly, and by far in the majority, are the community pipers who were ear-learned with or without anyone's idea of "correct" fingering and grace-noting, and whose repertoires were self-imposed and directed to satisfy personal and community tastes. Thirdly, there was a sub-set of the majority, traditional pipers who were functionally indistinguish-able from the traditional community pipers, except that they could read music. This subset, like the last of the Gaelic-speaking fiddlers of today, comprised people who at first learned by ear but subsequently, through whatever agency, learned or were taught how to read music (fiddle or bag-pipe) and therewith widened their repertoires. This group forms a bridge between the old Gaelic tradition and modern bagpiping.[4]

Whatever the technical abilities of the community pipers, and these var-ied widely, what the Gaelic-speaking piper in the Nova Scotia *Gàidheal-tachd* brought from the second half of the eighteenth century was a prime function, the production of step-dance music (work music, for haying or rowing, is doubtless part of the same rhythmical concept). This required con-fident and continuous music played to specific rhythms. Having music in you in Gaelic Cape Breton still means having a large repertoire and being able quickly to memorize new material by ear.[5] As with step-dance fiddling, musicality inevitably implies the ability to improvise, adapt, innovate, and, above all, keep going. Countless liberties are taken with compositions; for the non-playing dancer they may often be improvements. For the ear-learned traditional musician, the absence of a script freed music and spawned what in modern piping are officially accepted as "settings." No tune may ever be played the same way, but when function is the supreme dictate there is much greater room for spontaneous alteration. At its extreme there are almost new tunes, new "turns," or phrases that the musician adds or substitutes for no reason other than that they come into his mind and his fingers are appropri-ately linked to his musical thoughts.[6]

According to Allan Gillis, Alex the piper MacDonald was able to play pipe music in the traditional and in the modern styles, whichever his audi-ence preferred.[7] MacDonald and Archibald Beaton, Angus Campbell Beat-on, Willie the piper Gillis, Allan MacFarlane, and many others, fall into the literate but traditional category. Black Angus MacDonald (1849–1939) of Melrose Hill[8] in Inverness County, however was non-literate and deliberat-edly stayed that way.[9] As a man of about sixty he paid temporary lip service to literate music learning by obtaining a book of instruction, but he never took bagpiping literacy seriously and continued to pipe by ear.[10] Countless other pipers like him existed in immigrant Gaelic Cape Breton. They are the bedrock of New World Gaelic tradition.

BLACK ANGUS MACDONALD

Of a very large number of Gaelic-speaking Nova Scotia bagpipers, Black Angus MacDonald is by all public and private accounts a remarkable example of a Cape Breton Highland community piper. His life and music began in the immigrant period and lasted into the increasingly Anglicized twentieth century. He played the bagpipes until he was about eighty, so today competent memories of his actual playing belong to men and women of seventy and over and that of his playing only as an old man.

Through memories of Black Angus the value and function of the old Highland rural piper emerges along with the important corollary for modern students of the subject, the standards and discrimination of his audiences in the Gaelic community. Mary Gillis,[11] for example, daughter-in-law of the bard Malcolm Gillis (teacher, fiddler, and piper) in South West Margaree, immediately lumped Black Angus and Allan MacFarlane from Upper Margaree together as great pipers. While unable to use modern technical assessments of his playing, she had heard many pipers at her father-in-law's house and used the same standards she would have applied to a traditional Gaelic fiddler – standards that embody a superior sense of rhythm and timing than those of modern piping, although most Gaels have learned to discount that aspect of their critical faculty in the presence of modern self-styled experts.[12]

Three generations of the family left Brae Lochaber in Scotland in 1831, including the old widow Anne MacDonald of the Bohuntin and Crannachan families, seven of her eight children (including Archibald, Black Angus's father) and at least two of her grandchildren. Anne MacDonald's husband, Black Alasdair, who had died in Scotland, was a distant descendant of the Killiechonate MacDonalds.[13] From a social point of view the family's pride in its ninth-generation descent from the first MacDonald of Killiechonate, its nearer descent from Iain Dubh of Bohuntin, and its strong connection with the Crannachan family (all old Keppoch stock) is typical of the Brae Lochaber people who came out to the Mabou area.[14] Whatever their material condition, a sense of dignity was bred in the bone.

Black Angus was one of the nine children of Archibald MacDonald and Flora Campbell (daughter of a Brae Lochaber immigrant). Archibald was intensely musical and the family home was recognized from its early days until well into the twentieth century as a place of open hospitality and traditional music. Sarah Ann MacDonald (1886–1992) of Black River was unique in saying that he was a piper as well. His sons, Alexander, Sr, Alexander, Jr (it was not uncommon to give two sons the same name), Allan (a blacksmith), and Black Angus all played the violin. Black Angus was also a piper.[15] All of the family, with the exception of Flora, were stepdancers.

Their church attendance at Mabou shows piety and strong musical involvement through the pastorates of Frs Alexander MacDonald (a relative),[16] Kenneth MacDonald (the temperance priest who confiscated violins), and Dr John MacMaster, Black Angus's long-time friend and patron.

An intimate glimpse of the old home was given me by a neighbour, Florence Allan J. MacDonald (b.1904), of Judique.[17] She remembered going home as a girl to Mount Young from catechism at Brook Village and taking the shortcut by the kindly Black Angus's. Always she was invited in; Black Angus's habit was to play the pipes for half an hour outside the old home on the hill as a serenade to this visitor, then he'd go in and play the violin while they had a big tea off good china. Florence, who also knew Jimmie Dubh Gillis's piping well, said that Black Angus was much the better piper, although he played by ear while Gillis, an eccentric local teacher, was a note player.[18]

J.L. MacDougall wrote of Black Angus that he was the "best known piper in the County of Inverness ... His presence has enlivened many a festive gathering in Mabou, and the wail of his pipes, rendering the laments of the old land with that sure touch which belongs to him alone, has found an echo in many a heart as the body of some stalwart emigrant was carried to the cemetery where the Lochaber exiles take their last long rest."[19] Elsewhere a "piper Aonghus Dhu" is described as having preceded Fr Archibald Campbell, sj, and "twelve teams" to the church in Mabou for the beginning of the Scots priest's mission in 1907.[20] A decade earlier, in 1897, Black Angus and his brother Alexander, Jr were among the thirteen fiddlers listed at Fr MacMaster's first Mabou parish picnic of 20 and 21 July; Angus was described among the thirteen as a piper.[21]

To my knowledge Black Angus MacDonald's repertoire, J.L. MacDougall's "laments of the old land" notwithstanding, was limited to *ceòl beag* (the airs and laments as well as the strathspeys, reels, and jigs required for step-dancing). MacDougall is not known to have been knowledgeable about pibroch, and Alex Joe Rankin and Jemima Lydon's memories of Black Angus's piping at Mabou funerals in the 1920s suggest that he knew only *ceòl beag*. Sarah Ann MacDonald saw Black Angus piping for step-dancing on many occasions dating back to the 1890s. She said that he piped for the Scotch Four (which demanded step-dance strathspeys followed by step-dance reels) and mentioned his playing for what she called the "Single Four" (undefined). Neither she nor any other of my informants (see note 17) mentioned his having piped for the Eight-hand Reel, which is known to have survived into the 1920s in the rear of Judique and Glencoe, and which must have been very popular in Black Angus's younger day.[22]

The other popular group dance his neice saw him piping for was the Square Set (quadrille/Lancers), which required jig as well as reel timing (no strathspey). The Square Set became popular in rural Gaelic Nova Scotia after its introduction around 1890 (or earlier), according to Frank Rhodes.[23] Though the Square Sets had gradually been adapted to Highland tastes with the inclusion of traditional step-dancing setting steps in the 1950s, there is no reason to think that Black Angus played his reels to some non-step-dance rhythm.[24]

Thus, Black Angus's musical career straddles the thoroughly traditional period of the strathspey and reel and the beginnings of change with the quadrille and Lancers. If he had to adapt his music at all, it would only have been to add more jigs to his repertoire for the first two or three figures of the Square Set.

Photographs show that Black Angus held the bagpipes under his right shoulder and played with his right hand upper on the chanter. A photograph in my possesion of Black Angus and two other pipers, taken around 1930 in Glendale when he was about eighty, shows crooked fingers on the chanter.[25] He may have played that way all his life, or he may have developed arthritis or tendonitis. As a fiddler he used his right hand to bow – a far more reliable indicator of handedness than the way a piper fingers the chanter.

As to Black Angus's fingering technique, of all eleven informants only Willie the piper Gillis, former pipe-major of the Cape Breton Highlanders during the Second World War who had learned to read and play pipe music (having first learned by ear in Inverness), was prepared to assess Black Angus's technique by modern literate standards. Willie can only have been in his early teens when Black Angus was in his late seventies or early eighties and past his prime. Nonetheless, Willie noted that Black Angus played a one-finger D, which suggests that the old piper was interested primarily in dance music. In his explanation of what had become for him substandard fingering, Willie said that during his own youth in Inverness in the 1920s and 1930s, there were a hundred pipers of whom only five could play by note. The ear-pipers were far more popular because they could play fast enough and with the right timing for step-dancing. There is almost nothing left of this old Gaelic-speaking class of piper, and very few young pipers understand their function; fewer still are trying to replace them.[26] Black Angus, in common with all traditional ear-learned musicians, had a retentive memory for tunes in the hundreds.

In public Black Angus played far and near in the county at weddings and funerals, *céilidhs* and picnics, on the pipes and the fiddle. Some years after Fr MacMaster held his first picnic at Mabou, Black Angus fiddled for the Scotch Four at an early Creignish picnic.[27]

The fascinating aspect of Black Angus's piping career is his relationship with Fr Dr John MacMaster, his parish priest. In the early 1890s, after his return from doctoral studies in Rome, Fr John presented the Mount Young piper with the set of modern bagpipes he had bought for himself overseas; he is known to have piped once in public at Brook Village, but health appears to have discouraged him. Despite his efforts to stamp out the "black pots" (illicit stills) and the trepidation he aroused in some fiddlers in his extensive parish, he often summoned his old piper friend for music, and when Black

Angus was in his dotage the priest pressed local youngsters to cut and bring to him his winter wood supply. Fr John was not beyond taking him a bottle from time to time. In terms of social standing in the Gaelic community, the old piper was probably more prominent than his priest, which suggests an interesting and important social rapport.

ARCHIBALD BEATON

Very much less is known about the Mabou Coal Mines piper Archibald Beaton (c. 1840–c. 1925) other than that he was a good piper. D.D. MacFarlane's diary entry for Sunday ,18 October 1903 reads, "Was up to Malcolm Gillis 'Up. Margaree' this evening & heard Archy Beaton, Piper, from Mabou." While not informative, the entry perhaps conveys the local stamp of approval.[28] From what is known of Archibald Beaton the following three points are worth reiterating.

The first reflects confirmingly on what Manson had said about the growing interest in the modern Scottish piping fraternity about Highland piping overseas between 1880 and 1890. Although a bit later, Archibald Beaton, who had Beaton cousins in Prince Edward Island, showed up at a Caledonian Club piping competition held in Charlottetown in 1895. The late Dan Angus Beaton, a relative, described the Charlottetown piping competition as having been arranged to discover what had happened to piping in Atlantic Canada and had attracted local pipers from all over the area. Ships' passenger lists have not been made available, so even that slender chance of identifying them has had to be foregone. However, Dan Angus Beaton said that they declared Archibald, who had played late, a masterful player and "professor of piping."

Luckily the event was reported. The results of "The Scottish Gathering" held on Thursday, 1 August 1895 at the "driving Park" in Charlottetown confirm Dan Angus Beaton's claims. In the "Pipe Music" event, one of many that were restricted to "Scotchmen," first place was won by "A.A. Beaton, Cape Breton."[29]

The second point concerns musical literacy. Black Angus was musically illiterate. Almost certainly Archibald Beaton could read music. The likeliest source of instruction was Allan Cameron in North East Mabou, a Protestant immigrant who arrived in 1821 from Giusachan, by Glenfinnan.[30] Cameron was bilingual and literate in English; he was an immigrant fiddler and married Flora Beaton (before or after he converted to Catholicism).[31] Cameron taught his wife's brother's son, the still-remembered traditional local fiddler Donald John Beaton Son of the Tailor, and either or both men could have instructed Archie the piper.

There is nothing to suggest that the speed and timing of old Archie Beaton's piping, like the step-dance fiddling of his second cousin Donald Beaton, was anything other than traditional. (He would have been impossibly egregious had he played in any modern style, leaving what was a very important and powerful guiding fold, musically speaking). This means that the strathspey and reel he played to win the Charlottetown competition were played as step-dance pieces and were clearly acceptable to modern Scottish judges.[32]

The third point concerns the social make-up of Mabou Coal Mines and area. To begin with, Archie Beaton's work, apart from piping, included servicing Sandy Cameron's family telescope in the 1920s. This, the regular steamer run to Mabou, and the debating societies mentioned in D.D. Mac-Farlane's diary, indicate less detachment from modernity than is often imagined. Professor Archie's neighbours included the retired schoolmaster Malcolm MacLellan, who had had a classical education at Lord Selkirk's expense in southwest Scotland before emigrating.[33] The other child of a British military officer living in Mabou Coal Mines was Mary MacDonald (1795–1880), daughter of Captain Angus Tulloch MacDonald. She was married to John Beaton, the first Roman Catholic justice of the peace in the county. She is also said to have run a dancing school.[34] Captain Alexander MacDonnell "of Murlegan" lived on the west side of Mabou Harbour from about 1823 on, but I don't have his date of death.

Another cogent argument for the traditional nature of Professor Archie's piping is that his relative (a second cousin twice removed) and piping pupil Angus Beaton (1895–1971) was a traditional step-dance piper. Angus Beaton played the pipes for Scotch Fours and for (Gaelicized) Square Sets. Like Black Angus MacDonald, he was also a fiddler. Unlike Black Angus, however, Angus Beaton could take music from paper. He falls within the category of the musically literate traditional piper and was one of the last Gaelic community pipers in the parish. His piping was tape recorded at Broad Cove Chapel in 1948 by Fr John Angus Rankin[35] and the speed and timing of his piping, reels in particular, were distinctively traditional. Although cassette copies of the original reel-to-reel tape recording are not of good quality, there sounds to be very little in Angus Beaton's piping technique to distinguish it from modern piping. Nonetheless, to a Gaelic step-dancer the difference is immediately sensed.[36]

LITTLE FARQUHAR MACKINNON

Little Farquhar MacKinnon (1868–1941), the Presbyterian piper from Cobb Brook on East Lake Ainslie side,[37] is the focus for many of the points made about cultural conservatism in the Presbyterian communities. Where possible, data about him will be linked with that of Allan MacFarlane, a superior traditional piper from the neighbouring Roman Catholic community of Upper Margaree since that underlines the basic point that Scotch culture was happily maintained, apart from theology. In any case several of my informants were common to both pipers.[38]

Little Farquhar was an ear-piper who never learned to read music and who piped for both the old Scotch Four and quadrilles. His piping inspiration was his uncle, Big Farquhar, the piping precentor who in turn learned piping from the Big Batchelor (about both of whose teaching methods and piping nothing is known). An old photograph shows Little Farquhar holding the instrument under his left shoulder with his left hand upper on the chanter. Unlike Black Angus's fingers in one photograph, Little Farquhar's fingers were held straight on the chanter.

Edward Campbell, a Presbyterian school teacher who lived at East Lake, remembered dancing Scotch Fours at the Trout River schoolhouse to Little Farquhar's bagpiping, although he preferred dancing to fiddle music.[39] In 1982 Neil Dan MacInnis of Glenville, Little Farquhar's nephew, said that Little Farquhar loved to pipe for the Scotch Four and did so many times.[40] A gauge of the popularity of step-dancing is that the Reverend A.D. MacKinnon, a nephew of Little Farquhar, enjoyed step-dancing in his college days, according to his wife. (Although step-dancing was not integral to the quadrille at this stage, Florence Coleman, Edward Campbell's younger sister, remembered dancing Sets to Little Farquhar's piping at Archie Campbell's in Kirkwood 4 June 1982 and stubbing her toes on the pine knots. Peter MacMillan [b.c.1926] remembered Little Farquhar and Allan MacFarlane piping for Square Sets at the old Hamilton School (East Lake Ainslie) and at the hall at Trout River a few miles south.)

Mary Gillis, (20 May 1979), described Little Farquhar as "a fair piper" but said that "you could [step] dance to his music."[41] Archie MacPhail's story adds an oblique confirmation. MacPhail, who was raised by Campbell grandparents in Scotsville, lived near enough Little Farquhar to hear him piping out on his porch every night. Even after seventy years MacPhail, who lived in Boston from 1922–72, remembered that the piper's porch had a number of loose boards on which little Farquhar beat time, making an exaggerated noise that sounded just like a step-dancer's dancing.[42]

Typical of Highland community life, the *céilidh* house was as important a place in Presbyterian East Lake Ainslie as it was in Catholic Upper and South West Margaree to the north. At East Lake Ainslie it was fiddler Dan John MacDougall's house. A diary held by Charles and Jessie MacDonald shows that Hugh Fred MacKinnon, Little Farquhar's brother, piped there on 4 May 1937. According to Mary Gillis, when the various members of Malcolm Gillis's family were home in South West Margaree from Boston, they regularly went to *céilidh* at Dan John's.[43]

With the same easiness Little Farquhar often piped at Malcolm Gillis's in South West Margaree and elsewhere in the Catholic community. On 20 May 1979 Mary Gillis remembered a Scotch party on a cold February night at the

MacFarlane school at the iron bridge in Scotsville, not far north of Cobb Brook. When it was over the piper left with a group heading towards Upper Margaree. When they reached the little bridge at Sloy Brook, by the farm where Allan the piper and John Grant MacFarlane lived, Farquhar piped despite the cold, and Angus Allan Gillis the fiddler (1897–1978) and a number of others danced the cross.[44]

Although not in the same area, another important Protestant *céilidh* house was Neil Dan MacInnis's in Glenville. Neil Dan played the violin and danced and told stories. When he was asked how the ministers reacted Neil Dan said that one minister who used to visit the MacInnis home used discreetly to leave if people began to gather, knowing that the musical instruments were coming out and dancing was about to begin.[45]

Where musical literacy is concerned, the Catholic and Protestant communities north and south of Scotsville also enjoyed sharing. Long after Malcolm Gillis the bard was dead one of Dan John's daughters, Josie (MacDougal) Ross of North East Margaree, read piper/fiddler Gordon MacQuarrie's *Cape Breton Collection* in manuscript at his request before it was published. According to the late Walter Scott MacFarlane (one of piper Allan MacFarlane's relatives), Allan's tune "The Scotsville Reel" was checked by one of Dan John's daughters.[46]

ALLAN MACFARLANE

It seems unexpected that it would be the Catholic community of Upper Margaree and not that of Protestant Cobb Brook that would produce the literate traditional piper. It is the more surprising when one realizes that Allan MacFarlane[47] (1878–1938) had very little formal schooling. Different claims exist as to who taught him. His nephew, John Angus Collins, believed that he taught himself, but locally there was a flourishing piping brotherhood and several traditional pipers could be found within walking distance of Allan MacFarlane's home. Among them were Malcolm Gillis (literate) in South West Margaree, the Jamesons[48] (Canna people) and Angus MacLellan in Piper's Glen, as well as Angus Bàn MacFarlane (c. 1841–1931), Allan's father's first cousin, and Hughie Gillis, Angus Allan Gillis the fiddler's brother, in the Upper Margaree area. Then there were Hugh Gillis in Scotsville and the MacDonells in Kiltarlity.

How good a piper Allan MacFarlane was finds more measures than most other Nova Scotian pipers' music; he won prizes in Nova Scotia,[49] Maine, and Massachusetts and was in demand by the military in Nova Scotia for summer camps, but the unqualified approval of the Protestant Gaels of East Lake Ainslie is the most convincing evidence.

Clarence Moore the eccentric school teacher described Little Farquhar MacKinnon as untutored, not a "proper" piper, and preferred to discuss

Allan MacFarlane the moment he knew I had heard of him (Moore was perfectly aware of the distinction between a literate traditional Gaelic piper and a modern one).[50] Stanley Collins remembered being outside his house and hearing the piping, alternately, of his stepfather, Little Farquhar, and of Allan MacFarlane and said that it was "so easy" to tell them apart. Little Allan was a "real piper" and, according to Stanley Collins, a note player; he made his grace-notes properly while Farquhar didn't.[51] Collins's praise was unqualified.

Like many other traditional Scotch musicians, Allan MacFarlane played traditional step-dance music for the old Scotch Four and the quadrilles equally well on the fiddle and the pipes (right-handedly). In fact he favoured the violin until he got a newer set of bagpipes and then gave his attention to that instrument. Physically he was small and slightly deformed. While he is widely remembered for his piping,[52] there are no tape recordings of his playing. But he was compared favourably with John MacColl's pupil Sandy Boyd by several Inverness County Gaels who had heard both pipers.[53] The descriptive of him by Walter Scott MacFarlane, *"Am fear bu bhinne shein-neadh pìob"* ("The man who was the sweetest piper") is more than empty flattery.[54]

Another cross-denominational memory of Allan MacFarlane was given me by Mrs Margaret (Blue) MacLean (1902–79) of Blues Mills and Melford. When he was painting railway bridges near Orangedale he was invited to pipe at Kenneth Blue's home. Margaret Blue, who was a little girl at the time, remembered her Presbyterian father plying the piper with requests. She said that it would never have occurred to any of the children to laugh at Allan MacFarlane, although his deformities were obvious. She said he was treated with great respect as a memorable and special guest.[55] The point is that MacFarlane belonged to and represented the tastes of both Catholic and Protestant communities in the Nova Scotia *Gàidheal-tachd*.

Until Allan MacFarlane, there was little likelihood that any of the traditional pipers discussed here played or aspired to play classical pipe music. MacFarlane, the little deformed Upper Margaree musician who hardly went to school, was different. He wanted to play *"A' Ghlas Mheur"* ("The Finger Lock"), the one piece of *ceòl mór* that more than once, has been described in Scotch minds as the *sine qua non* of the accomplished Highland piper. Local Gaels like Malcolm Gillis and D.D. MacFarlane would certainly have known this fact but it is now impossible to say whether Allan MacFarlane's aspiration came from Inverness County, Nova Scotia, or outside.[56]

Of the pipers mentioned above, the important ones lived through the transition period of the 1880s and 1890s. They also lived through the Great War, the next major turning point. Suffice it to say that the essential Gaelic dance rhythms characterized all their music; most had the foundations etched into their minds while the old Scotch Four was the main community dance and the quadrille still lay in the future, and when the demands of the old class of dancing master still exerted an influence. The degree of variation in the music of these pipers can never be known, but just enough exists on tape of the twentieth-century pipers for us to have some idea of the richness that once was.

17 The Survival of Tradition in Nova Scotia

The Scottish piping world of 1900–20 was not one that found the ideas of old John Johnston, Coll, the least attractive; nor would it stop to consider that the Old and New World *Gàidhealtachds* still existed and harboured irreplaceable links with the older piping functions and tradition. It would have drawn a deep breath and raised a querulous eyebrow had it seen and heard Black Angus MacDonald of Mount Young or Allan MacFarlane piping for one of the Gillis step-dancers at an Inverness County picnic. It appears that the New World Gaeldom, through neglect and isolation, was truer to tradition for longer, but even so it should be remembered that in or near Glasgow there were still ear-learned pipers in the 1920s.[1] However, this kind of piper was disappearing fast in Scotland. Even in the Gaelic heartland the improver spirit was fermenting. In 1905 Gaelic speaker John MacDonald (Inverness) was sent by the Pibroch Society to South Uist to bring the ear-learned dance-music pipers up to literate scratch. As someone in the *Piping Times* praisingly remarked, "(MacDonald) is responsible more than anyone else for the present day standard of playing in South Uist."[2]

On the island, once a hotbed of traditional piping and Reel dancing, this urge to improve was encouraged by Major Finlay MacKenzie, who died in 1963 at age eighty-one, and who had been owner of the Loch Boisdale Hotel, which remains a piping centre. There is no report of anything other than enthusiastic acceptance of the great John MacDonald, whose name is still revered by Gael and non-Gael alike.[3] Highland games followed in South Uist in 1911, doubtless further driving in the wedge. After the First World War Pipe-Major Willie Ross, teacher of piping at Edinburgh Castle, continued John MacDonald's work in South Uist, teaching there in 1923 and 1924.

In 1925 he taught piping in Benbecula where Pipe-Major Willie Lawrie of the 8th Argylls had been sent to run a piping school in 1911–12.[4] However old-fashioned these luminaries' piping may seem today sometimes noticeably close in speed and timing to traditional Cape Breton Gaelic step-dance piping – there is no doubt that they all stressed fingering technique and relied on literate learning methods. Their efforts worked to displace from prominence the older sense of complete Gaelic musicality that had been the prime Gaelic prerequisite, and that had driven a thousand unselfconscious traditional dance-music pipers of earlier times.

In the present century this old living musical culture, what remained of it, was beyond the range of most modern and literately learned pipers' curiosity. If conscious of this kind of piping, they heard and saw it from the superior stance of the inevitably modern and improved.

Unquestionably the only areas of the world that could retain Gaelic traditionalism in the face of the piping renaissance that Stephen MacKinnon rightly described could have been the heartland Gaelic-speaking areas, home of unilingual Gaels, where the older consciousness was not easily challenged. Even in the heartland of the Scottish *Gàidhealtachd* itself, among the concentrations of old-style pipers in the most profoundly bagpipe-loving communities, there were concerted efforts to modernize piping. For all that, even if the overburden of modern notions of piping was heavily applied in Scotland, there are more and more indications that not all of the old Gaelic tradition was destroyed.[5] In the New World it certainly survived in the Gaelic heartland in Cape Breton and on the mainland of neighbouring Nova Scotia, but for most in the 1990s it has become a novelty. At a Broad Cove Scotch concert in 1991 I sat beside a Gael in his fifties who loves to stepdance in Square Sets and watched in vain for a reaction as Barry Shears played several strathspeys, followed by reels, in Cape Breton Scotch stepdance time, something few pipers could then do. The expectation of hearing step-dance music on the Highland bagpipe, for most Inverness County Gaels, no longer exists and an old link with the late eighteenth-century piping has been broken.

The complexities surrounding the intrusion of modern Scottish bagpiping and the survival of tradition in Gaelic Nova Scotia can best be outlined in two examples about three-quarters of a century apart, one from the Nova Scotia Gaelic-speaking Protestant community and the other from the Roman Catholic.

Kenneth MacKenzie Baillie (1859–1925),[6] a Pictou boy, was raised in his uncle's Gaelic household at Balmoral in eastern Colchester county, roughly at the westward limit of any Gaelic-speaking community in Nova Scotia at the time (Gaelic survived there until after WWI). Francis MacDonald, born in rural Cape Breton in 1932, was raised in Kiltarlity, Inverness County, Cape Breton, also in a Gaelic family. Both men learned to play the fiddle first but later took up the bagpipes, both under the influence of modern Scottish pipers who either were military pipers or had learned from a military piper.

Baillie was one of those rare characters who went to Britain to join the military (he enlisted in the Royal Marine Artillery in 1878). Overseas he met and married Catherine MacLennan from Inverness, and from her he learned the pipes. She was the daughter and piping pupil of Pipe-Major Sandy MacLennan (1807–1902) of the Cameron Highlanders, a *ceòl mór* as well as *ceòl beag* piper. Almost undoubtedly MacLennan had learned piping in the traditional way, as probably had his only daughter. In what style they taught is questionable, though both taught, she in Scotland and Nova Scotia. MacKenzie Baillie was too late to have been taught piping Nova Scotia by a Gairloch-born MacKay piper, although, had he stayed, he might have learned from a pupil of Angus MacKay (great-grandson of the Blind Piper) in Pictou County. As it was, his wife's father, Sandy MacLennan, was the grandson of a pupil of Angus MacKay, son of the Blind Piper, in Gairloch, Scotland. Baillie's influence on Maritime piping was not inconsiderable and among his Gaelic-speaking piping pupils was the Catholic Angus "the Ridge" MacDonald of Antigonish County; piping grew to be MacKenzie Baillie's major interest in life.

Francis MacDonald, now of Inverness, Cape Breton, joined the Second Battalion, Black Watch of Canada in 1954. He joined the battalion's pipe band in 1955, having had six months of daily piping tuition from Duncan Rankin, the pipe-major in Camp Gagetown, New Brunswick. When he enlisted MacDonald was already a traditional ear-learned Cape Breton stepdance fiddler whose sense of the Gaelic speed and timing of Scotch music had been firmly laid down in the tight social environment of rural Inverness County. Duncan Rankin, on the other hand, Francis's only piping teacher, was a Paisley man who, despite his Gaelic name, was a unilingual English speaker. Duncan Rankin had been a pupil of Willie Ross (it is not known where) and had competed in Scotland against his contemporary Sandy Boyd before the Second World War. Like Boyd, Rankin was literately learned and committed to modern, technique-oriented bagpiping.

Where MacKenzie Baillie made modern piping his dominant interest in his later years, MacDonald gave up piping when he left the Canadian Black Watch, preferring to concentrate on his fiddling. Today he is known first as a fiddler/composer and for his efforts to further the traditional Cape Breton Scotch form. Asked why he quit piping, he said that the range of the violin gave him greater musical freedom, although he had transposed pipe music for the violin. He also conceded that the rigours of a piping that had been taught in the modern fashion by Duncan Rankin, with the dependence on technique and without the imperatives dictated by traditional dance needs, had made playing the bagpipes less appealing to him.[7] As Black Angus and

Red Gordon MacQuarrie had earlier decided, the modern and the traditional forms of piping were, if not totally incompatible, at least uneasy partners. In essence the complex grace-notings in strathspeys and reels, even at times the presence of doublings, can make step-dance music hard to produce except by the exceptional.

Barry Shears's most recent transcriptions of step-dance pipe music include fewer grace-notings. Roderick Cannon remarked on the tendency of the top Scottish competition pipers to increase the grace-notings of (quick-step) march, strathspey, and reel tunes since competition in the *ceòl beag* categories began in the 1820s, and egregiously since mid-century. In the present century, which witnessed the change from the old "round" style of march playing to the modern clipped style, G.S. MacLennan, was responsible for a significant increase in *ceòl beag* grace-noting between 1910 and 1928, according to Archibald Campbell of Kilberry, presumably through his actual competition piping.[8]

It should be mentioned that Barry Shears himself was starting to change his fingering in an effort to duplicate the obscurer techniques of the old traditional Cape Breton Scotch pipers like Joe Hughie MacIntyre and Alex Currie. Although the research remains to be done and unfortunately can never be exhaustive, Shears suggested that the old pipers may have used what would be called "unorthodox" fingerings to produce tonal variations that modern pipers ignore in favour of the ingrained Joseph MacDonald standard. However, Shears's primary aim, at this stage, is to produce the overall musical cleverness by finding what he called the old pipers' "tricks" of fingering to achieve their technical (if not their tonal) ends. In particular, he described a tape-recorded version of the reel "The Sheepwife" that Alex Currie played, when he was in his heyday forty to fifty years ago. Shears described Currie's version as superior in musicality and technique to his own modern competition version. He said further that the only way he could reproduce the tune in Currie's form, and others like it from the deep well of preliterate Scotch tradition, was to listen to them again and again and, if necessary, experiment with unorthodox fingerings.[9]

Oddly, the presence of modern Scottish pipers in the Cape Breton *Gàidhealtachd*[10] in the twentieth century has not always been inimical to tradition, although their positive influence in that area has been very limited. Sandy Boyd's influence appears to have been much stronger, and more adverse, than Sandy Russell's a generation earlier. Boyd's example persuaded some Gaelic-speaking pipers to play in the modern style, although people like the late Alex Fortune of Glendale and Marble Mountain, while deeply appreciative of Sandy Boyd's piping, admired the technique but were well aware of the non-functional nature of his music. Younger pipers were less rooted in Gaelic tradition. Sandy Boyd's Cape Breton, obviously, was a much more English-speaking place than Sandy Russell's.

Russell, a Dundonian,[11] and always, as far as is known, a civilian piper, immigrated around 1900 and settled to coal mining at Inverness, Cape Breton. Among his piping pupils was Allan MacKay of Cape Mabou, whom Russell taught one summer while haying on the MacKay farm when the mine was closed. Allan in turn taught his nephew Archie Allan MacKay (later of the Cape Breton Highlanders).[12] Russell's informal influence reached the Inverness fiddler Donald Angus MacPherson,[13] who picked up tunes for the fiddle from the Scotsman's piping repertoire, just as Francis MacDonald used the literate repertoire he got in the Black Watch from Duncan Rankin on the fiddle.

Despite the anomalies, traditional piping did endure in the New World *Gàidhealtachd*, longest in the most Gaelic-speaking part, Cape Breton, less durably on the mainland (where the language is almost extinct) and on Prince Edward Island. There are two reasons for the persistence of tradition, and of a suspended pseudotradition outwith the Gaelic language (which describes the present state of affairs even in Cape Breton,[14] where tradition has yet finally to disappear).

The first was the overlooking of Gaelic tradition in rural Nova Scotia and the random nature of the intrusion of novel piping ideas where they occurred. Who these visitors and immigrant pipers were and what influence they exerted in the pre-World War I period is not well known. Stephen MacKinnon mentioned Willie MacLennan and others. More tantalizingly, the late Sister Sarah Ann Beaton recollected in 1982 the presence of the Scottish piper Manson at the Mabou picnic of 1897.[15] Sister Beaton was the only remaining witness to that picnic in 1982. Manson was based in Halifax, but little more can be added at this juncture.

The modern, post-World War II picture is clearer. Literately trained Scots pipers came to Gaelic Cape Breton, people like Sandy Russell (c. 1900), Sandy Boyd (1942), and several others, but they did not come as part of any prescribed system to upgrade piping. They came primarily to take advantage of less-depressed economic circumstances, knowing that their piping would stand them in good stead in Nova Scotia and all over the Dominion. People of the calibre of John MacDonald and Willie Ross, to my knowledge, never visited and were never "sent" to Nova Scotia to teach. Bear in mind further that Russell and Boyd, and most other piper-immigrants from Scotland, were unilingual English speakers and had no introduction to the deeper Gaelic world, a world that, as we have seen, could be highly reticent in its protection of itself.

The second was the process of the development of non-Gaelic dances in the province, which was quite different from that of Scotland in significant ways.

Generally speaking, the rural Gaelic communities of Maritime Canada were, not exposed to the Scottish variety or varieties of the quadrille, which was first danced openly in Edinburgh society in 1816. Undoubtedly these dances formed part of the English-speaking "society" dance card in Halifax, Sydney, Charlottetown, and Fredericton, but for a Gael in Scotchfort, Prince Edward Island, or Mabou or Heatherton (Pomquet Forks, Antigonish County), this was alien treading. In Gaelic Scotland quadrille dancing in Benderaloch first appeared in the 1880s and it was firmly resisted; always it was foregone in the Hebrides and many mainland areas. One can just as easily make sweeping statements about the absence of Hebridean dancing (a phenomenon still remembered by a few folk in Barra), which emerged from unknown origins through a MacLachlan in the 1870s. There is no record of these dances in Gaelic Nova Scotia, just as there is no record of country dancing like the "Gay Gordons" or "Strip the Willow" or the "Schottische."

Those absences in themselves ensured the continuance of traditional piping and fiddling for traditional Reel dancing – the most popular dancing – along with the diet of the Gaelic dancing master about which surprisingly little is known beyond the names of the dances or tunes that Margaret Gillis in South West Margaree called "hornpipes."

The only intrusive group dance that became a rage among the young in Black River, Mabou Coal Mines, Judique, and almost every other Cape Breton, Nova Scotian, and Prince Edward Island Gaelic community from c. 1890 was indeed the quadrille, but at the rural level it was an importation not from Scotland or upper-class British empire society but from the Boston area. Movement of people from Gaelic Cape Breton to the "Boston States" was intense, especially in the 1880s and 1890s, and lasted until the present.[16] The social links between Nova Scotian Gaels and Boston and its satellites remain, in many families, much stronger than comparable ties with any part of Canada.

In any case, the popularity of what is now called the Square Set in Gaelic Nova Scotia, if it didn't begin in the many Scotch and Scotch-and-Irish clubs in the Boston area, was thoroughly fostered there and was brought to the rural areas of Gaelic Cape Breton by returning, semi-urban, varyingly bilingual Gaels. At about the time of the First World War, according to Katie Margaret (Rankin) Gillis, the dance was so popular that children in Black River, Inverness County, practised the Square Set figures in the School hall at recess.[17] Black River was the rule rather than the exception. Older people like Archie MacPhail of Scotsville still reminisce about the old Boston halls, especially the Rose Croix, the Inter-Colonial, and the Winslow. New York also had its Scotch centre. The older folk remember the dances, the musicians (almost always ex-patriot or visiting Cape Bretoners), and the callers. Katie Margaret still chants some of the callers' more memorable lines.

The quadrilles that Maritime Gaels learned and brought back with them were different from upper class society quadrilles. From the Irish in New England came the jig timing of the first figure, and from a wider American popular taste (but certainly owing much to the Scotch population) came the reel timing of subsequent figures. By the time Maritime Gaels were going south for work, the Boston/American square dances had been vulgarized. Hence it was really only the jig timing that was to some extent novel to Scotch step-dancers. Jigs were by no means unknown in the eighteenth-century *Gàidhealtachd*, but they are associated with specific dances, as were the "hornpipes" Margaret Gillis and her people danced. Reel timing was an integral part of Scotch Gaelic life. With strathspey timing in equal measure, it comprised old Scotch Four (Reel); in the Eight-hand Reel, reel timing was the only timing used.

The Square Set, imported to Nova Scotia in several varieties, including the Saratoga Lancers, was a four-couple dance, and, given its remarkable popularity among the young at the turn of this century, it obviously did more than any bishop, priest, or teetotal League of the Cross[18] to wipe out the old "Wild Eight" (Frank Rhodes, in the *Fletts' Traditional Dancing in Scotland* [1964] attributed the disappearance of the old "wild" Eight-hand Reel in Cape Breton to episcopal interference).[19] The Square Set was popular because in many of its figures it was similar to the Eight and therefore fairly easy to learn. But more to the point, for the first fifty or sixty years of its existence in Gaelic Nova Scotia, it contained no step-dancing setting steps, which of course opened it up to many more dancers. The Four, which is built around step-dancing setting steps, along with individual step-dancing, remained as the firm and strong refuge of traditional Gaelic dancing. Both the Square Set and the Four employed traditional music played on the traditional instruments, the fiddle and the bagpipes.

The old strathspey timing came under the heaviest seige, and it is not surprising, since the Scotch Four has died as a spontaneous *céilidh* group dance,[20] that the strathspey continues most commonly as an audio feature of instrumental music. It is still an important timing for individual *céilidh* and exhibition step-dancing, but increasingly it is becoming a minor adjunct, in fact little more than an introduction to the reel that is the meat of any individual dancer's performance on stage or in the kitchen.[21] Nonetheless, the old traditional dancing of strathspey (individual step-dancing) and reel steps (individually and in the Square Set), slightly beefed up by variations on a basis jig shuffle in the first figure of the Square Set, continue little changed from the second half of the eighteenth century. Thus it is that the last of the old traditional Gaelic-speaking ear-learned bagpipers (often bagpiper-fiddlers) in what remained of the Nova Scotia *Gàidhealtachd* by 1945 were the most important and the most overlooked of Highland pipers anywhere. They were and are our last, quickly vanishing window on the music and dance culture of the late-eighteenth-century Highlands.

APPENDIX ONE

The Disarming Act, 1746*

An act for the more effectual disarming the Highlands in Scotland; and for more effectually securing the Peace of the said Highlands; and for restraining the Use of the Highland Dress; and for further indemnifying such Persons as have acted in Defence of His Majesty's Person and Government, during the unnatural Rebellion; and for indemnifying the Judges and other Officers of the Court of Justiciary in Scotland, for not performing the Northern Circuit in May, One thousand seven hundred and forty six; and for obliging the Masters and Teachers of Private Schools in Scotland, and Chaplains, Tutors and Governors of Children or Youth, to take the Oaths to His Majesty, His Heirs, and Successors, and to register the same.

Whereas by an Act made in the First Year of the Reign of His late Majesty King George the First, of Glorious Memory, intituled [sic] , An Act for the more effectual securing the Peace of the Highlands in Scotland, it was enacted, That from and after the First Day of November, which was in the Year of our Lord One thousand seven hundred and sixteen, it should not be lawful for any Person or Persons (except such Persons as are therein mentioned and described) within the Shire of Dunbartain, on the North side of the Water of Leven, Stirling on the North Side of the River of Forth, Perth, Kincardin, Aberdeen, Inverness, Nairn, Cromarty, Argyle, Forfar, Bamff, Sutherland, Caithness, Elgine, and Ross, to have in his or their Custody, Use, or Bear, Broad Sword or Target, Poignard, Whinger, or Durk, Side Pistol, Gun, or other warlike Weapon, otherwise than in the said Act was directed, under certain Penalties appointed by the said Act; which Act having by Experience been found not sufficient to attain the Ends therein proposed, was further enforced by an Act in the Eleventh Year of the Reign of His late Majesty, intituled, An Act for more effectual disarming the Highlands in that Part of Great Britain called Scotland; and for the better securing the Peace and Quiet of that Part of the Kingdom: And whereas the said Act of the Eleventh Year of His late Majesty being, so far as it related to the disarming the Highlands, to continue in Force only during the Term of Seven Years, and from thence to the End of the next Session of Parliament, is now expired: And whereas many Persons within the said Bounds and Shires still continue possessed of great Quantities of Arms, and there, with a great Number of such Persons, have lately raised and carried on a most audacious and wicked Rebellion against his Majesty, in favour of a Popish Pretender, and in Prosecution thereof did, in a traiterous and hostile Manner, march into the Southern Parts of this kingdom, took Possession of several Towns, raised Contributions upon the Country, and committed many other Disorders, to the Terror and great Loss of His Majesty's faithful Subjects, until, by the Blessing of God on his Majesty's Arms, they were subdued: Now, for preventing Rebellion, and traiterous Attempts in Time to come, and the other Mischiefs arising from the Possesssion or Use of Arms, by lawless, wicked, and disaffected Persons inhabiting within the said several Shires and Bounds; be it enacted by the King's most Excellent Majesty, by and with the Advice and Consent of the Lords Spiritual and Temporal, and Commons, in this present Parliament assembled, and by the Authority of the same, That from and after the First Day of August, One thousand seven hundred and forty six, it shall be lawful for the respective Lords Lieutenants of the several Shires above recited, and for such other Person or Persons as His Majesty, His Heirs, or Successors shall, by His or Their Sign Manual, from time to time, think fit to authorize and appoint in that Behalf, to issue, or cause to be issued out, Letters of Summons in His Majesty's Name, and under his or their respective Hands and Seals, directed to such Persons within the said several Shires and Bounds, as he or they, from time to time, shall think fit, thereby commanding and requiring all and every Person and Persons therein named, or inhabiting within the particular Limits therein described, to bring in and deliver up, at a certain Day, in such Summons to be prefixed, and at a certain Place therein to be mentioned, all and singular his and their Arms and warlike Weapons, unto such Lord Lieutenant, or other Person or Persons appointed by His Majesty, His Heirs, or Successors, in that Behalf, as aforesaid, for the Use of His Majesty, His Heirs, or Successors, and to be disposed of in such Manner as His Majesty, His Heirs, or Successors shall appoint; and if any Person or Persons, in such Summons mentioned by Name, or inhabiting within the Limits therein described, shall, by the Oaths of One or more credible Witness or Witnesses, be convicted of having or bearing any Arms, or warlike Weapons, after the Day prefixed in such Summons, before any One or more of His Majesty's Justices of the Peace for the Shire or Stewartry where such Offender or Offenders shall reside, or be apprehended, or before the Judge Ordinary, or such other Person or Persons as His Majesty, His Heirs, or Successors shall appoint, in Manner herein after directed, every such Person or Persons so convicted shall forfeit the Sum of Fifteen Pounds Sterling, and shall be committed to Prison until Payment of the said Sum; and if any Person or Persons, convicted as aforesaid, shall refuse or neglect to make Payment of the foresaid Sum of Fifteen Pounds Sterling, within the Space of One Calendar Month from the Date of such Conviction, it shall and may be lawful to any One or more of His Majesty's Justices of the Peace, or to the Judge Ordinary of the Place where such Offender or Offenders is or are imprisoned, in case he or they shall judge such Offender or Offenders fit to serve His Majesty as a Soldier or Soldiers, to cause him or them to be delivered over (as they are hereby impowered and required to do) to such Officer or Officers belonging to the Forces of His Majesty, His Heirs, or Successors, who shall be appointed from time to time to receive such Men, to serve as Soldiers in any of His Majesty's Forces in America; for which Purpose the respective Officers, who shall receive such Men, shall then cause the Articles of War against Mutiny and Desertion to be read to him or them in the Presence of such Justices of the Peace, or Judge Ordinary, who shall so deliver over such Men, who shall cause an Entry or Memorial thereof to be made, together with the Names of the Persons so delivered over, with a Certificate thereof in Writing, under his or their Hands, to be delivered to the Officers appointed to receive such Men; and from and after reading of the said Articles of War, every Person so delivered over to such Officer, to serve as a Soldier as aforesaid, shall be deemed a listed Soldier to all Intents and Purposes, and shall be subject to the Discipline of War; and in case of Desertion, shall be punished as a Deserter; and in case such Offender or Offenders shall not be judged fit to serve His Majesty as aforesaid, then he or they shall be imprisoned for the Space of Six Calendar Months, and also until he or they shall give sufficient Security for his or their good Behaviour for the Space of Two Years from the giving thereof.

And be it further enacted by the Authority aforesaid, That all Persons summoned to deliver up their Arms as aforesaid, who shall, from and after the Time in such Summons prefixed, hide or conceal any Arms, or other warlike Weapons, in any Dwelling-house, Barn, Outhouse, Office, or any other House, or in the Fields, or any other Place whatsoever; and all Persons who shall be accessary [sic] or privy to the hiding or concealing of such Arms, and shall be thereof convicted by the Oaths of One or more credible Witness or Witnesses, before any One or more of His Majesty's Justices of the Peace, Judge Ordinary, or other person or Persons authorized by His Majesty in Manner above mentioned, shall be liable to be fined by the said Justices of the Peace, Judge Ordinary, or other Person authorized by His Majesty, before whom he or they shall be convicted according to their Discretion, in any Sum not exceeding One hundred Pounds Sterling, nor under the Sum of

Fifteen Pounds Sterling, of lawful Money of Great Britain, and shall be committed to Prison until Payment; and if the Person so convicted, being a Man, shall refuse or neglect to pay the Fine so imposed, within the Space of One Calendar Month from the Date of the said Conviction, he shall, in case he be judged by any One or more Justice or Justices of the Peace, or the Judge Ordinary of the Place where such Offender is imprisoned, fit to serve His Majesty as a Soldier, be delivered over to serve as a Soldier in His Majesty's Forces in America, in the Manner before directed, with respect to Persons convicted of having or bearing of Arms; and in case such Offender shall not be judged fit to serve His Majesty as aforesaid, then he shall be imprisoned for the Space of Six Calendar Months, and also until he shall give sufficient Security for his good Behaviour, for the Space of Two Years from the giving thereof; and if the Person convicted shall be a Woman, she shall, over and above the foresaid Fine, and Imprisonment till Payment, suffer Imprisonment for the Space of Six Calendar Months, within the Tolbooth of the Head Burgh of the Shire or Stewartry within which she is convicted.

And be it further enacted by the Authority aforesaid, That if, after the Day appointed by any Summons for the delivering up of Arms in pursuance of this Act, any Arms, or warlike Weapons, shall be found hidden or concealed in any Dwelling-house, Barn, Out-house, Office, or any other House whatsoever, being the Residence or Habitation of or belonging to any of the Persons summoned to deliver up Arms as aforesaid, the Tenant or Possessor of such Dwelling-house, or of the Dwelling-house to which such Barn, Office, or Out-house belongs, being thereof convicted in Manner above mentioned, shall be deemed and taken to be the Haver and Concealer of such Arms, and being thereof convicted in Manner above mentioned, shall suffer the Penalties hereby above enacted against Concealers of Arms, unless such Tenant or Possessor, in whose House, Barn, Out-house, Office, or other House by them possessed, such Arms shall be found concealed, do give Evidence, by his or her making Oath, or otherwise to the Satisfaction of the said Justices of the Peace, Judge Ordinary, or other Person authorized by His Majesty, before whom he or she shall be tried, that such Arms were so concealed and hid without his or her knowledge, Privity, or Connivance.

And be it further enacted by the Authority aforesaid, That if any Person who shall have been convicted of any of the above Offences, of bearing, hiding, or concealing Arms, contrary to the Provisions in this Act, shall thereafter presume to commit the like Offence a Second Time, that he or she being thereof convicted before any Court of Justiciary, or at the Circuit Courts, shall be liable to be transported to any of His Majesty's Plantations beyond the Seas, there to remain for the Space of Seven Years.

And for the more effectual Execution of this present Act, be it further enacted by the Authority aforesaid, That it shall be lawful to His Majesty, His Heirs, or Successors, by His or Their Sign Manual, from time to time, to authorize and appoint such Persons as he or they shall think proper, to execute all the Powers and Authorities by this Act given to One or more Justice or Justices of the Peace, or to the Judge Ordinary, within their respective Jurisdictions, as to the apprehending, trying, and convicting such Person or Persons who shall be summoned to deliver up their Arms, in pursuance of this Act.

And to the end that every Person or Persons, named or concerned in such Summons, may have due Notice thereof, and to prevent all Questions concerning the Legality of such Notice, it is hereby further enacted by the Authority aforesaid, That such Summons, notwithstanding the Generality thereof, be deemed sufficient, if it express the Person or Persons that are commanded to deliver up their Weapons, or the Parishes, or the Lands, Limits, and Boundings of the respective Territories and Places, whereof the Inhabitants are to be disarmed as aforesaid; and that it shall be a sufficient and legal Execution or Notice of the said Summons, if it is affixed on the Door of the Parish Church or Parish Churches of the several Parishes within which the Lands (the Inhabitants whereof are to be disarmed) do lie, on any Sunday, between the Hours of Ten in the Forenoon, and Two in the Afternoon, Four Days at least before the Day prefixed for the delivering up of the Arms, and on the Market Cross of the Head Burgh of the Shire or Stewartry, within which the said Lands lie, Eight Days before the Day appointed for the said Delivery of the Arms; and in case the Person or Persons employed to affix the said Summons on the Doors of the several Parish Churches, or any of them, shall be interrupted, prevented, or forcibly hindered from affixing the said Summons on the Doors of the said Churches, or any of them, upon Oath thereof made before any of His Majesty's Justices of the Peace, the Summons affixed on the Market Cross of the said Head Burgh of the Shire or Stewartry as aforesaid, shall be deemed and taken to be a sufficient Notice to all the Persons commanded thereby to deliver up their Arms, within the true Intent and Meaning, and for the Purposes of this Act.

And to the end that there may be sufficient Evidence of the Execution, or Notice given of the Summons for disarming the several Persons and Districts, as aforesaid, be it further enacted by the Authority aforesaid, That upon the elapsing of the said several Days to be prefixed for the delivering up Arms, the Person or Persons employed to fix the Summons, as above mentioned, on the Market Cross of the Head Burghs of any Shire or Stewartry, shall, before any One of His Majesty's Justices of the Peace for the said Shire or Stewartry, make Oath, that he or they did truly execute and give Notice of the same, by affixing it as aforesaid; and the Person or Persons employed to affix the said Summons on the Doors of the Parish Church or Parish Churches, shall make Oath in the same Manner, and to the same Effect, or otherwise shall swear that he or they were interrupted, prevented, or forcibly hindered from affixing the said Summons as aforesaid; which Oaths, together with Copies or Duplicates of the Summons, to which they severally relate, shall be delivered to the Sheriff or Steward Clerk of the several Shires or Stewartries, within which the Persons intended to be disarmed do live or reside, who shall enter the same in Books, which he and they is and are hereby required to keep for that Purpose; and the said Books in which the Entries are so made, or Extracts out of the same, under the Hand of the Sheriff or Steward Clerk, shall be deemed and taken to be full and complete Evidence of the Execution of the Summons, in order to the Conviction of the Persons who shall neglect or refuse to comply with the same.

And be it further enacted by the Authority aforesaid, That if any such Sheriff or Steward Clerk neglect or refuse to make such Entry as is above mentioned, or shall refuse to make such Entry as is above mentioned, or shall refuse to exhibit the Books containing such Entries, or to give Extracts of the same, being thereto required by any Person or Persons who shall carry on any Prosecutions in pursuance of this Act, the Clerk so neglecting or refusing shall forfeit his Office, and shall likewise be fined in the Sum of Fifty Pounds Sterling; to be recovered upon a summary Complaint before the Court of Session, for the Use of His Majesty, His Heirs, or Successors.

And be it further enacted by the Authority aforesaid, That it shall and may be lawful to and for the Lord Lieutenant of any of the Shires aforesaid, or the Person or Persons authorized by His Majesty, His Heirs, or Successors, as aforesaid, to summon the Person or Persons aforesaid to deliver up his or their Arms, in Manner above mentioned, or to and for any One Justice of the Peace of the respective Shires above mentioned, or to the Judge Ordinary within their respective Jurisdicitons, or to such Person or Persons as shall be authorized by His Majesty, His Heirs, or Successors, for trying Offences against this Act, to authorize and appoint such Person or Persons as they shall think fit, to apprehend all such Person or Persons as may be found within the Limits aforesaid, having or wearing any Arms, or warlike Weapons, contrary to Law, and forthwith to carry him or them to some sure Prison, in order to their being proceeded against according to Law.

And be it further enacted by the Authority aforesaid, That it shall and may be lawful to and for his Majesty, his Heirs, and Successors, by Warrant under his or Their Royal Sign Manual, and also to and for the Lord Lieutenant of any of the Shires aforesaid, or the Person or Persons authorized by His Majesty, to summon the Person or Persons aforesaid to deliver up their Arms, or any One or more Justices of the Peace, by Warrant under his or their hands, to authorize and appoint any Person or Persons to enter into any House or Houses, within the Limits aforesaid, either by Day or by Night, and there to search for, and to seize all such Arms as shall be found contrary to the Direction of this Act.

Provided, That if the above mentioned Search shall be made in the Night-time, that is to say, between Sun setting and Sun rising, it shall be made in the Presence of a Constable, or of some Person particularly to be named for that Purpose in the Warrant for such Search; and if any Persons, to the Number of Five or more shall at any Time assemble together to obstruct the Execution of any Part of this Act, it shall and may be lawful to and for every Lord Lieutenant, Deputy Lieutenant, or Justice of the Peace where such Assembly shall be; and also to and for every Peace Officer within any such Shire, Stewartry, City, Burgh, or Place where such Assembly shall be; and likewise to and for all and every such other Person or Persons, as by His Majesty, His Heirs, or Successors, shall be authorized and appointed in that Behalf as aforesaid, to require the Aid and Assistance of the Forces of His Majesty, His Heirs, or Successors, by applying to the Officer commanding the said Forces (who is hereby authorized, impowered, and commanded to give such Aid and Assistance accordingly) to suppress such unlawful Assembly, in order to the putting this Act in due Execution; and also to seize, apprehend, and disarm, and they are hereby required to seize, apprehend, and disarm such Persons so assembled together, and forthwith to carry the Persons so apprehended before One or more of His Majesty's Justices of the Peace of the Shire or Place where such Persons shall be so apprehended, in order to their being proceeded against, for such their Offences, according to Law; and if the Persons so unlawfully assembled, or any of them, or any other Person or Persons summoned to deliver up his or their Arms in pursuance of this Act, shall happen to be killed, maimed, or wounded in the dispersing, seizing, and apprehending, or in the endeavouring to disperse, seize, or apprehend, by reason of their resisting the Persons endeavouring to disperse, seize, and apprehend them; then all and every such Lord Lieutenant, Deputy Lieutenant, Justice or Justices of the Peace, or any Peace Officer or Officers, and all and every Person or Persons, authorized and appointed by His Majesty, His Heirs, or Successors, in that Behalf, as aforesaid, and all Persons aiding and assisting to him, them, or any of them, shall be freed, discharged, and indemnified, as well against the King's Majesty, His Heirs, and Successors, as against all and every other Person and Persons of, for, or concerning the killing, maiming, or wounding any such Person or Persons so unlawfully assembled, that shall be so killed, maimed, or wounded as aforesaid.

And be it further enacted by the Authority aforesaid, That if any Action, Civil or Criminal, shall be brought before any Court whatsoever, against any Person or Persons for what he or they shall lawfully do in pursuance or Execution of the Act, such Court shall allow the Defendant the Benefit of the Discharge and Indemnity above provided, and shall further decern the Pursuer to pay to the Defender the full and real Expences that he shall be put to by such Action or Prosecution.

Provided nevertheless, and be it enacted by the Authority aforesaid, That no Peers of this Realm, nor their Sons, nor any Members of Parliament, nor any Person or Persons, who, by the Act above recited of the First Year of His late Majesty, were allowed to have or carry Arms, shall by virtue of this Act be liable to be summoned to deliver up their Arms, or warlike Weapons; nor shall this Act, or the above recited Act, be construed to extend to exclude or hinder any Person, whom His Majesty, His Heirs, or Successors, by Licence under His or Their Sign Manual, shall permit to wear Arms, or who shall be licensed to wear Arms by any Writing and Writings under the Hand and Seal, or Hands and Seals of any Person or Persons authorized by His Majesty, His Heirs, or Successors, to give such Licence from keeping, bearing, or wearing such Arms, and warlike Weapons, as in such Licence or Licences shall for Purpose be particularly specified.

And to the end that no Persons may be discouraged from delivering up their Arms, from the Apprehension of the Penalties and Forfeitures which they may have incurred, through their neglecting to comply with the Directions of the said Act of the First Year of His late Majesty's Reign, be it further enacted by the Authority aforesaid, That from and after the Time of affixing any such Summons as aforesaid, no Person or Persons residing within the Bounds therein mentioned, shall be sued or prosecuted for his or their having, or having had, bearing, or having borne Arms at any Time before the several Days to be prefixed or limited by Summons as aforesaid, for the respective Persons and Districts to deliver up their Arms; but if any Person or Persons shall refuse or neglect to deliver up their Arms in Obedience to such Summons as aforesaid, or shall afterwards be found in Arms, he and they shall be liable to the Penalties and Forfeitures of the Statute above recited, as well as to the Penalties of this present Act.

And be it further enacted by the Authority aforesaid, That One Moiety of the Penalties imposed by this Act, with respect to which no other Provision is made, shall be to the Informer or Informers; and the Other Moiety shall be at the Disposal of the Justices of the Peace, Judge Ordinary, or other Person authorized by His Majesty as aforesaid, before whom such Conviction shall happen, provided the same be applied towards the Expence incurred in the Execution of this Act.

And be it further enacted by the Authority aforesaid, That the above Provisions in this Act shall continue in Force for Seven Years, and from thence to the End of the next Session of Parliament, and no longer.

And be it further enacted by the Authority aforesaid, That from and after the First Day of August, One thousand seven hundred and forty seven, no Man or Boy, within that Part of Great Britain called Scotland, other than such as shall be employed as Officers and Soldiers in His Majesty's Forces, shall, on any Pretence whatsoever, wear or put on the Clothes commonly called Highland Clothes (that is to say) the Plaid, Philebeg, or little kilt, Trowse, Shoulder Belts, or any Part whatsoever of what peculiarly belongs

to the Highland Garb; and that no Tartan, or party-coloured Plaid or Stuff
shall be used for Great Coats, or for Upper Coats; and if any such Person
shall presume, after the said First Day of August, to wear or put on the aforesaid Garments, or any Part of them, every such person so offending, being
convicted thereof by the Oath of One or more credible Witness or Witnesses before any Court of Justiciary, or any One or more Justices of the Peace
for the Shire or Stewartry, or Judge Ordinary of the Place where such
Offence shall be committed, shall suffer Imprisonment, without Bail, during
the Space of Six Months, and no longer; and being convicted for a Second
Offence before a Court of Justiciary, or at the Circuits, shall be liable to be
transported to any of His Majesty's Plantations beyond the Seas, there to
remain for the Space of Seven Years.

And whereas by an Act made in this Session of Parliament, intituled, An
Act to indemnify such Persons as have acted in Defence of His Majesty's
Person and Government, and for the Preservation of the publick Peace of this
Kingdom during the Time of the present unnatural Rebellion, and Sheriffs
and others who have suffered Escapes, occasioned thereby, from vexatious
Suits and Prosecutions, it is enacted, That all personal Actions and Suits,
Indictments, Informations, and all Molestations, Prosecutions, and Proceedings whatsoever, and Judgements thereupon, if any be, for or by Reason of
any Matter or Thing advised, commanded, appointed, or done during the
Rebellion, until the Thirtieth Day of April, in the Year of Lord One thousand
seven hundred and forty six, in order to suppress the said unnatural Rebellion, or for the Preservation of the publick Peace, or for the Service or Safety of the Government, shall be discharged and made void: And whereas it is
also reasonable, that Acts done for the publick Service, since the said Thirtieth Day of April, though not justifiable by the strict Forms of Law, should
be justified by Act of Parliament; be it enacted by the Authority aforesaid,
That all personal Actions and Suits, Indictments and Informations, which
have been or shall be commenced or prosecuted, and all Molestations, Prosecutions, and Proceedings whatsoever, and Judgements thereupon, if any be,
for or by reason of any Act, Matter, or Thing advised, commanded, appointed, or done before the Twenty fifth Day of July, in the Year of our Lord One
thousand seven hundred and forty six, in order to suppress the said unnatural Rebellion, or for the Preservation of the publick Peace, or for the Safety
or Service of the Government, shall be discharged and made void; and that
every Person, by whom any such Act, Matter, or Thing shall have been so
advised, commanded, appointed, or done for the Purposes aforesaid, or any
of them, before the said Five and twentieth Day of July, shall be freed,
acquitted, and indemnified, as well against the King's Majesty, His Heirs,
and Successors, as against all and every other Person and Persons; and that
if any Action or Suit hath been or shall be commenced or prosecuted, within that Part of Great Britain called England, against any Person for any such

Act, Matter, or Thing so advised, commanded, appointed, or done for the Purposes aforesaid, or any of them, before the said Twenty fifty Day of July, he or she may plead the General Issue, and give this Act and the special Matter in Evidence; and if the Plaintiff or Plaintiffs shall become nonsuit, or forbear further Prosecution, or suffer Discontinuance; or if a Verdict pass against such Plaintiff or Plaintiffs, the Defendant or Defendants shall recover his, her, or their double Costs, for which he, she, or they shall have the like Remedy, as in Cases where Costs by Law are given to Defendants; and if such Action or Suit hath been or shall be commenced or prosecuted in that Part of Great Britain called Scotland, the Court, before whom such Action or Suit hath been or shall be commenced or prosecuted, shall allow to the Defender the Benefit of the Discharge and Indemnity above provided, and shall further decern the Pursuer to pay to the Defender the full and real Expences that he or she shall be put to by such Action or Suit.

And whereas by an Act passed in the Sixth Year of Her Late Majesty Queen Anne, intituled, An Act for rendering the Union of the Two Kingdoms more entire and complete; it is, among other Things, enacted, That Circuit Courts shall be holden in that Part of the United Kingdom called Scotland, in Manner, and at the Places mentioned in the said Act: And whereas by the late unnatural Rebellion, the Course of Justice in Scotland has been so interrupted, as rendered it impracticable to give up and transmit Presentments, in such due Time as Prosecutions might thereupon commence, before the Northern Circuit, to be holden in May this present Year, whereby there appeared a Necessity of superseding the said Circuit; be it therefore enacted by the Authority aforesaid, That the Judges of the Court of Justiciary, and all and every other Person and Persons therein concerned, are hereby indemnified for their not performing the said Circuit, as by the forecited Act they were obliged to do; any thing in the same Act, or in any other Law or Statute to the contrary notwithstanding.

And whereas a Doubt hath arisen with respect to the Shire of Dunbartain, what Part thereof was intended to be disarmed by the first recited Act made in the First Year of His late Majesty King George, and intended to be carried into further Execution by the present Act; be it enacted by the Authority aforesaid, That such Parts of the said Shire of Dunbartain, as lie upon the East, West, and North Sides of Lochlomond, to the Northward of that Point where the Water of Leven runs from Lochlomond, are and were intended to be disarmed by the aforesaid Act, and are comprehended and subject to the Directions of this Act.

And whereas it is of great importance to prevent the rising Generation being educated in disaffected or rebellious Principles, and although sufficient Provision is already made by Law for the due Regulation of the Teachers in the Four Universities, and in the publick Schools authorized by Law in the Royal Burghs and Country Parishes in Scotland, it is further necessary, that all Persons who take upon them to officiate as Masters or Teachers in Private Schools, in that Part of Great Britain called Scotland, should give Evidence of their good Affection to His Majesty's Person and Government; be it therefore enacted by the Authority aforesaid, That from and after the First Day of November, in the Year of our Lord One thousand seven hundred and forty six, it shall not be lawful for any Person in Scotland to keep a Private School for teaching English, Latin, Greek, or any Part of Literature, or to officiate as a Master or Teacher in such School, or any School for Literature, other than those in the Universities, or established in the respective Royal Burghs by publick Authority, or the Parochial Schools settled according to Law, or the Schools maintained by the Society in Scotland for propagating Christian Knowledge, or by the General Assemblies of the Church of Scotland, or Committees thereof, upon the Bounty granted by His Majesty, until the Situation and Description of such Private School be first entered and registered in a Book, which shall be provided and kept for that Purpose by the Clerks of the several Shires, Stewartries, and Burghs in Scotland, together with a Certificate from the proper Officer, of every such Master and Teacher having qualified himself, by taking the Oaths appointed by Law to be taken by Persons in Offices of publick Trust in Scotland; and every such Master and Teacher of a Private School shall be obliged, and is hereby required, as often as Prayers shall be said in such School, to pray, or cause to be prayed for, in express Words, His Majesty, His Heirs, and Successors, by Name, and for all the Royal Family; and if any Person shall, from and after the said first Day of November, presume to enter upon, or exercise the Function or Office of a Master or Teacher of any such Private School as shall not have been registered in Manner herein directed, or without having first qualified himself, and caused the Certificate to be registered as above mentioned; or in case he shall neglect to pray for His Majesty by name, and all the royal Family, or to cause them to be prayed for as herein directed; or in case he shall resort to, or attend Divine Worship in any Episcopal Meeting-House not allowed by the Law, every Person so offending in any of the Premises, being thereof lawfully convicted before any Two or more of the Justices of Peace, or before any other Judge competent of the Place summarily, shall, for the First Offence, suffer Imprisonment for the Space of Six Months; and for the Second, or any subsequent Offence, being thereof lawfully convicted before the court of Justiciary, or in any of the Circuit Courts, shall be adjudged to be transported, and accordingly shall be transported to some of His Majesty's Plantations in America for Life; and in case any Person adjudged to be so transported shall return into, or be found in Great Britain, then every such Person shall suffer Imprisonment for Life.

And be it further enacted by the Authority aforesaid, That if any Parent or Guardian shall put a Child or Children under his Care to any Private School that shall not be registered according to the Directions of this Act, or whereof the principal Master or Teacher shall not have registered the Certificate of his having qualified himself as herein directed, every such Parent or Guardian so offending, and being thereof lawfully convicted before any Two or more Justices of Peace, or before any other Judge competent of the Place summarily, shall, for the First Offence, be liable to suffer Imprisonment by the Space of Three Months; and for the Second, or any subsequent Offence, being thereof lawfully convicted before the Court of Justiciary, or in any of the Circuit Courts, shall suffer Imprisonment for the Space of Two Years from the Date of such Conviction.

And whereas by an Act passed in the Parliament of Scotland, in the Year of our Lord One thousand six hundred and ninety three, all Chaplains in Families, and governors and Teachers of Children and Youth, were obliged to take the Oaths of Allegiance and Assurance therein directed; and there may be some Doubt, whether by the Laws, as they stand at present, they are obliged to take all the Oaths appointed to be taken by Persons in Offices of publick Trust in Scotland: Therefore be it enacted by the Authority aforesaid, That from and after the First Day of November, in the Year of our Lord One thousand seven hundred and forty six, no Person shall exercise the Employment, Function, or Service of a Chaplain, in any Family in that Part of Great Britain called Scotland, or of a Governor, Tutor, or Teacher of any Child, Children, or Youth, residing in Scotland, or in Parts beyond the Seas, without first qualifying himself, by taking the Oaths appointed by Law to be taken by Persons in Offices of publick Trust, and causing a Certificate of his having done so to be entered or registered in a Book to be kept for that Purpose by the Clerks of the Shires, Stewartries, or Burghs in Scotland, where such Person shall reside; or in case of any such Governor, Tutor, or Teacher of any such Child, Children, or Youth, acting in Parts beyond the Seas, then in a Book to be kept for that Purpose by the Clerk of the Shire, Stewartry, or Burgh where the Parent or Guardian of such Child, Children, or Youth shall reside. And if any Person, from and after the said First Day of November, shall presume to exercise the Employment, Function, or Service of Chaplain in any Family in Scotland, or of a Governor or Teacher of Children or Youth, as aforesaid, without having taken the said Oaths, and caused the Certificate of his having duly taken the same, to be registered, as is above directed; every Person so offending, being thereof lawfully convicted before any Two or more Justices of Peace, or before any other Judge competent of the Place summarily, shall, for the First Offence, suffer Imprisonment by the Space of Six Months; and for the Second, or any subsequent Offence, being thereof lawfully convicted before the Court of Justiciary, or in any of the Circuit Courts, shall be adjudged to be banished from Great Britain for the Space of Seven Years.

Provided always, That it shall be lawful for every Chaplain, Schoolmaster, Governor, Tutor, or Teacher of Youth, who is of the Communion of the Church of Scotland, instead of the Oath of Abjuration appointed by Law to be taken by Persons in Offices civil or military, to take the Oath directed to be taken by Preachers and Expectants in Divinity of the established Church of Scotland, by an Act passed in the Fifth Year of the Reign of King George the First, intituled, An Act for making more effectual the Laws appointing the Oaths for Security of the Government, to be taken by Ministers and Preachers in Churches and Meeting-houses in Scotland; and a Certificate of his having taken that Oath shall, to all Intents and Purposes, be as valid and effectual as the Certificate of his having taken the Oath of Abjuration above mentioned; and he shall be as much deemed to have qualified himself according to Law, as if he had taken the Abjuration appointed to be taken by Persons in Civil Offices.

And be it further enacted, That from and after the said First Day of November, no Person within Scotland shall keep or entertain any Person or Chaplain in any Family, or as Governor, Tutor, or Teacher of any Child, Children, or Youth, unless the Certificate of such Person's having taken the Oaths to His Majesty be duly registered in Manner above directed; and if any Person shall keep or entertain a Chaplain in his Family, or a Governor, Tutor, or Teacher of any Child, Children, or Youth under his Care, without the Certificate of such Chaplain, Governor, Tutor, or Teacher's having respectively qualified himself, by taking the Oaths to His Majesty, being duly registered in Manner above mentioned, every such Person so offending, being thereof lawfully convicted before any Two or more of His Majesty's Justices of Peace, or before any other Judge competent, shall, for the First Offence, suffer Imprisonment by the Space of Six Months; and for the Second, or any subsequent Offence, being thereof lawfully convicted before the Court of Justiciary, or in any of the Circuit Courts in Scotland, shall suffer Imprisonment by the Space of Two Years.

And for the better preventing any Private Schools from being held or maintained, or any Chaplain in any Family, or any Governor, Tutor, or Teacher of any Children or Youth, from being employed or entertained contrary to the Directions of this Act, be it further enacted, That the Sheriffs of Shires, and Stewarts of Stewartries, and Magistrates of Burghs in Scotland, shall be obliged, and are hereby required, from time to time, to make diligent Enquiry within their respective Jurisdictions, concerning any Offences that shall be committed against this Act, and cause the same, being the first Offence, to be prosecuted before themselves; and in case of a Second, or subsequent Offence, to give Notice thereof, and of the Evidence for proving the same, to His Majesty's Advocate for the time being, who is hereby required to prosecute such Second or subsequent Offences before the Court of Justiciary, or at the Circuit Courts.

FINIS

* United Kingdom, *Statutes*, 19 Geo. 2, cap. 39, 1746, 587–602.

An Act to amend and enforce so much of an Act made in the nineteenth Year of his Majesty's Reign, as relates to the more effectual disarming the Highlands in *Scotland* ...*

III   And be it further enacted, That the Prohibition contained in the said Act of the first Year of his said late Majesty's Reign, or in the said Act of the nineteenth Year of his present Majesty's Reign, or in this Act, of having, keeping, bearing or wearing any Arms or Warlike Weapons, and the Pains and Penalties aforesaid, shall not extend or be construed to extend to any Officers or their Assistants, employed in the Execution of Justice, nor to prohibit or hinder any Person who is qualified to vote at Elections of Parliament Men, to serve for any of the above-named Counties; nor any Heretor or Life-renter, possessed of an Estate of four hundred, and less than one thousand Pounds *Scots* valued Rent, to have in his Custody, to be used by himself, Family or Servants, in the Manner allowed by the Laws now in Force, any Number of Arms, not exceeding three Firelocks, three Pair of Pistols and three Swords or Cutlasses; nor to prohibit or hinder any Heretor or Life renter, possessed of an Estate of one thousand or more, and less than three thousand Pounds *Scots* valued Rent, to have in his Custody, to be used by himself, Family or Servants, in the Manner allowed by the Laws now in Force, any Number of Arms, not exceeding seven Firelocks, seven Pair of Pistols and seven Swords or Cutlasses; nor to prohibit or hinder any Heretor or Life-renter, possessed of an Estate of three thousand or more, and less than six thousand Pounds *Scots* valued Rent, to have in his Custody, to be used by himself, Family or Servants, in the Manner allowed by the Laws now in Force, any Number of Arms, not exceeding twelve Firelocks, twelve Pair of Pistols and twelve Swords or Cutlasses; nor to prohibit or hinder any Heretor or Life-renter, possessed of an Estate of six thousand or more, and less than nine thousand Pounds *Scots* valued Rent, to have in his Custody, to be used by himself, Family or Servants, in the Manner allowed by the Laws now in Force, any Number of Arms, not exceeding twenty Firelocks, twenty Pair of Pistols, and twenty Swords or Cutlasses; nor to prohibit or hinder any Heretor or Life-renter, possessed of an Estate of nine thousand Pounds *Scots* valued Rent, or more, to have in his Custody, to be used by himself, Family or Servants, in the Manner allowed by the Laws now in Force, any Number of Arms, not exceeding thirty Firelocks, thirty Pair of Pistols, and thirty Swords or Cutlasses; nor to prohibit or hinder the Magistrates of any Burgh Royal, to have in their Custody a sufficient Number of Arms for keeping Guard within their Borough, according to the Directions of their respective magistrates; nor to prohibit or hinder any Person who shall be licensed to keep, bear or wear Arms, pursuant to the Directions of the said recited Act, from keeping, bearing or wearing such and so many Arms or Warlike Weapons, as in such Licence or Licences shall be for that Purpose particularly specified; nor to prohibit or hinder the Officers of the Army, having his Majesty's Commissions, and the Soldiers under their Command, to keep, use or bear Arms as formerly; nor the Lieutenants of Counties or their Deputies, or the fensible Men under their Command, to keep and receive Arms out of his Majesty's Magazines, and to use the same during the Time that their Militia or fensible Men shall be called out by lawful Authority.

IV   Provided nevertheless, That the several Persons before-mentioned, to whom a limited Number of Arms is hereby allowed, shall be obliged upon Summons, according to the said recited Act of the nineteenth Year of his present Majesty, to deliver up in the Manner directed by this and the said Act, all such Arms as they shall have in their Custody or Use, over and above the Number so limited.

*   United Kingdom, *Statutes*, 21 Geo. 2, cap. 34, 1748.

Letter from William MacKenzie, Piper, Second Battalion, 71st Regiment*

New York February 7th 1778

Dear Petter   This is to Enform you of my well being at presant hoping this [*sic*] lines will find you in the same and all other absent Friends, and as I send you this Letter in particular I hope you'll send me an answer Send me word concerning all friends especially your father & mother & your Brother & Sister Alexr & he's [*sic*] wife and my Grand father and my Ants [*sic*] and Chirstie my Ant is in Good health married on Donald M'Donald Soldr in Major Grant's Company 1st Battn 42 Regt and her husband is from ardnamurachan I am still in Capt Patrick Campbell's of Glenuir's Company I am Piper to the 2 Battn 71 Regt I am as well as ever I was in my Life my Pay is as Good as 1 Shilling & sixpence Per Day and I hope my fortune within two years will be as Good that I will have 200 Acres of free Ground of my own in this Country Concerning this War we alway's Get the Better of our enimy we make them Retreat like a hair before a Pack of Hounds and if it had not been for this war this is the Best Country in the World I hope Petter you'll take so much pains as to acquant [*sic*] my father & mother of my well being I was sorry when I was turnd at Crieff and could not Go to see my mother and I hope when you'll write to me you'll write the truth this is the 6 Letter I sent to you and I expect you'll see Hugh M'Intyre from Glenow send me concerning Parlan M'Farlan and hi's [*sic*] wife ------------------ turn over Remember me to William MacFarlan in Glenourchay and John his Brother is in Good health in Capt Chisolm's Company 1st Battn 71 Regt and send word to John how his wife is Petter Turner is in Coll M'Donald's Company and he is in Good health my kind compliments to his father & mother when I come first to America I heard of William M'Farlan but I heard no word of Duncan or Donald M'Farland

No more at presant [*sic*] but all countrymen in this country're in good health I am your real friend & well wisher

William MacKenzie

N.B. A private in the New Brunswickers (104th Foot) in 1811 was paid 1/-d per day. That 1/- a day was before "stoppages" and was a poor wage in contemporary North America (Morton, *A Military History of Canada*, 53).

*   Transcribed from Scottish Records Office, GD 170/3158.

Other Immigrant
Ceòl Mór Pipers

THE CAMPBELL PIPER TO BARCALDINE,
THE MACGILLIVRAY PIPER TO GLENALADALE,
AND COLIN FRASER

In the old and established family of the Campbells of Barcaldine and
Glenure, a family piper is known to have been getting ready to emigrate in
1791. A letter from an Alexander Campbell of Kinlochlaigh to Alexander
Campbell of Barcaldine (1745-1800) dated 31 August 1791[1] suggests a
replacement for Barcaldine's piper who was "going for America."[2] In May
1825 Archibald MacNab, thirteenth chief of MacNab, along with his personal piper, James MacNee,[3] went to Montreal to greet those of his Scottish
tenants who had decided to start a new life in the Ottawa Valley in Ontario.
John McTaggart, who travelled in Canada in 1826, 1827, and 1828, met
MacNab and saw his "tail" and the Highland piper strutting before. McTaggart reported the piper played the "Hacks o' Cromdale" and "The Campbells
Are Coming," both pieces of light music. In December 1837, when rebellion
threatened, MacNab reportedly wrote, in the *Bytown Gazette*, "to assure you
their War Pipe can still sound "The Pronach a'cach" – (the charge to battle)
... DONALD'S READY" (MacNab meant *brosnachadh catha*, battle inciting).[4]
Then, in 1840, when MacNab's immigrants in MacNab Township were driven to fight for fairness from their autocratic New World landlord, they were
led out in public by a Murdoch MacDonald who played "The Gathering of
the Clans."

Going to the New World was a guarantee of near anonymity, but such
anonymity was a simple continuation of the situation in Highland and Low-

land Scotland. Pipers were everywhere taken for granted and left unremarked until they competed or became involved in something unusual, and only then do they find mention in the published record. In Nova Scotia Fair Andrew MacGillivray's son John, an Arisaig man who had been Alexander MacDonald of Glenaladale's piper in the early nineteenth century and who emigrated in 1818, is remembered on both sides of the Atlantic for his songs, not his piping;[5] Kenneth Chisholm, the last piper to a Chisholm chief (c. 1790?), a man presumably of considerable musical talent, is remembered because he was killed by a falling tree in what is now Antigonish County. MacGillivray, according to a grandson in Antigonish, was a pupil of John MacKay (authority gave Skye, Raasay, as having perhaps been too particular a location),[6] and Kenneth Chisholm, according to the notes in MacKay's *Collection*, which reported his unusual death, was a pupil of Little John (MacRae), Lord Seaforth's piper.[7] Nothing is known of either man's music. If there was lore about these people it did not cross the Gaelic-to-English bridge, and now it is too late.[8]

In 1817, the year before MacGillivray arrived in Nova Scotia, George Ramsay, ninth earl of Dalhousie and lieutenant governor of Nova Scotia, travelled in the Strait of Canso area separating Nova Scotia from the province of Cape Breton and in what is now Antigonish County. His journals mention pipers in both places. On 9 September, having drifted on the current from Plaster Cove (Port Hastings) southward to Ship Harbour (Port Hawkesbury) waiting for a breeze, "an old Highlander tuned his pipes, & played to us as long as we could hear him."[9]

On 14 September, travelling overland to Guysborough, he visited the home of an Italian about six miles from Antigonish where he was entertained to "Italian song"; this he deemed "a very ludicrous contrast to our dancing musick, a Highland piper, occasionally relieved by a very wretched fiddler; still to that our reels were kept up with great Glee, snapping of fingers & the wildest, rudest & joyous expression of the Highland fling."[10]

Dalhousie's record prompts the question who was the piper, and there are two plausible answers. If Dalhousie was six or so miles to the east of Antigonish he could have been either in Pomquet (essentially Acadian French) or in Pomquet Forks, which was then a New World Strathglass, almost full of Chisholms, who had been arriving there since about 1790. If Kenneth Chisholm had settled at Pomquet Forks and was still alive, he may have been the piper. If the Italian's home was at Pomquet, then the piper was almost certainly one of the "Piper" Campbells of Pomquet (assuming that Pomquet meant Pomquet and was not an abbreviation of Pomquet Forks), although the date of the Campbell emigration is unknown. The "Piper" Campbells of Pomquet were Roman Catholic Lochaber people with deep roots in Keppoch country and with several marriage ties to the descendants of cadets of Keppoch, notably the *Sliochd an taighe* (People of the House) MacDonald family from Bohuntin. At least one Campbell from Tulloch (Keppoch country), Samuel, emigrated to Nova Scotia in 1803.[11] In any case, a Lochaber-born Campbell first cousin of the Pomquet "Piper" Campbells, Angus *Pìobair*, stayed with them before moving to Dunakin in Inverness County.[12] It is tempting to think that these Campbells were Mac a'Ghlasraichs.

How these Campbell pipers were related to the young Campbell piper to Glenaladale in 1745 (or, for that matter, to the piper Neil Campbell who married Betty MacEachen, daughter of Captain Hugh MacEachen of the Dubh Ghleannach, and settled at Alba Station in 1828 in Cape Breton) is in all likelihood beyond discovery, but it would be foolhardy now to assert that no relationship could have existed.[13]

Where Pomquet Forks (Heatherton) and its Scotch surroundings are concerned, almost nothing is known about Kenneth Chisholm and even less about the community pipers, other than that they existed. On 20 July 1846, when nearby St Andrews held its annual Temperance Society celebration, the sounds of church bells and cannon were accompanied by "the warlike notes of the pibroch."[14] Recently, on 29 March 1994, Mary Eliza (Chisholm) MacDonald died at the age of one hundred and two at Marydale, outside St Andrews. She was the daughter of the piper Big Colin Chisholm.[15] For at least part of his life Big Colin was a neighbour of the piper Allan Cameron, recently deceased, whose later music reflects, I am told, more the modern style than the older Gaelic tradition.

The emigrant Frasers who were traditional *ceòl mór* pipers are immediately associated with Australia rather than Nova Scotia or Canada, but there is at least one notable exception, Colin Fraser. His wider claim to fame lies in his having been piper and personal assistant to George Simpson, governor of the Hudson's Bay Company, on his journey by birchbark canoe convoy in the summer of 1828, from York Factory on Hudson's Bay to Fort Langley in what was then New Caledonia. Of Fraser it was written, "This decent young man ... lately from the Highlands ... on this voyage, accompanies the Governor in the double capacity of piper and assistant servant, &c."[16]

The edited journal of the company's chief factor, Archibald McDonald, includes McDonald's memories of Colin Fraser playing strathspeys in the governor's canoe: " 'The Campbells are coming, hooray, hooray' or some such music of our mountain land," and "a few marches," and, on one of the occasions when he appeared in "full Highland costume" (at Fort Saint James), " *Si coma leum cogadh na shea*" ("Peace: or War, if you will it otherwise"),[17] nothing if not a piece of classical piping.

Who Colin Fraser was in Highland Scotland remains to be found out. Any of the many Highland Scots in William MacGillivray's old North West Company, including MacGillivray himself, could have mentioned his name to Simpson. Whatever Fraser's path to the West, Phillip Scott Camsell, son of a later Hudson's Bay Company governor, told Canadian Broadcasting Corporation interviewer Bill McNeil that he knew Simpson had always travelled with a piper. Camsell remembered Colin Fraser's (paternal?) grandson, who lived at Fort Chipewyan at the west end of Lake Athabaska. His family, and probably he himself, were a mixture of Fraser and Cree.[18] Colin Fraser's pipe chanter was still held in the area in 1980, according to an article that appeared in the *International Piper*.[19] An earlier Canadian source, A.E. Garton from Eldorado, Saskatchewan, reported to the *Piping Times* that he had met Colin Fraser in 1936, at Fort Chipewyan.[20] He described Fraser, who was eighty-five in 1936, as a son of the piper to the governor of the Hudson's Bay Company who had gone clear across the country (i.e., Simpson). Fraser had his father's bagpipes, which he called the "Callum" pipes.

HECTOR JOHNSTON, PIPER TO COLL

A letter sent in 1906 from John Johnston (1836-1921) in Coll to a cousin in Nova Scotia states categorically that Hector (died c. 1870), the only son of Donald Johnston, farmer at Arinagour, Coll, was piper to the laird of Coll until he emigrated in 1824.[21] Hector Johnston presumably took over where Duncan M'Master (winner of the Edinburgh competition in 1805) left off, Duncan in turn having replaced Connduiligh Rankin, who joined the army in 1804 and went to Prince Edward Island in 1806. Connduiligh's father, Neil Rankin, quit piping in 1806 and died in 1819. Before he died, according to Henry Whyte, Neil Rankin took up the farm of Cliad in Coll.[22] John Johnston, who claimed to have heard the last of the Rankin pipers (whom he did not name), was the son of John Johnston, who was born in 1805 at Cliad and who must have known, or been acquainted with, both Hector Johnston and Neil Rankin.

Hector Johnston, like M'Master and Connduiligh Rankin, was piper to Alexander MacLean (1753–1835), fourteenth of Coll from 1786, younger brother of Donald MacLean (the "young Coll" who was host to Boswell and Johnson in 1773). Family information assembled in Pictou County by Thelma Johnson convincingly dates Hector Johnston's emigration to 1819 on the ship *Economy*.[23] He was a schoolteacher in River John before moving to Prince Edward Island around 1840; there he had a farm at Brudenell River that had originally been part of Lord Selkirk's grant. Thelma Johnson says that he took up teaching again, although local Brudenell historian Athol Robertson has never found any record of this.[24] However, like many of his kin in Scotland, Johnston took an active part in church affairs (he converted in Prince Edward Island from Presbyterianism to Baptism and was a deacon in Brudenell, which, as Thelma Johnson said, precluded his piping at least on Sunday).

Archibald Campbell of Kilberry published evidence that Hector Johnston was able to write pipe music.[25] Johnston and John Campbell (son of the author of the "Colin Campbell's Instrumental Book, 1797" (known undiscriminatingly as the "Campbell Canntaireachd") were each awarded £1 18s in 1817 "additional for music produced by them, and as having come from a distance." Kilberry noted that against Johnston's name was the notation "Writes music."[26] Kilberry had access to "some of the original records," held by the *Pìobaireachd* Society, from which Sir John Graham Dalyell drew for his *Musical Memoirs of Scotland* (1848) and from which the author(s) of the notes in Angus MacKay's *Collection* must have taken data. These records cover the period 1806–44 and appear to have been made and kept by the Highland Society of Scotland.

Two points emerge from this record. Firstly, the going premium for writing music "scientifically" in 1818 was a guinea, so the Highland Society of Scotland was prepared almost to double this amount in 1817 to attract musically literate Gaelic pipers from afar. This gives an indication of the society's priorities and the importance members put on steering traditional *ceòl mór* in the direction of literacy, a regency improver tendency that had an abundance of late-eighteenth- and early-nineteenth-century fiddle collections as models and motivation.

The second point concerns Hector Johnston's acquisition of musical literacy. The genealogy of the four Johnston families in Coll, c. 1810, mentioned by John Johnston is probably not without error, but it is obviously fairly accurate. The implication to be drawn from his family history is that Hector Johnston the piper and Lachlan Johnston (1787–1861) and his (Lachlan's) brother Roderick were first cousins. All of them emigrated to Nova Scotia, Hector and his cousin Roderick moving later to Prince Edward Island. Lachlan, who stayed in Nova Scotia, was considered by John Johnston's father, John (d. 1906), to have been an excellent scholar (they were at school together on Coll). There is no indication that he might have given his cousin musical instruction, but the point is that Hector Johnston, a schoolteacher in Nova Scotia, was a member of a family that had a good reputation for scholarship, if probably only at an undergraduate level.

Hector was believed by his family and their descendants in Pictou County to have been one of the best pipers, the man who had the "historic" set of pipes that, the family claimed, had been used during the 'Forty-five. A letter from John Johnston, Coll, dated 20 February 1907 to the Reverend David(?) Johnson in Prince Edward Island shows that Johnston was aware of the set and was anxious to obtain them:

Hector Johnston was family piper to the Chief of Coll for many years, and was a famous performer, having studied in the best Piping College, of the Country, that of Skye. You will perhaps smile at a Piping College, but such existed in the Highlands of Scotland for generations. At all events, our friend was a great Piper, and when he went to Nova Scotia, he carried the family Bagpipes with him which were an heirloom in the Coll Chief family for generations. I was making enquiries through Rev. A. McLean Sinclair, of Belfast, PEI, if these Bagpipes were in existence yet or could they be procured, as I knew Hector left a family. He replied that they were in exestence [sic], but were in the possession of others, as the widow of Hector sold them shortly after his death. I wonder if you know anything about them. I will feel very much obliged to you if you can find out from some of Hector's descendants where it is at present and if it could be obtained yet. I feel a great interest in this matter for the sake of old associations and for the fact that I was a great performer on the pipes myself, – perhaps the best of your name since Hector, himself died; and though I stopped playing generally for many years back, I feel I would stir up myself to play a "salute" on these pipes yet, could I lay hands on them. At all events, please try and find out where they are, if possible ...

Let me know also, if possible, about the descendants of Hector, the piper, referred to already, – I understand there are many.[27]

According to Thelma Johnson, Hector's wife told the family after Hector's death that the bagpipes had been destroyed in a fire in Prince Edward Island. The Pictou County Johnsons believed that Hector's widow had sold them, which may or may not be true, but at least the Reverend MacLean Sinclair verified the instrument's existence some time prior to 1907 and after Hector's death. In any case, a Prince Edward Island census shows that there were two sons and five daughters in Hector Johnson's family and none appears to have had any interest in piping.

Hector Johnston drew up his will on 18 September 1870 and in or about that year he sold the farm and moved to Charlottetown. Of all the Coll people whom John Johnston would have wanted to visit in the New World, Hector Johnston surely ranked highest. John Johnston must have heard from his own father, and doubtless from other relatives who either did not emigrate or who emigrated c. 1850, about Hector the piper, thus whetting his appetite for vanished piping information.

It is tempting to think that the novel additions he bequeathed to the world of *ceòl mór*, published in David Glen's *The Music of the Clan MacLean* (1900; Johnston took the trouble to travel to Glasgow from Coll to pass the music on), came from Hector Johnston in Brudenell River, but to date there is no evidence that John Johnston was in Prince Edward Island. A letter he wrote to a cousin, Alexander L. Johnston in Orillia, Ontario, dated 28 December 1905,[28] shows that in 1864 and 1865 he was in the Orillia area, where many of his Johnston relatives had settled. He piped at "cousin Lachy's" in Newmarket, "Canada West," and was greatly impressed at that New Year's *céilidh* by Lachy's brother John Johnston's fiddling. The 1907 letter to the "Revd. Sir" only shows that John Johnston knew about the famous set and about Hector and his family, but he might have had this information from many sources. Nothing suggests that John Johnston had actually visited his cousin Hector. The pipes, if they still exist, are unidentified.

Notes

1 William Matheson, "Duncan MacDonald (1882–1954)," 1.

CHAPTER ONE

1 Cultural retentiveness appears to have been the least in the New World (in Upper and Lower Canada, and in Australia for example), when a large proportion of the immigrants was made up of families of destitute Highlanders sent by assisted passage, and if the emigrations were later than c. 1850.
2 McDonell Dawson, *The Catholics of Scotland*, 520.
3 Ibid., 561–2.
4 Letter from Coll MacDonell, fourth of Barisdale, 1811, cited in Charles Fraser-Mackintosh, "Minor Highland Septs – The MacDonells of Barisdale," 98. After 1811 there was often scant economic option for the middle class but to move. MacLeod of Arnisdale shifted to the tack of Claigionn near Dunvegan, suggesting that there was at least some chiefly sympathy for a former tacksman.

The loss of *de facto* Gaelic politico-legal control increased the economic problems at lower levels of society. Coll MacDonell's correspondence of 1809, for example, shows also that the local fishery was suffering from the intrusions of "sixty to seventy boats on the coast this season from the south that did not use to frequent our lochs, and they are very much suspected by all the fishermen for stealing and destroying of nets." In another letter, probably a little later, Barisdale complained of "one thousand coasting boats there [at

Loch Hourn] last week." See Charles Fraser-Mackintosh, "Glengarry-Coll MacDonell of Barisdale," 152-3. British capitalism as prescribed in the Fisheries (Scotland) Act, 1756, *Statutes*, 29 Geo. 2, 1755–56, ungoverned by an effective system of policing, rather than exclusive local Scottish Gaelic subsistence in its own traditional fishery, was a major threat to the protein source of the common Gael.

5 A touching statement of the impact of emigrations from Dervaig, Mull, in Argyllshire is found in John McLean's *Notes of a Twenty-five Years' Service*, vol. 2: 289–90. McLean, a native Gaelic speaker, returned to Dervaig in September 1842, having been away for twenty-three years, most of them spent in the Canadian forests dealing in beaver pelts. He met his aging mother as a successful man and saw something of the old unchanging world:

These scenes were still the same, as far as the hand of Nature was concerned – there stood the lofty Benmore, casting his sombre shades over the glassy surface of Lochba, as in the days of yore; there were also the same heath-covered hills and wooded dells, well stocked with sheep and cattle; but the human inhabitants of the woods and dells – where were they? far distant in the wilds of America, or toiling for a miserable existence in the crowded cities of the Lowlands – a sad change! The bleating of sheep, the lowing of cattle, for the glad voices of a numerous population, happy and contented with their lot, loyal to their sovereign, and devotedly attached to their chiefs! But loyalty and attachment are but fancies, which in these utilitarian and trading days, are flat and unprofitable.

6 In 1732 a Captain Patrick MacKay took "a large body of people" from Edarachillis to Georgia with Oglethorpe (see Rev. Angus Mackay, *Book of MacKay*, 294). Between 1738 and 1740 Lauchlan Campbell organized the emigration of eighty-three Islay families to the north of the province of New York. Also, according to William Matheson, MacDonalds and MacLeods from Skye and Raasay settled along the York and Rappahannock Rivers in Virginia in the first half of the eighteenth century (see William Matheson, ed., *Songs of John MacCodrum*, 269).

7 Marianne McLean, *The People of Glengarry*, 123.

8 Alick Morrison, *The MacLeods*, section 3, 91–2.

9 Iain R. MacKay, "Glenalladale's Settlement," 19.

10 Ibid., 18.

11 William Matheson, ed., *The Songs of John MacCodrum*, in text and notes to "*Oran do na fogarraich*" ("Song to the Expelled") and "*Oran Fir Ghrìminis*" ("Song to the Tacksman of Griminish").

12 Among others it lost the last MacCrimmon Dòmhnul Ruadh, the famous piper.

13 Newte, *Prospects and Observations*, 236.

14 *A View of the Highlands &c* is mentioned by Keltie, *A History of the Scottish*

Highlands, vol. 2: 33, 42, 43. No author is named, but Colonel Thornton of Thornville-Royal, Yorkshire, was in Badenoch in September 1784.

15 Graham, *Colonists from Scotland*; also Bailyn, *Voyagers to the West*; and Bumsted, *The People's Clearance*.

16 According to Duncan Campbell, David Stewart (1772–1829), who was the son of pro-Hanoverian Robert Stewart of Garth (d. 1820), succeeded his older brother William as Stewart of Garth. See Duncan Campbell, *The Book of Garth*, 227, 236, 238.

17 Col. David Stewart, *Sketches*, vol. 1: 486ff.

18 The duke of Gordon's policy for traditional Keppoch lands south of the River Spean in 1770 appears to fit this model. First there was the removal of sub-tenants (i.e., tacksmen, since Keppoch himself was Gordon's tenant) from several holdings, setting up the later, early nineteenth-century removal of the common man, if not overseas then to minuscule crofts nearby (Stuart Macdonald, *Back to Lochaber*, 189–90). Gordon is said to have used higher rents to oust old MacDonald tacksmen families but since a Glencoe MacDonald family took one of the tacks, Gordon may have been exercising a vengeful animus against specific gentlemanly Catholic ex-Jacobite tenantry of long standing. However, not all the Keppoch middle class left in 1770 since, to Gordon, it was important to have officers to raise Gordon men on Keppoch lands. The point to be restated is that the old Gaelic social system was not everywhere extinguished by 1815.

19 In 1823, for example, MacNab of MacNab emigrated and obtained a township in Ontario.

20 John MacPherson, *Tales from Barra*, 129.

21 Brander, *The Emigrant Scots*, 139.

22 Somers, *Letters from the Highlands*, passim. The saddest aspect of the emigration subject is that, when at last in the 1880s when the Crofting Commission tackled the Highland land problem, it only addressed the problem of getting rights for Gaels who inhabited these "crofts." The real problem of the rights of Gaels to the *Gàidhealtachd* has always been avoided.

23 Samuel Johnson, *A Journey to the Western Islands*, 159.

24 Margaret MacKay, ed., *Revd John Walker's Report*, and also Walker, *An Economical History*.

25 Ships' records of Highland passengers sailing from Scotland to Maritime Canada and elsewhere at any time throughout the emigration years, are scarce – only a small percentage of those who sailed are included. Eighteenth-century statistics such as Webster's (1755) (found in Kyd, ed., *Scottish Population Statistics*) and Sinclair's *Old Statistical Account* are not completely accurate and the official censuses of the nineteenth century, spaced by a decade, are deceptive inasmuch as populations may be replaced from outside or may quickly make up losses to emigration or death by disease. Undoubtedly, as yet unnamed ships made sailings and known ships made unrecorded crossings with hundreds of people from the Scottish Highlands.

CHAPTER TWO

1 Smout, *A History of the Scottish People 1560–1830*, 241.
2 A thoughtful treatment of Scottish Jacobite thinking may be found in Audrey Cunningham's *The Loyal Clans*.
3 Some Scottish piper produced a fine piece of *ceòl mór* seldom played today called "*An Co-Aontachadh*" ("The Union"), a lament.
4 In signing the grand alliance recognizing King James III, Louis repudiated the 1697 peace treaty by which he had recognized William III as rightful British king.
5 Under (Sir) Robert Walpole alone the Whigs controlled English, Scottish, and Irish politics, from Westminster, 1721–42.
6 The Northumberland area was significantly supportive of the Jacobite cause.
7 Rob Roy MacGregor, the famous Highland Perthshire outlaw, had a hand, on the Jacobite side, in both the 1715 and 1719 risings and the double failures are still attributed in some degree to the fact that Rob Roy's superior allegiance was to the Hanoverian duke of Argyll. See Lang, *Companions of Pickle*, 98.
8 In the cases of the Glengarry and Clanranald chiefs the motive for staying out was fear of loss of property.
9 Keppoch lands were held late by virtue of military threat. In the New World, where protection of Catholicism was seldom necessary, the Catholic church had a tendency to arrogate to itself much more power than it had had in Gaelic Scotland where it existed in large part thanks to the protection of the militarily feared.
10 The systematic confiscation and subsequent loss of the contents of the charter chests of leading known and suspected Jacobite Highland families and the importance of the one-sided loss of documentation of what were the more politically and culturally conservative Highland families formed the topic of Dr James A. Stewart, Jr's talk entitled "Lost Highland Manuscripts and the Jacobite Rebellion of 1745–46" at the Tenth International Congress of Celtic Studies in Edinburgh in 1995. His original research may be found in his doctoral thesis "The Clan Ranald, the History of a Highland Clan," (Edinburgh University). In 1995 Stewart was in the History department at Hong Kong Baptist University.
11 Keltie, *History*, book 4: 66.
12 Cumberland had used the 42d Regiment at Fontenoy in 1745, even to the extent of acceding to the request of Lt Col Sir Robert Munro (of Foulis, Munro chief, veteran of Marlborough's wars) to let the men fight in traditional Highland fashion – charge, firearm discharge and then sword work (see Col. David Stewart, *Sketches*, vol. 1: 255). Cumberland was well aware of Highland battle techniques and bravery at Fontenoy.
13 20 Geo. 2, "An act to amend and enforce," is referred to in *Statutes*, 21 Geo.

2, cap. 34, 127, as follows: "An Act made in the twentieth Year of his present Majesty's Reign, enlarged, as to all Persons, not being Landed Men, until ..."

14 Millar, "Note on the Proclamation for Disarming," 216–22.

15 C.C. Pond, letter to author, 10 September 1996.

16 *The Scots Statutes Revised* (1899) 1:81.

17 See Article XX, "Heritable Offices, &c." in An Act for an Union of the Two Kingdoms of England and Scotland (*Statutes*, 6 Anne, 1706) in *Scots Statutes Revised* 1:4. For 1746 note also "All heritable jurisdictions of justiciary, all regalities and heritable bailieries and constabularies, were dissolved, and the powers former lay vested in them were ordained to be exercised by such of the king's courts as these powers would have belonged to if the jurisdictions had never been granted." See Lees, *History of the County of Inverness*, 203–4. (Neither Keppoch nor Lochiel held regalities).

18 Another indication of the fear that Highland Jacobites had caused the king and government in London was the huge increase immediately voted to William, duke of Cumberland, when his victory was known.

19 See chapter 6 for the officers in Fraser's Highlanders.

20 Rev. George Patterson includes "John MacKay, piper" in his Sutherlandshire list (see Patterson, *History of the County of Pictou*, 454).

21 John G. Gibson, "Piper John MacKay and Roderick McLennan." See also Angus MacKay, *A Collection*, 13. Elsewhere the piper is given as William MacKay.

22 *Hector* emigrant William MacKenzie (c. 1755–1844) of Loch Broom, younger son of Sir William MacKenzie of Ballone, was educated and bilingual. His friend and fellow passenger Alexander Cameron (alias Murray) also was bilingual but neither man organized or headed the *Hector* expedition. It was a commercial venture by Glasgow businessman John Pagan and his North American partner, the Scottish Dr Rev. John Witherspoon (1723–94), and headed by their emigration agent, John Ross, a former Dingwall merchant and later manager of the linen station at Loch Broom. The ship sailed late and the emigrants were not properly made aware of the facts of their situation (see Donald MacKay, *Scotland Farewell*, passim).

23 Genealogical data concerning the Gairloch MacKay piping family is by no means complete. In the Gairloch (Scotland) records several MacKays appear whose relationships, if any, to the piping family are unknown. For example, a "John MacKay Bein," native of Gairloch, Scotland, emigrated to Nova Scotia in 1804. He died 19 May 1862, aged seventy-eight. It is noteworthy also that a John MacKay, "piper," appears in the muster records of Banastre Tarleton's British Legion during the revolutionary war. He is the only man in any of Tarleton's musters so designated; he served in Lt Donald MacCrumen's company and died, presumably in New York, c. 1783. Nothing of his origin is given.

24 Even as Allan MacDonald, Glenuig, interprets *ceòl mór*, with the rapid playing of echo beats on E, and with the timing and rhythms of Gaelic song, the music remains noticeably more esoteric than dance music.

25 The direct influence of the MacCrimmons and the Gairloch MacKays did not end until the early nineteenth century.

26 Mackintosh of Mackintosh, *Notes Descriptive*, 35–6, cited also in Cheape, "The Piper to the Laird of Grant," 1, 173. Mackintosh, twenty-third chief, fought in America with his company of Fraser's Highlanders during the revolutionary war, at times alongside Banastre Tarleton's British Legion in which Lieutenant Donald MacCrumen served.

27 Alexander Nicolson, for example, wrote in 1930, "Just as the language and the dress of the Gael were proscribed in 1746, so also was the bagpipe, it being held to be an 'instrument of war'" (Nicolson, *History of Skye*, 266).

28 Disarming Act, *Statutes*, 19 Geo. 2, 1746, 587.

29 Ibid., 598.

30 Ibid., 588.

31 Ibid.

32 Ibid., 589. It is worthy of note that nobody has ever claimed that bagpipes were proscribed under the more explicit listing of 1716, and pipers were present at Sheriffmuir and elsewhere.

33 Disarming Act, *Statutes*, 19 Geo. 2, 1746, 595. The amending act of 1748 presented a sliding scale of actual numbers of firelocks, pairs of pistols, and swords or cutlasses that it was legal for any "Heretor or Life-renter" to possess. The number of weapons in these classes increased as one's worth rose from £400 Scots to over £9000 Scots.

34 Ibid., 591.

35 Ibid., 596.

36 Ibid., 588.

37 An Act to amend ... (*Statutes*, 21 Geo. 2, cap. 34, 1748), 127.

38 Disarming Act, *Statutes*, 19 Geo. 2, 1746, 596.

39 Ibid., 596 and 597.

40 22 Geo. 2, cap. 63, "An Act to Repeal ... the Use of the Highland Dress." This act refers to the original Disarming Act of 1746 and to the "Two several Acts, one made in the Twentieth, the other in the Twenty-first year of the Reign" of George II.

41 Iain Gray, archivist, Aberdeen City Archives, letter to John G. Gibson, 7 November 1996.

42 Carr, *Caledonian Sketches*, 453.

43 Disarming Act, *Statutes*, 19 Geo. 2, 1746, 588.

44 Donald MacDonald, *Ancient Martial Music*, 3. Elsewhere the citation given from the first edition runs: "After the Battle of Culloden, a powerful check was given to the spirit of the Highlanders; and, with their arms and garb, the Bagpipe was, for a long time, almost completely laid aside. In this interval much of

the Music was neglected and lost." Donald MacDonald was the son of John MacDonald, a Skyeman who is said to have been a MacArthur pupil.

45 Logan, *The Scottish Gael*, vol. 2: 288.

46 MacKay Scobie, *Pipers and Pipe Music*, 1 footnote.

47 Donald Macdonald, *Ancient Martial Music*, v.

48 Archibald Campbell, *The Kilberry Book*, 7.

49 David Johnson, *Scottish Fiddle Music*, 14, 24, listed four fiddle pibrochs that he dated to the first two decades of the eighteenth century. He added that Scottish "fiddlers" experimented with the form from c. 1710 to 1800. Allan MacDonald's work on vocal *ceòl mór* is pending (May 1997).

50 Kilberry's emphasizing the army's part in preserving traditional piping is in line with his family's long history of service in the Highland regiments.

51 Archibald Campbell, "The Highland Bagpipe," Part 2, in *Piping Times* 14, 11, (August 1962).

52 Collinson, *The Bagpipe*, 166–7.

53 Ibid., 171 footnote.

54 See Appendix 8, Disarming Act, *Statutes*, 19 Geo. 2, 1746.

55 Collinson, *The Bagpipe*, 172.

56 Ibid., 176–7. The argument is still made that cattle drovers were also exempted from the weapons clause of the Disarming Act, and if so, then they could only have enjoyed such exemption if "His Majesty, His Heirs, or Successors, by Licence under His or Their Sign Manual" permitted it. See Disarming Act, *Statutes*, 19 Geo. 2, 1746, 595. No such licence or copy is held by the Scottish Record Office (SRO) in either the Chancery or Exchequer records and to date (3 January 1997) I have not studied the English Privy Council or Privy Seal records (I am indebted to Dr N.J. Mills for searching the SRO material).

57 The first Fencible regiment was formed in 1759, six years after the disarming clause had ceased to have effect.

58 The published record shows that drover-pipers do not form a large group in Gaelic society during the Disarming Act years (1746–82).

59 Collinson, *The Bagpipe*, 172.

60 Two references to a *pìob bheag* (small pipe) appear in the song literature, first in J.L. Campbell, ed., trans., *Hebridean Folksongs*, in a waulking song called "*Dh'éirich mi gu moch Di-Luain*"("I rose Early Monday"). This was collected from a Barra woman and appears in vol. 3, 50. The second occurs also in a waulking song, in "*Rinn mi mocheirigh*," in Shaw, *Folksongs and Folklore of South Uist*, 251 and 252. It is also in K.C. Craig, *Orain Luaidh*.

61 A discussion of the effectiveness of the Society in Scotland for Propagating Christian Knowledge (SSPCK) in discouraging Gaelic, particularly from 1753–1766 when Gaelic was banned in its schools, lies outside my mandate.

62 James Reid's fate is described in the court transcipts for late 1746 and can also be found in Seton and Arnot's *Prisoners of the '45*, 266–7.

63 The Jacobites who were tried for high treason at Carlisle were not limited to

the garrison left there on the retreat north. Suspects were also taken there from Scotland and from Newcastle to be tried. Macgrigor was probably among those captured in Scotland. (All Jacobite Englishmen got extremely short shrift.)

64 Seton and Arnot, *Prisoners of the '45*, 94, 95.

65 Reid's crime of high treason is mentioned as such in *Scots Magazine* (November 1746): 543, and in the Edinburgh newspaper, the *Caledonian Mercury* no. 4076 (25 November 1746).

66 Cited in Seton and Arnot, *Prisoners of the '45*, 266-7.

67 Col. James Allardyce, *Historical Papers*, vol. 2 passim, citing the "Egerton MSS" papers of Council for the King, Sir John Strange which contain the depositions of the Carlisle prisoners (ibid., xxvii).

68 Two other pipers, Nicholas Carr and John Ballantine, were among the five who were tried at York and acquitted of treason. Both successfully claimed to have been impressed (legally compelled to serve in the army). Seton and Arnot, *Prisoners of the '45*, 22, 23, 102, 103.

69 Ibid., 22, 23, 80, 81, 94, 95, 102, 103, 302, 303. Besides Sinclair and Reid, another piper in Ogilvie's Regiment is known. Allan Stuart Donald served David Ogilvie, the fifth Earl of Airlie, as piper at Culloden. The piper's great grandson, George W. Donald born near Forfar in 1820, became locally a well-known Lowland songmaker (Rogers, *The Scottish Minstrel*, 461).

70 Carr was reported to have been the only piper in Glenbucket's Regiment. Without him, they marched to Derby and back to Carlisle "without any piper" (*Scots Magazine*, [October 1746]: 486). In fact Glenbucket's "regiment" was a company of men raised *inter alia* at the pulpit exhortation of Fr John Gordon in Rathven parish. They came from Glenlivet and Strathaven and served with their priest John Tyrie in the duke of Perth's regiment. One piper per company was normal procedure then and later. In 1781 Gordon of Glenbucket involved his piper and his fiddler in the celebrations, at Tomintoul, after Lord George Gordon, who had led the anti-Catholic riots in London, was found not guilty (Turreff, *Antiquarian Gleanings*, 276).

71 *Scots Magazine* 8 (October 1746): 485.

72 Col. James Allardyce, *Historical Papers*, vol. 2: 613. When Lord John Drummond entered Aberdeen on 8 February 1746, his mounted party were preceded by a mounted man with a French horn and followed by "a boy, richly mounted, beating a bass drum." See Turreff, *Antiquarian Gleanings*, 207).

73 Seton and Arnot, *Prisoners of the '45*, 308, 309.

74 Ibid., 308, 309. John Shaw, "fidler in Aberdeen," is first mentioned in a "List of prisoners in the [Aberdeen] Tolbooth for treasonable practices, 25 July 1746," no date of capture given but after 20 May 1746. Also in that list is "Jno Bruce Invercauld's fidler" (Iain Gray, archivist, Aberdeen City Archives, letter to author, 7 November 1996).

CHAPTER THREE

1 In 1911 Sir Henry Craik, KCB, MA(Oxon), LLD, MP for Glasgow and Aberdeen universities, after an exaggerated harangue on Cumberland's wickedness, claimed that the Highland population had been "decimated ... by the sword and fire and famine" after Culloden (Craik, *A Century of Scottish History*, 203). The same writer elsewhere noted that "it was due to Sir John Sinclair's restless and pervading influence that vast flocks of Cheviot sheep now occupied the mountains which a few years ago had been valueless, except as the homes of a numerous and ignorant, but withal an interesting, population" (ibid., 498).

2 Captured turncoats who had quit the Hanoverian army for Prince Charles's were summarily hanged, subject to military law.

3 Fergusson, *Argyll in the Forty-Five*, 96. For the history of the regimental name, 1712–51, see Farmer, *Regimental Records*, 118.

4 Sir James Fergusson, *Argyll in the Forty-Five*, 96.

5 Cited in Findlay, *Wolfe in Scotland*, 117.

6 Terry, *The Albemarle Papers*, vol. 1: 5, fn., and Blaikie, *Itinerary of Prince Charles*, 59.

7 *Scots Magazine* (May 1746): 230.

8 On 15 April 1746 royal assent was given to "An act for continuing an act of this present session of parliament, intitled, An act to impower his Majesty to secure and detain such persons as his Majesty shall suspect are conspiring against his person and government. – By this act, the suspension of the Habeas corpus is continued for six months longer" (*Scots Magazine* (May 1746): 243).

9 Craik, *A Century of Scottish History*, 220. Cumberland is also remembered as describing Duncan Forbes, the man who kept hundreds of Gaels from becoming active Jacobites, as "that old woman who talked to me about humanity" (Hill Burton, *Life of Lord Resident Forbes*, 382).

10 Besides the humiliating loss of Hawley's Hanoverian forces at Falkirk in mid-January, the brilliant retaking of the Campbell-occupied southern Highlands, and the enraging knowledge that the Jacobite rebellion had caused important losses to his major European campaign in Flanders, Cumberland quickly knew himself to have been the intended target for an assassin's bullet just before action began at Culloden. (The Highland deserter involved took a close-range shot at Albemarle, having mistaken him for Cumberland. Albemarle was not hurt.) Nonetheless, the assassination of the wounded on Culloden was as brutal, bestial, and reprehensible then as now and must have made even the most stupid of the executioners wonder what to expect in turn from their future enemies.

11 The Hanoverian horse at Falkirk in January 1746 had been shamefully routed by the Jacobite right wing and in their flight had ridden down their own infantry.

12 Marchioness of Tullibardine, *Military History of Perthshire*, 330.

13 Angus MacLeod, *The Songs of Duncan Ban Macintyre*, notes, 443–4 and 446.

A verse that Alasdair MacDonald wrote about Duncan Campbell's humanity in Arasaig and Moidart runs: "Then he would show compassion/ to the outlawed poor of every district;/ he would not execute the order/ put by the Butcher in his warrant."

14 Sir James Fergusson, *Argyle in the Forty-Five*, 221.

15 There was enforcement of military law, however. Before Culloden, on 24 February, a Lieutenant Fawlie "was broke" for pillaging the home of Oliphant of Gask. And at much the same time Ensign Daniel Hart of Sir Robert Munro's regiment was punished at Aberdeen for extorting five guineas. See *Scots Magazine* (March 1746). After Culloden Captain Hamilton of Cobham's Dragoons was investigated after many complaints had been made against him in Angus. He was exonerated as "zealous" (Findlay, *Wolfe in Scotland*, 117).

16 *Scots Magazine* (June 1746): 269. Attainder meant condemnation to death, in this instance by act of parliament, without other judicial procedure. It brought with it a loss of all civil rights and "corruption of the blood," meaning that the victim could not hold property or dispose of it.

17 At the risk of overcomplicating matters, it is only honest to report that while Cluny MacPherson's people turned in arms to Lord Loudon on 4 June 1746, the clan in Badenoch remained an armed and feared threat to the Hanoverian régime at least until 1755. With Cluny known to be "skulking" around home, this area, alone of the policed areas of Jacobite Scotland, was policed year round and Wolfe is on record as having tried his best to provoke a military response. This, Wolfe said with unhidden relish, would have given him "a sufficient pretext (without waiting for any instructions) to march into their country, *où j'aurais fait main basse, sans miséricorde*. Would you believe that I am so bloody?" (Findlay, *Wolfe in Scotland*, 210).

18 Angus Matheson, *The Appin Murder*, 8, 27, 44, 64.

19 Caroline ffrederick Scott, Major Lockheart of Cholmondley's Regiment, Captain Grant, son of Grant of Knockando, Colonel Cornwallis, Captain John Hay, RN, all ordered or condoned killing in the course of disarming Jacobites and wreaking economic havoc.

20 John Campbell, fourth earl of Loudon (1705–82), aide-de-camp to King George II, raised Loudon's Highlanders in 1745, occupied Lochaber in 1746, and served, briefly, in North America.

21 Sir James Fergusson, *Argyll in the Forty-five*, 179 (citing the Mamore MSS, 294).

22 Cited in Findlay, *Wolfe in Scotland*, 117.

23 MacGill, *Old Ross-shire and Scotland*, document no. 622, 245–6.

24 Ibid., document no. 624, 247.

25 While Knoydart people handed in arms it appears to have been a token gesture; Knoydart remained well armed in the mid-1750s to the irritation of Mungo Campbell, factor for the forfeited estate (see Marianne McLean, *The People of Glengarry*, 24).

26 MacGill, *Old Ross-shire and Scotland*, document no. 617, 244.

27 See also the *Celtic Magazine* 4, no. 40 (February 1879):127.

28 Sir James Fergusson, *Argyll in the Forty-Five*, 17.

29 The Cameron data is an official sworn list of losses, not a list of claims. It bears no signature and there is no notice of any potential court case. See SRO, E768/41/1-43, Forfeited Estates records. The Cameron list of losses is unique in the records of the forfeited estates.

30 That they were often wearing Highland dress is of no importance since the proscription on that did not take effect until December 1748.

31 Coren was severely reprimanded by Humphry Bland, then governor of Fort William. See, T.I. Rae, "Edinburgh Castle, 1751–1753," 55.

32 *Scots Magazine* (July 1746):342. Findlay wrote that Dejean's were "scattered in companies ... from Peterhead to Fochabers" (*Wolfe in Scotland*, 237).

33 J.T. Findlay (*Wolfe in Scotland*, 123, 124) specified six posts but adduced no evidence.

34 James Wolfe of Barrell's was responsible for the reconstruction of Inversnaid.

35 Cumberland left Scotland suddenly on 18 July 1746.

36 The Wolfe in question was James Wolfe's father, who served in Barrell's Blues (4th Foot) during the 'Forty-five and later as colonel of the 20th Foot.

37 Col. David Stewart, *Sketches*, vol. 1: 267–8.

38 Ibid., 246.

39 Ibid., 269.

40 Despite the occupying forces' shortcomings, Findlay restated, on no authority, the old saw that there was a widespread Highland demoralization that lasted for ten or twelve years after Culloden, which he traced to the "vindictive enactments of the reactionaries then in high places" (Findlay, *Wolfe in Scotland*, 134–5).

41 Cited in Sir James Fergusson, *Argyll in the Forty-Five*, 198.

42 Findlay, *Wolfe in Scotland*, 121, 122.

43 The building of roads by the British military was more effectively expanded with the passage of the Turnpike Act in 1751.

44 Walter Scott described Barisdale as classically educated but a plunderer. He wrote that "levying of black-mail was, before the 1745, practised by several chiefs of very high rank" whose claim was that they were assisting the government. Scott added that he had read a memoir of Cluny that showed him to have engaged in blackmail also (see Walter Scott, *Waverley*, 149).

45 Col. James Allardyce, *Historical Papers*, vol. 2:500–3.

46 Ibid., 500–1.

47 Ibid., vol. 1:306.

48 "Proposals offered to Major Gen[l] Blakeney for Covering that part of Inverness Shire lying South side of Murray firth, and the Shires of Murray, Bamff, Aberdeen, Mearns and Angus against the Depredations of the Highlanders of Rannoch, Lochaber, and Glengary," in ibid., vol. 2:493.

49 The preliminary signing of the Treaty of Aix-la-Chapelle took place in April 1748; the final signing was on 18 October 1748.

50 For a copy of King George's order to Humphry Bland, an order that deals only with "Arms, and warlike weapons," runs to over five pages in length, and bears Bland's signature, see Millar, "Note on the proclamation for disarming," 216–22. There is no mention of bagpipes or any other musical instrument. The original documents referred to by Millar are no longer accessible, if not lost.

51 Ibid., 215–6.

52 The procedure of regular reporting of companies' operations did not begin throughout the British army until the Seven Years' War.

53 The source of Col. James Allardyce's invaluable post reports, published in 1896 in his *Historical Papers*, vol. 2, was copies of reports sent to Henry Fox, Secretary at War, 1749–50; these in 1896 were held by the Forbes of Inverernan family. All efforts to locate these and any others that might exist through the Inverernan family have come to nothing. The eighteenth-century originals may exist in the Public Record Office, London. Also, post records for James Wolfe's 20th Foot, known to have manned posts in "disaffected" areas of the Highlands from Banff in 1751 and from Fort Augustus in the summer of 1752, are no longer extant, although those of Captain Rickson to Wolfe were available to Wolfe's biographer Robert Wright in 1864.

54 The exception to the summer policing was Lt Hector Munro who served year-round in Badenoch, not removing to winter quarters. With eighty men of the 34th Foot, Hector Munro unsuccessfully hunted for Cluny in Badenoch from 1751 to 1753, and their failure is made the more pathetic in that during the summer of 1752 James Wolfe deliberately stationed Trapaud and his men at Laggan to get the job done. (Captain Trapaud married Annie, daughter of Mungo Campbell, son of Barcaldine.)

55 Findlay, *Wolfe in Scotland*; Willson, *The Life and Letters of James Wolfe*; and Wright, *The Life of Major-General James Wolfe*.

56 Millar, "Note on the proclamation for disarming," 215–6.

57 W.C. MacKenzie, *History of the Outer Hebrides*, 473.

58 Adam, *John Home's Survey of Assynt*, xvi.

59 Pococke, *Tours in Scotland, 1747, 1750, 1760*.

60 Archibald Cameron was sent to Scotland to coordinate a projected Scottish Jacobite force and one to be led by James Keith using Swedish and Prussian forces. They were to meet at Crieff for an attempt to restore King James. The government was aware of the scheme but felt it had to keep its spy secret and thus allowed Cameron to go to the gallows.

61 Donald Ban "Liar" Cameron and John Ban MacConochy vic Ewan Duy (alias MacDonald) were hanged in 1753 for theft. Donald Gow was banished for life for stealing a sheep and Donald Cameron was transported for life for theft. Donald "Banlehin" was held at Killin and then hanged. See *Scots Magazine*, 1753 passim.

62   "Highland Reports, 1749–50," in Col. James Allardyce, *Historical Papers*, vol. 2:581.

63   Ibid.

64   Ibid., 540.

65   Ibid., 539.

66   In 1750 a William Gow, in Highland garb, was accosted at "the Cabrach" by a military party and struck the corporal. When Private Stables came to the corporal's assistance, Gow knocked him down. At that point a crowd milled threateningly around the soldiers. Then the solders shot Gow. Stables was sentenced to be executed 29 November 1751 for murder but was later pardoned. There is no explanation for the year's delay in reporting the infraction, sentencing, and pardon. See *Scots Magazine* 12 (July 1750):348; vol. 13 (April 1751):189; vol. 13 (September 1751):452; vol. 13 (November 1751):547.

67   "Highland Reports, 1749–50," in Col. James Allardyce, *Historical Papers*, vol. 2; 574–5. Allardyce cited the Egerton MSS, which contain the depositions of the Carlisle prisoners (ibid., xxvii).

68   Ibid., 560.

69   The winter report from Inversnaid Barracks dated 23 April 1750 includes a report from Peter Desbrisay of Bockland's Regiment of the capture by a corporal and some soldiers of a Highlander "carrying Arms in the shire of Stirling and parish of Buchanan." The man was taken before a JP called Neill Buchanan (a prominent local name), "who told the Corporal he would give him a receipt for the gun and enquire whether the man, lived within the bounds of the Disarming act. But the Corporal says he dismiss'd the Highlander, and has likewise inform'd that he return'd him the Gun. (Sign'd) Peter Desbrisay." Col. James Allardyce, *Highland Reports*, vol. 2:532. One instance of a weapon's having been returned to a kilted Highlander is hardly enough to allow any general pronouncement on the readiness or not of magistrates to prosecute under this dominant section of the Disarming Act, but the fact is that this decision cannot be overlooked as a freak. It is after all one of only three arms cases for the years 1749 and 1750.

70   Where the Lowlands are concerned, bachelor Lt Col James Wolfe of the 20th Foot stationed in Glasgow in May 1753 noted petulantly that the ladies were "cold to everything but a bagpipe" (Findlay, *Wolfe in Scotland*, 292).

At Lucky Vint's tavern at the west end of the village of Prestonpans in 1741, Mr Erskine of Grange treated Simon Fraser of Lovat and others to a dinner and afterwards to the piping of Hew Dalrymple (Lord Drummore)'s piper, Geordy Sym. Drummore's estate was in Inveresk and Prestonpans and Lovat was considering having his younger son Alexander educated in Prestonpans. Rev. Alexander Carlyle, who was there, said that Lovat "despised [Sym] ... and said he was only fit to play reels to Grange's oyster-women." However Lovat, a man of seventy-five insisted that Kate Vint, the landlord's daughter (and Drummore's mistress) stay and dance with him. See Burton, ed., *Autobiography of Carlyle*, 49–50).

Household records of the Gordon family in the northeast show that the third and fourth dukes of Gordon had a piper or pipers for a long time, probably from at least 1717 until 1776, and that pipers were associated with other prominent Gordon families, including "Glenbuchat." Pipers are also associated, at harvest time, with the Marchmont estate in Lowland Scotland where a John Marshall was the piper from 1746–1752 (from the unpublished researches of Dr B.L.H. Horn of the Scottish Record Office, supplied by Stuart Allan of the Historical Research Room, 13 January 1994).

71 Justiciary Court records, JC 11 GC 165 (1748–51), books 12 and 13.

72 "Mr. Bruce"(?) *The Highlands of Scotland in 1750*, xviii–xix (in introduction by Andrew Lang).

73 Charles Fraser-Macintosh, "Minor Highland Septs – the Macdonells of Barisdale," 93.

74 Wright, *The life of Major-General James Wolfe*, and Findlay, *Wolfe in Scotland*, 200.

75 MacGill, *Old Ross-shire and Scotland*, vol. 1, document no. 165, 67. See also document no. 627, 247. No proof has yet been found to substantiate the writer's citing the law against bearing arms in this case. Wearing Highland clothing, however, was illegal for almost all Scots.

76 Iain mac Theàrlaich Oig was John MacLean of Inverscadale, a tack in Ardgour. His song "*Oran an déidh Blàr Chuillodair*" ("A Song After Culloden Field") can be read in a number of books including John L. Campbell, ed., *Songs Remembered in Exile*, 254–60.

77 According to John MacKenzie, Rob Donn's song "Iseabail Nic-Aoidh" was admirably matched to a properly played version of the tune "Failte Phriunns'" (see Sar-Obair, 192). Dixon wrote that "he [John MacKenzie] and John Macrae of Raasay used to be judges of pipe music at the Edinburgh competitions." (Dixon, *Gairloch*, 190).

78 "The Prince's Salute," according to the notes appended to a written version of the tune in book 1 of the Piobaireachd Society's books, was made to commemorate Prince James's landing in Britain in 1715. Whether or not this is correct, the tune has for generations been treated as nostalgically Jacobite.

79 George J. Campbell ,"Ministers of the Presbytery of Tongue, 1726–63," 301.

80 "'*N uair a dh'fhàg e sinn mar phriosanaich,/Gun ghiodagan gun ghunnachan,/ Gun chlaidheamh, gun chrios-tarsainn oirnn,/ Chan fhaigh sinn prìs nan dagachan*." See "*Oran do'n bhriogais*" in Angus MacLeod, ed., trans., *Songs of Duncan Ban.*

81 Ibid., notes to "*Oran do'n Eideadh Ghàidhealach* ("Song to the Highland Dress")," 504.

82 John L. Campbell, ed., *Songs Remembered in Exile.*

83 In Boucé, reviser, *The Expedition of Humphry Clinker*, 241. The right that Smollett gave to the piper to bear arms accurately depends on the amended Disarming Act of 1748.

84 Alexander Fraser of Culduthel. An Alexander Fraser of Culduthel was commissioned captain in Fraser's Highlanders on 5 January 1757.

85 Capt. Simon Fraser, ed., *The Airs and Melodies*, tune 159, pp. 65, 109. Fraser, in keeping with the style of the day, presented the music with a harmony, a feature not found in traditional Gaelic music. He offered it in the key of D Major and extended the melody beyond the nine-note range of the pipe chanter for the convenience of literate parlour musicians.

86 MacKay Scobie, "Highland Military Dress."

CHAPTER FOUR

1 This was a fair measure of all of Scotland's acquiescence in the country's Hanoverian monarchy, duly buttressed by its Whig government.Those Highland Scots who were impressed in 1756 and later for wearing tartan also are eloquent proof that the occupying army had until then been incompetent in its efforts to catch and have convicted kilted or tartan-wearing Scots, or hadn't really been trying.

2 Lochgary, die-hard Jacobite in France, on the other hand, is said to have thrown a dirk at his son when he learned the latter had a company in Fraser's Highlanders. But such myopic inability to see the insignificance of Jacobite politics in European perspective was becoming rare.

3 These included Captain John MacPherson, brother of Cluny, John MacDonell of Lochgarry, Alexander Cameron of Dungallon, four Fraser captains, and Alexander MacDonell, Barisdale's son (who was killed at the Heights of Abraham, 1759).

4 Alexander Fraser, *The Royal Burgh of Inveraray*, 44.

5 No Scottish regiment was allowed to raise a second battalion from the Union of the Parliaments in 1707 until the death of George II in 1760.

6 Montgomerie's Highlanders were officered and manned predominantly from loyal Hanoverian clans.

7 Although of little significance where either Fraser's or Montgomerie's Highlanders are concerned, one Catholic opinion, Forbes Leith's, emphasized the important substrain in British politics that during that war six or seven thousand Roman Catholics served in the British army, and that most were sent to America (implying that, dead or alive, the government preferred that they should stay there).

8 Fischer (*The Scots in Germany*, 129) gave a glimpse of these strange-looking soldiers, with their "extraordinary love for their officers" and "their bagpipes."

9 Col. David Stewart, *Sketches*, 2:71.

10 Ibid., 332. Stewart wrote that Maclean raised this regiment in 1759 (ibid., 56) and that two hundred of them joined Keith's and Campbell's regiments in October 1760 under Prince Ferdinand of Brunswick (ibid., 73). See also Maxwell, ed., *Lowland Scots Regiments*, 327, and wo.2.33 fol. 157.

11 Findlay, *Wolfe in Scotland*, 226.

12 *Scots Magazine* (20 October 1759) vol. 21:553.

13 Col. David Stewart, *Sketches*, vol. 2: 335.

14 Recruiting for the Highland Brigade in Holland, which had absorbed hundreds of Highlanders, was suspended during the Seven Years' War.

15 This kind of restreaming indirectly caused three men to mutiny in the Black Watch and the 71st (Fraser's) in 1779 (see below).

16 See Ross, "Scottish Regiments Disbanded," 325. Ross cited WO1 614, and *Scots Magazine* 21 (October 1759):559. I have not been able to verify the *Scots Magazine* claim.

17 Maxwell, ed., *Lowland Scottish Regiments*, 324, citing Lt Gen. Beauclerk's correspondence in WO1, 613, passim, 1757.

18 Ibid., 324.

19 *Scots Magazine* 21 (June 1759):329.

20 Ibid., vol. 21 (August 1759):441.

21 Ibid., 440–1.

22 MacGill, *Old Ross-shire and Scotland*, document no. 165, vol. 1, 67; document no. 627. If it was an accurate report, this is the one case that suggests that the Disarming Act's seven-year limitation on having weapons was renewed.

23 *Scots Magazine* 21 (June 1759):329.

24 Fraser-Mackintosh of Drummon, *Letters of Two Centuries*, Letter 156, 275. It should be noted that *Fasti Ecclesiae Scoticanae* shows no record of a Church of Scotland minister in Laggan between 1649 and 1851.

25 Col. David Stewart, *Sketches*, vol. 2: lxxxv.

26 Ibid., lxxxv.

27 Prebble, *Mutiny*, 172–82, 504.

CHAPTER FIVE

1 James Grant, *The Scottish Soldiers of Fortune*, 281. Grant cited "Trans. Antiq. Soc. Scot." (*Transactions of the Antiquarian Society of Scotland*), giving no further information. The citation, taken from the "post scriptum" to a "Letter from Alexander Macnaughton, (of that Ilk) to the Earl of Morton, dated Falmouth, 15th January 1628," runs: "Our bagg pypperis & marlit Plaidis serwitt us to guid wise in the persuit of ane man of warr that hetlie followit us." Macnaughton signed himself "Alex Maknachtan." See, *Proceedings of the Society of Antiquaries of Scotland* 4, 3d series (1894): 443, 444. A footnote, ibid., 443, locates the original document among the Morton Papers.

2 The name Caddell appears several times in an early to mid-seventeenth-century (from 1608) Scottish military context in Holland. As far as can be judged in these instances, it was a Lowland name. See James Ferguson, ed., *The Scots Brigade*, passim).

3 J.F. Campbell, ed., *Popular Tales of the West Highlands*, vol. 4; 404, 405. See

also "Roll of MacNachtane's Soldieris schipped at Lochkerran, 11th December 1627" in Macphail, ed., *Highland Papers*, vol. 1: 114.

4 See *Transactions of the Society of Antiquaries, Scotland* 3. From the "Roll of M'Nachtane's Soldieris schipped at Lochkerran, 11th December 1627 ... the names of the Soldieris Schipped be the laird of M'nachtane in george massones schip at Lochkilcherane" (Macphail, *Highland Papers*, vol. 1, 114), it appears that "Allester caddell, pyper" had with him a boy. The MacNaughtons of Dunderawe were an old Gaelic Argyll-shire family and Sir Alexander MacNaughton is known to have been resolutely pro-Charles I.

5 Maxwell, ed., *The Lowland Scots Regiments*, 124, 125; James Grant, *Scottish Soldiers of Fortune*, 78, 79, 181, 189; Sir James and Sir John Hepburn in *Dictionary of National Biography*, vol. 9: 608–10.

6 Hepburn's Regiment was the remnant of Andrew Gray's Scots who went to Bohemia in 1620.

7 This at any rate is the view of the *Dictionary of National Biography*. Maxwell, ed., in *Lowland Scots Regiments*, 129, claimed that command devolved upon Monro of Foulis.

8 The Scots Brigade of Holland, (which came into existence to help the Estates General of Holland to fight the Spanish in the late sixteenth century), also continued to "beat the Scots march" until 1782. John Buchan associated the change from this old native drum cadence, in 1782, with the wholesale resignation of the Scots Brigade's officers. In 1794 they formed the Scots Brigade, or 94th Foot (see Buchan, *The History of the Royal Scots Fusiliers*, 60). The real motivation to quit was that, effective 1 January 1783, the brigade would no longer be British. See Maxwell, ed., *Lowland Scots Regiments*, 316.

9 See James Grant, *Scottish Soldiers of Fortune*, 283, 284.

10 There is only one case that comes to mind of a drum's being used by a Highlander in a Gaelic and Highland setting; it is linked to the beheading of a gentleman reiver, Dòmhnul Donn MacDonell of Bohuntin, in Keppoch, by his enemy, the chief of the Grants, around the end of the seventeenth century or beginning of the eighteenth. The reference is found in a song by "Donald Donn, son of the tacksman of Bohuntin, the night before he was put to death": "Better the bellowing of the stags,/ than swarthy Duncan and his drumming./ Back and forth from street to street,/ with his empty 'sound box' and his two [drum] sticks!" See John L. Campbell, ed., *Songs Remembered*, 251–3.

11 There was at least one Sinclair in Lord Reay's Regiment, Lt Col John Sinclair, who was killed at the battle of Neumark. He took over command when Monro of Foulis was in Scotland on a recruiting expedition. (Sinclair was replaced by William Stewart).

12 James Grant, *Scottish Soldiers of Fortune*, 178. See also Calder, *History of Caithness*, 276.

13 M.M. Haldane, "The Royal Scots," 135.

14 Ibid. John Campbell (1723–1806), marquis of Lorne, became fifth duke of

Argyll in 1770; he became colonel in 1765. Alexander MacDonell of Keppoch, who almost certainly at the time had a local Keppoch Mac a'Ghlasraich Campbell piper, served with the Royal Scots in the 1790s (see MacDonald and Mac-Donald, *Clan Donald*, vol. 2: 669, 670).

15 Walton, *History of the British Standing Army*, 11. "Est. Lists, Harl. MSS" refers to a section of nearly 8,000 volumes of manuscripts held by the British Library, Department of Manuscripts. Est. Lists presumably stands for establishment lists (I am indebted to Dr Frances Harris for this information).

16 Lord George Murray, Prince Charles Edward Stuart's general, began his military career in 1711 as an ensign in the Royals but deserted in 1715 to lead a battalion at Sheriffmuir. In 1745 the 2d battalion, Royals, fought against Prince Charles. In August 1745 Captain Scott headed the two companies that were detached from Perth to Fort William and ambushed by the Highlanders at High Bridge by Tirnadris and his twelve men (including the piper). They were paroled. The rest of the 2d Battalion were among Hawley's beaten army at Falkirk in 1746.

17 Quoted in Buchan, *Montrose*, 120.

18 Buchan, *History of the Royal Scots Fusiliers*, 15. (Buchan chose to call the regiment the Royal Scots Fusiliers, eschewing nominal accuracy for the majority of the regiment's existence.)

19 Quoted in Buchan, *Montrose*, 120.

20 Swinton, *Scots Guards*, vi.

21 During the early phase of the Thirty Years' War (1618–48) a company of pikemen and musketeers in Gustavus Adolphus's army contained one hundred and fifty men. Six such companies comprised nine hundred men (see Sinclair's regiment in Norway). Reading "12 Drumers and Pypers" to be six of each, then each company of Campbell of Lawers's regiment enjoyed one of each.

22 In the early 1670s drummers were classified and paid as such. "Two drummers are universally allowed in every Company of one hundred men, and more (as also of the caporals) according as the Company is strong. They ought to be skilful to beat a Gathering, a March, an Alarm, a Charge, Retreat, Travaille or Dian, and the Taptoo. If they can do that well, and carry a message wittily to an enemy, they may be permitted to be Drolls" (Turner, *Pallas Armata*, 219). The military meaning of "droll" is unclear.

23 Angus MacKay, *Collection*, 2, "Historical and Traditional Notes."

24 Another northern regiment that is likely to have had pipers during its short existence was Sir George Monro's. It was formed in 1674 and disbanded in 1676. Sir George was a cadet of the Monros of Obsdale and although his family and piping are not bound together by record, official or otherwise, their service under Lord Reay on the Continent in Gustavus Adolphus's wars puts them in close earshot of MacKay-raised pipers. It is by no means inconceivable that Sir George's troops included veterans of Lord Reay's men, though they would have been few.

25 Prebble, *Glencoe*, 216.

26 The regiment raised by Archibald Campbell (d. 1703), tenth earl and first duke of Argyll, was thoroughly Campbell. Its officers commanding companies included Campbells of Auchinbreck, Ardkinglas, three Barbrecks, Kames, Allengrange, and Glenlyon. The non-Campbell captains were allies, MacAulay, Lamont, and Bannatyne.

27 Swinton, "History of the Pipers," vii. The author did not cite his source(s).

28 Turner, *Pallas Armata*, 219.

29 Ibid., 218.

30 A wadset, according to John Home (*History of the Rebellion*, 93), was a security or pledge of land. The borrower of money who gave a pledge of land was called the reversor. The creditor who lent the money and received the pledge of land was called the wadsetter. The holding of land on wadset was also common in Lowland Scotland in the mid-eighteenth century. There, if a large acreage was involved, a wadsetter could vote in county elections like a landowner. In Gaelic Scotland the estates of Barisdale and Ardsheal were held on wadset and both were forfeited.

31 The term *capitaine* emerged in fourteenth-century French and the early French word *coronel* was supplanted by the term *colonnel* in literary French in the late sixteenth century, suggesting, perhaps, that Gaelic borrowed it earlier in the 1500s or before. See Quick, "English and Scots Military Loanwords."

32 For generations, for the sake of legal inheritance of Highland estates, conversion to Protestantism had been a *sine qua non* at least among certain members of the ruling family. In the 1770s, when the Penal Laws still discriminated harshly against Roman Catholics, it was essential for Catholic Highland officers who were entering the army and anticipating promotion (and a normal social life in the mess) to convert to Protestantism. Rev. Charles MacDonald cited the examples of Alasdair mac Dhòmhnuil MacDonald of Kinlochmoidart, Simon MacDonald of Morar (76th Regiment) and his brother Coll MacDonald (both of whom were nephews of the Roman Catholic Bishop Hugh MacDonald) and Colonel Gillis from Kinloch Morar (who rose from the ranks). See Rev. Charles MacDonald, *Moidart: or Among the Clanranalds*.

33 Highlanders of the 82d settled in what is now Pictou County.

34 Col. David Stewart, *Sketches*, vol. 1: 342.

35 While the lists of officers in Highland regiments give a good indication of the homes of the rank and file, including pipers, the actual geographical distribution of pipers' (and men's) homes cannot always be assumed. One reason is that officers' landholdings may have been spread outside their traditional areas. In the case of Fraser's Highlanders in 1776, for instance, men were raised from the parish of Fearn in Easter Ross, where at least one of the recruits was a Gaelic-speaking Graham; there may also have been Munros in that company. There were Munros in the 71st but which company they enlisted in is not certain. If Fearn produced a company, it probably included a local piper. The

explanation is that Fraser of Lovat, or a member of the family, leased a farm there which is why, one assumes, the name Simon appears in one Graham family around 1800. (Neither Mowat, *Easter Ross 1750–1850*, nor Timperley, ed., *A Directory of Landownership*, records any Fraser ownership in Easter Ross.) Similarly, Alexander, the duke of Gordon, raised a company in Fraser's Highlanders for his wife's brother, Hamilton Maxwell, in 1775. Generally, in cases where the military record is stubbornly silent and the secondary literature is of dubious value, the existence of piping will be seen to be fairly safely inferrable.

36 Piping was a common feature of Lowland Scottish and rustic northeastern English life, at least in the north of England until the second half of the eighteenth century.

37 Donald Gunn competed in the piping competition held at Falkirk in 1783 (Angus MacKay, "A Circumstantial Account," in *Collection*, 16). In 1779 the 77th dressed its pipers and drummers in green coats and belted plaids of the "red Murray tartan" (Marchioness of Tullibardine, *Military History of Perthshire*, 70). See also note 40 below.

38 The part played by Free Masonry in the English regiments must have mitigated against indiscriminate contempt and harshness by officers.

39 No less a personage than HRH William, duke of Cumberland, sanctioned Gaelic Scotch tactics at the battle of Fontenoy in Flanders (modern Belgium) on 11 May 1745. Colonel Sir Robert Munro of Fowlis, MP and chief of the Munros, was in command of Lord John Murray's Highlanders (the Black Watch). Before they attacked, Munro, sensing the need for a novel tactical initiative, had obtained permission from the duke of Cumberland "to allow them to fight in their own way. Sir Robert, according to the usage of his countrymen, ordered the whole regiment to clap to the ground on receiving the French fire, and instantly after its discharge, they sprang up, and coming close to the enemy, poured in their shot upon them to the certain destruction of multitudes, and drove them precipitately through their own lines." French reports of the battle mentioned the "Highland furies" but probably only because they (the French) won that day. There were Scotch Highlanders on both sides but there is no report of bagpipers. Capt. Francis O'Neill stated that the last time Irish pipers piped in war was at Fontenoy (11 May 1745), on the side of the French (see O'Neill, *Irish Minstrels and Musicians*). The source for the claim that Fraser's Highlanders would not fight at Quebec without pipe acompaniment is Rev. Walter Young in the preface to Patrick MacDonald, *Highland Vocal Airs*.

40 Stewart served in the 77th, Athole Highlanders, from 1778 and then drew half-pay; he continued his commissioned career in the Black Watch as an ensign in 1787, rising to captain in 1796; in 1804 he served as a major in the 28th battalion, 78th Ross-shire Highlanders.

CHAPTER SIX

1 Col. David Stewart, *Sketches*, vol. 1: 229ff.

2 Fraser-Mackintosh claimed that Lovat was captured at Druim a' chuirn, further east on the Meoble farm in South Morar.

3 Sir James Fergusson, *Argyll in the Forty-five*, 208.

4 *Piping Times* 22, no. 4 (January 1970):21. See also Alexander MacKenzie, *History of the Frasers of Lovat*, 475.

5 In his breakdowns of killed and wounded of the unranked soldier, Stewart of Garth normally gave "Drummers, and rank and file," or two columns, "Drummers," and "Privates." In the case of Montgomerie's Highlanders (77th), when a piper was involved, as happened in a campaign against the Cherokee during the Seven Years' War, the two columns became "Drummers and Pipers" and "Rank and File."

6 Col. David Stewart, *Sketches*, vol. 1: 354.

7 Ibid., 363. *Piping Times* 20, 12 (September 1968):9, gives Donald Cumming.

8 Ibid.

9 In his anxiety to ingratiate himself with the government, Simon Fraser did not scruple at being one of the Crown's prosecuting attorneys at the trial of James Stewart in 1752 at Inverary for the murder of Campbell of Glenure, a crime for which Stewart was hanged while known to be innocent.

10 Col. David Stewart, *Sketches*, vol. 2: 64.

11 David Graeme's Queen's Own Royal Regiment of Highlanders, which was raised in 1761 (the regiment that Bàrasdal Og joined), typically allowed two drummers per company (see "Proclamation authorising the raising of a Highland Regiment," in Kilgour, *Lochaber in War and Peace*).

12 Harper, *The Fraser Highlanders*, 123, 124, 125.

13 Ewen Cameron of Glen Nevis, in a letter to one of his uncles dated 17 February 1757, said that he had just happily accepted a lieutenant's commission in "Coll Fraser's Highland Regiment" and was setting out "a Recruiting soon for Strontian." (Kilgour, *Lochaber in War and Peace*, 315, citing the Callart Charter Chest).

14 Letter from William MacKenzie, SRO/GD 170/3158 in Appendix 7, *in toto*.

15 John Macdonald, "Journal of John Macdonald," cited in Rev. Angus Mackay, *Book of MacKay*, 217. Efforts to find the original MS have been unsuccessful.

16 Morton, *A Military History of Canada*, 53.

17 In Lord MacLeod's Highlanders, "off-reckonings" were deducted by the colonel from the men's pay to cover the costs of clothing. This system lasted until 1854 when a royal warrant demanded that the colonel be limited to charging only the actual cost of the clothing. In compensation for his loss the colonel was now paid £600 per annum, which gives some idea of how much the rich were appropriating from the rank and file.

18 The records of the Inverness Shire Highlands (97th Foot), a line regiment

(1794–96) typically list no pipers, although the regiment defintely had them. Their bagpipes were bought for them in Inverness by Sir James Grant of Grant who had letters of service to raise the regiment. The pipers were uniformed slightly differently from the ordinary soldier and one of them, unnamed, enjoys an unusual reputation. As part of a detachment to the navy he was aboard HMS Colossus (74) [74 guns] at the naval battle of Isle Groix (23 June 1795) when, kilted, he was ordered to "the maintopmast staysail netting ... where he skirled merrily for the three hours the ship was in action" (H.B. Mackintosh, *The Inverness Shire Highlanders*, 43).

19 This number included Alexander MacDonell (brother of Bàrasdal Og, mentioned above). He was killed at the battle of the Heights of Abraham in 1759.

20 Harper, *Fraser Highlanders*, 103. See also Col. David Stewart, *Sketches*, vol. 1:319.

21 Col. David Stewart, *Sketches*, vol. 2:64.

22 In a letter dated October 1751 to General Churchill, Colonel Crawfurd, in referring to a secret meeting that a number of Jacobites (including Pickle) had with Cluny MacPherson at Dalwhinnie in 1749, mentions Cluny's piper as well as the chief's younger brother as having acted as messengers between Glen Nevis and the MacPherson chief (see Lang, *Companions of Pickle*, 154).

23 Cited in Harper, *Fraser Highlanders*, 90.

24 MacKay Scobie, *Pipers and Pipe Music*, 7.

25 Capt. Simon Fraser, ed., *Airs and Melodies*, preface.

26 A Daniel Morison, surgeon, bought land in Quebec on 20 July 1764. See Roy, *Inventaire*.

27 Capt. Simon Fraser, ed., *Airs and Melodies*, 111, note to tune 185.

28 Ibid., 15.

29 Ibid., 102, in notes to tunes 40 and 41.

30 Ibid., 104, in note 69.

31 Ibid., 105.

32 David Johnson found a "Lord Kelly's strathspey" among the music in Aberdeen University Library, MS 2424, and gave the place and date as "Pitlochry, c. 1830" (Johnson, *Music and Society*, 214).

33 Col. David Stewart, *Sketches*, vol. 2:59.

34 Ibid., vol. 1: 295.

35 Ibid., 295–6; vol. 2:60. Grant and Archibald Montgomerie, who died in 1796, are good candidates for having been Stewart's informants.

36 Henry Monro, born in Ross-shire, settled at Granville in Annapolis County, Nova Scotia, where his two-thousand-acre land grant dates to 1765. He was a JP and member of the colonial legislature.

37 Col. David Stewart, *Sketches*, vol. 2: 335.

38 Fencible regiments in the British Army were raised to serve at home as defence forces. The Argyle and the Sutherland Fencibles were reduced in 1763 and the other three in 1783.

39 *Piping Times* 19, no. 11 (August 1967).

40 "A Circumstantial Account," in Angus MacKay, *Collection*, 15.

41 *Piping Times* 22, no. 4 (January 1970).

42 Angus MacLeod, ed., trans., *Orain Dhonnchaidh Bhàin*, 264, 265.

43 Maxwell, ed., *Lowland Scots Regiments*, 323, and 157, citing a list of officers, WO 2, 23, folio 157.

44 MacKay Scobie was from Sutherland and a descendant of the Scobies of Melness and Keoldale, a prominent military family. He began his military service in the Essex Regiment, but at the beginning of the Great War he succeeded in joining the Seaforth Highlanders. He was in part responsible for the editing of MacLennan's notices of pipers in the *Piping Times* (see also Rev. Angus Mackay, *The Book of MacKay*, 260).

45 MacKay Scobie, *Pipers and Pipe Music*, 7.

46 Ibid., 1.

47 According to Keltie, the honourable Captain William M. Maithland's and Captain Petrie's companies of the 1st Seaforth Highlanders in 1791 were "Highlanders" (see, Keltie, *A History*, vol. 2: 528, 529). Many more people bearing lowland names spoke Gaelic in the 1770s than do today.

48 From 1828 until 1856 three of the six head Seaforth pipers were Sutherland men. Neil Mathieson (b. 1804) was Pipe Major, 1840–48, 1852–56, Lachlan MacKay was acting P-M 1850–52, and John MacDonald ("*am pìobaire Frangach*"), acting P-M, 1854, 55, 56. The other three were Hugh Ross (P-M, 1828–1840) and Duncan MacPherson (P-M, 1848–1850), whose home areas were not given, and Ronald Kemp (acting P-M, 1854), the "stalwart from Glen Urquhart." See MacKay Scobie, *Pipers and Pipe Music*, 19–24.

49 Kilcoy had been Jacobite in 1745.

50 MacKay Scobie, *Pipers and Pipe Music*, 8.

51 George Geddie Patterson, *History of Victoria County*, 72.

CHAPTER SEVEN

1 The Royal Highland Emigrants were not numbered until 1778. The First Battalion was led by Lt Col Allan MacLean, who had commanded the 114th during the Seven Years' War, the second by Major John Small (Scotch Brigade, Black Watch, 21st and 84th), who, as an officer in the 42d, had caught Bàrasdal Og.

2 Col. David Stewart, *Sketches*, vol. 2: 167, 182.

3 The servant to Colin Campbell of Glenure ("the Red Fox") on 14 May 1752 in the wood of Lettermore in Appin was a John MacKenzie. See Angus Matheson, *The Appin Murder*, 6.

4 Duncan MacPherson was conceived and born during Cluny's outlaw period in Badenoch.

5 "A Circumstantial Account," in Angus MacKay, *Collection*, 15, 16.

6 "The MacIntyres, hereditary pipers to Menzies of Menzies," in ibid., 14.

7 Somerled MacMillan, *Bygone Lochaber*, 107–9.

8 "Na'm faicinn ur Suaicheantas/ 'G a nochda ri fuar chrann,/ Scal siunsair ga'r buaireadh cuir fearg oirbh." See *"Oran do na Gaël a bha sa cuir do America, san bhliadhna 1778. Air fonn,—'Bithidh claidhe air Iain san t-searmoin'"* (Song to the Gaels sent to America in the year 1778. To the melody,—'Iain will be wearing his sword in the sermon'"), in Stewart and Stewart, *Cochruinneacha Taoghta*, 524. My translations.

9 Col. David Stewart, *Sketches*, vol. 2: 156–9. Many men of the 74th settled in the Maritimes after the American war. On 24 May 1784 at Saint Andrew's, New Brunswick, one hundred and twenty-five men of the 74th (and a large number of women and children) were named by Captain Donald McLean and Lieutenant Duncan Stewart as being entitled to the King's Bounty. Names only are given, no descriptions musical or otherwise.

10 Robertson, *The King's Bounty*, 209.

11 "A Narative of the Proceedings of a Body of Loyalists in North Carolina —— Rec^d from Genl. 24th. March 1776 In Genl Howe's Letter of the 25th April 1776 1," Colonial Office (CO) 5, vol. 93. The handwritten document has no original pagination but covers fourteen foolscap, sheets from which the above citations are taken from pages 9, 12, and 14 (title). It is cited with permission from the Public Record Office, Kew.

12 Soirle MacDonald (c. 1739–1830) was a neighbour of Donald MacCrumen in North Carolina and Shelburne County, Nova Scotia. He returned to Skye in 1790 to take up *Baile Meadhonach* (Middle Farm) in Sartle, Staffin. Through his mother he was a great-grandson of Sir James MacDonald, second baronet of Sleat, and second cousin of Sir Alexander, seventh baronet (d. 1746). His maternal uncle, Capt. Hugh MacDonald, was stepfather of Flora MacDonald (see MacDonald and MacDonald, *Clan Donald*).

13 Banastre Tarleton was from Lancashire.

14 "A Circumstantial Account," in Angus MacKay, *Collection*, 13.

15 Murray Logan, *Scottish Highlanders and the American Revolution*, 130.

16 Sir Eyre Coote (born c. 1727) cannot have been a complete stranger to Highland piping since he was the commanding officer of the 37th Regiment at Fort George in 1773. That year he hosted Boswell and Johnson to a dinner at the fort but preferred the regimental "band of musick" to any bagpiper as a musical carminative. Coote, according to Brian Gardner (*The East India Company*, 86–90), was Irish. As a major under Clive he was the hero of the battle of Plassey (23 June 1757); as a colonel in 1761 he defeated the French army commander Tom O'Lally at Wandewash and then besieged him at Pondicherry. Coote died *en route* from Calcutta to Madras in 1783.

17 Col. David Stewart, *Sketches*, vol. 2: 136. Lord MacLeod had been an active Jacobite in the 'Forty-five. He was the son of the earl of Cromarty who was forfeited and attainted for his sympathies. Two loyal battalions, one headed by

Lord MacLeod and the other by his brother, George MacKenzie, were raised in 1777 with most of the men coming from Lord MacLeod's estate. Inasmuch as Stewart conspired with Coote in accepting the Englishman's terminology in referring to a set of bagpipes as a "pair," the two-tenor, or tenor-and-bass, drone set may have been in use. Among many sources for the Highlanders' adventures in India at the time, Stewart had his brother William of Garth, whose son William died of wounds suffered at the Siege of Mangalore (May 1783–January 1784).

18 Rev. Angus Mackay, *The Book of MacKay*, 217, 218. Macdonald had earlier been pipe-major of the Gordon Fencibles (1778); ibid.

19 Col. David Stewart, *Sketches*, vol. 2: 137. Stewart cited "Munro's Narrative."

20 Ibid., 137, 168.

21 Ibid., 172–75.

22 There had been widespread scurvy in 1782, to such an extent that the few able men left of the Seaforths were regimented with the 73d (ibid., 172, 173).

23 Ibid., 188.

24 Ibid., 188 and 189.

25 Ibid., 188.

26 Donald MacLeod, *Memoir of Norman MacLeod, D.D.*, 452. Campsie (*The MacCrimmon Legend*, 133) wrote that this MacLeod of MacLeod had resigned on being demoted to a lieutenant colonel.

27 The Bighouse Papers give Patrick Campbell as son of Duncan Campbell of Barcaldine and Glenure and a lieutenant in the 77th Atholl Highlanders. See "Selections from the Family Papers," 128.

28 Stewart (b. 1772) is listed among the "officers appointed later" as "Ensign David Stewart 14 April 1781." In the "remarks" column, "Second son of Garth. Never joined the 77th." See Marchioness of Tullibardine, *Military History of Perthshire*, 78. Stewart took an ensigncy in the 42d on 10 October 1787. (Col. David Stewart, *Sketches*, vol. 2: facing lxi in Appendix).

29 Marchioness of Tullibardine, *Military History of Perthshire*, 70. Identification of a specific Murray tartan in 1778, not known from any other sources to exist, detracts from the statement, although the Murrays may have had a simple preference for red tartans.

30 See, "Account," in MacKay, *Collection*, 17.

31 Among the former Jacobites who were commissioned in the 1757 Fraser's Highlanders were: Lt Col Simon Fraser, Captains John MacPherson (brother of Cluny), Simon Fraser of Inverallochy, Donald MacDonald (brother to Clanranald), John MacDonell Iain mac Dhòmhnuil of Lochgarry, Alexander Cameron of Dungallon, Thomas Fraser of Struy, Alexander Fraser of Culduthel, James Fraser of Belladrum, Captain Lieutenant Simon Fraser, and Lieutenants Hugh Cameron (unidentified) and Archibald Campbell of Glenlyon. The roster also included captain Ronald MacDonell, son of the Keppoch chief who was killed at Culloden, Lieutenant Charles Stewart, son of Col John

Roy Stewart, a Leeks MacDonell, and Ewen MacSorlie Cameron of Glen
Nevis.

32 Until 1804 commissions could be obtained in Highland regiments by raising
men. Stewart gave the requirement of the Second Battalion, 78th for that year:
lieutenant colonel – 100; major – 90; company captain – 50; lieutenant – 25;
and ensign – 20 (Col. David Stewart, *Sketches*, vol. 2: 292).

33 Lochgarry senior's forfeited estate was in northwest Perthshire. This was also a
probable source for volunteers. Lochgarry headed the Glengarry regiment in
the later part of the Jacobite campaign in 1746.

34 John MacDonald of Lochgarry's piper (perhaps only one of them) in 1790 was
the boy John Cameron who played Boisdale's Salute at the Edinburgh competition. "A Circumstantial Account," in Angus MacKay, *Collection*, 16.

35 MacLeod of MacLeod was sometime pupil of the Rev. Norman MacLeod of
Swordale. When, as a general, he returned to his estate in Skye in the summer
of 1799, he stopped *en route* at Fiunary and prevailed upon his old tutor,
Swordale, to let his son (Caraid nan Gaidheal) accompany him to Skye. They
were greeted by a multitude at Loch Bracadale and then by the tacksmen at
Dunvegan Castle, among whom was the laird of MacLeod's fellow British offi-
cer in the American war, Dòmhnul Ruadh MacCruimein, who struck up "*Fàilte
Ruairi Mhóir*" ("Rory Mor's Salute").

36 Those men – sergeants, corporals, drummers, and privates – of MacDonald's
Highlanders who preferred to stay in North America at the war's end sailed to
Nova Scotia in 1783. There were 108 of them, including six drummers, of
whom the piper Duncan McLean was the last named. They were granted land
on the east side of the Jordan River in what is now Shelburne County (see *New
Brunswick Historical Society Collections*, vol. 8: 296, 297). Their neighbour,
and the man who for a few years ran the ferry across Jordan Bay, was Dòmhnul Ruadh MacCruimein, late of Tarleton's Legion.

37 James Ferguson, *The Scots Brigade in Holland*, vol. 1: 93.

38 Col. David Stewart, *Sketches*, vol. 2: 335 and footnote. John Buchan (*Royal
Scots Fusiliers*, 60) gave a brief description of dissolution of the Royal Scots
(Scots Brigade) in 1782.

39 MacKay Scobie offered no proof for this statement.

40 While the few paragraphs that follow show only where Highlanders served in
sufficient numbers to give them a sense of homogeneity, at least at the company level, and perforce leave piping to the reasonable imagination, there is
yet something to be learned about the Disarming Act here.

41 Alexander MacKay was a son of George MacKay, third Lord Reay (d.1748).
Rev. Angus Mackay, *Book of MacKay*, 192, 194, notes MacKay's service with
the 25th, an Independent Company (1745–46), the 3rd, and the 52d Foot.

42 Walton, *History of the British Standing Army*, 462.

43 Ibid., 10, and footnotes on p. 11.

44 M.M. Haldane, "The Royal Scots (Lothian Regiment)," 135. The Royals were

regimental descendants of the Régiment d'Hebron. They were also known through the years as Régiment de Douglas, Dumbartaon's Regiment, and The Royal Scots Regiment of Foot (Royals, or Royal Scots).

45 Maxwell, ed., *Lowland Scots Regiments*, 78.

46 John Campbell, fourth earl of Loudon, had raised and was first colonel of Loudon's Highlanders in 1745. John Campbell, fifth duke of Argyll from 1770–1806, was the regiment's first lieutenant colonel.

47 Dr Ray MacLean, ed., *History of Antigonish County* (the edited historico-genealogical writings of Sagart Arasaig, Father Ronald MacGillivray), 2, 51, in the notes to the section headed "Highland Emigration Arisaig and Districts."

48 Duncan Robertson of Drumachuine had held a lieutenant's commission in Loudon's Highlanders in 1745, an honour he (in the company of various other turncoats, including Capt Ewen MacPherson of Clunie and Donald MacDonell of Lochgarry) betrayed to serve Prince Charles. For all the Robertsons' devoted Jacobitism, this was a foolhardy step since the Robertson chief in 1745, Alexander (c. 1670–1749), was about seventy-five, unmarried, and childless and the estate, which had already been forfeited from 1690 until 1731, was legally destined to descend to the Drumachuine branch of which he, Duncan, was the senior member (Col. David Stewart, *Sketches*, vol. 2: 50; Keltie, *A History of the Scottish Highlands*, vol. 2: 171, 172). Drumachine itself was a farm/estate in Atholl, Perthshire, and formed part of MacDonell of Lochgarry's holding, also in Atholl, from the duke of Atholl. After Culloden Lochgarry's estate reverted to the duke. Robertson of Drumachine, who held his land on wadset from Lochgarry, escaped, like Lochgarry, to France. The duke of Atholl subsequently went to the courts to try to establish his right to Drumachine (outcome unknown). The Lochgarry estate was granted in 1785 to John, the son of the attainted MacDonell of Lochgarry, and was rented by him from the duke of Atholl. (See Leneman, *Living in Atholl 1685–1785*).

49 Highland officers were not averse to raising Lowland Scots and Irishmen for their companies/regiments.

50 Correspondence of Lt Gen. Beauclerk. WO, 1, 613, 6 May 1757.

51 The Recruiting Act of 1756–57 (30 Geo 2, cap. 8) allowed the impressment of men who did not have certified exemption (the impressed were entitled to their discharge after five years if they asked for it). See Maxwell, ed., *Lowland Scots Regiments*, 324.

52 In 1756 "The 2d battalion of the 32d ... included a large number of Highlanders, who, having been convicted under the Disarming Acts of the crime of wearing the kilt, were condemned to wear breeks in his Majesty's 71st" (Maxwell, ed., *Lowland Scots Regiments*, 324).

CHAPTER EIGHT

1 It bears re-emphasizing that at the level of gentleman, or tacksman, the pipers involved were often, if not always, what may be called community pipers. Significantly, the term, which still awaits adequate definition, covers dance-music piping.

2 Many are known to have had pipers before and after 1746–83, including the Keppoch MacDonells, the Camerons, the Chisholms, and the Glenalladales.

3 Pipers were common on several Argyllshire Campbell estates, notably Breadalbane and Islay, and, although the Munro chiefs in Ross-shire have no tradition of patronizing pipers, the term *pìobaire* appears at least once in a Munro country place-name. Many Munro gentlemen, or tacksmen, raised Highland companies for service to the British Crown and why should they have been atypical? The famous Blind Piper of Gairloch is believed to have composed "Munro's Salute," although his lifelong patrons were MacKenzies of Gairloch. Lastly, when Sir James Grant of Grant was raising the Inverness Shire Highlanders (97th Foot) in 1794, the bagpipes Grant bought for his (unofficial) pipers came from James Munro, bagpipe maker, Inverness. (There are no known records of James Munro's business.) See H.B. Mackintosh, *The Inverness Shire Highlanders*, 31).

4 Murdoch MacDonald, son of Donald, was educated at Fearn in Easter Ross and graduated MA from St Andrew's University in 1722. He was tutor to MacKay of Rhenovie, minister of Durness, and married Anna Couper (d. 1784), daughter of the minister of Pittenweem. (Hew Scott, *Fasti Ecclesiae Scoticanae*, vol. 7: 102).

5 In a few instances, including Donald MacDonald, introductory runs (which are never played today) are reproduced, but the richness of Joseph MacDonald's embellishments was never duplicated in print by anyone else. Joseph MacDonald's "Compleat Theory" demands careful reading and an understanding that grasps the fact that the rational presentation of grace-notings, to which pipers adhere blithely today, was conceived as almost superfluous to the presentation of simply the main tune notes until the nineteenth century.

6 Joseph MacDonald, "Compleat Theory."

7 Ibid., title page. The 1971 reprint of the 1927 and 1803 editions also specifies "Directions and Examples for the proper Execution and Cutting of the Pipe Reels Composed by the same Masters in the Isles and Highlands." Alexander MacDonald, "A Compleat Theory."

8 To date I have found no record of Joseph MacDonald's time in Bengal, nor have I discovered how his manuscript survived.

9 Cannon, *A Bibliography of Bagpipe Music*, 19, 20, 21.

10 That many of the *bàrds* set their words to familiar melodies in eighteenth-century Highland Scotland, and still do, is a conservative feature of the oral tradition. In Gaelic Cape Breton one main reason for the persistent popularity of

traditional tunes is that they are good for step-dancing, a subtlety lost to modern Gaelic Scotland and increasingly to post-Gaelic fiddle players even in Cape Breton.

11 In the preface to his *Life of Robert Burns* (p. 4), James Currie wrote, "The jig so much in favour among the English peasantry, has no place among them." Currie's knowledge of the *Gàidhealtachd* is unknown and this claim belongs presumably to Burns's Ayrshire of c. 1773. See Fletts, *Traditional Dancing in Scotland*, 28.

12 de la Tocnaye, *Promenade autour de la Grande-Bretagne*.

13 Alexander MacPherson, *Glimpses of Social Life*, 47.

14 John MacKenzie, *Sar-Obair*, 61.

15 Capt. Simon Fraser, ed., *Airs and Melodies*, 111.

16 John Dixon, *Gairloch*, 179.

17 Gibson, "Genealogical and Piping Notes."

18 Hew Morrison, "Is toigh le seòras Leodach mise," in *Orain le Rob Donn*, 288, 289.

19 John Dixon, *Gairloch*, 178.

20 David Johnson, *Scottish Fiddle Music*, 23, 32, 248. (Johnson cited, "Sinkler, Margaret. Fiddle and keyboard book, 'written by Andrew Adam at Glasgow October the 31 day 1710.' NLS Glen 143," ibid., 248. Elsewhere Johnson gives NLS MS. 3296.)

21 Capt. Simon Fraser, ed., *Airs and Melodies*, 91, 94, 212. The slow strathspey is still a feature of the Gaelic fiddler in Cape Breton. Whether or not it was a feature of traditional piping I do not know.

22 Ibid., 102 (in notes to tunes 35, 36, and 48).

23 John Dixon, *Gairloch*, 177–8.

24 Assuming that he made those poem/songs attributed to him and also, for example, the very unlike pibrochs "*Crosanachd an Doill*" and "*Cumha Phàdruig Oig.*"

25 Annie MacKay, "All We Know about Our Grandparents."

26 Gaelic lingered into the twentieth century in out-of-the-way communities like Gairloch in Pictou County; the language's extinction occurred within living memory. The place-name Gairloch, however, is still given the Gaelic pronunciation, "Garloch," (the terminal "ch" often pronounced "ck").

27 Dr Neil Ross, CBE, DD, D.Litt, in a talk to the Gaelic Society of Inverness on 16 January 1925, "Ceòl Mór, The Classical Music of the Bagpipes," lumped the MacKays with the MacArthurs and the Rankins as having run teaching establishments. Ross was more explicit than John Johnston in adding that all were "minor off-shoots of the MacCrimmon school." Neil Ross was the father of Roderick Ross who compiled *Binneas is Boreraig*. See *TGSI* vol. 32, 165.

28 Young Rory MacKay is still believed by many to have had MacCrimmon training from Donald Mór MacCrimmon. Then, accepting that Rory MacKay was the first piping teacher of his son Iain Dall, the dance-music composer and player, and that Rory was piper to the MacKay chief (Huistean Du), then the

MacKay chief was probably not against dance-music piping, and there is a fair possibility that Rory's *ceòl beag* (along with his *ceòl mór*) knowledge was developed by Donaldo McCruimien.

29 See Joseph MacDonald, "Compleat Theory," under "Rest."

30 *Proceedings of the Society of Antiquaries* 14: 122.

31 The Highland Society of London's objectives included "the Preservation of the Ancient Music of the Highlands," the preserving and encouraging of the Celtic language, the rescue "from oblivion" of Celtic Literature, the restoration of the Highland dress, the resurrection of the harp in the Highlands and "the promoting of Agricultural Improvement" (Alastair Campbell, *Two Hundred Years*, 3–5).

Fiddling suffered as well as dance-music piping. Fiddlers, too, had been popular under the old Gaelic régime, from Sutherland to the marches with the Lowlands; they had been numerous in Martin Martin's time (fl. c. 1695); in some, probably most, Highland clan jurisdictions they also appear to have enjoyed favoured status in the service of a number of chiefs and other prominent Gaels into the early nineteenth century. After "improvement" had bitten deep and the emigrations had begun, this class of apparently untutored, traditionally ear-learned Gaelic musician was almost forgotten in Scotland. It may be that by the late 1830s traditional fiddlers and pipers were becoming rare in some parts of Gaelic Scotland because of massive emigration. In 1837, for example, a medical doctor who visited a ship at Cape Town bound for Australia recommended that a piper and a fiddler be included on every ship for the entertainment and health of the passengers (see Watson, *Caledonia Australis*, 59). To Cape Bretoners today this would seem almost incredible; they would assume that any emigrant ship of Scots Gaels bound for Nova Scotia until c. 1840 would contain a discernible proportion of instrumental musicians. But the concentration of attention in modern Scotland upon the literate and trained forms of fiddling and piping argues cogently that indeed such a fate befell traditional music.

32 John MacCulloch, *The Highlands and Western Isles*, vol. 2: 377, 378.

33 Ibid., 377. Neil Gow (d. 1807) was a famous eighteenth-century fiddler described by the Reverend W. Forsyth as "the best fiddler that ever knitted thairm wi' horse-hair" (see Forsyth, *In the Shadow of Cairngorm*, 255–6).

34 According to Stewart of Garth, MacCulloch published grotesquely incorrect facts about where Highlanders should be recruited; Garth put these errors down either to the ignorance of or dissembling among his informants, suggesting in the broadest terms that "a gentleman eminent in science and political economy, like Dr Macculloch" was hoodwinked and incompetent. See Stewart, *Sketches*, vol. 2: 442.

35 The apparent ignorance of members of the Highland Society of Scotland in Edinburgh of the value of the Campbell canntaireachd, c. 1816, paints an unflattering picture of their knowledge of Gaelic tradition, although in another instance their perception of the top pipers' repertoires is of great value.

36 Of the six Coll tunes in David Glen's book, "*Cas air Amhich, a Thighearna Chola*" is given as John Johnston's (appended are Johnston's particular full-note run introductions, which have become ᵍE/A to a grip on C, and a similar run introduction which has become ᵍE/G to an ᵈA). Other tunes that are probably Johnston's, if not necessarily exclusive to him, are "*Cumha Iain Ghairbh Chola*," "*Birlinn Thighearna Chola*," "*Cumha Mhic Ghilleathain Lochabuidhe*," "*Ribinn Gorm Chlann Ghilleathain*," and "*Spaidsearachd Chlann Ghilleathain*."

37 The dance-music bagpiping and the dancing of the tinkers in Highland Scotland, particularly the ethnic Gaelic tinkers, have yet to be compared to those of Gaelic Cape Breton. Of great interest would be the speed and timing of the dance music, and in dance the setting steps employed. Tinker pipers were often remembered, in the middle years of this century, as playing faster than their literately taught counterparts (and were often looked down upon for it). By "march" Johnston was talking about non-classical music. See NLS Acc. 7451, Box 1, Letter from John Johnston to Seton Gordon, 7 December, 1917.

38 NLS MS9623 f.235, Letter from John Johnston to the *Oban Times*, 3 September 1919.

39 Ibid., f.244, Letter from John Johnston to the *Oban Times*, 10 November 1919.

40 Angus MacKay describes him as "Alexander Bruce, Piper to Captain MacLeod of Gesto" (MacKay, *Collection*, 17).

41 NLS MS9623 f.244, Letter from John Johnston to the *Oban Times*, 10 November 1919.

42 Ibid. Alasdair Carrach (curly-haired, or possibly cross-grained, Alasdair, c. 1380–1445) was the youngest son of John, first lord of the Isles, and the first MacDonell of Keppoch, according to Dr Annie M. MacKenzie (ed.), in *Orain Iain Luim*, xxi.

43 The MS (c. 1812) of Donald MacDonald (1750–1840) includes a tune called "Alastair Charich's March"; Colin Campbell ("Instrumental Book") calls it "Argyle's March."

44 Bruford, "The Rise of the Highland Piper."

45 David Johnson, *Scottish Fiddle Music*, 123, 124.

46 James R. McLeod, "John McKay's Black House at Eyre," part 1, 19. McLeod cited no source for a quote that was attributed to John Ban MacKenzie but taken from J.F. Campbell's *Canntaireachd*, 33. Campbell reported from overhearing a conversation John Ban had with one of his piping pupils, a Duncan Ross, in which MacKenzie was describing his Raasay piping lessons from John MacKay, Raasay, in 1821.

47 By 1865 Coll had passed out of the control of its MacLean lairds and was well on the way to being dramatically depopulated.

48 Another suggestion from the mid-nineteenth century that there was some exclusivity of repertoire emerges from a reading of the notes on the MacPherson pipers Calum Pìobaire (d. 1898) and his son Jockan (d. 1933) in Roddie

Ross's *Binneas is Boreraig*. Whatever else they played, there is no doubt that the MacPherson piping family put a heavy emphasis on *ceòl mór* playing. It is quite possible that the various Cluny MacPhersons had the same attitude as the last Coll chieftains about light music, and for the same reasons, but it is only fair to mention that the MacPherson pipers claimed descent from the piping MacCrimmons, among whom the exclusivity theory may have meant something. Moreover, the MacPherson *ceòl mór* exclusivity is limited to the nineteenth century.

49 Neil Ross, "Ceòl Mór," 165.

CHAPTER NINE

1 Patrick MacDonald's *Highland Vocal Airs* apparently set out to continue Joseph MacDonald's plan for his book on piping by publishing, almost exclusively, Highland pipe music of the dance music sort.

2 The Highland Society of London was formed in 1778. Its first president was Simon Fraser of Lovat, whose second regiment of Fraser's Highlanders was then serving in America. The society's mandate has already been excerpted but it should be restated that this gentleman's society was devoted not only to cultural conservation but to the radical notion of improvement in traditional music and in agriculture. It quickly became the proud fosterer of part of Scotland's identity. An attempt to revive the harp came to nothing. See note 31, chapter 8, citing Alastair Campbell, *Two Hundred Years*.

3 The 77th Regiment (1778–83) was also known as the Athol Highlanders. David Stewart of Garth, who began his military career as an ensign in this regiment, described the corps as being "like a family, of which General Murray was the common father and friend" (Col. David Stewart, *Sketches*, vol. 2: 168). Murray was the duke of Athol whose piper, David Ross, competed in the Edinburgh competition in 1784.

4 Son or grandson of Sir John Clerk of Pennicuik (1676–1755). Sir John was the player and composer of mainstream European classical music.

5 Lord Drummore, the judge, Jupiter Carlyle's neighbour at Prestonpans in 1741, belonged to the Dalrymple family. Geordy Sym(e), his piper, was a man whom Simon Lord Lovat said was only fit to play reels for the dancing of oyster-women. However, at the local tavern, Lucky Vint's, in or near Prestonpans, Simon danced with Kate Vint, the landlady's daughter (and Drummore's mistress). There is no description of what he danced. Drummore is marked on current Ordnance Survey maps as being near Cockenzie.

6 After almost a century of political union with England, of being referred to as "North Britain," Scotland's economic situation may have improved but the country, Lowland and Highland, then as now, bristled with important notions of its cultural distinctiveness. It is not surprising that something as essentially

Gaelic as *ceòl mór* was symbolically important even for Lowlanders. English piping was reduced to vulgar status even in Yorkshire by the 1770s.

7 According to a hand-written MS by G.C.B. Poulter in the possession of Dr Hugh MacCrimmon, Guelph, Ontario, a Norman MacCrimmon born in Lowerkill, Skye, piped in the 1824 piping competition at Edinburgh. Angus MacKay's record of the competition results does not include his name.

8 *Scots Magazine* 46 (October 1784): 552, 553.

9 MacCrumen's fellow British Legionnaire, Soirle MacDonald (later of Sartle and then Quintolan), is believed to have emigrated in 1770 (see MacQueen, *Skye Pioneers*, 125).

10 *Piping Times* 22, no. 2 (November 1969).

11 Gibson, "Genealogical and Piping Notes," 94–8.

12 Watson, *Gaelic Poetry 1550–1900*, 104–11.

13 A.R.B. Haldane, *Drove Roads*, passim.

14 Lt Dòmhnul Ruadh MacCruimein's last holding on MacLeod lands was in Glenelg. There Alexander Campbell found him in 1814, among neighbours of his own name, and listened in awe to his playing of a prelude and then of "*Fàilte a' Phrionnsa*" ("The Prince's Salute"). Campbell may have had an intimate liking for piping nurtured in the Callander of his boyhood but more likely he got, or greatly improved on, what he knew in Keppoch country (he was the second husband of Sarah [Cargill] MacDonell, and lived from 1806–10 at Clianaig, part of the old Keppoch estate, stepfather to the two sons of Raonul Òg, late chief of Keppoch, and unhappy neighbour of both Aonghus Bàn Innse and his son Gilleasbuig Aonghuis Bhàin). In that case Campbell's assessment of MacCrimmon's piping may have been based on Keppoch impressions. See Stuart Macdonald, *Back to Lochaber*.

15 One scholar (a non-piper) wrote that "the latter [*ceòl beag*] was almost certainly developed by the pipers of the newly-raised Highland regiments in the late eighteenth and early nineteenth centuries, beginning in the period when only soldiers could play the pipes without the fear of prosecution under the Disarming Act" (Bruford, "The Rise of the Highland Piper).

16 MacLeod, "John McKay's Black House," 21. MacLeod cited the 1838 edition of Angus MacKay's *Collection*.

17 Angus MacKay died insane in 1859. He had been certified mad in 1854.

18 John Maclean, "Am Pìobaire Dall," 283–306; Gibson, "Genealogical...

19 *Piping Times* 5, no. 6 (March 1953).

20 Capt. Neil MacLeod of Gesto (a tack in Skye), lover of classical piping and friend of Iain Dubh MacCrimmon, had published a book of twenty of Iain Dubh's pieces of *ceòl mór* in 1828. MacLean also ignored Joseph MacDonald's "Compleat Theory."

21 Ruairidh MacLeod, "'The Best Piper of His Time," 66–73.

22 John Maclean, "Am Pìobaire Dall," 305, 306.

CHAPTER TEN

1   *Scots Magazine* 46 (1784): 552, 553.
2   Flett and Flett, "Some Early Highland Dancing Competitions," 345–58.
3   de Saint Fond, *A Journey through England and Scotland.*
4   John Ban MacKenzie is known to have piped for Reels in Edinburgh in 1819. Shaw, *Pigeon Holes,* 116.
5   Since the Four-hand Reel was very popular in Edinburgh at the time, and had been during Topham's visit in the 1770s, one must presume that what may have been peculiar to the *Gàidhealtachd* about this dance, as can be inferred from what Joseph MacDonald wrote (see above), was the setting steps. Various Gaelic travelling figures are believed to have existed at the turn of the nineteenth century, from twentieth-century evidence in the Cape Breton *Gàidhealtachd.*
6   Angus MacKay, "A Circumstantial Account," in *Collection,* 19.
7   Fletts, "Some Early Highland Dancing Competitions," 354. The assumption has been, and is here, that the dancing in 1832 was still essentially Gaelic traditional, uncontrived by any choreographer, and that the instrumental band was not a band of bagpipes.
8   Letter from the Highland Society of Scotland, in Archibald Campbell, *The Kilberry Book,* 7, 8.
9   Ibid., 7, 8.
10 Fletts, "Some Early Highland Dancing Competitions," 354 (citing Dalyell, *Musical Memoirs*). There is a coincidence, if not a correlation, to be remarked upon between out-migration from the highlands and the moves away from Gaelic tradition in the highly organized Highland Society piping and dancing competitions after the French defeat at Waterloo. The changes in the competition dancing and in its accompaniment occurred in roughly the last thirty years of the Highland Society's tenure in Edinburgh, dating from the last years of the French wars. The competitions became triennial in the mid-1820s, by which time emigration, forced and voluntary, of Gaels to Canada and elsewhere was in full flood. This is explored later in greater depth. For now, suffice it to say that the Regency period had hoisted the first nostalgic banner of Gaelic caricature. With fascinating pointers in the record to instances of lingering old-fashioned Gaelic piping tradition, that process continued and intensified as the twentieth century approached.
11 Burton, ed., *Autobiography of the Rev. Dr. Alexander Carlyle,* 53, 54. Cited in Emmerson, *Social History of Scottish Dance,* 116.
12 Writing about his grandfather, Rev. Norman MacLeod (minister of Morvern and the father of Caraid nan Gàidheal), Rev. Donald MacLeod said that "not unfrequently the minister would tune his violin, and, striking up some swinging reel or blythe strathspey, would call on the lads to lay aside their books, and the girls their sewing, and set them to dance with a will to his own hearty

music. Family worship, generally conducted in Gaelic, for the sake of such servants as knew little English, ended the day" (see Rev. Donald MacLeod, *Memoir of Norman MacLeod*, 19).

13 If, as Joseph MacDonald wrote of the "Compleat set of Jigs & Reells" composed for the bagpipes, these were used for dances that were unique to the Highlands and Isles, then how did the setting steps of Lowland Reels differ? Alternatively, had Highland setting steps become the vogue in Lowland Scotland by the 1770s?

14 David Johnson, *Music and Society in Lowland Scotland*, 6, 68.

15 How widely the strathspey had spread in the *Gàidhealtachd* by the early eighteenth century is unknown.

16 The relationship between Captain John MacDonald of Glenaladale and the Roman Catholic church in St John's Island (Prince Edward Island) as described by Kenneth MacKinnon in "Captain John MacDonald and the Glenaladale Settlers" puts the matter into the appropriate perspective.

17 Alexander Allardyce, ed., *Scotland and Scotsmen*, 393.

18 MacCulloch, *The Highlands and Western Isles*, vol. 3: 6, 25.

19 *MacTalla* 5, no. 36 (13 March 1897): 278. My translation. In 1993 a dwindling number of Gaelic-speaking, fiddling, and dancing Catholic priests still existed in the shrinking *Gàidhealtachd*. From the main Gaelic and once-Gaelic part of Nova Scotia, clerical fiddlers include Fr Angus Morris, Fr Colonel MacLeod, and Fr Francis Cameron; among the Gaelic singers are Frs Hugh MacDonald and Hugh MacMillan. Fr Eugene Morris is a well-known step-dancer and so was the late Fr Alexander MacDonell. In the late nineteenth century one famous Cape Breton priest in Mabou who had a reputation as a represser of fiddling and dancing had no cultural axe to grind; his mission was to stamp out alcoholism and public body contact.

20 John Campbell (Iain mac Cailein Mhoir 'ic Dhòmhnuil), piper to Frederick Campbell of Shawfield and Isla, taught his employer's son, J.F. Campbell (Iain Og Ile, or Iain Og nan Oran), Gaelic in the late 1820s. He was also the source of Gaelic stories that made a lasting impression on the boy's mind. It is most probable also that J.F. Campbell learned Gaelic dance steps from the piper and at the get-togethers that the older man took his charge to in Isla. Unfortunately, the piper-storyteller died in 1831 when he was only thirty-six, before J.F.C. could plumb his cultural depths. Campbell won fourth prize at the 1815 competition in Edinburgh.

21 In one instance the thoroughness of his reporting has to be questioned. Campbell was a good artist and in 1848 he made a drawing of three Highland pipers at Inverness to portray the current dress. Each piper is shown holding his instrument under the right shoulder, which is unusual. Having the right hand upper on the chanter was common enough to be unremarkable, but right-shoulder pipers are rarer and may always have been. The same phenomenon is found in the coloured representation of a kilted Highland piper at the end of Joseph

MacDonald's "Compleat Theory," and the explanation, founded on artistic style, that is offered further on in this book is probably wrong. In Campbell's case there is the possibility of a printer's alteration or error.

22 Similarly, Osgood H. MacKenzie (1842–1922), who arranged for the collection of Gaelic stories in Gairloch for J.F. Campbell, was deliberately taught Gaelic (and French) as a child. He too relied on a school teacher as his collector-assistant.

23 There is almost no doubt but that *canntaireachd*, whether used by pipers or singers in the Outer Hebrides, was still used into the twentieth century, although it may indeed have become extinct in Argyll in Iain Og Ile's time. The reader's is referred to Frans Buisman's "From Chant to Script," "More Evidence on Colin Campbell," and "Melodic relationships."

24 J.F. Campbell, *Canntaireachd*, title page, 9, 12, 33, 34.

25 Craik, *A Century of Scottish History*, 456. However nostalgic and rosy a view this may have been, it points to the existence of an enlightened Christian Gaelic middle and upper class. It isn't difficult to see the sort of social distress that might have been caused when this system was displaced over the century from 1750 to 1850 by a relatively insensitive capitalist system dependent upon several social artificialities.

26 The ancient poems of Ossian, collected, edited, and published by James MacPherson (1760–63) caused a stir in Europe. Samuel Johnson derogated them as fake. Napoleon Bonaparte is said to have carried them with him on his campaigns.

27 See a draft letter of J.F. Campbell to story collector Hector MacLean, 19 May 1859, cited in *Lamplighter*, 26.

28 Ardeonaig on Loch Tay had a Gaelic-speaking minister, Iain mac Caluim (Rev. John McCallum), until the first decade of the twentieth century. See Iain Mac-Calum *Cunntas Aithghearr*.

29 Hall, *Travels in Scotland*, vol. 2: 436.

30 MacCulloch, *The Highlands and Western Isles*, vol. 2: 377.

31 Col. David Stewart, *Sketches*, vol. 1: 81, 82.

32 Ibid., 81.

33 Ibid., 486ff.

34 Ibid.

35 J.F. Campbell, ed., *Popular Tales of the West Highlands*, vol. 1: xv.

36 Burt, *Letters*, vol. 2: letter 23.

37 Col. David Stewart, *Sketches*, vol. 2: appendix M, xxii and xxiii.

38 Gilleasbuig mac Iain Fhrangaich 'ic Aonghuis Bhorrodal, d. c. 1828.

39 Rev. Charles Macdonald, *Moidart*, 259. The size of his home may have had something to do with it, although according to the ruling Clanranald in 1989 it was only a fairly modest three-room dwelling, presumably of only one floor.

40 Christina Byam Shaw, ed., *Pigeon Holes*, 101, citing Eileanach's MS diary.

41 From "*Oran Ghlinn Urchaidh*": Bu chridheil bhith 'sa' gheamhradh ann,/ Air

bainnsean gheibhte spurt:/ Fonncheòl réidh na pìobaireachd,/ Cha bhiodh sgìos mu a sgur;/ Fuaim nan teud aig fidhleirean/ A sheinneadh sìos na cuir;/ 'S an luinneag féin aig nìghneagan/ Bu bhinne mhìlse guth. Angus MacLeod, ed., trans., *The Songs of Duncan Ban MacIntyre*, lines 2238–45.

42   Dwelly's dictionary describes the Rough Bounds as lying between Loch Suin-eart in the South and Loch Hourn in the North.

43   Christina Byam Shaw, ed., *Pigeon Holes*, 81. Eileanach's older brother, Sir Francis MacKenzie, twelfth of Gairloch (1798–1843), according to Christina Byam Shaw, editor of Eileanach's diary, "played the fiddle." Ibid., 109.

44   Capt. Simon Fraser, ed., *Airs and Melodies*, 102.

45   Ibid., 105.

46   Mackintosh, *Notes Descriptive*, 36.

47   Osgood MacKenzie, *A Hundred Years in the Highlands*, 161.

48   Newte, *Prospects and Observations*, 174.

49   "The Complaynt of Scotland," 1548, in Leyden, *Preliminary Dissertation..*

50   Knox, *A Tour*, 136.

51   See *Leaves from the Journal*, 129 and 130. By 1868 P. Cotes had for some years been piper to Farquharson of Invercauld.

52   This is an implausible claim in light of known pipers' having been retained by Breadalbane in his Perthshire estate until the nineteenth century, and in the MacGregor "college." Given Perthshire military losses at Culloden and in later British army battles, Rob Roy's old henchman's claim is probably wishful thinking.

53   Burt, *Letters*, vol. 1: 217, letter 11.

54   Aeneas Mackintosh, *Notes Descriptive*, 34.

55   Pennant, *A Tour*, 89.

56   Aeneas Mackintosh, *Notes*, 34. To date, no evidence of this custom has come to light in Cape Breton.

57   Pennant, *A Tour*, 190.

58   MacCulloch, *The Highlands and Western Islands*, vol. 2: 35.

59   In Skye, ministerial proscription of music and dance, at least in one parish, began in the early 1820s when Rev. Roderick MacLeod, who was bent on reforming the Moderate Church and who brooked no official chidings or orders to desist, described bagpipe music as "seductive." He was concerned with dance-music bagpiping, which was plentiful in the parish of Duirinish in the early nineteenth century.

60   A classic example of this neglect is sharply etched in the writing of Alexander MacKenzie, editor of the *Celtic Magazine*, who took the time to track a son of the last MacKay piper to the Gairloch MacKenzies to his home in New Glasgow, Nova Scotia, during the winter of 1879–80.

MacKenzie had a keen and persistent mind and a good breadth of vision. His several histories of Highland clans were not mere regurgitations and show considerable ability. He had been aware, if from nowhere else than from Angus

MacKay's notes on the Gairloch MacKay pipers in the *Collection*, that the last of the great Gairloch pipers had emigrated to Nova Scotia in 1805, taking with him two sons, both pipers. MacKenzie was curious enough to visit the younger of these two sons, Squire John MacKay, JP (?1792–1884), yet what he reported of the meeting was pabulum about the old man's fine mind and consummately Ross-shire-accented Gaelic. Anything he learned of Gairloch MacKay piping he obviously felt was better left unsaid. The old squire may indeed have been a commanding and dominating character in any conversation, but MacKenzie was a prominent man who should have been dependable enough to keep him on the subject of piping long enough to find out at least what *canntaireachd* system the family had used, whether the Blind Piper had been taught by Pàdruig Og MacCruimein, to whom the MacKays had taught piping and how, and what tunes the famous Blind Piper and others of them had made.

As the younger of two sons the squire probably had not received as much piping attention as his older brother Angus (c. mid-1780s–1868) but he had learned, giving the instrument up as a man. His mind was particularly attentive and his memory excellent, as MacKenzie recalled. What's more, as the younger son he was longer in close contact with his father than anyone else in the family, starting the new farm in the forest wilderness in the early 1800s. He must have had a fund of piping information and no insurmountable reason to keep it to himself. With him, unfortunately, died the last reliable hope of answers to all of those simple questions that are nonetheless so important. (According to a New Glasgow lawyer-neighbour, Charlie Manning, who died in 1983, many of the family papers that had belonged to Squire John Mackay's son Norman (1846–1929) were deliberately destroyed some time in this century.) Incidentally, although the first MacKay to live in Gairloch, the Ruairidh mentioned in Angus MacKay's *sloinneadh*, had a strong military rôle to play in Gairloch society in times of turmoil, none of the family are linked in any capacity with the British army. To date no Gairloch MacKay piper of this family is known to have served any Britannic majesty in any of the Highland regiments, including the Seaforths.

61 Mackay Scobie, *Pipers*, 5.
62 Ibid., 50.
63 Ibid., 30ff.
64 Ibid., 8, citing Anderson, *Seaforth Songs*.
65 The critical shift away from Gaelic tradition in the mainland part of the Seaforth estate is difficult to date. Where the traditional populations remained it was doubtless gradual, but the loss of their chief in 1781 must have heralded the onset of non-Gaelic ideas, if they hadn't already taken root (as the emigrations from Kintail in the 1770s suggest). The Humberston MacKenzie brothers must have emphasized the break with Highland tradition. A move away from traditional piping and other aspects of gaelic culture may have been slightly

accelerated when Humberston MacKenzie became president of the Highland Society of London.

66 M'Crie, *The Correspondence of the Rev. Robert Wodrow*, vol. 2: 146.

67 "Journal of Captain Ronald Campbell, Grenadier Company, 72nd Regiment," 2 Vols, folio MS, cited indirectly from Keltie, *A History of the Scottish Highlands*, vol. 2: 531.

68 MacKay Scobie, *Pipers and Pipe Music*, citing "Journal of Lieut Ronald Campbell."

69 "Bheir sinn ceòl dannsaidh eile dhaibh"; see Gardyne, *Life of a Regiment*, n.p.

70 Col. David Stewart, *Sketches*, vol. 2: lxxxix.

71 Gardyne, *Life of a Regiment*, 296, 360ff., citing information originally received by Archibald Campbell from Col John Cameron of Fassifern in 1813–14. It is not known whether the correspondence is extant.

72 Keltie, *A History of the Scottish Highlands*, vol. 2: 707 and 708. Lord Cathcart had been Lt Donald MacCrimmon's commander in the British Legion in the American revolutionary war. The piper-officer appealed to him in 1807 for a renewed commission in the British army.

73 See Gardyne, *Life of a Regiment*, 424. It is not known whether Louisa Tighe's letter of 13 January 1889 is extant.

74 H.B. Mackintosh, *The Inverness Shire Highlanders*, 43.

75 Ibid., Appendix D, 71, 72, citing the letters of Lt William Rose.

76 One of the prizes taken after the Isle Groix action was the eighty-four gun *Le Tigre*, which later saw action with Nelson in the Mediterranean and the Atlantic. One of her impressed seamen for 9 May 1804–February 1812 was Roderick MacLennan of Gairloch, a great-grandson of Iain Dall, the Blind Piper and cousin of Squire John (New Glasgow) who avoided turning him in as a haugable deserter. See Gibson, "Piper John MacKay."

77 Gardyne, *Life of a Regiment*, 39.

78 David Johnson, *Scottish Fiddle Music*, 217.

79 "Stewart, James" in "Notices," *Piping Times* 27, no. 6 (March 1975): 29.

CHAPTER ELEVEN

1 *Archæologia Aeliana*, 4th Series, vol. 9, 1932.

2 See Joseph MacDonald, A Compleat Theory, 30.

3 Patrick MacDonald, *Highland Vocal Airs*, 7.

4 The example that Collinson gave, attributed to a Donald Gorm (d. 1617), occurs in Shaw's *Folksongs and Folklore*. It runs thus: "*Ruidhleadh mu seach air an ùrlar,/ Le pìob mhór nam feadan dùmhail,/ Le pìob bheag nam feadan siùbhlach*" (from "*Rinn mi mocheirigh gu éirigh*"). A similar song crops up in *Hebridean Folksongs III Waulking Songs*, from the song "*Dh'éirich mi gu moch Di-Luain.*"

5 Dixon, *Gairloch*, 179.

6 Three of his daughters, married to Donald, Murdock, and Colin Fraser, had respectively six, six, and five children by 1811.

7 Alexander NacKenzie, "The Editor in Canada," 71.

8 Joseph MacDonald, *Compleat Theory*, 30.

9 Dalyell, *Musical Memoirs*.

10 Dr Fraser set out successfully to find traces of the two-drone bagpipe in Gaelic Scotland in the 1880s and 1890s.

11 MacDonald wrote, "Some of the immigrants came to Cape Breton with two tenors, no bass drone. I played a set of these at a MacDonald house at Oiseau View, French Road. The same pipes were played at the battle of Waterloo, 1815" (J.M. MacDonald, "Piping in Cape Breton").

12 See Joseph MacDonald, "Compleat Theory." In the painting of the Joseph MacDonald piper, thought by many to be a self-portrait, each drone emerges from a separate stock, but there is only one tuning slide on the bass drone. Inaccurate use of the negative image has led to the belief that MacDonald held the pipes under his right shoulder and played right hand upper on the chanter while his tutorial instruction give "higher hand left hand." This and other eighteenth century artistic examples of right-shoulder pipers were explained by W.G.F. Boag as the "Bickham Piper" syndrome: Boag wrote that depictions of right-shoulder pipers in the eighteenth century followed an artistic style that began with the "Bickham Piper" of the Black Watch, which was made in 1743; Boag noted that "for the next 20 or 30 years, all illustrations of pipers were based on the Bickham and have the pipes under that arm" (personal correspondence, Boag to Gibson, 14 February 1980. See also Cheape, "Stock Imagery in Piping," *Common Stock* 9, no. 2 (December 1994).

13 See Joseph MacDonald, *A Compleat Theory*, 27.

14 The painting by Richard Waitt of the Grant piper suggests that a cylindrical-bore pipe chanter may have been used in Grant country in 1714. However to my knowledge no such eighteenth-century chanters have survived and the only Highland small-pipes known to have existed were made in Edinburgh, between 1840 and 1850 by Thomas Glen (see Baines, *Bagpipes*, 128).

15 *Tha'n gaothair air stopadh,/Tha'n dà dhos na'n tromshuain.* From "Elegy to Red John MacQueen, Piper in South Uist, while living, by Archibald MacDonald, the Uist Bard," my translation. Stewart and Stewart, *Cochruinneacha Taoghta de Shaothair nam Bard Gaëlach*, 388.

16 Piping tapes belonging to Barry Shears, Halifax, show that the Cape Breton piper Joe Hughie MacIntyre (1891–1968) sometimes played *edres* in place of doublings on E with excellent effect. Some of his music, including the *edre*, may be found in Shears, *Cape Breton Collection*.

17 Rev. Alexander MacRae, *History of the Clan MacRae*, 381, 382.

18 The pipers of the Royal Inniskilling Fusiliers, c. 1870, and of the Royal Ulster Rifles in 1948 played a two-drone (base and tenor) separate stock bagpipe and

the pipers of the Royal Irish Fusiliers in 1922 played a two-drone (base and tenor) common stock bagpipe. Price, ed., *Royal Irish Rangers*.

19 Bands of music such as the one in Fraser's Highlanders in the 1757–63 period were one avenue for the introduction of modern musical ideas, but so little is known of them in Highland regiments that an assessment of their influence is still premature.

20 Patrick MacDonald, *Highland Vocal Airs*, 10.

21 John Ramsay of Ochtertyre's opinions and observations, even about Highland Scots, are well thought of by modern scholars. While he and Lord Kames visited Inverary Castle several times dispensing advice on improvement (See Freda Ramsay, ed., *Day Book of Daniel Campbell*, 105), the degree of his understanding of Highland society appears to have been superficial. He also thought fit to advise Robert Burns on improving his writing style.

22 John McLachlan's *The Piper's Assistant* (May 1854) offers "quicksteps" in split common, common, 2/4, 3/4, 6/8 and 9/8 time.

23 Nicolson, *Gaelic Proverbs*, 189, 190.

24 Bain, *Les voyageurs français en Écosse*, 42.

25 Wardell, *With "The Thirty-Second,"* 110.

26 Ibid., 111.

27 By 21 August 1808, the date of Vimiera, the 1st Battalion, 71st, had received a draft reinforcement of about two hundred men from its second battalion in Scotland, men who had been raised in Glasgow in 1804 and who were known unofficially as the "Glasgow Highland Light Infantry." The possibility that some Highlanders spoke Lallans is regarded by some, unreasonably, as incorrect. The *Piping Times* describes "Clark, George" as born in Tougue, Reay, in 1784. He transferred to the 71st from the North Lowland Fencibles in 1800 and he was at Vimiera, 21 August 1808. *Piping Times* 20, 11 (August 1968):21–2.

28 Angus MacKay, *Collection*, 18.

29 John Glen, *Early Scottish Melodies*, 137.

30 Logan, *The Scottish Gael*, 289.

31 *Scots Magazine* 46 (1784): 552–3. "Report of the annual competition of the Highland Society of London held Tues. 19 Oct 1784 at the Assembly Hall."

32 Angus MacKay, "A Circumstantial Account," in *Collection*, 16.

33 *Scottish Genealogist* 29 (December 1982): 4.

34 Angus MacKay, *Collection*, 15.

35 George Moss wrote in the 1980s that two Strathglass pipers who joined the British army as pipers in the mid-nineteenth century did so as completely adequate pipers, having learned at home in the traditional way. One was an ancestor of Moss's. "An Da Phiobair" in *Tocher* 26.

36 See Decreet of Removing, 16 May 1795, Scottish Record Office, SC 29/7/2.

CHAPTER TWELVE

1 By the middle of the nineteenth century spirits must have been deeply inured
   to economically motivated clearances. In 1841, some sixty years after the root-
   ing out of powerless Gaels had begun, there was a parliamentary *Report of the
   Select Committee on Emigration (Scotland)* and an Agent General for Emigration report entitled *Emigration to Relieve Distress in the Highlands.* Procrustes
   would have smiled. The United Kingdom has yet to acknowledge its shameful
   acquiescence in such inhumanity. As late as the 1920s a deputation of Highland
   clerics visited Nova Scotia to study the possibility of getting farmland for
   Scotch Gaels.

2 A prominent exception was the transplanting of Strathglass traditional *ceòl mór*
   piping to Australia. Unfortunately, to my knowledge, no identifiable trace of it
   has survived.

3 Alastair Campbell, *Two Hundred Years*, 5.

4 The Frenchman Pierre-Nicolas Chantreau, however, had also been exposed to
   the other idea and wrote in the same place, "*Parce-que cet instrument* était
   autrefois *en prédilection dans les montagnes et les îles de l'Ecosse ... il
   adoucissait leurs peines et charmait leurs ennuis*" ("Because this instrument
   was formerly much favoured in the mountains and islands of Scotland ... it
   softened their troubles and lightened their boredom"; my translation, emphasis
   added). See Chantreau, *Voyages*, book 3: 85–6, cited in Bain, *Les Voyageurs
   Français*, 46.

5 Bain, *Les Voyageurs français*, 166, citing Duclos, *Itinéraire et Souvenirs*, my
   translation.

6 MacLeod, *Caraid nan Gàidheal*, 226, 227, my translation.

7 Ibid., 382, my translation.

8 John Campbell (1796–1862), second marquis of Breadalbane, succeeded his
   father John in 1834.

9 Somerled MacMillan, *Bygone Lochaber*, passim.

10 Alexander Allardyce, ed., *Scotland and Scotsmen*, 393. Most of Ramsay's man-
    uscript was written in the last quarter of the eighteenth century but with
    unidentified additions made up to 1813. This interclass familiarity is widely
    reported elsewhere also.

11 Ibid., 396. While not wishing to confound my argument I should add that Ram-
    say may only have been aware directly of Gaelic Scotland from his trips with
    Lord Kames to Inveraray in Argyll to advise on improvement (Freda Ramsay,
    ed., *Day Book of Daniel Campbell*, 105). Otherwise he probably was eloquent-
    ly restating received information current in the Lowlands but with which there
    is little reason to quibble.

12 Col. David Stewart, *Sketches*, vol. 2, Appendix s, xxxi.

13 Ibid., xxix, xxx. In 1773 Samuel Johnson was surprised at the education of
    many of the Highlanders whom he met, people living in what often were to

him very humble circumstances but who knew Latin and Greek as well as Gaelic and English and, often, French. Ironically (because an earlier Argyll was the earliest of the Highland improvers), George Douglas Campbell (b.1823), eighth duke of Argyll, remembered members of the old school of Gaelic gentlemen-tacksmen in Argyll and his description of them was as laudatory as Stewart of Garth's. See United Kingdom, *Crofters Commission*, Appendix A, 384.

14 Col. David Stewart, *Sketches*, vol. 2, Appendix S, xxxi.

15 In 1847, according to Robert Somers, there were no Cameron tacksmen living on the Locheil estate and Loch Arkaig-side (Cameron of Locheil land) had gone from being home to about a thousand Gaels to being home for none. The Cameron of Fassifern holding (from Locheil) was a sheep farm with twenty thousand animals and there are hints that the Fassiefern family had also become acquisitive and was clearing Gaels elsewhere. See Somers, *Letters*, Letter 25, 123. The acquisition by a Cameron of Meoble in South Morar, old Clanranald country, is one example. Another is Callart (bought, from another Cameron, in 1796). Another Cameron, Captain Allan, was a factor in North Uist at the time of large emigrations from there. The Camerons are probably more typical of the powerful families than not. See Somerled MacMillan, *Bygone Lochaber*, passim.

16 Alexander Smith described neighbouring land controllers in Skye, one a traditionalist and the other an improver. "McIan" belonged to the old Gaelic school, caring for his tenants, not scrupling over cash rent and ready to accept labour in its place; the other, an outsider and a man of business, was all for cash on the barrel-head and was in the process of clearing many of his people in the name of improvement. See Alexander Smith, *A Summer in Skye*, passim. McIan is given elsewhere as Charles Macdonald of Ord, Black Watch veteran of Corunna, Quatre Bras, and Waterloo (Alexander Cameron, *History and Traditions of Skye*, 156).

17 The MacDonald of Lathaig in Eigg whom Necker de Saussure visited in 1822 was a proud and imperious descendant of arch-Gael Alasdair mac Mhaighstir Alasdair of the 'Forty-five. He cleared many of his tenantry from Cleadale on the simple expedient of making way for a relative. De Saussure went to Eigg, having been advised that MacDonald was a traditionalist and an anachronism. "Upon the whole," he wrote, "nothing was more singular than his whole deportment; it was the tone, the manners of an epoch which had long passed away, and of a generation almost extinct" (*Voyage to the Hebrides*, 52–3). Lathaig was deeply fond of piping and sang a number of tunes, with variations, for his guest. Lathaig's antithesis is his cousin Captain John MacDonald of Glenaladale, himself a man in no doubt as to his high social station in anyone's company. In the early 1770s he led an emigration of many of his extended family and others to Isle St Jean (Prince Edward Island) rather than continue to endure unwanted pressures.

18 According to Lt Col C. Greenhill Gardyne (*Life of a Regiment*), who joined the
    92d Highland Regiment in 1851, the Gaelic-speaking middle class that Ochter-
    tyre and Garth had mentioned, were by 1850 rare anachronisms.

19 Incoming improver farmers crop up at different times in different places and
    often made it a condition of their entry that the existing people be cleared. The
    process of stripping the land of its native people went on until within living
    memory of 1993. The improver mentality invokes something of the Gaels' capac-
    ity for futile contempt at the uncultured: "*Gun iomradh air dualchas,/ Air cru-
    adal, no tapachd,-/ Chuir a'Chuibhle mun cuairt dhi/ Car tuathal is tarsuinn;/
    Sìol nam bodachan giùgach/ A bhiodh 'sna dùnain 'gan cartadh, Seòladh àrd os
    ar cionn-sa/ Bho'n a thionndaidh a'chairt ud*" ("There's no word of heredity,/ Or
    of hardiness or heroism,/ Perverse and unlucky,/ The wheel of fortune has
    turned;/ A race of churls, cringing,/ Whom we'd dump on the middens,/ Now
    sails high above us/ Since the cards are changed"). From "Oran an déidh Blàr
    Chuil-lodair" by Iain Mac Theàrlaich Oig, John MacLean of Inverscadale in Ard-
    gour. See John L. Campbell, ed., *Songs Remembered in Exile*, 7, 8, 256.

20 A casual idea of the number of Lowlanders serving in the Highland regiments
    during the Crimean War and the Indian Mutiny (1857–58) may be found in
    Cromb's *The Highland Brigade*. The Gaelic-speaking officers' necessary use of
    English hastened the process of bilingualization of Gaelic recruits.

21 A useful analogy is found in the telling of the old Gaelic tales. In the 1850s
    Gael John Francis Campbell (1821–85) saw the empty glens and began collect-
    ing Gaelic tales because he believed that, with the passing of the old Gaelic
    world, they would soon disappear. Campbell cautioned his collectors to avoid
    the ministers and teachers and all people of middling influence because they
    had a vested interest in being ignorant of folk affairs. Ironically, Eachan MacIl-
    leathain (Hector MacLean) the Baile Ghrannd, Isla, a teacher, and Thomas
    Cameron, the schoolteacher in Gairloch, were among Campbell's finest collec-
    tors. An appreciation of MacLean appears in Friseal, *Leabhar nan Sonn*, 7–34.
    A Cameron contribution is acknowledged in J.F. Campbell, ed., *Popular Tales*,
    vol. I: 152.

22 The farm Somers called Immergraden in Glenelg was a "club farm" in 1847. It
    had four tenants who paid an annual rent of £120. They cultivated "on the old
    system – keeping eight or nine cows each and only a few sheep." Somers found
    club farms elsewhere in Gaelic Scotland, notably in Keppoch. See his *Letters*,
    92 and passim.

23 Burleigh, *Church History*, 291. The two Lowland clerical observers I have
    mentioned, Carlyle and Erskine, were of different opinions. Alexander
    "Jupiter" Carlyle was a Moderate; Dr John Erskine was an evangelical.

24 In the 1760s several Moderate Highland ministers, led by the Reverend Hugh
    Blair, minister of St Giles in Edinburgh (1758–1800) and professor of rhetoric
    and belles lettres at Edinburgh University, were eagerly part of a scheme
    inspired by David Hume to collect Ossianic stories in the Highlands in defence

of James MacPherson's published claim to have collected Dark Ages heroic Gaelic verse from literate and illiterate sources in Gaelic Scotland. See James Grant, *Thoughts*, 379–99.

25 Baptist and Congregationalist ideas were entering Scotland c.1800 but appear to have had little effect in Gaelic Scotland, although a tiny Baptist presence seems to have existed in the Uig area of Skye.

26 Col. David, *Sketches*, vol. I: 126.

27 Somers, *Letters*, Letter III. The MacKenzies of Gairloch followed their tenantry and joined the Free Church but in Gairloch, as doubtless elsewhere, an old-fashioned and typically warm relationship between landlord/landowner and most tenants was not dissolved after the Disruption and persisted long into the nineteenth century.

28 In 1843 there were only 101 Gaelic-speaking Free Church ministers to go round; there were 150 vacancies with only thirty-one unattached ministers to serve them. The revised ideas of social righteousness, of shining moral distinctiveness from the old Kirk, cannot have taken root immediately everywhere, even with the presence of the top twelve ministers (and eighty others) itinerating and evangelizing in the ministerless Highland parishes. Where there was traditional sympathy for the landlord, his hostility to the new denomination, which after all had split over the issue of the landlord's right to place clergy where he wished, may have caused resistance to Free Church ideas. See "DMcL," "Free Church of Scotland," 87. In some parts of Skye, music and dance were condemned from 1805 by Donald Munro (1773–1830), SSPCK catechist and blind Skye fiddler who was converted by John Farquharson; Munro got rid of his own fiddle immediately.

29 In Tiree in 1968 the *seannachaidh*, Dòmhnul Chaluim Bàin (Donald Sinclair, 1885–1975), was able to remember and to explain why some of the old lorists had given up their attachment to traditional song and story. He called them "Christians." Cregeen, "Donald Sinclair," 61.

30 The SSPCK was formed in 1701.

31 Kenneth MacKinnon, *The Lion's Tongue*, 45–55. In 1822 there were about 495 schools in Highland Scotland: the Church of Scotland, 171; SSPCK, 134; Edinburgh Society, 77; Glasgow Society, 48; and the Inverness Society, 65 (ibid., 48).

32 Friseal, *Leabhar nan Sonn*, 41–2, my translation.

33 Ibid., 42, my translation.

34 John MacKenzie, "Dughall Bochannan," 167. Without offering a title, author, or other detail, MacKenzie cited a memoir of Bochannan that appeared in a publication of Bochannan's diary in 1836.

35 "A Circumstantial Account," in Angus MacKay, *Collection*, 17. The publication in question is Joseph MacDonald's *A Compleat Theory* (1803).

36 Ibid. The prize was awarded to Donald MacDonald in 1806 for rendering *ceòl mór* in staff notation. William MacKay, piper to the Celtic Society, was paid in

1821, 1822, and 1835 for writing pipe music scientifically. Published collections soon followed.

37 I have not included the two volumes of Robert Purdie (see Roderick Cannon, *Bibliography*, 21, 60, 61) or the music included in James Logan's *Scottish Gael*, vol. 2: 1–7, also set lower than the chanter scale.

38 Roderick Cannon, *Bibliography*, 127 and passim.

39 Three boy pipers are mentioned in Angus MacKay, "A Circumstantial Account," as having taken part in the Edinburgh *ceòl mór* competitions between 1781 and 1798; two won prizes: John MacGregor "tertius," age twelve, winning third prize in 1792, and Donald MacLean, a boy, came third in 1798. Many more may have competed. "A Circumstantial Account," in Angus MacKay, *Collection*, 15–17.

40 Roderick Cannon, *Bibliography*, passim.

41 Twentieth-century collections of ceòl beag generally include more marches than the faster and more difficult strathspeys and reels. This reflects the military's influence and the decline in the use of the bagpipe for traditional Gaelic dancing.

42 MacDonald stated that the more complex grace-note clusters were by no means used in all *ceòl mór*. Angus Fraser ("*Ceol-Suaicheantas Morair Bhraidh'-Albainn*") wrote, "The *Bàrr-lu* or close duodecupling was the tune anciently played to announce a decisive victory in the field, called, *Buaidh làraich*, – and also to announce a repulse of the enemy, called, *Ruaig Chòmhraig*."

43 Part of the only known copy of the second edition of William MacKay's *Tutor* shows interpolated grace-note clusters. Later editions are known to have been improved by Angus MacKay (see Cannon, *Bibliography*).

44 "The few tunes which contain doublings ... seem to have been borrowed from Donald MacDonald's collections (nos. 304 and 306 above)" (Roderick Cannon, *Bibliography*, 132, 133).

45 In 1799, "in the course of the performance, Madame Frederick of the Theatre Royal, dressed in an appropriate garb, danced Strathspeys, Jiggs, and other dances, with her accustomed dexterity and effect" ("A Circumstantial Account," in Angus MacKay, *Collection*, 17).

46 At the 1784 competition in part two each piper had to play the tune "*Glassviar*" ("*A' Ghlas Mheur*," "The Finger Lock"), a tune the competent playing of which was widely believed, with physiological justification, to be the mark of a good piper. See *Scots Magazine* 46, (1784): 553.

47 Prebble, *The King's Jaunt*, passim. Prince George, the Prince Regent (George IV from 1820–30), became chief of the Highland Society of London in 1817 (Neville McKay, "History of the Office of Piper to the Sovereign," *Folk Music Journal* 7, no. 2 (1996): 190).

48 In 1838 a prize was given to Daniel Munro from Ross-shire for the best "ornamental dress." It is tempting to think that Munro's "ornamental dress" was a forerunner of modern "Highland" dress.

49 Archibald Campbell, "The History and Art of Angus MacKay." Campbell also associated Angus MacKay with the "comparatively modern development of the quickstep march as a serious branch of the Highland piper's art" (ibid.).

50 It is also quite possible that listeners could not detect the deviations in the pipers' playing.

51 For example, John Johnston on Coll told Seton Gordon with pride that he was musically illiterate and publicly and privately decried the evil influences of literacy on *ceòl mór* (with the exception of David Glen's work). See Gordon, *Hebridean Memories*, 109; and John Johnston's letters to Seton Gordon, NLS Accession 7451, Box 1. See also my correspondence with George Moss.

52 John MacKenzie, compiler of *Sár-Obair nam Bàrd*, native of Gairloch and sometime judge of the Edinburgh piping competitions, called Glengarry's games "the gymnastic games at Fort William" (*Sar-Obair*, 299, under "Ailean Dall"). MacKenzie lived at Mellon Charles in 1806 and at Inverewe in 1848; both are in Gairloch.

53 Glengarry's society of true Highlanders, however, shared with the Northern Meeting a social exclusivity. Glengarry's was an élite group of the socially prominent, including Stewart of Garth, that did not include ordinary Gaels, except as entertainers and sportsmen at its outdoor games.

54 Capt. Simon Fraser, ed., *Airs and Melodies*, xi, 5, 101. How many of these tunes survived in Gaelic Nova Scotia is open to speculation.

55 Dalyell, *Musical Memoirs*, 106.

56 Fraser's sources were his paternal grandfather, who had been an officer in the first Black Watch, and MacKay of Bighouse in Reay country.

57 Capt. Simon Fraser, ed., *Airs and Melodies*, 107.

58 "*Air dhuinn greis bhi gabhail òrain,/ 'S tacan eil' ri sgeulan gòrach;/ Chuir Rob Cam a' phìob an òrdugh,/ 'S thoisich cuid ri dannsa.*" See Creighton and MacLeod, *Gaelic Songs in Nova Scotia*, 248–9.

59 "*Seach bhi cleasachd measg nan Gàidheal; ceòl na pìoba, cainnt na Gàidhlig', sid a ghnàth a b'anns' leam.*" Ibid., 249. My translation.

60 The signal cultural significance of Catholic South Uist is shown as early as the 1760s and 1770s. Compared to North Uist, South Uist was beginning to be seen as a valuable reservoir for Gaelic culture by people such as John MacCodrum. See William Matheson, ed., *The Songs of John MacCodrum*. From inquiries made in Gaelic Nova Scotia a similar cultural retentiveness existed in other Catholic areas.

61 Unfortunately no description of the Reel setting steps has come down to us, although there is little reason to believe that they had changed from the 1840s and thus there is little doubt that those were identical to the setting steps which now survive as unique anachronisms in Gaelic Cape Breton.

62 Christina Byam Shaw, ed., *Pigeon Holes of Memory*, 81.

63 Osgood MacKenzie, *A Hundred Years in the Highlands*, 194.

64 Gairloch a century earlier had been a stronghold of Episcopalianism. In the

1850s one of John Francis Campbell's Gaelic story gatherers in Free Church Gairloch noted that *céilidhs* and tale telling were discouraged and disappearing.

65 Christina Byam Shaw, ed., *Pigeon Holes of Memory*, 116. The John MacKenzie in question was the soon-to-be-famous rising star of piping John Ban MacKenzie, referred to above, who was to win prizes at the Edinburgh competition in 1821 (third), 1822 (second), and 1823 (first).

66 "'S rachainn leat dha'n chaisteal dùinte,/ Far am faighinn modh is mùirne,/ Daoin' uaisle mu bhòrda dùmhail,/ Ruidhle mu seach air an ùrlar,/ Fidhlear-achd bu ragha ciùil dhaibh." ("And I'd go with you to the closed castle,/ Where respect and joy would be mine,/ Gentlemen around the creaking table,/ Reels alternating on the floor,/ Fiddling was their favourite music"; my translation). See John L. Campbell, ed., *Songs Remembered in Exile*, 170, 171, citing "'Mhic 'ic Ailein, tha mi'n déidh ort."

67 MacDermid, "The Religious and Ecclesiastical Life."

68 MacRae, "Revivals in the Highlands," 67.

69 The possible persistence of a remnant and impoverished Episcopal church in parts of Skye may have accounted for cultural retentiveness into the 1890s.

70 Flett and Flett, *Traditional Dancing in Scotland*, 3. Dr Alexander D. Fraser came upon old traditional dance steps c.1890 in Caroline Hill, Skye. (A Carolina Hill is shown on the 1:50,000 Ordnance Survey map of North Skye, lying less than a mile south of Skeabost to the west of the River Snizort.) Traditional steps meant traditional music but Fraser offered no description of either.

71 An educated Scottish opinion holds that Pipe-Major Willie Ross, head of the Army School of Piping, always retained a preference for traditional styles of *ceòl mór* playing, which he dutifully limited to his preliminary tunings (personal communication, letter from Bridget MacKenzie, 10 July 1997).

72 John MacCulloch, *The Highlands and Western Islands*, vol. 2: 377–8.

73 The MacGregors' absence from the prize lists from c.1815 suggests that the increasingly artificial standards of the competitions were unaccommodating to them. A modernist might suggest their inadequacy to meet "higher" standards.

74 Cromb, *The Highland Brigade*, 198.

75 George fifth duke of Gordon (from 1827) was the first colonel of the 92d (Gordon Highlanders), 1796–1806, and colonel of the 42d from 1806 to 1820. In 1840 the Inverlochy estate, including tracts of traditional Keppoch Mac-Donell lands, belonged to the first Lord Abinger. He was succeeded by his son, Robert Scarlett.

76 M'Innes piped the members from the masons' lodge in Fort William to old Inverloch Castle. See Kilgour, *Lochaber in War and Peace*, 58. (Kilgour cited masonic records for 10 February 1840.) Angus M'Innes was one of a list of competition pipers at the Theatre Royal in Edinburgh who "appeared but were unsuccessful" at the fourth triennial competition in 1838. He is described as "Piper to the Most Noble the Marquis of Huntly" (Angus MacKay, *Collection*,

20) and may have had military piping experience. He lived in 1840 at Inverroy, to the west of Keppoch House in Glen Spean. The early masonic lodge in Fort William was associated with the British army stationed there and dates at least to 1736. I have not had access to the lodge's records.

77 See letter in the *Oban Times*, 10 November 1919 (NLS MS 9623 f. 244).

78 *Piping Times* 20, no. 9 (June 1968). John Campbell was a post carrier and registrar at Invermoriston and probably owed his stable employment to his musical talent. A John Campbell won first prize at the Edinburgh piping competition in July 1819. Unfortunately no rank or other designation is given for him.

79 See, MacFarlane, "Tenants in Brae Lochaber," which is based on research by Dr I.S. MacDonald, Falkirk. Dr MacDonald has assured me that the descriptive "piper" occurs as MacFarlane gave it in Scottish Records Office SC28/16/3, and Dr N.J. Mills at the SRO kindly informed me that the McGlaserich Campbells are mentioned also in SRO SC29/7/2, pp. 239–240, 14 April 1795, and in SC29/7/6 pp. 477–478, 18 May 1804.

80 Dughalach, *Orain Ghàidhealacha*, and *Orain, Marbhrannan*.

81 A John MacFarlane, whose brother William was "in Glenourchay" in 1775, was in Captain Chisholm's company, first Battalion, 71st, serving in New York, according to the piper William MacKenzie of Patrick Campbell of Glenuir's company, second Battalion 71st (see Appendix 3). In his "*Oran Ghlinn Urchaidh*" ("Song of Glen Orchy") Duncan Ban MacIntyre paints a very musical picture of the place, lots of piping and fiddling at the weddings.

82 "Marbhrann do Mhac-'Ic-Raonuill na Ceapaich." Dughalach, *Orain, Marbhrannan*, 2.

83 Somers, *Letters from the Highlands*, 137 and 138. Keppoch club-farm communities were at the two Bohuntin villages and Bohenie in Glen Roy, at Achluachrach and Murlaggan, and on Walker's estate (a little to the east, and south of the river Spean), at Monessie and Achnacoichine.

84 Somers, *Letters from the Highlands*, 192.

CHAPTER THIRTEEN

1 After the Highland and Island Emigration Society came into being, it helped five thousand Highlanders sail to Australia between 1852 and 1857.

2 Gaelic was still spoken by a few of the descendants of the Lewis immigrants to the Megantic area of the Eastern Townships of Quebec in 1972 and possibly also in the Bruce Peninsula in Ontario.

3 The reverse influence, of novel dances upon traditional music in Gaelic Nova Scotia, will be touched upon in a later chapter.

4 The discovery of Archibald Campbell's tantalizing remarks about the brilliant piping of Dòmhnul Ruadh Mac Cruimein at Glenelg c. 1814 was not made until the twentieth century by R.W. Munro. (According to Munro, Campbell's record was later publicized by Seton Gordon in *Piping Times*, credit omitted.

See R.W. Munro correspondence, 31 July 1933). Nobody notices that Campbell said that the last great MacCrimmon piper "had a style of fingering peculiar to himself."

5 Gaelic-speaking fiddlers include Fr Francis Cameron, John Donald Cameron,
   Cameron Chisholm, Alex Francis MacKay, Donald MacLellan, Theresa
   MacLellan, and Greg Smith.

6 Devine, "The Flight of the Poor," 645. Devine's study deals with emigration,
   often coerced emigration, from 1846–56, which was almost exclusively of the
   poor Gael, but he added that the "social composition of the emigrant parties to
   Canada finally remains to be determined" (ibid., 656). One exception is the list
   of two hundred and eight Gaels who emigrated from Rum in 1828 and who
   came ashore in Ship Harbour (modern Port Hawkesbury) in Nova Scotia (see
   J.L. MacDougall, History of Inverness County, 126–31).

7 J.L. MacDougall (d. 1928 at seventy-seven); (Fr) A.D.MacDonald (1907–56).

8 An example of the removal and replacement, albeit piecemeal, of all of the tenantry of an Upper Strathearn estate in Perthshire following the hardships of the
   terrible harvest of 1826 points to the prevalence of laissez-faire ideas all over
   Scotland (see Drummond, Perthshire in Bygone Days, 41).

9 In the decade 1840–50, per estate figures show that ten thousand Highland
   Scots took advantage of the landlords' thoughtfulness.

10 The destinations in Canada for the deportees were mainly Ontario and Quebec (to, inter alia, British American Land Company lands in what are now
   the Eastern Townships of Quebec). The flow continued into the twentieth century.

11 The Bornish (South Uist) community-type settlement on the stony Thom soils
   of the Creignish Hills at River Denys Road in 1826 attracted South Uist people
   in the 1840s. Its rapid decline and depopulation began c. 1950 with the decision not to run electricity lines there.

12 The same stubborn persistence, into the early years of the twentieth century,
   of relics of the older traditional way of life can, to a certain extent, be assumed
   from the endurance of the Highland cattle economy, relying on drovers and
   lowland and other cattle markets. See note 16, chapter 12.

13 Stuart Macdonald, Back to Lochaber, 286, 287. Macdonald cited Borrow's
   A Tour in Scotland and Shorter's The Works of George Borrow. A less-valid
   rival claim was made later by Josephine MacDonell in An Historical Record.

14 See, MacKinnon and Morrison, The MacLeods – The Genealogy of a Clan,
   35–8, and J.L. MacDougall, History of Inverness County, 345–6. The social
   information is only found in The MacLeods. MacDougall didn't know, or overlooked the subject; his interest and knowledge, after all, were more in Catholic
   families. (Major General Norman MacLeod, 1754–1801, was the man whom
   Lt Donald MacCrumen greeted in Skye with "Fàilte Ruairidh Mhoir" ["Rory
   Mor's Welcome"] in 1799, in the presence of a young Norman MacLeod, later
   author Caraid nan Gaidheal.)

15 Ewen Campbell, son of Archibald, returned to Scotland where he trained as a minister, taking the charges of Knock in Lewis in 1864 and of Lochs, where he remained from 1870 until he died in 1889. Two of Ewen Campbell's sisters' sons, John Campbell MacKinnon from New Canada (Cape Breton), and Neil MacKay from Head Lake (Ainslie), also became ministers. MacKinnon was ordained in Knoydart on 2 May 1883. MacKay served in Prince Edward Island and New Brunswick and was a temperance man. (There was a shortage of Church of Scotland clergy in Gaelic Scotland after the many defections to the new Disruption denomination.)

16 MacRae, *Revivals in the Highlands*, 67.

17 Dr Hugh is still remembered as the man who put John L. Sullivan on his back in an American bar for the American's foolish policy of not making customers' change.

18 See Hugh Macdonald, "Macdonald and Mackinnon Families," introduction; in the second edition a shortened version of this information occurs on page 19. Lauchann Mac Thearlaich Oig (Lachlan son of young Charles), who flourished around 1700, was of the chiefly family of MacKinnon in Skye, according to John MacKenzie, *Sar-Obair nam Bárd*, 80.

19 Royle, *Death Before Dishonour*, passim. General Sir Hector MacDonald (1853–1903), KCB, DSO, ADC, LLD, Gordon Highlanders, hero of Afghanistan and Omdurman, later commander of troops in Ceylon and ADC to King Edward VII, committed suicide in Paris. He is buried in the Dean Cemetery in Edinburgh. He was born in Mulbuie, Easter Ross, seventh son of William MacDonald (Inverness-shire) and Ann Boyd. Nothing is known of his co-lateral kin. He left one son, Hector Duncan MacDonald (ibid, passim).

20 Duncan Campbell of Lochnell (d. 1837), formerly of the Foot Guards, was appointed lieutenant colonel commandant of the 91st Princess Louise's Argyleshire Highlanders on 10 February 1794. See Goff, *Historical Records of the 91st*, and Dunn-Pattison, *The History of the Argyllshire Highlanders*.

21 J.L. MacDougall, *History of Inverness County*, 140.

22 Donald MacCrimmon had been MacLeod's piper in the late 1760s and early 1770s.

23 MacDonald, who had been an ensign in Tarleton's Legion and who shared MacCrimmon's fugitive hardship after the loss at Widow Moore's Creek Bridge in 1776, also returned to Scotland from the Shelburne area of Nova Scotia. He took the small Trotternish tack of Sarthill and later moved to Quintolan (see MacDonald and MacDonald, *Clan Donald*, and MacQueen, *Skye Pioneers*, where MacDonald is given as captain).

24 MacCrimmon's most likely link with the royal family was through his former colonel, Banastre Tarleton (1754–1833), who had as his mistress for about sixteen years Mary Robinson (1758–1800), who had previously been the mistress of George IV, son of King George III (see Hibbert, *George IV Prince of Wales*). Patrick appears to have left no issue.

25 Lockhart, *Memoirs*, vol. 3, 231.
26 MacLeòid, *Sgialachdan á Albainn Nuaidh*, 14, my translation. Unfortunately, Calum MacLeod did not mention where or from whom he obtained the information about the piper who emigrated from Lowergill. Nobody knows what became of him in the New World and the tune apparently has not survived.
27 Manson, *The Highland Bagpipe*, 261.
28 According to James Cameron, *Pictonians in Arms*, 62, he was John MacKay, a railway engineer who moved to the southern United States in the mid-1850s. Elsewhere his dates are given as 1821–89.
29 From an interview with Marjorie Hawkins conducted in Windsor, Nova Scotia, 22 May 1981.
30 An Angus MacKay, b. Ross-shire, d. Pictou County, Nova Scotia, 21 May 1868, and who is described as son of John MacKay "farmer," appears in a list of deaths PANS, RG32 "D"(1864–77), vol. 65, sheet 51, no. 170.
31 Alexander MacKenzie, "The Editor in Canada," 71.
32 In *Celtic Magazine* 3, no. 25 (November 1877): 40 John Henry Dickson's address is given as "Inveran Lodge." He kept a piper.
33 This mysterious claim is probably the origin of Collinson's small-pipe theory for the evasion of the Disarming Act. That Red John would even need piping tutoring outside of his piper father Angus's family in Gairloch may be partially explained by Angus's death as a youngish man in the early 1770s.
34 John MacDonald of Glenaladale established several socially and educationally prominent Roman Catholic relations in Prince Edward Island in the 1770s. In the Glengarry settlements in Upper Canada there were prominent Catholic community leaders who had left in the 1770s and settled initially in New York state (MacDonells of Leek, Aberchalder, Scotus).
35 At the highest levels of society political factors dictated a different pattern, but even there intermarriages between particular clans over long periods, Camerons with Campbells and MacLeans, for example, were common.
36 Gaelic lore and story, including the *Cù Glas Mheoble* ("The Grey Dog of Meoble"), supplied by Dougal MacDonald to Dr John Shaw, is lodged at St Francis Xavier University, Antigonish, Nova Scotia. Local genealogies overlooked MacDonald's ancestry. Meoble, a Clanranald holding, has been depopulated for generations.
37 See Catherine MacDonald et al., *The Clanranald Connection*, and MacDonald and Colin, *Fair Is the Place*, passim.
38 R.A. MacLean, *The Casket*, 24.
39 The custom of bilingual chiefs fostering their heirs in the homes of the Gaelic-speaking middle class did much to standardize speech patterns and accent. The essential stamp of status at that level was the knowledge of English.
40 MacLeòid, "*An t-Eilthireach*," n.p. My translation.
41 South Morar was called in Gaelic *Morar 'ic Dhùghail*; hence the recurrence of the name Dougal in the principal family.

42 Cited in Drummond, *Perthshire in Bygone Days*, 258.

43 There is as yet no study of the (greater?) Gaelic cultural retentiveness in those Nova Scotian Church of Scotland parishes, especially in Pictou County, which stayed within the established Church of Scotland fold. A study of the presence and influence of a Gaelic merchant middle class in the county is also wanting. (The Reverend Norman MacLeod, 1780–1866, Assynt in Wester Ross, West River, Pictou County, Saint Ann's, Cape Breton, and Waipu, New Zealand, admittedly a man with a profoundly immoderate bias, presented a picture of Presbyterian Pictonians as profanely acquisitive. Squire John MacKay's description leaves music and dance alone but otherwise is often one that was typical of the Roman Catholic communities in Cape Breton.)

44 Hoodie remembered his playing "Keppoch's Rant." See Hugh Macdonald, *Macdonald and Mackinnon Families*, 13, 23.

45 This tenacious conservativism belatedly triumphed when the Reverend Iain MacMillan, filial grandson of Isobel MacMillan (b. 22 September 1903) of Twin Rock Valley on East Lake Ainslie side learned to step-dance from Fr Eugene Morris, a Roman Catholic priest from Port Hood, Inverness County. (Isobel MacMillan is a Gaelic speaker. Her grandson isn't.)

46 Dr Hugh (Hoodie) MacDonald is reported as having told a CBC interviewer, date unknown, "I remember a man named Farquhar MacKinnon, a tall man, 6 feet 6 inches, who played the violin. He could teach any kind of music: pipes, singing, everything. We'd walk three miles to his house just to hear him play the violin. And then when he finished, we'd walk next door to hear his son, Little Farquhar play the pipes!" (Little Farquhar will be discussed in chapter 15.) McNeil, *Voice of the Pioneer*, 192.

47 I have not had the opportunity to study the influence of the Education Act (Scotland) of 1872 on educational policy pertaining to Gaelic in Nova Scotia, but many of the last Gaelic-speaking generations remembered vividly the shock of having to speak nothing but English in their first year at school. People like Seumas MacKay in Kingsville harboured a profound lifelong resentment at what he considered a harsh and arrogant policy.

48 Nova Scotia, *Revised Statutes*, 50, 59.

49 Chief Justice John G. Marshall (1786–1880) was a strict Methodist and a defender of temperance (see, PANS, MGI, vol. 1456, "The John George Marshall Papers," Doc. 5, "On Temperance").

50 Justices of the Peace, until Confederation in 1867 and afterwards in the Highland counties, were local worthies who received no pay for their work.

51 To the South in Judique Fr Allan MacLean (1804–77) danced, piped, and fiddled (*MacTalla* 5, no. 36 [13 March 1897]: 278).

52 John "Baron" MacDonald's son Allan used the violin in church "giving the notes himself" to his choir. See Alexander D. MacDonald, *Mabou Pioneers*, 413. (Black Angus MacDonald the piper/fiddler and his brothers, Alexander, Alexander, Jr, and Allan Gobha, also played fiddles and a cello in the choir.)

53 According to Angus Rankin (b. c. 1920), South West Mabou Ridge, it wasn't until the time of Fr Bryden (resident parish priest from 1937–48), that the quadrille, or Square Set, was officially condoned in Mabou. By that time moonshining and illegal importation of distilled liquor were much harder to carry on, although the social uses for alcohol were undiminished.

54 Pope Pius X specified dance music and opera music as the musical elements to be removed from the liturgy. The Church was to get back to the Gregorian art and polyphonic art of the sixteenth century. He wanted to restore "primitive purity to the liturgical chant" (see report of a papal interview given to M. Charles Bordes, *Charlottetown Herald* 41, no. 33 (14 August 1912).

55 Prominent among them are the late Fr John Angus Rankin, Fr Francis Cameron, Fr Malcolm MacDonell, Fr Eugene Morris, and Fr Allan MacMillan.

CHAPTER FOURTEEN

1 Alexander Campbell, "A Slight Sketch," 196.

2 Ibid., 196. Alexander Campbell's life in Keppoch, married to the widow of Ranald MacDonell of Keppoch, certainly exposed him to Keppoch piping but it is risky to presume that he had sufficient knowledge to make hard and fast assessments of MacCrimmon's technique.

3 Diana Henderson, *Highland Soldier*, 166.

4 The opinion of retired Lieutenant Donald Campbell of the 57th Regiment, in 1862, is corroborative. He wrote that "such meetings of Highlanders [who were bagpipers] are now held under patronage ... But I greatly suspect, since the piper has become a domestic musician that he finds it his interest to cultivate the tastes of strangers." See Donald Campbell, *A Treatise*, 128, 129.

5 Ibid., 214. To deduce, as Sinclair of Ulbster had earlier done, that pipers no longer existed because they weren't joining the armed forces is one of many fallacious views met with in piping thought during the Napoleonic era; however, by the middle of the nineteenth century depopulation on a vast scale, in my opinion, genuinely vindicated Fordyce's similar fear; by then there were fewer Gaelic pipers. Henderson cites Fordyce, "Digest of Services."

6 The use of *crannan*, meaning "drum," occurs twice in extant Gaelic poetry/song, both times in MacLean context. In the seventeenth century Alasdair mac Mhaighstir Alasdair did not include it in his 1741 dictionary (Watson, *Bàrdachd Ghaidhlig*, 206, 319). Bagpipes and drums, however, cannot be linked in Highland Scotland except in the British military.

7 The pipers' social function, both in the mess and in the surrounding community (if there were any cultural compatibility), is another matter.

8 Diana Henderson, *Highland Soldier*, 96ff., 259 and Ewart, *Soldier's Life*, vol. I: 151, 152, 163–5.

9 See Ewart, *Soldier's Life*, n.p.

10 Diana Henderson, *Highland Soldier*, 247.

11 Queen Victoria's interest in Gaelic tradition appears to have been kind, naïve, and ingenuous, although her published writings overlook clearances. Part of the royally inspired cachet of modern "highland" middle-class society in the second half of the nineteenth century was the keeping of pipers. Later, Sir Duncan Campbell of Barcaldine, author of *Records of Clan Campbell*, had a family piper in 1912, and so did the Campbell of Dunstaffnage family (see *Records of Clan Campbell*, 41.)

12 Ibid., lxxxi, 215. Another example, from c. 1866 in Putteala (Kashmir), shows that the services of John MacKay, pipe-major of the 93d Regiment (Sutherland Highlanders), were purchased by the local maharajah who had been entranced by the strathspeys and reels of the regiment's twelve pipers. MacKay spent five years in the maharajah's employment, trained fourteen local men as pipers, got them Glen pipes, and eventually returned home to set himself up in business in Aberdeen (Munro, *Reminiscences of Military Service*, 318, 319, and Diana Henderson, *Highland Soldier*, 251).

13 Scobie served to start with in the Essex Regiment. A generation later, Bruce Seton, son of the Sir Bruce who, with Arnott, published *Prisoners of the 'Forty-five*, was a middle-class piper and lieutenant in the Second Battalion, Black Watch. He composed "The Sprig of Ivy," a four-part march in two-four time (see William Ross, *Collection*, book 5, 8). There are countless other examples of gentlemen pipers, including HRH Edward VIII.

14 General Charles Simeon Thomason (1833-1911), Royal Engineers (Bengal), collector and publisher of *Ceòl Mór*, although musically literate as a boy, learned his chanter fingering from the Elchies head gardener, Mackie, about whose technique nothing is known. One of Thomason's later teachers, in Chatham, over eighteen months between 1852 and 1854. was Sandy MacLennan, Highland Light Infantry (ret.). See B.D. MacKenzie, "General Thomason," 60.

15 Judging solely by one tape of Willie Ross's piping, undated, the great piper could and did play strathspeys at a speed and with a rhythm that were very close to traditional Cape Breton strathspey playing for step-dancing. The reel in the set (following "Balmoral Castle") lacked those qualities. See also endnote 71, chapter 11.

16 See Roderick Cannon, *Bibliography of Bagpipe Music*.

17 Roderick Cannon's *Bibliography* shows William MacKay's book to be anything but common today, but that is by no means to say that once upon a time it wasn't.

18 Roderick Cannon, *The Highland Bagpipe*, 152.

19 When Strathglass men Hugh Fraser and Duncan Chisholm joined the 79th Regiment in the nineteenth century, they did so as pipers, acceptably formed by the local musical tradition. They were sent to Fort George "where they learned the job of Army piper. As regards piping, they were better taught already than their instructors, but there were many other things to be learned" (Moss's trans-

lation). Moss was obscure about the date of enlistment but the story suggests that pipers had an official status, i.e., it was 1854 or after. See Moss, *"An Da Phiobair,"* 114, 115.

20 A. Duncan Fraser, *Some Reminiscences*, 38.

21 Antigonish *Casket*, 24 June 1852.

22 McAfee, "79th Regiment," 28, 29.

23 Todd, *The Seventy-ninth Highlanders*, 302, 303.

24 The uniform of the whole army had been changed in 1856 (Keltie, *History of the Scottish Highlands*, section 3, 659).

25 A Donald Ross was the author of an elegy, *"A measg gach call a thàinig oirnn,"* for Donald MacCodrum (c.1785–1852), an emigrant to Cape Breton in 1831 and a relative of the *bàrd* John MacCodrum (see William Matheson, ed., *The Songs of John MacCodrum*, xlviii, xlix, citing *MacTalla* 11, no. 9).
A Donald Ross lived at "Celtic Cottage" in Dartmouth, Nova Scotia in December 1878. He was the author of "A Sutherland Highlander's Welcome."

26 At least one David Glen pipe chanter is still held in Inverness County, Cape Breton (probably with matching Glen drones) and a set of Glen pipes, bought in 1858, went to John MacQuarrie in Antigonish County. They remain in the family. David Glen (b. 1850) took over his father Alexander's business in 1872 or 1873. David was highly thought of by John Johnston on Coll as a man knowledgeable of traditional *ceòl mór*.

27 R.G. Hardie & Co., which incorporated Peter Henderson Ltd, will not divulge the records of the old P. Henderson company, so the extent of Henderson business with Nova Scotia cannot be accurately given.

28 John Glen, *Early Scottish Melodies*, 91, cited in Roderick Cannon, *A Bibliography of Bagpipe Music*, 32, 41, 63.

29 The 42d (Black Watch) sent detachments to Prince Edward Island, Cape Breton, and Annapolis in the summer of 1851, recalling those two hundred men to Halifax early in 1852 for embarkation to Scotland.

30 The notable exception is the school teacher son of the Highfield, Antigonish County piper John MacGillivray (Glenaladale's piper until 1818). Twenty-one-year-old James Paul MacGilvray enlisted as a trooper in the 2d Regiment of Life Guards on 3 September 1846. He died a trooper, of chronic peritonitis in the regimental hospital at Hyde Park Barracks, 25 August 1850 (no cause given). Another, Alexander MacMillan of Kempt Road in southern Cape Breton, served in the Crimean campaign (and composed *"Oran do'n Chogadh Ruiseanach"* ("Song to the Russian War") to commemorate his experiences). MacKenzie Baillie, the piper from Pictou County, also joined the British army, but later than the Crimea (see below).

31 Diary of Col J.W. Wedderburn, Black Watch Regimental Archives (BWRA) 28/714/1, cited in Diana Henderson, *Highland Soldier*, 226.

32 Flett and Flett, "Some Early Highland Dancing Competitions," 349, 350.

33 Roderick Campbell, Cuilchonich, Aultbea (Gairloch), and John Nicolson, a

grandson of Iain Dubh MacCruimein, are both known from published sources to have played the fiddle and the pipes.

34 Diana Henderson, *Highland Soldier*, ff96, 259, citing the diary of Col. J.W. Wedderburn, 42d, BWRA 28/714/1 (24 June 1852).

35 MacKay Scobie, *Pipers and Pipe Music*, 19, 20.

36 Ibid., 24, 25.

37 Donald MacLeod (d. 1875, age eighty-four), who had fought at Quatre Bras in the 42d, settled at Lansdowne, Pictou County. Neil MacVicar, another veteran of the Napoleonic Wars, a piper and a fiddler, settled in Cape Breton. Alexander MacRae of the 71st became a customs official in Quebec and Roderick Campbell of the 74th settled earlier in the Maritimes where he died in 1826, age thirty-eight.

38 MacKay Scobie, *Pipers and Pipe Music*, 30, citing Col. G.W. Anderson's *Stories of Sport*. Anderson recollected once telling old Kenneth that it was a pity that such a musically sensitive mind hadn't taken up the more harmonious and more emotionally expressive fiddle, only to get the following reply: "Ta feedil, pha iss ta feedil to ta piobmhor? Can ta feedil speak to you as ta pipes will, my pretty man, when the ball cartridge will be loose in your pooch and your snider shoe-block is het? And will your feedils or your tam brass bands be able to give you wan plaw when the paignet is on ta snider and it is 'Capper Fay gu pra', or eternal tamnation? No py cot, ta pipes is ta best what effer" (MacKay Scobie, *Pipers*, 30).

39 Information from personal communications. Colin Strelley from Kincraig, one of my piping teachers, was a pupil at Edinburgh Academy. He became a professional soldier, serving as an officer in the Seaforth Highlanders in India and Europe. The registrar of Edinburgh Academy in 1995 was unable to confirm James Sutherland in any official or unofficial capacity at the school. Strelley described I.H. MacKay Scobie as a Gaelic speaker from the Strathnaver area. It was from Scobie that Strelley got his first practice chanter during the Great War.

40 Shears, *The Gathering of the Clans Collection*, 12, 22.

41 Pipe-Major Stephen MacKinnon (1885–1958), "The Bagpipe in Canada."

42 According to Col Paul P. Hutchison, a Highland gathering was held at Tinques on 6 July 1918. The retreat was played by twenty-four massed pipe bands, including the 13th (later the Black Watch of Canada), the 15th Scottish, and the 51st Highland Division. See Hutchison, *Canada's Black Watch*, 120.

43 Pipe-Major Stephen MacKinnon, b. Kilbarchan, pupil of MacDougall Gillies (Cameron school), emigrated to Canada in 1911 where he settled in the West. He served as a piper in the Canadian Black Watch during the First World War and was later pipe-major of the Canadian National Railways Pipe Band at Montreal. According to another Canadian Black Watch piper, Donald William MacLeod (c. 1890–1983), who served at the Somme, Vimy, and Amiens, nineteen pipers were killed at Mons, he alone surviving (see McCrimmon and MacLeod, *Lochinvar to Skye*, 291).

44 McIntyre, "The Cape Breton Highlanders," 52.

45 George Sutherland, personal communication, Soldier's Cove, 25 August 1980.

46 Gordon MacDonald was from Sydney or New Waterford. According to Suther-land he had some Gaelic, which he could read and write but not speak very well. Sutherland said he was the first Cape Breton Highlander to be killed, near Naples. Another who remembered him, Carl Kooper of Cleveland, Cape Bre-ton, said that Gordon MacDonald learned to pipe from an Iron Mike Campbell (personal communication, telephone, 11 November 1976.)

47 MacKenzie had Allachan Aonghuis Dhuibh's set of Henderson pipes, which he got from the MacNeils in Christmas Island, the family that had cared for Mac-Farlane in his last few years.

48 Neil MacKay, personal communication, Dunvegan, 6 December 1994.

49 See, Cannon, *The Highland Bagpipe*, 151–63.

50 Dunoon, Argyllshire, centre of the Presbytery of Dunoon, is about thirty miles roughly west of Glasgow and at the turn of the century must still have had a Gaelic-speaking element in its population in villages such as Strachur.

51 Laidlaw is referring to himself and to piper Jack Muir (1891–1976), who is buried in River Denys, Cape Breton. Muir joined the Stonehouse band in 1910.

52 Private correspondence, James Laidlaw to John G. Gibson, 12 January 1977.

53 James Laidlaw, private correspondence with author, 28 January 1977.

54 Roderick Cannon, *The Highland Bagpipe*, 49, photo inter 36 and 37.

55 Flett and Flett, *Traditional Dancing*, 260–66.

56 Ibid., 28–9, citing MacTaggart, *Scottish Gallovidian*. The one apparent flaw in this argument, assuming the East Lothian "treepling" of c. 1900 that the Fletts implied to have been very similar to Gaelic Scotch step-dancing (and various other rustic step-dancings/cloggings), and assuming it to have been of similar antiquity, is that Joseph MacDonald wrote that the Scotch Gaelic dancing of c.1760 was unique. MacDonald lived for a time in Haddington, East Lothian, where it seems reasonable to assume he would have been exposed to vernacu-lar dancing and seen at least some similarity.

57 For a short and speculative treatment of the origins of the civilian pipe band in Scotland, dating perhaps to the 1880s, see Roderick Cannon, *The Highland Bagpipe* in chapter cited in note 49 above.

CHAPTER FIFTEEN

1 The *Encyclopædia Britanica* gives the following history of first Highland Games in Scotland: Braemar and the Strathdon (Lonach Gathering), c.1835; Ballater, Aboyne, Oban (Argyll Gathering), and Dunoon (Cowal Gathering), between 1864 and 1871, thereafter expanding to include about forty games. Obviously the British army's part in the popularizing of Highland Games in the 1850s is not insignificant.

2 Glengarry organized games that are associated with Inverlochy, but they were also held at Invergarry (Joseph Mitchell, *Reminiscences of My Life*, I, 73).

3 The appearance in 1801 of Joseph Strutt's book *The Sports and Pastimes of the People of England*, introduced to the improver and soon-to-be scientific age a well-researched history of English country sports over the centuries. It is unreasonable to suppose that a work of this calibre did not have a salutary effect both in England and English Scotland as organization gradually replaced sporting spontaneity.

4 The *Eastern Chronicle* of 26 July 1866 contained the announcement that the third annual "Caledonian Club Gathering" (also described as the third "Annual Gathering of the Caledonian Club, and International Competition in Highland Games") would be held on 15 August 1866, in Charlottetown, Prince Edward Island. This notice was subscribed by E.J. Mcdougall, the Caledonian Club's secretary, Alyce Taylor Cheska gave an uncited report that the Caledonian Club of Prince Edward Island held its first Highland Games in 1838. Cheska also noted that the Caledonian Society of Cape Breton held their first games in 1848. See Cheska, "The Antigonish Highland Games."

5 Edward Dwelly, citing Alexander Carmichael, noted that "odas" died out in Harris in 1818, in South Uist in 1820, in Benbecula in 1830, and in North Uist in 1866. In Gaelic Cape Breton an echo of the same Celtic fascination with horses survives today. Within living memory that fascination was much stronger; in the first half of the twentieth century, the common sport of racing specially shod horses on the ice off Port Hood, off Sporting Mountain in Bras d'Or, in Antigonish Harbour, and elsewhere, shows that an ancient attachment did not die. Dwelly, *Gaelic-English Dictionary*, 703.

6 Allan MacDonald of Kingsburgh, Skye, and North Carolina was a wrestler of repute in his day, one of a number, and the sport is known to have been popular in Harris at an earlier date (see William Matheson, ed., *The Songs of John MacCodrum*, 293).

7 Presumably, since his father was Murdoch, he was a Gael who could have been identified as Aonghus mac Mhurchaidh.

8 Reverend John Skinner (1721–1807), author of "Tullochgorm," "John o' Badenyon," and "The Ewie wi' the crookit horn," and William Marshall, JP (1748–1833), the Scottish violin composer and patronized protégé of the duke of Gordon, were members of the Episcopal church, which, maybe more than the Moderates in the Kirk, appears to have fostered music and dance in the second half of the eighteenth century. The reaction of episcopal clergy to traditional Gaelic pleasures in the times of Church revivalism from c.1800 in its Highland parishes remains unstudied.

9 Sage, *Memorabilia Domestica*, 15.

10 MacLeod, *Caraid nan Gàidheal*, 399–405.

11 *Casket* I, no 24 (30 December 1852).

12 This tune is associated in modern Highland memory with the massacre of

Glencoe (1692). The words convey a warning to get out. See A. Sinclair, *An t-Oranaiche*.

13 Donald A. Fergusson, ed., *Fad air falbh as Innse Gall*, 57, and *MacTalla* 11, no. 14 (9 January 1903): 112; the latter contains Big Painter MacDonald's song.

14 "Get up auld wife, and shake your feathers,/ Dinna think we are beggars,/ We're jist bairns come oot to play,/ Get up and gie us oor hogmanay." A fuller version of this song, with an air, may be found in *Tocher* 12, p. 121 (1973). The latter was sung by Dr Ian M. Campbell as a boy in Findochty, Banffshire, c. 1950. He learned it from his father.

15 MacQueen, *Skye Pioneers*, 69, 71. For an earlier instance of the custom, see Campbell, *Witchcraft and Second Sight*.

16 Redmond, *The Caledonian Games*, 37. The large migration of Nova Scotian Gaels to New England from c. 1800 heightened cultural contact but as yet no influence of games there has been studied.

17 *Acadian Recorder*, Friday, 12 June 1868.

18 Cheska, "The Antigonish Highland Games," 59.

19 Redmond, *The Caledonian Games*, 17.

20 Cited in ibid., 110. The New York Caledonian Club's records for 1868 show that the "Eleventh Annual Pic-Nic" failed to raise enough to cover expenses. The twelfth annual event raised $1,976.73 (ibid., 64–5). The Boston *Globe* (30 August 1888) advertised the Point of Pines annual picnic and games of the Boston Caledonian Club with the usual regular attractions (ibid., 65). Whether or not the picnic aspect was separate from the Highland Fling and sword dance (which were boring people) is unclear. If it was separate, then Gaels had quit attending because the truer traditional, but undefined, picnic elements of these gatherings had been dispensed with and the pseudo-Highland dances meant little to them. Redmond cited the *Scottish-American Journal*, 9 September 1885.

21 *Casket* 47, no. 37 (15 September 1898).

22 The late John Collins of Scotsville said that Allan MacFarlane, his uncle, had piped at a Highland games in The Margarees in 1924, the least likely place for such an event. It may have been a very commonplace happening, like the many picnics of the time. It may have been informal enough to have escaped the notice of a stringer for the *Casket*. Collins, long an American resident, may have confused the terms Highland games and picnic.

23 Military brass bands were in demand for various events around the province of Nova Scotia. For example, the 63d Halifax Rifles band played at the two-day bazaar in Antigonish in September 1875; see *Casket* 24, no. 9 (23 September 1875).

24 Redmond, *The Caledonian Games*, 64–5, citing *Harper's Weekly* (10 July 1867).

25 J.L. MacDougall, *History of Inverness County*, 503.

26 *Casket* 11, no. 1: 2. This earlier Halifax gathering must have been held in 1860. The piper's grandson, Angus MacQuarrie of Arasaig, Antigonish County, told me that it was a sporran that he had won. Personal communication, Antigonish, November 1994.

27 *Casket* 11, no. 11 (25 September 1862). The first prize went to Hugh Fraser (twelve dollars), the second to John Patterson (nine dollars).

28 The community of Grulin, part of the Lathaig farm on Eigg, was cleared on Whitsun 1853 of twelve of its fourteen families as part of the deal cut by the owner of Eigg, Dr MacPherson, and the incoming Lowland tenant, Stewart. The last Gaelic tenant of Lathaig had been Angus MacDonald (born c. 1829) who had assumed a heavy debt, never cleared it, and emigrated to Wisconsin in 1853. His last shepherd, a man who stayed on to shepherd depopulated Grulin for a year or two under Stewart, was a Hector MacQuarrie. Hugh MacKinnon, "The MacDonalds of Laig."

29 John MacQuarrie, son of Archibald, died of pleurisy, 30 January 1874.

30 Angus MacQuarrie, personal communication, Antigonish, 9 November 1994.

31 Cheska, "The Antigonish Highland Games," 57.

32 *Casket* 12, no. 15 (22 October 1863), cited in Cheska, "The Antigonish Highland Games," 57.

33 *Casket* 11, new series, no. 25 (1 January 1863): 2.

34 There appears to have been no unselfconscious wearing of tartan in the homes and at rural work in Gaelic Nova Scotia from around 1800. No visitor to the province remarked on any dress other than homespun trousers and jackets. The custom of buying "Highland" clothing and prizes in Scotland for Maritime Highland games existed in the 1860s and persisted into the twentieth century.

35 See, Elliott, *The Legislative Assembly of Nova Scotia 1758–1983*, 140, 141.

36 Another Roman Catholic MacKinnon family in Inverness produced the burnt piper, *am pìobaire loisgte*, John MacKinnon. These MacKinnons were from Rum and a living descendant, John Paul MacKinnon of Harbourview (b. 1929), a one-time step-dance piper, is a nephew of the burnt piper.

37 Ormond, *A Century Ago*, 22.

38 Neill McNeill's twenty-seventh family in his "list of the papists in Eigg" ("Census of the Small Isles 1764–65") is that of Donald McGuary (fifty-six) and his wife Cathrina McIsaack (fifty). They and their family, Lauchlan, Donald, Cathrina, and John, are included in the subsection "Laig in Eigg papists." Of the six MacKinnon families given in McNeill's census one contained two sons named John (aged twenty-one and seven) and another one son so named (aged seven). Both families, and another, "Hough's," had a family servant.

39 I am indebted to Ronald MacDonald, Antigonish, for the name of John MacQuarrie's father, John's date of death (from pleurisy), and for the information that Bishop MacKinnon helped resolve McQuarrie's land problem. The MacGillivray piper also lived in Highfield.

40 The popularity of the Four-hand Reel is still remembered in Antigonish Coun-

ty. I know nothing of the Eight-hand Reel there but it too must have enjoyed some popularity, if Inverness County is anything to go by.

41 *Casket* 16, no. 52 (30 July 1868): second page of available document.

42 The winner was "Alex. McDonald, Antigonishe," presumably Alasdair Mac-Donald, the Keppoch Bard (b. Glenuig, 1820, d. Méinn Cnoc-an-Fhuarain, 1904). See *Eastern Chronicle*, 13 September 1866, and MacLeòid, *Bàrdachd a Albainn Nuaidh*, 30 and 31–40.

43 *Eastern Chronicle*, 13 September 1866.

44 Spedon, *Rambles among the Blue-noses*, 197.

45 *Eastern Chronicle*, 9 August 1866.

46 Cheska noted that Glengarry had the first Highland Society in Canada, established in 1818. (Cheska, "Antigonish Highland Games," 55).

47 Under the heading "*Chlann an Gael/Gualibh ri Gualibh*" ("Children of the Gael Shoulder to Shoulder"), the *Casket* 24, no. 48 (22 June 1876) advertised the upcoming Arisaig Highland Society's annual "Athletic Games." In the notice the society stated that it would pay the "expenses &c" of the man who emerged from the games as the province's new hammer-throwing champion, to compete at the Prince Edward Island games "next August."

48 *Eastern Chronicle*, 13 September 1866.

49 Possibly the Dòmhnul mac Iain MacKenzie mentioned above, from New Gairloch, pupil of John MacPherson (neighbour and piping pupil of Angus MacKay.

50 *Eastern Chronicle*, 4 September 1867, 2.

51 The McCrimmons had emigrated from Glenelg.

52 McCrimmon and MacLeod, *Lochinvar to Skye*, 197.

53 Ibid., 139.

54 Members of the regiment shut out the opposition in piping, reel dancing, and the Highland Fling in both years. They also had other successes.

55 Lord and Lady Minto attended the 1901 games in Charlottetown, for example.

56 *Charlottetown Herald*, 19 July 1899.

57 Ibid., 16 August 1899.

58 Ibid., 24 August 1898.

59 Step-dancing competitions in Judique in the 1920s are still remembered. They were part of a specifically picnic-and-good-works atmosphere rather than Highland games.

60 The 78th (Ross-shire Buffs) were stationed in Halifax, Nova Scotia, from 14 May 1869 until 25 November 1871.

61 Roderick Cannon (*The Highland Bagpipe*, 80) identifies Pipe-Major R. MacKenzie as Pipe-Major Ronald MacKenzie, a nephew of John Ban MacKenzie and an excellent player of *ceòl mór*.

62 *Acadian Recorder*, 26 August 1869.

63 Ibid., 8 September 1870.

64 Manson, *The Highland Bagpipe*, 297.

65 Pipe-Major Stephen MacKinnon, "The Bagpipe in Canada," 5.

66 Ibid.

67 John Johnston, Coll, wrote that he had "heard McDougall Gillies play several times. He is quite clever in Reels, and Marches, but as for Piobaireachds he may be called nil of course, as to old playing." From a letter from John Johnston to Seton Gordon, 7 January 1918, NLS 7451/1.

68 Major C.I.N. MacLeod told me, in Antigonish in 1972, that Sandy Boyd's playing of *ceòl mór* deviated from his teacher John MacColl's.

CHAPTER SIXTEEN

1 James N. MacKinnon, *Pioneer Scotch Settlers*, 18.

2 Donald was one of the boys of the family of Donald, son of Alasdair. See Mac-Dougall, *History*, 405.

3 Ibid., 520. Allan MacCormack the immigrant piper was described by his great-grandson John R. MacCormack, as Ailean mac Niall 'ic Iain Oig 'ic Dhòmh-nuill 'ic Dhùghail 'ic Niall (Allan son of Neil son of Young John son of Donald son of Dougall son of Neil), a *sloinneadh* that would take his ancestry back to the mid-seventeenth century. Clanranald had brought Neil MacCormack from Donegal to Moidart as a boat builder c.1690 (John R. MacCormack, personal communication, Saint Mary's University, Halifax, Nova Scotia, 28 September 1996). MacDougall (*History*, 521) added that three of Allan MacCormack's grandsons gained prominence, one as a parish priest, one as a doctor in Boston, and the third as a Sydney police chief. John R. MacCormack added unprompted that one of his paternal ancestors had been a justice of the peace and that one of the immigrant's sons and grandsons had been fiddlers. One of the fiddlers had been in the habit of sailing over Loch Bàn to learn from a MacQuarrie fiddler in North Ainslie. The bard Alasdair MacDonald mentioned a Duncan MacCormick in Beannacha Luinge; see John MacKenzie, *Sar-Obair*, 140.

4 Some sort of basic literacy in the nine notes the pipes play could never have been hard to obtain and there were pipers from this sub-set in Nova Scotia from immigrant times. Using the basic written notes of dance music is no guarantee of the corruption of tradition.

5 Angus Rankin of Mabou Ridge (personal communication, 10 October 1994) introduced an interesting and revealing aspect of the power of illiteracy. He told the story of literate Beaton traditional piper Angus Campbell Beaton (Aonghus Iagain Raonuil) who played tunes on the pipes from written music and being surprised at the rich embellishments his brother Donnie (Dòmhagan Iagain Raonuil) immediately grafted onto the same music on the violin, which he had absorbed completely by ear.

6 The fact that Barry Shears thought that Alex Currie the piper had made up the tune "Fire in the Forest" (as Currie said it was called) as he was playing is a pointed indication that invention of a new tune on the wing, certainly of new

phrases, was and is quite conceivable. Alex Currie (b. 5 August 1910) of Frenchvale, Cape Breton County, was one of the last of the old traditional pipers alive in 1997. His father's paternal grandfather was from South Uist. His piping has always been Scotch step-dance music.

7 Gillis, "From Kitchens to Pipebands," 20, 21, 22. Alex the piper MacDonald, a patrilineal great grandson of Captain Allan MacDonald of South West Margaree, was also known as the Indian teacher (he did not speak Micmac). For one or two years Alex MacDonald taught at the school in Rear Little Judique, and while Duncan Archie J. MacIsaac (1902–96), who was the last of his pupils living, remembered his piping, he did not remember ever seeing anyone step-dancing to it (Duncan MacIsaac, personal communication, 6 September 1994, Judique).

8 Melrose Hill is a now-deserted part of a settlement known broadly as Mount Young, east of Mabou.

9 Marcella (MacDonald) Chisholm (1906–93), a schoolteacher, was often at Black Angus's old two-storey Melrose Hill home as a child. She recollected riding in the horse and buggy with Black Angus to Brook Village and his reciting Robert Burns to her. She said he was well read (meaning in English). With that kindly, almost contradictory Highland nationalistic feeling, Black Angus appreciated Robert Burns and quoted him. Marcella Chisholm, personal communication, Port Hood, 14 April 1982.

10 Willie the piper Gillis, personal communication, Inverness Legion, 25 March 1982. Gillis also noted that Black Angus had attributed his capable fingering to the daily milking of cows.

11 Wife of John, son of Malcolm the bard, Calum Eoghann.

12 It would be unfair not to mention that prominently positive attitudes at times may, in the case of Black Angus, have been flavoured by his known patronage by Fr John Francis MacMaster in Mabou. In general, however, Black Angus's popularity was so widespread that there is no doubt that he was exceptional, by rural Gaelic standards.

13 Among the spouses of Anne MacDonald's children who are known to have emigrated married were Catherine Cameron, John "Baron" MacDonald, and Angus Campbell ("the Fair-haired smith.") In 1831 Killiechonate was in the Inverlochy estate owned by the Marquis of Huntly, Col George Gordon. North of the Spean River, including Glen Roy (*et ergo* Bohuntin, Crannachan, Achvady, etc.) belonged to anti-Jacobite MacIntosh of MacIntosh who, after 1746 one assumes, was able, fearlessly, to collect his rent.

14 A neighbour, Jean (Adams) Smith (b. 1922) of Hillsborough, remembered Black Angus's visits to the Adams house at election time (the polls were in Hillsborough); to her, spontaneously, he was "the old gentleman" (Jean Adams, personal telephone communication, 24 March, 1994).

15 Pipers who were also fiddlers, and vice versa, were common in the Nova Scotia *Gàidhealtachd* in the nineteenth century.

16 Reckoning by descent from Iain Dubh of Bohuntin, Anne MacDonald was Fr Alexander MacDonald's paternal aunt. Using the Crannachan family as a focus they were first cousins.

17 Florence Allan J. MacDonald, personal communication, Judique, 11 August 1987. Apart from Florence, my informants were Dan Angus Beaton (1903–96), Blackstone; Donald Angus Beaton (1912–82), Mabou; Marcella (MacDonald) Chisholm (1906–93), Port Hood; Mary Gillis (b. 1902), South West Margaree; Willie the piper Gillis (1914–95), Inverness; Jemima (MacInnis) Lydon (b. 1923), Broad Cove Banks and Braintree, Massachusetts; Angus Bernard MacDonald (b. 1913), Marble Hill; Angus Cù MacDonald (b. 1910), Mabou; John Alex MacDonald (1893–1983), Creignish; Sarah Ann MacDonald (1886–1992), Black River; Donald MacKay (b.1911), St Peter's, Nova Scotia; John Alex MacNeil (b. 1920), Black River; Alex Joe Rankin (1908–86), Judique and Port Hood; and Isobel (MacDonald) Young (1886–1985), Brook Village. All of them, among the hundreds, heard Black Angus's piping. Marcella (MacDonald) Chisholm and Angus Bernard MacDonald, brother and sister, were grandchildren of a sister of Black Angus the piper, and Sarah Ann MacDonald (Saddler), their aunt, one of the most valuable informants, was a niece.

18 James D. Gillis, b. 1870, lived as an old man with Florence Allan J.'s parents in Mount Young. See James D. Gillis, *A Little Sketch*.

19 J.L. MacDougall, *History of Inverness County*, 572.

20 *The Casket* 55, no. 41 (10 October 1907).

21 Alexander D. MacDonald, *Mabou Pioneers*, 424. Also present was the piper Archibald Beaton from Mabou Coal Mines and his second cousin, Donald Beaton, the still-remembered old fiddler.

22 Frame homes in the New World forest setting, often of two stories, were larger and roomier than those vacated in West Highland Scotland, and there is every reason to believe that the period from the setting up of local sawmills saw the flourishing of the Scotch Four in its beloved *céilidh* setting and had a special place in the marriage rite. It was danced to the fiddle, the pipes, the chanter, and to singing, indoors and out.

23 Rhodes, "Dancing in Cape Breton Island."

24 No Cape Breton Scotch fiddler has ever played reels to anything other than traditional step-dance timing and Black Angus was also a fiddler. Nothing known about the rustic quadrille/Lancer suggests that any rhythmic or timing imposure was laid upon the traditional musician, with the possible exception of a slight speeding up of the music.

25 Shears, *The Gathering of the Clans Collection* and above. The source of the photograph was Angus Cù MacDonald, Mabou, via JGG.

26 John Paul MacKinnon of Harbourview is a former step-dance piper. A small number of young non-Gaelic-speaking Scots are reviving traditional piping but largely outwith the *céilidh* atmosphere and more as a novelty and as part of the commercial revival of Keltic music.

27 Coming to prominence in the late nineteenth century, parish picnics and
    bazaars were used to raise money for a church, school, or other project. Alex
    Joe Rankin (personal communication, Port Hood, 26 April 1982) remembered
    Black Angus piping at the 1925 Judique picnic, the year the new stone church
    was begun. John Alex MacDonald (personal communication, Creignish, 19
    July 1982) remembered his fiddling for the Scotch Fours at the "special stage"
    at a picnic at Creignish c.1900 (the new church was built in 1899).

28 D.D. MacFarlane (1861–1950), the South West Margaree school teacher, Gael-
    ic poet, and lifelong friend of fellow teacher Malcolm Gillis, for whom he
    often supplied. See MacFarlane's unpublished diaries, St Francis Xavier Uni-
    versity archives, AAJC MG 75/1 SG F38. Malcolm Gillis was a celebrity in the
    Scottish Gaelic world by virtue of his songs (see Bernard Gillis, comp.,
    Smeòrach nan Cnoc 's nan Gleann).

29 Charlottetown Herald, new series vol. 24, no. 32, (7 August 1895). Members of
    the Caledonian Club had foregathered at the club's rooms on Queen Street,
    Charlottetown, and marched in procession, headed by pipers, to the field
    where, during the day, "the artillery band was present during the afternoon,
    playing well" (a typical military brass band). The report mentions that "there
    were also several pipers in attendance," perhaps referring to, or including, the
    contingent that Dan Angus Beaton claimed was there from Scotland.

30 Cameron's presence in Ardgower but so near Glenaladale's Clanranald patri-
    mony is interesting as it may further substantiate the notion of the westward
    spreading of Cameron landholders in the late eighteenth or early nineteenth
    century. A Cameron, for example, was in Meoble when Dougal MacDonald's
    ancestor left for Low Point, Inverness County.

31 Allan Cameron played the violin "in the choir" of Mabou church, according to
    his great grandson Sandy Cameron (b. 1918). Sandy Cameron, personal com-
    munication, North East Mabou, 1994.

32 It is unlikely but not inconceivable that he played a non-step-dance slow strath-
    spey. Fr Hugh A MacDonald (born c. 1913) remembered his mother, a Gillis
    from Mabou Harbour who died in the 1970s, telling him that one day while she
    was scrubbing the floor two of the three tunes that Gilleasbuig was known to
    have played at Charlottetown popped into her mind. She sang them to Hugh A.
    who, as recently as May 1994, sang them to Angus Rankin of Mabou Ridge.
    The march was one of Gilleasbuig's own compositions. Fr. MacDonald didn't
    remember the name of the strathspey but the reel was "The Smith of Chillie-
    chassie." According to Fr MacDonald, Archie Beaton was a literate piper.
    Angus Rankin, personal communication, telephone, Mabou Ridge, 1994.

33 Rev. A.A. Johnston, History of the Catholic Church in Eastern Nova Scotia,
    vol. 1, 483. Malcolm MacLellan was one of two teacher sons of Captain
    Archibald MacLellan from Morar (who settled in Cape George, Antigonish
    County). Malcolm MacLellan's daughter Jane was married to John Beaton and
    living in Mabou Coal Mines.

34 Mary Hughie (Beaton) MacDonald (1896–1983), better known as Màiri Alasdair Raonuil, personal communication, Mira, Cape Breton, 1976. Mary Hughie's fiddling was profoundly traditional; she was from Mabou Coal Mines and also step-danced. Katie Margaret (Rankin) Gillis did not confirm the dancing school information. Katie Margaret Gillis, personal communication, Mabou Harbour, 10 October 1994.

35 John Angus Rankin (d. 1995) was a descendant of John "the immigrant" Rankin of Mabou Coal Mines.

36 Other traditional step-dance pipers include Joe Hughie MacIntyre, some of whose taped music is transcribed in Shears, *Gathering of the Clans Collection*.

37 Unless it is a well-known place, like Trout Brook, Head Lake, or Scotsville, I have used East Lake Ainslie to cover a larger area than it properly should.

38 The following are the principal informants for Little Farquhar: Edward Campbell (1911–95), Trout River; Florence (Campbell) Coleman (b. 1914), Trout River and Franklin, Massachusetts; Stanley Collins (b. c. 1912); Alice (MacLean) Freeman (b. 1937), Scotsville and Inverness; Mary Gillis (b. 1902), South West Margaree; Neil Dan MacInnis (1893–1993), Glenville; Rev. Archibald D. MacKinnon (1898–1985), East Lake Ainslie; John M. (John Neillie) MacLean (b. 1903), Head Lake; Archie McPhail (b. 1900), Scotsville; Clarence Moore (1905–82), schoolteacher, lake Ainslie, east side.

39 Edward Campbell (personal communication, Trout River, by East Lake Ainslie, 11 June 1979). Campbell preferred to dance to violin music because he was conscious of a limitation to pipe music, which, as he said "cut down the number of steps you could dance." Of all my informants, Edward Campbell was the most insistent that Scotch traditional music and dance had come to East Lake Ainslie with the immigrants, that it had persisted, and that it had not been grafted on later from neighbouring Catholic communities in the New World. The same strongly held opinion is occasionally heard from Pictou County Scots who remember the last days of the living culture and language there.

40 Neil Dan MacInnis was a great admirer of his uncle Farquhar MacKinnon. He had Little Farquhar's old set of bagpipes, but would not show them to me in 1982. He said, however, that they had been brought out from Scotland by Farquhar's paternal grandfather Donald MacKinnon, who was himself a piper. Neil Dan was the only source for this detail (Neil Dan MacKinnon, personal communication, Glenville, 26 September 1978). Clarence Moore added that the pipes were said to have been played at Waterloo, a not uncommon claim for old sets in Cape Breton (Clarence Moore, personal communication, Lake Ainslie, 9 May 1977.)

41 Mary Gillis, personal communication, South West Margaree, 20 May, 1979.

42 Archie McPhail, personal communication, Scotsville, 29 October 1994. A feature of traditional Scotch fiddling, and once of piping, is the accompanying beating of time. Isobel MacMillan (b.1902) Twin Rock Valley, told me at her home, unprompted or led, that she vividly remembered the Protestant piper

Robert Campbell from the rear of Scotsville, sitting down to pipe, beating time vigorously with both feet. (Campbell went to Boston around 1914 and never returned.) Isobel MacMillan (daughter of Allan Cameron of Kiltarlity, a strict Sunday keeper) was a non-dancer (personal communication, Twin Rock Valley, 29 October 1994).

43 Mary Gillis, personal communication, South West Margaree, 9 July 1994.

44 Dancing at crossroads and at bridges, "dancing the cross," was a feature of Gaelic rural life in Inverness County.

45 Neil Dan McInnis, personal communication, Glenville, September 1978. I neglected to ask which minister this was but in East Lake Ainslie Ewan MacKillop, the last minister before many Presbyterian churches joined the United Church of Canada in 1925, was the only one remembered as unusually stern and he clearly made little impression upon his musical parishioners.

46 Walter Scott MacFarlane (d. 1979), Inverness, Cape Breton, 20 April 1977. See also MacQuarrie, *Cape Breton Collection*, 7. Charles MacDonald thought the daughter would have been Josie.

47 Allan's *sloinneadh* was Allachan Aonghuis Dhuibh 'ic Iain 'ic 'Illeasbuig (MacPharlain). He was a descendant, through the wife of his MacFarlane immigrant ancestor, of the MacDonells of Scotus in Knoydart.

48 See Bernard Gillis, comp., *Smeòrach nan Cnoc 's nan Gleann*, 123, which includes a poem/song about the Jamesons mentioning all the pipers, male and female, in the family.

49 In a piping competition in Sydney in the 1930s Black Jack MacDonald, a World War I Cape Breton Highlanders military pipe-major, won the march but Allan MacFarlane won the strathspey and reel. (Personal communication from a later Cape Breton Highlanders pipe-major and pupil of Black Jack, George Sutherland [dec.], Soldier's Cove, 25 August 1980.) (Sutherland described Black Jack as a literate piper).

50 Clarence Moore, personal communication, Lake Ainslie, 9 May 1979.

51 Stanley Collins, personal communication, Cobb Brook, 11 June 1994.

52 One random memory belonged to Neil Williams (1918–97) of Melford. He remembered Allachan piping for the step-dancing of a Protestant Gael, Finlay MacCuspic, at a Glendale concert in the early 1930s, as well as in a small Catholic Margarees pipe-band got together for the same event (the photograph in my possession of Black Angus MacDonald, Allan MacFarlane, and Angus Johnnie Ranald Beaton used in Barry Shears's book was probably taken at this concert). Neil Williams, personal communication, Melford, Cape Breton, 23 March 1977.

53 Neil Allan MacLean (1897–1992), of Scotsville, descendant of the MacLean immigrant Presbyterian dancing master, said of a pipe tune he recognized being played by Sandy Boyd that the only piper he had ever heard play it better was Allachan Aonghuis Dhuibh MacFarlane. Although I interviewed Neil Allan MacLean my notes are missing. I have this information from John M.

MacLean, Headlake, 11 June 1994. Mary Gillis said that Allachan's piping was "much sweeter" than Sandy Boyd's but "not so loud" (personal communication, South West Margaree, 29 May 1979). *Fìor Ghàidheal* (True Gael) Johnnie Williams of Melford, summed up his thoughts one day in the 1970s, "Sandy Boyd needn't be bragging, or any of them late-models." (In fairness, had Sandy Boyd been able to play step-dance music he would have been remarkable.)

54   Taken from the Gaelic chorus of "Blow the Bugle" by W.S. MacFarlane, an elegy for Allachan MacFarlane.

55   Margaret MacLean, personal communication, Melford, 6 December 1976.

56   If MacFarlane's inspiration sprang from within Inverness County's Gaelic community, then the place of classical piping in Gaelic Nova Scotia will have to be reassessed.

CHAPTER SEVENTEEN

1   John MacGregor, an ear piper from the Loch Fyne area, told Archie MacNeil (b. 1879) when lodging at the MacNeils in Glasgow that he had often played the pipes for Lord Archibald Campbell of Inveraray Castle in the late nineteenth century (see Archie MacNeill, "Early Piping Days."

2   Anon., "Pipe-Major John MacDonald." Reverend (Fr) Allan MacDonald (1859–1905), Eriskay, knew the older traditional reel-dance piping and celebrated it in song: "*Pìob 'ga spreigeadh, binn a fead leam,/ Is cha b'e sgread na fidhle;/ Cridhe toirt breab as, 's e 'ga freagairt/ Ann am beadradh inntinn./ Air an fheasgar bhiodh na fleasgaich/ A' comh-fhreasgairt tìm dhi:/ Leam bu ghas-da bhidh 'nam faisge/Dol an teas an rìghlidh*" ("Pipe inciting, sweet its whistle to me/ and it wasn't the screech of the fiddle;/ Heart taking a pulse from it and its answering/ in the caressing of the mind./ Of an evening the young men would be/ all keeping time to her: to me 'twere excellent to be nearest driving in the heat of the reel"). My translation. See MacDonald, "Eilean na h-Òige," in Watson, *Bàrdachd Ghàidhlig (Gaelic Poetry)*, 3, lines 57–64.

3   One of John MacDonald's pupils was Seton Gordon, the man who, in some of his published books, exposed the existence of some of the older Gaelic tradition more effectively perhaps even than any letters John Johnston wrote to the *Oban Times* on the subject.

4   See MacAulay, "The MacKenzies of Loch Boisdale," and the obituary for Finley MacKenzie in *Piping Times* 16, no. 4 (January 1964).

5   According to Cameron MacQuarrie (principal of Mabou Consolidated School), when he and his father-in-law, traditional Inverness County step-dancer Gael Willie Fraser, were in South Uist in the summer of 1996 people for whom Willie step-danced in old folks' homes recognized the style of dancing as once common there. The recent discoveries of a small number of older, native Scottish step-dancers by Maggie Moore show that the old speeds and timings of Gaelic music survived.

6   Shears, *Gathering of the Clans Collection*, vol. 1: 3, 4.

7   Francis MacDonald, personal communication, Inverness, 1994.

8   Cannon, *Highland Bagpipe*, 142.

9   Barry Shears, personal telephone communication, Halifax, 17 December 1995.

10 From this class I have excluded late immigrants who were Gaelic-speaking pipers from the Scottish *Gàidhealtachd*, people like the MacMaster piper who settled in the rear of Judique in the 1860s and the Gillis brothers from Morar, Alex and Allan, who were pipers during the First World War and who settled in the Mabou-Port Hood area of Inverness County, although all may have been influenced by modern piping.

11 In *Canntaireachd*, John Francis Campbell included with the top names associated with piping and "the old forgotten language of MacCrimmen," the "Piper o' Dundee." Presumably this was John MacLennan of the Dundee police whose influence must have reached much further than that of his brilliant nephew William (1860–92).

12 MacKay is the last living member of the Cape Breton Highlanders pipe band of World War II.

13 Donald Angus MacPherson's mother was Christie MacNeil, Gaelic composer and singer (Corinne (MacPherson) MacDonald, one of Christie MacNeil's son Donald Angus's daughters, personal communication, Inverness, 5 December 1994. Corinne is also the wife of Francis MacDonald). The Cape Mabou MacKays, Ailean Bàn and his son Donald, are mentioned in J.L. MacDougall, *History of Inverness County*, 334.

14 There are far fewer than a thousand native speakers of Gaelic left in Cape Breton. They are all bilingual and most of them are over fifty.

15 Gibson, "Mabou in its Halcyon Days" in the Sunflower, an insert in the weekly newspaper *Scotia Sun*, 19 May 1982. I am indebted to Sister Claire I. Beaton, Mabou, for the use of her copy. She is a relative of Sister Sarah Ann.

16 Kenneth E. Nilsen reported an early Boston Scot's exaggerated opinion that there were more Gaels in the Boston area than in the New World homeland (see Nilsen, "The Nova Scotia Gael in Boston," 84).

17 Katie Margaret Gillis, personal communication, Mabou Harbour, 10 October 1994.

18 The *Total Abstainer*, "official organ of the League of the Cross," began publishing in 1907 and became known to many as the League of the Corks. The *Trumpet*, "pledged to temperance, liberty, and law," published vol. 1, no. 1, on 25 October 1869, n.p.

19 Joseph MacDonald (c.1760) used the term "wild Reells" in his manuscript "Compleat Theory." The wording: "This mode of Cutting being frequently met with in the wild Reells is a Sufficient Specimen ..." is the same as in the 1803 publication and appears on page 32 of the 1971 reprint.

20 Efforts to revive it on the summer concert stage have failed to attract the attention of EveryGael and the old dance is now all but dead.

21 Custom demands that once into the reels the fiddler never play strathspey timing for a step-dance performance; the break is always to the faster timing.

1 The letter is in SRO GD 170/1604/2.
2 Alexander Campbell, seventh of Barcaldine (and second of Barcaldine and
Glenure) was the oldest son of the Killin JP Duncan Campbell, who thwarted the
efforts of the occupying forces to obtain convictions of men caught wearing Highland dress around 1750. Alexander Campbell was also the brother of Captain
Patrick Campbell ("of Glenuir") whose company piper in the Second Battalion,
71st, in February 1778 in New York, was William MacKenzie the piper. See Letter
from William Mackenzie, Piper, GD 170/3158. The letter is given in Appendix 3.
3 By the mid-1830s MacNab also kept an *amadan* (fool) called Lipsy.
4 Read and Stagg, *Rebellion of 1837*, 260 and 261. December 1837's *Gazette* is
unavailable in Nat. Lib. Can.
5 Apart from his own songs, MacGillivray is commemorated as "Bràthaich" the
piper in Alasdair MacKinnon's poem "*An dubh Ghleannach*" about Glenaladale's *birlinn*. See John MacKenzie, *Sar-Obair*, 346-7. The Glenaladale whose
boat was praised was the man who had built the first Glenfinnan monument.
6 Dr Ray MacLean, ed., *History of Antigonish*, 25.
7 The 1817 census for Antigonish (PANS RG1, vol. 445, no. 15, and RG1, vol.
447), county of Sydney, Nova Scotia, taken on 2 July, shows a "Kennith
Chisholm" as head of a family of six. Two were Scots-born, the rest were listed
in the "Acadian" column. There was a man of over fifty and one "woman." One
of the Acadian-born was a man between the ages of fifteen and sixty, dating the
emigration to at the latest 1802. This is the only Kenneth Chisholm on this census record; none appears in Dorchester (Antigonish), St Andrews or "Trac-
cadie" in the count of 1827. An 1801 passenger list for the *Dove of Aberdeen*
(PANS F 106/P5/M22 shows a Kenneth Chisholm, his wife and a child, from
Strathglass. The ship was bound for Pictou, Nova Scotia.
8 After 1863, Pomquet Forks was renamed Heatherton, the community's current
name. The last local Gaelic speaker, Alex J. Chisholm, died recently in a nurs-
ing home in Antigonish.
9 Whitelaw, ed., *Dalhousie Journals*, 53.
10 Ibid., 57.
11 Alexander D. MacDonald, *Mabou Pioneers*, 311, where Samuel Campbell is
given as being from Tulloch, a convert to Catholicism. Among the Tulloch people listed in a "Decreet of Removing" in 1795 (SRO SC 28/7/2) was a "Samuel
Campbell, alias McGlaserich"; another, "Samuel MacGlaserich alias Campbell," received a removal order from Inverroy and Boline (SRO SC 28/16/3).
Both orders were issued at the behest of Aeneas Mackintosh. See MacFarlane,
"Tenants in Brae Lochaber."

12 Alexander D. MacDonald, *Mabou Pioneers*, 309.

13 Donald Campbell (c. 1727– ?), piper to arch-Jacobite Alexander MacDonald of Glenaladale, moved to Campbell country after Culloden. His son Colin was the author of "Colin Campbell's Instrumental Book," 1797, which gave classical piping a large number of tunes in *canntaireachd* (vocable) form. Donald's grandson, John (d. 1831 aged thirty-six) was the language and culture teacher of John Francis Campbell "of Isla." Donald's home is unknown but the nearest Jacobite Campbells to Glenaladale were the Mac a'Ghlasraichs in Keppoch. See Buisman, "From Chant to Script," *Piping Times* 39, no. 7 (April 1987); "More Evidence on Colin Campbell," *Piping Times* 47: nos. 11 and 12 (August and September 1995); and "Melodic relationships in Pibroch," *British Journal of Ethnomusicology* 4, (1995).

14 Rev. A.A. Johnston, *History of the Catholic Church in Eastern Nova Scotia*, vol. 2: 256, 257.

15 For a photograph of Big Colin Chisholm and his son Duncan Big Colin, see Shears, *The Gathering of the Clans Collection*, 6.

16 Malcolm MacLeod, ed., *Peace River: A Canoe Voyage*, passim.

17 Ibid., 24.

18 CBC Radio interview reported in Bill McNeil, *Voice of the Pioneer*, 108, 109.

19 Capt. John MacLellan, "Tenth Hereditary Piper to the Clan MacLeod," *International Piper* 3, no. 1 (May 1980): n.p.

20 Letter from A.E. Garton, *Piping Times* 17, no. 10 (July 1965): 27, 28.

21 Letter from John Johnston, Coll, to A.L. Johnston in Nova Scotia, dated 19 March 1906, in the possession of Thelma Johnson, Scotsburn, Pictou County, Nova Scotia.

22 Whyte, *The Rankins Pipers*.

23 Thelma Johnson's prime source for family history was her paternal aunt, Pearl (Johnson) Henderson, who in turn had her information from her father (Thelma's paternal grandfather), James Johnson (1854-1936). James was bedridden during his last year and took pains to pass on what he knew.

24 Athol Robertson, personal communication, Montague, Prince Edward Island, summer 1994.

25 Archibald Campbell, *The Kilberry Book of* Ceòl Mór, 11.

26 Ibid.

27 From a copy of a letter in the possession of Miss Thelma Johnson, Pictou County. The letter is from John Johnston, Coll, to a relative, a 'Revd. Sir' (probably Rev. David Johnson) in Canada, 20 February 1907.

28 Letter from John Johnston to cousin Alexander Johnston, Orillia, is owned by Thelma Johnson.

Bibliography

ARCHIVAL MATERIAL

Archives Nationales du Québec, Québec City

"Journals of James Thompson Senior."

Conan House Archives, Gairloch, Ross-shire

Privately held family and estate records of the Mackenzies of Gairloch.

Dalhousie University Archives, Halifax, Nova Scotia

MS2/82-T-I-A-I, Archibald MacMechan Papers. Anonymous article, "John MacKay ... The Blind Piper of Gairloch."

Edinburgh University Library.

Campbell, Alexander. "A Slight Sketch of a Journey made through parts of the Highlands and Hebrides; undertaken to collect materials for Albyn's Anthology." MS La.III.577 and La.II.51, fol.172–6.

Fraser, Angus. "Angus Fraser MSS." Therein "Ceol-Suaicheantas Morair Bhraidh'-Albainn – The distinguished Family Tune of The Lords of Breadalbane. An ancient Gaelic Melody." (The shelf mark for the Angus Fraser MSS is Gen.614 but in December 1996 no song about the lairds of Breadalbane was identified.)

"Lady Evelyn Stewart Murray Collection," 240 Gaelic tales collected in 1891, held by School of Scottish Studies, Edinburgh University.

MacDonald, Joseph. "Compleat theory of the Scots Highland Bagpipe with all the Terms of Art in which this instrument was originally taught by its first masters & composers in the islands of Sky & Mull." Laing MS 111, 804.

British Museum, London

"Bruce, Mr" (?). "The Highlands of Scotland in 1750," from Manuscript 104 in the King's Library, British Museum, with an introduction by Andrew Laing.
Egerton MSS. Papers of Sir John Strange, council to the King, held by the British Museum. See Egerton ms. 2000 in British Museum. *Catalogue of Additions to Manuscripts* ..., 943. London: British Museum, 1967.

National Library of Scotland (NLS)

Adv. 50 MS 50 1 14 ff. 163–4. Draft letter from J.F. Campbell to story collector Hector MacLean, 19 May 1859.
NLS M221, MSS 3733-6, Campbell Papers (John Campbell of Mamore).
NLS Accession 7451. "Papers and Correspondence of Seton Gordon MBE," Box 1, General Correspondence 1913–39. Letter from John Johnston, Totamore, Coll, to Lieut. Seton Gordon RN Vol. Res., Naval Centre, Kingstown, Ireland, February 1918.
NLS Glen 298. MacDonald, Donald. "A Collection of the ancient martial music of Caledonia called Piobaireachd as performed on the great Highland Bagpipe." MS. c. 1812.
NLS/313/3478. Sutherland Estate Papers.
NLS MS 3714 and MS 3715. "Campbell Canntaireachd." Vol. 1: "Colin Campbell's Instrumental Book, 1797." Vol. 2: "John Campbell's Book 4th June, 1820."
NLS MS 3743. "Specimens of canntareachd." Holograph by Angus MacKay. Transcript of early Colin Campbell work known broadly from later versions as the "Campbell Canntaireachd."
NLS MS 9623, ff. 235 and 244. Letters from John Johnston, Coll, to the *Oban Times*, 3 September and 10 November 1919.
NLS MSS 3753–4. MacKay, Angus. MSS. Two volumes of pìobaireachd.
NLS Mus. Box 9.594. Menzies, Captain Robert. "A Preceptor for the great Highland Bagpipe."

Public Archives of Nova Scotia (PANS)

PANS, MG20 674 7. MacKay, Squire John, JP, "Reminiscences of a Long Life." Subsequently published by the *Oban Times*, 1935.
PANS, F.106\P5\M22. A published passenger list of the ship *Dove of Aberdeen*, 1801).
PANS, MG1, vol. 1456. "The John George Marshall Papers." Document 5, "On Temperance."

PANS, RGI, vol. 445, no. 15 and RGI, vol. 447. Censuses for the County of Sydney, 1817 and 1827.

PANS, RG32, "D"(1864–77), vol. 65, sheet 51, no. 170. Death record for an Angus MacKay, b. Ross-shire, d. Pictou County, Nova Scotia, 21 May 1868.

Public Record Office, London, England (PRO)

PRO KB 8. "Baga de Secretis." Appendix 2 to the fifth report of the Deputy Keeper of Public Records, London, vol. 69: 193, 1746.

British Military and Naval Records, Series C. Musters of the British Legion. Copies held by Public Archives of Nova Scotia, Halifax, Nova Scotia.

PCC Foreign Parts, Prob 11, Piece 1915, p. 173 RH–174 RH. "Transcript of Will of Patrick McCrummen" (Lt Donald MacCrummen's son), 1839.

PRO Colonial Office 5, vol. 93: 287, English records, Box 12, folder 18. McLean, Capt. Alex^r. "A Narrative of the proceedings of a Body of Loyalists in North Carolina ... Rec^d from Genl 24$^{th.}$ March 1776 In Genl Howe's Letter of the 25th April 1776 1." Filed in correspondence dated 25 April 1776.

PRO Treasury 50, Bundle 5, North Carolina Historical Commission, English Records, Treasury Papers, Miscellanea, North and South Carolina Refugees, 1781–82.

PRO State Papers Domestic, George 2, Bundle 79, Folio 26 and Bundle 91, Folio 77.

PRO War Office (WO)1, 613, passim, 1757. Correspondence of Lieutenant General Beauclerk.

WO 2. 33, folio 157. A list of officers in the 114th regiment.

St Francis Xavier University Archives, Antigonish, Nova Scotia

AAJC MG 75/1 SG F 38. MacFarlane, D.D. (1861–1950). Unpublished diaries.

Scottish Military Archives.

Black Watch Regimental Archives (BWRA), 28/714/1, 24 June 1852. "Diary of Colonel J.W. Wedderburn."

Royal Highland Fusiliers Regimental Archives (RHFRA), D/1/11. "Digest of Services, 74th Highlanders, vol. 1, 1787–1852." Containing material from Lt Col John Fordyce.

Argyll and Sutherland Highlanders Regimental Archives, Stirling Castle. The Descriptive Roll Book of the 93rd Sutherland Highlanders 1799–1831

Scottish Record Office (SRO)

SRO JC 11 GC 165 (1748–51). Books 12 and 13 of the Scottish Justiciary Court records.

SRO SC29/7/2. "Decreet of Removing Duncan Robertson Tacksman of Wellhouse and setter of the lands after mentioned, against Alexander MacLean Piper in Well-house ..."

Horn, Dr B.L.H. unpublished researches in family records of the Gordon ducal family and the Marchmont estate records, *inter alia*. Made available by Stuart Allan, Historical Research Room, SRO.

SRO GD 170/1604/2. Letter from Alexander Campbell, Kinlochlaigh, to Alexander Campbell of Barcaldine, 13 August 1791.

SRO GD 170/3158. Letter from William MacKenzie, piper, 2d Battalion, 71st Regiment, to Petter.

SRO E 786/11/8. Memorial of Mungo Campbell.

SRO E 786/41/1–43. Records of the Forfeited Estates.

SRO RH 2/4/87, 73–5. Ship's passenger list for the *Dove of Aberdeen*, 1801.

SRO 112/1/803. Specimen of Campbell *pìobaireachd* notation signed "Errors Excepted, By Colin Campbell Piper to the Earl of Bredalbin at Neither [*sic*] Lorn Argyle Shire."

SRO Register of Criminal Letters (1751–80).

Parliamentary Acts

An Act for an Union of the Two Kingdoms of England and Scotland (6 Anne), 1706.

An Act for rendring the Union of the Two Kingdoms more intire and complete (6 Anne), 1707.

Act to Attaint, 19 Geo. 2, cap. 26, 1746.

An Act for the more effectual disarming the Highlands in Scotland (Disarming Act), 19 Geo. 2, cap. 39, 1746.

Act of Indemnity, (for Hanoverians), 19 Geo. 2, 1746.

An Act more effectually to prohibit Episcopal meeting homes in Scotland, 1746.

Act suspending Habeas Corpus, 1746.

Tenures Abolition Act, 1746 (Short Titles Act, 1896).

Sales to the Crown Act, 1746 (Short Titles Act, 1896).

Vesting Act, 20 Geo. 2, cap. 41, 1747.

An Act for taking away and abolishing the Heretable Jurisdictions in that Part of Great Britain called Scotland; and for making Satisfaction to the Proprietors thereof; and for restoring such Jurisdictions to the Crown; and for making more effectual Provision for the Administration of Justice throughout that Part of the United Kingdom, by the King's Courts and Judges there; and for obliging all Persons acting as Procurators, Writers or Agents in the Law in Scotland to take the Oaths; and for rendering the Union of the two Kingdoms more complete (The Heritable Jurisdictions (Scotland) Act, 20 Geo. 2, cap. 43), 1747.

Act for taking away the Tenure of Ward Holding in Scotland, and for converting the same into Blanch and Feu Holdings, 20 Geo. 2, cap. 50, 1747.

An Act affecting penalties for the Wearing of Highland Dress, 20 Geo. 2, cap. 51, 1747.

An Act to enlarge the Time limited by an Act of the last Session of Parliament, for restraining the Use of the Highland Dress, 20 Geo. 2, cap. 51, 1747 (cited in 21 Geo. 2, cap 34, section VII, 1748).

Act for the King's Most Gracious General and Free Pardon (also known as Act of Grace), 20 Geo. 2, cap. 52, 1747.

An Act to amend so much of an Act made in the nineteenth Year of his Majesty's Reign, as relates to the more effectual disarming the Highlands in Scotland ... 21 Geo. 2, cap. 34, 1748.

Annexing Act, 25 Geo. 2, cap. 41, 1752.

The Fisheries (Scotland) Act, 1756 (Short Titles Act), 29 Geo. 2, 1755–56.

An Act for the speedy and effectual Recruiting of his Majesty's Land Forces and Marines, 29 Geo. 2, cap. 4, 1756.

Recruiting Act of 1756–57, 30 Geo. 2, cap. 8, 1757.

PRIVATE CORRESPONDENCE

Boag, William G.F. (1923–92), Assistant to the Keeper, Scottish United Services Museum, Edinburgh Castle (NMS). Letter to the author, 14 February 1980.

Cooke, Peter, School of Scottish Studies, University of Edinburgh, to the author, 22 February 1987.

Cumming, James, secretary, Society of Antiquaries of Scotland, to Sir Alexander Dick of Prestonfield, 13 November 1781. Held by the library of the Society of Antiquaries of Scotland.

Emerson, Lelia (MacKay), Newburyport, Massachusetts. Letters to the author, 24 February 1982 and 31 March 1983.

Gray, Iain, Archivist, Aberdeen City Archives. Letters to the author, 7 November 1996 and 7 February 1997. Mr. Gray's letters contain references to Enactment Books, 1741–1749 and 1749–1758, "containing bonds of good behaviour by those found guilty of misdemeanours in the Baillie Court" of Aberdeen; Minutes of the Baillie Court of Aberdeen, 1748–1758; and List of prisoners in the (Aberdeen) Tolbooth for treasonable practices, 25 July 1746, as reported to Lord Justice Clerk;

Iredale, David, c/o *Scots Magazine*, Dundee. Letter to the author, 8 January 1997.

Johnson, Thelma I. Scotsburn, Pictou County, Nova Scotia. Letter to the author, 27 March 1992.

Johnston, John, Coll, Scotland. Letter to Alexander L. Johnston, Orillia, Ontario, 28 December 1905, in the possession of Thelma Johnson, Scotsburn, Nova Scotia.

Johnston, John, Coll. Letter to A.L. Johnston in Nova Scotia, 19 March 1906, in the possession of Thelma Johnson.

Johnston, John, Coll. Letter to a relative (Rev. David Johnson?) in Canada, 20 February 1907, in the possession of Thelma Johnson.

Laidlaw, James, Scarborough, Yorkshire. Letters to the author, 12 January 1977 and 28 January 1977.

MacKay, Clara G, Malden, Massachusetts. Letter to the author, 25 November 1981.

MacKenzie, Bridget, Dornoch, Sutherland, to the author, 10 July 1997.

MacLeod, Ruairidh H. Auchtermuchty, Fife. Letter to the author, 6 September 1981.

Moss, George (1903–90), Kessock, by Inverness. Letters to the author, 4 May and 5 February 1980.

Munro, R.W., Grianach, Nethy Bridge, Inverness-shire. Letter to the author, 31 July 1993.

Other Sources

Agnew, Sir Andrew, Bart, of Lochnaw. *The Hereditary Sheriffs of Galloway Their "forebears" and Friends their Courts and Customs of their Times with Notes of the Early History, Ecclesiastical Legends, the Baronage and Place-names of the Province.* 2 vols. Edinburgh, 1893.

Allardyce, Alexander, ed., *Scotland and Scotsmen in the 18th century.* N.p., 1888.

Allardyce, Col James, LL.D. (ed), *Historical Papers Relating to the Jacobite Period 1699–1750.* 2 vols. Aberdeen: New Spalding Club, 1895 and 1896.

Anderson, Col G.W. *Seaforth Songs, Ballads, and Sketches.* Dublin, 1890.

– *Stories of Sport and Service in the (1st Battalion) Seaforth Highlanders.* Dublin, 1896.

Anderson, William James, ed. *A Short, Authentic Account of the Expedition against Québec in the Year 1759.* Québec, 1872.

Anonymous. *A View of the Highlands &c.* N.p., c. 1784.

Anonymous. "Pipe-Major John MacDonald [South Uist]." *Piping Times* 11, no. 2 (November 1958):18, 19.

Army School of Piping. "Historical and Traditional Notes on Piobaireachd." N.p., 1964.

Army List, 1763.

Askew, Gilbert. "The Origins of the Northumbrian Bagpipe." in *Archæologia Aeliana* (Newcastle-upon-Tyne) 9, 4th series (1932).

Bailyn, Bernard. *Voyagers to the West: A Passage in the Peopling of America on the Eve of the Revolution.* New York: Alfred A. Knopf, 1986.

Bain, Margaret I. *Les Voyageurs Français en Ecosse 1770–1830 et leurs Curiosités Intellectuelles.* Paris: H. Champion, 1931.

Baines, Anthony. *Bagpipes.* Oxford: Oxford University Press, 1960.

Balfour, Captain Charles B. "The Scots Guards." In *The Lowland Scots Regiments, their origin, Character and Services previous to the Great War of 1914,* edited by Herbert E. Maxwell. Glasgow: J. Maclehose and Sons, 1918.

Bartlett, I. Ross. "Scottish Mercenaries in Europe 1570–1640: A Study in Attitudes and policies." *Scottish Tradition* (Canadian Association for Scottish Studies, University of Guelph, Guelph, Ontario) 13 (1984–85).

Bass, Robert D. *The Green Dragon: The Lives of Banastre Tarleton and Mary Robinson*. New York: Holt, 1957.

Beaton, Elizabeth A., and Sheila W. Macintyre, eds. *The Burgesses of Inveraray, 1665–1963*. Edinburgh: Scottish Record Society, 1990.

Berthoff, R.T. *British Immigrants in Industrial America*. Cambridge, MA: Harvard University Press, 1953.

Black, Ronald, William Gillies, and Roibeard Ó'Maolalaidh, eds. *Celtic Connections: Proceedings of the Tenth International Congress of Celtic Studies*. Vol. 1. East Linton: Tuckwell Press, 1997.

N.a. *Spanish John*. Edinburgh and London: Blackwood and Sons, 1931.

Blaikie, Walter Biggar. *Itinerary of Prince Charles Edward Stuart from his landing in Scotland July 1745 to his departure in September 1746 Compiled from the Lyon in Mourning Supplemented and corrected from other contemporary sources*. 1897. Edinburgh: Scottish Academic Press, 1975.

Borrow, George H. "A Tour in Scotland." 1858. In *The Works of George Borrow*, edited by C.K. Shorter. London, New York, 1924.

Boswell, James. *Journal of a Tour to the Hebrides with Samuel Johnson* (1773). Reprint. Everyman edition, edited by Ernest Rhys. London and New York: Dent and Dutton, 1909.

Brander, M. *The Emigrant Scots*. London: Constable, 1982.

Brander, Michael. *The Scottish Highlanders and Their Regiments*. London: Seeley, 1971.

Brewer, John. *The Sinews of Power – War, Money and the English State, 1688–1783*. Cambridge, MA: Harvard University Press, 1990.

British Museum. *Catalogue of Additions to the Manuscripts in the British Museum in the years 1854–75*. Reprint. London: British Museum, 1967.

Bruce, Mr (?). *The Highlands of Scotland in 1750 from Manuscript 104 in the King's Library, British Museum*, with an introduction by Andrew Lang. Edinburgh and London: William Blackwood and Sons, 1898.

Bruford, Alan. "The Rise of the Highland Piper." Unpublished expanded version of a talk given to the International Celtic Congress, Oxford, 1983.

Buchan, John. *The Massacre of Glencoe*. New York: G.P. Putnam's Sons, 1933.

– *The History of the Royal Scots Fusiliers (1678–1918)*. London and New York: T. Nelson and Sons, 1925.

– *Montrose*. 3d reprint. London: Thomas Nelson and Sons, 1928.

Buchanan, Donald. *Reflections of the Isle of Barra*. London: Sands & Co, 1942.

Buisman, Frans. "From Chant to Script, Some Evidences of Chronology in Colin Campbell's Adaptation of Canntaireachd." *Piping Times* 39, no. 7 (April 1987).

– "More Evidence on Colin Campbell and the Development of the Campbell Notation: MS. SRO 112/1/803." *Piping Times* 47, nos. 11 and 12 (August and September 1995).

– "Melodic Relationships in Pibroch." *British Journal of Ethnomusicology* 4 (1995): 17–39.

Bulloch, John Malcolm, ed. *The House of Gordon.* 3 vols. Aberdeen: New Spalding Club, 1903, 1908 and 1912.

Bumsted, J.M. *The People's Clearance; Highland Emigration to British North America.* Winnipeg: University of Manitoba Press, 1982.

Burleigh, J.H.S. *A Church History of Scotland.* London: Oxford University Press, 1973.

Burns, David. "John MacGregor of Fortingall and His Descendants." *Scottish Genealogist* 29, no. 4 (December 1982).

Burrill, Gary Clayton. *Away – Maritimers in Massachusetts, Ontario, and Alberta: An Oral History of Leaving Home.* Montreal and Kingston: McGill-Queen's University Press, 1992.

Burt, Captain Edward. *Letters from a Gentleman in the North of Scotland (1727–1736).* 2 vols. London, 1754.

Burton, J.H., ed. *Autobiography of the Rev. Dr Alexander Carlyle, Minister of Inveresk containing Memorials of the Men and Events of His Time.* Boston: Ticknor and Fields, 1861.

Burton, John Hill. *Lives of Simon Lord Lovat and Duncan Forbes.* London: Chapman & Hall series, 1847.

Byrne, Cyril J., Margaret Harry, and Pàdraig Ó'Siadhail, eds. *Celtic Languages and Celtic Peoples.* Proceedings of the Second North American Congress of Celtic Studies. Halifax, NS: St Mary's University, 1992.

Calder, James T. *Sketch of the Civil and Traditional History of Caithness, from the Tenth Century.* Glasgow: T. Murray and Son, 1861.

Cameron, Alexander. *The History and Traditions of the Isle of Skye.* Inverness: E. Forsyth, 1871.

Cameron, James M. *Pictonians in Arms, a Military History of Pictou County.* Published by the author through arrangement with the University of New Bruswick, Fredericton: 1969.

– *Pictou County's History.* New Glasgow, NS: Pictou County Historical Society, 1972.

Campbell, Alastair of Airds. *Two Hundred Years – The Highland Society of London.* London: Highland Society of London, 1983.

Campbell, Alexander. *Albyn's Anthology or a Select Collection of the Melodies & Vocal Poetry Peculiar to Scotland & The Isles Hitherto Unpublished.* Edinburgh: Oliver and Boyd, 1816. Reprint. Norwood, PA: 1976.

Campbell, Archibald. "The Highland Bagpipe." *Piping Times* 14, no. 11 (August 1962).

– "The History and Art of Angus MacKay" in Piping Times, vol. 2, nos 5, 6 and 7, February, March and April 1950.

– *The Kilberry Book of Ceòl Mór.* 3d edition. Glasgow: John Smith & Son, on behalf of the Piobaireachd Society, 1969.

– "The MacGregor Pipers of the Clann an Sgeulaiche." *Piping Times* 2, nos. 10–12 (July, August and September) 1950.

Campbell, Colin. "71st Fraser's Highlanders in Massachusetts, 1776–1780." *New England Historical and Genealogical Register* 112, no. 447 (July 1958) 200–13;

112, no. 448 (October 1958):265–75; 113, no. 449 (January 1959):3–14; and 113, no. 450 (April 1959):84–94. Boston: New England Historic Genealogical Society.

Campbell, Donald. *A Treatise on the Language, Poetry, and Music of the Highland Clans: with Illustrative Traditions and Anecdotes, and Numerous Ancient Highland Airs.* Edinburgh: D.R. Collie and Son, 1862.

Campbell, Duncan. *The Book of Garth and Fortingall.* Inverness, 1888.

Campbell, Duncan. *Reminiscences and Reflections of an Octogenarian Highlander.* Inverness: Northern Counties Newspaper and Printing and Publishing Company, 1910.

Campbell, Sir Duncan of Barcaldine Bt. *Records of Clan Campbell in the Military Service of the Honourable East India Company 1600–1858.* New York: Longman's Green and Co., 1925.

Campbell, Dr Ian M. "Rise Up Gweedwife." *Tocher* 12, (Winter 1973): 121.

Campbell, Dr John. *A Full and Particular Description of the Highlands, its situation and produce, the manner and customs of the natives ... to which is annexed a scheme which, if executed ... will [bring] the most disaffected amongst them &c.* London, 1752.

Campbell, John Francis. *Popular Tales of the West Highlands Orally Collected with a Translation.* 4 vols. Edinburgh, 1860, 1862.

– *Canntaireachd: Articulate Music, dedicated to the Islay Association, by J.F. Campbell, Iain Ileach. 14th August, 1880.* Glasgow: Archibald Sinclair, 1880. Facsimile edition. Edinburgh, 1989.

Campbell, John Gregorson. *Witchcraft and Second Sight in the Highlands and Islands of Scotland.* Glasgow: James MacLehose and Sons, 1902.

Campbell, John Lorne, ed. and trans. *Hebridean Folksong: A Collection of Waulking Songs by Donald MacCormick.* Tunes transcribed by Francis Collinson. Oxford and Toronto: Clarendon Press, 1969.

– *Hebridean Folksong, 2, Waulking Songs from Barra, South Uist, Eriskay and Benbecula.* Tunes transcribed by Francis Collinson. Oxford: Clarendon Press, 1977.

– *Hebridean Folksongs 3, Waulking Songs from Vatersay, Barra, Eriskay, South Uist and Benbecula.* Tunes transcribed by Francis Collinson. Oxford: Clarendon Press, 1979.

Campbell, John Lorne, with Compton MacKenzie and Carl H. Borgstrom. *The Book of Barra.* London: G. Routledge and Sons, 1936.

Campbell, John Lorne, ed. *Songs Remembered in Exile – Traditional Gaelic Songs from Nova Scotia Recorded in Cape Breton and Antigonish County in 1937 with an Account of the Causes of Hebridean Emigration, 1790–1835.* Most tunes transcribed by Séamus Ennis. Aberdeen: Aberdeen University Press, 1990.

Campbell, Patrick. *Travels in the Interior Inhabited Parts of North America in the years 1791 and 1792.* Edited with introduction by H.H. Langton and W.F. Ganong. Toronto: Champlain Society, 1937.

Campbell-MacLachlan, Archibald Neil. *William Augustus, Duke of Cumberland being a Sketch of His Military Life and Character, Chiefly as Exhibited in the General Orders of H.R.H., 1745–1747.* 1876.

Campsie, Alistair Keith. *The MacCrimmon Legend – The Madness of Angus Mac-Kay*. Edinburgh: Canongate Publishing, 1980.

Cannon, Richard. *Historical Record of the Nineteenth, or The First Yorkshire North Riding Regiment of Foot*. London, 1848.

– *Historical Record of The Seventieth, or The Surrey Regiment of Foot; containing an Account of the Formation of the Regiment in 1758*. London, 1849.

– *Historical Record of the Thirty-First, or, The Huntingdonshire Regiment of Foot; containing an Account of the Formation of the Regiment in 1702, and of its Subsequent Services to 1850; to which is appended An Account of the Services of the Marine Corps, from 1664 to 1748; The Thirtieth, Thirty-First, and Thirty-Second Regiments having been formed in 1702 as Marine Corps, and Retained from 1714 on the Establishment of the Army as Regiments of Regular Infantry*. London, 1850.

Cannon, Roderick. *Joseph MacDonald's Compleat Theory of the Scots Highland Bagpipe*. N.p. The Piobaireachd Society, 1994.

Cannon, Roderick D. *A Bibliography of Bagpipe Music*. Edinburgh: John Donald Publishers, 1980.

– *The Highland Bagpipe and Its Music*. Edinburgh, John Donald Publishers, 1988.

Carmichael, Alexander. *Carmina Gadelica, hymns and incantations with illustrative notes on words, rites and customs, dying and obsolete; orally collected in the Highlands and Islands of Scotland*. 6 vols. Edinburgh: Oliver and Boyd, 1928–71.

Carnon, R.J.F, and Stuart Maxwell, eds. *The Book of the Old Edinburgh Club*. Vol. 32. Edinburgh: T. and A. Constable, 1966.

Carr, Sir John. *Caledonian Sketches, or a Tour Through Scotland in 1807: to which is prefixed an explanatory address to the public, upon a recent trial*. London, 1809.

Celtic Magazine 3, no. 25 (November 1877): 40, advertising the address of John Henry Dickson.

Chantreau, Pierre-Nicolas. *Voyage dans les trois Royaumes d'Angleterre, d'Écosse et d'Irlande fait en 1788–1789*. Vol. 3. Paris, 1792.

Cheape, Hugh. "The Piper to the Laird of Grant." *Proceedings of the Society of Antiquaries of Scotland* 125, (1995): 4–10.

– "Portraiture in Piping." *Scottish Pipe Band Monthly*, no. 6 (January 1988): 1163–73.

Cheska, Alyce Taylor. "The Antigonish Highland Games: A Community's Involvement in the Scottish Festival of Eastern Canada." *Nova Scotia Historical Review* 3, no. 1 (1983): 51–63.

Church of Scotland, The Principal Acts of the General Assembly, convened occasionally at Edinburgh, upon the 22. day of January, in the year 1645. N.p., n.d.

Church of Scotland. Printed Acts of the General Assembly 1690–1717. N.p., n.d.

"C.M.P." "The bagpipe and the Gael." *Guth na Bliadhna*, book 5, no. 3 (Summer 1908): 271.

Codicil to the will of Simon Lord Lovat. *Piping Times* 22, no. 4 (January 1970).

Cole, Jean Murray. *Exile in the Wilderness – The Biography of Chief Factor Archibald McDonald 1790–1853*. Don Mills, ON: Burns and MacEachern, 1979.

Collinson, Francis. *The Bagpipe – The History of a Musical Instrument.* London and Boston: Routledge & Kegan Paul, 1975.

Cooke, Peter. "Text, Transcriptions and Notes." in George Moss, *Scottish Tradition*, with accompanying cassette, "Scottish Tradition Cassette Series 6, Pibroch." Edinburgh: School of Scottish Studies, University of Edinburgh, 1982.

Coombe, William. *The Tour of Dr Prosody in Search of the Antique and the Picturesque, through Scotland.* London, 1821.

Cox, J. Charles, ed. *The Sports and Pastimes of the People of England from the earliest period ... by Joseph Strutt 1801.* London: Methuen and Co, 1903.

Craig, David. *On the Crofters' Trail – In Search of the Clearance Highlanders.* London: Cape, 1990.

Craig, K.C., ed. *Orain Luaidh.* Glasgow: A. Matheson, 1949.

Craik, Sir Henry. *A Century of Scottish History from the Days before the '45 to those within Living Memory.* Edinburgh and London: Blackwood and Sons, 1911.

Craven, J.B. *Dioceses of Argyll and the Isles (records of 1560–1860).* Kirkwall: William Peace and Son, 1907.

Crawford, Scott A.G.M. "The Origins of Scottish Highland Games." *Scottish Journal of Physical Education* 12, no. 4 (November 1984).

Cregeen, E.R. "Donald Sinclair." *Tocher* 18, School of Scottish Studies, Edinburgh University 1975, 41–65.

– ed. *Inhabitants of the Argyle Estate, 1779.* Edinburgh: Scottish History Society, 4th series, vol. 1, 1963.

– "The tacksmen and Their Successors; A Study of Tenurial Re-organisation in Mull, Morven and Tiree in the Early 18th century." *Scottish Studies* 13 (1969): 93–144.

Creighton, Helen, and Calum MacLeod. *Gaelic Songs in Nova Scotia.* Reprint. Ottawa: National Museums of Canada, 1979.

Cromb, James. *The Highland Brigade: Its Battles and Its Heroes.* Edited and brought down to the end of the Boer War, 1902, by David L. Cromb. Stirling: Eneas Mackay, 1902.

Culloden Papers Comprising an Extensive and Interesting Correspondence from the Year 1625 to 1748. Compiled from MSS in the possession of Duncan George Forbes of Culloden, Esq. London, 1815.

Cunningham, Audrey. *The Loyal Clans.* Cambridge: Cambridge University Press, 1932.

Currie, James. *The Life of Robert Burns with His General Correspondence; also a Criticism of his Writings, and Observations on the Scottish Peasantry by Dr. Currie.* London: Jones and Co., 1800.

Dalrymple, Sir John. *Memoirs of Great Britain and Ireland from the Dissolution of the Last Parliament of Charles II ... to the Battle of La Hogue.* 2d edition. London: W. Strahan & T. Cadell, 1771–88.

Dalyell, Sir John Graham. *Musical Memoirs of Scotland, with Historical Annotations.* Edinburgh, 1849.

Damon, S. Foster. *The History of Square Dancing.* Barre, MA: Barre Gazette, 1957.

Davidson, Major Hugh. *History and Services of the 78th Highlander Ross-shire Buffs 1793–1881. Compiled from the Manuscripts of the Late Major Colin Mackenzie and Official and Other Sources.* 2 vols. Edinburgh: W. and A.K. Johnston, 1901.

de Saussure, Necker. *Voyage to the Hebrides.* N.p., 1822.

– *Voyages en Ecosse.* 1822. Ann Arbor & London: University Microfilms Inc.

Devine, Thomas M. "The Flight of the Poor: Highland Emigration to Canada in the Mid-Nineteenth Century." In *Celtic Languages and Celtic Peoples*, edited by Cyril J. Byrne, Margaret Harry, and Pàdraig Ó'Siadhail. Proceedings of the Second North American Congress of Celtic Studies. Halifax, NS: St Mary's University, 1992.

Diary of an inhabitant of East Lake Ainslie. In the possession of Charles and Jesse MacDonald, East Lake Ainslie.

Dictionary of Canadian Biography. Vol. 8. "Rankin Coun Douly (Condulli) (Conduiligh MacRaing)," 740–2. Toronto: University of Toronto Press, 1985.

Dixon, John H. *Gairloch in North-west Ross-shire – Its Records, Traditions, Inhabitants, and Natural History with a Guide to Gairloch and Loch Maree and a Map and Illustrations.* Edinburgh, 1886.

DMcL (possibly HDMcL, Hugh D. MacLennan). "Free Church of Scotland." In *The Companion to Gaelic Scotland,* edited by Derick Thomson, 86–9. Oxford: Blackwell, 1983.

Drummond, P.R. *Perthshire in Bygone Days: One Hundred Biographical Essays.* London: W.B. Whittingham and Co., 1879.

Duclos, B. *Itinéraire et Souvenirs d'Angleterre et d'Écosse, 1814–1826.* 4 vols. Paris, 1834.

Dughalach, Ailean. *Orain, Marbhrannan agus Duanan Ghaidhealach.* Untranslated. N.p.: Alastair MacIntosh, 1829.

– *Orain Ghàidhealacha; maille ri co' chruinneachadh òran is dhàn le ùghdairibh eile.* Untranslated. N.p., 1798.

The Duke of Atholl. "The 77th Regiment of Foot or Atholl Highlanders." In *Military History of Perthshire*, edited by Marchioness of Tullibardine. Glasgow: R.A. and J. Hay, 1908.

Duncanson, John Victor. *Rawdon and Douglas – Two Loyalist Townships in Nova Scotia.* Belleville, ON: Mika Publishing, 1989.

Dunn-Pattison, R.P. *The History of the 91st Argyllshire Highlanders now the 1st Battalion Princess Louise's (Argyll and Sutherland Highlanders).* Edinburgh and London: Blackwood and Sons, 1910.

Dwelly, Edward. *The Illustrated Gaelic-English Dictionary.* 7th ed. Glasgow: Gairm Publications, 1971.

Elliott, Shirley B., ed. and rev. *The Legislative Assembly of Nova Scotia 1758–1983, a Biographical Directory.* Halifax, NS: Government Services Information Services, 1984.

Emmerson, George S. *Rantin' Pipe and Tremblin' String, a History of Scottish Dance Music.* Montreal: McGill-Queen's University Press, 1971.

– *A Social History of Scottish Dance.* Montreal: McGill-Queen's University Press, 1972.

Ewart, Lt Gen. John A. *The Story of a Soldier's Life; or Peace, War and Mutiny.* 2 vols. London, 1881.

Ewing, Rev. William, ed. *Annals of the Free Church of Scotland 1843–1900.* 2 vols. Edinburgh: T. and T. Clark, 1914.

Farmer, John S. *The Regimental Records of the British Army, A Historical Résumé Chronologically Arranged of Titles, Campaigns, Honours, Uniforms, Facings, Badges, Nicknames, Etc.* London: Grant Richards, 1901.

Faujas de Saint Fond, B. *A Journey through England and Scotland to the Hebrides in 1784.* Edited with notes by Archibald Geikie. Revised version of the English translation. N.p., 1907.

– *Voyage en Angleterre, en Écosse et aux îles Hébrides, ayant pour objet les Sciences, l'Histoire naturelle et les Mœurs.* 2 vols. Paris, 1797.

Ferguson, James, ed. "Papers Illustrating the History of The Scots Brigade in the Service of the United Netherlands 1572–1782 Extracted by permission from the Government Archives at The Hague." In *Publications of the Scottish History Society*, edited by James Ferguson. Vols. 32, 35 and 38. Edinburgh, 1899, 1901.

Ferguson, Joan P.S. *Scottish Family Histories.* Rev. ed. Edinburgh: Her Majesty's Stationery Office, 1986.

Fergusson, Donald A., ed. *Fad air falbh as Innse Gall leis comh chruinneachadh Cheap Breatunn (Beyond the Hebrides).* Halifax, NS: Printers Lawson Graphics Atlantic, 1977.

– *From the Farthest Hebrides.* Toronto: MacMillan of Canada, 1978.

Fergusson, Sir James of Kilkerran. *Argyll in the Forty-five.* London: Faber and Faber, n.d.

Ferrar, Major M.L. *A History of the Services of the 19th Regiment ... from its Formation in 1688 to 1911.* London: Eden Fisher and Co., 1911.

Findlay, J.T. *Wolfe in Scotland in the '45 and from 1749 to 1753.* London: Longmans, Green and Co., 1928.

Fionn (Henry Whyte). *The Martial Music of the Clans with Historic, Biographic, & Legendary Notes regarding the Origin of the Music, also portraits of Highland chiefs & Distinguished Clansmen, with their Seats, Arms, etc. etc.* Glasgow: J. MacKay, 1904.

Fischer, Th. A. *The Scots in Germany: Being a Contribution towards the History of the Scot Abroad.* Edinburgh: John Donald Publishers, n.d. (1902?).

Fleming, James A., ed. *The Scots Statutes Revised, volume 1, The Public General Statutes Affecting Scotland 1707–1819, 6 Anne to 60 George III. & 1 George IV.* Edinburgh: William Green and Sons, Law Publishers, 1899.

Flett, J.F., and T.M. Flett. *Traditional Dancing in Scotland.* London: Routledge and Kegan Paul, 1964.

– "Some Early Highland Dancing Competitions." *Aberdeen University Review* 36, no. 115 (Autumn 1956): 345–58, Aberdeen.

Flinn, Michael, ed. *Scottish Population History from the 17th Century to the 1930s.* Cambridge: Cambridge University Press, 1977.

Forbes, Robert, A.M. *The Lyon in Mourning or a Collection of Speeches Letters Journals etc. relative to the Affairs of Prince Charles Edward Stuart by the Rev. Robert Forbes A.M. Bishop of Ross and Caithness 1746–1775.* Edited by Henry Paton. 3 vols. Edinburgh: Scottish Academic Press, 1975.

Forsyth, the Reverend W. *In the Shadow of Cairngorm – Chronicles of the united Parishes of Abernethy and Kincardine.* Inverness: Northern Counties Publishing Co., 1900.

Fraser, A. Duncan. *Some Reminiscences and the Bagpipe.* Edinburgh, 1907.

Fraser, Alexander. *History of the Frasers of Lovat.* Inverness, 1896.

Fraser, Alexander (Alasdair Friseal). *The last laird of MacNab: an Episode in the Settlement of MacNab Township, Upper Canada.* Toronto: Imrie, Graham and Co., 1899.

Fraser, Alexander. *The Royal Burgh of Inveraray.* Edinburgh: Saint Andrew Press, 1977.

Fraser, Capt. Simon, ed. *The Airs and Melodies peculiar to the Highlands of Scotland and The Isles, communicated in an original pleasing & familiar style, having the lively airs introduced as medleys to form a sequence to each slower movement; with an admired plain harmony for the piano forte, harp, organ or violoncello, and Chiefly acquired during the interesting Period from 1715 to 1745, through the Authentic Source narrated in the Accompanying Prospectus.* 1816. Reprint. With introduction by Paul S. Cranford. Sydney, NS: 1982.

Fraser, Sir William. *Papers from the Collection of Sir William Fraser K.C.B., LL.D.* Edited by J.R.N. MacPhail. Edinburgh: Edinburgh University Press for T. and A. Constable, 1924.

Fraser, William LL.D. *The Chiefs of Grant.* 2 vols. Edinburgh, 1883.

Fraser-Mackintosh, Charles. "Glengarry – Coll MacDonell of Barisdale." In Charles Fraser-Mackintosh. *Antiquarian Notes.* 2d series. Inverness: N.p., 1897.

– "Minor Highland Septs – The MacDonells of Barisdale." *Transactions of the Gaelic Society of Inverness* 13 (1886–87): 84–102.

– *Antiquarian Notes.* 2d series. Inverness: n.p., 1897.

– *Letters of Two Centuries chiefly Connected with Inverness and the Highlands, from 1616 to 1815.* Inverness, 1890.

Friseal, Alasdair. *Leabhar Nan Sonn Gearr-aithris air Curaidhean na Craoibhe Ruaidhe is air Diulanaich Iomraiteach La an Diugh.* Untranslated. 2d ed. Toronto: Uilleam Briggs, 1897.

Gardner, Brian. *The East India Company – A History.* New York: Dorset Press, 1990.

Gardyne, Lt Col C. Greenhill. *Life of a Regiment, the History of the Gordon Highlanders from its Formation in 1794 to 1816.* Edinburgh: D. Douglas, 1901.

Geikie, Archibald, ed. *The Life of Sir Roderick I. Murchison.* 2 vols. London, 1875.

Gibson, John G. "Genealogical and Piping Notes from 'Squire' John MacKay's 'Reminiscences of a Long Life (c. 1794–1884)." *The Scottish Genealogist Quarterly Journal of the Scottish Genealogy Society* 30, no. 3 (September 1983): 94–8.

– "Piper John MacKay and Roderick McLennan: A Tale of Two Immigrants." *Nova Scotia Historical Review* 2, no. 2 (December 1982): 69–82.

– "Mabou in Its Halcyon Days," "Sunflower" (insert of the *Scotia Sun* weekly newspaper), Port Hawkesbury, NS, 19 May 1982.

Gibson, John Sibbald. *Lochiel of the '45 – The Jacobite Chief and the Prince.* Edinburgh: Edinburgh University Press, 1994.

Gillies, Rev. William A. *In Famed Breadalbane – The Story of the Antiquities, Lands, and People of a Highland District.* Reprint. Strathtay: Clunie Press, 1987.

Gillies, William, ed. *Alba agus a'Ghàidhlig.* Edinburgh: Edinburgh University Press, 1989.

Gillis, Allan. "From Kitchens to Pipebands Alex 'the piper' MacDonald – piper of transition." *Am Bràighe* (Summer 1993): 20–2.

Gillis, Bernard, comp. *Smeòrach nan Cnoc 's nan Gleann Comh-Chruinneachadh Bardachd a chaidh a dheanamh am Margairi an Iar-Dheas, Ceap Breatainn.* Glasgow: Alasdair Maclabhruinn Agus a Mhic, 1939.

Gillis, James D. *A Little Sketch of My Life.* Halifax, NS: N.p., n.d.

Glen, David. *The Music of the Clan MacLean compiled & arranged under the Auspices of the Clan MacLean Association & dedicated to Colonel Sir Fitzroy Donald MacLean, Bart. C.B. Chief of the Clan.* Edinburgh: David Glen, 1900.

Glen, John. *Early Scottish Melodies.* Edinburgh: J. and R. Glen, 1900.

Glen, Robert. "Notes on the Ancient Musical Instruments of Scotland." *Proceedings of the Society of Antiquaries* 2, new series (1880): 114–25.

Goff, G.L., arranger. *Historical Records of the 91st Argyllshire Highlanders.* London, 1891.

Gordon, Seton Paul. *Hebridean Memories.* London: Cassell and Co., 1923.

– *Highland Summer.* London: Cassell and Co., 1971.

Government of Nova Scotia. *The Revised Statutes of Nova Scotia.* Halifax, NS: Queen's Printer.

Graham, I.C.C. *Colonists from Scotland: Emigration to North America, 1707–1783.* Ithaca, NY: Cornell University Press, 1956.

Grant, Elizabeth. *Memoirs of a Highland Lady, 1797–1827.* London: Albemarle Library, 1960.

Grant, I.F. *The MacLeods: The History of a Clan 1200–1956.* London: Faber and Faber, 1959.

Grant, James. *The Scottish Soldiers of Fortune, their Adventures and Achievements in the Armies of Europe.* London, 1890.

Grant, James. *Thoughts on the Origin and Descent of the Gael: with an account of the Picts, Caledonians, and Scots; and observations relative to the authenticity of the poems of Ossian.* Edinburgh: Archibald Constable and Co., 1814.

Grove, Lilly. *Dancing.* London, 1895.

Gunn, Mark Rugg. *History of the Clan Gunn.* Glasgow: Alex. McLaren and Sons, 1969.

Haldane, A.R.B. *The Drove Roads of Scotland.* London: Nelson, 1952.

Haldane, M.M. "The Royal Scots (Lothian Regiment)." In *The Lowland Scots Regiments, their Origin, Character and Services previous to the Great War of 1914,* edited by Herbert E. Maxwell. Glasgow: J. Maclehose and Sons, 1918.

Hall, Rev. James. *Travels in Scotland, by an Unusual Route.* 2 vols. London, 1807.

Handley, James E. *Scottish Farming in the Eighteenth Century.* London: Faber and Faber, 1953.

Harper, J.R. *The Fraser Highlanders.* Montreal: Society of the Montreal Military and Maritime Museum, 1979.

Harper, J. Ralph. *The 78th Fighting Frasers, A Short History of the Old 78th Regiment of Fraser's Highlanders 1757–1763.* Chomedey, PQ: Devsco Publishing, 1966.

Hassall, Arthur. *The Balance of Power 1715–1789.* London and New York: Macmillan, 1914.

Hawkins, Marjorie (MacKenzie), Hector L. MacKenzie, and John R. MacQuarrie. *Gairloch, Pictou County, Nova Scotia.* N.p.: N.p., 1977.

Henderson, Diana M. *Highland Soldier – A Social Study of the Highland Regiments, 1820–1920.* Edinburgh: John Donald Publishers Ltd, 1989.

Henderson, George. *Dàin Iain Ghobha.* 2d ed. 2 vols. Glasgow and Edinburgh, 1896.

Hereditary Ear-Pipers to the Duke of Atholl. *Piping Times* 27, no. 6 (March 1975).

Heron, Robert. *Observations made in a Journey through the Western Counties of Scotland; in the Autumn of M,DCC,XCII. Relating to the Scenery, Antiquities, Customs, Manners, Population, Agriculture, Manufactures, Commerce, Political Condition, and Literature of these Parts.* 2 vols. Perth, 1793.

Hibbert, Christopher. *George IV Prince of Wales 1762–1811.* London: Longman, 1972.

Holland, Lord, ed. *Memoirs of the Reign of King George the Second by Horace Walpole, Youngest Son of Sir Robert Walpole, Earl of Orford.* Rev. ed. London, 1847.

Home, John. *John Home's Survey of Assynt.* Edited by R.J. Adam. Scottish History Society, 3d series, vol. 52. Edinburgh: T. and A. Constable, 1960.

Home, John, Esq. *The History of the Rebellion in Scotland in 1745.* Edinburgh, 1822.

Hutchison, Col Paul. *Canada's Black Watch – The First Hundred Years, 1862–1962.* Montreal: Black Watch (RHR) of Canada, 1962. Reprint. 1987.

Jameson, Captain Robert. *Historical Record of the Seventy-ninth Regiment of Foot or Cameron Highlanders.* Edinburgh and London: Blackwoods, 1863.

Johnson, David. *Music and Society in Lowland Scotland in the Eighteenth Century.* London: Oxford University Press, 1972.

– *Scottish Fiddle Music in the 18th Century – A Music Collection and Historical Study.* Edinburgh: John Donald Publishers, 1984.

Johnson, Samuel. *A Journey to the Western Islands of Scotland.* Introduction and notes by J.D. Fleeman. Oxford, 1985.

Johnston, the Reverend A.A. *A History of the Catholic Church in Eastern Nova Scotia.* 2 vols. Antigonish, NS: Saint Francis Xavier University Press, 1960, 1971.

Keltie, Sir John Scott, ed. *A History of the Scottish Highlands, Highland Clans and Highland Regiments.* 2 vols. Edinburgh and London, 1875.

Kilgour, W.T. *Lochaber in War and Peace, being a Record of Historical Incidents, Legends, Traditions, and Folk-lore with Notes on the Topography and Scenic Beauties of the Whole District.* Paisley: A. Gardner, 1908.

King, J.B. "'Waterloo' MacLeod." In John R. MacQuarrie, *Lansdowne Sketches: Battery Hill, Wilkins Grant, Upper New Lairg.* 2d ed. Pugwash, NS: Published by the author, 1975.

Kitzmiller, John M. II. *In Search of "Forlorn Hope," a Comprehensive Guide to Locating British Regiments and Their Records (1640–WWI).* 2 vols. Ogden, UT: Manuscript Pub. Foundation, 1988.

Knox, John. *A Tour through the Highlands of Scotland and the Hebride Isles in 1786.* London, n.d.

Kyd, J.G. *Scottish Population Statistics.* Edinburgh: Scottish History Society, 1952.

Lang, Andrew, *The Companions of Pickle; being a Sequel to 'Pickle the Spy.'* London, 1898.

– *Pickle the Spy, or the Incognito of Prince Charles.* 3d ed. London, 1897.

Lawrance, Robert Murdoch. The Bagpipe in History and Anecdote. Aberdeen: William Smith and Sons, The Bon-Accord Press, 1928.

Lees, J. Cameron. *History of the County of Inverness (Mainland).* London: W. Blackwood, 1897.

Leith, William Forbes. *Memoirs of Scottish Catholics during the XVIIth and XVIIIth Centuries.* 2 vols. London: Longmans, Green and Co, 1909.

Leneman, Leah. *Living in Atholl – A Social History of the Estates 1685–1785.* Edinburgh: Edinburgh University Press, 1986.

Lewin, Henry Ross. The Life of a Soldier. A Narrative of Twenty-seven Years' Service ... by a Field Officer. N.p., 1834. Also published as *With "The Thirty-Second" in the Peninsular and other Campaigns.* Dublin: J. Wardell, Hodges, Figgis and Co., 1904.

Leyden, John. *Preliminary Dissertation to the Complaynt of Scotland.* Edinburgh, 1801.

Lindsay, Ian G., and Mary Cosh. *Inveraray and the Dukes of Argyll.* Edinburgh: Edinburgh University Press, 1973.

Lockhart, John Gibson. *Memoirs of the Life of Sir Walter Scott.* 7 vols, Edinburgh, 1837, 1838.

Logan, James. *The Scottish Gaël; or, Celtic Manners, as Preserved among the Highlanders.* 2 vols. London, 1831.

Lord Cockburn. *Circuit Journeys by the Late Lord Cockburn.* Edinburgh: David Douglas, 1888.

MacAulay, Alexander. "The MacKenzies of Loch Boisdale." *Piping Times* 13, no. 10 (July 1961).

– "The Art and History of the MacDougalls of Aberfeldy." *Piping Times* 16, no. 4 (January 1964).

MacAulay, Donald, and Donald McClure, eds. *Scottish Language.* Proceedings of the First International Conference on the Languages of Scotland, University of Aberdeen, 26–29 July 1985. Aberdeen: The University Press, n.d.

MacCalum, Urr. (Rev.) Iain. *Cunntas Aithghearr air Iain Wesley agus Sgriobhaidhean Eile.* Untranslated. Glasgow: Gilleasbuig Mac-na-Ceardadh, 1911.

MacCulloch, John. *A Description of the Western Islands of Scotland, Including the Isle of Man.* 3 vols. London, 1819.

MacCulloch, John. *The Highlands and Western Isles of Scotland containing Descriptions of their Scenery and Antiquities, with an Account of the Political History and Ancient Manners, and of the Origin, Language, Agriculture, Economy, Music, Present Condition of the People &c. &c. &c. founded on a Series of Annual Journeys between the Years 1811 and 1821, and forming an Universal Guide to that Country, in letters to Sir Walter Scott, Bart.* 4 vols. London, 1824.

MacDermid, "The Religious and Ecclesiastic Life of the Northern Highlands 1750–1843." PhD thesis; University of Aberdeen, n.d.

MacDonald, Rev. A., and Rev. A. MacDonald. *Clan Donald.* 3 vols. Inverness: Northern Counties Publishing Co., 1900.

MacDonald, Alasdair (the Big Painter). "Is mo luaidh na fir." Song published in *MacTalla* 11, no. 14 (9 January 1903): 112.

MacDonald, Alexander. *Ais-Eiridh na Sean-Chanoin Albannaich.* Untranslated. Edinburgh, 1751.

– "Beannacha Luinge, maille ri brosnacha fairge, a rinneadh do sgioba birlinn Thighearna Chlann-Raonuill." Untranslated. In John MacKenzie, Esq. *Sar-Obair* ... 136–42. New edition. Edinburgh: N. MacLeod, 1904.

MacDonald, Alexander. "The Glenmoriston Bard." *Transactions of the Gaelic Society of Inverness* 12 (1885–86): 226–43.

MacDonald, Alexander. *Story and Song from Loch Ness-side, Inverness.* 1914. Reprint. Inverness: Gaelic Society of Inverness, 1982.

MacDonald, Alexander D. *The Mabou Pioneers.* Re-issue. Antigonish, NS: Formac Publishing Company, n.d.

MacDonald, Father Allan. "Eilean na h-Oige." In *Bardachd Ghaidhlig. Gaelic Poetry 1550–1900*, edited by William J. Watson. Reprint. Inverness: An Commun Gaidhealach, 1976.

MacDonald, Catherine, John Colin MacDonald, John J. MacEachern, and Catherine MacDonald, eds. *The Clanranald Connection – A Commemorative Sketch of Clanranald People in Inverness County, Nova Scotia.* Booklet. N.p., n.p., August 1983.

MacDonald, Rev. Charles. *Moidart or Among the Clanranalds.* Oban: Duncan Cameron, 1889. Reprint. Edinburgh: James Thin, 1989.

MacDonald, the Reverend D. *Cape North and Vicinity – Pioneer Families History and Chronicles including Pleasant Bay, Bay St Lawrence, Aspy Bay, White Pointe, New Haven and Neil's Harbour.* N.p., n.p., 1933.

MacDonald, Donald. *A Collection of Quicksteps, Strathspeys, Reels & Jigs.* Edinburgh, 1828.

– *A Collection of the Ancient Martial Music of Caledonia called Piobaireachd.* Edinburgh, c. 1822. Reprint. Wakefield, UK: EP Publishing, 1974.

MacDonald, Hugh N. *Macdonald and Mackinnon Families (a Biographical Sketch).* Handwritten manuscript, dated 21 August 1937. Privately held, East Lake Ainslie, Nova Scotia.

MacDonald, Hugh N. *Macdonald and Mackinnon Families (A Biographical Sketch).* 2d ed. Truro, NS: N.p., 1937.

MacDonald, J.M. "Piping in Cape Breton." *Piping Times* 21, no. 2 (November 1968).

Macdonald, John. "MS Journal of John MacDonald." Unlocated. Cited in Rev. Angus Mackay. *The Book of MacKay.* Privately printed by William Rae, Wick, 1906.

MacDonald, Joseph. *A Compleat Theory of the Scots Highland Bagpipe.* 1803. Reprint. Wakefield, UK: S.R. Publishers, 1971.

MacDonald, Mildred, and John Colin. *Fair Is The Place – An account of Two Clanranald Families at Judique, Cape Breton.* Sydney, NS: City Printers, n.d. (1985).

MacDonald, Norman. *Canada, Immigration and Colonisation 1841–1903.* Toronto: MacMillan of Canada, 1966.

MacDonald, Patrick. *A Collection of Highland Vocal Airs Never hitherto published. To which are added a few of the most lively Country Dances or Reels of the North Highlands & Western Isles. And some Specimens of Bagpipe Music.* Edinburgh, 1784.

Macdonald, Stuart. *Back to Lochaber – A Search for Historic Events, Travels, Tales and Customs.* Edinburgh, Cambridge and Durham: The Pentland Press, 1994.

MacDonell, Colonel John, of Scottos. *Spanish John; being a Narrative of the Early Life of Colonel John McDonell of Scottos, Written by Himself.* Edinburgh and London: Blackwood and Sons, 1931.

MacDonell, Josephine, of Keppoch. *An Historical Record of the Branch of "Clann Domhnuill" called The MacDonells of Keppoch and Gargavach.* Glasgow: Archibald Sinclair, 1931.

MacDonell, Margaret. *The Emigrant Experience – Songs of Highland Emigrants in North America.* Toronto: University of Toronto Press, 1982.

MacDougall, J.L. *History of Inverness County.* Belleville, ON: Mika Publishing, Canadiana Reprint Series, No. 43, 1922, 1976.

MacFarlane, Robert. "Tenants in Brae Lochaber." Unpublished MS. Brits, South

Africa c.1995. Obtained from Ann MacDonell, Braevig, Spean Bridge, 1995, through Mary Campbell, Glenora, Inverness County, Nova Scotia. The cited contents of those legal documents under the headings SRO SC 28 and SC 29, which pertain to the MacGlaserich Campbells, were authenticated by the researcher Dr Ian S. MacDonald, Falkirk.

MacFarlane, Walter Scott. "Blow the Bugle." An unpublished elegy for Allan MacFarlane (d. 1938) the piper.

MacGill, William. *Old Ross-shire and Scotland from the Tain and Balnagown Documents.* Inverness: Northern Counties Newspaper and Printing and Publishing Company, 1901.

Mac Gill-eain, Somhairle. "Domhnall Donn of Bohuntin." In Somhairle Mac Gill-eain. *Ris a' Bhruthaich – The Criticism and Prose Writings of Sorley MacLean by Somhairle Mac Gill-eain.* Edited by William Gillies. Stornoway: Acair, 1985.

– *Ris a' Bhruthaich – The Criticism and Prose Writings of Sorley MacLean by Somhairle Mac Gill-eain.* Edited by William Gillies. Stornoway: Acair, 1985.

MacGillivray, Rev. Ronald (Sagairt Arasaig). "A History of the County of Antigonish, Nova Scotia." Published serially in *Casket*, 1890–92. Reprint. *History of Antigonish.* Edited by R.A. MacLean. Antigonish, NS: Casket printing and Publishing Company, 1976.

MacGregor, John. *Our Brothers and Cousins: A Summer Tour in Canada and the States.* London, 1859.

MacInnes, Daniel W. and Anthony Davis. "Some Religious Implications of the 1764–1765 Census of the Small Isles." A talk delivered by Professor MacInnes at "Scotia and Nova Scotia," a conference held at Saint Mary's University, Halifax, Nova Scotia, 26–29 September 1996.

MacIntyre, Duncan Ban. "Ode to Gaelic and the Great Pipe in the year 1783." In *Orain Dhonnchaidh Bhàin – The Songs of Duncan Ban MacIntyre,* edited and translated by Angus MacLeod, 282–5. Edinburgh: Scottish Gaelic Texts Society (vol. 4), 1952.

Mackay, Rev. Angus. *The Book of MacKay.* Privately printed by William Rae, Wick, 1906.

MacKay, Angus. *A Collection of Ancient Piobaireachd or Highland Pipe Music, many of the pieces being adapted to the piano forte with full instructions for those desirous of qualifying themselves in performing on the National Instrument. to which are prefixed some sketches of the principal HEREDITARY PIPERS and their ESTABLISHMENTS with historical & traditional notes respecting the origin of the various pieces. Dedicated by permission to the Highland Society of London.* Includes N.a. "A Circumstantial Account of the Competitions for the Prizes given by the Highland Society in London, to the best Performers on the Great Highland Bagpipe, from the year 1781," 15–20; N.a. "Account of the Hereditary Pipers," 7–14; and N.a. "Historical and Traditional Notes on the Piobaireachds," 1–14. Wakefield, UK: EP Publishing, 1972.

MacKay, Annie. "All We Know About Our Grandparents." Holograph longhand MS privately held by Sandy MacKay, Lyon's Brook, Pictou County, Nova Scotia.

MacKay, Donald. *Scotland Farewell: The People of the Hector.* Toronto and Edinburgh: McGraw-Hill Ryerson/Paul Harris Publishing, 1980.

MacKay, Iain R. "Glenalladale's Settlement, Prince Edward Island." *Scottish Gaelic Studies* (University of Aberdeen) 10, part 1 (August 1963): 16–24.

MacKay, William. *Urquhart and Glenmoriston.* Inverness, 1893.

MacKenzie, Alexander. "The Editor in Canada." *Celtic Magazine* 5, no. 49 (November 1879).

– *History of the Chisholms, with Genealogies of the Principal Families of the Name.* Inverness, 1891.

– *The History of the Clan MacKenzie.* Bound copies of *Celtic Magazine* articles from November 1877–79. Held by St Francis Xavier University Library, Antigonish, Nova Scotia.

– *History of the Frasers of Lovat.* Inverness, 1896.

– *History of the MacDonalds and Lords of the Isles.* Inverness, 1881.

MacKenzie, Annie M., ed. *Orain Iain Luim: Songs of John MacDonald Bard of Keppoch.* Edinburgh: Scottish Gaelic Texts Society, 1964.

MacKenzie, Archibald A. *The MacKenzies' History of Christmas Island Parish, the original 1926 edition revised and updated by His Son Archibald A. MacKenzie.* Sudbury, ON: Mackenzie Rothe Publishers, 1984.

MacKenzie, B.D. "General Thomason and Ceòl Mór." *Transactions of the Gaelic Society of Inverness* 57 (1990–92): 58–72.

MacKenzie, John, Esq. "Dughall Bochannan." In John MacKenzie, Esq. *Sar-Obair* ... 167–181. New edition. Edinburgh: N. MacLeod, 1904.

MacKenzie, John, Esq. *Sar-Obair nam Bard Gaelach: or, The Beauties of Gaelic Poetry, and Lives of the Highland bards; with Historical and Critical Notes, and a Comprehensive Glossary of Provincial Words.* New edition. Edinburgh: N. MacLeod, 1904.

MacKenzie, Osgood Hanbury. *A Hundred Years in the Highlands.* New edition. London: Geoffrey Bles Ltd, 1952.

MacKenzie, William C. *History of the Outer Hebrides.* Paisley: A. Gardner, 1903.

MacKinnon, Rev. Dr Donald, and Alick Morrison. *The MacLeods – The Genealogy of a Clan.* Section one. "MacLeod Chiefs of Harris and Dunvegan." Edinburgh: Clan MacLeod Society, 1969.

MacKinnon, Hugh. "The MacDonalds of Laig." *Tocher* 10, University of Edinburgh, School of Scottish Studies.

MacKinnon, James N. *A Short History of the Pioneer Scotch Settlers of St Andrews, Sask.* Regina: Saskatchewan Archives Board, n.d.

MacKinnon, Kenneth. "Captain John MacDonald and the Glenaladale Settlers." In *Celtic Language and Celtic Peoples,* edited by Cryil J. Byrne et al. Proceedings of the Second North American Congress of Celtic Studies. Halifax, NS: St Mary's University, 1992.

MacKinnon, Kenneth. *The Lion's Tongue. The Story of the Original and Continuing Language of the Scottish People.* Inverness: Club Leabhar, 1974.

MacKinnon, P.-M. Stephen. "The Bagpipe in Canada." *Canadian Geographical Journal* (April 1932).

Mackintosh, Sir Aeneas, Bart. *Notes Descriptive and Historical Principally Relating to the Parish of Moy in Strathdearn and the Town and Neighbourhood of Inverness.* N.p., 1892.

Mackintosh, H.B. *The Inverness Shire Highlanders or 97th Regiment of Foot 1794–1796.* Elgin: J.D. Yeadon, 1926.

Mackintosh, Margaret. *The Clan Mackintosh and the Clan Chattan.* Edinburgh and London: W. and A.K. Johnston, 1948.

MacLaren, George. *The Pictou Book: Stories of Our Past.* New Glasgow: Hector Publishing, 1954.

MacLean, John. "Am Piobaire Dall." *Transactions of the Gaelic Society of Inverness* 41 (1951–52): 283–306.

MacLean, John of Inverscadale. "Oran an déidh Blàr Chuil-lodair." in *Songs Remembered in Exile* ... edited by John Lorne Campbell, most tunes transcribed by Séamus Ennis. Aberdeen: Aberdeen University Press, 1990.

MacLean, J.P. *An Historical Account of the Settlements of Scotch Highlanders in America prior to the Peace of 1783 together with Notices of Highland Regiments and Biographical sketches.* Cleveland: Helman-Taylor Co., 1900. Reprint. Baltimore: N.p., 1968.

MacLean, J.P. *The History of Clan MacLean.* Cincinnati: R. Clarke and Co., 1889. Reprint. N.p., n.p., 1986.

MacLean, R.A. *The Casket 1852–1992 – From Gutenberg to Internet: The Story of a Small-Town Weekly.* Antigonish, NS: Casket Printing and Publishing Company, 1995.

MacLellan, Captain John. "Tenth Hereditary Piper to the Clan MacLeod." *International Piper* 3, no. 1 (May 1980).

MacLennan, John. "'A Dictionary of Pipers and Piping' 'Notices of Scottish Highland Pipers ... originally compiled by Lieutenant John MacLennan and Revised and Added to by Major I.J. MacKay Scobie, F.S.A. (Scot.)' 'with further additions by Archbald Campbell, Kilberry.'" *Piping Times* 20, no. 10 (July 1968).

MacLennan, Ronald George. *The History of the MacLennans.* Inverness: John G. Eccles Printers, 1978.

MacLeod, Angus, ed. and trans. *Orain Dhonnchaidh Bhàin – The Songs of Duncan Ban MacIntyre.* Edinburgh: Scottish Gaelic Texts Society, No. 4, 1952.

MacLeod, Rev. Donald. *Memoir of Norman MacLeod, D.D.* Toronto, 1876.

MacLeod, Norman. *Caraid nan Gàidheal (The Friend of the Gael.) A choice selection of the Gaelic Writings of the late Norman MacLeod, D.D., of St. Columba Parish, Glasgow ... with a memoir of the author by his son, the late Norman MacLeod, D.D., of the Barony Parish, Glasgow, selected and edited by Rev. A. Clerk, LL.D, (minister of Kilmallie).* New Edition. Edinburgh: Norman MacLeod, 1899.

MacLeod, Ruairidh Halford. "'The Best Piper of His Time' MacCrimmon.'" *Clan MacLeod Magazine* 9, nos. 54 and 55 (1982): 66–73.

MacLeod, Ruairidh Halford. "Early MacCrimmon Records." *Piping Times* 29, no. 5 (February 1977).

– "The MacCrimmons and the '45." *Piping Times* 29, no. 6 (March 1977).

– "The End of the MacCrimmon College." *Piping Times* 29, no. 8 (May 1977).

MacLeòid, Calum Iain. *Bardachd a Albainn Nuaidh.* Untranslated. Glasgow: Gairm, 1970.

– *An t-Eilthireach Original Gaelic Poems and Melodies.* Glace Bay, NS: Brodie Printing Service, 1952.

– *Sgialachdan á Albainn Nuaidh.* Untranslated. Glasgow: Gairm, 1969.

MacMillan, Rev. Allan J. *To the Hill of Boisdale, A Short History and a Genealogical Tracing of the Pioneer Families of Boisdale, Cape Breton, and the Surrounding Areas.* Sydney, NS: City Printers, 1986.

MacMillan, Somerled. *Bygone Lochaber – Historical and Traditional.* Glasgow: Printed by K. and R. Davidson, 1971.

MacNeil, Neil. *The Highland Heart in Nova Scotia.* Reprint. Toronto: Saunders, 1969.

MacNeil, Stephen R. *All Call Iona Home.* Antigonish, NS: Formac Publishing, 1979.

MacNeill, Archie. "Early Piping Days." *Piping Times* 12, no. 6 (March 1960):16–22.

Macphail, J.R.N., ed. *Highland Papers.* Edinburgh: Scottish History Society, vol. 1, 1914.

MacPherson, Alexander. *Glimpses of Church and Social Life in the Highlands of Olden Times.* London and Edinburgh: Blackwoods, 1893.

– *Old Church and Social Life in the Highlands.* Edinburgh, 1893.

MacPherson, John. *Tales from Barra, told by the Coddy (John MacPherson, North Bay, Barra, 1876–1955).* Foreword by Compton MacKenzie. Introduction and notes by John Lorne Campbell. Edinburgh: W. and A.K. Johnston, 1960.

MacPherson, Norman. "Notes on Antiquities from the Island of Eigg." *Proceedings of the Society of Antiquaries of Scotland* 12, part 2 (1876–77): 577–97.

MacQuarrie, Gordon F., compiler and arranger. *The Cape Breton Collection of Scottish Melodies for the Violin Consisting of Marches, Slow Airs, Strathspeys, Reels, Jigs, Hornpipes, Etc. Mostly Original, and Containing 152 Selections.* Edited by J. Beaton. Originally printed in 1940. 2d printing. Medford, MA: J. Beaton, 1975.

MacQuarrie, John R. *Lansdowne Sketches: Battery Hill, Wilkins Grant, Upper New Lairg.* 2d ed. Pugwash, NS: Published by the author, 1975.

MacQueen, Malcolm A. *Skye Pioneers and "The Island."* Winnipeg: Stovel Co, 1929.

MacRae, Rev. Alexander. *History of the Clan MacRae with Genealogies.* Dingwall, Scotland, 1899.

MacRae, Alexander. *Revivals in the Highlands and the Islands in the 19th Century,* Stirling: Eneas McKay, n.d. (1906?).

MacRae, Finlay. "An Old Bagpipe." *Piping Times* 30, no. 5 (May 1978).

Manson, W. L. *The Highland Bagpipe – Its History, Literature and Music.* Paisley: A. Gardner, 1901.

Marchioness of Tullibardine, ed. *A Military History of Perthshire.* Glasgow and Edinburgh: R.A and J. Hay, 1908.

Martz, Louis L. *The Later Career of Tobias Smollett.* New Haven: Yale University Press, 1942.

Matheson, Angus. *The Appin Murder – A Traditional Account reprinted from Vol. XXXV of the Transactions of the Gaelic Society of Inverness.* Inverness: Club Leabhar, 1975.

Matheson, William. "Duncan MacDonald (1882–1954)." *Tocher* 25, School of Scottish Studies, University of Edinburgh (Spring 1977): 1.

Matheson, William, ed. *The Songs of John MacCodrum, Bard to Sir James MacDonald of Sleat.* Edinburgh: Scottish Gaelic Texts Society, vol. 2, 1938.

Mathews, Hazel C. *The Mark of Honour.* Toronto: University of Toronto Press, 1965.

Maxwell, Herbert E, ed. *The Lowland Scots Regiments, their Origin, Character and Services previous to the Great War of 1914.* Glasgow: J. Maclehose and Sons, 1918.

McAfee, Michael J. "79th Regiment, New York State Militia." Under the heading "Uniforms and History." *Military Images* 11, no. 2 (September-October 1989): 28–9.

McCombie-Smith, W. *Memoirs of the Family of McCombie and Thoms.* Edinburgh: W. Blackwood and Sons, 1890.

McCrimmon, Madeleine, and Donaldson R. MacLeod, *Lochinvar to Skye – 1794–1987* (alternate title, *Lochinvar to Skye, A History of the Areas along the Roads East and West of McCrimmon*). N.p. (Ontario): Lomar Printers, 1988.

McDonell Dawson, Aeneas. *The Catholics of Scotland – From 1593, and the Extinction of the Hierarchy in 1603, till the Death of Bishop Carruthers in 1852.* London, Ontario, 1890.

McIntyre, Leo. "The Cape Breton Highlanders." In *More Essays in Cape Breton History*, edited by R.J. Morgan, 50–61. Windsor, NS: Lancelot Press, 1977.

McKay, Neville T. "A History of the Office of Piper to the Sovereign." *Folk Music Journal* (English Folk Dance and Song Society) 7, no. 2 (1996): 188–204.

McLachlan, John, ed. *The Piper's Assistant – A new Collection of Marches, Quick-steps, Strathspeys, Reels & Jigs.* Edinburgh, May, 1854.

McLean, John. *Notes of a Twenty-Five Years' Service in the Hudson's Bay Territory.* 2 vols. London: Richard Bentley, 1849. Facsimile edition. 1 vol. Edited by W.S. Wallace. New York: Greenwood Press, 1968.

McLean, Marianne. *The People of Glengarry, Highlanders in Transition, 1745–1820.* Montreal: McGill-Queen's University Press, 1991.

McLeod, James R. "John McKay's Black House at Eyre, Raasay." Part 1. *Piping Times* 45, no. 5 (February 1993).

McLeod, Malcolm, ed. *Peace River. A Canoe Voyage from Hudson's Bay to the Pacific, by the late Sir George Simpson; (Governor, Hon. Hudson's Bay Company) in 1828. Journal of Canoe Voyage from Hudson's Bay to the Pacific by the late Sir George Simpson, Governor of the Honorable Hudson's Bay Company. Journal of the late Archibald McDonald, Esquire, Chief Factor, Honorable Hudson's Bay Company, who accompanied him.* Montreal and Toronto, 1872. Facsimile edition. Toronto: Coles Canadiana Collection, 1970.

McNaspy, C.J., trans. *The Motu Proprio of Church Music of Pope Pius X – A New Translation and Commentary.* Toledo, OH: Georgian Institute of America, 1948.

McNeil, Bill. *Voice of the Pioneer.* Toronto: MacMillan of Canada, 1978.

McNeill, Neill. "Census of the Small Isles 1764–65, at Canna 20th March 1765." Appendices 2 and 3 transcribed by Catherine MacInnes and Catherine and Alan Blair. Used as part of Daniel W. MacInnes's talk at Saint Mary's University, Halifax, Nova Scotia, 26–29 September 1996. The census is unpublished and has no pagination.

M'Crie, Rev. Thomas, ed. *The Correspondence of the Rev. Robert Wodrow, edited from MSS in the Library of the Faculty of Advocates* (widely known as *The Wodrow Correspondence – 1715–22*). Vol. 2. Edinburgh, 1843.

McTaggart, John. *The Scottish Gallovidian Encyclopedia; or, The Original, Antiquated, and Natural Curiosities of the South of Scotland.* London, 1824.

– *Three Years in Canada: An Account of the Actual State of the Country in 1826-7-8. Comprehending Its Resources, Productions, Improvements, and Capabilities; and Including Sketches of the State of Society, Advice to Emigrants, &c.* London, H. Colburn, 1829.

McWhannell, D.C., and Alastair Campbell of Airds. "The Macgillechonnels – a family of hereditary boatbuilders." Unpublished MS. Dundee and Inverary, 1995.

Menary, George. *Life and Letters of Duncan Forbes Lord President of the Court of Session.* London: A. Maclehose & Co., 1936.

Menzies, D.P. *The "Red and White" Book of Menzies – Leabhar dearg 'us geal na Meinerich – The History of Clan Menzies.* Glasgow, 1894.

Millar, A.H. "Note on the Proclamation for Disarming of the Highlands in 1746." *Proceedings of the Society of Antiquaries of Scotland* 30 (1895–96): 210–22.

Miller, Kerby A. *Emigrants and Exiles – Ireland and the Irish Exodus to North America.* London: Oxford University Press, 1985.

Mitchell, Dugald. *A Popular History of the Highlands and Gaelic Scotland from the Earliest Times till the Close of the 'Forty-five.* Paisley: A. Gardner, 1900.

Mitchell, Joseph. *Reminiscences of My Life in the Highlands.* Vol. 1. 1883. Reprint. Newton Abbott, Devon: David and Charles, 1971.

Monro, Robert. *Monro, his Expedition ... with the Scots Regiment (called Mac-Keyes Regiment), ... discharged in severall duties and observations of service*

first under the ... King of Denmark, during his warres against the Emperour;
afterward under the ... King of Sweden ... London: W. Jones, 1637.

Monroe, John D. *Chapters in the History of Delaware County, New York.* N.p.:
Delaware County Historical Association, 1949.

Morehouse, F. "Canadian Migration in the Forties." *Canadian Historical Review* 9,
(December 1928).

Morgan, R.J., ed. *More Essays in Cape Breton History.* Windsor, NS: Lancelot
Press, 1977.

Morrison, Alex, and Ted Slaney. *The Breed of Manly Men – The History of the
Cape Breton Highlanders.* Sydney, NS: N.p., 1994.

Morrison, Alick. *The MacLeods – The Genealogy of a Clan.* Edinburgh: Clan
MacLeod Society, 1974.

Morrison, Hew. "Notices of Ministers of the Presbytery of Tongue from 1726 to
1763: From the Diary of the Rev. Murdoch MacDonald of Durness." *Transactions of the Gaelic Society of Inverness* 11 (1884–85).

Morrison, Hew, ed. *Orain le Rob Donn bard ainmeal na h-Ard Tuath.* Untranslated.
3d edition, revised and enlarged, with a history of Rob Donn in English. Edinburgh: John Grant, 1899.

Morton, Desmond. *A Military History of Canada*, 3d ed. Toronto: McClelland and
Stewart, 1992.

Moss, George, "An Da Phiobair" ("The Two Pipers"). Translated by George Moss.
Tocher 26, (Autumn 1977): 114–19.

– "Scottish Tradition Cassette Series 6, Pibroch." School of Scottish Studies, University of Edinburgh, 1982.

Mowat, Ian R.M. *Easter Ross 1750–1850: The Double Frontier.* Edinburgh: Donald, 1981.

Munro, Surgeon-General. *Reminiscences of Military Service with the 93d Sutherland Highlanders.* London: Hurst and Blackett, 1883.

Munro, R.W. "Archibald Munro, Piper to Glengarry." *Clan Munro Magazine*, no. 9
(1965).

Murray, Amy. *Father Allan's Island.* Edinburgh and London: Moray Press, 1936.

Murray Logan, G. *Scottish Highlanders and the American Revolution.* Halifax, NS:
McCurdy Printing Co., 1976.

National Library of Scotland. *Lamplighter and Story-teller, John Francis Campbell
of Islay 1821–1885.* Exhibition catalogue 25. 1985.

New Brunswick Historical Society. *Collections.* No. 8. "The Disbanded Soldiers at
Shelburne" taken from Benjamin Marston's Papers. Saint John, NB: Barnes and
Co., 1909.

Newte, Thomas. *Prospects and Observations on a Tour in England and Scotland:
Natural, Oeconomic and Literary.* London, 1791.

Nicolson, Alexander. *A Collection of Gaelic Proverbs and Familiar Phrases based
on MacIntosh's Collection.* 2d ed. revised. Edinburgh: MacLachlan and Stewart,
1882.

Nicolson, Alexander. *History of Skye – A Record of the Families, the Social Conditions, and the Literature of the Island.* Glasgow: A. Maclaren and Sons, 1930.

Nilsen, Kenneth E. "The Nova Scotia Gael in Boston." *Harvard Celtic Colloquium* 6 (1986): 83–100.

"Notices of Pipers." Piper John Campbell from Invermoriston. *Piping Times* 20, no. 9 (June 1968).

O'Baoill, Colm. *Bàrdachd Chloinn Ghill Eathain.* Untranslated. Edinburgh: Scottish Gaelic Texts Society, 1979.

– *Eachann Bacach agus Baird Eile de Chloinn Ghill-Eathain.* Untranslated. Edinburgh: Scottish Gaelic Texts Society, 1979.

O'Neill, Francis. *Irish Minstrels and Musicians with numerous Dissertations on Related Subjects.* Darby, PA: Norwood Editions, 1973.

Old Edinburgh Club. *The Book of the Old Edinburgh Club.* Edinburgh: Printed by T. and A. Constable 1966.

"Orain Le Maighstir Ailein" ("Songs with Father Allan"). *MacTalla* (Sydney, Cape Breton) 5, no. 36 (13 March 1897).

Ormond, Douglas Somers. *A Century Ago at Arichat and Antigonish and Other Familiar Surroundings: Reminiscences of Mary Belle Grant Ormond (1860–1947).* Hantsport, NS: Lancelot Press, 1985.

Oswald, James. *The Caledonian Pocket Companion.* 12 books. London: J. Simpson and J. Oswald, 1743, 1745, 1751, 1759.

Owen, John B. *The Eighteenth Century 1714–1815.* Totowa, NJ: 1975.

Patterson, Rev. George. *A History of the County of Pictou, Nova Scotia.* Montréal, 1877. Reprint. Toronto: James Campbell and Son, 1977.

Patterson, George Geddie. *The History of Victoria County* (Nova Scotia). N.p., 1885.

Paul, Sir James Balfour. "The 2d Dragoons Royal Scots Greys." In *The Lowland Scots Regiments ...* , edited by Herbert E. Maxwell 35–66. Glasgow: J. Maclehose and Sons, 1918.

Pennant, Thomas. *A Tour of Scotland and Voyage to the Hebrides, 1772.* Chester, UK, 1774.

– *A Tour in Scotland 1769.* 3d ed. 3 vols. 1771.

Phillipson, N.T., and Rosalind Mitchison, eds. *Scotland in the Age of Improvement – Essays in Scottish History in the Eighteenth Century.* Edinburgh: Edinburgh University Press, 1970.

Piobaireachd Society. *Pìobareachd.* Books 1 to 13. Glasgow: Aird and Coghill, book 2, 1963, book 9, n.d.; Bell, Aird and Coghill, books 1, 3–8, 1968, book 11, n.d.; London: Lowe and Bryden Printers, book 10, 12, n.d.; West Central Printing Co., book 13, n.d.

Pococke, Bishop R. *Tours in Scotland, 1747, 1750, 1760.* Edinburgh: Scottish History Society, 1887.

Poulter, G.C.B. Unpublished MS on MacCrimmon genealogy. Held in 1996 by Dr Hugh MacCrimmon, Guelph, Ontario.

– *History of the Clan MacCrimmon, compiled by G.C.B. Poulter.* Camberley, UK: Clan MacCrimmon Society, 1938.

Poulter, G.C.B., and C.P. Fisher. *The MacCrimmon Family. Origin; music; Iain Odhar; Padruig Mor; Padruig Og; the descendants of Donald Donn from 1740 to 1936.* Camberley, UK: W.H. Smith and Son, 1936.

Prebble, John Ross. *Culloden.* London: Secker and Warburg, 1961.

– *Glencoe.* New York: Holt, Reinhart and Winston, 1966; London: Secker and Warburg, 1966.

– *The King's Jaunt – George IV in Scotland, August 1822:'One and twenty daft days.'* London: Collins, 1988.

Price, A.V., comp. and ed. *The Royal Irish Rangers (27th 83rd and 87th) Standard Settings of Pipe Music.* London: Paterson's Publications, 1975.

Quick, I. "English and Scots Military Loanwords in Scottish Gaelic." In *Scottish Language,* edited by Donald MacAulay and Donald McClure. Aberdeen: The University Press, n.d.

Rae, T.I. "Edinburgh Castle, 1751–1753." in *The Book of the Old Edinburgh Club.* Vol. 32. Edinburgh: N.p., 1966.

Ramsay, Freda, ed. and annot. *The Day Book of Daniel Campbell of Shawfield 1767 with Relevant Papers Concerning the Estate of Islay.* Aberdeen: Aberdeen University Press, 1991.

Ramsay, John of Ochtertyre. "Of the Influence of Poetry and Music upon the Highlanders." In Patrick MacDonald. *A Collection of Highland Vocal Airs* ... Edinburgh, 1784.

– MSS of John Ramsay. Published in Alexander Allardye, *Scotland and Scotsmen in the 18th Century.* N.p., 1888.

Rankin, Hugh F. *The North Carolina Continentals.* Chapel Hill, NC: University of North Carolina Press, 1971.

Rankin, Reginald, ed. *Mabou Pioneer II.* Port Hawkesbury, NS: N.p., 1977.

Rea, F.G. *A School in South Uist, Reminiscences of a Hebridean School-master.* Edited by John Lorne Campbell. London: Routledge and Kegan Paul, 1964.

Read, Colin, and Ronald J. Stagg, eds. *The Rebellion of 1837 in Upper Canada – A Collection of Documents.* Toronto: the Champlain Society, 1985.

Redmond, Gerald. *The Caledonian Games in Nineteenth Century America.* Madison, NJ: Fairleigh Dickinson University Press, 1971.

– *The Sporting Scots of Nineteenth Century Canada.* Madison, NJ: Fairleigh Dickinson University Press, 1982.

Reith, John. *Life of Dr John Leyden.* Galashiels: A. Walker and Son, n.d. (1923).

Rhodes, Frank. "Dancing in Cape Breton Island Nova Scotia." Appendix In J.F. Fletts and T.M. Flett. *Traditional Dancing in Scotland.* London: Routledge and Kegan Paul, 1964.

Roberts, Michael. *Gustavus Adolphus – A History of Sweden 1611–1632.* 2 vols. London and New York: Longmans Green, 1958.

Rogers, Rev. Charles. *The Scottish Minstrel – The Songs of Scotland Subsequent to Burns with Memoirs of the Poets.* Edinburgh, 1873.

Robertson, Marion. *The King's Bounty; A History of Early Shelburne, Nova Scotia.* Halifax, NS: Nova Scotia Museum, 1983.

Ross, Andrew. "Scottish Regiments Disbanded." In *The Lowland Scots Regiments* ... , edited by Herbert E. Maxwell. Glasgow: J. Maclehose and Sons, 1918.

Ross, D.K. *The Pioneers and Churches, the Pioneers and Families, of Big Brook and West Branch E.R. and Surrounding Sections Including, Lorne, Glengarry, Elgin, Centerdale, Hopewell, Marshdale, Foxbrook.* Hopewell, ns: N.p., n.d. (1957?).

Ross, Donald. "A Sutherland Highlander's Welcome to the Governor General of Canada." *Celtic Magazine* 5, no. 49 (November 1879):39–40.

Ross, Neil. "Ceòl Mór, the Classical Music of the Bagpipes." *Transactions of the Gaelic Society of Inverness* 32 (1924–25): 158–171.

Ross, Roderick. *Binneas is Boreraig.* 5 vols. Edinburgh: MacDonald Printers, 1959–67.

Ross, William. *Pipe-Major W. Ross's Collection of Highland Bagpipe Music Book 5.* London: Paterson's Publications, n.d. (1950?).

Roy, Pierre-George. *Inventaire des Concessions en Fief et Seigneurie Fois et Homages et Aveux ... de la Province de Québec par Pierre-George Roy.* 4 vols. Beauceville, PQ: L'"Eclaireur," 1927, 1928.

Royle, Trevor. *Death before Dishonour – The True Story of Fighting Mac.* New York: St Martin's Press, 1982.

Sage, Rev. Donald. *Memorabilia Domestica or, Parish life in the North of Scotland.* Edinburgh: W. Rae, Wick and John Menzies and Co., 1889.

Sanger, Keith. "Auchinbreck's Harper." *Notes and Queries of the Society of West Highland and Island Historical Research*, no. 30 (February 1987).

– "MacCrimmon's Prentise-A Post Graduate Student Perhaps?" *Piping Times* 44, no. 6 (March 1992).

Scobie, I.H. MacKay. "Highland Military Dress: A Short Historical Review." *Transactions of the Gaelic Society of Inverness* 30 (1921): 223–39.

– *An Old Highland Fencible Corps.* Edinburgh and London: Blackwood and Sons, 1914.

– *Pipers and Pipe Music in a Highland Regiment – A record of Piping in the 1st Seaforth Highlanders, originally the Earl of Seaforth's or 78th (Highland) regiment, afterwards the 72nd or Duke of Albany's Own Highlanders.* Dingwall: Ross-shire Printing and Publishing Company, 1924.

Scots Guards Standard Settings of Pipe Music. London: Paterson's Publications, 1954.

Scots Magazine. Various issues, 1746, 1751, 1753, 1756, 1759, new series 1992.

Scott, Hew. *Fasti Ecclesiae Scoticanae.* New ed. 8 vols. Edinburgh: Oliver and Boyd, 1915–50.

Scott, Walter. *Rob Roy.* Preface by W.M. Parker. London: Everyman's Library, 1966.

– *Waverley.* Preface by James C. Corson. 1814. London: Everyman's Library, 1969.

"Selections from the Family Papers of the MacKays of Bighouse." Includes "Prefatory Notes by the Editor of the 'Northern Chronicle'" to "Contemporary Letters
on the Rebellion of 1745." *Transactions of the Gaelic Society of Inverness* 21,
(1896–97).

Seton, Sir Bruce, and Jean Gordon Arnot, eds. *Prisoners of the '45.* 3 vols. Vol. 14
of the 3d Scottish History Series. Edinburgh: Constable, 1928, 1929.

Shaw, Christina Byam. *Pigeon Holes of Memory – The Life and Times of Dr John
Mackenzie (1803–1886) edited from his Manuscript Memoirs.* London: Constable, 1988.

Shaw, Margaret Fay. *Folksongs and Folklore of South Uist.* London: Routledge and
Kegan Paul, 1955.

Shears, Barry. *The Gathering of the Clans Collection.* Vol. 1. Halifax, NS: Privately
published. Bounty Press, 1991.

Shorter, C.K., ed. *The Works of George Borrow.* Vol. 16. London and New York:
N.p., 1924.

Sinclair, A. *An t-Oranaiche.* Untranslated. Glasgow, 1879.

Sinclair, Rev. A. MacLean, ed. *Clàrsach na Coille.* Untranslated. Glasgow, 1881.

– *The Gaelic Bards from 1715–1765.* Charlottetown, 1892.

Sinclair, Donald. Recorded interview with Eric Cregeen. *Tocher* (School of Scottish
Studies, Edinburgh University) 18 (Summer 1975): 61.

Sinclair, Sir John, ed. *The Statistical Account of Scotland.* Edinburgh, 1791–99.
Also cited as "Old Statistical Account."

Sinton, James, ed. *Journal of a Tour in the Highlands and Western Islands of Scotland in 1800 by John Leyden.* Edinburgh & London: Blackwoods, 1903.

Skelton, Constance Oliver, and John Malcolm Bulloch. *The House of Gordon.* Vol.
3. Aberdeen: New Spalding Club, 1912.

Skene, W.F. *Celtic Scotland.* Edinburgh, 1880.

Skinner, James Scott. *My Life and Adventures.* Introduction by Graham Dixon.
Aberdeen: City of Aberdeen Arts and Recreation Division in association with
Wallace Music, 1994.

Smith, Alexander. *A Summer in Skye.* London and New York, 1866.

Smollett, Tobias. *The Expeditions of Humphrey Clinker.* Revised by Paul-Gabriel
Boucé with editing and introduction by Lewis M. Knapp. London: Oxford University Press, 1988.

Somers, Robert. *Letters from the Highlands on the Famine of 1846.* 1848. Reprint.
UK: Melven Press, 1985.

Spedon, Andrew Learmonth. *Rambles among the Blue-noses; or, Reminiscences of
a Tour through New Brunswick and Nova Scotia during the Summer of 1862.*
Montreal, 1863.

Squires, Capt. W. Austin. *104th Regiment of Foot (The New Brunswick Regiment)
1803–17.* Fredericton, NB: Brunswick Press, 1962.

Stanley, Laurie. *The Well-Watered Garden: The Presbyterian Church in Cape Breton
1798–1860.* Sydney, Cape Breton: University College of Cape Breton Press, 1983.

Stenhouse, William. *Illustrations of the Lyric Poetry and Music of Scotland.* Edited by David Laing. 2 vols. Edinburgh, 1853.

Stephen, Sir Leslie, and Sir Sidney Lee, eds. *The Dictionary of National Biography.* Vol. 9. London: Oxford University Press, 1973.

Stewart, Rev. Alexander. *Nether Lochaber: The Natural History, Legends, and Folk-lore of the West Highlands.* Edinburgh, 1883.

– *Twixt Ben Nevis and Glencoe: The Natural History, Legends, and Folk-lore of the West Highlands.* Edinburgh, 1885.

Stewart, Alexander, and Donald Stewart. *Cochruinneacha Taoghta de Shaothair nam Bard Gaëlach.* Untranslated. Edinburgh, 1804.

Stewart, Colonel David of Garth. *Sketches of the character, Manners, and Present State of the Highlanders of Scotland: with Details of the Military Service of the Highland Regiments.* 2 vols. Edinburgh, 1822.

Stewart, James A. "The Clan Ranald, the History of a Highland Clan." Unpublished doctoral thesis. University of Edinburgh, Department of History, 1982.

– "Lost Highland Manuscripts and the Jacobite Rebellion of 1745–46." In *Celtic Connections: Proceedings of the Tenth International Congress of Celtic Studies,* edited by Ronald Black, William Gillies, and Roibeard Ó'Maolalaigh. Vol. 1. East Linton: Tuckwell Press, 1997.

Swinton, Captain John, Scots Guards. "History of the Pipers of the Regiment, together with an account of their customs." In *Scots Guards Standard Settings of Pipe Music.* London: Paterson's Publications, 1954.

Tayler, Alistair, and Henrietta Tayler, eds. *1745 and After.* In essence the "Narrative" of John William O'Sullivan, one of the seven men of Moidart. London: Thomas Nelson and Sons, 1938.

Tayler, H., ed. *A Jacobite Miscellany – Eight Original Papers on the Rising of 1745–1746.* Oxford, 1948.

Terry, Charles Sanford. *The Albemarle Papers – Correspondence of William Anne, 2d Earl of Albemarle, Commander in Chief Scotland. 1746–47.* Vol. 1. Aberdeen: Spalding Club, 1902.

Thomason, Charles S. *Ceol Mor: written in a new and abbreviated system of musical notation for the piobaireachd as played on the Highland bagpipe.* Part III. Glasgow: John MacKay, 1897.

Thomson, Derick, ed. *Companion to Gaelic Scotland.* Oxford: Blackwell, 1983.

Thornton, Col. Thomas. *A Sporting Tour through the Northern Parts of England, and great part of the Highlands of Scotland.* London, 1804.

Timperley, Loretta R., ed. *A Directory of Landownership in Scotland 1770.* Edinburgh: Scottish Record Society, 1976.

Todd, William. *The Seventy-ninth Highlanders New York Volunteers in the War of Rebellion 1861–1865.* Albany, NY: Press of Brandow, Barton and Co., 1886.

Tolman, Beth, and Ralph Page. *The Country Dance Book.* New York: A.S. Barnes, c. 1937, 1976.

Topham, Edward. *Letters from Edinburgh ... Letters written from Edinburgh during the years 1774 and 1775 containing various remarks on the Amusements, the Manners and Laws of the Scots.* London, 1776.

Turner, Sir James. *Pallas Armata, Military Essays of the Ancient Grecian, Roman, and Modern Art of War. Written in the Years 1670 and 1671, Originally published in 1683.* Reprint. Westport, CT: Greenwood Press, 1968.

Turreff, Gavin. *Antiquarian Gleanings from Aberdeenshire Records.* 2d ed. Aberdeen, 1871.

United Kingdom. House of Commons. *Journals of the House of Commons.* Vol. 26, 1750–54.

– Crofters Commission. *Report.* Vol. 32, Appendix A. London, 1884.

– *Statutes at Large. Vol. 6: From the Ninth Year of the Reign of King George the Second to the Twenty-fifth Year of the Reign of King George the Second. Vol. 6.*

– *From the Twenty-sixth Year of the Reign of King George the Second to the Sixth Year of the Reign of King George the Third. Vol. 7,* London, 1786.

Victoria Regina. *Leaves from the Journal of Our Life in the Highlands, from 1848 to 1861.* Edited by Arthur Helps. London: Smith, Elder and Co., 1868.

– *More Leaves from the Journal of a Life in the Highlands from 1862 to 1883.* 4th ed. Toronto: A.H. Hovey and Co., 1884.

Walker, John. *Revd John Walker's Report on the Hebrides of 1764 and 1771.* Edited by Margaret MacKay. Edinburgh: John Donald Publishers, 1980.

Walker, Rev. John. *An Economical History of the Hebrides and Highlands of Scotland.* 2 vols. Edinburgh, 1808.

Walton, Colonel Clifford C.B. *History of the British Standing Army. A.D. 1660 to 1700.* London, 1894.

Wardell, John, ed. *With "The Thirty-second" in the Peninsular and other Campaigns by Harry Ross-Lewin of Ross Hill, Co. Clare.* Abridged version. Dublin, 1904. Originally published as *The Life of a Soldier, by a Field Officer.* 3 vols. Dublin, 1834.

Warrand, Duncan, ed. *More Culloden Papers.* Vol. 4, February 1744–February 1746. Inverness: R. Carruthers and Sons, 1929.

Watson, Don. *Caledonia Australis Scottish Highlanders on the Frontier of Australia.* Sydney, Australia: Collins, 1984.

Watson, William J. *Bardachd Ghaidhlig. Gaelic Poetry 1550–1900.* Reprint. Inverness: An Commun Gaidhealach, 1976.

Wedderburn, Robert (1510?–52?). *The Complaynt of Scotland.* 2 vols. Edinburgh: Scottish Text Society, 4th series, 1979.

White, Arthur S. *A Bibliography of Regimental Histories of the British Army.* London: Society for Army Historical Research in conjunction with the Army Museums Ogilby Trust, 1965.

Whitelaw, Marjory, ed. *Dalhousie Journals.* Ottawa: Oberon Press, 1978.

Whyte, Henry ("Fionn"). *The Rankins Pipers to the MacLeans of Duart, and later to the MacLeans of Coll.* Glasgow, 1907.

Wilkinson, Brig-Gen. Montagu Grant. "The King's Own Scottish Borderers." In *The Lowland Scots Regiments* ... , edited by Herbert E. Maxwell. Glasgow: J. Maclehose and Sons, 1918.

Willson, Beckles. *The Life and Letters of James Wolfe.* London: William Heinemann, 1909.

Wimberley, Captain D. "Papers from the Bighouse Charter Chest." Published in part 1 as "Selections from the Family Papers of the MacKays of Bighouse, Consisting Mainly of Letters Addressed to John Campbell of Barcaldine, some time one of the Government Factors on the Forfeited Estates after the '45." *Transactions of the Gaelic Society of Inverness* 21, (1896–97): 120–71.

Woodhouselee MS – A Narrative of Events in Edinburgh and District during the Jacobite Occupation, September to November 1745. Edinburgh: Chambers, 1907. In *A Jacobite Miscellany* ..., edited by H. Taylor. N.p.: Oxford, 1948.

Wright, Robert. *The life of Major-General James Wolfe founded on Original Documents and illustrated by his Correspondence including numerous Unpublished Letters contributed from the Family Papers and Noblemen and Gentlemen, Descendants of his Companions.* London, 1864.

Young, Reverend Walter Erskine. "Preface." In Patrick MacDonald. *A Collection of Highland Vocal Airs* ... Edinburgh, 1784.

Youngson, A.J. *After the Forty-Five – The Economic Impact on the Scottish Highlands.* Edinburgh: Edinburgh University Press, 1973.

Index